Routledge Handbook of International Criminology

The *Routledge Handbook of International Criminology* brings together the latest thinking and findings from a diverse group of both senior and promising young scholars from around the globe. This collaborative project articulates a new way of thinking about criminology that extends existing perspectives in understanding crime and social control across borders, jurisdictions, and cultures, and facilitates the development of an overarching framework that is truly international.

The book is divided into three parts, in which three distinct yet overlapping types of crime are analyzed: international crime, transnational crime, and national crime. Each of these perspectives is then articulated through a number of chapters which cover theory and methods, international and transnational crime analyses, and case studies of criminology and criminal justice in relevant nations. In addition, questions placed at the end of each chapter encourage greater reflection on the issues raised, and will encourage young scholars to move the field of inquiry forward.

This handbook is an excellent reference tool for undergraduate and graduate students with particular interests in research methods, international criminology, and making comparisons across countries.

Cindy J. Smith is a retired faculty member of the University of Baltimore, Maryland, USA, the former Chief of the International Center at the National Institute of Justice (2006–8), and a Senior Fulbright Research Scholar in Turkey (2005–6). She was the Director of the Master's in Criminal Justice program (2001–5), and Chair of the International Division of the American Society of Criminology (2005–9). Her research interests include terrorism, human trafficking, corrections, sex offenders, and comparative methodology.

Sheldon X. Zhang is Professor of Sociology at San Diego State University. His research interests include criminal enterprise, transnational organized crime, community corrections, and program evaluation. He has authored three books and his articles have appeared in *Criminology*, *British Journal of Criminology*, *Research in Crime and Delinquency*, *Criminology and Public Policy*, and *Crime and Delinquency*.

Rosemary Barberet is an associate professor in the Sociology Department at John Jay College of Criminal Justice (CUNY), where she directs the Master's program in International Crime and Justice. Her publications have dealt with victimology, crime measurement, and comparative methodology. She is the recipient of the 2006 Herbert Bloch Award of the American Society of Criminology.

Routledge Handbook of International Criminology

Edited by
Cindy J. Smith, Sheldon X. Zhang, and Rosemary Barberet

Routledge
Taylor & Francis Group
LONDON AND NEW YORK

SPECIAL EDITION, 2014

First published 2011 by Routledge
2 Park Square, Milton Park, Abingdon, Oxon, OX14 4RN

Simultaneously published in the USA and Canada
by Routledge
711 Third Avenue, New York, NY 10017

Routledge is an imprint of the Taylor & Francis Group, an informa business

British Library Cataloging in Publication Data
A catalogue record for this book is available from the British Library

Library of Congress Cataloging in Publication Data
Routledge Handbook of International Criminology / edited by Cindy J. Smith, Sheldon X. Zhang, and Rosemary Barberet.
p. cm.
1. Criminology. 2. Crime. I. Smith, Cindy J. II. Zhang, Sheldon.
III. Barberet, Rosemary. IV. Title: Handbook of International Criminology.
HV6025.R68 2011
364 – dc22 2010040654

ISBN: 978–0–415–77909–8 hbk
ISBN: 978–0–203–86470–8 ebook

Typeset in Bembo
by Keystroke, Station Road, Codsall, Wolverhampton

Printed and bound in India by Bhavish Graphics.

We dedicate this collective body of knowledge
to the man who started the path in 1983
with his *International Handbook of
Contemporary Developments in Criminology*,
Elmer H. Johnson

In his memory

Contents

Plates

Figures

Tables

Boxes

Notes on contributors

Editor biographies

Cindy J. Smith, Ph.D., is a retired faculty member of the University of Baltimore, Maryland, USA. She is the former Chief of the International Center at the National Institute of Justice (2006–8), a Senior Fulbright Research Scholar in Turkey (2005–6), Director of the Master's in Criminal Justice Program (2001–5), and Chair of the International Division of the American Society of Criminology (2005–9). Her research interests include terrorism, human trafficking, corrections, sex offenders, and comparative methodology.

Sheldon X. Zhang, Ph.D., is Professor of Sociology at San Diego State University. His research interests include community corrections and reintegration, and transnational organized crime. His works have appeared in such journals as *Criminology*, *British Journal of Criminology*, and *Crime and Delinquency*. He has published two books on human smuggling topics: *Chinese human smuggling organizations – families, social networks, and cultural imperatives* (Stanford University Press, 2008) and *Smuggling and trafficking in human beings: all roads lead to America* (Praeger, 2007).

Rosemary Barberet, Ph.D., is an associate professor in the Sociology Department of John Jay College of Criminal Justice in New York City, USA., and directs the Master's Program in International Crime and Justice. She has spent most of her academic career in Europe (Spain and England) and is fluent in Spanish and French. Her publications have dealt with youth crime, victimology, crime indicators, and comparative methodology. From 2001–5 she chaired the International Division of the American Society of Criminology (ASC). In 2006 she received the Herbert Bloch Award of the ASC, as well as the Rafael Salillas Award of the Sociedad Española de Investigación Criminológica.

Contributor biographies

Freda Adler, Ph.D. is a visiting professor and the Director of the Master of Science Program in Criminology at the University of Pennsylvania, and Professor Emeritus at Rutgers University. She is a world renowned leader of international criminology. The Freda Adler Distinguished International Scholar Award of the Division of International Criminology of the American Society of Criminology is named in honor of her work in advocating for an international perspective in all work and her knowledge building to internationalize criminology around the world. Her publication list is extensive with over 130 books and papers.

Mario Arroyo Juarez, Ph.D., is an expert in security and crime reduction. He holds a Ph.D. in Sociology from the National Autonomous University of Mexico (UNAM), and an MSc. in criminal justice policy from the London School of Economics and Political Science, UK. Currently, he is a researcher on strategic intelligence at the Tecnológico de Monterrey in Mexico.

Jana Arsovska, Ph.D., a native of Macedonia, is an assistant professor at the Sociology Department at John Jay College of Criminal Justice (CUNY) in New York City, USA. She holds a Ph.D. degree in criminology from the Catholic University of Leuven in Belgium where she studied ethnic Albanian organized crime. She has published widely on Balkan criminal networks.

Roderic Broadhurst, Ph.D., is Professor at the Australian Research Council Centre of Excellence in Policing and Security (CEPS), School of Regulation, Justice and Diplomacy, College of Asia and the Pacific, Australian National University. He is currently engaged in research for CEPS on "illicit organizations" and "investigative practices" as well as on crime in Cambodia, Hong Kong, and China.

Anne Brunton, Ph.D., has professional qualifications in law and a background in social policy. She has experience of working with vulnerable groups such as care leavers, drug users, and young offenders. Until recently she was Director of the British Society of Criminology and an associate lecturer in criminology at the London School of Economics and Political Science. She is now a senior lecturer in criminology and policing at Buckinghamshire New University.

Ko-lin Chin, Ph.D., is Professor II (Distinguished) at the School of Criminal Justice at Rutgers University-Newark. He is the author of *Chinese subculture and criminality: non-traditional crime groups in America*; *Chinatown gangs: extortion, enterprise, and ethnicity*; *Smuggled Chinese: clandestine immigration to the United States*; *Heijin: organized crime, business, and politics in Taiwan*; and *Golden triangle: inside Southeast Asia's drug trade.*

Kyung-shick Choi, Ph.D., is an assistant professor in the Criminal Justice Department at Bridgewater State University, USA. He also facilitates the UN Virtual Forum against Cybercrime as a lecturer. He received his Ph.D. in criminology from Indiana University of Pennsylvania, USA. His scholarly interests focus on the study of cybercrime and theory testing.

Kim-Kwang Raymond Choo, Ph.D., is a senior research lecturer at the University of South Australia, and the recipient of a number of awards including the 2010 Australian Capital Territory Pearcy Award, 2010 Consensus IT Professional Award, a 2009 Fulbright Scholarship, and the 2008 Australia Day Achievement Medallion. He was nominated as one of 100 Emerging Leaders in *The Weekend Australian Magazine*/Microsoft's Next 100 series.

Yiu Kong Chu, Ph.D., is an honorary assistant professor in the Department of Sociology of the University of Hong Kong. He is one of the founding members of the Asian Association of Police Studies and the Hong Kong Juvenile Delinquency Research Society. He is conducting research on organized crime and policing.

Innocent Chukwuma is a leading researcher on police, policing, and criminal justice reform in Nigeria, having served as a consultant to the United Nations Office on Drugs and Crime (UNODC), the European Union (EU), and many other agencies, as well as the founder of CLEEN Foundation in West Africa. He is currently the William H. Bloomberg Visiting Lecturer in Public Management at the Harvard Kennedy School, USA.

Nicole Crutcher, upon completion of her master's degree in 2000, began her career with the federal government in Canada, first in research at the Correctional Service of Canada before moving to the Research and Statistics Division of Justice Canada. Her research expertise is in sentencing, drug offending, and high-risk offenders.

Corinne Davis Rodrigues, Ph.D., is an associate professor in the Sociology and Anthropology Department, Director of the Center for Urban Studies, and researcher at the Center for Studies in Criminality and Public Safety at the Federal University of Minas Gerais, Brazil. Her current research focuses on intra-urban variations in Brazilian crime.

Jan van Dijk, Ph.D., was Director of the Research and Documentation Centre of the Dutch Ministry of Justice, where he launched the International Crime Victims Survey. From 1998 to 2005 he worked for the United Nations in Vienna and Turin. He was president of the World Society of Victimology from 1997 to 2000. In 2008 he received the Sellin-Glueck Award of the American Society of Criminology. He currently holds the Pieter van Vollenhoven Chair in Victimology and Human Security at the University of Tilburg (the Netherlands).

Obi N. I. Ebbe, Ph.D., is a professor of criminology and sociology at the University of Tennessee at Chattanooga. He is a graduate of Western Michigan University and received a Ph.D. in sociology from Southern Illinois University at Carbondale in 1981. He has published numerous articles in refereed journals and six books. He is a recognized expert in political criminology and international criminal justice systems.

Gipsy Escobar is an assistant professor in the Criminal Justice Department at Loyola University, Chicago, USA. Her research interests include the study of collective violence, urban crime, social disorganization, and criminal justice in Colombia. Before moving to the USA, she worked with the Colombian government designing and implementing criminal justice policies.

David P. Farrington, O.B.E. is Professor of Psychological Criminology at the Institute of Criminology, Cambridge University, UK. His major research interest is in developmental criminology, and he is Director of the Cambridge Study in Delinquent Development, which is a prospective longitudinal survey of over 400 London males from age 8 to age 48.

Yakov Gilinskiy, Ph.D. is Professor at St. Petersburg's Juridical Institute of the Academy of the General Prosecutor's Office of Russia; Dean of the Faculty of Law at the Baltic University of Ecology, Politics, and Law, and Head of the Department of Criminal Law at the Russian State Educational University.

Charlotte E. Gill is a postdoctoral fellow in the Center for Evidence-Based Crime Policy, Department of Criminology, Law and Society, George Mason University. She recieved her Ph.D. from the Jerry Lee Center of Criminology, University of Pennsylvania in 2010. She has been the Managing Editor of the Campbell Collaboration Crime and Justice Group since 2006.

Joanna Heskia holds a law degree from the Pontificia Universidad Católica de Chile and did postgraduate studies in applied social sciences and criminology at the University of Exeter, UK. She has published on community penalties, precautionary measures, restorative justice, and litigation procedures. She is a professor at Pontificia Universidad Católica de Chile and Alberto Hurtado University. She is also a consultant to UNICEF and OAS.

Martha K. Huggins, Ph.D., Charles A. and Leo M. Favrot Professor of Human Relations, is a sociologist at Tulane University in New Orleans. A scholar of Brazil for over three decades, her research – which focuses on crime, social control, and human rights – has produced seven books (two of which were also published in Brazil) and numerous academic articles on Brazil. She is now writing *Policing Katrina*, a book exploring the best and the worst of post-Katrina disaster policing.

Joon Oh Jang, Ph.D., is the Director of the Public Relations and International Cooperation Center, Korean Institute of Criminology, and is an adjunct professor at Yonsei University in Korea. He holds a Ph.D. and master's degree in sociology from the University of Kansas, USA. He was Vice President of the Korean Society of Criminology from 2006 to 2008, and President from 2010.

Matti Joutsen, Ph.D., is Director of International Affairs at the Ministry of Justice of Finland. He continues to be closely involved in work on the UN Convention against Transnational Organized Crime and the UN Convention on Corruption.

Kristiina Kangaspunta, as the Executive Officer of the United Nations Interregional Crime and Justice Research Institute (UNICRI), is heading the Applied Research Programme of the Institute. Previously, she worked with UNODC as the Chief of the Anti-Human Trafficking Unit. She moved to UNODC from the European Institute for Crime Prevention and Control, affiliated with the United Nations (HEUNI).

Jacqui Karn, Ph.D., is at The Police Foundation in the UK. She was a senior analyst at the International Centre for the Prevention of Crime in Montreal, Canada. Previously she worked for the UK Ministry of Justice and Nacro, a crime-reduction charity. She has held a postdoctoral fellowship at the London School of Economics and published *Narratives of neglect*, which was shortlisted for the British Society of Criminology Book Prize 2008.

Chenda Keo is completing a Ph.D. in criminology at the Australian National University. His research explores people-trafficking dynamics within the Great Mekong Subregion based on traffickers' experience, perspective, and modus operandi. He had worked with non-governmental organizations and UN agencies in Cambodia for over eight years at the managerial and technical level.

Jade Lindley studied Criminology and criminal justice in her undergraduate and master's degrees. She is currently undertaking a doctoral thesis exploring transnational organized crime. Her research interests are multidisciplinary, combining criminology, international law, human rights and diplomacy. She is currently working as a research analyst at the Australian Institute of Criminology.

Anna Markina is a lecturer at the Institute of Public Law in the Faculty of Law at the University of Tartu, Estonia. She has worked on organized crime, and recently on juvenile delinquency. Her present research focuses on trafficking in human beings. She is also a part of the International Self-Report Delinquency Study research consortia.

Veronica Martinez Solares is a Ph.D. candidate. She is an international consultant in criminal justice policy issues. As researcher and board member at the International Organization for Victim

Assistance, her academic specialties include victim support, crime prevention, and policing improvement. She has a Ph.D. in Law from the National Autonomous University of Mexico.

William F. McDonald, Ph.D., is Professor of Sociology and Co-Director of the Institute of Criminal Law and Procedure at Georgetown University in Washington, D.C., USA. His scholarship covers crime victims, police, prosecutors, defense counsel, courts, pre-trial processes, sentencing, immigration, globalization, and international cooperation.

Juanjo Medina, Ph.D., is Senior Lecturer in Criminology at the University of Manchester, UK, and has held positions at the Violence Institute of New Jersey, USA, and the University of Seville, Spain. His research focuses on gangs, violence against women, and crime-reduction policy and politics, with an emphasis on comparative aspects.

Stephen Mihorean is the Director of the Research and Statistics Division of the Department of Justice, Canada. His professional interests include the economic and social costing of crime, international comparisons, and machinery of government analyses. Stephen completed his graduate studies in sociology at Queen's University at Kingston.

Riccardo Montana, Ph.D. (Cardiff), LLM (Cardiff), LLB (Pavia University), is a researcher and lecturer at Kingston University Law School and a supervisor in Law at Homerton College. He taught previously at Cardiff University.

David Nelken, Ph.D., is Distinguished Professor of Legal Institutions and Social Change at the University of Macerata, Italy; Distinguished Research Professor of Law at Cardiff University, UK; and Visiting Professor at the Mannheim Centre of Criminology, London School of Economics. He received a Distinguished Scholar Award from the American Sociological Association and the Sellin-Glueck Award from the American Society of Criminology. His latest book is *Comparative criminal justice: making sense of difference* (Sage, 2010).

Ali Ozdoğan, Ph.D., is a Division Chief with the Turkish National Police, and an adjunct professor in the Turkish Police Academy. He earned his Ph.D. at the American University, Washington, D.C, USA. He has published on terrorism and intelligence. He is the author of *On wiretapping*.

Prasanna Poornachandra, Ph.D. in criminology, heads the International Foundation for Crime Prevention and Victim Care (PCVC), a not-for-profit organization based in Chennai, India, that provides services for victims of domestic violence and sexual abuse. Her main research interests are violence against women and police behavior.

Blythe Bowman Proulx, Ph.D., is an assistant professor of criminal justice in the Wilder School of Government and Public Affairs at Virginia Commonwealth University, USA. Her research interests include antiquities trafficking, biosocial criminology, and inmate litigation (Section 1983 claims).

Judy Putt, Ph.D., is currently a senior research fellow at the Tasmanian Institute of Law Enforcement Studies, University of Tasmania, Australia. Her current research interests include rural and remote policing, transnational and organized crime, and community safety in indigenous communities. She has published on violence against women, juvenile justice, missing persons, crime in the fishing industry, people trafficking, and substance misuse. She is the former Head of Research at the Australian Institute of Criminology.

Sławomir Marek Redo, Ph.D., is the author of three books and co-editor of three books, including *For the rule of law: criminal justice teaching and training @cross the world* (Helsinki – Seoul 2008) and has published about 50 articles on various crime prevention and criminal justice issues, mostly from the area of the United Nations studies. In 1999–2002, he was the Senior Crime Prevention and Criminal Justice Expert in the Regional UNODC Office for Central Asia (Tashkent, Uzbekistan).

Harry M. Rhea is Assistant Professor of Criminal Justice at the Richard Stockton College of New Jersey, USA. He is currently completing a Ph.D. in international criminal law at the Irish Centre for Human Rights, National University of Ireland, Galway. His book, *The United States and international criminal tribunals: an introduction*, will be published in 2011. Rhea's research interests are centered on international criminal law, human rights law, and the law of war.

Rosemary Serra, Ph.D., is Ricercatore Universitario in Social Research Methodology and Techniques at the Faculty of Training Sciences at the University of Trieste (Italy) and Co-director of the Doctoral School of Integrated Sciences for Territorial Sustainability. Her research interests are focused on the conditions of at-risk populations—including children, women, and the elderly—as well as social networks, migration, non-profit and volunteer work, the development of local communities, and family issues.

Dina Siegel, Ph.D., is Professor of Criminology at Utrecht University in the Netherlands. She received her Ph.D. in cultural anthropology from the VU University, Amsterdam. She has published on the Russian mafia, human trafficking, crime in the diamond sector, XTC industry, underground banking, and the role of women in criminal organizations. Her most recent publications include: *The mazzel ritual: customs, culture and crime in diamond trade* and *Organized crime: culture, markets and policies*.

Russell G. Smith, Ph.D., has qualifications in law, psychology, and criminology from the University of Melbourne and a Ph.D. from King's College London. He is currently Principal Criminologist at the Australian Institute of Criminology and President of the Australian and New Zealand Society of Criminology.

André Solecki is a quantitative researcher in the Department of Justice's Research and Statistics Division, Canada. He completed his thesis in sociology, specializing in quantitative methodologies, at Carleton University in 2007. His areas of research include impaired driving and illicit substances regulation.

Melvin R. J. Soudijn, Ph.D. is Senior Researcher at the National Crime Squad of the Netherlands Police Agency. He has published on Chinese human smuggling, organized crime, art crime, crime prevention, and drug trafficking. His current research is primarily focused on money laundering.

Jiang Tingyao, Ph.D., works at the China University of Political Science and Law. She obtained her doctoral degree in criminal law and justice. She has studied and published in the area of

Chinese, Russian, Canadian, and American organized crime. She studied as a visiting scholar at the University of Montreal in Canada.

Mustafa Cosar Unal, Ph.D. is Chief Superintendent in the Turkish National Police (TNP), Department of Intelligence (DI). He gained his Ph.D. in public policy/administration from University of Maryland Baltimore County. He specializes in terrorism, ethno-terrorism, and counterterrorism policies. Between 2000 and 2002 he worked for the United Nations in Bosnia and Herzegovina.

Matthijs F.J. Vijlbrief is Researcher at the National Crime Squad of the Netherlands Police Agency. In addition, he has several years' experience in the field of crime analysis. His current research is primarily focused on synthetic drugs and the organized crime groups that operate in this field.

Christopher E. S. Warburton, Ph.D. is a member of the Economics Department at John Jay College, City University of New York, where he teaches courses in economics, crime, and research methods. His recent publications include "War and exchange rate valuation" and "International trade law and trade theory".

David L. Weisburd is Walter E. Meyer Professor of Law and Criminal Justice and Director of the Institute of Criminology at the Hebrew University Law School, and Distinguished Professor of Criminology, Law and Society at the Center for Evidence Based Policy, George Mason University, Virginia, USA. He is the 2010 recipient of the Stockholm Prize in Criminology.

Liu Xiu, Ph.D., is an assistant professor at Chengdu University of Technology in China. He received his Ph.D. from China University of Political Science and Law. As a research scholar, he studied criminology at San Diego State University in 2009. He has spent several years conducting research on criminal law and criminology. He has published about 20 papers on crime and law.

Jianhua Xu, Ph.D., is a postdoctoral fellow in the Department of Sociology at the University of Hong Kong. His research interests include crime and policing in China, cultural criminology, social exclusion and crime, victimology, and qualitative methods. Xu is currently exploring how social exclusion affects the production of crime in migrant workers in China.

Lening Zhang, Ph.D. is Professor in the Department of Sociology/Criminal Justice and Director of the Rural Center for Applied Social, Health and Behavioral Research, Saint Francis University, Pennsylvania, USA. He has published about 60 articles and co-edited a book on crime and social control in China.

Foreword

Knowledge in international and comparative criminal justice and criminology has grown considerably since Gerhard O. W. Mueller and I first started teaching at Rutgers in 1974. In the early days, the publisher of our textbook, *Criminology* (1991), thought it was unnecessary to devote a whole chapter to comparative and international criminology. When Elmer H. Johnson edited the *International Handbook of Contemporary Developments in Criminology* in 1983, world criminology and comparative criminal justice were struggling for their place among other disciplines. Johnson described the field as being handicapped by "ethnocentricity." His two-volume text provided seven chapters on the state of criminology throughout the world (e.g. the United Nations, international organizations, feminist and radical criminology perspectives) and forty country chapters. The authors were invited to focus on, "What is criminology?" The responses varied widely based on contributors' placement in education and in the field.

Change, however, has occurred over the last thirty years since Johnson's text. Criminology and criminal justice have moved into the spotlight in many ways. In the United States, the international divisions of both the Academy of Criminal Justice Sciences and the American Society of Criminology have grown from a handful to one of the largest divisions of each organization. The luncheons that provide the networking opportunities for academics have grown from a table of close friends to a reception of over one hundred. In Europe, the British Society of Criminology (1985) and the European Society of Criminology (2000) were founded. In similar fashion, other countries and regions developed professional societies, including the Indian Society of Criminology (1970) and the Asian Criminological Society (2009). Articles on comparative or international research, virtually impossible to publish in the past, now appear in a growing number of internationally focused journals. Criminologists are increasingly being consulted on policy issues. The change started to become visible in the 1970s in the United Nations where Mueller served as the Chief of the Crime Branch, reaching out to academics and non-governmental organizations for knowledge building and assistance and in the American Society of Criminology's work with the United States Attorney General Janet Reno during my presidency. Yes, we have made great strides, but we have not moved along rapidly enough to keep up with the globalization of crime. Other academic and practitioner fields, such as business, economics, and health care, have been racing forward. Unfortunately, Johnson's ethnocentricity is still very much alive in many countries and many universities in the field of criminology and criminal justice. Only a handful of universities have degree programs in international criminology or criminal justice and many universities around the world do not recognize criminology as a field of study.

International criminology can no longer be seen as a luxury for those who have achieved sufficient status to enable them to travel or as a perk given as a reward for some other activity. Rather, changes need to be made in this growing area of concern. It requires retooling to meet the needs of those who have not had the good fortune to be mentored by international criminologists. It requires that students seek out an international mentor and take advantage of international educational opportunities, such as the study abroad semester, the summer course abroad, an international internship, a placement at the United Nations, or the Fulbright program. Universities across the country are rapidly including these overseas opportunities in their curriculum offerings to ensure that their students are given an advantage in obtaining future career goals.

This text is an important step in this preparatory process. The book is divided into three parts. The first part, *Methods and theories*, introduces the reader to the challenges of research and theory building in comparative/international settings. The progress and problems are well documented and thought provoking. Part II, *Special topics*, offers a comprehensive insight into the broad range of our rapidly increasing transnational crime problems and the attempt on the part of international bodies to deal with them. The third part, *Criminology and criminal justice in context*, offers a unique discussion of worldwide criminology. Here we get a most intriguing look at the state of the art of criminology in twenty countries spread around the globe (with the authors' wise caution that definitions and cultural contexts dictate the need for careful comparison). Each of the chapters ends with five research questions that will guide the readers to areas of research that will enable them to move forward in our pioneering efforts in this challenging new perspective.

The foremost scholars in the field of international/comparative criminology have assembled chapters that, when taken together, yield a comprehensive update and thorough analysis of the globalization of crime. It answers many questions, but it raises more. It calls on us to further assess international criminology and to map out its future directions.

Freda Adler
Director, Master of Science in Criminology, University of Pennsylvania
Visiting Professor, Department of Criminology, University of Pennsylvania
Professor Emeritus, Rutgers University

Acknowledgments

This text includes pictures taken by the Dutch police. We are grateful they were willing to share them with us. The editors would like to thank Gerhard Boomgaarden for his inspiration and ever patient demeanor as we moved through the process of coordinating over 50 authors in 48 chapters. Also, we would like to thank Jennifer Dodd for her attention to detail and assistance in keeping the book on track. We thank Lindsey Hall and the many proofreaders for improving this book. Finally, we would like to thank our partners and families for tolerating our endless hours spent at the computer instead of attending to them.

1

Progress of international criminology

Cindy J. Smith, Sheldon X. Zhang, Rosemary Barberet

Criminology has changed tremendously in the past few decades, most of which can be summarized in one word: internationalization. Spurred by the advent of the internet, digital media, and ease of transnational travel, researchers from around the world have increasingly come into contact physically and virtually at a level that was never possible before. These increased and intensified interactions have ushered in a period in crime research in which no one can ignore or overlook what is going on elsewhere.

Crime has been international for a long time. Slavery and sea piracy have existed since antiquity (Felsen and Kalaitzidis, 2005). However, for a long time, scientific inquiry into crime and justice policies was mainly ethnocentric, constrained by researchers' cultural and geographical boundaries. To some extent this mirrored the reach of the criminal justice system, which was largely a domestic venture (see Joutsen, Chapter 12). We no longer have the simplicity of assuming that a crime committed here and now is a local and isolated incident. Examples vary widely, including kidnapping, homicide, drug distribution, and human trafficking. What is considered local or regional has become relative, and geographical boundaries are receding rapidly due to ubiquitous digital media and global commerce. While localized crime continues to occur, the torrents of individuals, groups, and corporations from different countries and cultures clash and produce additional crimes of great intricacy and complexity.

So what is international criminology, as opposed to local or nation-state-based criminology? Multiple terms have been used to describe this research endeavor that is non-local. Adjectives that qualify this brand of research include global, transnational, bi-national, cross-national, trans-border, and comparative. Comparative criminology and criminal justice studies are probably the better known of them all, where we compare cattle theft in two or more nations, pool cross-national data, or examine police practices in one or more nations, or even compare immigrant group behavior in one country. Different researchers will offer up different definitions, all of which can claim some validity. Suffice it to say, there is no definitive definition because it is still evolving, and we do not pretend that we have all the answers to settle the debate once and for all in this book. However, we do want to make significant progress in this book towards a more clarified and uniform definition of what the subject matter is and how we can collectively pursue and build a common knowledge base.

There are two ways to define international criminology. From the perspective of subject matter, international criminology includes the study of: 1) international crime (i.e. activities that are so horrendous that they threaten the very basic human existence – such as genocide), and 2) transnational crime (i.e. activities that are specified in the Palermo convention, so for a particular crime if:

> *(a)* It is committed in more than one State;
> *(b)* It is committed in one State but a substantial part of its preparation, planning, direction, or control takes place in another State;
> *(c)* It is committed in one State but involves an organized criminal group that engages in criminal activities in more than one State; or
> *(d)* It is committed in one State but has substantial effects in another.
>
> *(United Nations, 2000; Article 3(2))*

Based on this definition, it is difficult to identify a crime that can be considered purely domestic (e.g. trafficking of young girls by a local man) or purely international (e.g. trafficking of young girls in one country into another country by a foreign organization), because the local crime has foreign impact and the international crime has a local impact, albeit varying in degree of impact. As a result, it is impossible for researchers to avoid the global perspective in their work.

Although subject matter (or crime type) carries significant influence over a study's general conceptual orientation, it is inadequate in defining international criminology. We believe a much more sensible way to define international criminology is to emphasize the meaningful context with which a researcher contextualizes his/her work and upon which he/she projects the findings. *International criminology is a culturally sensitive and globally mindful approach to crime and social control problems where they happen to be.*

A key element that runs through our examples and main ingredients of this definitional effort is the global and geographically transcending nature of the scientific inquiry. International criminology aims to create a knowledge base that reflects and appreciates political and cultural complexity in a global context, while pointing out the shared and common patterns of human behavior. To put it differently, our scientific inquiry embraces cultural and political diversity, and promotes a nuanced appreciation of different interpretations and applications of research findings. More importantly, we pursue a research agenda that is not only about what or why certainly crime happens, but what it means or implies to people in one context as well as in others.

To some extent, criminology within each nation-state has gone through similar growth in the past century. What researchers found in one particular city early in the 1900s has been applied, modified, replicated, and expanded by other researchers elsewhere in their study of criminal activities. The famous Chicago School is such an example. We are envisioning a further expansion in this century where researchers from different parts of the world, with few geographical and communication constraints, engage in studies with implications beyond their immediate location. It is in this global transcending environment we seek common as well as unique patterns about crime and social control policies.

In this spirit, we attempt to include as diverse a set of examples as possible but constrained only by the physical space allotted by the publisher. Examples in this text include Chapter 21, which discusses how organized criminal groups in the post Cold War era are working together internationally. They are creative and innovative, permeating criminal acts not previously associated with organized crime and dividing the world between the mafias. We must understand how to intervene before their tentacles are permanently embedded throughout the world. On the other hand, Chapter 22 describes how loosely tied Chinese criminal organizations migrated to different corners of the world, taking advantage of emerging criminal enterprises. Thus, even a seemingly isolated incident may be connected to a greater organization.

This text articulates this relatively new way of thinking about criminology that challenges the existing knowledge built on the traditional nation-state-based justice system and monocultural production of criminological knowledge. We embrace the intricacies of complex cultural and law violating behaviors and conceptualize our research from a perspective that finds various legal and social transgressions not easily defined through one's own cultural lenses. For instance, amidst transnational crimes we find in each country or culture its own unique crime problems, as well as problems in common with many other countries. Transnational crime crosses national borders and is often exacerbated by borderless technologies. Examples include some acts of terrorism, drug or people trafficking, piracy of intellectual property, and cybercrime. On the other hand, international crime is legally defined as when a crime affects humanity regardless of where it is perpetrated, such as war crimes and crimes against humanity. It is reasonable to think that these crimes might fall under international law, such as the Rome Statute of the International Criminal Court. However, all of these crimes also may fall within domestic jurisdiction. It is with this framework that this text provides an introduction or overview of international criminology and its components. The detail in this text is sufficient to introduce and discuss the contours of this framework, but the general topic is so broad that each component could fill its own book.

Some of the specific questions addressed in this handbook include: What has been our understanding and response to international criminology? What do we know about international crime? How does our crime compare to their crime? Do we know what causes these crimes? Do we have theories that cross borders and cultures? Do we have laws that cross borders and cultures? Are our research methods adaptable to international crime research, which includes comparative crime research? What has been the response to international, transnational, and domestic crime? Is one country responding more effectively than another? Do we understand the transferability of our "successful" programs? These questions are not yet adequately addressed in the current knowledge found in textbooks and journal publications.

One oft-cited shortcoming of the existing "international criminology" texts is that they were written by the Anglo-Saxon academics (e.g. United States, United Kingdom, Canada, and Australia), without the benefit or full knowledge of the differences in cultures and the input from our fellow scholars around the world. Although this is not to downplay the significance of our fellow English-speaking authors, the lack of representation of perspectives or voices native to other parts of the world is rather glaring in our current state of knowledge on international criminology (see also Barberet, 2007). This text makes a remedial attempt at addressing this gap.

Diversity

Much like the world described in this book, this text is strong in its diversity. First, the text is diverse in the topics it covers, research methods, and international and national crime. It covers some of the most cutting-edge international crime topics (e.g. cybercrime), as well as the more traditional topics, such as terrorism and drugs. The 20 country assessments of the state of criminology and the criminal justice system include countries from North and South America, Europe, Asia, Australia, and Africa. Second, the authorship of this text is truly international. Among the 54 authors, only 14 are from the US and many have a mother tongue other than English. Additionally, the gender mix is approaching equal. This brings a culturally diverse perspective to the topics discussed.

This text was written with three guiding principles. First, to foster a future generation of international criminologists, teams of authors were preferred with a seasoned author paired with a newer international author. Eleven chapters were co-authored with this in mind, providing an opportunity for mentoring newer scholars while ensuring high quality and state-of-the-art information is included in the text. Second, the text was written for readers at the third year of undergraduate school or beyond with the intention of raising their awareness for possible academic careers, as well as for the purpose of providing libraries with a clearly written handbook for the uninitiated scholar. The chapters provide the state-of-being of each topic in context and conclude with five research questions that will help to guide future research. Third, this text comes at a time when universities are increasing their international breadth with students, both in the classroom and through the use of online courses where geographic location does not dictate the nationality of the student population. Therefore, its diversity responds to the increasing diversity of the student population worldwide.

The state of criminology

Criminology is lagging behind other disciplines in terms of internationalizing its research and broadening the cultural awareness of its students and faculty. The world has globalized, creating new business and crime opportunities. Business began to globalize in the seventeenth century and modernized through the technology boom after World War II. Crime opportunity expanded to these new markets, incorporating new methods. Our response to crime around the world is slowly changing. Our research in international criminology is at a snail's pace.

Three major changes have been instrumental in the recent rapid change in globalization. Transportation (e.g. airline industry), technology (e.g. borderless technologies such as the internet), and communication (e.g. mass media, mobile phones, and satellite) have changed the way the world does business and interacts. Unfortunately, the same conditions that changed the economic and social interactions between and within countries also have changed crime (Howard *et al.* 2000; Smith, 2009).

Crime research in an international context implies comparison, often between and among nations. However, social, political, and cultural differences in international research often lead to definitional challenges. The same criminal behavior may be counted differently and the judicial environments of different legal systems may produce different outcomes. For instance, in the US attempted murders are counted as aggravated assault, but they are treated as other homicides in England and Australia (Lynch, 1995).

Definitional issues aside, different justice systems also respond to crime and criminals differently. For instance, plea bargains are widely practiced in the US criminal justice, in which the accused may accept a lesser charge or even admit to an entirely different crime. Such a practice allows the prosecution to shorten the legal proceedings and cut down workload, while the accused avoids the uncertainty of a trial for the charged offense. However, such a practice would be unthinkable in many other legal systems.

International organizations that routinely gather crime data, such as the United Nations, European Sourcebook and, until recently, INTERPOL, caution against inappropriate use (i.e. making country comparisons), because of differences in the way that crime is defined, reported, measured, and reacted to in different countries (United Nations, 2006). In the United States, the most commonly referenced national crime data are produced from two sources: the Uniform Crime Reports (UCR) and the National Crime Victimization Survey (NCVS). There are few venues where cross-national crime data are routinely gathered and published.

The United Nations Office on Drugs and Crime (UNODC) is probably the only organization that gathers and publishes cross-national crime data, since INTERPOL stopped releasing its data. Through the UN Survey of Crime Trends and Operations of Criminal Justice Systems the UNODC provides crime data pooled from Member States and its own survey mechanism. Spreadsheets of various crime data are readily available for download at the UNODC website (http://www.unodc.org/unodc/en/data-and-analysis/crimedata.html). Of all crimes, homicide probably has the most comparable definition. UNODC presents statistics of homicide in a more refined analysis than all other crime statistics, which are simply kept in spreadsheet formats for download purposes.

Thus, the state of criminology is lagging behind other disciplines in terms of internationalization. That is to say, the world of technology and business have expanded rapidly, creating new crime, and the academic discipline is struggling with definition, differing responses to crime, minimal data collection across nations, and almost no comparable international data collection. This text attempts to shed light on these issues.

Format of the book

The text is divided into three parts: (1) research methods, (2) international crime topics, and (3) country specific case studies. The goal of the part on research methods is to discuss the main analytical strategies researchers have employed to examine crime problems nationally, as well as in an international comparative or transnational context. Comparative research methods are more comprehensive than the traditional methods commonly taught in the Western world. In addition to a solid implemented research design, comparative research methods place the research and subjects in a contextual framework (Howard, et al. 2000; Smith, 2009). Simply stated, comparative research methods highlight the contextual similarities and differences between the research subjects. This enables the findings to be generalized to the relevant group, as opposed to generalizing to a greater population made up of various cultural groups, each having its own norms, moral, and values. Chapter 21 by Arsovska is an example of this contextualization as she discusses the United Nations' origins of the definition of organized crime. Without the understanding of this context, researchers are led to criticize the definition when it is the only way to make the Convention against Transnational Organized Crime applicable to all member states. The first chapter in the research methods section (Chapter 3) includes a discussion of the challenges of doing criminal justice and criminology research during an era when it is not respected and not considered mainstream. The next two chapters, Chapters 4 and 5, provide the qualitative and quantitative perspectives of international research. Chapter 6 provides a slightly different perspective, using an update on a decade of research through the Campbell Collaboration. In Chapter 7, Karn examines how crime prevention and evaluation fit into criminology and criminal justice.

> Though understanding if and why a policy worked is crucial, the need to evaluate it in a way that will convince others in these limited terms has the potential to guide policy development not towards what works but what can be evaluated . . . A key problem for policy exchange internationally is that initiatives with limited aims and limited approaches, particularly situational approaches, suit this form of evaluation, putting pressure on those attempting to implement "evidence-based policy" to advocate such approaches. (p. 73)

Chapter 8 discusses theory building and its transferability between cultures. Chapter 9 provides an example of the knowledge base that is built when data are available. The final chapter, Chapter 10, places three more pieces into the methods puzzle: definition, contextualization, and partnership.

Part II of this text includes 17 special topics chapters with a mix of both traditional and contemporary crime topics. With traditional crimes being committed through technology from anywhere in the world, the international and transnational crime types continue to grow. Thus, Part II could have hundreds of chapters as crime becomes less geographically bound under national jurisdiction. Additionally, Part II could have numerous chapters related to prevention, intervention, and criminal justice systems. In other words, each country may have specific problem crimes. However, these crimes are also shared with neighboring countries where cultures are similar and only arbitrary boundaries of nation states divide the issue into countries. Thus, the crimes may be transnational, as well as domestic. After the introductory chapter, the topics include two chapters on the United Nations, one on international criminal courts and 12 on crime-specific topics (e.g. cybercrime, immigration, trafficking of drugs and human beings, gangs). The final chapter discusses one aspect of the criminal justice system – the role of prosecutors in the demand from the public and policymakers for increased punitiveness for immigrant crime. The chapter discusses how the Italian prosecutors have been somewhat immune to these pressures and the impact on the other components of the criminal justice system.

In Part II, authors provide a case study of the specific transnational or borderless topic. For example, Kangaspunta (Chapter 18) provides an overview of the state of trafficking in persons, including the UN Protocol and its implementation by various countries, ending with a discussion of the relative success of countries of finding victims and prosecuting traffickers while articulating the routes and investigative activities, providing both depth and breadth of the topic. A more detailed lead-in for each chapter is provided in the introduction chapter at the beginning of Part II, from which readers can acquire a quick overview of these special topics.

Part III of this text places criminology and criminal justice in the country context. Each of the 20 countries is a case study describing indicators of its national profile (infrastructure, people), the administration of justice, the state-of-being of criminology, and a brief summary of the institutions that can foster and encourage international criminology (i.e. professional organizations, funding agencies). These chapters are more structured in content and theme. They can be used to compare countries and criminal justice systems with the cautions discussed in this text.

Because of space limitations, we were forced to choose a set of countries that to some extent "represent" the main classification of nations along a broad socio-political axis. The case studies can be grouped into three tiers based on income: countries with rich academic traditions in criminological and criminal justice research (e.g. Australia, Canada, Estonia, Great Britain, Hong Kong, Italy, South Korea, Netherlands), middle countries (e.g. Brazil, Chile, Mexico, Russian Federation, Turkey), and developing nations (e.g. Cambodia, People's Republic of China, Colombia, Ghana, India, Nigeria, Sierra Leone). A brief introduction is included at the beginning of this section to provide a quick overview of the essential themes of the country profiles.

Response to internationalization

As a comprehensive reader on international criminology, this book provides undergraduate and graduate students with the foundation of where to go to find information, how to integrate an international perspective into criminology where it has been ignored or excluded for many years, and how to discuss the issues that are found in good research. Similarly, it provides the more experienced scholar with a resource book that is useful for undertaking international criminological research.

In 1983, Elmer H. Johnson wrote *International Handbook of Contemporary Developments in Criminology*, a ground-breaking work at the time, when international criminology was in its infancy. Many of the questions Johnson asked his authors (p. 24) were repeated in the request to the authors in this text (e.g. What research is being conducted? By whom? What is the state of criminology?). Some progress has taken place. For example, a plethora of international journals has cropped up over the last few years. This enables scholars to publish their single-topic original research articles. Unfortunately, too few international scholars have prepared too few up-and-coming scholars. This is partially the result of the lack of recognition of international research and the related reward structure. Most of the new international journals are not indexed, as a result of the economic impact of adding new journals to the existing indexing structure operated by private industry. This limitation results in the hesitation of new scholars to enter the field, knowing that their work will carry less weight in the reward structure (see Chapter 3 for a full discussion). Sadly, the "insularity" (i.e. "the tendency to be convinced without careful consideration that the beliefs of one's own ethnic group are superior to those of other groups" Johnson, 1983, p. xiii) still exists in criminology today and is quite evident in the superiority of the quantitative focus of the Western world to the detriment of accurate and relevant findings. The solution to this problem is the contextualization of the findings found in the qualitative data largely ignored in Western criminology. However, until the informal power and reward structures are modified, budding criminologists will emulate yesterday's insularity.

The problem of insularity is further complicated by linguistic barriers. With the most dominant journals published in English, research findings and viewpoints from non-English speaking countries do not get adequate exposure. The hesitance and sometimes reluctance are palpable in international conferences where English is the only working language. Meaningful debate and exchange of ideas are only limited by the level of comprehension and communication of the English language.

The group of international criminologists is growing, but still quite small relative to the traditional criminologist numbers. One measure of the number of prepared criminologists over the last seven years is the average membership of the Division of International Criminology, hovering at 325 out of approximately 2,500 members of the American Society of Criminology. Although not every criminologist with an international perspective is a member of this group, it is indicative of the proportions. These members represent criminologists, anthropologists, sociologists, and legal scholars. However, generally the field is lacking in numbers and in an integrated interdisciplinary approach to international criminology.

The number of academic programs teaching criminology as a discipline is growing, and the same is with the number of programs including one or two courses on international criminology (Cordner *et al.*, 2000). Therefore, students are getting a small sprinkling of international criminology. The US has lagged behind other English-speaking countries in developing the field of international criminology. For example, the UK has many master's-level international criminology courses in its curriculums. Unfortunately, there is little guidance on how to conduct international criminology research if a student has the desire. This text will fill part of this void in the literature.

Limitations

Constrained by the length of the book and the volume of topics that could be addressed under the heading of international criminology, many topics were either briefly discussed or left out of the book entirely. This does not indicate that they are any less important. In fact, it is more likely that the omitted topics are exactly where we have a limited knowledge base, thus making them even more important than those discussed in detail in the text. For example, only one chapter could be devoted to discussing theories of crime and their relative transferability from one culture to another (see Chapter 8). However, Western theories are discussed in volumes. For example, Strain Theory has been developed and used to explain crime in the Western world. It is possible that it has been applied in developing countries, but there is very limited empirical testing and no coherent body of literature that draws together international crime theory. Other topics were not included, such as the impact of religion on criminal justice, or only briefly touched upon, such as research ethics of human subjects protection, not because they are unimportant, but because the literature is scant and expert researchers in these topics unknown. Still other topics were discussed, but limited in scope by the length of the chapters, such as finding equivalent measures in qualitative and quantitative methods in an international context.

Partnerships between researchers across countries and between researchers and practitioners are only briefly discussed in Chapter 10. Partnership knowledge is only slightly better than in 1983, albeit Johnson discussed the merits and difficulties within the field, equating partnerships with practitioners to applied versus pure research and the resulting respectability of applied research. This debate continues. Despite its limited range of topics, we believe this text represents a major step forward in developing and promoting criminology that is truly international in scope and/or comparative in nature. Students and young scholars can be assured that they are exposed to the most current knowledge available in the field.

Looking forward – next steps

Each chapter concludes with relevant research questions for the respective topic, outlining the research needs of the field in terms of the next steps. Students and young scholars alike can learn about the most pressing issues that remain unstudied or understudied in the field of international criminology. One can use these suggested topics to quickly formulate research agendas and plot strategies.

References

Barberet, R. (2007). The internationalization of criminology? A content analysis of presentations at the American Society of Criminology Conferences. *Journal of Criminal Justice Education*, 18(3): 406–27.

Cordner, A. Dammer, H., and Horvath, F. (2000). A national survey of comparative criminal justice courses in universities in the United States. *Journal of Criminal Justice Education*, 11: 211–23.

Felsen, D. and Kalaitzidis, A. (2005). A historical overview of transnational crime. In P. Reichel (Ed.) *Handbook of transnational crime and justice*, pp. 3–19. Thousand Oaks, CA: Sage.

Howard, G. J. Newman, G., and Pridemore, W. A. (2000). Theory, method, and data in comparative criminology (from measurement and analysis of crime and justice.) *Criminal Justice 2000* (4): 139–211. Washington, DC: National Institute of Justice, Office of Justice Programs, US Department of Justice. Online at http://www.ncjrs.gov/criminal_justice2000/vol4_2000.html (accessed May 20, 2007).

Johnson, E. H. (ed). (1983). *International handbook of contemporary developments in criminology: general issues and the Americas*. London: Greenwood Press.

Lynch, J. (1995). Crime in international perspective. In James Q. Wilson and Joan Petersilia (Eds.) *Crime*, pp. 11–38. San Francisco, CA: ICS Press.

Smith, C. J. (2009). Comparative methods: going beyond incorporating international comparative research methods with traditional methods. *International Journal of Comparative and Applied Criminal Justice*, 32(2): 211–28. Official Journal of the Division of International Criminology of the ASC.

United Nations (2000) *Convention against transnational organized crime*. December. Palermo, Italy.

—— (2006). *Fundamental principles of official statistics*. United Nations Statistics Division. Online at http://unstats.un.org/unsd/methods/statorg/FP-English.htm (accessed September 6, 2010).

Part I
Methods and theories

2

Introduction to international research challenges

Cindy J. Smith

Considering the existing breadth of challenges in international research on crime and the complexities of conducting research across time, space, and cultures, the spectrum of potential topics to be included was endless. This section of the text could focus on the various components of the research design, but there is not a universal understanding of the components of the research design. For example, mainstream criminologists articulate the components of the research design in the following ways:

> In the most generic sense, research may be categorized as quantitative or qualitative. In traditional texts, the research design may be categorized based on its experimental degree (e.g., experimental, quasi-experimental, and non-experimental), or as a progression or goal of research, which reflects a hierarchical nature, articulated as exploratory, descriptive, and explanatory designs. Finally, traditional research designs may be categorized based on data collection strategies, such as surveys, case studies, and secondary data designs. Another perspective to research design is categorized based on the nature of the data, such as cross-sectional and longitudinal designs.
>
> *(Smith, 2009, p. 215)*

If we were to use this cadre of topics, the book would be too lengthy. And international research methods – where populations to be studied are not homogeneous – must include more detailed discussions, such as data challenges, comparable measures, comparative methods, transferability, cultural versus national perspectives, and partnerships. Selecting the most important topics for this section thus became a task in prioritizing issues of comparable or equal importance. As a result of the limited space in the book, the authors were asked to cover broadly the challenges in the field of criminology, including qualitative, quantitative, and theoretical perspectives.

The goal of Part I is to discuss the main analytical strategies researchers have employed to examine crime problems nationally, as well as in a comparative and transnational context. Part I begins with Medina's discussion of the roadblocks to crime research as a result of the lack of global acceptance of criminology as a discipline, thus moving the research and the researchers to the periphery in many parts of the world. As discussed in Chapter 1, international criminologists are even further in the periphery.

Chapters 4 and 5 present the qualitative and quantitative debates. Huggins charges that the focus on quantitative criminology is US centric and narrowly centered on crimes of the underclass. Qualitative research provides insight into a more comprehensive criminology, including the crimes of the state. However, in Chapter 5, van Dijk contends that through the advent of computer technology, quantitative comparative studies are increasing rapidly and globalization has resulted in comparable datasets, especially among victim surveys.

There is a debate among criminologists about whether efforts in evaluation should focus on the outcomes or the implementation. Of course, the best methods dictate that proof of program fidelity should be determined through an implementation evaluation and only then can outcomes be useful. In Chapter 6, Farrington, Weisburd and Gill present the progress made in research based on the Campbell Collaboration. They answer questions such as what works to reduce crime and what is most cost effective, through the systematic review of high-quality evidence-based evaluation studies.

In Chapter 7, Karn presents the issues in the lesser discussed and more recently developed topic of crime prevention. Crime prevention takes a proactive rather than a reactive approach to crime, which does not complement the punitive policy making in a post 9/11 era. The discussion outlines the concepts of crime prevention and then speaks directly about the implications for policy transfer, especially from developed to developing countries.

Part I ends with a study of applying Western theory and methods to the Eastern culture of China. If any Western theory holds any universal truth about its ability to explain or predict criminal behavior, then it also must be verified in different cultural contexts. However, testing Western criminology theories and methods directly in non-Western countries invariably requires linguistic and cultural familiarity. Zhang suggests that this is only appropriate if the researcher knows and understands the local cultural context. Chapter 9 presents the progress in crime research that has occurred as a result of worldwide data collection. Chapter 10 highlights commonly missing pieces in today's research and challenges future researchers to improve the quality of research findings by incorporating these additional concepts.

In sum, we believe Part I of the *Handbook* goes beyond the more mundane discussions of the problems of comparison that have been dealt with in the literature on international criminology to date, and will provoke reflection among experienced readers as well as those newer to the field in the planning and appreciation of future research in international criminology.

References

Smith, C. J. (2009). Comparative methods: going beyond incorporating international comparative research methods with traditional methods. *International Journal of Comparative and Applied Criminal Justice*, 32(2): 211–28. Official Journal of the Division of International Criminology of the ASC.

3

Doing criminology in the "semi-periphery" and the "periphery"

In search of a post-colonial criminology

Juanjo Medina

Introduction

This chapter aims to reflect on some of the challenges facing criminologists doing criminological research "in the periphery"; that is, outside those countries with a more established and solid criminological community and research tradition. Being from the semi-periphery and maintaining strong links with it, I have spent most of my academic life working in the North Transatlantic "core," namely the US and the UK. It should be clear from the outset that my own understanding of the challenges facing criminology outside the core has been powerfully colored by my own personal experiences and those of researchers closer to me. In this sense I am more familiar with the challenges encountered in my own home country (Spain), and other Spanish-speaking countries, as compared to the US and the UK than elsewhere. Nevertheless, I also believe that the challenges facing Spanish-speaking criminologists are not unique, but representative in many ways of many other national realities.

Often in the social sciences the apparent impartiality and neutrality of the rules of the game we aspire to follow in the production of knowledge blind us to the ingrained social and economic inequalities that shape the structure of our field and the consequently biased specificities of knowledge associated with this structure. Although awareness towards some forms of "written out criminological knowledge" (that produced by minority scholars or females) has increased in recent times, criminology remains structured in such a way that knowledge produced in the periphery continues to be neglected and often considered of an insufficient standard. That this has taken place despite the significance of post-colonial theory in other areas of the social science contributes to the reputation of criminology among non-criminologists social scientists as a rather conservative or middle-of-the-ground enterprise. This chapter intends to develop a greater appreciation for this "written out" criminology and for the scholars who work in these environments.

Before I begin describing some of the challenges, it is worthwhile briefly discussing the ideas of the "core," "periphery" and "semi-periphery". The concepts of core and periphery were popularized and developed by Wallerstein (2004) in his world systems theory. Wallerstein suggested that the world economy is organized around two interdependent regions (core and periphery) hierarchically related, in which the powerful and wealthy "core" societies dominate and exploit "weak" and poor peripheral societies. In his account, technology and science play a central role in this positioning and the peripheral countries are constrained to experience a type of development reproducing their subordinate status. According to Wallerstein's account semi-peripheral states act as a buffer zone between core and periphery. Wallerstein used these concepts to highlight the profound economic differences across the world and to challenge the idea of modernization as a driver of development.

I use these terms in a rather loose way, not as absolute categories but as representing different points in a continuum, and not in the strict Wallerstein sense. It is clear that the US is the country, followed by the UK, with a more established criminological community as represented by a number of indicators (the number of universities offering degrees, the number of PhD students, and the number of journals), and that therefore sits clearly in what we could call the "core." This is, for example, clearly reflected in the data of attendance to the European Society of Criminology conference. Since its first annual meeting in Lausanne in 2001 and with the exception of the Tubingen annual meeting in 2006, the largest contingent of criminologists attending the meeting have come from the UK, often with a proportion of two to one with the second country in the list. Equally, although this is a European conference, criminologists from the US have always figured as one of the top five most represented countries in this conference (Nobli and Crocitti, 2008).

Even if we admit that the US and the UK represent the core, the semi-periphery and the periphery are more diffused categories. For example, where do you locate Canada, Australia or the Netherlands? If we were to talk of a semi-periphery in criminology given its current level of development we could possibly locate most of continental Europe and some other English-speaking countries, and then a "periphery" where our discipline is even more diluted in a landscape where historically criminology may have a more troublesome past of justifying authoritarian repression (Aniyar de Castro, 1987; Huggins, 1998) or colonial domination (Agozino, 2004).

Different degrees of academic institutionalization: problems for recognition and stable careers

Disciplines are intellectual categories, cultures and institutional structures (Wallerstein, 2003). In this latter sense, as institutional structures (e.g. departments in universities, specialized degrees, scholarly journals, national associations, shelves in bookstores), a review of the situation of criminology across different countries reveals a continuum of development with the core countries at one end with fully developed structures and periphery countries on the other, striving for institutional recognition and organizational autonomy.

In the US and the UK some consider this discipline has grown so much that it needs to be reconsidered (Garland, 2008). Indeed, one of the first challenges that scholars outside the core countries face is gaining recognition for their work and an institutional space where they can carry out their work. This limited institutionalization has repercussions for achieving a sense of respect for their work and it also implies limited reward in the development of one academic career. The problem of inadequate recognition for the discipline is magnified in countries with a more bureaucratic, rigid and formalistic university environment where, such as in Italy or Spain, academic subjects fall within bureaucratically established areas crucial for recruiting faculty as well as attracting government funding (Maffei and Merzagora Betsos, 2007, p. 465). Criminology in these institutions does not have the formal recognition as an academic discipline in its own right.

In countries where criminology is not a recognized discipline, criminological research is often carried out as a "part time" enterprise (Barberet, 2005), subject to low pay, in the context of criminal law, and surrounded by colleagues with little knowledge of the culture, development and recognition of the discipline. Scholars in criminology are ostracized from their "parent" disciplines and often have to justify the relevance of their existence to their peers. Criminologists often have to migrate to the UK and the US to continue their careers (Oberwittler and Hofer, 2005). Those who stay may pay the price of personal isolation and greater difficulty in gaining academic promotions and appointments, because they are judged by others with little criminological knowledge. In Spain, for example, many colleagues of my generation are still in contracts with pay and stability equivalent to those of graduate teaching assistants despite their remarkable achievements. Not surprisingly, in these contexts scholars interested in criminology have a vested interest in advocating for greater recognition by university authorities and government funding (Redondo Illescas, 2001; Medina Ariza, 2002).[1] Research is still carried out by these scholars, who face adverse environments while pursuing the satisfaction of being national pioneers no matter what field they explore. However, these challenges hamper the stability required by researchers to produce work that can compete internationally.

Different degrees of the "governmental project": the role of administrative criminology

The relationship between science and policy in the field of criminology is without doubt a complex one that is played out in different ways in different countries. However, the level of commitment by the state towards the development of knowledge about crime and criminal justice often goes a long way in explaining why criminology has become institutionalized in some countries but not in others.

When writing about the origins of British criminology, Garland (1997, p. 12) contended that "modern criminology grew out of the convergence of two quite separate enterprises: the 'governmental project' and the 'Lombrosian project.'" The first was linked to state efforts to develop a more efficient and equitable crime control system and the second was orientated towards developing a better understanding of crime. It was only the combination of these two that proved essential to the academic institutionalization of criminology. Equally, across the world the institutionalization of criminology as an academic discipline and recognized field of research has been closely linked to the interest of different states in producing knowledge about the functioning of their respective criminal justice systems.

It is perhaps no accident that in the two countries with the largest and most productive criminological communities, the UK and the US, crime features prominently as a cultural phenomenon that is taken seriously by citizens and politicians (Garland, 2001). These are also the countries in which policy makers and government administrators are also, at least rhetorically, committed to the notion of "evidence based policy" or of "experimenting society."

One factor common in the US and the UK is the strong government support for criminological research. This support is evidenced by the many government agencies, such as the Home Office Research and Statistics Directorate, the Bureau of Justice Statistics or the National Institute of Justice, which carry out internal research or fund external projects. Although the political, theoretical and methodological agenda of these institutions, as well as their practices, is often questioned by criminologists of a critical disposition as being too conservative in nature and narrowly focused, this "administrative criminology" produces a large body of information, resources and governmental positions that simply do not exist in most other countries.

In other words, although administrative criminology can be manipulated (Hope, 2004) and create problems of its own for crime control policy and for academic researchers (Walters, 2003), it also helps to create a vibrant field of criminology in these countries. These government research institutions have developed rich data about their criminal justice institutions, crime prevention schemes and their respective crime problems. Critically they may also have contributed to a culture of "relative" transparency among criminal justice agencies that encourages data quality and outcome measures. Van Swaaningen's (2006) account of the role of the Dutch Ministry of Justice's Research and Documentation Centre (WODC) and the Netherlands Institute for the Study of Crime and Law Enforcement clearly illustrate the important role these institutions play in shaping the field of criminology at the national level.

On the other hand, government-sponsored criminological research cannot be taken for granted. As Liu (2009) points out, "frequently, governments consider crime-related data to be politically sensitive and are reluctant to disclose them to researchers." In most countries around the world there are few agencies comparable to the Home Office Research and Statistics Directorate or the National Institute of Justice. This has significant implications for the type of statistical information that is being gathered, its transparency and quality standards on data collection methods.[2] The absence of government involvement restricts funding to research projects. Such absence tends to diminish the rhetorical weight of criminologists in policy and political decision making.

The rich data generated by government agencies in the UK and the US do not automatically translate into good policy. In fact, it is rather puzzling to realize how incredibly punitive, regressive and counterproductive criminal justice policies are in the UK and the US despite the amount of information available to policy makers in these two countries. This contradiction demonstrates that the "experimenting society" and the "Maryland" approach to criminal justice policy are based on a rather candid view of the world of politics. Evidence-based policy often turns into policy-driven evidence (Matthews, 2009).

The paradoxical result of this is that in countries with a more established criminological tradition we can witness the development of critical interpretations of "administrative" or governmental criminology. In the periphery, "critical" or "public" criminologists are the ones who often have to carry out the basic "positivistic" descriptive research about the function of the criminal justice system that we often associate with administrative criminology. In contexts where discussions about crime policy do not even consider data about the realities of the criminal justice system, generating these data to inform debates has a strong critical edge and often becomes one of the main tasks of academic researchers hoping to elevate the tone of the policy debate and to ground it in the everyday realities of criminal justice. This has implications as well for the limited international recognition and relevance granted to the work of these scholars that will normally be perceived as too descriptive, basic or of little relevance to the Anglo-American experience.

It's the money, stupid . . .

Data from the Organisation for Economic Co-operation and Development show that there is significant variation across countries in their civil research and development expenditure. It is difficult to access cross-national data on social science research expenditure and even more so on criminological research expenditure. In this context, it is difficult to judge claims by researchers based in different countries complaining about the lack of access to sufficient research funds (Kerezsi and Levay, 2008; Olafsdottir and Bragadottir, 2006; O'Donnell, 2005; Barberet, 2005). This is a common complaint among researchers no matter how abundant research funds are in their own respective country, particularly given the increased competitiveness for these resources. Yet the lack of clear and comparable quantitative indicators cannot prevent us from highlighting the relevance of differential expenditure on criminological research by both private and public institutions as an additional challenge facing criminologists in the periphery. There is no question that (1) these differences exist, even if it is hard to quantify them, and that (2) they do have a significant impact on the type of research one can do and its impact. The literature on research productivity has documented a strong and clear correlation between receiving grants or special funding support for research and success on scholarly publication (Teodorescu, 2000).

Differences in funding vary significantly from country to country. For example, the Economic and Social Research Council, the main public body funding social science research in the UK, formally considers a "small grant" anything below £100,000, which is subject to the expedited review process of 14 weeks. These small awards are often tailored more towards younger researchers. However, in Spain, the Ministry of Education rarely provides grants for social science research projects over €40,000 and only after several months of deliberation. These awards need to be split among medium-sized teams of researchers (Barberet, 2005). These funding differences constrain research designs and dramatically condition the type of research questions examined. Complex data-gathering projects integrating individual and community level measures or qualitative and quantitative components, quantitative or the more ambitious qualitative longitudinal designs and project evaluations with sufficient statistical power and sample size become almost impossible to achieve in these national contexts. There is simply not enough money to support these expensive but state-of-the-art research designs. These methods are also linked to the increasing theoretical and analytical complexities of the field. The inability to use such sophisticated methods places researchers in a disadvantageous position.

That is not to say that one can only do research with these expensive designs. As we say in Spanish "*el hambre agudiza el ingenio*" (hunger makes you sharper). These limitations indeed force researchers to use creative solutions. It may mean that the standards of what is considered acceptable evidence or a good study may be flexible. There may be more quasi experiments with small sample sizes, ethnographic studies conducted by lone researchers, small-scale surveys with less fancy methods of data collection and limited quality control, or manual collection of archival data. Some of these studies may be very good. However, such small-scale studies will in general make it more difficult (1) to publish in journals where the standards are higher and subject to methodological fashion, (2) to interest people to attend your conference presentations and (3) more generally, to acquire an international recognition as anything other than an expert for one's home country.

Publishing and language

With limited budget and access to government-sponsored criminal justice data, even electronic data such as the National Archive of Criminal Justice, scholars working in the periphery face an uphill struggle to produce work of sufficient quality to reach international standards of recognition. Even when successfully meeting these challenges, researchers face additional difficulties in getting their work published in internationally ranked journals that Anglo-American criminologists do not experience. This is particularly problematic in the new globalized context where higher education operates. As recognized by many, "governments around the world are holding their own academics, sociologists included, accountable to 'international' standards, which means publishing in 'Western' journals, and in particular American journals" (Burawoy, 2005, p. 284).[3]

Clearly language barriers are an important challenge. Of the 31 journals for which an impact index is computed in the ISE Web of Knowledge and classified as criminological in the *Journal Citation Reports*, only two admit articles in a language other than English. English is indeed the international language of science. Being able to speak and write in English is simply a requirement that those who want to do science must accept. The existence of a lingua franca indeed facilitates communication among researchers and can be a driver for cross-fertilization. Unfortunately this renders the work of many scholars from non-English-speaking countries invisible to the international readership. Younger scholars from non-English-speaking countries are more fluent in English than their predecessors and this may be less of a problem in the future. But this has indeed been a factor that historically has limited the influence of criminological research outside English-speaking countries. Not surprisingly some criminologists from non-English-speaking countries have demanded editorial policies in criminological journals be more sensitive to these linguistic issues (e.g. more support to papers with poor English, multilingual journals and acceptance of translated papers originally published in a language other than English).[4] But rarely have these calls been heard, even in the case of journals representing international professional societies.

More problematically not only do the majority of criminological journals in the *Journal Citation Reports* use English, but the overwhelming majority of them (26 out of 31) are published in either the US or the UK and their editorial boards are composed of criminologists mostly based in American or British universities. This fact illustrates the degree to which the Anglo-American experience with crime and crime control has shaped current criminological knowledge and debates. This, in itself, has implications for those aiming to publish in these journals – they are expected to both know and care greatly for the Anglo-American experience. An American researcher is not expected to explain common acronyms (e.g. UCR, NCVS). Equally, when writing about criminal justice in these two countries, one need not provide background details about the history or the configuration of the particular criminal justice institution simply because both editors and writers are presumed to be familiar with the cultural environment. This, however, is a common problem facing those in the periphery. They are often asked (1) to explain what to them is the obvious and (2) to situate their findings in relation to issues and debates that affect primarily the Anglo-American context. The end result is that most of what gets published in these journals is quite parochial in scope and of questionable relevance to most of the world. Burawoy (2005, p. 289), in his advocacy for a public sociology, argued that along this process "national sociologies lose their engagement with national problems and local issues" with these external demands.

The indifferent "core" criminology? The unidirectional transference of knowledge

Much has been written recently in criminology about the transfer of policy ideas and their underpinning theories, with a primary focus on the "transatlantic crossings" from the US to Europe (Wacquant, 1999; Newburn, 2002; Jones and Newburn, 2002) and other parts of the world (Huggins, 1998; Brogden and Nijhar, 2005). This emerging literature on policy transfer of criminal justice ideas often reflects a concern with the entrepreneurial exportation of policy and theoretical models from the American "juggernaut" that to European sensibilities is somehow unpalatable, too conservative or simply inadequate to explain their own contexts. As Brogden and Nijhar (2005, p. 81) point out in reference to community policing, Anglo-American inventions are exported overseas as the only valid models, denying the legitimacy of other alternatives. Indeed, as highlighted by many, one of the dangers of comparative criminal justice and criminology is that of ethnocentrism: "assuming that what we do, our way of thinking about and responding to crime, is universally shared or, at least, that it would be right for everyone else" (Nelken, 2009, p. 291). Implicit in the ambivalence about or direct opposition to the transferability of such concepts as broken windows policing or research on youth gangs in Europe is the recognition of the danger of ethnocentrism. Yet the structural factors as highlighted earlier and the strength of Anglo-American criminology make the transfer of knowledge about crime and crime control largely unidirectional from the core to the periphery.

There is also a certain degree of *orientalism*, which envisions all countries outside the US and the UK as fundamentally similar to one another and fundamentally dissimilar from the US and the UK. Karstedt (2001) has written about the common tendency to treat cultures as monolithic entities and how as a result cultural comparisons in criminology suffer from exaggerations of differences. For instance, Anglo-American criminologists tend to talk about Asian exceptionalism in relation to crime and crime control. The same reasoning can also be applied to some of the current writing on punitiveness and the way that European countries are often clustered together under a "welfare" model that supposedly prevents high levels of incarceration (Nelken, 2009; Larrauri, 2008). This way of thinking about the periphery demands that scholars outside the US and the UK demonstrate through their research the danger of extreme relativism as well as parochialism (Nelken, 2009).

This is not a global indictment of Anglo-American criminology. Their wealth of ideas has certainly energized theoretical and empirical work elsewhere and that, in itself, is not a bad thing. Moreover, many Anglo-American criminologists are truly interested in developments from other countries and have aimed to foster a greater multidirectional cross-national understanding. Some of the efforts of the International Division of the American Society of Criminology or other international societies, such as the International Society of Criminology or the European Society of Criminology are good examples.[5] Thanks to their efforts, for example, concepts such as restorative justice have become mainstream within the field. A global indictment this is not, but clearly there is a state of academic dependency in social sciences where researchers and practitioners from the periphery depend on their counterparts in the North Atlantic for ideas, concepts, methods, theories (Alatas, 2003) and, critically, for recognition. This situation also extends to criminology and is perpetuated by "certain features of the global division of labor in the social sciences" (Alatas, 2003, p. 460). Burawoy's following comment about the present and future of sociology is highly pertinent in this context and can be extrapolated to the field of criminology:

> Without conspiracy or deliberation on the part of its practitioners, United States sociology becomes world hegemonic. We, therefore, have a special responsibility to provincialize our own sociology, to bring it down from the pedestal of universality and recognize its distinctive character and national power. We have to develop a dialogue, once again, with other national sociologies, recognizing their local traditions or their aspirations to indigenize sociology. We have to think in global terms, to recognize the emergent global division of sociological labor.
>
> *(Burawoy, 2005, p. 284)*

On the other hand, criminologists outside the core can be ethnocentric and parochial in their own way. In fact, they themselves may often be complicit in this unidirectional and uncritical transference of knowledge. That, in itself, is part of the problem. The powerful seduction of the ideas generated in the core often leads researchers in the periphery simply to conform themselves with checking whether "they apply to their national contexts," thus reducing the contribution of the periphery to a sort of laboratory for external validity. In sum, the strength and wide diffusion of the theoretical and policy ideas of Anglo-American criminology requires that researchers in the periphery are vigilant to guard against artificially reconstructing their own national contexts according to these marketed exports.

The relevance of international and cross-national collaborations

Cross-national research can and should be one way to challenge the parochialism of national criminologies. In addition, in countries where the institutional space occupied by criminology is limited and national funding for its research activities is sparse, collaborations with researchers from other countries, particularly when aimed at obtaining external funding, become a key engine for driving research. There has been a number of such collaborations that have contributed to cross-national links among researchers, forums for international discussions on specific topics, and data and research protocols in ways that may alleviate some of the difficulties noted above. The *International Crime Survey* (van Dijk *et al.*, 2008) and the *International Self-Report Delinquency Study* (Junger-Tas *et al.*, 2009) are prime examples of such collaborations. These enterprises not only have generated national quantitative crime data in countries where the governments devote few resources for this type of research, but also have created unique opportunities for participating scholars in the periphery to raise their profile both nationally and internationally. These studies have indeed highlighted the fact that scholarly productivity outside the core "is highly dependent on accessing professional international networks" (Teodorescu, 2000).

One of the problems of these collaborations is that up to this point these studies have been more directed towards countries in the semi-periphery than those in the periphery. So far, Anglo-American researchers have primarily carried out collaborations with European colleagues or those in other English-speaking countries where criminology has some presence. Most of the world, particularly post-colonial societies, have received little attention from Anglo-American criminologists and those attempting to develop criminological research in the periphery are particularly isolated. Africa, for example, remains an almost invisible continent to criminologists from the North Atlantic. The traditional polar division between sociology as the social science for developed societies and anthropology as the social science that focuses on the periphery (Wallerstein, 2003) still casts a long shadow when it comes to criminology.

A legitimate question that also needs to be asked is whether some of the existing international collaborations represent what Wallerstein (2004) calls forms of *unequal exchange* that both typify and perpetuate relations of subordination between the core and the periphery. Do these collaborations allow for local development of ideas? Or rather, do they treat the collaborators as field managers for essentially a core intellectual project? Who benefits the most from these research collaborations in terms of research productivity and scientific recognition? Do these research collaborations treat seriously the problem of acculturation of concepts based on the Anglo-American experience? Are these cross-national collaborations testing true cross-national questions or simply generating the export of particular ways of thinking about crime and its control originated in the core? Unfortunately the answer to these questions often suggests that unequal exchange in international collaborations within the field of criminology is the norm rather than the exception.

Conclusions: public criminology in the comparative context

Some of the contemporary debates about the future of sociology and social sciences (e.g. the *Gulbenkian Commission Report* of 1996, current debates about public sociology) have emphasized the need to think globally, to recognize non-Western experiences, the hegemonic position of the North Atlantic social sciences and the unequal global division of labor within social sciences. In criminology, however, most debates remain provincially anchored in the Anglo-American experience as ever (Garland, 2008; Loader and Sparks, 2008). This is partially explained by the fact that criminology still concerns itself mostly with rather local matters – street crime and its control.

What are the possible solutions to this state of affairs? Some of the problems highlighted here are big problems and are rather hard to solve. The global unequal division of labor within social sciences is hard to deal with in a context in which resources remain in a few hands. This is something that increasingly affects the higher education sector. Yet some measures can be taken to resist these inequalities. Professional associations, for instance, can play an important role in this regard. These inequalities can be contested by increasing academic and professional associations' support to open access to electronic journals, thus reducing the economic burden on research institutions and scholars outside the core. Why shouldn't we advocate for the free digital access to the journals of our professional associations? For that matter, we could demand our professional journals develop editorial policies that (1) diminish the hegemonic position of the English language by accepting translations of material originally published in other languages and by providing support to authors whose English is less than ideal, (2) develop a less parochial interest with the realities of the North Atlantic, and (3) reduce not the rigorous methodological standards but the nonsensical methodological fetishism.[6] The publication of special issues related to geo-political regions in the periphery could be a way to achieve some of these goals.

Issues of unequal exchange in international collaborations can and should be addressed by our professional associations. Why can these professional associations not develop specific protocols or ethical guidelines in these regards to prevent situations of exploitation? Also, some professional societies, such as the Law and Society Association, (1) offer special membership discounts to scholars from lower-average income countries as classified by the World Bank, (2) encourage ordinary members to contribute to a fund to support annual meeting attendance of these scholars, and (3) have a special program to sustain international collaborations. Why do criminological associations such as the American Society of Criminology[7] and the European Society of Criminology not follow this lead? These initiatives could be complemented with specific training workshops aimed at young scholars from these countries. These proposals, albeit modest, are certainly good starting points. Some authors have argued that the global problems in social sciences should lead to a restructuring of the field that dispenses with the disciplinary boundaries that were inherited from past centuries (Wallerstein, 2003). Garland (2008) recently questioned the way that criminology has become institutionalized in the core insofar as it raises a number of significant problems (e.g. isolation from debates in other social sciences, narrowing of theoretical and empirical concerns, etc.). This is indeed a big debate. Unfortunately such a debate could be collective suicide for struggling scholars who strive to establish themselves in countries with little institutional recognition of criminology.

Problematic as it might be, institutionalization to some degree is required for scholars to be able to develop a research career. Perhaps we should be more open to different ways of thinking about institutionalization, rather than simply taking the American or British example as the only way forward. But what would those alternatives look like? As someone who has spent most of his professional life trying to think about the right balance between his advocacy for a greater space for criminological research and better informed policy in his own home country, I am afraid I continue to have more doubts and questions than answers. One thing is clear: these are questions should become part of a global criminology agenda not dominated by the Anglo-American experience.

Future research questions

1. Some countries clearly seem to have more thriving criminological communities than others. This chapter proposes some factors that may underpin this variation, but what other variables (e.g. level of democracy, economic development, etc.) may explain the more successful development of criminology as a scientific discipline across countries? Could you use the principles of fuzzy-set analysis (Ragin, 2000) for a cross-national comparative analysis of this question?

2. Clearly Anglo-American journals publish primarily Anglo-American contributions. But is it possible to empirically demonstrate a publication bias against contributions from other countries or regions?
3. As we have seen, a number of researchers from the periphery and the semi-periphery migrate to US and UK universities in order to develop their careers as criminologists. Does this migration affect the impact of their research outputs (as measured, for example, by citation metrics: ISI Web of Knowledge or through Publish or Perish)? How does the impact of their research outputs compare with that of researchers from their countries that do not migrate?
4. The general studies of intellectual diasporas suggest that researchers that work abroad from their home countries can play an important role as translator of ideas. What role do criminologists working abroad play in the development of research or policy initiatives in their own home countries?
5. Although the US remains a force to be reckoned with in the international arena, we are witnessing a significant change in the landscape of international economic relations where countries such as China, India and Brazil are becoming increasingly influential. What is the likely impact that these changes may have in the academic field of criminology?

Notes

1 This makes the support of the European Society of Criminology of its working group on undergraduate criminology benchmarks critical for the development of these institutional spaces outside the core.

2 For example, a great deal of American criminology, particularly of a macro character, is based on the use of these statistics that are easily accessibly from the internet (via ICPSR or equivalent). In many other countries, however, these statistics are simply not accessible to researchers.

3 Actually, the problem is even more serious than this suggests. It is not only that publication in "American" journals is rewarded but the fact that publication in languages other than English is actually penalized. The use of criteria such as the h-index (that undercounts publications in languages other than English) means that those who spend their time trying to achieve a dual publication record do so at the risk of getting low scores in these metrics.

4 The unequal global division of labor within criminology means that the only papers that get translated are those produced by Anglo-American scholars into the national journals of the periphery in languages other than English.

5 But even these organizations operate under constraints of the global division of labor. Out of the 17 co-authors of the books winning the ASC International Division Award, 10 are US/UK scholars or work in US/UK universities, five work in either Australia or the Netherlands, and only two are based outside further from the "core."

6 As Braithwaite (2005: 347–8) has argued, our so-called methodological high standards often are nothing but particular disciplinary obsessions: "So psychologists insist on an artificial experiment in circumstances when naturalistic qualitative work or a piece of survey research would be better to evaluate the hypothesis. Economists insist on econometrics to test a theory that could be tested, and would be more rigorously tested, by the psychologist's preferred approach of a randomized controlled trial. Sociologists ignore recent advances in econometrics because being competent across them is expected of economists but not sociologists, or they use unvalidated single-item measures of attitudes in circumstances where psychology would rightly expect scaling of multiple items. Anthropologists stick with ethnography to answer quantitative questions. Sociologists of Foucauldian persuasion defend sloppy historical research of the sort Foucault himself did, ignoring accessible primary sources because they claim they are doing a history of the present rather than the past! Sociologists of law do research without reading cases . . ."

7 The International Division does give free and reduced membership to its Division based on country of residence after one becomes a member of the ASC, but the ASC refuses to do it at the ASC level.

References

Agozino, B. (2004). Imperialism, crime and criminology: towards the decolonisation of criminology. *Crime, Law and Social Change*, 41: 343–58.

Aniyar de Castro, L. (1987). *Criminología de la Liberación*. Maracaibo: Ediluz.

Alatas, S. (2003). Academic dependency and the global division of labour in the social sciences. *Current Sociology*, 51(6): 599–613.

Barberet, R. (2005). Spain. *European Journal of Criminology*, 2(3): 341–68.

Braithwaite, J. (2005). For public social science. *British Journal of Sociology*, 56(3): 345–53.

Brogden, M. and Nijhar, P. (2005). *Community Policing. National and International Models and Approaches*. Cullompton: Willan Publishing.

Burawoy, M. (2005). 2004 American Sociological Association Presidential Address: For a Public Sociology. *British Journal of Sociology*, 56(2): 259–94.

van Dijk, J., van Kesteren, J., and Smit, P. (2008). *Criminal Victimisation in International Perspective. Key Findings from the ICVS and EU ICS*. The Hague: Dutch Ministry of Justice.

Garland, D. (1997). Of crimes and criminals: the development of criminology in Britain. In Reiner, R., Morgan, R., and Maguire, M. (Eds). *The Oxford Handbook of Criminology*. 2nd edn. Oxford: Oxford University Press.

—— (2001). *The Culture of Control. Crime and Social Order in Contemporary Society*. Oxford: Oxford University Press.

—— (2008). Criminology in a culture of control. Paper presented at the 60th Annual Meeting of the American Society of Criminology, St. Louis.

Hope, T. (2004). Pretend it works. Evidence and governance in the evaluation of the Reducing Burglary Initiative. *Criminal Justice*, 4(3): 287–308.

Huggins, M. (1998). *Political Policing. The United States and Latin America*. Durham: Duke University Press.

Jones, T. and Newburn, T. (2002). Policy convergence and crime control in the USA and the UK: streams of influence and levels of impact. *Criminal Justice*, 2(2): 173–203.

Junger-Tas, J., Marshall, I. H. Enzmann,D., Killias, M., Steketee, M., and Gruszczynska, B. (eds). (2009). *Juvenile Delinquency in Europe and Beyond*. Springer.

Karstedt, S. (2001). Comparing cultures, comparing crime: challenges, prospects and problems for a global criminology. *Crime, Law, and Social Change*, 36: 285–308.

Kerezsi, K. and Levay, M. (2008). Criminology, crime and criminal justice in Hungary. *European Journal of Criminology*, 5(2): 239–60.

Larrauri, E. (2008). Questions from the South. *European Society of Criminology Newsletter*, November, pp. 2 and 18.

Liu, J. (2009). Asian criminology: challenges, opportunities, and directions. *Asian Criminology*, 4: 1–9.

Loader, I. and Sparks, R. (2008). Doing criminology in a "hot" climate. Paper presented at the 60th Annual Meeting of the American Society of Criminology (St Louis, November 12–15).

Maffei, S. and Merzagora Betsos, I. (2007). Crime and criminal policy in Italy. *European Journal of Criminology*, 4(4): 461–82.

Matthews, R. (2009). Beyond "so what?" criminology. *Theoretical Criminology*, 13(3): 341–62.

Mediña Ariza, J. (2002). Reflexiones críticas sobre la futura licenciatura en criminología. *Revista Electrónica de Ciencia Penal y Criminología*, 04–15: 1–30.

Nelken, D. (2009). Comparative criminal justice. Beyond ethnocentrism and relativism. *European Journal of Criminology*, 6(4): 291–311.

Newburn, T. (2002). Atlantic crossings. "Policy transfer" and crime control in the USA and Britain. *Punishment and Society*, 4(2): 165–94.

Nobli, G. and Crocitti, S. (2008). Who attends ESC conferences? *European Society of Criminology Newsletter*, May, pp. 3 and 14.

Oberwittler, D. and Hofer, S. (2005). Crime and justice in Germany. *European Journal of Criminology*, 2(4): 465–508.

O'Donnell, I. (2005). Crime and justice in the Republic of Ireland. *European Journal of Criminology*, 2(1): 99–131.

Olafsdottir, H. and Bragadottir, R. (2006). Crime and criminal policy in Iceland. *European Journal of Criminology*, 3(2): 221–53.

Ragin, C. (2000). *Fuzzy-set Social Science*. Chicago: University of Chicago Press.

Redondo Illescas, S. (2001). Erase una vez una cenicienta llamada criminología. *Criminoticias*. Sevilla: Universidad de Sevilla.

van Swaaningen, R. (2006). Criminology in the Netherlands. *European Journal of Criminology*, 3(4): 463–501.

Teodorescu, D. (2000). Correlates of faculty publication productivity: a cross-national analysis. *Higher Education*, 39: 201–22.

Wacquant, L. (1999). How penal common sense comes to Europeans: notes on the transatlantic diffusion of the neoliberal doxa. *European Societies*, 1(3): 319–52.

Wallerstein, I. (2003). Anthropology, sociology and other dubious disciplines. *Current Anthropology*, 44(4): 453–65.

—— (2004). *World-systems Analysis: An Introduction*. Durham: Duke University Press.

Walters, R. (2003). New modes of governance and the commodification of criminological knowledge. *Social and Legal Studies*, 12(1): 5–26.

4

International criminology

Qualitative research on polluted actors

Martha K. Huggins

In studying Brazil for over three decades, I have observed several things about United States academic positivist quantitative criminology that differentiate it from my own qualitative research conducted from a critical criminology[1] perspective. Positivist quantitative research in the United States is US centric, whereas I study deviance and crime in Brazil and in other "foreign" States. United States positivist quantitative criminology focuses on legally defined "criminality," while critical criminology examines conditions often not even defined as "criminal." As such they are not usually treated as illegal by State agents. Most United States positivist criminological research focuses on crimes of the powerless, using official criminal justice system data – what Alexander Liazos (1972) called a "Nuts, Sluts, and Preverts" approach to social problems. Those in the critical criminology tradition focus most on State crimes and associated actors; further rendering criminal justice system data unreliable.

This chapter illustrates field research in "criminology," both as narrowly defined by quantitative practitioners and using a broader definition that includes many "human rights" topics. Examples of such research are primarily taken from women's research in *Women fielding danger: negotiating ethnographic identities in field research* (Huggins and Glebbeek, 2008b) and from *Violence workers: torturers and murderers reconstruct Brazilian atrocities* (Huggins *et al.*, 2002).

Quantitative and qualitative research

Pointing to crucial differences between qualitative and quantitative positivist[2] research, Charles Ragin *et al.* (2004a) explain that, "Qualitative data are suggestive rather than definitive, illuminating rather than convincing, 'soft' rather than 'hard'" (p. 16), adding that qualitative research focuses on discovery and theory construction, while keeping a flexible analytic frame. *Discovery*: "qualitative researchers often want to find out 'how' things happen (or happened);" a common goal is "mak[ing] the facts understandable" (Ragin *et al.*, 2004b, p. 23). *Theory building*: Qualitative research is often "framed as . . . sources of ideas, evidence, and insights for theory construction, rather than as systematic techniques for theory testing" (ibid., p. 24). *Analytic frame flexibility*: keeps research open to serendipity.

Qualitative criminological research: epistemology, definition, "data"

Epistemologically, qualitative research is founded on a reluctance to accept "taken-for-granted" preconceptions and definitions of the social world, studying it "as seen" by variously positioned and differently empowered respondents.

Positivist research, in contrast, relies on, "conventional [read: positivist] ways of framing and answering research questions. . . . [which] often rest on an acceptance of conventional understandings that hide what we should be studying" (Becker, 2009, p. 520).

Applying this to criminology, Loschper (2000, p. 1) argues that, "'crime' is a matter of judgment . . . concerned with the interpretations and definitions of situations and actions . . . [an] analysis . . . not possible with quantitative methods."

Pointing to the inductive, iterative nature of qualitative field research, Greenhalgh and Taylor (1997, p. 1) remind us that its research processes and outcomes are "dependent on the subjective experience[s] of both the researcher and the researched." Quantitative criminologists can claim that such an assertion, in its application, leads to "researcher contamination" of qualitative findings – a positivist epistemological assessment that grows out of its formally impersonal "scientist" premises.

Such assessments would be inconsequential but for the paradigmatic dominance of quantitative research in US criminology. Howard Becker (2009) argues that quantitative positivist epistemology has negatively influenced evaluations of qualitative research, limiting the ability of qualitative researchers to obtain US National Science Foundation (NSF) funding.

Theoretical and "scientific" givens are deliberately placed front and center in positivist research proposals, developed as fixed research designs that emphasize hypothetical–deductive theory testing. Qualitative researchers[3] "usually don't know enough [at the start of a research project] to formulate good hypotheses," says Becker (2009, p. 550). And while quantitative research formally separates data collection and analysis, arriving at the meaning of data during the "data analysis" phase of a study, qualitative research uses data gathered at one point, to guide observations at the next step, with data interpretations on-going rather than at the end of research (Becker, 2009, p. 547).

Criminology's subject-matter

Qualitative criminology often questions quantitative criminology's adherence to theory testing through scientifically detached research using statistics generated by criminal justice organizations. As Becker points out:

> We make best use of theory when we refuse to base our research designs on what organizational personnel tell us, or on what "everybody knows", . . . and instead build theories on unexpected observations made in the field.
>
> *(Becker, 2009, p. 549)*

On "detached scientific" data collection, Denzin and Lincoln (2000, p. 523) argue that research is most robust when it, "seeks to construct analyses that show how respondents *and* the social scientists who study them jointly construct . . . realities . . ." (emphasis added). And Loschper (2000, p. 1; see also Cicourel, 1968; Kitsuse and Cicourel, 1963) cautions against reliance on statistics generated by criminal justice organizations because such data determine if an incident is noticed, if it is registered as a case, and if the case is classified as "criminal" on its way through the criminal justice institutions. Officially registered offenses do not represent the "reality of deviance." They point to official constructions of crime that grow out of criminal justice system classifications.

By applying these observations to the study of crime, whether national or international, a researcher can broaden criminology's subject-matter to areas that US positivist criminology would explicitly and implicitly treat as outside its scope. For example, some neglected "human rights" topics are potentially compatible with "criminology" – genocide, rape in war, and torture.[4] Studying such subjects, of course, raises questions about the appropriate role for an interviewer who deposes such atrocities:[5] "objective observer" who maintains distance from subjects and subject-matter, or "subjective participant" in the world view of an atrocity perpetrator or victim (see Huggins *et al.*, 2002, Ch. 4; Clendinnen, 1998; Gunn, 1997).

Perhaps US positivist criminology's relative neglect of human rights topics can be explained by its US-centric research focus, as well as by its assumptions about criminology's "appropriate" subject matter and "data." However, even qualitative criminologists have neglected many topics related to international human rights. This may also stem from US qualitative criminology's US centricity. Or international qualitative criminologists may be hindered by the very nature of qualitative field research: Since it is hands-on, person-to-person, and field-site-rooted, some qualitative research can be dangerous for researcher and researched, as well as ethically complicated.[6] In addition, perhaps the difficulty of obtaining data inhibits some qualitative research on human rights subjects. As a qualitative criminologist, I often study subjects without available or reliable secondary sources – for example, why and how police become torturers. Doing such research in spite of such hurdles grows out of my international focus and an epistemological rationale that places a premium on interviews for understanding underlying institutional, organizational, and personal processes and for capturing changes over time.

Yet there are subjects that, as a qualitative criminologist, I could or would not study for safety and ethical reasons: in-situ torture, genocide in process, women being raped in war. Setting aside the ethical reasons for not studying such atrocities in process, Skidmore argues that researcher assessments of danger changes across the life cycle:

> As a childless doctoral student . . . in Rangoon [Burma] . . . research activities that might land me in jail . . . or lead to my deportation . . . were "acceptable risks". . . . Now a mother of two, I can no longer enter Burma without defining safety and danger in terms of my children. . . . [For their sake] I have the responsibility to conduct research in a manner that doesn't endanger me.
>
> *(2008, p. 310)*

The remainder of this chapter focuses on these and other field research issues raised by conditions and outcomes encountered and negotiated by field researchers in US national and international settings. Most of the reported research is not in "criminology" as narrowly defined; most deals with topics related to the criminology of "human rights" violations. All such research points to things that are valuable for research in international qualitative criminology.

Research dynamics: "pollution" and "purity" in the field

Focusing on two broad and related categories of under-illustrated qualitative research – "polluted topics" and "spoiled identity pollution" – this discussion is framed by the anthropological notions of "pollution" and "purity." Pollution, the opposite of purity (see Douglas, 2002), is often described as:

- defiling through its spread from one person or situation to another;
- controlled or eliminated through rituals that keep "polluted" persons or situations from contaminating "purity."

Whether a qualitative field researcher actually thinks that some people and situations have the capacity to "pollute" is not the point; rather, "pollution" and "purity" are tools for highlighting certain aspects of a researcher's interactive relationships with "interlocutors"[7] – the latter of whom we study as research actors. The research interaction thus involves two people (researcher and interlocutor) with possibly different definitions of self and "other," decency and morality, and justice. In research on deviance and crime such definitions might vary greatly between researcher and researched. Yet as the following discussion will illustrate, an important outcome for each field site interaction is to achieve an "approximation" of differences – a temporary (and usually tenuous) balance between how much the researcher is willing to change in order to interact positively and productively with the interlocutor, and how far the latter will go to achieve this. Such a field site "approximation," which often impacts whether research will move forward, has been under-illustrated by qualitative researchers.[8]

Framing qualitative field research practice as a dynamic, involving reducing "pollution" and increasing "purity," is especially useful for criminologists because we *are* routinely involved with subject-matters and people considered socially "polluted" – i.e. "immoral" and/or "dangerous." How many of us have been asked: "How can *you* study *such things*?" "Are you safe studying *those* people?" The tone of these questions suggests an attitude that the people or situations being researched are so "damaged" as to impart "impurities" and "danger" to the researcher. Perhaps qualitative criminologists are more likely to receive these sorts of questions than quantitative researchers because, in seeking interviewees' taken-for-granted worlds, we enter into their lives and world views – sometimes discovering that we cannot, or do not want, to be part of them through approximation, even if only tangentially and temporarily.

Likewise, interviewees often see interviewers as "polluting," and so resist giving up their secrets. These issues are compounded for international qualitative criminologists because we encounter layers of social beliefs and expectations different from our own, with no easy formula for working with and within them. An interlocutor's deviance may be just a small part of the differences between "them" and "us." As a consequence, qualitative international researchers are often confronted with how much they can or want to change their presentation of self in order to neutralize what interviewees see as a researcher's "polluting" potential. Interviewees in addition must decide how much they can disclose before losing their preferred sense of who they are. In a "successful" interview "approximation" each side becomes a little less "pure" and a little more "polluted."

Schwandner-Sievers, researching in conflict-riven Albania and Kosovo, found herself with three local possibilities for her "acceptable" field site persona:

> I could be treated as a "vulnerable woman," "fictive kin," or as an "honored foreign guest". . . . As a vulnerable [woman] . . . [I] "need[ed] protection" under a host household. . . . [As a] "fictive kin" [there were] obligations and (gendered) limits. [As] an "honored foreign guest" . . . [I would be] seen as having a "likeness to men".
>
> *(2008, p. 190)*

Schwandner-Sievers learned to balance her identities – those she preferred, those interlocutors preferred, and those she was negotiating with them. However, Schwandner-Sievers was questioning who she was becoming. While she disliked being "shaped by patriarchy, [this] nonetheless [was] greatly facilitating [her] research" (2008, p. 186).

Under-illustrated "topic pollution"

Researchers cannot effectively study a situation until they select a topic, a decision often hemmed in by assumptions about "topic pollution."[9] Clendinnen (1998: 88), after Primo Levi (1988), argues that a "moral-sensitivity exclusion" among some Holocaust researchers leads them "not to even attempt to understand Nazis, based on the belief that to do so risks moral contamination." Studying certain kinds of deviance and crime from a statistical standpoint can use the "distance" created by secondary statistics to protect from pollution by those being studied. Scholars of qualitative epistemology and practice do not have such protections.

Howard Becker (1967) asks, "When do we accuse ourselves and our fellow sociologists of bias?" Answering his own question, Becker argues that such an accusation is likely to arise when the research gives credence, in any serious way, to the perspective of the subordinate group in some hierarchical relationship. In the case of deviance, the hierarchical relationship is a moral one. The superordinate parties represent the forces of approved and official morality; the subordinate parties are those who, it is alleged, have violated that morality.

Labeling this a "hierarchy of credibility," Becker (1967) asserts that research giving insider voice to deviants and criminals can lead to the charge that a researcher is "biased" for accepting the deviant group's "illegitimate" point of view. But, for Becker, "the question is not whether we should take sides, since we inevitably will, but rather whose side we are on" (p. 239). A socio-cultural "hierarchy of credibility" renders one position more credible than others, with serious implications for how research is assessed.

But are the different "sides" to a conflict or other situation always clear-cut? Can "sides" be dynamic and shifting? As a human rights advocacy researcher documenting Indonesian military abuses against East Timor's liberation groups, Fredriksson (2008) saw "people . . . suffering and dying in a small country under violent Indonesian occupation" and knew "whose side" she was on (p. 152). Later, during East Timor's post-occupation period, the "sides" became blurred: some former Indonesian loyalists had been forcibly inducted as children into Indonesian military service. Were these children "perpetrators" or "victims"? (p. 161; see also Huggins *et al.*, 2002, pp. 23–5). Later, in newly independent East Timor, Fredrikkson discovered yet another "side": those coping with the "unhealed physical and psychological wounds," including Frederikkson herself (p. 169).

Robben (1995) argues that there is often "more sympathy for [research that] unmask[s] the abusers of power than [for] doubt[ing] . . . the words of their victims" (p. 84). But, how about a victimizer's abuse of power being explained in a manner seemingly favorable to the abuser? Can "perpetrators" be "victims" as well, as Huggins *et al.* (2002) discovered in research on torturers? Thus, while Becker correctly argues that taking sides is inevitable in research, the "sides" are neither fixed – "perpetrator" or "victim" – nor incapable of changing as new findings arise. However, taking sides is not without consequences for the researcher or for assessments of a researcher's "objectivity."

Researching "topic pollution" despite "contaminated" data

Can the voices of those assumed to have "spoiled identities" ever be considered "credible"? If, as Becker (1967. p. 241) argues, "In any system of ranked groups, . . . members of the highest group have the right [to be seen as credible]," then "data" derived from those with "spoiled identities" – in Goffman's (1986) words, those embodying "stigma" – cannot possibly be "credible."[10] Scully (1984) and Presser (2008) are among US criminology's qualitative researchers whose interviews with US rapists and murderers, respectively, have provided valuable information about how such actors define, rationalize, and legitimize their violence. What rapists and murderers communicate as their "truth" speaks volumes about their world views and its relationship to their explanations of criminality (see also Huggins *et al.*, 2002, Ch. 11; Cohen, 1993).

Can such actors tell the "truth"? Within research settings, "truth" and "lies" collide and become puzzles to be understood. As I found with Brazilian torturers (Huggins and Glebbeek, 2003, p. 381), each new interview situation involved "real-but-shifting as well as fictional identities on the part of both interviewer and interviewee. . . . An interviewer cannot express all that she really feels and expect an interviewee to give up what she needs [from him]. Likewise, interviewees cannot disclose everything that they are and still protect their hidden identities and secrets." (Huggins and Glebbeek, 2003, p. 381; see also Simmel, 1950).

Fredriksson learned in Indonesian-occupied East Timor that "truth" is a two-way street:

> During my interviews . . . I was certainly lied to, sometimes suspected of being a liar (or something worse), and sometimes tricked into accepting a respondent's political or personal agenda. Looking back . . . I would say that outright lies and other subtle forms of subterfuge were relatively rare. In the field, when one knows a country, its people and their customs, it is possible to develop a fairly accurate sense about truth-telling and lying.
>
> *(Fredriksson, 2008, p. 168)*

Sehgal (2008, p. 339), in research on women of the violent Hindu Nationalist Movement, discovered that "right-wing informants have a vested interest in communicating partial, distorted, and misleading accounts." Blee discovered that "accounts by those who have participated in campaigns for racial and religious supremacy . . . often are laced with deceptive information, disingenuous denials of culpability, and dubious assertions . . ." (1993, p. 597; see also Cohen, 1993, p. 13). But this does not mean that "informants are deliberately lying, indeed, they may really believe their distorted and partial versions of reality" (Blee, 1993, p. 599).

Under-illustrated "spoiled-identity" pollution

Smyth and Mitchell (n.d.) argue that those studying deviant or criminal groups must balance "feeling vulnerable[,] to being perceived as either in sympathy with the views of . . . ['un-loved'] groups, or as too prejudiced against them to be capable of understanding them." Focusing qualitative research on criminology's version of Nigel Fielding's (1982) "un-loved groups"[11]– rapists, serial murderers, pedophiles, torturers – introduces how a researcher handles negative feelings about such actors. Glebbeek (Huggins and Glebbeek, 2008a, p. 365) wondered whether she could be objective: "with [Guatemalan] police [who] had been responsible for great atrocities – murders, mutilations, torture, disappearances?" Blee discovered in her study of Ku Klux Klan women that

> it is one thing to understand the world through the eyes of an informant with whom you have some (even a little) sympathy, but a very different matter to think about developing rapport with someone . . . whose life is given meaning and purpose by the desire to annihilate you or others like you.
>
> *(2002, p. 13)*

How are field researchers to deal with interlocutor beliefs that evoke fear and even disgust in themselves? I (Huggins *et al.*, 2002) could not let my revulsion of torture creep into the interview situation or interviewees would cut short the interview. I opted to deal with my reactions to their "poisonous accounts" (see Sanford, 2002) outside the interview setting, alone in my hotel room. Inside the interview, I mediated what I was hearing by becoming introspectively analytical about interviewees' disclosures (see also Fredrikkson, 2008). Sehgal also "attempted to intellectualize what [she] was hearing and seeing":

> in part, by focusing on the interview as a "technique" and, in part, by explaining to myself sociologically what I was seeing and hearing. I had to think fast to ask the right question, while . . . processing my troubling feelings about the interlocutor's responses and developing a follow-up question. . . . When all these techniques failed, I would become physically ill and/or feel intellectually paralyzed, unable to . . . analyze my field notes and interview transcripts.
>
> *(2008, p. 343)*

Presser (2008) decided to back-stage, negotiate around, and reorder some of her own political standpoints and values. Pointing to the imprisoned male interviewees' hegemonic gender and class expectations, Presser (ibid., p. 267) recognized that, "The men's self-constructions effectively reproduced binary distinctions between men and women, victims and offenders, and good and evil," which Presser worked against in her own social, academic, and political life. In Presser's mind, in "such constructed differences lay the basis for social injustice, violence and inequality [which] . . . threaten safety." Yet Presser (p. 267) felt she had to "participate . . . in their 'difference-making'" because, in her words, "It benefited me to the extent that, in the short run, it seemed to ensure my safety . . . [for] the men . . . [to] 'do' . . . goodness with me in the interviews." But Presser was uncomfortable with presenting herself "as sympathetic to the men's claims of being misunderstood and mistreated; in several cases my [expressed] sympathy was false" (p. 268).

In fact, women researchers find gender assumptions and expectations require constant negotiation.[12] As Arendell (quoted in Sharp and Kramer, 2006, p. 318) has argued, in "qualitative research [,] . . . *who* the researcher is, in terms of race, class, and gender, . . . [is] important to the dynamics of face-to-face interviews" (emphasis added).[13] All the researchers in *Women fielding danger* (Huggins and Glebbeek, 2008b) discovered that in interactions between researcher and researched gender superseded and shaped other ascribed statuses and most achieved ones.

Researching un-loved groups

If a "hierarchy of credibility" were applied to research on groups considered "polluted," it could be assumed that a researcher – in most cases having more power than interlocutors – would be able to translate this into control over the research dynamic. Yet this is not necessarily the case for women researchers. Knowing that entering secret police worlds would require flexibility and stealth, Glebbeek leaned toward employing an interview "give and take":

> a few jokes and "chit chat" offered a greater possibility of getting my questions answered. . . . [The necessity for these] extensive preliminaries . . . [was a] reminder of . . . interviewees' power over an interviewer.
>
> *(Huggins and Glebbeek, 2008, p. 365)*

Glebbeek decided that she should be:

> sensitive to what I was "supposed" to know and when I was "supposed" to know it. This seemed to buy me the opportunity to ask more sensitive questions later, when my discretion had time to be established.
>
> *(Huggins and Glebbeek, 2008, p. 365).*

Sometimes researchers of "un-loved" actors must accept an interviewee's prevarications. During an interview with Bruno, a Brazilian torturer, Huggins:

> knew that [his statement was untrue] but . . . did not feel it within my research role to contradict Bruno. [Yet] by encouraging Bruno to continue, I [was becoming] incorporated into . . . Bruno's "face maintenance" . . . [This] . . . moved the interview toward more of Bruno's secrets [albeit] through a new collaborative synthesis [with] Bruno . . . what Habenstein (1970) labels "research bargaining."
>
> *(Huggins and Gleeback 2008a, p. 372)*

In research on some "un-loved groups," "no neutrals" are allowed, including the researcher:

> Whether or not you take sides, those actively involved in the situation are going to define whose side they think you are on. They will act toward you on the basis of this definition, regardless of your professions of neutrality.
>
> *(Sluka, 1995, p. 287)*

Ethics in motion

Research "ethics" cannot be confidently laid out in a précis prior to getting into the field, nor can they be resolved with finality for a university Internal Review Board (IRB), even though that is exactly what the latter institutions explicitly require. Ethical challenges – expected and unexpected – emerge and change each day and with each interview: Ethics are always "in motion." Researchers must know and exercise responsibility with respect to their own and interlocutors' safety by protecting interviewees and their testimonies. How this is accomplished in the field – that's the rub!

Research ethics are shaped in the field by a dialectic that includes a field site's (often changing) politico-geography, the identity negotiations within it, and the on-going results of such negotiations; these are structured by the behavioral opportunities available to researcher and researched. Some ethical challenges may of course be predicted prior to research, although they may not develop in the field as expected. Most ethical perils emerge *in situ*, in ways not even imagined during field research preparation.

Glebbeek encountered dramatic and unexpected ethical problems with no easy resolution:

> During a surprise visit to a police precinct building, a man rushed up to me and began screaming in my face . . . I suddenly noticed that the man's hands were cuffed at his back – an arrestee who had escaped from the precinct's makeshift detention area . . . A precinct policeman . . . grabbed the arrestee and hit him violently in the face with the butt of his revolver. I was profoundly shocked and disturbed, but there was little that I could do about it. I felt that ethically I should have taken the side of the mistreated prisoner, but . . . this would harm my research relationship with precinct police. I thus ignored the situation and left . . . but resolved to incorporate this incident into my assessment of Guatemalan Civil Police reform
>
> *(Huggins and Glebbeek, 2008, pp. 369–70)*

Glebbeek felt as if she had betrayed her own "personal and research ethics" in order to accomplish research goals.

As time passed, Glebbeek encountered an even more troubling ethical dilemma: Her opinions about police interviewees were becoming positive, demonstrating what I call the "perpetrator-as-victim" dilemma:

> I had to ask myself how someone studying a police institution with a long history of violence and repression could become in any way partial to that institution? I had not anticipated that objectivity itself – e.g. seeing interviewees as people first and listening openly to their accounts – would pull me into the interviewee's point of view.
>
> *(Huggins and Glebbeek, 2008a, p. 370)*

While grappling with these ethical issues, some qualitative researchers discover yet another unexpected one: In the process of studying an un-loved group, the researcher becomes a "victim." "Emotional blow-back" can follow from listening to and working within the socio-political spaces of "un-loved" groups. As Gunn (1997) has argued, in contrast to the permissibility of empathic witnessing in research with atrocity survivors – where an interviewer can accept taking simultaneously the roles of observer and victim and be morally transformed by such embodied involvement in atrocity survivors' accounts – the researcher working with morally indefensible "un-loved groups" can be impacted negatively by what she hears. Sehgal (2008, pp. 343–4), after two weeks undercover at a Hindu Nationalist Movement's paramilitary training camp, had "unwittingly internalized elements of the Hindu nationalist worldview [that] . . . required considerable time and energy to neutralize." Unable to effectively read her field notes and assess their meaning," Sehgal (ibid., p. 345) had learned painfully about the "psychological costs" of studying un-loved groups (see also Klatch, 1988, p. 83; Lee-Treweek, 2000, p. 115). Similarly, the emotional "blow-back" experienced by Glebbeek (2008, p. 370) from researching Guatemalan police violence delayed her in assessing her field notes:

> Even far away in The Netherlands, writing about Guatemalan police illegalities, I felt as if I were betraying police informants' trust – an irrational way of thinking that illustrates the conflicts inherent in adopting "progression to friendship" in research on violence perpetrators. Continually I had to ask myself how someone studying a police institution with a long history of violence and repression could become in any way partial to that institution? I had not anticipated that objectivity itself – e.g., seeing interviewees as people first and listening openly to their accounts – would pull me into the interviewee's point of view . . . Simply [to] objectify and demonize the violent police we study – as they have done to their victims . . . would certainly provide a check on developing feelings of humanity toward them. But . . . demonizing and objectifying those we study would violate the most basic rules of research and ethical practice.
>
> *(Huggins and Glebbeek, 2008a, p. 370)*

Skidmore (2008, p. 305) was likewise impacted by her "affective field site" in military Burma, where "normal geographic familiarity is overlaid by a topography of *emotionally experienced* locations, [and] the familiar routines and assumptions about personal safety are revealed to be comforting fictions that can no longer provide a psychological refuge." Returning from a year's research, Skidmore recalls that:

> it then took me more than another year . . . to stop covering my mouth with my hand when speaking about Burma's military regime. I also needed time to stop sliding my eyes toward street corners to see who might be loitering before I entered and left buildings. Each time

> I leave the "affective field" I need to consciously stop using secrecy as a methodology for living.
>
> *(2008, p. 320)*

Skidmore could not "even . . . think of writing about . . . field experiences . . . [because this] caused fear. . . ." Even ten years "after that initial doctoral fieldwork . . . I continue to feel the weight of the regime's implicit threats of violence towards me" (2008, p. 321)

Conclusion

As qualitative research scholars and professionals our research outcomes are often measured *against* what quantitative criminology defines as "purity" – i.e. positivist epistemology and practice. Yet, as this chapter has illustrated, qualitative research makes unique contributions to the study of deviance and crime through a process that balances roles, identities, and research practices within the realities of field-site political geography and human choices and options. Our findings are "us"; "we" are our findings – two "facts" about qualitative research that cannot be quantified, but should be narrated and meticulously documented. Yet rarely do qualitative researchers include the richness of their research "negotiations" in the "methods sections" of their articles or books. "What? – include in a research monograph's 'methods section' the fits and starts of 'identity approximation'; our feelings of fear and doubt; how we negotiated ethics in motion? Would that not suggest that our work is 'unscientific'?" Yet as Campbell (2001, p. 15) argues, "feelings . . . beliefs, and values . . . shape . . . research and are a natural part of inquiry . . . Emotions influence our research, and our research can affect us emotionally." Qualitative criminologists offer this insight to researchers of all stripes.

International qualitative criminology, particularly through collaborative qualitative research in a variety of international settings, will disclose patterns and processes that could modify criminological research findings from the US. The outcomes of such collaborations will add force to purely national qualitative findings, making what may seem "exclusive" or "atypical" to one national setting become a patterned regularity. In fact, only in this way can criminology overcome its narrow and parochial concerns.

Future research questions

1. If a focus on State crimes and associated actors renders criminal justice system data unreliable, can criminologists deem it reliable for non-State crimes?
2. Should the subject-matter of criminology be extended to include subjects related to human rights? Would this impact research in international criminology? How?
3. In international criminological research, whose voice is more marginalized, the victim's or the offender's?
4. Can field research risks be managed? If so, how? If not, why not?
5. How does what Huggins defines as the "approximation" of differences between interlocutor and researcher affect data validity and reliability?

Notes

1 My critical criminological work is based on a social class conflict analysis, associated with Karl Marx's theory of class and the State, and as revised by Latin American scholars. I have increasingly brought feminist and Afro-centrist theories into my work, while linking these to Marx's theory of class and the State.

2 In this chapter the terms "quantitative" and "positivist" are used interchangeably, even though it should be recognized that not all quantitative research achieves all of the standards of positivist science (see also the next note).
3 While recognizing that not all quantitative or qualitative researchers fully observe each of their paradigm's ideal standards, there is still evidence that the National Science Foundation has favored versions of "pure" quantitative over qualitative research proposals.
4 See Huggins, 2010.
5 One strategy for breaking the secrecy surrounding State-linked violence, a method that I (Huggins *et al.*, 2002, Ch. 4) label "deposing atrocity," involves an intentional play on words. It suggests simultaneously the two meanings of depose – in legal terminology, "to testify," and in political terms, "to remove from a position of authority." Accomplishing the first version of deposition leads the interviewer to solicit deponents' explanations, justifications, and accounts of atrocity – getting them to testify about what they have done, how they did it, and why they carried it out. Deposing atrocity also requires overthrowing the authority of secrecy that silences interviewer and interviewee. For the interviewer, this is facilitated by taking the role of an "onlooker witness," a phrase coined to indicate that the researcher is simultaneously inside and outside the interviewee's account.
6 Quantitative criminologists could access a good deal of data about subjects now studied as "human rights." I do so routinely to supplement qualitative studies.
7 Interlocutor is used here interchangeably with "the people we are studying." The term "subjects" is avoided because the latter violates an important principle of qualitative research; it can suggest that those we study are subjects of our detached research. The term "interlocutor" sees those we study as participants in a conversation; as actors rather than acted upon in research.
8 This point has been made by Rebecca Campbell as well in *Emotionally involved: the impact of researching rape* (Campbell, 2001).
9 An extension of this category is that some theoretical perspectives or approaches are deemed "polluted," a claim sometimes directed at those taking a critical criminology approach to deviance or crime.
10 I find ironic that, in the case of State-sponsored torture at Abu Ghraib, that *only* the accounts of a few sacrificed lower-ranked torture actors and facilitators have become public memory through video tapes and trials. The more powerful upper-level facilitators of Abu Ghraib torture – who ordered, promoted, and sometimes even directly participated in it – have been able to control the definition of "truth" such that any information threatening their secrets and leading to their punishment is protected in the interest of "national security" (see Huggins, 2010).
11 This term's definition is being modified in this chapter to also include, besides right-wing extremist groups, common criminals.
12 Race, class, and caste differences are also relevant.
13 While Arendell's (1997) and Sharp and Kramer's (2006) research involves women researching men, the research published in *Women fielding danger* (2008) illustrates that gender also "counts" when women interview women (see Viterna, 2008; Sehgal, 2008).

References

Arendell, T. (1997). Reflections on the researcher–researched relationship: a woman interviewing men. *Qualitative Sociology*, 20(3): 341–68.

Becker, H. S. (1967). Whose side are we on? AASP Presidential address. Online at http://www.leonardbeeghley.com/docs/SYG%206125/Becker,%20whose%20side%20are%20we%20on.pdf (accessed November 20, 2010).

—— (2009). How to find out how to do qualitative research. Online at http://ijoc.org/ojs/index.php/ijoc/article/viewFile/550/329 (accessed November 20, 2010). See also in *International Journal of Communication*, 3: 545–53.

Blee, K. M. (1993). Evidence, empathy, and ethics: lessons from oral histories of the Klan. *Journal of American History*, 80(2): 596–606.

—— (2002). *Inside organized racism: women in the hate movement*. Berkeley: University of California Press.

Campbell, R. (2001). *Emotionally involved: the impact of researching rape*. New York: Routledge.

Cicourel, A. V. (1968). *Social organization of juvenile justice*. New York: Wiley.

Clendinnen, I. (1998) *Reading the Holocaust*. New York: Cambridge University Press.

Cohen, S. (1993). Human rights and crimes of the state: the culture of denial. *Australian and New Zealand Journal of Criminology*, 26: 97–115.

Denzin, N. K. and Lincoln, Y. (2000). *Handbook of qualitative research*, 2nd edn. Los Angeles, CA: Sage.
Douglas, M. (2002). *Purity and danger: an analysis of the concepts of pollution and taboo*. New York: Routledge.
Fielding, N. (1982). Observational research on the National Front. In Blumer, M. (Ed.) *Social research ethics*, pp. 80–104. New York: Holmes and Meier Publishers.
Fredriksson, L. (2008). Human rights in East Timor: advocacy and ethics in the field. In M. K. Huggins and M. L. Glebbeek (Eds.) *Women fielding danger: negotiating ethnographic identities in field research*, pp. 147–72. New York: Roman and Littlefield.
Goffman, E. (1986). *Stigma: notes on the management of spoiled identity*. New York: Touchstone.
Greenhalgh. T. and Taylor, R. (1997). How to read a paper: papers that go beyond numbers (qualitative research). *BMJ: British Medical Journal*, 315 (7110): 740–3.
Gunn, J. V. (1997). Autobiography in the "Emergency Zone": reading as witnessing. Paper presented at the Modern Languages Association conference, Toronto, 29 December.
Habenstein, R. (1970). The ways of pathways. In R.W. Habenstein (Ed.) *Pathways to data: field methods for studying ongoing social organizations*. Chicago, IL: Aldine Publishing.
Huggins, M. K. (2010). Modern institutionalized torture: is it "organized crime"? In R.J. Michalowski and W. Chambliss (Eds.) *State crime in the global age*. Cullompton: Willan Press.
Huggins, M. K. and Glebbeek, M. L. (2003). Women studying violent male institutions: cross-gendered dynamics in police research on secrecy and danger. *Theoretical Criminology*, 7(3): 363–87.
—— (2008a). Studying violent male institutions: gender dynamics in police research – Brazil and Guatemala. In Huggins, M. K. and Glebbeek, M. L. (Eds.) *Women fielding danger: negotiating ethnographic identities in field research*, pp. 353–77. New York: Roman and Littlefield.
—— (Eds.) (2008b). *Women fielding danger: negotiating ethnographic identities in field research*. New York: Roman and Littlefield.
Huggins, M. K., Haritos-Fatouros, M., and Zimbardo, P. (2002) *Violence workers: torturers and murderers reconstruct Brazilian atrocities*. Berkeley, CA: University of California Press.
Kitsuse, J. I. and Cicourel, A. V. (1963). A note on the uses of official statistics. *Social Problems*, 11: 131–9.
Klatch, R.E. (1988). The methodological problems of studying a politically resistant community. *Studies in Qualitative Methodology*, 1: 73–88.
Lee-Treweek, G. (2000). The insight of emotional danger: Research experiences in a home for older people. In G. Lee-Treweek and S. Linkogle (Eds.) *Danger in the field – risk and ethics in social research*. London: Routledge.
Levi, P. (1988). *If this is a man and the truce*. London, UK: Abacus Press.
Liazos, A. (1972). The poverty of the sociology of deviance: nuts, sluts, and preverts. *Social Problems*, 20(1): 103–20.
Loschper, G. (2000). Crime and social control as fields of qualitative research in the social sciences. *FQS. Forum: Qualitative Social Research*, Sozialforschung. Institute for Qualitative Research and the Center for Digital Systems, Freie Universität Berlin. Volume 1 #1, January. Online at http://www.qualitative-research.net/index.php/fqs/article/viewArticle/1119/2483 (accessed November 20, 2010).
Presser, L. (2008). Power, safety and ethics: cross-gender research with violent men. In M. K. Huggins and M. L. Glebbeek (Eds.) *Women fielding danger: negotiating ethnographic identities in field research* (pp. 251–70). New York: Roman and Littlefield.
Ragin, C., Nagel, J. and White, P. (2004a). Workshop on Scientific Foundations of Qualitative Research. Washington: National Science Foundation. Online at http://www.nsf.gov/pubs/2004/nsf04219/nsf04219.pdf (accessed November 20, 2010).
—— (2004b). Appendix 2: Workshop Agenda National Science Foundation Workshop on the Scientific Foundations of Qualitative Research. Washington: National Science Foundation. Available online from the NFS website (accessed November 20, 2010).
Robben, A. C. G. M. (1995). The politics of truth and emotion among victims and perpetrators of violence. In C. Nordstrum and A.C.G.M. Robben (Eds.) *Fieldwork under fire: contemporary violence and survival*. Berkeley: University of California.
Sanford, V. (2002). Gendered observations: activism, advocacy, and the Academy. In Huggins, M. K. and Glebbeek, M. L. (Eds.) *Women fielding danger: negotiating ethnographic identities in field research*, pp. 123–46. New York: Roman and Littlefield.
Schwandner-Sievers, S. (2008). Securing safe spaces: Field diplomacy in Albania and Kosovo. In M. K. Huggins and M. L. Glebbeek (Eds.) *Women fielding danger: negotiating ethnographic identities in field research*, pp. 173–98. New York: Roman and Littlefield.

Scully, D. (1984). Convicted rapists' perceptions of self and victim: role taking and emotions. *Gender and Society*, 2(2): 200–13.

Sehgal, M. (2008). The veiled feminist ethnographer: Fieldwork among women of India's Hindu Right. In M. K. Huggins and M. L. Glebbeek (Eds.) *Women fielding danger: negotiating ethnographic identities in field research*, pp. 325–52. New York: Roman and Littlefield.

Sharp, G. and Kramer, E. (2006). The safety dance: confronting harassment, intimidation, and violence in the field. *Sociological Methodology*, 36(1), 317–27.

Simmel, G. (1950). *The sociology of George Simmel.* Glencoe, IL: Free Press.

Skidmore, M. (2008). Secrecy and trust in the affective field: conducting field work in Burma. In M. K. Huggins and M. L. Glebbeek (Eds.) *Women fielding danger: negotiating ethnographic identities in field research*, pp. 301–23. New York: Roman and Littlefield.

Sluka, J.A. (1995). Reflections on managing danger in fieldwork: dangerous anthropology in Belfast. In C. Nordstrum and A.C.G.M. Robben (Eds.) *Fieldwork under fire: contemporary violence and survival*, pp. 276–94. Berkeley: University of California Press.

Smyth, L. and Mitchell, C. (n.d.) Researching conservative groups: rapport and understanding across moral and political boundaries. Online at http://works.bepress.com/cgi/viewcontent.cgi?article=1001&context=lisa_smyth (accessed November 20, 2010).

Viterna, J. (2008). Negotiating the muddiness of grassroots research: managing identity and data in rural El Salvador. In M. K. Huggins and M. L. Glebbeek (Eds.) *Women fielding danger: negotiating ethnographic identities in field research*, pp. 271–97. New York: Roman and Littlefield.

5

Quantitative criminology

Crime and justice statistics across nations

Jan van Dijk

Background and introduction

In the second half of the twentieth century criminologists became sensitized to the cultural and legal relativity of the concept of crime. Court and police statistics on crime came to be seen as social constructions, not necessarily reflecting an objective reality of crime. More specifically, criminologists became aware that police figures are heavily influenced by national legal definitions, recording practices of the police and the readiness of victims to report their experiences to the police. Considering the variation in these definitions and practices across countries, these insights were the kiss of death for comparative international criminology. Between 1970 and 2000 fewer studies comparing levels of crime of different countries were conducted than before (but see Barberet, 2009). For modern criminologists the epidemiological approach seemed to have run out of steam.

Two factors have spurned a revival of international comparative criminological research. First, administrative statistics of police forces, courts and prisons have in most developed countries been fully computerized, thereby enhancing both the completeness and reliability of official statistics on crime and justice. Statistics on numbers of police officers, recorded homicides, convictions and prisoners are currently available for scholarly analysis from a large number of countries (see http://www.unodc.org; http://www.wodc.nl (European Sourcebook); http://www.prisonstudies.org). Second, many governments have commissioned regular sample surveys among the public on their experiences with victimizations by common crime (crime victimization surveys). The resulting survey-based statistics, reflecting problems of crime as perceived by the public at large, provide a new source of information on crime and attitudes toward crime and justice. Questionnaires and other methods of standardized victimization surveys are well suited for comparative purposes (see the International Crime Victims Survey at http://rechten.uvt.nl/ICVS).

This chapter presents a sample of results of the new generation of empirical studies in comparative international criminology. First, survey-based data on the available measures of conventional or common criminality are presented, commenting on the strengths and weaknesses of international police figures and results of crime victimization surveys for comparative work. The next section presents comparative, international data on complex, non-conventional crimes such as organized crime and corruption. Third, prisoner rates from a large number of countries are presented, one of the few types of international statistic on the operation of criminal justice systems that can reliably be used for comparisons. The final section briefly discusses some emerging theoretical perspectives on the determinants of crime and on penal policies in an international, comparative perspective.

Police figures and victimization rates

Victimization surveys have primarily been designed as a source of statistical information on the volume and trends of common crime collected independently from police records. The surveys yield estimates of the total numbers of crime experienced by the public (victimization rates), which can be compared with numbers of officially recorded offences. Several developed countries conduct independent annual victimization surveys at a national scale, including Australia, England and Wales, France, Italy, the Netherlands, Scotland, Sweden, Switzerland and the USA. In the case of the International Crime Victim Surveys (ICVS), data about crime at the macro level is collected in a standardized way to allow comparisons across countries. The first round of ICVS surveys was in 1989, followed by surveys in 1992, 1996 and 2000. The last round of surveys was completed in 2004 and 2005. For full results and detailed information on the methods of the ICVS we refer to the reports with key findings (van Dijk *at al.*, 2008). In 2010 the survey was repeated in six countries, using web-based interviewing. The European Union has scheduled a fully-fledged European Security Survey to be conducted in all 27 member states for 2013.

The ICVS results provide an opportunity to study concurrence between the survey-based ranking and those according to international police figures. Howard and Smith (2003) examined the relationships between police figures of the UN Crime Survey, European Sourcebook of Crime and Criminal Justice Statistics and INTERPOL and between these three official measures of crime and ICVS victimization rates. Their analysis was limited to Europe and North America. Their results show that for the group of countries under study official measures collected by the UN, the European Sourcebook or INTERPOL are reasonably consistent amongst themselves but show little or no resemblance to rankings based on victimization survey research among the public. They also concluded that analyses of the social correlates of crime showed fundamentally different, even opposing results, depending on the data sources used, thus putting in doubt most of the existing knowledge on the macro-causes of crime based on official crime data.

A further test of the usefulness of recorded crime as a measure of the relative level of crime should include data on countries from all regions of the world and not just from Europe and North America. Both the UN crime survey and the ICVS contain a measure for "total crime." For 39 countries data are available on the overall ICVS victimization per 100 respondents in 2000 and the total numbers of crimes per 100,000 recorded by the police in 2002. Figure 5.1 depicts both the number of recorded crimes per 100,000 inhabitants and the percentage of the public victimized by crime according to the ICVS (van Dijk, 2007).

In the 39 countries with information from both sources, on average 28 percent of the respondents to the ICVS were victims of at least one crime of those included in the survey. Victimization rates in the majority of countries (23) were close to the average (between 23 and 33 percent), while 6 were well below (Azerbaijan, Philippines, Croatia, Japan, Spain and Portugal) and 10 markedly above. Among them, the countries where citizens were most frequently victimized were Colombia, Swaziland, Estonia, Uganda, South Africa, Zambia and the Czech Republic. In contrast, the highest levels of police-recorded crime were observed in Sweden, United Kingdom, Finland, Belgium, Denmark, Netherlands and Canada, while in Colombia, Uganda and Zambia, which as just mentioned appeared in the group of countries with the highest rates of victimization, police-recorded levels of crime are comparatively low. It can be observed

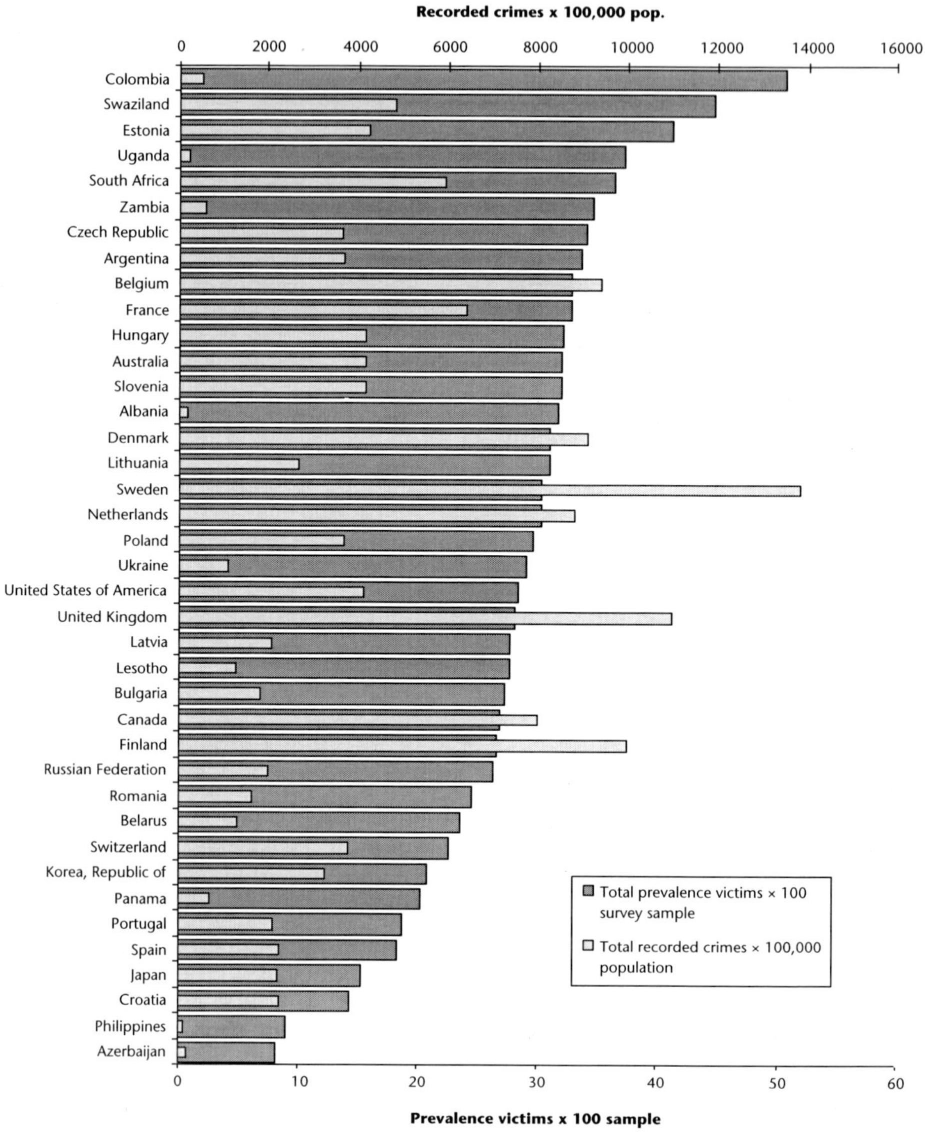

Figure 5.1 Total crime, by countries

that 4 out of 6 countries with the highest victimization rates were in Africa, while among the 6 countries with the highest levels of police-recorded crime 5 belong to the 15 Member States of the European Union before enlargement.

From a European perspective, it is worth noting that new members of the European Union, such as Romania, Bulgaria and Lithuania, show relatively low police figures and moderately high victimization rates. This finding suggests that dark numbers are comparatively high among these former communist nations. In these countries victims are less inclined to report crimes to the police and recording practices are relatively restrictive.

The results show that there is no correlation between the actual level of victimization by crime and the rates of crime recorded by the police among these 39 countries (r = 0.212; n = 39; n.s.). Some countries with exceptionally high numbers of recorded crimes also show comparatively high victimization rates (South Africa) but many others, such as Finland, Canada and Switzerland, do not. The comparison of these two measures shows that rates of total recorded crimes cannot be reliably used as measures of common crime in a comparative perspective. In response to these criticisms INTERPOL has decided to withdraw its long-running series of international police figures from its public websites. Since homicide statistics are less strongly affected by differences in legal definitions, reporting patterns and recording practices, they continue to be used for comparative analyses (LaFree and Tseloni, 2006). For comparisons of other frequently-occurring types of crimes, results of standardized victimization surveys are the preferred source.

Trends in common crime

Hereunder, data from the most recent round of the ICVS conducted in 2004/2005 in 30 industrialized countries and six main cities in developing countries are presented. Almost 16 percent of the population of the 30 participating countries has been a victim of any crime in 2004. The overall victimization rates per country are shown in Figure 5.2. The four countries with the highest overall prevalence victimization rates in 2004 are Ireland, England and Wales, New Zealand and Iceland. Other countries with comparatively high victimization rates are Northern Ireland, Estonia, the Netherlands, Denmark, Mexico, Switzerland and Belgium. All of these countries have overall victimization rates that are statistically significantly higher than the average of the 30 participating countries. The USA, Canada, Australia and Sweden show rates near the average. Compared to past results, these countries have dropped several places in the ranking on overall victimization. Countries with victimization levels just under the mean include Norway, Poland, Bulgaria, Scotland, Germany, Luxembourg and Finland. The lowest levels were found in Spain, Japan, Hungary, Portugal, Austria, France, Greece and Italy. The latter eight countries all have victimization levels significantly below the average of participating countries. They can be regarded as low-crime countries in this context. This group is fairly heterogeneous, both geographically and in terms of affluence (GDP per capita). Finland, Greece and Poland are comparatively less urbanized than other European countries.

Figure 5.2 also displays the results of surveys conducted in 32 main cities concerning victimization by any crime. The results confirm that levels of victimization by common crime are universally higher among city populations than among national populations. Lisbon forms the only exception to this criminological rule. The mean victimization rate of the participating cities in developed countries is 19.9 percent, whereas the mean national rate is 15.8 percent. In almost all countries, risks to be criminally victimized are a quarter to a third higher for main city inhabitants than for others.

On average, city rates are higher in developing countries (28.4 percent) than in developed countries (19.9 percent). This difference is most pronounced for victimization by personal crimes, especially robbery (van Dijk, 2007). The 2004/5 ranking of cities in terms of victimization puts Phnom Penh and Maputo on top. Relatively high rates are also found in London and Buenos Aires. Tallinn, Amsterdam, Reykjavik, Belfast, Dublin and Johannesburg have rates above the global mean. Victimization rates near the global city average of 21.7 percent are found in New York, Copenhagen, Stockholm, São Paulo and Oslo. The five participating cities with the lowest victimization rates are Hong Kong, Lisbon, Budapest, Athens and Madrid.

Trend data over the past 20 years are available for 15 Western countries. Overall trends in victimization show a curved trend since 1988 with a peak in the early or mid-1990s. The survey

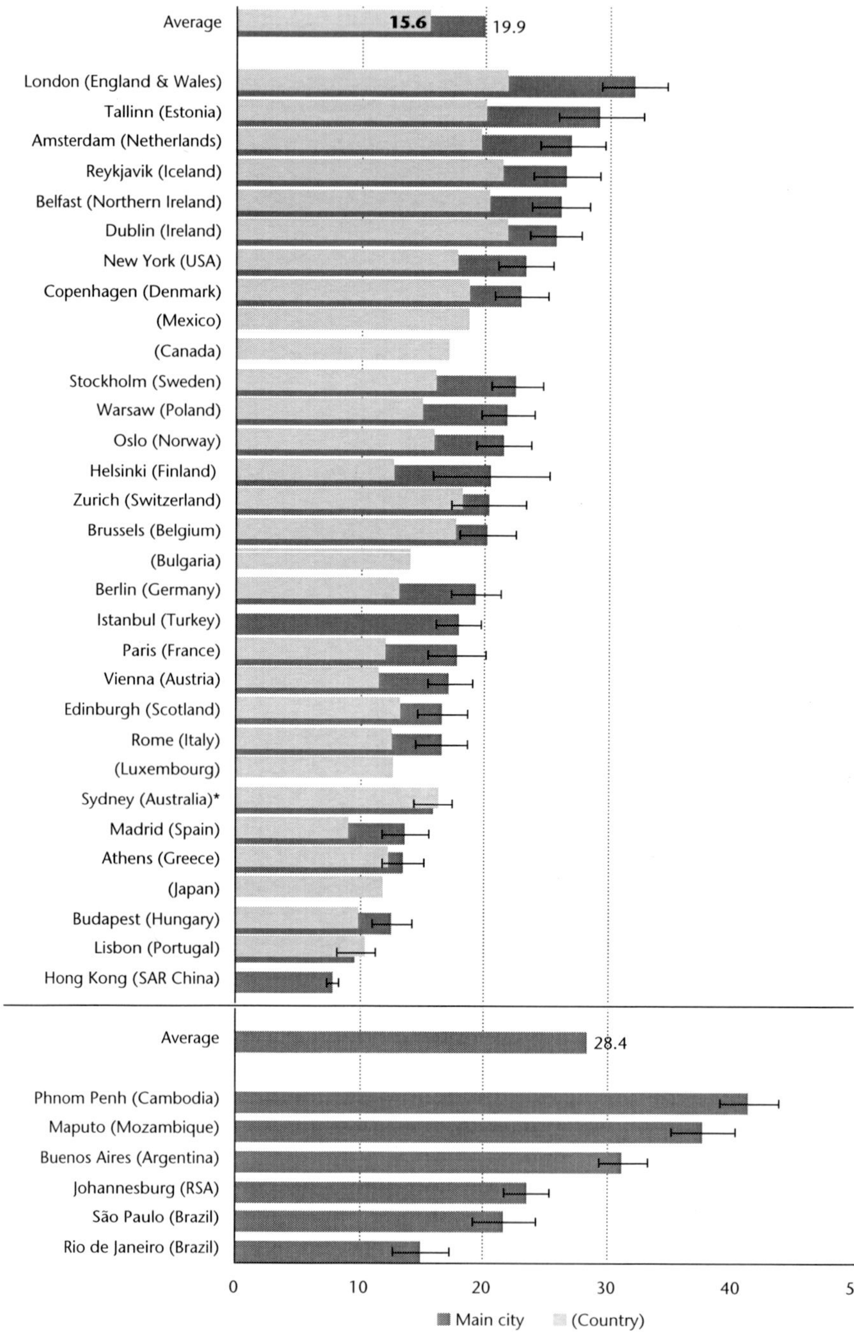

Figure 5.2 Overall victimization for ten crimes; one year prevalence rates in 2003/4 (percentages) of capital cities and national populations of 28 countries.

* Australian victimization rate is based on nine crimes; sexual offenses were not included; the overall victimization is one percent point lower as a result.

also showed that levels of fear of property crime are declining together with victimization rates and that levels of satisfaction with the police among the general public have gone up. The latest round of the ICVS confirms that most Western countries have emerged from a decade-long crime epidemic and that the public has started to become aware that this is indeed the case.

Measuring organized crime with the use of statistical indicators

One important limitation of victimization surveys, including the ICVS, is their focus on common crimes victimizing ordinary citizens. No information is collected about other types of crime harming the community rather than individual persons, such as environmental crimes, organized crime and high-level corruption. Developing indicators for these crimes is a further challenge for comparative criminology.

The first requirement of measuring organized crime in an international context is agreement on its definition. Although definitions in national law show great variation, criminologists describe organized crime as criminal activities for material benefit by groups that engage in extreme violence, corruption of public officials, including law enforcement and judicial officers, penetration of the legitimate economy (e.g. through racketeering and money-laundering) and interference in the political process These elements are not only incorporated in anti-mafia laws of some countries, including the USA, Italy and Hungary, but are also used as operational definitions by the FBI and the European police community.

One of the most common types of organized crime is racketeering including the collection of protection money from businesses. Through victimization surveys among business executives, reliable information can be collected on the extent of extortion practices in business communities in different countries. Since 1997 the World Economic Forum (WEF) has carried out annual surveys among business executives of larger companies to identify obstacles to businesses, which includes a question on the prevalence in the country of organized crime defined as "mafia-oriented racketeering, extortion" (World Economic Forum, 2003 and 2004; see http://www.weforum.org/en/media/publications). Data are available on the prevalence of organized crime according to business executives of 102 countries. An analysis was conducted of the results from the seven rounds of WEF surveys conducted between 1997 and 2003. National scores proved to be very consistent across years. To reduce sampling error, the scores of the annual surveys were averaged. The resulting mean scores for 1997–2003 are based on sample sizes of 500 or more. The national scores reflect the perceived prevalence of organized crime in the period 1997 to 2003 according to business executives.

Another source of cross-national data on perceived organized crime is risk assessments made by international consultancy companies. The London-based consultancy company Merchant International Group (MIG) assesses investment risks in over 150 countries, including the prevalence of different types of organized crime (MIG, 2004).[1] The risk assessments concerning organized crime from MIG were found to be strongly correlated to the perceptions of business executives of the WEF surveys. To facilitate further statistical exploration, a composite index was constructed based on the averaged rankings of countries on the WEF surveys of 1997 to 2003 and the assessments of organized crime prevalence of MIG. The resulting Organized Crime Perception Index (OCPI) refers to the level of different types of organized crime activities, such as extortion and drugs, arms and people trafficking, as perceived by potential victim groups and/or independent experts.

As mentioned above, instrumental violence, corruption of public officials and money-laundering are regarded as other defining characteristics of organized crime. It is indeed hard to imagine a country where organized crime is rampant without significant amounts of these three mafia-related phenomena. Statistical indicators were selected for the prevalence of each of these three defining characteristics of organized crime. Police-recorded homicides can be roughly divided into emotional attacks on intimates and cool-blooded killings executed by organized crime. The perpetrators of the first category are in most cases arrested. The perpetrators of the second category are not. To develop a proxy measure of "mob-related violence," rates of unsolved homicides were calculated by deducting numbers of convictions for homicide from the numbers of police-recorded homicides.[2] The resulting country rates of unsolved murders per 100,000 population were found to be fairly strongly correlated to the national scores on the OCPI ($r = .57$; $n = 63$; $p < 0.05$). Similarly, a proxy indicator of "high level corruption" was derived from studies of the World Bank Institute and indicators of money-laundering and the extent of the black economy were taken from the WEF surveys among business executives. All three indicators proved to be strongly correlated to the scores on the OCPI as well. These findings support the construction of a composite organized crime index combining the five interrelated proxy indicators: perceived prevalence of organized crime, especially racketeering, unsolved homicides, grand corruption, money-laundering and the extent of the black economy.

Table 5.1 depicts the mean scores on the Composite Organized Crime Index (COCI) of world regions. To allow a more detailed diagnosis of regional problems with organized crime, the picture presents both the absolute scores of regions on the composite index as well as the rank numbers on the five source indicators used.

The ranking of regions according to the composite index and those according to the five constituting indicators show a high degree of consistency. Outliers are the relatively high-rank numbers on informal sector and money-laundering of Central America. Among the high-crime regions, West and Central Africa show relatively low-rank numbers on homicides. The latter result could point to a shortcoming in the available statistics – homicide statistics for Nigeria are, for example, missing. It could also reflect that organized crime groups in the region are less prone than elsewhere to the use of extreme violence.

Country scores

The combination of data from different sources allows the calculation of scores for a large number of individual countries. The rank numbers of countries for different indicators are mostly in the same range as the COCI rank, but many deviations can be found. Deviations of single indicators from the COCI rank can point to specific features of organized crime in the country or to deficiencies in some of the measures. In some cases the diagnosis at the country level can only be very tentative due to lack of sufficient information on the source indicators, notably on the numbers of unsolved homicides.

Figure 5.3 shows the global map of organized crime, based on the OCPI. As said, the rates of individual countries should not be taken at face value, but be used as a basis for further enquiry. In Asia rates are the worst in parts of South Asia (Pakistan, Bangladesh). But also China and India are rated unfavourably (even more than Italy with its notorious problems in the South). In the international literature on organized crime India is rarely the focus of attention. Research on Chinese organized crime is mainly focused on Chinese expatriates. Limited available research findings on homeland China point to collusion between corrupt communist party members and local gangs in remote areas (Zhang, 2001). More research on the role of the organized crime–corruption in these two emerging superpowers seems warranted.

In Africa, Nigeria, Angola and Mozambique stand out with the highest scores. Nigerian organized crime activity in both the country and the region has been well documented (UNODC, 2005). A detailed account of how organized crime threatens to penetrate state and

Table 5.1 Regional mean scores on Composite Organized Crime Index (COCI) and data on source indicators: perceived organized crime prevalence, grand corruption, money-laundering, extent of shadow economy and the rates of unsolved murders per 100,000 population

	Average of the composite organized crime index	*Organized crime perception (rank)*	*Informal sector (rank)*	*Unsolved homicides (rank)*	*High-level corruption (rank)*	*Money laundering (rank)*
Oceania	33	1	1	1	2	1
West and Central Europe	35	2	2	2	4	3
North America	44	4	4	4	6	4
East and South East Asia	45	5	3	7	3	6
Central America	50	4	13	3	8	13
Near and Middle East	50	7	6	11	1	2
World	54	—	—	—	—	—
South Asia	54	13	8	8	7	11
North Africa	55	6	5	6	—	5
East Africa	55	11	9	—	11	9
Southern Africa	56	9	12	5	12	10
South America	58	10	14	10	13	12
South-East Europe	58	14	10	12	9	14
West and Central Africa	60	12	11	15	5	8
East Europe	70	16	16	14	14	16
Central Asia and Transcaucasian	70	15		13	15	—
Caribbean	70	8	15	—	16	15

Source: van Dijk (2007).

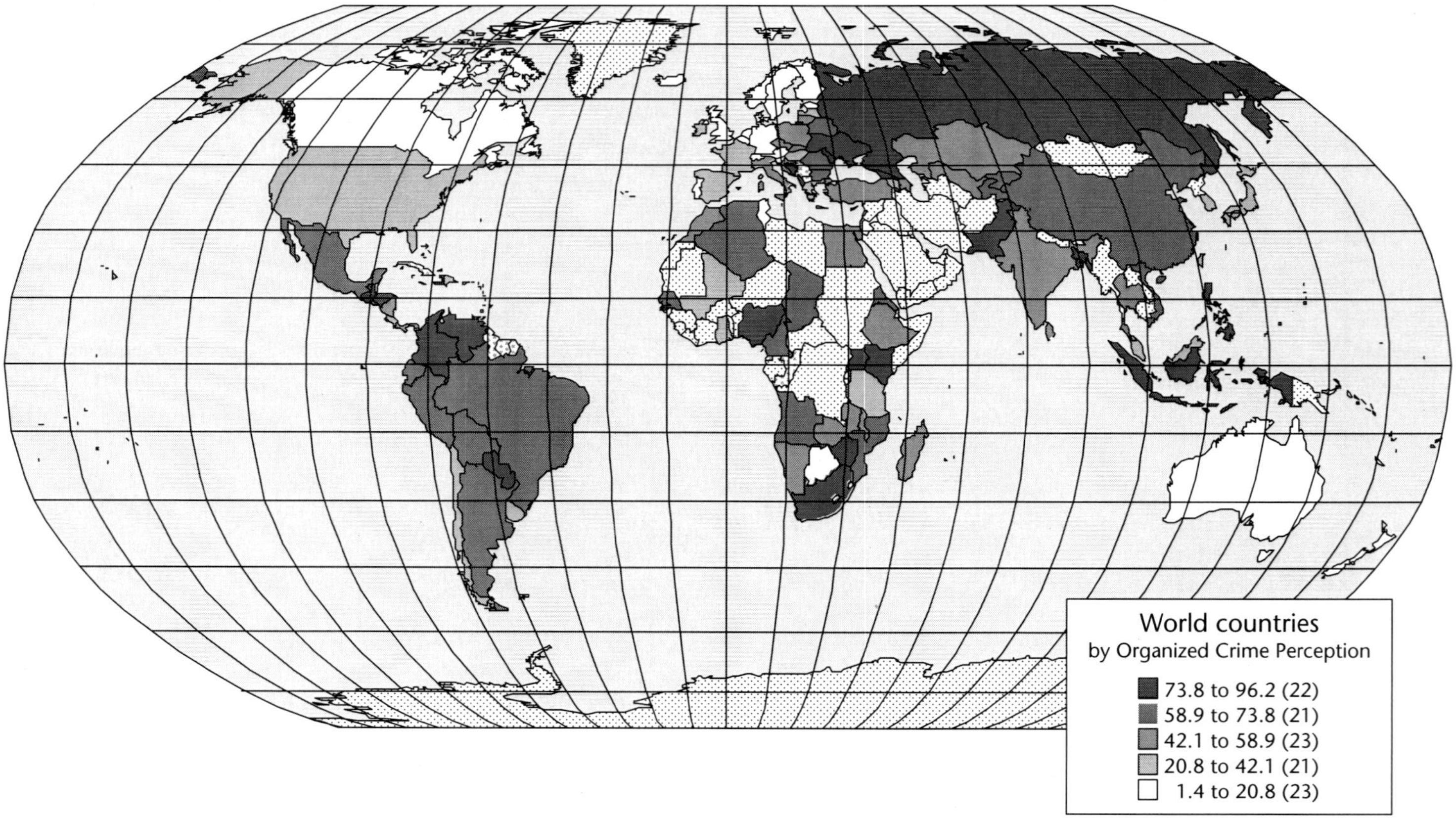

Figure 5.3 Global maps with scores on Organized Crime Perception Index

businesses in Southern Africa, notably in Mozambique, is given in Gastrow (2003). In Latin America, Haiti, Paragua, Guatamala, Venezuela and Colombia show the highest scores. High scores are also observed in Jamaica. None of these scores will come as a surprise to informed readers.

Within Europe, organized crime prevalence increases diagonally from the North West to the South East, with levels being low in England and Germany, higher in Spain and Italy and by far the highest in Russia, Albania and Ukraine. The annual surveys of the WEF point at incremental improvements in some of the new Member States of the European Union.

Trends in prisoner rates

Statistics on the operations of the criminal justice system are strongly influenced by legal definitions and procedural technicalities determining the processing of cases through the system. This feature greatly complicates meaningful international comparisons. One of the statistics that seems relatively unaffected by legal niceties of national laws and systems is the number of detainees as a rough indicator of the punitiveness of criminal justice across countries. On the basis of the figures of the World Prison List, collated by British criminologist Roy Walmsley, the world prisoner rate was approximately 158 per 100,000 population in 2007–8. This figure indicates that at that time, over 10 million people were being held in penal institutions around the world, either as pre-trial detainees or after having been convicted. According to informed estimates, the official Chinese numbers exclude 850,000 people in "administrative detention" ordered by the prosecutors outside court procedures (Walmsley, 2007). If these estimated dark numbers of Chinese prisoners are added, the world total inmates can be estimated at 10.6 million. This amounts to the total population of a medium-sized country such as Belgium or Portugal. It means that the global prisoner rate is circa 166 per 100,000 people.

Because many prisoners stay in prison for less than one year, the total number of persons admitted into a prison in the course of a year (admission rate), is higher than the number incarcerated at any date. In many countries, the prison admission rate is three times higher than the prisoner rate. The total number of people admitted to prisons per year can be estimated at 20 million worldwide.

Over the past three years prison populations have continued to grow in many parts of the world. Prison populations have risen in 71 percent of countries included in the World Prison List. The largest prison populations according to now available data, are to be found in China (2.4 million including pre-trial detainees and those in "administrative detention"), the USA (2.29 million in 2008), Russian Federation (0.89 million), Brazil (0.44 million), India (0.37 million), Mexico (0.22 million), Thailand (0.17 million in 2005), South Africa (0.16 million) and Iran (0.166 million).

Imprisonment is, besides capital punishment, the most severe form of punishment. The rates of prisoners per 100,000 population can be used as a proxy indicator of the punitiveness of national criminal justice systems. Table 5.2 shows the national prisoner rates per 100,000 of selected countries.

At the country level, rates per 100,000 are highest in the US. In 2008, the rate has risen to 756. Other categories of corrections, such as parole and probation, show equally high figures in the US (Uggen *et al.*, 2006). High rates of prisoners are also found in countries of the former Soviet Union, such as Russia (606), Belarus (544), Kazakhstan (522) and Turkmenistan (489), as well as in Southern Africa (e.g. South Africa, 402) and the Caribbean (e.g. Bahamas, 410). In Asia, Thailand and Singapore stand out with comparatively high rates. At the low end stand

Table 5.2 *World ranking according to number of prisoners per 100,000 population in 2004–6 (latest available)*

15 countries with high rates								
1	United States	701	6	Belize	459	11	Bahamas, The	410
2	Russian Fed.	606	7	Suriname	437	12	South Africa	402
3	Belarus	554	8	Dominica	420	13	Thailand	401
4	Kazakhstan	522	9	Ukraine	415	14	Kyrgyz Republic	390
5	Turkmenistan	489	10	Maldives	414	15	Singapore	388
15 countries with moderately high rates								
18	Estonia	361	68	Mexico	156	75	Spain	138
27	Cuba	297	70	New Zealand	155	108	Germany	98
33	Tunisia	252	74	United Kingdom	141	130	Sweden	73
38	Iran	226	91	China (est. at 166)	117	134	Finland	70
39	Poland	218	92	Canada	116	151	Japan	53
15 countries with low rates								
164	Congo, Rep.	38	169	Mali	34	174	Comoros	30
165	Guinea	37	170	Micronesia	34	175	Indonesia	29
166	Iceland	37	171	Nigeria	33	176	India	29
167	Sudan	36	172	Gambia, The	32	177	Nepal	29
168	Angola	36	173	Solomon Islands	31	178	Burkina Faso	23

Source: Walmsley (2007).

countries in Western–Central Europe, Southern Europe, South Central Asia (e.g. India, 29; and Indonesia, 29) and Western Africa (e.g. Nigeria, 33).

Expanding use of imprisonment

Prison populations have grown since the late 1980s in most parts of the world. Growth figures vary from 20 percent in Western Europe to 60 percent or more in the USA, Mexico, Brazil and Colombia. In the USA, the number of people incarcerated has risen by 290 percent since 1980 (Waller, 2006). Rising crime rates may explain in part these movements in prison populations. In many countries rates of serious crimes have, however, been fairly stable or decreasing over the last ten years, as was the case in the USA and most European countries. Part of the rise in the prison population is, therefore, attributed by experts to an increasing belief among sentencing decision makers that prison is preferable to its alternatives or perceived to be so by the public (Waller, 2006). Reviews of factors behind recent major increases in prison populations indicate that the growth is mainly the result of changes in sentencing policies: greater use of imprisonment, longer sentences and more restricted use of parole or conditional release (Walmsley, 2007).

In Eastern and Central European countries there was a marked increase in crime after the political transformations in the early 1990s and this seems to have resulted in the increased use of imprisonment. Since the mid-1990s, crime rates have been mainly stable while the prisoner rate continued to rise. One of the reasons for this could be that the public, media and subsequently the politicians continue to be alarmed by the increased level of crime, generating a generalized toughening of public attitudes towards offenders.

Theoretical explorations

Criminologists can use valid and reliable country data on crime and justice to test theories on the macro causes of crime and correlates of penal policies. Policy makers can use such information for the purpose of benchmarking their country's performance in terms of crime and crime control in an international perspective.

The results of the ICVS have, first of all, refuted the conventional notion of the USA as a high-crime nation. Levels of common property crime and assaults in the USA lie below that of many European countries. Among Western nations, Australia, United Kingdom, the Netherlands and Ireland stand out with the highest prevalence of simple assaults. This position is associated with the highest consumption of beer in liters per head. In Southern Europe beer consumption is much lower and so are rates of victimization by assaults. USA shows moderate scores on beer consumption and simple assaults. It stands out, though, with comparatively high levels of assaults and robberies at gun point. International comparison suggests that the high rates of serious violence in the USA are linked to its uniquely high level of ownership of firearms, especially hand guns (Hepburn and Hemenway, 2004). In the USA over a third of all households own one or more firearms. Elsewhere in developed countries ownership rates range between 1 percent in the United Kingdom and the Netherlands to 4 percent in Australia and 11 percent in Canada.

Probably the most common theoretical notion on crime is that it is driven by social problems such as extreme poverty and economic inequality. This has always been one of the tenets of the milieu school, expressed in the famous citation of French criminologist Lacassagne that each society possesses the crime rate that it deserves (Alexandre Lacassagne, 1903; Wikipedia, n.d.). Available empirical evidence for the poverty–crime link seems, however, mixed. Support for this hypothesis can be found in the high rates of violent crime and robberies in many of the largest cities in Africa and South America. Some of the poorer Asian nations, however, such as India, Philippines and Indonesia, belong to the safest places on earth. The low-crime situation in metropoles, such as Djakarta and Bombay, flies in the face of the poverty–crime link. Among the developed countries variations in crime levels in 2004/5 do not fit the hypothesis either. The ten countries with the highest rates of common crime comprise several very affluent countries, such as Switzerland, Ireland and Iceland. Trends in crime over time also put into question conventional wisdom about poverty as the main driver of common crime. In the Western world crime booms seem to have been propelled by the increased opportunities of crime created by postwar economic growth (Cohen and Felson, 1979) rather than by economic slumps. Recent crime booms in Switzerland, Ireland and Iceland are cases in point. These three countries have each in recent years undergone rapid economic growth.

Considering the poverty–crime link, many are concerned about the impact of the current financial and economic crisis on levels of crime. In our view, the drop in property crime of recent years was caused by improved self-protection by potential victims in response to increased risk awareness (van Dijk, 2007). The economic crisis may persuade people to be even more careful with their possessions and thereby curtail opportunities of crime. Through this mechanism the crisis may sustain rather than disturb the ongoing drop in crime.

Levels of organized crime are unrelated to levels of common crime. A high degree of urbanization is associated with high levels of common crime, but not of organized crime. The variation across nations of organized crime requires a separate explanation. International data reveal that high levels of organized crime almost invariably go together with ill-functioning state institutions and economic stagnation. These universal findings suggest that organized crime, bad governance and poverty are mutually reinforcing forces. Organized crime tends to erode the integrity of those holding a public office, including those responsible for upholding the rule of law. Through the pervasive bias of legislation, policy decisions and jurisprudence, market efficiencies are undermined and both local and foreign investors lose confidence in the legal and regulatory functions of the state and stay away. Many developing countries are trapped in vicious cycles of rampant organized crime, grand corruption and lack of investment. These insights from comparative international criminology underline the vital importance of the rule of law in the advancement of sustainable economic growth. To promote sustainable development, developing countries and countries with economies in transition should follow the striking examples of prosperous nations, such as Singapore, Hong Kong and Botswana. These model countries have all grounded their economic policies on well-functioning security and justice sectors with special attention for anti-graft commissions.

Finally, the striking variation in national imprisonment rates are often used as a direct measure of the severity of sentencing in a country. Actually, they may also be the result of higher levels of serious crime and/or the outcome of more effective action in solving such crimes and bringing to justice those who have committed them. When interpreting prisoners' rates, it is important to take into account the seriousness of the national crime problem. Homicide rates are a reliable indicator of the overall level of violent and organized crime in a country. In order to put the national imprisonment rates in perspective, van Dijk (2007) related the imprisonment rates per 100,000 population to the rates of homicides per 100,000 population. These data allow nations to benchmark their imprisonment rate with those of countries that experience similar homicide rates. For example, the USA, a country housing a quarter of the world's total prison population, ranks first on imprisonment and 46th on homicide rates. Possible candidate countries for a benchmarking exercise would be Australia and Finland whose homicide rates are roughly similar (rankings of 59 and 64 respectively) but whose rankings on prisoners rates are incomparably lower (64 and 95) than the top position of the USA. Homicide rates are not dramatically lower in the United Kingdom or Spain either, two other countries with much lower imprisonment rates. Benchmarking with these countries might provide useful insights for the USA. If the USA would move somewhat in the direction of the prisoner rates of a country such as the United Kingdom, such policy would potentially produce savings of several tens of billions of government expenditures per year. The benchmarking will, among other things, reveal that levels of (serious) crime are falling in these reference countries as fast as in the USA. They seem as successful as the USA in controlling or reducing crime, while maintaining much lower prisoner rates. Such benchmarking might also be of interest to countries with medium–high prisoner rates, such as the United Kingdom. It seems interesting to examine in more detail and depth why the United Kingdom ranks 52 on prisoner rates and Sweden 92, while the UK homicide rates are lower than those of Sweden.

Using ICVS data on victimization, fear of crime and public attitudes, Norris (2009) has investigated which nations are most similar in terms of crime and justice measures. His results confirm that an existing typology of nations applied in studies of public administration, the Family of Nations Typology, is applicable to the domain of crime and justice. Anglophone nations form a distinct cluster characterized by, inter alia, moderately high crime rates and high punitiveness. Other distinct clusters are the Nordic countries, including Austria and Switzerland and the mid continental European countries. As in previous analyses, Japan, with its low victimization rates and high punitiveness, was found to be an outlier.

In a focused analysis of the correlates of punitiveness, van Kesteren (2009) has shown that on a global scale high punitiveness is strongly related to economic inequality. The latter factor explains why the cluster of Anglophone countries is characterized by high punitiveness. The uniqueness of the Anglophone countries in terms of crime and justice seems somehow related to their comparatively high degrees of economic inequality.

In the coming years more international statistics on crime and justice will become available. The United Nations is committed to continue its regular worldwide collection of statistics on inter alia homicides and human trafficking and on the operation of criminal justice systems. A new round of the ICVS was conducted in 2010. In Europe, the European Union has started to publish harmonized statistics on police-recorded crimes (Tavares and Thomas, 2008) and is preparing the launch of a regular standardised victimization survey in all 27 member states. Theoretical reflection on these new sources of information on crime and justice in an international perspective is still in its infancy. The utilization of the data sources listed poses a challenge to criminologists willing to think out of the box of established realities and policies of their home countries.

Future research questions

1. Based on similarities and differences in the crime and justice profiles of your home country and one or more other nations of interest, using common crime, organized crime and level of imprisonment, what could these countries learn from each other?
2. Why can statistics of police-recorded offences not be reliably used for comparisons of levels of crime across countries?
3. What are the main differences between developed countries (the North) and developing countries (the South) in terms of both common crime and organized crime? What are the possible explanations for the gap in security?
4. What is the relationship between affluence and level of common criminality at the country level, focusing on various world regions?
5. Identify nations suffering from homicide rates of the same magnitude as the USA with significantly lower prisoner rates. What are the possible explanations for the divergence in the level of imprisonment?

Notes

1 The Merchant International Group Limited's monthly Global Risk Trends include information on trends in corruption and organized crime in selected countries (http://www.riskline.com).

2 Both types of data were drawn from the seventh round of the crime and criminal justice surveys of UNODC.

References

Barberet, R. (2009). The legacy of INTERPOL crime data to cross-national criminology. *International Journal of Comparative and Applied Criminal Justice*, 33(2): 193–210.

Cohen, L. E. and Felson, M. (1979). Social change and crime rate trends: a routine activity approach. *American Sociological Review*, 44: 588–608.

van Dijk, J. J. M (2007). *The world of crime; breaking the silence on problems of security, justice, and development across the world.* Thousand Oaks, CA: Sage Publications.

van Dijk, J. J. M., Smit, P. and Kesteren, J. Van (2008). *Criminal victimization in global perspective; key findings of the ICVS 2004–2005 and the EU ICS.* Meppel: Boom Legal Publishers; and The Hague: Research and Documentation Center, Ministry of Justice.

Gastrow, P. (2003). *Penetrating state and business. Organized crime in Southern Africa.* Vol. 1. Pretoria: Institute for Security Studies.

Hepburn, L. M. and Hemenway, D. (2004). Firearm availability and homicide: a review of the literature. *Aggression and Violent Behavior*, 9: 417–40.

Howard, G. J. and Smith, T. R. (2003). Understanding cross-national variations of crime rates in Europe and North America. In K. Aromaa, S. Leppa, S. Nevala and N. Ollus (Eds.), *Crime and criminal justice systems in Europe and North America, 1995–1997*, pp. 23–65. Helsinki: HEUNI.

Kaufmann, D., Kraay, A., and Mastruzzi, M. (2004). *Governance matters III: Governance indicators for 1996–2002*. Policy Research Working Paper 3106. Washington, DC: World Bank. Online at http://www.worldbank.org/wbi/governance/pubs/govmatters3.html (accessed November 23, 2010).

van Kesteren, J. N. (2009). Public attitudes and sentencing policies across the world. *European Journal of Criminology and Criminal Policy*, 15: 25–46.

LaFree, G. and Tseloni, A. (2006). Democracy and crime: a multilevel analysis of homicide trends in 44 countries, 1950–2000. *Annals of the American Academy of Political and Social Science*, 605, Thousand Oaks: SAGE Publications, pp. 26–49.

Merchant International Group Limited (MIG). (2004). Grey area dynamics, organized crime figures 2004. Special analysis commissioned by UNICRI.

Norris, P. A. (2009). Families of nations, victimisation and attitudes towards criminal justice. *International Review of Victimology*, 16: 229–55.

Tavares, C. and Thomas, G. (2008). Statistics in focus, crime and criminal justice. Luxembourg: Eurostat.

Uggen, C., Manza, J., and Thompson, M. (2006). Citizenship, democracy, and the civic reintegration of criminal offenders. In S. Karstedt and G. LaFree (Eds) *Democracy, Crime, and Justice, Annals of the American Academy of Political and Social Science*, 605: 281–310.

United Nations Office on Drugs and Crime (UNODC). (2005). *Crime and development in Africa*. Vienna: UNODC.

Waller, I. (2006). *Less law, more order. The truth about reducing crime*. Westport: Praeger.

Walmsley, R. (2007). World Prison Population List. 7th and 8th edns. London: King's College, International Centre for Prison Studies.

Wikipedia (n.d.) Alexandre Lacassagne. Online at http://en.wikipedia.org/wiki/Alexandre_Lacassagne (accessed December 3, 2010).

Zhang, X. (2001) The emergence of "black society" crime in China. *Forum on Crime and Society*, 1: 53–73.

6

The Campbell Collaboration Crime and Justice Group

A decade of progress

David P. Farrington, David L. Weisburd and Charlotte E. Gill

What works to reduce crime? How should offenders be dealt with so that they do not reoffend? What methods of preventing crime are most cost-effective? These are all questions to which citizens, as well as government officials, policy makers, practitioners, researchers, teachers, and the news media, deserve good answers. All such persons should have ready access to the most rigorous and up-to-date evidence on the effectiveness of interventions designed to reduce crime and offending. The best evidence on what works should be quickly accessible to those who need it.

Much practice in crime and justice, as in fields such as medicine and education, is based on long-term traditions and clinical experience. Although tradition and experience often provide the only guidance for criminal justice practitioners, there is a growing consensus among scholars, practitioners, and policy makers that crime control practices and policies should be grounded as much as possible in the results of scientific research (Cullen and Gendreau, 2000; MacKenzie, 2000; Sherman *et al.*, 2006). Support for evidence-based policy in criminal justice may be seen as part of a more general trend toward the use of scientific research for establishing rational and effective practices and policies in many fields. This trend is perhaps most prominent in the health professions where the idea of evidence-based medicine has gained strong government and professional support. A central component of the movement toward evidence-based practice and policy is the reliance on systematic reviews of prior research and evaluation studies.

In the past, there have been many efforts to review the literature on "What Works," of which some of the most famous have been by Martinson (1974), McGuire (1995), and Sherman et al. (1997). Most of these efforts have included narrative rather than systematic reviews of the literature. In this chapter, we will first discuss both narrative and systematic reviews, to bring out the difference between them. We will then describe an international network that aims to produce and make accessible the best evidence on what works in crime and justice: the Campbell Crime and Justice Group (CCJG). This network of scholars, policy makers, practitioners, and others from around the world is preparing rigorous systematic reviews of high-quality research on the effects of criminological interventions.

These systematic reviews are being maintained and updated in light of new studies, insightful criticisms, or new methodological developments. They are readily accessible on the Internet: see http://www.campbellcollaboration.org. Through international collaboration, the Crime and Justice Steering Committee (CJSC) aims to ensure that relevant evaluation studies conducted all over the world will be taken into account in its systematic reviews, and that the evidence from such reviews will be made accessible globally through language translation and worldwide dissemination.

Deciding what works from narrative reviews

Deciding what works to reduce crime and delinquency requires us to examine the results of prior evaluation studies whenever they are available. This is better than drawing conclusions about what works from our personal experience, from anecdotal evidence, from widespread beliefs, or from a single study that was well funded or heavily publicized. Given such advantages, it is no surprise to find that criminologists have been reviewing what works for at least 50 years. Although the methods have varied, reviewers have followed the same general set of tasks: identify and gather relevant reports of evaluation studies, assess them, and come to a summary conclusion about what works.

Beginning in the 1970s, the traditional methods used in these reviews began to be seriously criticized. One criticism focussed on the general lack of explicitness of reviews: most suffered from a lack of detail about how the reviewer conducted the research. Information was often missing about why certain studies were included while others were excluded from the review. Sometimes this lack of detail was caused by space limitations imposed on reviewers by journal or book editors. The report of the review often did not describe what literature searches were carried out in order to locate relevant evaluation studies. It was often difficult for the serious reader to determine how the reviewers came to their conclusions about what works. Too often, the reader was forced to accept and trust the reviewer's expertise and was not given sufficient information to permit replication of the reviewer's methods.

A second criticism focussed on the methods used. Most of the reviewers did not attempt to control for problems that could potentially bias their review toward one conclusion rather than another. At its worst, a reviewer advocating a particular conclusion could selectively include only studies favoring that viewpoint in the review. For example, a reviewer in favor of strict gun control laws could ignore evaluations that found little effect of such laws. Such intentional distortion was fortunately rare in academic reviews.

More common than intentional distortion was the failure to deal with potential biases that could compromise the results of a review. For example, some reviewers examining what works relied on easy-to-obtain journal articles as the only source of reports of evaluations. One advantage of journal articles over other documents is that they have usually passed a rigorous peer review process. Unfortunately, research in other fields suggests that relying on journal articles can bias the results towards concluding that interventions are more effective than they really are. This is because researchers in many fields are more likely to submit their papers to journals when they find a positive effect of an intervention and are more likely to bury the manuscript in their file drawer when they do not. Both authors and journal editors are biased against papers reporting no effect, sometimes falsely assuming that such papers do not contribute to knowledge. This is called publication bias (see Rothstein *et al.*, 2005).

Another criticism is that inexplicit and unsystematic review methods cannot cope with the incredible increase in research worldwide. For example, the number of journals that now publish materials relevant to crime and justice is enormous compared to just a few years ago. Relying on journals available in a library or on papers collected in office files will no longer ensure coverage of all available studies. The Internet now makes hundreds – if not thousands – of evaluation reports readily accessible to prospective reviewers. In the same way that it would be difficult to make sense of a large, growing and scattered collection of police reports or prison folders without orderly methods, it is also difficult to make sense of the burgeoning and scattered number of relevant evaluation studies without some systematic method for doing so.

Characteristics of systematic reviews

What are systematic reviews? These are reviews that use rigorous methods for locating, appraising, and synthesizing evidence from prior evaluation studies (see Farrington and Petrosino, 2000; Littell *et al.*, 2008). They contain methods and results sections, and are reported with the same level of detail that characterizes high-quality reports of original research. Other features of systematic reviews include:

1. *Explicit objectives.* The rationale for conducting the review is made clear.
2. *Explicit eligibility criteria.* The reviewers specify in detail why they included certain studies and rejected others. What was the minimum level of methodological quality for inclusion in the review? Did they consider only a particular type of evaluation design such as randomized experiments? Did the studies have to include a certain type of participant, such as children or adults? What types of interventions were included? What kinds of outcome data had to be reported in the studies? All criteria or rules used in selecting eligible studies are explicitly stated in the final report.
3. *The search for studies is designed to reduce potential bias.* There are many potential ways in which bias can compromise the results of a review. The reviewers must explicitly state how they conducted their search of potential studies to reduce such bias. How did they try to locate studies reported outside scientific journals? How did they try to locate studies in foreign languages? All bibliographic databases that were searched should be made explicit so that potential gaps in coverage can be identified (and reviews can be replicated).
4. *Each study is screened according to eligibility criteria, with exclusions justified.* The searches always locate many citations and abstracts to potentially relevant studies. Each of the reports of these potentially relevant studies must be screened to determine whether it meets the eligibility criteria for the review. A full listing of all excluded studies and the justifications for exclusion should be made available to readers.
5. *Assembly of the most complete data possible.* The systematic reviewer will generally try to obtain all relevant evaluations meeting the eligibility criteria. In addition, all data relevant to the objectives of the review should be carefully extracted from each eligible report and coded and computerized. Sometimes, original study documents lack important information. When possible, the systematic reviewer will attempt to obtain this from the authors of the original report.
6. *Quantitative techniques are used, when appropriate and possible, in analyzing results.* Although there is still some confusion about the meaning of these terms, it is useful to distinguish between a systematic review and a meta-analysis. A meta-analysis involves the statistical or quantitative analysis of the results of prior research studies (see Borenstein *et al.*, 2009; Lipsey and Wilson, 2001). Because it involves the statistical summary of effect sizes and their correlates, it requires a reasonable number of intervention studies that are sufficiently similar to be grouped together. For example, there may be little point in reporting a weighted mean effect size based on a very small number of studies. Nevertheless, quantitative methods can be very important in helping the reviewer determine the average effect size of a particular intervention and in what circumstances it works best.

   A systematic review may or may not include a meta-analysis. For example, a reviewer may only find a few studies meeting the eligibility criteria. Those studies may, for example, differ just enough in the operational definition of the intervention or in the way they were conducted to make formal meta-analysis inappropriate and potentially misleading. It is important not to combine apples and oranges in calculating a weighted mean effect size.

7. *Structured and detailed report.* The final report of a systematic review is structured and detailed so that the reader can understand each phase of the research, the decisions that were made, and the conclusions that were reached. In principle, it should be possible for an independent scholar to replicate both the review and the results.

From Cochrane to Campbell

An important model for the development of systematic reviews has come from the Cochrane Collaboration, which seeks to prepare, maintain, and make accessible systematic reviews of research on the effects of health care interventions (see http://www.cochrane.org). The Cochrane Library, with over 1,200 completed and maintained reviews on a variety of treatments, is now widely recognized as the single best source of evidence on the effectiveness of health care and medical treatments, and it has played an important part in the advancement of evidence-based medicine.

In 1999, the founder of the Cochrane Collaboration, Sir Iain Chalmers, organized an effort with University of Pennsylvania Professor Robert Boruch to create a similar infrastructure for reviews on what works in areas such as education, social welfare, and criminology (see Petrosino *et al.* 2003b). This resulted in the establishment of the Campbell Collaboration, named after the influential methodologist, psychologist, and evaluation theorist Donald T. Campbell (1917–96). At a meeting in Philadelphia attended by over 80 persons from 12 different countries, the Campbell Collaboration was inaugurated in February 2000, to prepare, maintain, and make accessible systematic reviews of research on the effects of social, educational, and criminological interventions.

At that February 2000 meeting, the Campbell Collaboration established a Crime and Justice Group (CCJG) and a Steering Committee (CJSC) to coordinate the work of this Group (see Farrington and Petrosino, 2001; Petrosino *et al.*, 2003a). The original CJSC consisted of ten members from seven different countries. The CJSC managed to secure some funding from the British Home Office to support a part-time coordinator for three years. The first CJSC meeting was held in Paris in April 2000, coinciding with a meeting of the Board of Directors of the International Society for Criminology (ISC). This was partly to emphasize the international remit of the CCJG and partly because four members of the CJSC were on the ISC's Board of Directors. It was agreed that the institutional home of the CCJG would be at the University of Pennsylvania.

At the first meeting, it was decided to commission reviews on 15 key topics, such as the effectiveness of boot camps, child skills training, CCTV, neighborhood watch, and hot spots policing. The aim was to select narrowly defined topics where there was likely to be only a small number (e.g. 20–50) of high-quality evaluations, nevertheless covering a wide range of criminological interests in total. Instead of waiting for researchers to propose topics, the CJSC proactively approached well-known scholars to do the first few reviews. This ensured that key topics were covered, that results could be speedily obtained, and that a good reputation was established quickly. Those who undertook systematic reviews were asked to agree to the following requirements:

1. A commitment to undergo a rigorous editorial review process not only from researchers but also policy makers, practitioners, and citizens to ensure that the review meets high scientific standards and is also written to be understandable to non-academic audiences.
2. A commitment to maintain transparent and open review processes so that users can comment and criticize each stage of the review, from its proposal through to its completion.

3. A commitment to use the most rigorous search methods available to ensure that all relevant studies are considered for inclusion or exclusion and not just those reported in easily accessible journals and books.
4. A commitment to cover literature from around the world and not just the English-speaking world.
5. A commitment to code and computerize key features of each evaluation study reviewed (so that anyone accessing the review can organize the studies according to such features as sample size, design, or effect size).
6. A commitment to report the final review explicitly so that readers could understand decisions made at each stage, justifications for those decisions, and how conclusions were reached.
7. A commitment to make the review available to broader audiences than readerships of peer-reviewed academic journals through electronic publication and dissemination into policy, practice, and media outlets.
8. A commitment to update the systematic review to incorporate new evidence, respond to criticisms, or use more advanced methods, on a regular basis.

Major challenges

Several major challenges were identified. The first (perhaps most important and controversial) was what criterion of methodological quality should be set for including evaluation studies in systematic reviews. Several CJSC members argued that only randomized experiments should be reviewed, since these were able to demonstrate effects most convincingly (with highest internal validity). However, setting the "gold standard" of randomized experiments would inevitably exclude almost all evaluations based on areas (as opposed to individuals), covering the effects of interventions such as neighborhood watch or CCTV. Also, when David Farrington, Anthony Petrosino, and Lawrence Sherman made a presentation to the Committee of Directors of Criminological Institutes in November 2000, some of those present were concerned that the methodological standard should not be set so high that important evaluations were excluded. Directors said that they needed the best available evidence and that conclusions saying that "we know nothing because all studies are flawed" were very unhelpful.

The second challenge was funding. The very welcome Home Office funding covered the salary of the part-time coordinator and some CJSC meeting expenses but not the cost of reviews. Without funding, it seemed unlikely that busy scholars could give Campbell reviews high priority in their workload. For example, one potential reviewer responded that he thought that the systematic review was very important and would love to do it, but could not do it without resources. Funding was needed not only for reviews and meeting expenses but also for refereeing proposals and completed reviews, administrative and organizational support, translation costs, and setting up a registry of studies.

A third challenge, related to incentives for reviewers, was the worry that academics would not give Campbell reviews high priority if they did not produce publications. Academics need publications in scholarly journals in order to get tenure, promotion, and recognition. It was therefore suggested that reviewers should be encouraged to complete not only a detailed electronic Campbell review but also an (inevitably less detailed) review for a scholarly journal. Of course, this raised problems of copyright and duplication that needed to be resolved. It was thought that journal editors might be reluctant to publish systematic reviews if a more detailed version was available on the Internet. It was hoped that, in due course, Campbell reviews on the Internet might have sufficient prestige themselves to carry weight in tenure and promotion decisions.

A fourth challenge was the coordination of reviews, both with other parts of the Campbell Collaboration and with the Cochrane Collaboration. Representatives of the CJSC and the Campbell Methods Group met in July 2000 to discuss standards for proposals (protocols) and other methodological issues. The work of the CCJG had moved forward very quickly, and we could not afford to wait for these topics to be resolved by the Campbell Collaboration. There was also the problem that similar topics, such as the treatment of sex offenders, were being reviewed by the Cochrane Developmental, Psychosocial and Learning Problems Group. We decided to go forward with our own reviews, which were likely to differ from Cochrane reviews, which focussed more on medical and health care issues.

The fifth challenge was how the CJSC could cope with the work needed to maintain the high quality of systematic reviews. This involved refereeing both protocols and final versions of reviews, as well as building up the network and infrastructure of the CCJG. It was clear that organizing the CCJG would generate an enormous amount of day-to-day work, as all the different activities built up. This was why we decided to move forward initially with a relatively small number of reviews and to learn from experience. We were concerned that large-scale publicity, inviting people to volunteer to do particular reviews, might open the floodgates and attract more reviews than the CJSC could cope with. However, we had to open the process to unsolicited review proposals and wider participation by the research community as soon as possible. We could not take the risk that we might be viewed as a closed in-group.

The sixth challenge was how to regularize the CJSC, which was essentially appointed on an ad-hoc basis for three years (until 2003). The overall Campbell Collaboration Steering Committee needed to work out procedures for appointing and replacing CJSC members and the co-chairs, ensuring that the CJSC included a wide variety of expertise and countries and that it had the capacity to supervise reviews and reviewers effectively.

A seventh challenge was that the people who are most knowledgeable and motivated to carry out a systematic review were often those who had worked on the particular topic, but arguably they were not unbiased and might have a stake in the conclusions. One way of dealing with this challenge was to encourage collaborations between reviewers who had and had not previously worked on a particular topic. Also, there was a need for workshops to train people in how to do systematic reviews.

There were other issues to be resolved. To build a registry of studies, it was necessary to agree on a common core of items to be coded and computerized in all reviews. Another issue was to what extent all reviewers should be encouraged to carry out a meta-analysis or other quantitative summary of conclusions. It was thought that, ideally, cost–benefit information should be included in all reviews, where available (see Farrington *et al.*, 2001; Welsh *et al.*, 2001). Another issue was whether Campbell reviews should include policy recommendations. Also, ideally, the CJSC should develop a master plan (a systematic classification and organization of all possible intervention topics for review), and aim to fill the gaps with solicited reviews.

Developments since 2000

The major problem for the CJSC, and indeed for the Campbell Collaboration, has been funding. Unlike the Cochrane Collaboration, which had guaranteed funding from the UK National Health Service, the Campbell Collaboration has found it very difficult to obtain continued funding. It is currently funded by the Norwegian government (the Directorate for Health and Ministry for Education and Research), and it is hoped that this funding might provide some stability for a few years. Currently, the Campbell Collaboration provides some support for the CCJG editor-in-chief and payments for referees, while the Jerry Lee Foundation provides support for the CCJG managing editor. There are no funds for meeting expenses; CJSC members have to fund themselves. It is easier to get funding for reviews, which can be viewed as a product to be purchased by funding agencies, than for infrastructure expenses.

Other challenges have been overcome. The establishment of the *Journal of Experimental Criminology* has provided an important publication outlet for Campbell reviews. Procedures for the evolution of the CJSC have been agreed. For example, a new co-chair will be appointed in 2012 and another in 2014. A subcommittee for mapping the field has developed a systematic classification of criminological topics to identify gaps in knowledge and reviews that should be commissioned. A dissemination subcommittee investigates how best to publicize CCJG reviews. Several reviews have been well publicized in national media and have had an impact on public policy in different countries. This is true, for example, of the review of the effectiveness of CCTV in reducing crime, which has been well publicized in the UK, Denmark, and Sweden.

The completion of systematic reviews has not been achieved as speedily as we had hoped. Nevertheless, as of February 2010, there are 25 systematic reviews from the CCJG published on the Campbell Collaboration website, on the following topics:

1. "Scared Straight" and other juvenile awareness programs for preventing delinquency.
2. The effects of correctional boot camps on offending.
3. The effectiveness of counter-terrorism strategies.
4. The effects of non-custodial employment programs on the recidivism rates of ex-offenders.
5. Incarceration-based drug treatment programs.
6. The effects of custodial versus non-custodial sentences on reoffending.
7. Hot spots policing.
8. Police-led drug enforcement strategies.
9. Cognitive-behavioral programs for juvenile and adult offenders.
10. Programs for serious (violent and chronic) juvenile offenders in secure corrections.
11. Cost–benefit analysis and cost-effectiveness of sentencing.
12. The effectiveness of family programs implemented up to age five in reducing later antisocial behaviour and delinquency.
13. Court-mandated interventions for individuals convicted of domestic violence.
14. The effects of improved street lighting on crime.
15. The effects of problem-oriented policing on crime and disorder.
16. The effects of second responder programs on repeat incidents of family abuse.
17. Mentoring programs to affect juvenile delinquency and associated problems.
18. The effects of closed-circuit television surveillance on crime.
19. The effectiveness of neighborhood watch.
20. The effects of parental imprisonment on children's antisocial behavior, crime, and mental health problems.
21. Cyber abuse prevention for children, youth, and parents.
22. The effects of drug substitution programs on reoffending.
23. School-based programs to reduce bullying and victimization.
24. Formal system processing of juveniles: effects on delinquency.
25. Effectiveness of programs designed to improve self-control.

Thirteen more reviews are in progress, with an approved protocol. There are other reviews on the Campbell website that are of interest to criminologists but have been completed by the Education or Social Welfare Groups, such as the effectiveness of multisystemic therapy.

The international dimension

The Campbell Collaboration, the CCJG, and the CJSC are international bodies. For example, as of February 2010, the CJSC included 19 members from 11 different countries, covering North America, Northern and Southern Europe, Israel, Australia, China, and Japan. However, there are no members from other areas such as Africa and South America. CJSC members have tried to encourage high-quality research in their countries. For example, our Japanese member has constructed a Japanese-language website, and our Chinese member has been very active in encouraging Chinese evaluation research.

All CJSC meetings are conducted in English and all reviews are published on the Campbell website in English. However, a series of systematic reviews have been published in both Swedish and English by the Swedish National Council for Crime Prevention (see http://www.bra.se). Also, a number of systematic reviews have been published in two special sections of the Spanish-language journal *Psicothema* (in 2006 and 2008). In addition, articles about the work of the CCJG have been published in different languages (e.g. Tsutomi *et al.*, 2002).

Published CCJG reviews have been completed by scholars from several different countries, including the USA, the UK, Israel, Switzerland, Spain, and Australia. Efforts are made in the reviews to include research from all over the world, and CJSC members frequently help in translating reports in languages other than English. For example, the review of anti-bullying programs (Farrington and Ttofi, 2009) analyzed studies from 16 countries (including Czechoslovakia and South Africa) and translated reports in German, Italian, and Spanish.

Undoubtedly, more could be done to include non-English language research and researchers within the umbrella of the CCJG. It would be desirable to complete a scoping project to identify countries where there is high-quality evaluation research that is not published in the English language, and then attempt to secure funds for translating reports from these countries into English. Indeed, the CJSC made an application to the European Union Crime Prevention Network for funds for such a scoping project in Europe, but this application was not successful. Nevertheless, a priority aim for the future development of the CCJG should be to become even more international in scope.

Doing a systematic review

All criminologists are encouraged to conduct systematic reviews with the CCJG. The first step is to submit a proposed title to the CCJG managing editor, who is currently Charlotte Gill. This is refereed and, if accepted, is registered in the Campbell Collaboration Library of Systematic Reviews. The main reason for not accepting a proposed title would be overlap or duplication with an existing title. The second step is to complete and submit a draft protocol (a detailed description of how the systematic review will be completed). This should include the background to the review (hypotheses tested, operational definitions of interventions and outcome variables), the objectives of the review, strategies for searching the literature, selection criteria for including or excluding studies, and strategies for data extraction, coding, and analysis. This is also refereed and revised in the light of the referees' comments, before it is published on the Campbell website. David Wilson currently acts as editor-in-chief of the CCJG refereeing process.

The third step is to complete the systematic review. This is also refereed (by the Campbell Methods group as well as by criminologists) and again is likely to require revisions before it is published in the Campbell Library. These rigorous refereeing processes are designed to ensure that the published reviews are of high quality. Once a review is published on the Campbell website, anyone can post comments on it, and authors are encouraged to update the review every two to three years. Campbell Collaboration policy is that each review should have at least two authors, in order to reduce bias and facilitate tests of the reliability of inclusion/exclusion decisions and coding of key features of evaluation studies.

The information that is extracted and coded from each included study should comprise at least the following: principal investigators, full citations to all evaluation reports, funding, publication dates, design of the study, characteristics of experimental units (for example, age and gender of participants, prior crime rates of areas), sample size, hypotheses tested, interventions, implementation details, how extraneous variables were controlled so that it was possible to disentangle the impact of the intervention, who were the program delivery personnel, what were the control conditions (since it is rarely possible to have a truly untreated control group), who knew what about the intervention (since double-blind trials are desirable), measurement of outcome variables (for example, official records and/or self-reports of crime), before and after measures of offending, length of follow-up period, and measures of effect size and variability of effect size. Authors of reviews are encouraged to code all variables independently, so that the reliability of coding can be assessed.

Decisions about what studies to include in a systematic review can be highly controversial, because they involve assessments of methodological quality. Authors of excluded studies may feel that their research has been negatively assessed or even "cast into outer darkness" (as one person has told us). Methodological quality standards for evaluation research have been discussed by Farrington (2003) and Weisburd (2003). We hope that Campbell Collaboration reviews will lead to an improvement in the quality of the primary evaluation research. In general, randomized experiments have the greatest internal validity. However, randomized experiments that evaluate criminological interventions are relatively uncommon (see Farrington and Welsh, 2005, 2006). Also, randomized experiments based on a small number of units (e.g. less than ten areas randomized) would not adequately control for extraneous variables and would not have high internal validity. If Campbell Collaboration reviews were restricted to randomized experiments, they would be relevant to only a small fraction of the key questions for policy and practice in criminology. Therefore, for topics where there are few or no randomized experiments, reviewers also select high-quality quasi-experimental evaluations for inclusion. The aim is to reach the most defensible conclusions based on the best available research.

Conclusion

We believe that the aim of the CCJG is a noble one: to make available to everyone the best possible information about what works in reducing crime and offending. We are proud of what has been achieved in our first decade, but we are very conscious that we need to get more systematic reviews completed and on the Campbell Collaboration website. We hope very much that sufficient funding will be forthcoming to increase the number of published reviews significantly in the next decade, and especially to make the coverage of the CCJG even more international in scope.

One of the main aims of conducting a systematic review is to draw conclusions about the best available knowledge about the effects of a criminological intervention, possibly accompanied by methodological caveats or "health warnings." To the extent that existing research is inadequate, in internal validity or in any other feature, this should be stated by the reviewer, and recommendations should be made about needed research in the future. It is hoped that systematic reviews will identify gaps in knowledge and key questions that need addressing, and also that they will lead to increased attention to methodological issues and to an improvement in the methodological quality of intervention research in criminology.

We hope and expect that systematic reviews will become more widely conducted in criminology, not only for evaluating the impact of interventions but also in other areas such as assessing the adequacy of theories and the strength of predictors of offending or recidivism. We expect that only a minority of systematic reviews in criminology will be conducted under the umbrella of the Campbell Collaboration, partly because of the very time-consuming and rigorous refereeing procedures that have to be undergone. Nevertheless, we hope that in due course Campbell reviews will be widely recognized as providing the most rigorous, high quality, easily accessible, and up-to-date evidence on the effectiveness of criminological interventions. We invite all criminologists to join us in this exciting venture.

Future research questions

1. What are the most effective methods of reducing offending and reoffending by individuals?
2. What are the most effective methods of reducing crime rates in areas?
3. What are the financial costs and benefits of different crime prevention methods?
4. What should be the priority topics for systematic reviews of the effectiveness of criminological interventions?
5. How can systematic reviews be improved so that they have more impact on policy makers and practitioners?

References

Borenstein, M., Hedges, L. V., Higgins, J. P. T., and Rothstein, H. R. (2009). *Introduction to meta-analysis*. Chichester, UK: Wiley.

Cullen, F. and Gendreau, P. (2000). Assessing correctional rehabilitation: policy, practice, and prospects. In J. Horney (Ed.) *Polices, processes, and decisions of the criminal justice system: criminal justice 3*. Washington DC: US National Institute of Justice.

Farrington, D. P. (2003). Methodological quality standards for evaluation research. *Annals of the American Academy of Political and Social Science*, 587: 49–68.

Farrington, D. P. and Petrosino, A. (2000). Systematic reviews of criminological interventions: the Campbell Collaboration Crime and Justice Group. *International Annals of Criminology*, 38: 49–66.

—— (2001). The Campbell Collaboration Crime and Justice Group. *Annals of the American Academy of Political and Social Science*, 578: 35–49.

Farrington, D. P. and Welsh, B. C. (2005). Randomized experiments in criminology: What have we learned in the last two decades? *Journal of Experimental Criminology*, 1: 9–38.

—— (2006). A half-century of experiments on crime and justice. In M. Tonry (Ed.) *Crime and Justice*, vol. 34 (pp. 55–132). Chicago: University of Chicago Press.

Farrington, D. P. and Ttofi, M. M. (2009). *School-based programs to reduce bullying and victimization*. Campbell Systematic Reviews 2009:6. Available from http://www.campbellcollaboration.org.

Farrington, D. P., Petrosino, A., and Welsh, B. C. (2001). Systematic reviews and cost–benefit analyses of correctional interventions. *Prison Journal*, 81: 339–59.

Lipsey, M. W. and Wilson, D. B. (2001). *Practical meta-analysis*. Thousand Oaks, CA: Sage.

Littell, J. H., Corcoran, J., and Pillai, V. (2008). *Systematic reviews and meta-analysis*. Oxford, UK: Oxford University Press.

McGuire, J. (Ed.).(1995). *What works: reducing reoffending*. Chichester, UK: Wiley.

MacKenzie, D. L. (2000). Evidence-based corrections: identifying what works. *Crime and Delinquency*, 46: 457–71.

Martinson, R. (1974). What works? Questions and answers about prison reform. *The Public Interest*, 10: 22–54.

Petrosino, A., Farrington, D. P., and Sherman, L. W. (2003a). The Campbell Collaboration Crime and Justice Group: early development and progress. *Journal of Offender Rehabilitation*, 38: 5–18.

Petrosino, A., Boruch, R. F., Farrington, D. P., Sherman, L. W., and Weisburd, D. (2003b). Toward evidence-based criminology and criminal justice: systematic reviews, the Campbell Collaboration, and the Crime and Justice Group. *International Journal of Comparative Criminology*, 3: 42–61.

Rothstein, H. R., Sutton, A. J., and Borenstein, M. (Eds.). (2005). *Publication bias in meta-analysis: prevention, assessment, and adjustments.* Chichester, UK: Wiley.

Sherman, L. W., Gottfredson, D. C., MacKenzie, D. L., Eck, J., Reuter, P., and Bushway, S. (1997). *Preventing crime: what works, what doesn't, what's promising.* Washington, DC: US Department of Justice, Office of Justice Programs.

Sherman, L. W., Farrington, D. P., Welsh, B. C., and MacKenzie, D. L. (Eds.) (2006). *Evidence-based crime prevention* (rev. edn.). New York: Routledge.

Tsutomi, H., Farrington, D. P., and Petrosino, A. (2002). The Campbell Crime and Justice Group in Progress (in Japanese). *Japanese Journal of Sociological Criminology*, 27: 113–18.

Weisburd, D. L. (2003). Ethical practice and evaluation of interventions in crime and justice: the moral imperative for randomized trials. *Evaluation Review*, 27: 336–54.

Welsh, B. C., Farrington, D. P., and Sherman, L. W. (Eds.) (2001). *Costs and benefits of preventing crime.* Boulder, CO: Westview.

7

A question of good governance?

Developments in crime prevention internationally

Jacqui Karn

This chapter aims to provide an introduction to developments in crime prevention internationally. The chapter will firstly explore the importance of trends in governance for debates around crime prevention. It will then outline the language and politics of prevention in Europe and North America that have influenced exchange of policy internationally. A brief outline of the challenges faced by developing countries in which high crime levels exist will then inform a discussion of the implications for policy transfer to developing countries of approaches developed in resource-rich countries, and will outline some influential home-grown approaches to violence prevention in Latin America. The chapter will close with a discussion of some of the challenges and opportunities presented by comparative research on crime prevention internationally.

Crime prevention and the governance of security

Contemporary crime prevention as a field of expertise developed, particularly during the 1980s, in Europe, North America and Australia, in somewhat different ways, influenced by distinct political, socio-economic and cultural environments. The pattern of its development is increasingly complicated by the international exchange of ideas, and shifts in policy and practice that have blurred the lines distinguishing between them (Crawford, 2009b). Crime prevention often suffers as a result from vague and confusing conceptualization. Broadly, crime prevention is a concern to prevent crime rather than always act in response to it, often constituted as the opposite of repression (law enforcement) at the international level. The development of crime prevention approaches has been described as marking an "epistemological break" in thinking about policies to address crime that moves away from a narrow concern with criminal justice responses (Garland, 2000). Though overly optimistic about the shift that crime prevention represents, in view of the continued resort to punitive approaches worldwide, contemporary developments in crime prevention are reflective of some important shifts in thinking about how to govern, away from an assumption of state monopoly of public services, including the provision of security, towards *governance*, particularly through "partnership" between public, private and third sector (community and non-profit-making) (Shearing and Johnston, 2003) and a multi-disciplinary, cross-departmental approach to crime prevention.

A focus on addressing the complex and multiple causes of crime opens the floodgates to the consideration of a wide variety of areas of public policy with a potential impact on crime and violence, and a similarly broad range of potential actors. Many working in areas of social policy with wider welfare aims have feared that extending a crime prevention aim to areas such as education, health, housing and social work will stigmatize those with whom they work, particularly if targeted on the basis of risk of offending. Pressures to focus resources on high crime areas and at-risk groups, rather than provide universal welfare, also presents some particular ethical problems for developing countries, with cities with vast slums areas without sanitation, water supply and electricity, where health, housing and lack of access to education present pressing problems and long-term barriers to poverty reduction. In such a situation directing resources on the basis of crime rates is difficult to justify (Dixon, 2006).

Equally, with highly contested understandings of what causes crime and violence, and the best methods to address those causes, prevention presents a particular challenge for partnership working across different areas of public policy. While social policies may hope to impact on the causes of crime and violence in the long term, the pressures to reduce rates of victimization in the short term, and to demonstrate results, can shift political attention to more conventional reactive or highly visible approaches, policy becoming influenced by electoral and party politics. Sustaining effective partnerships to tackle these dilemmas, without dominance of particular agencies, involving civil society and businesses in decisions while managing interests and expectations and negotiating complex political and financial power relationships between the center and the local, are in practice a significant challenge for a governance approach. This is further complicated in developing contexts by lack of resources, public distrust, corruption and lack of organizational or civil society capacity on which to build partnership approaches. Capacity building to govern, financially and organizationally, may be a crucial step in the delivery of prevention.

Exploring developments in crime prevention internationally is thereby necessarily caught up with debates about shifts in the governance of security. International organizations have increasingly posed normative questions of what then makes for *good* governance of security, and, furthermore, whether good governance in itself creates safe societies. This thinking is reflected in attempts by UN organizations to create norms and standards to guide delivery of crime prevention, outlining principles of crime prevention[1] and urban governance.[2] Implicit in the development of these norms is a move beyond considering what methods are used to prevent crime towards a question of whether the promotion of equality, democracy and human rights can produce safer societies. Increased attention to crime as a barrier to development in the last decade, and significant lessons from violence reduction initiatives in Latin American cities and the UN Habitat Safer Cities program, have shaped this international approach to crime prevention. Equally, promotion of "good practice" in crime prevention has increasingly stressed the need for adaptation to local contexts and capacity (reflecting considerable variation in state resources and civil society organization) and the central role of regional and local, particularly municipal, governments (UN Habitat, 2007, 2009; ICPC, 2010).

Though there is considerable academic debate about the homogenization of crime prevention policy and the dominance of certain models of crime prevention (Stenson and Edwards, 2004; Crawford, 2009b) in richer countries (e.g. Europe, North America and Australia), there is less awareness of developments in the prevention of crime, particularly of violence, in the developing world. The challenges of high rates of violence and crime victimization faced by developing countries, particularly in sub-Saharan Africa and South and Central America, and the ways in which reductions in crime and violence can be achieved in the most difficult of circumstances, raise some important questions for crime prevention. Not only do these contexts demand scepticism about the relevance of approaches developed in resource-rich countries, but they can also offer important lessons for practice and fruitful ground for theory development, not least because some of the most successful examples have coincided with a shift in governance in the context of democratic transition.

Conceptualizing crime prevention

Conceptualization of contemporary crime prevention has been dominated by understandings of its development in richer countries. Influential public health distinctions between primary, secondary and tertiary level interventions (Brantingham and Faust, 1976), or more recently, *universal*, *selective* and *indicated* (Institute of Medicine, 1994)[3] reflect that Western individualistic understandings tend to assume the targets of interventions will be individuals, rather than families, institutions, neighborhoods or whole cities, and that these will be offenders rather than victims (Crawford, 1998). A second key distinction made between social and situational approaches reflects distinct understandings of crime aetiology, but is also closely associated internationally with their development in particular political/cultural contexts in Europe and North America. Social crime prevention is characterized by a concern with affecting social processes and circumstances addressing the social and economic causes of offending behavior. Situational approaches focus on the reduction of opportunities for crime, particularly through physical alterations to environments and design, variously associated with "target hardening" and "designing out crime." Tonry and Farrington (1995) have further distinguished between "developmental" and "community" approaches to social crime prevention which are, respectively: approaches that intervene to reduce individual risk factors in childhood development associated with later criminality; and prevention that aims to alter social conditions in community settings, such as increasing residents' capacity to exert informal social control. These means of conceptualizing crime prevention have been enormously influential, and are reflected in international definitions of crime prevention.[4]

Despite these limitations the distinction between social and situational remains relevant for analysis of policy and policy transfer internationally because their distinct understandings of crime causation can mean that they also appeal to particular political orientations (Crawford, 2009b). The following section will explore some of the ways in which socio-political/cultural contexts have influenced the development of crime prevention in the North. This is not intended to provide a comprehensive picture of development, and is a broad brush, but it sets the context for understanding the politics of policy exchange.

The language and politics of prevention in the North

The term "crime prevention" is often used interchangeably in the North with other terms, such as community safety and urban security, but has some important connotations in different countries. The two dominant models of crime prevention, situational and social, have simplistically tended to be associated with Anglo-American and French developments, at two extremes, which developed in very different political contexts. The particular context of policy development is reflected in the language used to refer to crime prevention practice in these countries.

In many Anglophone countries the term "crime prevention" has become narrowly associated with police-led, situational approaches to reducing opportunities for street crime, reflecting the development of policy associated with "routine activities" theory in the UK and US in the 1980s (Stenson and Edwards, 2004). The term "crime prevention" tends thereby to be associated with measures to "target-harden," through the use of burglar alarms, locks, street lighting, CCTV and other methods of security and surveillance technology, and product or building design to hinder theft. These technical approaches have been coupled with policies to manage public space by improving the appearance, and excluding disorderly activities from public spaces associated with "broken windows" and "zero tolerance" approaches. Neo-liberal trends in governance in both countries, with market-driven understandings of individuals as consumers of security, "responsibilizing" individuals for their own safety and neo-conservative punitivism, with its call for moral renewal of civic virtues (Garland, 2000; Crawford, 2009a), shaped the development and implementation of these crime prevention approaches.

In the UK, after the election of New Labour (1997), there was a shift in language with "community safety" gaining currency as a term better able to encompass a wider array of initiatives to address broader issues of disorder and multi-agency involvement in preventing crime (Crawford, 1998). Partnerships, however, tended to be dominated by police and local authorities, leading a situational and urban management agenda, while performance monitoring limited local autonomy and community participation in decision-making (Karn, 2007). In addition, community was conceptualized in policy as the victims, whose lives were blighted by the intimidation of a disruptive minority (Crawford, 2003), echoing the neo-conservatism of the previous administration. Though social prevention activities, such as education/training, mentoring and diversionary leisure activities for "at risk" youth, have been implemented, in practice community safety in the UK has continued to be dominated by extensive use of situational crime prevention and CCTV, and included exclusionary measures, such as Anti-Social Behaviour Orders, restricting an undefined number of behaviors, with particularly damaging consequences for the criminalization of young people.

Crime prevention approaches in France, though developing at around the same period, followed a very different path in the context of a socialist government and inspired by the Bonnemaison model proposed by a commission of city mayors following urban riots in Lyon (1982). The model proposed a local approach to urban policy which has remained at the core of French crime prevention, though this local role has in practice been undermined by the centralized nature of the French state (Wyvekens, 2009). In contrast to Anglo-American developments, the police played only a minor role in prevention. Policy favored social prevention initiatives intended to have direct and indirect effects on individual opportunity and wider living conditions to address root causes of crime (e.g. inequality, unemployment/low paid work, poor housing). Initiatives included recruiting older youth to act as paid youth workers (*animateurs*) in ghetto suburbs, connected to resident and local government prevention committees intended as a form of urban participatory governance to promote urban renewal and citizenship, as well as security. The 1990s saw an attempt to reconnect prevention with law enforcement, through a language of *urban security*, using partnerships developed through local security contracts (*contrats locaux de securité*) with criminal justice agencies. However, security continued to be seen as the preserve of the criminal justice system and their involvement in local urban partnerships remained minimal. Nevertheless, a social prevention approach characterized concurrent independent police and judicial initiatives, such as the *police de proximité* and *justice de proximité*, intended to bring the criminal justice system closer to people, until called to a halt by the Sarkozy administration in 2002. Since 2002, criminalization and exclusion of disruptive behavior, particularly in public spaces, greater use of CCTV (on transport and in Paris), increased powers for the police and a toughening of youth justice and sanctions for repeat offenders by the political right have shifted prevention policy away from French social prevention roots. Nevertheless, there remains, though in slightly new forms, a focus on urban (i.e. physical) renewal (i.e. of public space) and local initiatives to reduce conflict and positively reinforce responsible shared use of public space (*co-production*). This latter, with its emphasis on mediation and inclusive interaction, remains a distinct model of thinking about inclusive management of conflict in the use of public space, in considerable contrast to broken windows or zero tolerance approaches with their emphasis on exclusion.

Developments in other countries in Europe and North America were less ideologically driven and political reverses and international policy exchange over time has meant that most countries, as in the UK and France, are now better characterized as having a mixed approach to prevention drawing on a number of influences.[5] However, there are concerns that there is a trend towards increased dominance of situational approaches and a "new orthodoxy" of developmental prevention (Farrington, 2007). In addition, the introduction of extensive surveillance, alongside anti-terrorism powers, is undermining civil rights (Crawford, 2009b). Nevertheless there remain some distinct differences between countries in political receptiveness to situational crime prevention, surveillance and developmental approaches, which appear to resonate most with neo-liberal politics of market individualism and risk management. A more positive point of convergence appears to be an acknowledgement that crime prevention is most effectively delivered at the local level; the recognition of a principle of subsidiarity (see glossary, p. 74 for definition). The shift towards a language of community, local governance and urban security is in large part a reflection of this trend towards a local/municipal ethos (Crawford, 2009a, 2009b). Some similar trends can be seen in policies in developing countries, which are partly attributable to policy exchange.

The influence of international policy exchange

International exchange has particular significance in exploring trends in crime prevention in developing countries, which are often reliant on aid agencies for funding of projects promoting examples of "good practice" from evidence of implementation in the North. The influence, and relevance, of these approaches to prevention developed in resource-rich countries for other contexts are an increasingly important debate (Pelser, 2002; Shaw, 2009; Holtman, 2008). There is growing recognition of the need for South–South exchange of practice, particularly where facing similar resource challenges.[6] These developments echo a trend away from imposing models on the South, particularly through donor agencies' funding requirements, that do not reflect national or local priorities or capacity to deliver them.[7] Though pressures persist to use evidence-based policies that largely draw on research conducted in the North, there is growing acknowledgement at the international level that any emulation of practice requires adaptation to cultural and socio-political/economic circumstances in low- and medium-income countries (Shaw, 2009). Successes in violence reduction seen in the South, particularly in certain Latin American cities, have also begun to be recognized by international organizations as offering valuable lessons for crime prevention for the North.

International organizations,[8] city alliances[9] and crime observatories[10] have played an increasing role in facilitating the exchange of policy ideas across countries and cities. The production of norms and standards by UN organizations both draws on these global exchanges and plays a large part in influencing them. The province of Queretero in Mexico, for example, explicitly based its provincial crime prevention strategy on UN guidelines (Shaw, 2009).

Although international policy exchange again tempts debates about harmonization of policy globally, it is important to recognize the difference between rhetoric and practice, and that strategies do not necessarily translate into practice. Equally, local and national politics, and institutional and civil society capacity to implement policies, play a considerable part in the receptiveness of governments, local authorities and practitioners to crime prevention ideas. While there may be emulation of policies from other contexts and high-level networks of policy exchange, interpretation, adaptation and innovation are more important themes in understanding policy exchange, particularly where there is clear acknowledgement of differences in the challenges to be faced. Crucially, prevention approaches in the South, particularly in Sub-Saharan Africa and Latin America, are also developing in very different political circumstances to those in the North, and have only begun, in the last decade, to place crime and violence prevention at the forefront of policy, often as part of policies to promote economic development, and in the wake of democratic transition.

Violence and crime prevention for development: an emerging international agenda

In the last decade, there has been increasing recognition at the international level of the impact of everyday violence on countries' prospects for economic growth and development and the achievement of Millennium Development Goals (Geneva Declaration Secretariat, 2008). Increasingly security is described as a crucial part of development, if not a precursor to it. This has been driven by a public health approach to violence, which reframes violence (e.g. death, injury and other related health consequences) as a preventable issue of public health threatening economic development and democratic participation, particularly in certain regions of Sub-Saharan Africa, Latin America and the Caribbean (World Health Organization, 2008).

The global distribution of violence

Homicide rates have been an influential, if crude,[11] proxy measure for comparing levels of violence internationally. These make striking statistics that highlight the scale of the problems in some regions, far removed from that of contemporary experience in the North. Countries in Sub-Saharan Africa and Central and South America with the highest rates of homicide include the following, in rank order: El Salvador, Colombia, Guatemala, Jamaica, South Africa and Venezuela, ranging from 59 (El Salvador) to 37 (Venezuela) per 100,000 in 2005, compared to an average rate of under 3 in Western Europe (Geneva Declaration Secretariat, 2008) with significant proportions associated with firearms (UNODC, 2008).[12] Regional homicide rates reflect entrenched and endemic levels of violence though they also mask wide variation nationally and locally. Homicide rates also probably underestimate the extent of violence, being unable to reflect non-lethal violence.[13] Police data suggest that there has been a rise in non-lethal violence in Latin America and Southern Africa, with rates of robbery considerably higher than in richer countries, though considerably under-reported (UN Habitat, 2007).

A key trend associated with rising crime and violence in Sub-Saharan Africa, South America and the Caribbean is both the growth and inequality of their cities. Although growth rates have slowed, developing countries continue to have the highest rates of urbanization, absorbing five million new residents every month (i.e. 95 per cent of the world's urban population growth) (UN Habitat, 2009, p. xi). This is a huge challenge for cities already struggling to provide adequate services and infrastructure for their populations. In many parts of the developing world unplanned "slum" areas are growing faster than planned areas and in some cities, particularly in Sub-Saharan Africa, slum dwellers constitute the majority of the urban population (UN Habitat 2007, 2009). Although high rates of violence have tended to be assumed to be related to rapid growth (UN Habitat 2007), a more important trend is a global growth in levels of urban inequality, with particularly high levels evident in cities of Africa, and Latin America, compared to Europe and Asia (UN Habitat, 2009). Latin American and Caribbean cities are among the most unequal in the world. Within the African continent, urban inequalities are highest in southern Africa,[14] with South Africa in particular still exhibiting patterns that are the legacy of apartheid.

Violence prevention for development

This context raises the question of the relevance of prevention approaches developed in circumstances of far lower rates of victimization and comparatively more equal societies. The relevance of approaches aimed to reduce "fear of crime" in the context of low rates of victimization are particularly questionable (Shaw, 2009). Policies of "reassurance policing," for example, are clearly irrelevant to countries with globally high rates of victimization and histories of ineffective, militarized, often brutal and corrupt (e.g. ex-colonial, ex-apartheid, ex-regime) policing. In Africa, for example, the chances of a murder resulting in a conviction are only around 11 per cent (18 per cent South Africa) compared to 56 per cent in the US and 61 per cent in the UK (UNODC, 2005). In some contexts the actions of the police contribute to local homicide rates; in the *favelas* of Rio de Janeiro, for example, police and security forces were responsible for 1,098 of the 7,000 homicides in 2005 (Ramos, 2006). Tackling corruption and police brutality and illegality are important efforts in these contexts, central to transition to democracy and to reducing a sense of impunity and fear of security services. Nevertheless, it is increasingly recognized that criminal justice actors cannot reduce criminality alone, or produce a sense of security. Moreover, even if criminal justice systems could be improved in effectiveness, with victimization at the rates currently recorded, criminal justice systems would groan under the weight of the numbers of people coming through it, and with poor outcomes (Holtman, 2008). There is an increasing recognition internationally that a balance of criminal justice reform, crime prevention and urban policy approaches are needed to improve security, and that citizen involvement and empowerment in the "co-production" of security are crucial. This understanding, while resonating with trends in the North has also drawn on (and influenced) key experiences of violence reduction/prevention in the South, particularly in certain Latin American cities, that have developed in the context of democratic reform, explicitly promoting equality, democracy and human rights.

The language and politics of violence prevention in Latin America

Though political and interpersonal violence has been a feature of the history of many parts of South and Central America, political attention has only recently been paid to the impact of everyday insecurity and violence in the region, particularly in the wake of processes of democratization. In the 1990s, many parts of Latin America began to observe a growth in violence, associated with organized drug trafficking and the proliferation of firearms, alongside rapid urbanization and displacement. Recognition of high rates of homicide and insecurity, and demand for the reform of regime policing, as a part of democratic transition, shaped many of the debates around security in the region.

The context of transition to democracy has also opened the way for a new language of security, to promote a move away from militarized and repressive policies of national (internal/external) security of previous authoritarian regimes, and better reflect democratic aims (González, 2003). The term *seguridad ciudadana* (citizen security) developed (in opposition to *national* security), particularly influenced by a concept of *human security* (see glossary, p. 74) with a focus on individual and collective security, holding states accountable for the protection of their citizens (ibid.). The term is also contrasted with *seguridad pública* (public security), which, though in practice used interchangeably, tends to assume state monopoly of security. *Seguridad ciudadana* has become associated with concepts of co-production, with cooperation between state, civil society and business, and with the participation of citizens in decision-making and urban citizenship (*ciudadanía*) (Velasquez, 2007). Though resonant of some Western, particularly French, approaches to prevention, the language, politics and practice of *seguridad ciudadana* illustrates an approach to the governance of security with a Latin American flavor.

The division between public security and citizen security approaches is also shaped by debates around security in the region which have tended to be drawn along strongly party political lines for and against "*mano dura*" policies pursued by the political right in many countries to control gangs and organized crime, using "tough" policing and criminal justice sanctions. This approach has been increasingly criticized as counter-productive, having increased violence in gang-controlled areas and created further distrust and hatred of the police. *Seguridad ciudadana*, on the other hand, has tended to be associated with prevention approaches, and with the political left. Swings in electoral politics has, as in the North, thereby considerably affected the emphasis placed on crime prevention, nationally and locally, and on what type of prevention. Similarly, this has also meant a blurring of the lines between what is meant by *seguridad ciudadana* and *seguridad pública*, and the former can be used in reference to policies that reflect a conventional emphasis on police effectiveness/enforcement, and increasingly, situational crime prevention, area patrols and surveillance. There is, in many parts of the region, a continued emphasis on state security, or on private security (UN Habitat and Universidad Alberto Hurtado, 2009), echoing the inequality of access to security in other developing countries (Shearing and Johnston, 2003). The development of crime/violence prevention is therefore patchy and fragmentary.

Nevertheless, parts of Latin America have also seen considerable delegation of powers to municipalities, as a result of democratic reform and policies of decentralization (Satterthwaite, 2009), which has facilitated some of the most sustained examples of successful reductions in violence, through innovation in urban governance, often with key mayoral figures at their helm standing outside mainstream national politics. Cities such as Bogotá and Medellín in Colombia have seen spectacular reductions in homicide rates through various municipal programs over the long term involving a mixture of police reform, conflict resolution, urban regeneration and social development/prevention. Medellín, for example, experienced the highest rate of homicide in the world at 381 per 100,000 in 1991, which though halving over the next ten years, remained one of the highest rates of homicide globally. However, between 2002 and 2007, following local interventions, rates in the city fell from 174 to 29 per 100,000, a startling achievement. Bogotá also saw falls from a peak in 1993 of 80 homicides per 100, 000 to 19 by 2007, with reductions in rates maintained to date. Although the various projects and initiatives undertaken in these cities make it impossible to ascribe one reason for these falls, these achievements are characterized by the key role of their elected mayors in initiating local analysis of violence problems as chiefs of police, through the creation of multi-agency Security Councils (based on French models of *contrats de sécurité*), and a long-term strategy covering all aspects of the governance of security from prevention to the judicial system (Acero Velásquez and Cardona, 2009; Abello Colak (2010); Beckett and Godoy (2010)), largely removing urban crime and disorder from national electoral politics.

Central to the approach in Bogotá was the idea of developing a culture of citizenship (*Cultura Ciudadana*) seeking to develop shared and voluntary norms of *convivencia*, rather than to impose and exclude, as a means of rebuilding the legitimacy of the local state. Although including support for police, the strategy focussed on strengthening alternative conflict resolution mechanisms and reinforcing "co-production" of security and norms of civility in public spaces. Social prevention initiatives were also undertaken with vulnerable groups such as homeless adults and children, children involved in violence and drug addiction, migrants displaced by violence and those involved in the sex industry. Reductions in rates of homicide have been maintained to date.

Mayors in Medellín focussed their efforts on investing in housing, transport, education and green space in informal settlements with highest rates of violence, often controlled by armed groups to re-establish confidence in local government and reduce inequality (Dávila, 2009). Key to this was the ability of the municipality to work with civil society organizations, whose presence in and legitimacy within their neighborhoods, having sustained their independence from armed groups in preceding years, gave the local authority a means to establish contact with communities. These approaches, though supported by the center, stand in marked contrast to the highly militarized approaches to security at the national level and reflect a local urban approach to promoting peace in the context of ongoing conflict.

Though successful city-level developments in Latin America vary, as these Colombian examples illustrate, they share characteristics, in their decentralized city-level multi-agency approach, emphasizing conflict resolution/mediation, citizenship and inclusion, reduction of inequality and promotion of confidence in local authorities. Most importantly they stress democratic engagement in co-production which shapes the "responsibilization" of citizens, not only as responsible for their own safety, but for that of each other; a corporatist model as opposed to individual. Good governance and the promotion of human rights is at the heart of these developments, driven by the context of democratic transition and public distrust of enforcement approaches and corruption. As such, they provide important lessons, not only for other Latin American cities, or other high violence contexts, but also for some approaches in the North, criticized for their complacency towards rights.

These examples are in many respects exceptions within their region and reflect diversity of practice, rather than typical cases. Coercive, reactive and often brutal and corrupt practices remain a central concern in the region, and there remains considerable resistance to decentralization from political elites. However, these examples echo emerging international trends in thinking about crime prevention, drawing in part on experiences like these, based on four key influences:

- a public health approach to violence prevention;
- urban policy approaches to reducing inequalities (through social development and investment in infrastructure);
- conflict resolution/mediation and inclusive approaches to developing norms of shared use of public space;
- and democratic participation in urban governance.

In particular this moves beyond highly individualized conceptions of the targets of violence prevention to see addressing inequality, cultural change and city-level policy as aspects of violence prevention. A key influence in these models, is an approach to violence through the lens of conflict, and an openness to conflict mediation and democratic participation approaches, particularly in the management of public space, but also as a means of building an inclusive culture of civility by channelling conflict within democratic process (González, 2003). In essence this works on an assumption that democratic engagement and good governance will reduce violence.

Challenges and opportunities for international crime prevention

This chapter has outlined some key developments and trends in crime prevention internationally, using contextualized examples to draw out some of the key points of convergence and divergence between them. A central message from these examples is that though there are some important points of convergence internationally in thinking about the nature of governance, these have emerged in very different socio-political contexts and are driven by different political imperatives (democracy, decentralization and market-driven responsibilization).

International exchange tends to attempt to learn from experiences in different contexts as examples of "good practice" for replication or emulation (with adaptation), often decontextualizing and depoliticizing their development. This limits understanding of why and how policies have been successful in the political, social and cultural contexts in which they were implemented. This decontextualization is exacerbated by pressures to evaluate prevention initiatives in narrow ways that compare a limited number of outcomes with a control group that does not lend itself to whole city, or multi-agency approaches. Though understanding if and why a policy worked is crucial, the need to evaluate it in a way that will convince others in these limited terms has the potential to guide policy development not towards what works but what can be evaluated. A key problem for policy exchange internationally is that initiatives with limited aims and limited approaches, particularly situational approaches, suit this form of evaluation, putting pressure on those attempting to implement "evidence-based policy" to advocate such approaches. The trend towards developmental approaches, based on an assessment of, and reduction of, risks also provides a poisoned chalice for those advocating social approaches to prevention, over-exaggerating the predictive power of risk assessment and over-concentrating on individual risk factors.

The challenge for proponents of an approach to crime prevention that draws on international experience of social development for crime prevention, rather than a narrow literature on experiences in the North, and to counter trends towards surveillance, risk-management and early intervention, is not only the difficulty of evaluating prevention but the lack of evaluation of initiatives undertaken in the South, and of contextualized comparative research. This chapter hopes to inspire others to take up the gauntlet of comparative research on urban governance and prevention which presents some important challenges and opportunities for criminology and for practice. The following suggests some initial ideas for avenues for comparative research, though is by no means exhaustive.

Future research questions

Research in this area requires a multi-disciplinary approach and a sharing of expertise from many directions, including geography, urban policy, public health, development studies, economics and other areas of social policy, and most importantly a contextualized approach to research and theory development, drawing on local knowledge and expertise. In doing so, however, there is an opportunity not only to make sense of high rates of victimization in these contexts and of the varying practices to address them, but also to re-examine criminological theories developed in the North and some of the assumptions that inform them.

1. How far can strain and social control theories, developed in the context of industrialization, urban expansion and consumerism in the North, be applied to societies of extreme inequality, and poverty in the South? What are the implications for social policy and crime prevention?
2. How far do situational or social crime prevention approaches developed in richer countries have relevance for (high violence/crime) developing countries?
3. Do approaches to crime prevention developed in the context of transition to democracy have relevance for established democracies of the North/West?
4. In what ways have prevention approaches developed in resource-rich contexts been adapted successfully in those where capacity for delivery is limited, and what do we mean by "success" in such contexts?
5. How far have local, urban and multi-sector approaches to crime prevention enabled participation of citizens in the governance of security, and does participation promote more inclusive approaches to crime prevention?

Glossary

Human security is an emerging paradigm for understanding global vulnerabilities which focuses on the security of individuals, used at the international level, particularly within the UN, as a concept providing a human rights based understanding of global security. It can refer to a wide range of environmental, social, economic and social issues that impact on individual security. The United Nations Development Programme's 1994 Human Development Report is considered a key publication in the development of the concept, with its argument that insuring "freedom from want" and "freedom from fear" for all individuals is the key to addressing the problem of global insecurity.

Subsidiarity: Responsibility for policy at the most appropriate level for delivery. Advocated as one of the principles of good governance by UN Habitat.

Notes

1 The UN guidelines for crime prevention can be summarized around themes of promoting human rights and building a culture of lawfulness and rule of law; socio-economic development and inclusion; community-centered action; government leadership and partnership; sustainability and accountability; and evidence-based practice (Redo, 2008; Shaw, 2009).

2 UN Habitat's "Campaign for Good Governance" developed proposed norms of *good* urban governance particularly emphasizing subsidiarity (responsibility for policy at the most appropriate level for delivery); sustainability (tackling inequality of access to resources); accountable, transparent and effective services; and public participation in decision-making.

3 Primary/universal interventions are aimed at general populations. Secondary/selective prevention is aimed at groups/individuals "at risk" because of risk factors identified with likelihood of involvement in criminality. Tertiary/indicated approaches include initiatives directed at known offenders to reduce likelihood or impact of further offending.

4 The UN Guidelines for the Prevention of Crime define crime prevention broadly as "strategies and measures that seek to reduce the risk of crimes occurring, and their potential harmful effects on individuals and society, including fear of crime, by intervening to influence their multiple causes." The guidelines distinguish between social crime prevention, including early intervention; community-based crime prevention; situational and victim-oriented crime prevention; and re-integration of offenders.

5 For further exploration of other European models see Crawford's edited collection (2009a).

6 The UN Office on Drugs and Crime (UNODC) has established a program for "South–South Regional Cooperation for Determining Best Practices for Crime Prevention in the Developing World" particularly promoting exchange between Africa and the Caribbean.

7 The Paris declaration on aid effectiveness of 2005 stresses the importance of recipient country ownership, priorities and timetables rather than that of donor countries or organizations.

8 E.g. the European Union Crime Prevention Network, the Council of Europe, the UN Crime Prevention and Criminal Justice Program Network (including the International Centre for the Prevention of Crime), UN Habitat (Safer Cities Program) and the *Facultad Latinoamericana de Sciencias Sociales* (FLACSO).

9 E.g. the European Forum for Urban Safety (EFUS), Metropolis and the Mercociudades Network.

10 E.g. the *Observatorio CentroAmericano sobre Violencia* (OCAVI) and the International Juvenile Justice Observatory (IJJO).

11 Though problematic, official statistics on homicide rates (from police and public health statistics) are comparable between contexts (being simple to define) and more likely to be reported than other forms of crime/violence.

12 Data from 45 out of the 86 countries contributing to the UN Crime Trends Survey suggests that globally around 60 per cent of homicides are committed with firearms (based on data from 2002–4) ranging from a high of 77 per cent in Central America to a low of 19 per cent in Western Europe.

13 The World Health Organization estimates that approximately ten times more people are injured than killed by violence (WHO, 2008).

14 North African cities tend to be more equal than Sub-Saharan.

References

Abello Colak, A. (2010). Civil society and security transformation in Medellín: challenges and opportunities. Global Consortium on Security Transformation: *New Voices Series*, No. 2. Online at http://www.securitytransformation.org/images/publicaciones/175_New_Voices_Series_2_-_Civil_Society_and_Security_Transformation_in_Medellin._Challenges_and_Opportunities.pdf (accessed December 9, 2010).

Acero Velásquez, H. and Cardona, S. (2009) *Medellín, Bogotá: Del autoritarismo y anarquía a la garantía civilista de los derechos ciudadanos. Mejoría de la seguridad ciudadana.* Available at http://www.oecd.org/dataoecd/30/39/41413443.pdf (accessed November 20, 2010).

Beckett, K. and Godoy, A. (2010). A tale of two cities: a comparative analysis of quality of life initiatives in New York and Bogotá. *Urban Studies*, 47(2): 277–301.

Brantingham, P. and Faust, F. (1976). A conceptual model of crime prevention. *Crime and Delinquency*, 22: 284–96.

Crawford, A. (1998) *Crime prevention and community safety: politics, policies and practices.* Essex, UK: Longman.

—— (2003). Contractual governance of deviant behaviour. *Journal of Law and Society*, 30: 479–503.

—— (2009a) The preventive turn in Europe. In A. Crawford (Ed.) *Crime prevention policies in comparative perspective.* Cullompton: Willan.

—— (2009b). Situating crime prevention policies in comparative perspective: policy travels, transfer and translation. In A. Crawford (Ed.) *Crime prevention policies in comparative perspective.* Cullompton: Willan.

Dávila, J. (2009). Being a mayor: the view from four Colombian cities. *Environment and Urbanization*, 21: 37–56.

Dixon, B. (2006). Development, crime prevention and social policy in post-apartheid South Africa. *Critical Social Policy*, 26: 169–91.

Farrington, D. (2007). Childhood risk factors and risk focused prevention. In M. Maguire, R. Morgan and R. Reiner (Eds.) *The Oxford Handbook of Criminology.* 4th edn. pp. 602–40. Oxford: Oxford University Press.

Garland, D. (2000). *The Culture of Control.* Oxford: Oxford University Press.

Geneva Declaration Secretariat. (2008). *Global Burden of Armed Violence.* Geneva: Geneva Declaration Secretariat.

González, P. (2003). *Seguridad ciudadana, cuadernos de seguridad y defensa 2.* Guatemala: FLACSO.

Holtman. B. (2008). Presentation at AFSSA Convention, 25–8 August. Online at http://www.safesouthafrica.org.za (accessed November 20, 2010).

International Centre for the Prevention of Crime (ICPC) (2010). *Second international report on crime prevention and community safety: trends and perspectives.* Montreal: ICPC.

Institute of Medicine. (1994). *Reducing risks for mental disorders: frontiers for preventive intervention research.* Washington DC: Institute of Medicine.

Karn, J. (2007). *Narratives of neglect: community, regeneration and the governance of security.* Cullompton: Willan.

Pelser, E. (2002). *Crime prevention partnerships: lessons from practice.* Pretoria: Institute for Security Studies.

Ramos, S. (2006). *Juventude e violencia.* Presentation at the Seminario de Prevencao a Violencia e la Criminalidade, Belo Horizonte, 9–10 November. Cited in Shaw (2009).

Redo, S. (2008). Six United Nations guiding principles to make crime prevention work. In M. Coester and E. Marks (Eds.) *International perspectives of crime prevention: contribution from the 1st annual international forum.* Mönchengladbach: Forum Verlag Godesberg.

Satterthwaite, D. (2009). What role for mayors in good city governance? *Environment and Urbanization*, 21: 3–17.

Shaw, M. (2009). International models of crime prevention. In A. Crawford (Ed.) *Crime prevention policies in comparative perspective.* Cullompton: Willan.

Shearing, C. and Johnston, L. (2003). *Governing security: explorations in policing and justice.* London: Routledge.

Stenson, K. and Edwards, A. (2004). Policy transfer in local crime control: beyond naïve emulation. In T. Newburn and R. Sparks (Eds) *Criminal justice and political cultures.* Cullompton: Willan.

Tonry, M. and Farrington, D. (1995). Strategic approaches to crime prevention. In M. Tonry and D. Farrington (Eds.) *Building a safer society. Crime and justice: a review of research*, vol.19. Chicago: University of Chicago Press.

UN Habitat (2007). *Global report on human settlements 2007: enhancing urban safety and security.* Nairobi: UN Habitat.

—— (2009). *The state of the world's cities: harmonious cities.* Nairobi: UN Habitat.

UN Habitat and Universidad Alberto Hurtado (2009). *Guía para la prevención local: hacia políticas de cohesión social y seguridad ciudadana*. Nairobi: UN Habitat.

United Nations Office on Drugs and Crime (UNODC) (2005). *Crime and development in Africa*. Vienna: UNODC.

—— (2008). Tenth UN crime trends survey (2005–6) Intentional homicide Vienna: UNODC. Online at http://www.unodc.org/documents/data-and-analysis/CTS10%20homicide.pdf (accessed November 20, 2010).

Velasquez, E. (2007). La gouvernance de la seguridad ciudadana. In R. Arnauldo and L. Martin (Eds.) *Consolidación de los Gobiernos Locales en Seguridad Ciudadana*, Région Toscana: URB-A1: 61–87.

World Health Organization (2008). *Preventing violence and reducing its impact: how development agencies can help*. Geneva: World Health Organization.

Wyvekens, A. (2009). The evolving story of crime prevention in France. In A. Crawford (Ed.) *Crime Prevention Policies in Comparative Perspective*. Cullompton: Willan.

8

Transferring Western theory

A comparative and culture-sensitive perspective of crime research in China

Lening Zhang

Introduction

China is emerging as a world economic power. Social research, including crime research, cannot ignore this big, emerging nation. Pre-reform China had very low crime rates and enjoyed a reputation of being a "crime free" society (Fairbank, 1987; Rojek, 1996). However, since the nation implemented economic reform and the open-door policy in the late 1970s, the Chinese have been experiencing surging crime waves (Liu, 2006). According to official statistics, the crime rate was 55.91 per 100,000 in 1978 and it reached 355.5 per 100,000 in 2005 (Zhang *et al.*, 2008). Consequently, China is experiencing an unfortunate "cost" of modernization similar to the experience of other developing nations (Shelley, 1981, 1986).

Although researchers believe that the changing China is offering a unique opportunity for crime research, conducting such research confronts special difficulties and barriers because of its unique political and social systems (Johnson, 1986; Liang and Lu, 2006; Peerenboom, 2001; Troyer *et al.*, 1989). Traditionally, crime research and crime data have been considered highly sensitive because Chinese authorities have believed that crime should not be part of a socialist society. The authorities are concerned that publicizing and revealing crime information would damage the country's image and become a source of "international embarrassment" (Bennett, 2004, p.12). Consequently, similar to other socialist countries (Robertson, 2006), official crime statistics were not open to the public in the past. Although this socialist tradition has changed since China implemented the open-door policy, the barriers for crime research are still formidable (Liang & Lu, 2006).

Because China enjoyed very low crime rates before the economic reform, criminology as an academic discipline and crime research was not well developed (Zhou and Cong, 2001). One easy remedy to this situation is to apply well-developed Western theories and methods to the Chinese context. However, these theories (e.g. social disorganization theory) and methods (e.g. self-report surveys) have been developed and used in Western societies where democracy, individualism, freedom of speech, and protection of privacy prevail. The application of the theories and methods requires knowledge and understanding of the unique Chinese context which has a different social, political, and cultural system such as the traditional emphasis on collectivism and respect for authority (Bracey, 1989; Dutton, 1992; Zhang *et al.*, 1996).

The purpose of this chapter is to share our research experience in China, what we have done, and how we did it. The chapter will also discuss the challenges and barriers in doing crime research in China. Finally, the chapter will conclude with a summary of the lessons that we have learned for comparative studies of crime and criminal justice, which provide valuable information for students who are interested in comparative studies of crime.

Comparative studies of crime

Comparative studies of crime involve research on crime across different cultural and social settings. Although this kind of research may be traced back to the Enlightenment period (Smith, 2009), it has been conducted in the US since the late 1960s and the early 1970s (e.g. Bayley, 1969, 1976; Clifford, 1978; DeFleur, 1969; Friday, 1971; Miller, 1978). However, major advances in this type of research have occurred only in recent years (see Bennett, 2004 and Howard *et al.*, 2000 for detailed reviews). As Robertson has observed (2006, p.137), the growth has been promoted by "both negative and positive occurrences." Negative occurrences refer to the significant increase in transnational crime problems such as terrorism, drug/human trafficking, and smuggling. The positive factors involve increasing access to data for conducting comparative crime research in countries that had prohibited such research in the past, such as China and the states of the former Soviet Union. In his presidential address to the Academy of Criminal Justice Sciences (ACJS), Bennett (2004, p. 18) predicts that "the continued globalization of business, economics, politics, and cultures will create a demand for global criminology and criminal justice research."

One notable comparative study is the International Crime Victim Survey (ICVS) sponsored by the United Nations Interregional Crime and Justice Research Institute. The ICVS entails the implementation of a standardized survey in participating countries (Nieuwbeerta, 2002). Since 1989, over 140 surveys have been completed in over 70 countries. Beijing, China, was one of the sites during the 1992–4 ICVS survey. The ICVS Beijing survey was co-sponsored by the China Department of Justice (CDJ) and conducted by the CDJ Research Institute on Crime Prevention. It randomly selected a sample of 2,000 residents from the urban districts of Beijing. Researchers from the CDJ Institute conducted face-to-face interviews in households using the ICVS standard questionnaire that had been translated into Chinese.

Although the ICVS Beijing survey demonstrates the feasibility of using the victim survey method to study the crime situation in the Chinese context and provides illuminating descriptive data, its utility is limited in several important respects. The questionnaire contains very few theoretically informed items that can be used to assess the applicability and generalizability of well-established criminological theories across different countries. The standardized instrument does not allow researchers to develop variables that reflect the unique social and cultural characteristics of the country surveyed. For example, each of urban Chinese communities has a neighborhood committee which is a mass organization and supported by Chinese governments. The operation of neighborhood committees represents a unique type of semi-public control at the neighborhood level that does not exist in Western urban communities. These variables may be critical for understanding the country's crime situation and for modifying established theories or developing new theories.

Our research experience

Our research experience came from a large-scale survey of criminal victimization in the city of Tianjin, China. The Tianjin survey was funded by the National Science Foundation and conducted in 2004. Tianjin is one of the four largest municipalities in China, the others being Beijing, Shanghai, and Chongqing. Tianjin (together with these other three largest cities) has the same administrative status as that of any provinces in the country, which is directly under the control of the central government in Beijing. Tianjin is located along the Hai He River. Its ports, some distance away, are located on the Bohai of the Pacific Ocean. The Tianjin municipality borders Heibei province to the north, south, and west, the municipality of Beijing in a small portion to the northwest, and the Bohai Gulf to the east. At the end of 2009, the population of the Tianjin municipality was 10.43 million, of which 9.39 million were holders of Tianjin *hukou* (permanent residence). Among Tianjin permanent residents, 5.62 million were urban and 3.77 million were rural. (The source is the official site of Tianjin government http://www.tj.gov.cn/english.)

The survey entailed a multi-stage cluster sampling design. Tianjin had 15 administrative districts and three counties at the time when the survey was conducted. The sample was drawn from the six traditional districts located in the central urban area of the municipality. They include Heping, Nankai, Hongxiao, Hexi, Hebei, and Hedong districts. Each district has approximately six to ten City-Street Offices. We first randomly selected 2 City-Street Offices from each of the selected districts, yielding a total of 12 City-Street Offices which are the agencies of Chinese government at the grassroots level.

Among the 12 selected City-Street Offices are two large offices that include a relatively large number of neighborhood committees. Five neighborhood committees were randomly selected from each of these large City-Street Offices, while four neighborhood committees were randomly drawn from each of the remaining ten City-Street Offices. A total of 50 neighborhood committees were thus obtained through a combination of purposive and random selection. Members of the research team met the supervisor in each of the selected neighborhood committees to explain the purpose and importance of the survey, the financial sources of the survey, and compensation for costs associated with administration. Upon securing agreement for assistance, the research team requested a complete list of households in that neighborhood.

Fifty-one households were selected for the survey in each of the 50 selected neighborhoods in hopes of reaching the target of 2,500 households. Using the household roster provided by the neighborhood committee in each selected neighborhood, the research team conducted systematic sampling. A starting point was randomly determined and every eighth household from each neighborhood was selected until the specified number of households was obtained. The research team defined a criterion date to select a specific respondent from a selected household with more than one person 18 years old or older. The individual with a birthday closest to the criterion date was chosen to be the respondent.

Data were collected through anonymous, self-administered questionnaires at convenient sites within the neighborhood (e.g. recreational areas). With the assistance of the neighborhood committees, the research team contacted the respondents to schedule the questionnaire administration. A total of 2,474 valid questionnaires were obtained, which represents a response rate of 97 percent. This response rate might appear to be suspiciously high, but the ICVS survey in Beijing was also able to get cooperation from virtually all selected households (Zhu *et al.*, 1995).

The theoretical underpinnings for the survey are routine activities/lifestyle theories and neo-social disorganization theory, modified and elaborated to reflect characteristics of the Chinese context. The overarching objective is to draw upon recent developments in Western crime research to conduct analyses of the individual, household, and neighborhood determinants of criminal victimization in China. Such analyses allow us to compare the protective and risk factors of criminal victimization in China and in the United States using the standard measures, and to examine the effects of the variables that capture unique features of Chinese society. Therefore, the research design involved two efforts. The first one was to adopt the standard Western variables and measures in the survey with a careful consideration of whether they are applicable to the Chinese context. The second effort was to develop variables and measures that could capture the unique features of the Chinese context.

Research findings

The research findings are clustered in two aspects: assessing the application and generalizability of Western concepts and theories; and examining unique variables/measures that reflect the unique characteristics of the Chinese context. For the first aspect, the data yield interesting findings that are similar to and different from those discovered in the West. For instance, although the degree of involvement in activities that are commonly included in Western research as "risk factors" is rather low in Tianjin (e.g. low dining out on a regular basis and few traveling outside of the city for work or leisure except on rare occasions), indicators of these two features of lifestyles yield similar effects on the victimization risk as discovered in Western research. Venturing out of the household for leisure and work tends to increase risks of becoming a victim of crime (Messner *et al.*, 2007). Also, consistent with the Western literature, females exhibit greater risks of personal theft and lower risks of assault. Young people are at relatively high risk of personal theft and robbery, while the elderly are vulnerable to swindles. Education is positively associated with personal theft and robbery, consistent with the view that educated people are more likely to engage in lifestyles that entail risk (ibid.).

Bicycle theft as a property crime has been prevalent in China since the economic reform in the late 1970s. We applied routine activities/lifestyle theories to examine the protective and risk factors of bicycle theft (Zhang *et al.*, 2007a). The findings indicate that neighborhood poverty level and neighborhood deviance/crime level exhibit significant positive effects. These significant variables were conceptualized as indicators of capable guardianship or indicators of proximity to potential offenders, and thus the results demonstrate the applicability of routine activities/lifestyle theories.

Residents' safety and security are a major issue in crime research. Findings from our studies of fear of crime in Chinese urban communities have also replicated the gender difference in the fear of crime found in the West (Liu *et al.*, 2009; Zhang *et al.*, 2009). Females report higher levels of fear than do males. Our studies also indicate that physical strength and ability of self-defense are negatively associated with the reported level of fear of crime in Chinese urban communities. These findings are also consistent with the perspective of routine activities/lifestyle theories.

We adopted the general conceptual framework established in the West to study Chinese residents' crime reports to police by concentrating on three groups of potential correlates: incident-specific correlates (e.g. the seriousness of offenses), individual-specific factors (e.g. gender, age, education, and employment status), and environment-specific factors (e.g. neighborhood disadvantage and social cohesion) (Zhang *et al.*, 2007b). Consistent with the Western research, our findings indicate that offense seriousness is significantly associated with Chinese residents' reporting of robbery, assault, personal theft, and household burglary to the police. The more serious the offense, the more likely that victims would report to the police. In addition, we observed a non-linear, negative relationship between neighborhood disadvantage and reporting of crime. Respondents who resided in highly disadvantaged neighborhoods were much less likely to report incidents of household burglary to the police. This pattern has also been reported in Western research.

Finally, we applied routine activities/lifestyle theories and social disorganization theory to assess the protective and risk factors in Chinese residents' victimization of household burglary

(Zhang *et al.*, 2007c). Our findings generally supported these theories. The results revealed that indicators of target attractiveness (household income) and guardianship (length of residence and "somebody home") exhibit significant effects on the risk of household burglary. A high household income was associated with an increased risk of residential burglary, whereas reports that somebody is usually at home and lengthy residence in a neighborhood are related to a decreased risk. Also, our findings on the effects of collective efficacy and public control were consistent with those discovered in Western research. Neighborhoods with a high level of collective efficacy tended to exhibit lower risks of household burglary and neighborhoods in which the police were highly visible were characterized by relatively low levels of household burglary.

In sum, although China has a different social and cultural context, our studies found similar results to those discovered in the Western research and demonstrated the general applicability of Western concepts and theories. However, our findings also differed from some found in the West. For instance, inconsistent with Western research, our data indicated a negative effect of residential mobility on the risk of being victimized in household burglary (Zhang *et al.*, 2007c). We attributed such an opposite finding to the dramatic change of urban China in housing and social mobility. During the rapid change in urban China, newly developed neighborhoods are more attractive with houses that have much higher quality and larger spaces. The opportunity to move to these new communities largely depends on residents' economic, political, and social resources. As a result, these newly developed neighborhoods are likely to be populated by high-status residents.

In contrast to the well-established patterns in Western urban communities, our studies also found that the young and the educated exhibited higher levels of fear of crime in urban China than the older and the less educated (Liu *et al.*, 2009; Zhang *et al.*, 2009). We attributed these differences to the unique family and community context, as well as the Chinese educational system. We also observed a somewhat anomalous finding. Household income is negatively related to victimization risk in bicycle theft which is contrary to the general premise of routine activities/lifestyle theories that high income is associated with target attractiveness. Perhaps higher-income households improved their security measures to protect their bicycles and thus income reflected guardianship as well as target attractiveness, with the former outweighing the later.

China represents a unique social and cultural setting. Therefore, in addition to the application of Western concepts and theories to the Chinese context, we also made an effort to develop variables/measures to capture the unique characteristics of Chinese society that might be relevant in crime research. For instance, Chinese society is viewed as neither individual-based nor society-based, but relation-based. This unique cultural characteristic contrasts sharply with the typical Western individualistic orientation, as reflected in weak personal ties, infrequent interaction, and low intimacy. Therefore, we conceptualize *Guanxi* (commonly defined as a personal network that involves instrumental and affective bonds of individuals) as a unique variable that may influence Chinese residents' perception of their safety and security (Zhang *et al.*, 2009). Chinese people rely on their *Guanxi* or personal networks for virtually every aspect of their life and *Guanxi* serves as a unique form of social capital in Chinese society.

Using the Tianjin data, we assessed the role of *Guanxi* in the reported level of fear of crime when other conventional and important variables were controlled (Zhang *et al.*, 2009). *Guanxi* was found to be a significant predictor of the reported level of fear of crime in urban China. This finding demonstrates an important task in comparative studies of crime: conceptualizing factors that may be uniquely relevant to the particular social–cultural context and examining the impact of these factors in such a context. The results of such assessment and examination would advance our knowledge and understanding of crime phenomena across different social–cultural settings.

Another example is our study of the effect of row houses (*Ping Fang*) on the risk of bicycle theft (Zhang *et al.*, 2007a). Row houses are single-story buildings with a shared courtyard. They were the dominant house type in urban China before the economic reform. Since the 1980s, many row houses have been demolished to make rooms for high-rise apartment buildings to improve residents' housing conditions. The Chinese usually place their bicycles outside their houses because of limited living space. The layout of row houses with shared courtyards makes it easy for residents to watch and guard their bicycles and those of their neighbors. In contrast, it is difficult for residents in apartment buildings to monitor and guard their bicycles if they park them outside of the buildings or in hallways of the apartment buildings. We thus conceptualized house type (row houses versus apartment buildings) as an important indicator of household guardianship for the risk of bicycle theft. We hypothesized that residents who lived in row houses were less likely to be victimized in bicycle theft. The results of our analysis support the hypothesis.

Summarily, our study indicates that Western theories have mixed results when applied in China. Some Western concepts and variables are applicable to the Chinese context and others are not. More importantly, the real findings of our study indicate that variables must be developed and selected in context. Their meaning is based only on their related context. The development and test of these variables would make significant contribution to the field.

Research challenges

As noted above, crime is still a sensitive topic for research in China. The Chinese government has strict control over such research activities. In addition, public officials are often suspicious of the intentions of foreign researchers. It is therefore difficult to imagine any realistic scenario wherein Western researchers would successfully implement an original data collection project dealing with crime in China without the support and cooperation of local contacts. Consequently, the first challenge in doing crime research is to gain access and support from government control agencies and to seek local collaborators. No formal and systematic research on crime can be conducted without such access and collaboration.

The second challenge is related to research design. The basic principles of survey research presumably remain the same regardless of the social context, but some procedures and techniques that can be readily used in Western countries may not work in a different social and cultural setting such as China. Researchers may thus be required to make acceptable compromises between the ideal and the feasible. For example, in the development of our survey instrument, we relied heavily on past criminal victimization surveys in the West. Question wording for a large number of theoretically relevant variables was readily available in English because they have been used and tested in a good number of Western surveys. However, when they are used in the Chinese setting, it requires a large amount of effort to ensure the meaning of the survey questions can clearly fit knowledge and understanding of the Chinese respondents. Our original questionnaire was written in English, but it obviously had to be translated into Chinese. To ensure that the questions were readable and appropriate in Chinese, we worked closely with our local collaborators on the translation. Following standard practices, we used the method of "back translation" (Behling and Law, 2000) to enhance confidence in the Chinese version of the instrument.

The issue of protecting human subjects posed a number of challenges, in both the Chinese and US settings. China does not have formal legislation for the protection of human subjects in research and established institutional mechanisms to ensure such protection. To minimize the risk of harm and to satisfy requirements for US government-funded research projects, we provided training on the protection of human subjects to our Chinese collaborators similar to that offered in the US. We established standard protocols to secure Institutional Review Board (IRB) approval in the US. In the course of securing IRB approval, we discovered that some procedures that are quite practical in the US are not easily implemented in the Chinese context. We thus devised alternative strategies to meet the IRB requirements. For example, it is a standard procedure that all questionnaires should be sealed in a large envelope to ensure the confidentiality when a self-administration section is completed. However, these large envelopes are quite expensive in China. We had to compromise with our local collaborators to use old boxes to achieve the task.

Ensuring the validity of responses to a survey is a paramount concern in any survey research project, but the Chinese context poses some distinctive obstacles. The self-report method for victimization surveys has been developed in a Western socio-cultural setting characterized by individual autonomy and freedom to express personal opinions and views. Such independence and freedom of expression may have a significant impact on the quality of the data collected. In contrast, collectivism has traditionally been the essence of the Chinese culture. In this cultural context, an individual is encouraged to conform to the society, community, group, or family. It is generally not desirable to express opinions or beliefs openly that are contrary to those of other members of the social collectives (Zhang and Shavitt, 2003). These cultural traits are potentially problematic for survey research because they may make Chinese respondents reluctant to share their own viewpoints. They may be inclined to express what others in their groups and communities believe. To the extent that this is the case, the basic assumption of surveys that participants are willing to report their own views and opinions may be suspect.

In an attempt to minimize the impact of this cultural trait, we included text on the questionnaire assuring respondents that the answers would be treated confidentially and would only be used for purposes of the research. We also requested that our Chinese collaborators emphasize confidentiality before administering the questionnaires. They also made sure that respondents did not converse with one another when filling out the questionnaires.

Another feature of Chinese society that posed a potential problem is the lack of a self-consciously "scientific" tradition in social research. The notion of "doing science" in the study of social phenomena has not been firmly established, especially in criminology. Studies of crime and criminal justice that have appeared in Chinese professional journals and books usually involve general discussions or speculations without a sound theoretical framework and empirical analysis (Zhou and Cong, 2001). Such traditional practices foster a somewhat cavalier approach to the importance of conforming to rigorous scholarly standards and procedures. Consequently, we made conscientious efforts (e.g. laying out a detailed framework and enumeration of procedures for each step of the survey implementation) to ensure the strict enforcement of academic standards and research protocols when the surveys were conducted in China.

Conclusion

As many scholars have argued, comparative studies of crime will be much needed in the years ahead because of globalization in economic, social, and political areas. China, as an emerging economic power in the world, provides a strategic setting for crime research because the nation has been experiencing profound social changes and rising levels of crime. Our research experience in China demonstrates the value and benefit of conducting comparative studies of crime despite the significant challenges and barriers. The findings from our research enhance our understanding of Western concepts, theories, and methods from a different social and cultural setting. They inform us that the general conceptual framework and theories are likely to be applicable to a different social and cultural context – China, which implies that crime phenomena in different countries do share commonalities. At the same time, we also found differences contingent on the unique characteristics of Chinese society. These findings can extend our knowledge and understanding of crime phenomena across different social and cultural settings.

Also, the unique characteristics of a country such as China deserve special attention in developing new concepts and theories of crime to advance the concepts and theories established in the West. Our findings in a few new variables demonstrate the value and benefit of the development of new concepts and theories, although such development is more difficult and challenging.

Doing comparative studies of crime is challenging and will encounter special barriers. From our experience, the proper execution of crime research in a different cultural setting relies on several factors. First, researchers need to have a good understanding of the political, social, and cultural context of the host country. Such understanding involves a broad knowledge ranging from familiarity with the political/administrative system and social structure to an awareness of its tradition in social research. In addition, the importance of extensive contacts with government officials and local researchers cannot be overstated. Our experience underscores the benefits of linking up with experienced and fully engaged collaborators on-site.

The second factor is related to having a good balance between science and feasibility. In the course of collaboration with local researchers, flexibility and compromise are necessary to achieve success without sacrificing much scientific rigor. Scientific rigor is not exact duplication, but duplication of exact meaning through modified contextual frameworks. Making adjustments in research design and implementation to accommodate the social and cultural setting requires ability and considerable skill that a researcher needs to cultivate.

Finally, it is also important to build mutual trust and respect with local collaborators for effective collaboration. The local collaborators may have different academic background with a different cultural tradition. Disagreements and even conflict are likely to occur in the course of research. To handle these situations effectively, researchers must be convinced of the "good faith" of others and be willing to compromise as needed. These compromises are most easily achieved among scholars who have a genuine respect for the role and contributions of all involved.

In sum, our research experience in China demonstrates the value and benefit of comparative studies of crime and reveals special challenges and barriers for doing such studies in a different social and cultural context. It is worth the effort to meet the challenges and overcome the barriers to do the studies if we are willing to adopt a global perspective to develop and advance our knowledge and understanding of crime phenomena. Our research experience in China provides an example that is valuable for students who are interested in comparative studies to see how the challenges can be met and how the barriers can be overcome. Comparative studies of crime will receive greater attention as the world becomes more interconnected in the years ahead.

Future research questions

1. How will you test social disorganization theory in a different cultural setting such as China?
2. How will you analyze the difference and similarity of people's experience of being victimized in sex offenses in China and the United States?
3. How will you approach a comparative study of legal and social services provided to victims in China and the United States?
4. How will you discover cultural differences in China and the United States regarding people's view on capital punishment?
5. How will you compare the risk of being victimized in personal theft in China and the United States?

References

Bayley, D. H. (1969). *The police and political development in India*. Princeton: Princeton University Press.

—— (1976). *Forces of order: police behavior in Japan and the United States*. Berkeley: University of California Press.

Behling, O. and Law, K. S. (2000). *Translating questionnaires and other research instruments: problems and solutions*. Thousand Oaks, CA: Sage.

Bennett, R. R. (2004). Comparative criminology and criminal justice research: the state of our knowledge. *Justice Quarterly*, 21: 1–21.

Bracey, D. H. (1989). Policing the People's Republic of China. In R. J. Troyer, J. P. Clark, and D. G. Rojek (Eds.) *Social control in People's Republic of China*, pp. 131–40. New York: Praeger.

Clifford, W. (1978). Culture and crime in global perspective. *International Journal of Criminology and Penology*, 6: 61–68.

DeFleur, L. B. (1969). Alternative strategies for the development of delinquency theories applicable to other cultures. *Social Problems*, 17: 30–39.

Dutton, M. R. (1992). *Policing and punishment in China*. London: Cambridge University Press.

Fairbank, J. K. (1987). *The Great Chinese Revolution: 1800–1985*. New York: Harper and Row.

Friday, P.C. (1971). Problems in comparative criminology: comments on feasibility and implications of research. *International Journal of Criminology and Penology*, 1: 151–60.

Howard, G. J., Newman, G., and Pridemore, W. A. (2000). Theory, method, and data in comparative criminology. *Criminal Justice 2000*, 4: 139–211. Washington, DC: National Institute of Justice, US Department of Justice.

Johnson, E. H. (1986). Politics, power and prevention: the People's Republic of China case. *Journal of Criminal Justice*, 14: 449–57.

Liang, B. and Lu, H. (2006). Conducting fieldwork in China: observations on collecting primary data regarding crime, law, and the criminal justice system. *Journal of Contemporary Criminal Justice*, 22: 157–72.

Liu, J. (2006). Modernization and crime patterns in China. *Journal of Criminal Justice*, 34: 119–30.

Liu, J., Messner, S. F., Zhang, L., and Zhuo, Y. A. (2009). Socio-demographic correlates of fear of crime and the social context of contemporary urban China. *American Journal of Community Psychology*, 44: 93–108.

Messner, S. F., Lu, Z., Zhang, L. and Liu, J. (2007). Risks of criminal victimization in contemporary urban China: an application of lifestyle/routine activities theory. *Justice Quarterly*, 24: 496–522.

Miller, W. R. (1978). *Cops and bobbies: police authority in New York and London, 1830–1870*. Chicago: University of Chicago Press.

Nieuwbeerta, P. (2002). Introduction. In P. Nieuwbeerta (Ed.) *Crime victimization in comparative perspective: results from the International Crime Victims Survey, 1989–2000*, pp. 1–10. The Netherlands: Boom Juridische uitgevers.

Peerenboom, R. (2001). Seek truth from facts: an empirical study of the enforcement of arbitral awards in the People's Republic of China. *American Journal of Comparative* Law, 49: 249–327.

Robertson, A. (2006). The significance of language, culture, and communication in researching post-Soviet crime and policing. *Journal of Contemporary Criminal Justice*, 22: 137–56.

Rojek, D.G. (1996). Changing directions of Chinese social control. In C. B. Fields and R. H. Moore, Jr. (Eds.) *Comparative criminal justice: traditional and nontraditional systems of law and control*, pp. 234–49. Prospect Heights, IL: Waveland Press.

Shelley, L. (1981). *Modernization, age structure and regional context: a cross-national study of crime*. Carbondale, IL: Southern Illinois University Press.

Shelley, L. (1986). Crime and modernization reexamined. *Annales Internationales de Criminologie*, 24 : 7–21.

Smith, C. (2009). Comparative methods: going beyond incorporating international comparative research methods with traditional methods. *International Journal of Comparative and Applied Criminal Justice*, 32: 211–28,

Troyer, R. J., Clark, J. P., and Rojek, D. G. (1989). *Social control in People's Republic of China*. New York: Praeger.

Zhang, J. and Shavitt, S. (2003). Cultural values in advertisements to the Chinese X-Generation: promoting modernity and individualism. *Journal of Advertising*, 32: 21–31.

Zhang, L., Zhou, D., Messner, S. F., Liska, A. E., Krohn, M. D., Liu, J., and Lu, Z. (1996). Crime prevention in a communitarian society: Bang-Jiao and Tiao-Jie in the People's Republic of China. *Justice Quarterly*, 13: 199–222.

Zhang, L., Messner, S. F., and Liu, J. (2007a). Bicycle theft in contemporary urban China: a multi-level assessment of risk and protective factors. *Journal of Research in Crime and Delinquency*, 44: 406–26.
—— (2007b). An exploration of the determinants of reporting crime to the police in the city of Tianjin, China. *Criminology*, 45: 959–84.
—— (2007c). A multilevel analysis of the risk of household burglary in the city of Tianjin, China. *British Journal of Criminology*, 47: 918–37.
—— (2008). A critical review of recent literature on crime and criminal justice in China: research findings, challenges, and prospects (Introduction). *Crime, Law and Social Change*, 50: 125–30.
Zhang, L., Messner, S.F., Liu, J., and Zhou, Y.A. (2009). *Guanxi* and fear of crime in contemporary China. *British Journal of Criminology*, 49: 472–90.
Zhou, L. and Cong, M. (2001). Criminology in China: perspectives and development. In J. Liu, L. Zhang, and S.F. Messner (Eds.) *Crime and social control in a changing China*, pp. 57–64. Westport, CT: Greenwood.
Zhu, H., Lixian, W., Jialun, L., Jianan, G., and Lu, Z. (1995). The International Crime (Victim) Survey in Beijing. In U. Zvekic and A. Alvazzi del Frate (Eds.) *Criminal Victimization in theDeveloping World*, pp. 67–87. Rome: United Nations Interregional Crime and Justice Research Institute.

9

The legacy of INTERPOL crime data to cross-national criminology

Rosemary Barberet

Introduction

Crime data from INTERPOL are the oldest dataset of cross-national indicators of crime maintained by an international organization. Created in 1923, the International Criminal Police Commission (ICPC, later abbreviated to ICPC-INTERPOL and now known as INTERPOL) was founded to facilitate police cooperation among countries, even where diplomatic ties do not exist. INTERPOL's International Crime Statistics were first published in 1950. In 2006, INTERPOL decided to cease collecting and disseminating crime data, and 2005 was the last year data were collected, covering 2004. INTERPOL Resolution AG-2006-RES-19 noted problems with the accuracy and reliability of INTERPOL's statistics; that the agency was not equipped to improve the quality of its statistics; that the number of members and National Central Bureaus who contributed statistics was insufficient; that, consequently, the statistics were not useful for international police cooperation; and, that "the publication of the statistics is likely to create difficulties in the way they are used."

Van Dijk (2008, p. 39) has called for a moratorium on international police figures, arguing that "[t]he decision of INTERPOL in 2006 to remove its historical series of crime statistics from its public website is to be applauded and should serve as a model for the police community." Van Dijk claims that "it is in the best interest of the international police community to fully convert to crime surveying as the method of data collection on crime." Police-generated crime statistics, he argues, are only good as indicators of input of police forces and criminal justice systems. They cannot be used comparatively or even longitudinally, since they are tainted by reporting and recording biases and differences in legal definitions across countries (ibid., p. 41).

This article questions this "INTERPOL data obituary" by systematically reviewing the research in which INTERPOL data were analyzed, very little of which was cited by van Dijk or others who have recently examined the quality of INTERPOL data (Rubin *et al.*, 2008). In doing so, its aims are to approximate how much published research literature has used INTERPOL data; the methods of research, including the sample of countries, years, and crimes chosen; the practice of researchers in checking for reliability and validity; the analytical strategies; sources for independent variables; theoretical contributions; consistent and contradictory findings; and policy recommendations. What can be said about the value of the research that was produced with INTERPOL data, and what can we learn from this literature about how to use INTERPOL and other international data sources in the future?

INTERPOL crime data have always presented a number of advantages over other data sources (e.g. WHO, UNCS, ICVS) and have been the data more often used by many crime researchers around the world. Some of these advantages are also disadvantages. First, it was the oldest series, published biannually from 1950 and then annually as of 1993. As of 2000, it was published free of charge on INTERPOL's website and was available in Arabic, English, French, and Spanish. This longevity and transparency, ironically, brought its own demise, since the politicization of crime resulted in the unwillingness of countries to have their "dirty laundry," or crime statistics, aired. Second, although participation in INTERPOL's crime statistics program was voluntary, INTERPOL is one of the largest international agencies in the world currently with 187 member countries. Rubin *et al.* (2008, p. 60), upon examining response rates to INTERPOL from 1959 to 2004, found that the proportion of reporting members declined since 1985. Nevertheless, it often provided researchers with data from more countries and a more diverse collection of countries in terms of socioeconomic development than other data sources. The International Crime Statistics data collection sheet included categories of offenses and offenders, and crime definitions were simple. Collaborating institutions were given certain latitude to use their own crime definitions and fit their statistics into the INTERPOL crime categories. Minimal change occurred over the years to this series. But it was this simplicity that researchers criticized as deceiving, because it masked the definitional and reporting problems that occurred at the national level.

The INTERPOL data represented police and judicial statistics. They contained information on murder ("any act performed with the purpose of taking human life, in whatever circumstance, excluding abortion but including infanticide"), serious assault, theft (including aggravated theft, robbery, burglary, theft of motor vehicles), fraud, counterfeit currency offenses, drug offenses, and sex offenses, including rape. Offense data included the total number of cases known to the police, the percentage that were attempts, the clearance rate, and the rate of each offense per 100,000 population. INTERPOL also recorded data on the total number of offenders and the percentage of known offenders who were females and/or juveniles and who were not citizens of a particular country (Howard *et al.*, 2000; Haberfeld and McDonald, 2005). INTERPOL made no effort to validate its data or to tabulate them for users.

Thus far, one of the more popular datasets in the literature that uses INTERPOL data has been the Correlates of Crime Archive (COC) compiled by Richard R. Bennett of American University, which covers the years 1960–84 and holds indicators on 52 nations, sampled purposefully from seven regions of the world. The dataset includes crime data from INTERPOL as well as other indicators of theoretical interest in explaining crime. Bennett is currently updating the COC Archive for the last time to include data up to 2003 (Bennett, personal conversation, 2009). A more extensive but less popular database among crime researchers is Archer and Gartner's Comparative Crime Data File (CCDF), with data on 110 nations and 44 cities, covering varying but generally broader time periods. The CCDF uses "native" categories of crime for the countries and cities in the database, and as such, single-nation research is more appropriate and feasible with the CCDF than pooled analyses or comparisons among nations. The CCDF uses INTERPOL data along with other data. It has not been updated since it was created in 1984.

The criticisms of the INTERPOL data have been the same of all official data, particularly police data. All datasets have flaws that result in decreased validity and reliability, and INTERPOL data were no exception. Similar to domestic measures of police-recorded crime, INTERPOL data were subject to underreporting and underrecording. And similar to domestic measures of police-recorded crime in federal systems (such as the UCR in the United States), INTERPOL data were also subject to flaws that resulted from legal definitions that vary nationally and sub-nationally and from misinterpretation of its data reporting rules. Finally, reporting of data by

INTERPOL member states was voluntary, thus varying response rates determine the sample of countries in the INTERPOL dataset. INTERPOL data quality was affected by missing data, including key categories such as the percentage of attempts versus completed crimes and anomalies that were most often seen from year to year. Bennett and Lynch (1990) concluded that INTERPOL data were as appropriate as other cross-national datasets "for studies seeking aggregate descriptions of world crime or analytic explanations of cross-national crime rates" (p. 153) and noted that in any event, there was no real way to assess the validity of crime reports, because all data gathering strategies measure different phenomena (ibid. p. 153, note 1). But even the analytical strategies recommended by Bennett and Lynch were conditioned by the sample of countries (Gottschalk *et al.*, 2006), which was often a product of countries with the least missing data.

Methods

The aim of this study was to locate research literature that used INTERPOL data from 1950 to 2008. Research literature here implied books or journal articles of an empirical nature in the social or behavioral sciences, excluding textbooks and unpublished dissertations. Although some "gray literature," such as government reports, surfaced in the literature search, no special effort was made to locate it. Literature reviews of collections of empirical studies using INTERPOL data, such as LaFree (1999), were included, as were citations that countered or debated previous citations (e.g. the controversy over Rushton's race and crime analysis). Besides a search at the John Jay College of Criminal Justice Lloyd Sealy Library, the following databases were used: ICPSR Correlates of Crime Archive; Criminal Justice Abstracts (1968–2008); PsychINFO (1887–2008); World Political Science Abstracts (1975–2008); Sociological Abstracts (1952–2008); and Econlit (1969–2008). In addition, the author searched the database at the United Nations Vienna Documentation Centre, which serves the United Nations Office on Drugs and Crime, in April 2009. The keyword used for all fields was INTERPOL. Literature was excluded if INTERPOL data were not used in analysis. Due to the nature of the databases, all but two of the pieces of research were in English, and few book chapters were found. The reference lists for those sources that did include INTERPOL data were also examined to locate additional literature.

Findings

Sample description

Eighty-nine studies were found, published between 1967 and 2008. The number of studies published grew from one in the 1960s to eight in the 1970s and 22 in the 1980s, before peaking with 35 studies in the 1990s. From 2000 to the present, 23 studies were published. Those authors with three or more citations include Arthur, Barber, Bennett, Krohn, LaFree, Messner, Neapolitan, Rushton, Savage, and Wellford. Journals that featured two or more studies included criminology or criminal justice journals (*British Journal of Criminology*, *Canadian Journal of Criminology*, *Criminology*, *International Criminal Justice Review*, *International Journal of Comparative and Applied Criminal Justice*, *International Journal of Offender Therapy and Comparative Criminology*, and *Justice Quarterly*), and to a lesser extent, sociology journals (*Sociological Quarterly*, *Comparative Social Research*). A little more than half (48) were single-authored publications.

Aims: why use INTERPOL data?

The aims of using INTERPOL data in the literature examined were very broad. The bulk of criminological research used INTERPOL data in macro-analyses of crime. In its simplest form, the INTERPOL dataset was used as a background against which to frame a study with a larger purpose. For example, Yang (1994) uses INTERPOL data to frame his larger study of crime in China. INTERPOL data were also used for descriptive single, regional, or multicountry studies. Newman's massive *Global Report on Crime and Justice* (1999) used INTERPOL data to compare country figures from the UN Crime Survey, particularly on homicide. Oftentimes INTERPOL data were used to supplement another incomplete data source. Austin and Kim (1999), in examining education and crime in sub-Saharan Africa, claim that INTERPOL data were the only comparative data source for that region of the world. Along with descriptive research is the use of INTERPOL data in methodological research to discern the difference in using the various data sources available or to validate other crime indicators. Fourteen of the 89 studies can be placed in this category. Messner (1992) explored alternative forms of compensating for missing data and Gottschalk *et al.* (2006) examined the importance of the sample of countries chosen. Neapolitan (1996) argued for the importance of theoretically relevant variables, controlling for attempts as opposed to completed crimes and purposefully planning the sample of countries used as opposed to letting the sample self-select by eliminating countries with missing or anomalous data. Bennett and Lynch (1990), along with Aebi *et al.* (2002), looked at the differences in datasets and the correlation among them; Marshall and Block (2004) argued for composite indices. Rubin *et al.* (2008) audited 2002 data from INTERPOL as well as the UN UNCTS to examine missing countries and missing data and to categorize and count data anomalies. The most popular use of INTERPOL data was to conduct cross-national explanatory research of crime trends and test theory. INTERPOL data played an important role in theory testing in the field of homicide studies, as well as in modernization theory. They had also been used by researchers outside of criminology who used international crime data as part of non-criminological theory testing. In 1990 J. Philippe Rushton sparked a huge debate when, using INTERPOL data, he argued that he had found support for his evolutionary theory about racial inferiority. Ten of the citations in the literature located for the present chapter deal with either Rushton's work or reanalyses of his data. Surprisingly, despite much theory testing in the literature using INTERPOL data, policy-related aims were largely absent in the literature examined. We will return to this in the discussion.

Methods: how were INTERPOL data gathered for inclusion in analysis?

INTERPOL data were used in a variety of ways in the research examined. They were used within established datasets (Correlates of Crime Dataset, CCDF) or gathered by the author or authors. They were used in combination with other data (UNCS, WHO, ICVS, European Sourcebook), alone and independent of other datasets, longitudinally, cross-sectionally, for multiple countries, or for a single country. More than half the studies (50) used INTERPOL as their only crime data source. The variation was great. Fourteen of the 89 citations were cross-sectional studies that used INTERPOL data from only one year. The rest either conducted longitudinal analyses or used means of various years of INTERPOL data. Only one study analyzed a single location (Arthur, 1992), although two other studies were comparative relative to one country (Fujimoto and Park, 1994, for Japan, and Yang, 1994, for China). The rest analyzed multiple countries' data, ranging from 4 to 140 locations. Similarly, various combinations of crimes were used. Homicide-only or "murder"-only studies accounted for 22 of the total. The vast majority of studies used INTERPOL offense data. INTERPOL's offender data were used less often and mostly by researchers who were interested in women or juveniles.

How did researchers cope with incomplete, missing or anomalous INTERPOL data?

Researchers using INTERPOL data were generally aware of the incomplete or fluctuating nature of INTERPOL data. Nevertheless, 24 of the 89 studies made no adjustments for fluctuating or missing data. For those researchers who did adopt strategies, they undertook the following measures: selection of only some crime types; creation of index variables; elimination of attempts where possible; elimination of outliers; selection of only some years; selection of only some nations or self-selection; mean substitution for missing values; and computation of multiyear averages. They also complemented or compared with data from other datasets. Neapolitan (1996), Messner (1992), and Gottschalk *et al.* (2006), were the only authors who examined the effects of these various strategies. Neapolitan argued for the purposeful selection of country samples, as did Gottschalk *et al.*, who argued for the importance of context in general. Messner found that for moderate- and high-reporting countries, estimates using averages did not change the findings greatly. But for low-reporting nations, estimates using averages change the findings.

Analytical strategies

The analytical strategies found in the literature included descriptive comparisons of crime rates, ANOVA, correlational studies, and multiple regression. In the vast majority of studies, INTERPOL data were used for the dependent variable or variables. Only recently has research featured INTERPOL data as independent, as opposed to dependent variables. Ruddell and Urbina (2004) and Ruddell (2005) used the INTERPOL homicide data as a predictor of punishment across nations.

Sources for independent variables

Although the literature made frequent mention of the limitations of the INTERPOL data as a dependent variable, it was rare to find any mention of the quality of the data for the independent variables. Sources for independent variables in explanatory studies were varied including Polity III, *Handbook of Political and Social Indicators*, World Bank, *United Nations Demographic Yearbook*, *United Nations Statistical Yearbook*, the Dimensions of Nations data, *Human Development Report*, CIA *World Factbook*, Amnesty International, International Monetary Fund, *Economist World in Figures*, and *Handbook of International Data on Women*, as well as data published by individual authors (e.g. Kurian, Walmsley).

Theoretical contributions

INTERPOL data have been used to test a wide variety of theories. These include routine activities/opportunity; deterrence; modernization/Durkheimian/Anomie theory; strain or relative deprivation; conflict; gender theory female emancipation; medical care and social welfare; radical conflict, legitimation of violence; race and crime; minority threat; evolutionary; subculture of violence; and social control. The literature leads to both consistent and contradictory findings. The more consistent findings have to do with the positive relationship across nations between inequality and homicide, the lack of support for the female emancipation hypothesis as causing female crime, and the qualified support for modernization theory, which has undoubtedly received the most attention.

Discussion

This data-driven review of the literature that has used INTERPOL data from 1967 to the present is revealing in a number of ways. First, there is a real legacy in academic criminology thanks to INTERPOL data. The research reviewed spans four decades and 89 published studies. For many of the more prominently published and productive authors, these studies marked their careers. This was also the first opportunity for cross-national analyses to make their way into mainstream, high-ranking criminology journals. Although one cannot accept all the research without a critical eye, a majority of the research conducted has been cross-national, trend based, and theory driven. The fact that the bulk of the studies were published from the 1980s onwards can be explained by the increased use of computers in social research, which made quantitative analysis of large datasets easier; the compilation of the two cross-national datasets (COC and CCDF), which saved time and effort; and the academic trend towards quantitative theory testing. In the past three decades, INTERPOL data have been used to their fullest, and a true research tradition in macro-social criminology evolved out of their use. What is most striking about the legacy of INTERPOL data is that no study ever appears to use exactly the same dataset more than once, and it is impossible to control for all the variables that one would like. This variability is an advantage of INTERPOL data, as well as to researchers' search for appropriate independent variables, and thus a tribute to the creativity of secondary data analysts in criminology. It is also the dataset's downfall, in that the lack of standardization of indicators, country samples, selection of crimes or offenders, years, and independent variables means that INTERPOL data have supported a great many findings. Virtually every theory has found a modicum of support. This may not be a problem of the dataset, of course, but of the state of development of criminological theory.

What data sources are left for cross-national analyses? To date, the ICVS has not undergone as many sweeps as would allow good trend analysis and still does not feature permanent institutional support. WHO data cover homicide only. UNCTS data are the only versatile dataset left. But Rubin *et al.* (2008), in their audit of 2002 INTERPOL data, showed that INTERPOL's data were more regularly reported and with fewer anomalies than UNCTS data.

Perhaps we need to explore what the discontinuance of the collection of crime data by INTERPOL tells us about the usefulness of research published to the international policymaker. As an underfunded agency, INTERPOL prioritizes crime fighting and intelligence sharing over data gathering. Crime has also become politicized, so it is easy to understand that member states would become more and more uncomfortable submitting reports that could easily be used for international league tables by uncritical analysts. INTERPOL has never been a research organization: INTERPOL did little to check on the crime figures submitted by member states or even compile the data in a way to be useful to analysts. The dataset did little to accommodate the changing face of crime: over the years, categories were only modified slightly and new crime types had never been introduced in order to modernize the series. INTERPOL does not seem to have used its own data: a review of articles in the *International Criminal Police Review* from 1950–2001, an INTERPOL publication that has been discontinued as well, revealed no article except Bowker (1981) (reprinted in the *International Journal of Comparative and Applied Criminal Justice*) that used INTERPOL data in a sophisticated way. One has to question, then, how useful these data were to INTERPOL and whether any of the academic criminological research published was ever read by or deemed useful to INTERPOL, the data owner and supplier. None of the 89 articles in this literature made any mention of disseminating its research to INTERPOL or, with the exceptions of Bennett and Archer and Gartner, of any direct relationship at all with the data provider for the creation of their own datasets.

Criminologists are partly to blame for this. Most of the research cited in this chapter is useful only to academic criminologists. Policy aims were absent in virtually all of the articles or books listed herein, and virtually no policy recommendations were drawn in the conclusions sections either. Only Braithwaite and Braithwaite (1980), Neumayer (2003), and Savage and Vila (1997) chose to recommend such things as a more equal society, humanitarian state policies, and increased social welfare spending, respectively, while most of the methodological analyses (e.g. Bennett and Lynch, 1990, and Rubin *et al.*, 2008) argued for more and better data. Are the variables analyzed far too abstract and general to generate policy recommendations? Surely not. Even the simplest variables, such as sex, primary school enrollment, or income inequality, are of use in international criminal justice policymaking.

Conclusion

Unfortunately, INTERPOL data now remain as a source of data for a specific period in history. Our discipline has been nourished and shaped by those data. But because INTERPOL data no longer exist, that does not mean they are useless. The data from the Correlates of Crime Dataset continued to be used for research even as recently as 2008.

We need to become more involved in encouraging international organizations to continue gathering this data and encouraging our own governments to fund this data collection and contribute our national data to the international datasets. Besides victimization and self-report surveys, official data present a number of advantages, and their collection encourages governmental accountability. We need to contribute our methodological expertise to the better collection of international crime data. Why have scholars not been active in supporting data collection efforts at INTERPOL and making their research policy relevant to INTERPOL in exchange for using their data? INTERPOL has no mechanism to allow scholars to play an organized role, but by playing a more active role at the United Nations, as criminologists, we can ensure that member states know the value and relevance of providing good data for the use of the international community of scholars and policymakers. In recent years, the United Nations Office on Drugs and Crime has published manuals on the gathering of crime statistics, conducted technical assistance projects, and held expert meetings designed to improve response rates and data quality for the UNCTS (see, E/CN.15/2009/13, E/CN.15/2008/7, E/CN.15/2007/2, and A/CONF.203/3 at http://www.unodc.org). Nevertheless, in the face of resistance from many member states to the provision of their crime data, criminologists' voices must be heard. We also need to rethink how we design our secondary data research, how we can contextualize it in time and space, and how it can be translated into relevant policy recommendations. If all of this occurs, we stand a chance to save the remaining official data sources for comparative criminologists of the next generation.

Future research questions

1. What policy implications can be drawn from the criminological research that has used international data?
2. How can governments be encouraged to participate in international crime-data gathering exercises?
3. What would be a good strategy for maintaining quality control over crime data gathered at the international level and encouraging its proper use by researchers?

4. Are crime data more politicized than other types of data (e.g. health, economic data) and if so, why?
5. Why do legal definitions of crime vary around the world?

Acknowledgment

Permission granted to reproduce this abridged version of "The legacy of INTERPOL crime data to cross-national criminology," *International Journal of Comparative and Applied Criminal Justice*, 33(2): 193–210 (2009).

References

Dijk, J. van (2008). *The world of crime: breaking the silence on problems of security, justice, and development across the world.* Thousand Oaks, CA: Sage Publications.

Haberfeld, M. and McDonald, W. F. (2005). International cooperation in policing. In P. Reichel (Ed.) *Handbook of transnational crime and justice*, pp. 286–309. Thousand Oaks, CA: Sage.

Howard, G. J., Newman, G., and Pridemore, W. A. (2000). Theory, method and data in comparative criminology. In *Measurement and analysis of crime and justice: criminal justice 2000,* pp. 139–211. Washington, DC: National Institute of Justice.

International Criminal Police Organization (2006). Proposal to discontinue the production of crime statistics. Resolution No. AG-2006-RES-19. 75th INTERPOL General Assembly, Rio de Janeiro, Brazil.

LaFree, G. (1999). Homicide: cross-national perspectives. In D. Smith (Ed.), *Studying and preventing homicide: issues and challenges*, (pp 115–39. Thousand Oaks, CA: Sage Publications.

Rubin, M. M., Culp, R., Mameli, P., and Walker, M. (2008). Using cross-national studies to illuminate the crime problem: one less data source left standing. *Journal of Contemporary Criminal Justice*, 24: 50–68.

References used in analysis

Aebi, M. F., Killias, M., and Tavares, C. (2002). Comparing crime rates: the International Crime (Victim) Survey, *The European Sourcebook of Crime and Criminal Justice Statistics*, and INTERPOL statistics. *International Journal of Comparative Criminology*, 2(1): 22–37.

Anderson, T. L. and Bennett, R. (1996). Development, gender and crime: the scope of the routine activities approach. *Justice Quarterly*, 13(1): 31–56.

Archer, D. and Gartner, R. (1984). *Violence and crime in cross-national perspective.* New Haven: Yale University Press.

Arthur, J. (1991). Development and crime in Africa: a test of modernization theory. *Journal of Criminal Justice*, 19(6): 499–513.

—— (1992). Social change and crime rates in Puerto Rico. *International Journal of Offender Therapy and Comparative Criminology*, 36(2): 103–19.

—— (1997). Influences of social and economic conditions on crime in East Africa. *International Journal of Comparative and Applied Criminal Justice,* 21(1): 51–77.

Austin, R. L. and Kim, Y. S. (1999). Educational development and homicide in Sub-Saharan Africa. *Homicide Studies*, 3(1): 78–98.

—— (2000). A cross-national examination of the relationship between gender equality and official rape rates. *International Journal of Offender Therapy and Comparative Criminology*, 44(2): 204–21.

Barber, N. (2000). The sex ratio as a predictor of cross-national variation in violent crime. *Cross Cultural Research*, 34(3): 264–82.

—— (2004). Single parenthood as a predictor of cross-national variation in violent crime. *Cross-National Research*, 38(4): 343–58.

—— (2006). Why is violent crime so common in the Americas? *Aggressive Behavior*, 32(5): 442–50.

Bennett, R. R. (1982). The effect of police personnel levels on crime clearance rates: a cross-national analysis. *International Journal of Comparative and Applied Criminal Justice*, 6(2): 177–93.

—— (1991a). Development and crime: a cross-national, time-series analysis of competing models. *Sociological Quarterly*, 32(3): 343–63.

—— (1991b). Routine activities: a cross-national assessment of a criminological perspective. *Social Forces*, 70(1): 147–63.

Bennett, R. R. and Bennett, S. B. (1983). Police personnel levels and the incidence of crime: a cross-national investigation. *Criminal Justice Review*, 8: 32–40.

Bennett, R. R. and Shelley, L. (1985). Criminalité et développement économique: Une analyse internationale longitudinale. *Annales de Vaucresson*, 22: 13–31.

Bennett, R. R, and Lynch, J. P. (1990). Does a difference make a difference? Comparing cross-national crime indicators. *Criminology*, 28(1): 153–82.

Bennett, R. R. and Basiotis, P. (1991). Structural correlates of juvenile property crime: a cross-national, time-series analysis. *Journal of Research in Crime and Delinquency*, 28(3): 262–87.

Bennett, R. R. and Lynch, J. P. (1997). Status inequality and property crimes: the effect of design, scope and specification. *International Criminal Justice Review*, 7: 1–30.

Bowker, L. H. (1981). The institutional determinants of international female crime. *International Journal of Comparative and Applied Criminal Justice*, 5(1):11–28.

Braithwaite, J. and Braithwaite, V. (1980). The effect of income inequality and social democracy on homicide. *British Journal of Criminology*, 20(1): 45–53.

Brantingham, P., and Easton, S. T. (1998). *The costs of crime: who pays and how much?* 1998 update. Vancouver, CAN: Fraser Institute.

Camara, M. and Salama, P. (2004). Homicidios en America del Sur: Los pobres son peligrosos? *Revista de Economia Institucional*, 6(10): 159–81.

Cernovsky, Z. Z. and Litman, L. C. (1993). Re-analyses of J. P. Rushton's crime data. *Canadian Journal of Criminology*, 35: 31–6.

Chon, D. S. (2002). *The relationship between national homicide rates and medical care: a cross-national assessment.* New York: LFB Scholarly.

Christiansen, K. O. (1967). *The post-war trends of crime in selected European countries*. Copenhagen: Kriminalistiriske Institute.

Clifford W. and Mukherjee, S. (1979). *Crime trends and crime prevention strategies*. Canberra: Australian Government Publishing Service.

Deane, G. D. (1987). Cross-national comparison of homicide: age/sex-adjusted rates using the 1980 US homicide experience as a standard. *Journal of Quantitative Criminology*, 3(3): 215–27.

Dijk, J. van, Mayhew, P., and Killias, M. (1990). *Experiences of crime across the world: key findings of the 1989 International Crime Survey*. Deventer, The Netherlands: Kluwer.

Fujimoto, T. and Park, W. (1994). Is Japan exceptional? Reconsidering Japanese crime rates. *Social Justice*, 21(2): 110–35.

Gabor, T. and Roberts, J. V. (1990). Rushton on race and crime: the evidence remains unconvincing. *Canadian Journal of Criminology*, 32(2): 335–43.

Gottschalk, M., Smith, T., and Howard, G. J. (2006). Explaining differences in comparative criminological research: an empirical exhibition. *International Journal of Comparative and Applied Criminal Justice*, 30(2): 209–34.

Hagerty, M. R. (1999). Testing Maslow's hierarchy of needs: national quality of life across time. *Social Indicators Research*, 46(3): 249–71.

Hartnagel, T. F. (1982). Modernization, female social roles, and female crime: a cross-national investigation. *Sociological Quarterly*, 23: 477–90.

Hartnagel, T. F. and Mizanuddin, M. (1986). Modernization, gender role convergence and female crime: a further test. *International Journal of Comparative Sociology*, 27: (1–2): 1–14.

Hinton, M. S. (2005). A distant reality: democratic policing in Argentina and Brazil. *Criminal Justice*, 5(1): 75–100.

Howard, G. and Smith, T. (2003). Understanding cross-national variations of crime rates in Europe and North America. In K. Aromaa, S. Leppd, S. Nevala, and N. Ollus (Eds.), *Crime and criminal justice systems in Europe and North America 1995–1997*, pp. 23–65. Helsinki, Finland: HEUNI.

Huang, W. S. W. (1993). Are international murder data valid and reliable? Some evidence to support the use of INTERPOL data. *International Journal of Comparative and Applied Criminal Justice*, 17(1): 17–29.

Huang, W. S. W. and Wellford, C. F. (1989). Assessing indicators of crime among international crime data series. *Criminal Justice Policy Review*, 3(1): 28–47.

Jacobs, D. and Richardson, A. M. (2008). Economic inequality and homicide in the developed nations from 1975 to 1995. *Homicide Studies*, 12: 28–45.

Kalish, C. B. (1988). *International Crime Rates*. Washington, DC: US Bureau of Justice Statistics.

Kick, E. L. and LaFree, G. D. (1985). Development and the social context of murder and theft. *Comparative Social Research*, 8: 37–58.

Kirkcaldy, B. D. and Brown, J. M. (2000). Personality, socioeconomics and crime: an international comparison. *Psychology, Crime and Law*, 6(2): 113–25.

Krahn, H., Hartnagel, T. F., and Gartrell, J. W. (1986). Income inequality and homicide: cross-national data and criminological theories. *Criminology*, 24(2): 239–95.

Krohn, M. (1976). Inequality, unemployment and crime: a cross-national analysis. *Sociological Quarterly*, 17: 303–13.

—— (1978). A Durkheimian analysis of international crime rates. *Social Forces*, 57(2): 654–70.

Krohn, M. and Wellford, C. (1977). A static and dynamic analysis of crime and the primary dimensions of nations. *International Journal of Criminology and Penology*, 5: 1–16.

LaFree, G. and Kick, E. L. (1986). Cross-national effects of developmental, distributional and demographic variables on crime: a review and analysis. *International Annals of Criminology*, 24: 213–36.

Landau, S. F. (1984). Trends in violence and aggression: a cross-cultural analysis. *International Journal of Comparative Sociology*, 55: 133–58.

Lee, M. R. and Shihadeh, E. S. (1998). Labor market structure, unemployment, and crime: the indirect effect of low-skills jobs on homicide and theft in 26 countries. In Jeffery T. Ulmer (Ed.), *Sociology of crime, law, and deviance,* Vol. 1, pp. 49–64. Stamford, CT: Jai Press.

McDonald, L. (1976). *The Sociology of Law and Order.* Boulder, CO: Westview.

Mackey, W. C. and Mackey, B. (2003). The presence of fathers in attenuating young male violence: Dad as social palliative. *Marriage & Family Review*, 35(1–2): 63–75.

Marshall, I. H. (1982). Women, work, and crime: an international test of the emancipation hypothesis. *International Journal of Comparative and Applied Criminal Justice*, 6(1): 25–37.

Marshall, I. H. and Block, C. R. (2004). Maximizing the availability of crossnational data on homicide. *Homicide Studies*, 8: 267–310.

Mehrtens, F. J. (2004). Laissez-faire vs. regulated capitalism: a cross-national analysis of social costs. *Sociological Spectrum*, 24: 341–68.

Messner, S. F. (1980). Income inequality and murder rates: some cross-national findings. *Comparative Social Research, 3*: 185–98.

—— (1989). Economic distribution and societal homicide rates: further evidence on the cost of inequality. *American Sociological Review*, 54(4): 597–611.

—— (1992). Exploring the consequences of erratic data reporting for cross-national research on homicide. *Journal of Quantitative Criminology*, 8(2):155–73.

Neapolitan, J. L. (1994). Cross-national variation in homicides: the case of Latin America. *International Criminal Justice Review*, 4: 4–22.

—— (1995). Differing theoretical perspectives and cross-national variation in thefts in less developed countries. *International Criminal Justice Review*, 5: 17–31.

—— (1996). Cross-national crime data: some unaddressed problems. *Journal of Crime and Justice*, 19(1): 95–112.

—— (1998). Cross-national variation in homicides: is race a factor? *Criminology*, 36(1): 139–56.

Neumayer, E. (2003). Good policy can lower violent crime: evidence from a cross-national panel of homicide rates, 1980–97. *Journal of Peace Research*, 40(6): 619–40.

—— (2005). Inequality and violent crime: evidence from data on robbery and violent theft. *Journal of Peace Research*, 42(1): 101–12.

Newman, G. (Ed.). (1999). *Global report on crime and justice.* New York: Oxford University Press.

Ortega, S. T., Corzine, J., and Burnett, C. (1992). Modernization, age structure, and regional context: a cross-national study of crime. *Sociological Spectrum*,12(3): 257–77.

Roberts, J. V. and Gabor, T. (1990). Lombrosian wine in a new bottle: research on crime and race. *Canadian Journal of Criminology*, 32(2): 291–343.

Rubin, M. M., Culp, R., Mameli, P., and Walker, M. (2008). Using cross-national studies to illuminate the crime problem: one less data source left standing. *Journal of Contemporary Criminal Justice*, 24: 50–68.

Ruddell, R. (2005). Social disruption, state priorities and minority threat: a cross-national study of imprisonment. *Punishment and Society*, 7(1): 7–28.

Ruddell, R. and Urbina, M. G. (2004). Minority threat and punishment: a crossnational analysis. *Justice Quarterly*, 21(4): 903–31.

Rushton, J. P. (1990). Race and crime: a reply to Roberts and Gabor. *Canadian Journal of Criminology*, 32(2): 315–34.

—— (1994). Race and crime: a reply to Cernovsky and Litman. *Canadian Journal of Criminology*, 36: 79–82.

—— (1995a). Race and crime: international data for 1989–90. *Psychological Reports*, 76: 307–12.
—— (1995b). *Race, evolution and crime*. New Brunswick, NJ: Transaction.
—— (1995c). Race and crime: an international dilemma. *Society*, 32: 37–41.
Rushton, J. P. and Whitney, G. (2002). Cross-national variation in violent crime rates: race, r-K theory and income. *Population and Environment*, 23(6): 501–11.
Savage, J. and Vila, B. (1997). Lagged effects of nurturance on crime: a cross-national comparison. *Studies on Crime and Crime Prevention*, 6(1): 101–20.
—— (2002). Changes in child welfare and subsequent crime rate trends: a cross-national test of the lagged nurturance hypothesis. *Applied Developmental Psychology*, 23: 51–82.
Savage, J., Bennett, R. R. and Danner, M. J. (2008). Economic assistance and crime: a cross-national investigation. *European Journal of Criminology*, 5: 217–38.
Shichor, D. (1985). Effects of development on official crime rates. *Sociology and Social Research*, 70(1): 96–7.
—— (1990). Crime patterns and socioeconomic development: a crossnational analysis. *Criminal Justice Review*, I(1): 64–78.
South, S. J. and Messner, S. F. (1987). The sex ratio and women's involvement in crime: a cross-national analysis. *Sociological Quarterly*, 28(2): 171–88.
Stack, S. (1984). Income inequality and property crime. *Criminology*, 22(2): 229–57.
Steffensmeier, D., Allan, E., and Streifel, C. (1989). Development and female crime: a cross-national test of alternative explanations. *Social Forces*, 68(1): 262–83.
Vigderhous, G. (1978). Methodological problems confronting cross-cultural criminological research using official data. *Human Relations*, 31(3): 229–47.
Wellford, C. F. (1974). Crime and the dimensions of nations. *International Journal of Criminology and Penology*, 2(1): 1–10.
Wolf, P. (1971). Crime and development. An international comparison of crime rates. *Scandinavian Studies in Criminology*, 3: 107–20.
Yang, C. (1994). Public security offences and their impact on crime rates in China. *British Journal of Criminology*, 34(1): 54–68.

10

Research methods overview

The missing pieces of rigorous research

Cindy J. Smith

Introduction

Thus far in this handbook, the authors have presented discussions of the key components of research methods that traditionally come to mind (i.e. qualitative methods in Chapter 4, quantitative methods in Chapter 5, and theory in Chapter 8). Additionally, in Chapter 3 they have discussed the state of criminology and criminal justice as a field of study that exists in the periphery in the majority of countries. And, authors have focused on two very different, yet overlapping, perspectives from which one can view research methods, that is from an evaluation perspective in Chapter 6 and a crime prevention perspective in Chapter 7. Finally, Chapter 9 provides one example of how knowledge has been built, using publically collected data, albeit with considerable debate about the usefulness of the knowledge because of the limitations of these data. To complete the picture in this puzzle of research methods, there are three missing topics. First, there is the need for documentation and use of more comprehensive research methods than is found in much of the current Western literature. Second, there is the need for comprehensive contextualization. And, finally, this chapter concludes with a brief discussion of the merits of developing partnerships to enhance the research.

This chapter is an introduction to these critical pieces of the puzzle that, without them, may lead to misinformation and inaccurate knowledge building. To date, much of the research that has consumed the peer-reviewed journal articles and other publications has not adhered to strict scientific rigor, so much so that the knowledge base might be described as built as a house of cards. That is to say, think of building a house from a deck of playing cards where each card stands on its edge and its only support is to lean on another card on its edge (a graphic description of this process is presented in Plate 10.1, Step 1). The edge represents the amount of fact in the article and the face represents the amount of *thought* in the publication. In other words, the wide area of thought is built on slim evidence, which may or may not be accurate or useful. As the house is built, one layer of *thought* built on top of the next layer of *thought*, the knowledge base appears to grow higher and higher (see Plate 10.1, Step 2). Unfortunately, when scientifically rigorous research disproves one of the slim "facts," the house of cards tumbles, thus leaving the entire knowledge base in question with only veins of knowledge (see Plate 10.1, Step 3).

One example of this house-of-cards concept is found in the terrorism literature (although there are as many other examples as there are topics in crime research) where Cynthia Lum and

Plate 10.1 House of cards

her colleagues (2006) reviewed 20,047 publications. Of these, 354 were found to have hinted at using some data resulting in some level of scientific rigor. Only seven of the publications met the standard used by the Campbell Collaborative for rigorous program evaluation. Think about the house built with 20,000 cards and the resulting knowledge base tumbling when rigor is applied. What do we know about terrorism? What veins are represented by the edges of the flat pile of cards? (See Smith and Picarelli (2008) for a framework in which to place the answer to this question.) So, it would seem that *thought* pieces might be a waste of time and effort. But before we err on the side of the Martinson tragedy (discussed later in this chapter), there should be some discussion about why researchers spend their valuable time on *thought* pieces. This would be a field of research in and of itself. Suffice it to say that the reward structure of publish or perish in the university system, the lack of available research dollars in the field, the lack of available data and the related high cost of collecting it, and the demand on practitioners to *do something* as a result of widely publicized and horrific events, such as 9/11 in New York, train bombings in Madrid, etc., have significant draw for academics to engage in research activities, though not perfect but efficient in producing publications. And, these *thought* pieces are not necessarily bad. For example, O'Brien and Bera (1986) offered a typology of juvenile sex offenders with anecdotal data supporting it. This typology has guided research since that time. Their thought led the way for future research. And, much of this handbook consists of *thought* pieces that summarize the state of the art in a way that is useful to a particular audience. It is only negative when the piece has only slim evidence that is later found to be wrong. It would assist those who are searching for meaningful findings if publications were categorized into groupings, such as *thought* pieces summarizing research for particular audiences, data-based research, and *thought* with limited data pieces. Understanding that there are weaknesses even in the most rigorous research, this chapter begins with the problems in research methods, then moves into answering some of the other questions that will help us see more of the picture in the puzzle.

What are the problems with research methods?

The problems begin with the lack of a shared lexicon of the term *research methods*. At a very basic level, research methods and research methodology are used interchangeably when, in fact, they are very different. Research methods are the plan and the steps of the research. Research methodology is the study of methods. Other terms, such as comparative research and research design, also are used interchangeably when referring to research methods. Comparative research does not have a clear definition among criminologists. Hantrais (1995) describes comparative methods as synonymous with international methods, Bechtel (2004) summarized it as comparing one country to another, and Barberet (2004) suggests it is multiple cultural comparisons. Although there are many reasons for the deficiency in definition, part of this problem is the lack of understanding or appreciation of the impact of the global situation on crime and part of it is the lack of scientific training of criminologists (Smith, 2009). The current state of the definition includes multiple terms, such as the comparative perspective denoting a global view (Howard *et al.*, 2000), the comparative approach articulating the type of research (Ragin, 1994), and comparative research comparing similarities and differences (Mills *et al.*, 2006). Although Durkheim (1938) broadly defined comparative research in 1938 as: "Comparative sociology is not a particular branch of sociology; it is sociology itself, insofar as it ceases to be purely descriptive and aspires to account for facts" (p. 139), the definition continues to be elusive (Smith, 2009). This confusion in definition is not only in what is taught as comparative research methods, but extends from the widely used research methods taught and used in today's criminology in countries such as the US, Canada, UK, and Australia (hereafter called Western methods).

Western methods have similar problems with clarity in definition, particularly in the use of the term research design when discussing various methods.

> In the most generic sense, research may be categorized as quantitative or qualitative. In traditional texts, the research design may be categorized based on its experimental degree (e.g., experimental, quasi-experimental, and non-experimental), or as a progression or goal of research, which reflects a hierarchical nature, articulated as exploratory, descriptive, and explanatory designs. Finally, traditional research designs may be categorized based on data collection strategies, such as surveys, case studies, and secondary data designs. Another perspective to research design is categorized based on the nature of the data, such as cross-sectional and longitudinal designs.
>
> *(Smith, 2009, p. 215)*

The limited Western methods seem to differ by the attention to detail from the broader, more inclusive research methods often found in comparative methods. For example, scientifically rigorous comparative methods spend considerable effort contextualizing each step in the research process to ensure comparability between the issues under investigation (e.g. measures) and to make exact replication possible. It should be noted here that it is possible that not all Western methods lack this attention, but it is not reflected in the publication. This may be because of space limitations. However, research that is not replicable is not useful. Thus, these details must be included or the house of cards example applies to the building of knowledge.

Using only one of these perspectives of methods (e.g. cultural comparisons) or definitions of design (e.g. experimental degree), except for Durkheim's all encompassing definition, limits the growth of scientifically rigorous research in the field of criminology and criminal justice (see Smith, 2009 for a detailed discussion of these limitations). For example, suggesting that comparative methods only apply when comparing two countries suggests that each country is homogeneous within its borders, which is not the case for any country. Even worse, this assumption results in developing a faulty knowledge base. In today's globalized world, it is imperative that research – all research – include an international perspective. An international perspective "incorporates a world view, mindful of geographic, political, and cultural boundaries/differences" (Smith, 2009, p. 215). Unfortunately, much of the research published in the most respected journals in the field does not have this international perspective, thus missing the context that is so important to developing replicable research. Therefore, the field must come together with a shared lexicon to ensure effective communication and increase the rigor and/or documentation of the applied rigor to ensure replicable research. *Comparative methods is the overarching term under which researchers must include a global perspective and incorporate comprehensive methods that ensure comparability through the documentation of various design types used*. Using this framework would move the field a considerable distance forward in terms of building a shared lexicon and comprehensive documentation resulting in improved communication. Once the communication problems are resolved, the next step is to develop the practice of comprehensive contextualization in all research.

What is comprehensive contextualization?

Comprehensive contextualization is the result of comparative methods (as defined in the previous section). Comparative methods have the "added attention to the concepts, measures, or alternative (e.g., scientific rigor) that results in the ability to account for facts in a global, contextualized framework, rather than simple description" (Smith, 2009, p. 213). It is the complete description of all procedures and design used to conduct the research and the context in which that research project is implemented. Thus, the findings are fully contextualized. The process of detailing each step attributes to the scientific rigor and the ability to replicate the study. The final step of contextualizing the findings requires the most attention because it is used by the media, policy makers, practitioners, and researchers.

Placing research in context has two levels. First, there is the process of contextualizing the methods and findings. Second, there is the process of using findings without context (see Martinson, 1974 and subsequent references to his article). Both cause problems because not contextualizing methods and findings results in a faulty knowledge base, and taking findings out of their context leads to faulty knowledge building in subsequent studies.

When methods and findings are not contextualized, the resulting knowledge base is flawed. How might this occur? First, the researcher may not have considered all of the nuances of comparative research. The key to comparative methods is concept equivalence. For example, are all participants of the same culture? Do they share a common language? Do they share a common lexicon? Are the questions of a survey written in such a way that a 70-year-old would interpret the question in the same way as a 16-year-old? Does the question avoid jargon that changes between generations? Second, if the methods and findings are not adequately documented, there is no way of knowing if the researchers took into consideration such things as differences in cultures or variation in meanings of words when an instrument is translated into a different language. A more complete discussion of this is found in Smith (2009).

For example, Huggins and Glebbeek (2003) (two women) studied male violence in male-dominant policing institutions in Latin America. The authors described what they learned about cross-gender methods while conducting their primary research. Their article is rich with contextualization of the issues that may have impacted their ability to gather information and thus develop reliable findings in the original studies and of the ethical dilemmas during the research. Huggins, a light-skinned female with academic credentials, was conducting interviews in a society that values light skin and is less suspicious of academics than journalists, which opened doors that may have otherwise remained closed (ibid., p. 373). Additionally, Huggins experienced many ethical dilemmas, including when one interviewee was so distraught the day after the interview that he was contemplating suicide (ibid., p. 382). One ethical obligation would be to reach out for help for the interviewee, but the ethics of confidentiality in research prevent this without the express permission of the interviewee. These examples demonstrate the depth of the contextualization necessary to ensure that the findings reported in the studies were accurate, albeit to the extent of the authors' nuanced understanding of the research environment. The resulting knowledge base is therefore enriched.

When research findings are taken out of context, findings may be misinterpreted and this faulty knowledge provides the foundation for future research hypotheses and support of arguments. For example, in the early1970s Martinson and his colleagues were funded by the state of New York to review the literature on correctional rehabilitation to determine "What works?" in corrections. The review of 231 publications with sufficient scientific rigor to be included in the study revealed mixed results, but generally that there was no way to know if the programming worked ("no clear pattern to indicate the efficacy of any particular method of treatment") (Martinson, 1974, p. 47)). The final report with the full details and contextualization was withheld for some time, but Martinson published an article in *The Public Interest* in 1974 with sufficient contextualization that suggested the following three findings: 1) treatment in corrections was based on the blind premise of rehabilitation – that the flaws in prisoners were changeable or that we know how to change the flaws ("Our present treatment programs are based on a theory of crime as a 'disease' – that is to say, as something foreign and abnormal in the individual which can presumably be cured") (1974, p. 48)); 2) programs were not fully implemented – that there was no way of knowing what *dose* was needed or administered ("It may be simply that our programs aren't yet good enough – that the education we provide to inmates is still poor education, that the therapy we administer is not administered skillfully enough . . .") (ibid., p. 47)); and 3) researchers used research methods lacking scientific rigor – that resulted in not knowing if the program did not work because of the program or because the methods were so inadequate ("It is just possible that some of our treatment programs *are* working to some extent, but that our research is so bad that it is incapable of telling") (ibid.)). These findings were taken out of context by many criminal justice stakeholders and reported widely as "nothing works." The report and article do not say "nothing works," but provide various results. In fact, the report provides rather damning accusations of academic inadequacies in program development, implementation and evaluation and is supported by data for which Martinson paid a personal price in his relationships with many colleagues.

The ramifications of the lack of full contextualization can be extensive. An examination of the literature since Martinson's report reveals that he is the most misquoted – taken out of context – author in our field. Martinson and his colleagues did not find that "nothing works." Yet, the literature is replete with these claims. As a result of taking these findings out of their context, treatment was virtually removed from corrections for nearly three decades during a time of rapid prison expansion. Martinson spent considerable time discussing and disseminating the findings until his untimely death by suicide (Miller, 1989). The house of cards has been built by careless academics that have misquoted this study's findings. But probably more important is the attention that has not been paid to what Martinson did find – that academics working in the criminal justice field have not developed, implemented and evaluated programs with sufficient scientific rigor, as evidenced by the recent review of the terrorism literature (Lum *et al.*, 2006) or a similar comprehensive review of the human-trafficking literature (Gozdziak and Bump, 2008). But, to avoid the same mistake, we need to acknowledge the improvements that have been achieved and are found throughout this volume (see, for example, Barberet in Chapter 9 or Farrington *et al.* in Chapter 6). Thus, future researchers must be careful to develop solid research plans with full documentation and contextualization, as well as build the studies on findings that include the full contextualization. One way to encourage comprehensive studies and the inclusion of the nuances of research situations is to partner with practitioners and multidisciplinary partners.

Developing partnerships

Developing partnerships, particularly those in foreign countries, requires considerable work and patience, but has its rewards. Partnerships have evidence of being more effective and productive than single-author research (Dugery and Knowles, 2003; Jacobs, 1996). Sustainable lifetime partnerships are developed through a sound incremental process where relationships are built and the resulting research benefits from mutual participation (e.g. researcher and practitioner partnership) and understanding (e.g. policymaker understanding the findings of the research and researcher understanding the policymaker's needs). The literature on partnerships indicates that developing new partnerships almost always requires deliberate efforts (Dugery and Knowles, 2003), often motivated by external funding or other rewards (ibid.), should benefit both partners as well as communities (Letona, 1999), and are established to solve current problems (ibid.). Although research on social science partnerships is limited, other disciplines are better developed. Broadly, successful partnerships include the following:

1) Trust and respect are foundational for any partnership (Lafferty and Filicko, 2000, p. 3).
2) "Partners tend to select each other due to common needs, goals and/or shared belief that the team approach can be more productive and effective than working alone" (Lafferty and Filicko, 2000, p. 3). Conversely, those who fail are often found to have differing goals and beliefs.
3) Researchers need to recognize practitioner norms, values, and goals (Letona, 1999).
4) Partners are equal but different. They should possess complementary traits, qualities, and resources (Lafferty and Filicko, 2000, p. 4).
5) Synergy is developed between the partners, resulting in overall involvement (Boris and Steuerle, 1999).
6) Power and knowledge are shared and there is demonstrated accountability *to* the partnership and the community (Bloom *et al.*, 2009)

In addition to these general characteristics of a partnership, criminology and criminal justice as a multidisciplinary course of study benefits from research that involves a multidisciplinary team.

Further research should be conducted on each of these partnership characteristics to determine its usefulness in the criminology/criminal justice field. However, one example of the fourth item in a comparative research context is the parallel study where two or more researchers are conducting one study across multiple sites where language and culture varies (see Smith, 2009 for a discussion). Each researcher possesses a different language and understands the related culture, but implements the same protocol that has been adjusted for the language and culture. The process, when rigorously applied provides equivalent data that can be compared. The methods (e.g. full description of translation and back translation) and findings are then contextualized. Partnerships add yet another dimension, time and expense to research, but other disciplines have found them to result in more productive and useful results (Lafferty and Filicko, 2000).

Summary

This chapter provides additional pieces to the puzzle of research methods that are necessary in a comparative context: shared lexicon, contextualization and partnerships. The lack of strict adherence to definitions of terms used in research methods has caused considerable confusion in the field. The interchangeability of terms has added to the weaknesses found in the research methods. This chapter discusses the need for and impact of contextualization. It provides a brief discussion of contextualizing the methods and findings of a study to ensure that the knowledge base grows with a solid foundation, using two current examples of contextualization. The 1974 summary (Martinson, 1974) of *The Martinson report* is used to demonstrate what occurred when one statement was taken out of context, and the long shadow cast over the field of corrections. Martinson's not so famous quote from this study, "with few and isolated exceptions, the rehabilitative efforts that have been reported so far have had no appreciable effect on recidivism" (Martinson, 1974, p. 22) became the infamous "nothing works" doctrine. The literature is replete with examples of otherwise well-informed academics using "nothing works" in place of the more accurate quote. In addition to contextualization, this chapter emphasizes the importance of partnerships in research endeavors, a method used to enhance research and use of its findings.

Future research questions

1. Identify the evolution of the research methods terms over the last five years. What term best describes each process in the development of the methods?
2. Based on each step in the research process (e.g. survey/instrument development, data collection, design development), what contextualization must be present to provide adequate information for the replication of future studies?
3. What is the minimum amount of context that must accompany prior findings to ensure development of a solid knowledge base?
4. What is the relationship of each of the known partnership characteristics in producing valid research findings?
5. Which journals publish the best comparative and contextualized research? What are the strengths and weaknesses of the articles in terms of contextualization?

References

Barbaret, R. (2004). Mainstreaming comparative methodology in criminal justice/criminology research methods courses. *International Journal of Comparative Criminology*, 4(1): 112–26.

Bechtel, J. (2004). *High tech crimes: new crimes, new tools and new research methods?* Paper presented at annual meeting of the American Society of Criminology: Nashville, TN.

Bloom, T., Wagman, J., Hernandez, R., Yragui, N., Hernandez-Valdovinos, N., Dahlstrom, M., and Glass, N. (2009). Partnering with community-based organizations to reduce intimate partner violence. *Hispanic Journal of Behavioral Sciences*, 31(2): 244–57.

Boris, E. and Steuerle, C. (Eds.) (1999). *Nonprofits and government: collaboration and conflict*. Washington, DC: Urban Institute.

Dugery, J. and Knowles, J. (eds). (2003). University + community research partnerships: a new approach. Charlottesville, VA: Pew Partnership for Civic Change.

Durkheim, E. (1938). *The rules of sociological method*. Translated by Sarah Solvey and John Muellet. Edited by George E. G. Catlin (8th edn.) NY: Free Press.

Gozdziak, E. M. and Bump, M. (2008). *Data research on human trafficking: bibliography of research-based literature*. Institute for the Study of International Migration. NIJ Grant-2007-VT-BX-K002.

Hantrais, L. (1995). Comparative research methods. *Social Research Update*, 13. Online at http://sru.soc.surrey.ac.uk/SRU13.html (accessed May 20, 2007).

Howard, G. J., Newman, G., and Pridemore, W. A. (2000). Theory, method, and data in comparative criminology (from measurement and analysis of crime and justice.) *Criminal Justice 2000*, (4): 139–211. Washington, DC: National Institute of Justice, Office of Justice Programs, US Department of Justice. Online at http://www.ncjrs.gov/criminal_justice2000/vol4_2000.html (accessed May 20, 2007).

Huggins, M. K. and Glebbeek, M. L. (2003). Women studying violent male institutions: cross-gendered dynamics in police research on secrecy and danger. *Theoretical Criminology*, 7(3): 363–87.

Jacobs, R. (1996). Partnership research: pulling rabbits from hats. *Human Resource Development Quarterly*, 7(2): 117–19.

Lafferty, S. A. and Filicko, T. (2000). A profile of creating partnerships: drawing lessons from scholar-practitioner collaborations. A paper presented at the 26th Annual Social Theory, Politics, and the Arts Conference, October 13–15, 2000. Washington, DC. Online at http://www.cpanda.org/data/a00043/Profile.pdf (accessed December 4, 2010).

Letona, M. (1999). *The government nonprofit relationship: towards a partnership model*. Washington, DC: Nonprofit Sector Research Fund.

Lum, C., Kennedy, L. W., and Sherley, A. (2006). *The effectiveness of counter-terrorism strategies: a Campbell Systematic Review*. The Campbell Collaboration. Online at http://www.rutgerscps.org/publications/Lum_Terrorism_Review.pdf (accessed November 24, 2010).

Martinson, R. (1974). What works? Questions and answers about prison reform. *Public Interest*, 35: 22–54.

Mills, M., van de Bunt, G. G., and de Bruijn, J. (2006). Comparative research: persistent problems and promising solutions. *International Sociology*, 21(5): 619–31.

Miller, J. (1989). The debate on rehabilitating criminals: is it true that nothing works? *The Washington Post*, NY. Online at http://www.prisonpolicy.org/scans/rehab.html (accessed September 6, 2010).

O'Brien, M. and Bera, W. H. (1986). Adolescent sexual offenders: a descriptive typology. *Preventing sexual abuse: a newsletter of the National Family Life Education Network*, 1: 2–4.

Ragin, C. 1994. *Constructing social research: the unity and diversity of method*. Thousand Oaks, CA: Northwestern University, Pine Forge.

Smith, C. J. (2009). Comparative methods: going beyond incorporating international research methods with traditional methods. *International Journal of Comparative and Applied Criminal Justice*, 33(2): 211–28.

Smith, C. J. and Picarelli, J. (2008). Terrorism: where are we today? *International Journal of Comparative and Applied Criminal Justice*, 32(1): 1–8; Official journal of the Division of International Criminology of the American Society of Criminology.

Part II
Special topics

11

Introduction to special topics in international criminology

Sheldon X. Zhang

The task of deciding what to include in this section was a difficult one. There are simply too many interesting and pertinent topics to cover. Additionally we were under a strict word limit imposed by the publisher. We could follow the convention by including topics commonly covered in other international or comparative criminology texts. However, changes in global politics and commerce in the past two decades have added much complexity to criminal activities of an international and transnational nature. Criminal organizations and enterprising agents are marching along with legitimate commerce to discover and exploit new territories of business opportunities. One major advantage of transnational crimes, over legitimate businesses, is that the participants unite easily under a single motivation and can reach agreements with few restrictions. There are no bureaucracies to overcome and no international conventions to follow.

In Part II, we instead let our contributors decide what they felt most comfortable and valuable to present in their pieces. Our instruction was simple – each piece must reflect the latest state of knowledge on the selected topics and contain the most current materials for our targeted audiences. We are confident that the goal has been accomplished. Readers will find that the chapters included are about the most pressing subject matters in international criminology. The range and quality of the chapters also reflect well the multifaceted research portfolios among the contributing authors, a group of senior and promising young scholars from around the world.

In contrast to the other two parts in this volume, authors here were allowed the maximum leeway in framing their research questions and presenting their analyses. Still, these chapters continue the main theme from Part I, but with case studies that add details and substance to the frameworks established in the previous section. They can serve as supplemental materials to criminology instructors who are looking for specific transnational criminal activities, or who are exploring the implications of crime control policies in an international context. Topics covered in Part II are not only transnational in nature but also international in their implications. At the end of each chapter the authors have provided five prompting questions for students who want to develop thesis topics or engage in future research endeavors. Many of these questions are also suitable for young scholars who are still exploring and framing their own research interests.

For those who just want to get the essentials of these chapters in just a few minutes, here are a few quick glimpses of what one might expect to find. The chapters in this part largely fall into two groups – (1) international collaborations and efforts in studying and controlling crimes of transnational and international nature; and (2) particular transnational criminal activities confronting many nations. These chapters are arranged in a somewhat mixed manner to avoid monotony. Although a gross injustice to their rich analyses and empirical data, we nonetheless hope to entice the reader to go deeper into the themes of these chapters.

The international criminal system

Joutsen (Chapter 12) begins with a discussion of the challenges in achieving consensus among member states of the United Nations on crimes that are condemned by all nations, describing the complex process of negotiating and securing consensus on crime control conventions. Redo, in Chapter 13, presents the sometimes opaque structure of the United Nations in its striving for collective efforts in dealing with crime and social control across countries. Criminology here is always international because member states initiate and fund the UN research agendas. Harry M. Rhea (Chapter 14), on the other hand, illustrates how the international court can complement national courts to tackle transnational and international crimes. Although still limited in its jurisdiction, the idea of an international justice system is slowly but steadily gaining acceptance in the global community. This is important because some transnational or even domestic crimes are so heinous that the perpetrators must be prosecuted on behalf of the entire mankind.

Particular transnational criminal activities

Some of the transnational criminal activities have long been covered by criminologists, such as the trafficking of drugs and human beings. Others are relatively new to the research community, such as cybercrime and identity theft. In Chapter 15, Russell Smith argues that technological advances have largely erased territorial barriers for criminal activities. The financial industry and transnational commerce have created tremendous opportunities for identity thieves, because goods and services are ultimately consumed by individuals. The nation-state-based justice system is no longer adequate to deal with transnational criminal activities. By the same token, criminologists must look beyond their own countries to study crime and criminal behavior. Similarly, Broadhurst and Choo (Chapter 16) explore the many aspects of the virtual world where crimes are easily committed and law enforcement is still lagging due to the nation-state legal system. Cyber space is full of vulnerabilities such as malware and hacker-installed backdoors. Compromised computers (i.e. zombies) are then used as tools to launch additional attacks or to acquire confidential information from unsuspecting users. The scientific community has been slow to gauge the scope and depth of the cybercrime environment.

The majority of the chapters, however, are about the brick-and-mortar activities involving organized criminals. Dina Siegel in Chapter 20 describes how conflict (or blood) diamonds are systematically smuggled and comingled with legitimate supplies and the world diamond merchants' struggle with an imperfect certification process, which has thus far failed to prevent the entry of conflict diamonds and cut off the financial sources to much of the armed conflicts in Africa. In Chapter 21, Arsovska describes a future where organized crime will command much attention from countries around the world. The topic of organized crime is difficult to define and to measure. Researchers are often forced to rely on police reports or media accounts, not to mention encountering barriers due to different legal jurisdictions, transnational context, and language/cultural differences. Still, researchers must serve as critical voices in this understudied field and strive to influence policy makers with their research. Effective anti-crime policies must rely on collaborative efforts that are truly interdisciplinary.

In Chapter 22, Chu counters that despite widespread speculations Hong Kong Triads have not come to dominate international criminal projects. Enterprising agents in the Chinese communities around the world can and often team up to organize criminal transactions as long as they have the required resources. Triads have no competitive advantages in overseas ventures, despite the high earning potentials. Triads have neither the business know-how nor the necessary connections. Unal's timely piece on terrorism (Chapter 26) provides a nuanced analysis of political violence, which has captured the world's attention and triggered collective government movements from around the world since 9/11 events in the U.S. and the bombings of the Madrid train station in 2004 and the London transit system in 2005. From definitional challenges to differences in government response strategies, Unal strives to provide a balanced perspective that is practical as well as philosophical.

These are just a few examples of the gems in Part II. There are others that warrant a careful read as opposed to just a few lines here. For instance, Proulx in Chapter 19 illustrates the coexistence of both licit and illicit markets for antiquities and how the looting of archeological sites not only disrupts normal antiquities trade, but also funds terrorist activities. Soudijn and Vijlbrief in Chapter 24 illustrate how ecstasy is produced in the Netherlands and the trafficking groups are able to exploit legal and logistical loopholes to manufacture and transport the illicit product.

In sum, these chapters reflect the latest knowledge on the selected topics, and are written to convey broad perspectives and a deep appreciation of the complexity of the criminal activities across borders and nationalities. We hope these articles will spark interests among students and junior researchers alike and inspire them to develop their own research topics.

12

The impact of United Nations crime conventions on international cooperation

Matti Joutsen

Introduction: crime and criminal justice as an international concern

Three United Nations (UN) conventions have been prepared on criminal justice issues: the 1988 Convention against Illicit Traffic in Narcotic Drugs and Psychotropic Substances, the 2000 Convention against Transnational Organized Crime (with its three protocols), and the 2003 Convention against Corruption. Each has contributed to a more uniform and streamlined regime of international cooperation in criminal matters. This chapter places the three conventions within the context of the evolution of international cooperation.

Criminal justice has traditionally been regarded as a sovereign matter. Each country is used to deciding on its own what it regards as criminal, and on how it should respond to criminal acts. After all, for many centuries few people traveled beyond even the next village, and few crimes affected anyone but those who were directly involved. Those responsible for public order and the meting out of justice had little reason to be concerned with what happened elsewhere. As a result, criminal justice was almost entirely territorial, in the sense that it was concerned only with acts or omissions committed in the country in question.

During the 1700s and early 1800s, developments in, for example, commerce and transportation increased the amount of such cross-border activity as piracy, smuggling, cross-border forays by bandits, and the slave trade. Some States took unilateral action in order to arrest and bring the offenders to justice even if they were to be found abroad. At times this took the form of blatant incursions into foreign territory, with or without the support of law enforcement colleagues on the other side of the border. Examples were seizures of suspected pirate or slave-trade ships on the open seas or even when they sailed in the territorial waters of a foreign state.

However, unilateral action was an unsatisfactory response to a growing problem. Unilateral action creates unnecessary tensions between nations. Furthermore, under international law, States may not intervene in the domestic affairs of other States. For this reason, some States began to resort to informal measures such as the work of private detectives, and to informal contacts between police officers on both sides of a border.

The limitations of the simple territorial approach to law enforcement and adjudication began to become more and more apparent during the 1800s, when a growing number of offenders could and would take deliberate advantage of national borders in order to avoid apprehension. Transnational crime became a practical problem.[1] Countries with close contacts with one another began to consider bilateral agreements and other arrangements for cooperation in criminal justice.

The earliest arrangements to emerge were informal, bilateral arrangements on the sharing of information between law enforcement forces (at first on an ad hoc, i.e. case-by-case, basis, and later on also on a regular basis) and other forms of law enforcement cooperation. The first formal arrangements between law enforcement agencies emerged during the early 1900s, usually between neighbouring countries with considerable cross-border traffic, such as Belgium and France.

Attempts at judicial cooperation emerged more slowly. Such cooperation can be based on bilateral and multilateral agreements and arrangements or directly on national law. Bilateral agreements, which were the first to emerge, tend to vary considerably depending on the specific needs and legal systems of the States in question.[2] The end result is a patchwork quilt design, with an individual State having a wide variety of agreements with other States. This can easily be very frustrating to the individual practitioners, who must use different forms and different procedures, depending on the State with which they are dealing.[3]

Multilateral agreements (conventions) have several signatories. Since all of the States involved have to agree on the text of the multilateral agreement, their negotiation can become quite complex and time-consuming. Because of the number of States involved, the agreements often also set up a Secretariat and various measures designed to promote implementation, which in turn requires more negotiation and more resources. Despite these difficulties, the present trend seems to be towards greater use of multilateral agreements, either regional (such as within the framework of the Organization of American States, or the Council of Europe) or global (where the pre-eminent examples are the United Nations conventions). One reason for this trend is the realization that crime problems are becoming more and more global; States must find ways of cooperating even with States that have different legal systems. It is easier to negotiate (and later on, update) one multilateral agreement, than dozens of bilateral agreements. A second reason is the search for improved coverage: extending the geographical scope of a multilateral agreement makes it more difficult for an offender to evade justice by operating in, or escaping to, a State that is not a party to such an agreement.

The earliest forms of organized judicial cooperation between different countries were based on bilateral agreements on extradition or the service of summons. In time, other forms of procedural cooperation were incorporated into agreements; examples of such forms are the hearing of witnesses, other collection of evidence (such as the provision of official records), the transfer of proceedings, cooperation in the enforcement of judgments, and the transfer of convicted persons.

In respect of extradition, the first multilateral instrument did not emerge until 1933. This was the Convention on Extradition prepared within the framework of the Organization of American States.[4] More than 20 years later, two influential multilateral conventions emerged with the framework of the newly established Council of Europe: the European Convention on Extradition of 1957, and the European Convention on Mutual Assistance in Criminal Matters of 1959.[5] Subsequently, multilateral conventions on extradition and/or mutual legal assistance have been prepared within the framework of other international organizations and structures, such as the Arab League, the Union Africaine et Malagache, the Economic Community of West African States, the Commonwealth of States, the Benelux countries, the Nordic countries, the European Union, and the Southern African countries.

A second line of development was attempts to get countries to agree on how to define certain offenses. The first serious and ultimately successful effort along these lines was in respect of slavery. A combination of different factors led to the emergence of a strong anti-slavery movement in England during the 1800s, and to the ultimate success of the English authorities in getting a significant number of other countries to join in these efforts. The first formal multilateral agreement on taking action against slavery was the so-called Brussels Conference Act of 1890. It was followed in 1926 by the Geneva Slavery Convention (Andreas and Nadelmann, 2006, pp. 27–33).

Another form of crime which attracted early attention was drug trafficking, where the first multilateral conventions were the International Opium Conventions of 1912 and 1925, and the Convention for Limiting the Manufacture and Regulating the Distribution of Narcotic Drugs in 1931.[6]

Following the Second World War, and especially since the 1950s, transnational criminal justice evolved considerably more rapidly. The network of bilateral agreements expanded and intensified, with both the United States and the USSR leading the way in negotiating such agreements with dozens of countries around the world.

Another impetus to transnational criminal justice was given by the integration of criminal justice elements into the foreign policy of some countries, in particular the United States. Over 100 years after England promoted anti-slavery around the world as part of its foreign policy, the United States injected a clear foreign policy aspect into its "war on drugs" which began in the 1960s. The rash of skyjackings soon after (during the 1970s) by its very nature required a transnational response (see Andreas and Nadelmann, 2006, pp. 106–7).

The changing role of the UN in crime prevention and criminal justice

The role of the UN should be seen against the backdrop of this rapid evolution of transnational criminal justice. One of the main purposes of the UN, as grandly expressed by article 55 of the UN Charter, is "to create the conditions for stability and well-being which are necessary for peaceful and friendly international relations, based on mutual respect, equality and self-determination." The UN is also specifically charged with the promotion of universal respect for, and observance of, human rights and fundamental freedoms.

Since crime in general is a major concern of all countries, it should come as no surprise that crime-related issues have found their way onto the UN agenda. Within the UN system, the primary responsibility for crime prevention and criminal justice lies with the Economic and Social Council. Within the UN Secretariat, in turn, these issues are dealt with by the UN Office on Drug and Crime, although related issues are also dealt with by, for example, the Office of the United Nations High Commissioner for Human Rights. Many politically sensitive crime issues, such as war crimes, genocide, and terrorism, are now and then debated directly in the General Assembly of the UN. In addition, the General Assembly at times sets up special bodies to deal with specific issues, such as the drafting of new international agreements.

The work of the UN on crime prevention and criminal justice takes a number of different forms. For the first few years of UN activity in this field, the focus was on the collection and exchange of information, research, and the development of international standards and norms. This focus was largely a reflection of the constituency of the UN, and the decision-making structure in the UN program on crime prevention and criminal justice. The first Member States of the UN were primarily Western industrialized countries, and the persons who took part in the discussions were often practitioners, interested in trading ideas with their colleagues from other countries sharing the same immediate concerns (see Clark, 1994 for a description of the evolution of the UN program).

As a result of their work, a large number of UN standards and norms have been produced, beginning with the Standard Minimum Rules for the Treatment of Prisoners (1956). These standards and norms cover a broad range of criminal policy issues, from the independence of the judiciary, a code of conduct for law enforcement officials, the role of lawyers and the role of prosecutors, to the administration of juvenile justice, the treatment of victims of crime, and capital punishment.

Another aspect of this early UN focus was primarily on crime and criminal justice as a domestic concern: juvenile delinquency, violent crime, policing, prison administration and non-custodial sanctions, and so on. This was in keeping with the general attitude of countries, described earlier in this chapter, according to which crime was primarily regarded as a local or at most national issue.

The emergence of UN crime conventions

Within the UN in general, considerable attention has been devoted to the negotiation and implementation of international agreements, since this type of "hard law" provides a stable base for international cooperation. The topics have covered a wide range, from the international sale of goods, to the law of the seas, to fundamental human rights.

Within the UN crime prevention and criminal justice program, however – and in line with what has been mentioned before – there was for a long time little work related to international treaties. The one significant exception to this concerned drugs.[7]

The 1988 Drug Convention. The reason for this one exception was that the UN was able to build on earlier international work. The agreements mentioned above that had been negotiated at the beginning of the century were essentially replaced by the 1961 Single Convention on Narcotic Drugs. This Convention established new mechanisms and obligations. It assigned certain functions to new UN bodies, the Commission on Narcotic Drugs and the International Narcotics Control Board. The Convention also required States to provide annual estimates of drugs used for various purposes, to abide by restrictions on manufacture, production and import, to criminalize the possession, supply and transport of drugs, and make them extraditable offenses.

The 1961 Single Convention was amended by a Protocol in 1972. However, this protocol did not change the substantive scope of the Convention, which continued to encompass cannabis, coca and opium, and drugs with similar effects. Developments during the 1950s and especially during the 1960s focused attention on a new form of drugs, psychotropics: perhaps first and foremost psychedelics (such as LSD), but also amphetamines and barbiturates.

Moreover, calling upon States that were parties to these agreements to criminalize drugs proved to be insufficient, without parallel agreements on various forms of procedural cooperation. When work began on a convention that would expand the substantive scope of the 1961 Single Convention to include also psychotropics, the negotiations were for the first time extended to include procedural provisions (for example on police cooperation, and on extradition and mutual assistance). The result was the 1988 United Nations Convention against Illicit Traffic in Narcotic Drugs and Psychotropic Substances, which today remains the basic international agreement on drugs.

The 2000 UNTOC Convention. The 1988 Convention, the first global convention to combine substantive and procedural provisions, almost immediately became the template for further negotiation of conventions. Italy, with its long experience with organized crime, began international lobbying for a corresponding UN convention that would deal with an entirely new and far broader field, transnational organized crime. Italy hosted the World Ministerial Conference on Organized Transnational Crime in 1994, only a few years after the 1988 Convention had entered into force. From that point, matters proceeded very quickly. Poland formally introduced a draft for the convention at the autumn 1996 session of the General Assembly.[8] Only four years later, amid much pomp and ceremony, the United Nations Convention on Transnational Organized Crime (UNTOC), with separate protocols on trafficking in persons, the smuggling of migrants, and trafficking in firearms, was formally opened for signature.

Those who have been involved in the negotiation of multilateral conventions know that the process tends to be a long and arduous one. Getting countries interested in an idea takes time, consensus has to be reached on the general outline of the convention and on the basic concepts, legal differences have to be worked out, political difficulties may bog down the discussion for years, and even the practical issues take time.

For the UNTOC process to go from start to finish in six years is highly unusual. Counting the various informal sessions held during the negotiations, a total of some 80 working days were devoted to the Convention (an average of only two days per article). This speed cannot be explained by the simplicity of the task, the clarity of the concepts, or the lack of any political disagreements. On the contrary, there were a large number of problems to be overcome, ranging from the vagueness of the key concept of "transnational organized crime," to the fact that three protocols had to be negotiated at the same time, and to the almost endless political disagreements that surfaced along the way.

The speed can also not be explained by any general consensus that a convention was even needed. Before Poland introduced its draft, there had in fact been considerable resistance to the preparation of a convention, particularly among Western European and North American countries. This hesitancy had been due to a variety of reasons. Those who were sceptical of the need for a new convention argued that the concept of organized transnational crime is too vague, that it appears in too many forms to be dealt with except on a high level of generality, and that existing instruments on extradition and mutual assistance (if promoted and properly implemented) could already provide an adequate basis for international cooperation. The focus, in their view, should be on the development and strengthening of practical measures. The sceptics also noted that negotiating a convention is an expensive process, for both the countries involved and for the UN. The resources needed for this would inevitably be taken away from other projects, perhaps just as deserving.

Once Poland introduced its proposal, however, the political pressure to negotiate the convention became overwhelming. Organized crime is something that constantly makes the headlines, and people know where they stand on this issue: they are against it. Individual criminal justice practitioners and victims are doubtless earnest in their conviction that not enough is being done on the local, national or international level to prevent and control organized crime. Consequently, the idea that the UN should develop an international convention on this subject soon took on a life of its own, and UNTOC with its three protocols emerged.

The 2003 UNCAC Convention. The dust had barely settled on the negotiating tables where the UNTOC Convention had been hammered out, when work began on a UN convention on corruption. The genesis of the United Nations Convention against Corruption (UNCAC) differs from that of UNTOC. UNTOC did not have any direct forbears, any multilateral conventions on organized crime that would have served as a model. UNCAC, in turn, had several predecessors:

- The 1996 Inter-American Convention against Corruption of the Organization of American States;
- The 1997 Convention on Combating Bribery of Foreign Public Officials in International Business Transactions of the Organization for Economic Cooperation and Development (OECD);
- The 1998 Convention on the Fight against Corruption Involving Officials of the European Communities or Officials of Member States of the European Union;
- The 1999 Criminal Law Convention on Corruption and the 1999 Civil Law Convention on Corruption of the Council of Europe;

- The 2001 Southern African Development Community Protocol against Corruption; and
- The 2003 African Union Convention on Preventing and Combating Corruption.

All of these conventions – UNCAC included – had emerged within a relatively short period of time, the seven years from 1996 to 2003. We can surmise that a tipping point was reached sometime during the 1990s, when States realized that corruption cannot be dealt with solely on a national basis. International conventions were seen to be the necessary next step in dealing with the problem. It is likely that when work began in one forum on the drafting of a convention (the Inter-American Convention and the OECD Convention),[9] this influenced the decision to begin work also elsewhere (the European Union, the Council of Europe, Southern Africa and Africa – as well as within the framework of the UN).

The impact of the UN conventions on criminal justice

The three UN crime conventions have influenced international cooperation in at least three respects:

- As global conventions, they have considerably expanded the geographical scope of cooperation.
- They provide common definitions of certain key offenses, and require (or, in some cases, at least encourage) State parties to criminalize these acts.
- They have standardized and contributed to the development of procedural forms of cooperation.

Global scope. The UN Conventions are specifically global instruments, open to countries around the world. Most earlier agreements were bilateral or at most regional. The UN Conventions provide a relatively clear basis for cooperation between countries at opposite ends of the earth, regardless of their legal system or the underlying principles of the operation of their criminal justice system. As of January 1, 2010, the 1988 Convention has a grand total of 184 parties, UNTOC has 153 parties (and its three protocols have somewhat fewer), and UNCAC has 143 parties. All three thus have considerable geographical scope.

Criminalization requirements. The major significance of the 1988 Convention was the integration of procedural provisions on international cooperation with substantive provisions on a specific form of crime, drug offenses. The 1988 Convention calls for criminalization of a range of criminal offenses, including the organization, management, or financing of drug offenses (article 3). According to article 6, the offenses criminalized by the 1988 Convention are by definition extraditable offenses, and the Convention itself can be regarded as providing the necessary legal basis for extradition and mutual assistance. Article 5 contains provisions on confiscation, article 7 on mutual assistance, article 8 on the transfer of proceedings, and article 11 on controlled delivery. One notable aspect of the 1988 Convention is that a State party may not refuse to render mutual legal assistance on the grounds of bank secrecy. Traditionally, this had been a commonly used reason for refusing assistance.

The 1988 Convention also introduced, for the first time for most of the States which became parties to it, the requirement to criminalize money laundering. One of the main motivations for the commission of crime is illegal profit (Bassiouni and Gualtieri, 1997; Gilmore, 1993; Bernasconi, 1995; Savona, 1997). Domestic criminal law has traditionally sought to ensure that offenders could not benefit from the proceeds of crime. In international cooperation, on the other hand, the focus has been on apprehending fugitives and bringing them to justice. Less attention had been paid, at least until recent years, to requests that other States take measures and provide assistance in relation to confiscation of the proceeds of crime.

UNTOC requires that State parties criminalize four types of conduct. These are, respectively, participation in an organized criminal group (article 5), money laundering (article 6), corruption (article 8), and obstruction of justice (article 23). In particular, the first two of these articles marked a considerable shift in thinking in many countries. The definition of participation in an organized criminal group proved difficult, since few countries had anything in their laws that would cover the concept. The definition ultimately represented a marriage of the common law concept of conspiracy with elements of the Italian and US concept of a racketeering influenced criminal organization. article 8, in turn, was essentially a widening of the definition of money laundering used in the 1988 Convention: while the 1988 Convention limited its scope to the laundering of the proceeds of drug crime, UNTOC referred more broadly to the proceeds of crime.

UNTAC contains a number of criminalizations. The provisions on money laundering and obstruction of justice (articles 23 and 25) are broadly similar to those to be found in UNTOC. Understandably, UNCAC goes into greater detail than UNTOC in requiring the criminalization of corruption offenses, such as bribery, and misappropriation or other diversion of property by a public official (articles 15, 16(1), and 17). In addition, UNCAC contains definitions of some acts that State parties are encouraged to criminalize, although there is no obligation to do so. This non-mandatory approach is the result of the fact that, during the negotiations, many States were dissatisfied with what they saw as the vagueness of such definitions of offenses as trading in influence (article 18), abuse of functions (article 19), and illicit enrichment (article 20). In addition, some State parties opposed making bribery in the private sector (article 21) a mandatory offense.

To illustrate the impact of the three conventions on procedural cooperation, it may be helpful to attempt to describe what cooperation was typically like before the conventions entered into force (referred to here as "traditional cooperation") and compare this with the "new, improved" cooperation to which the three conventions contributed. These two regimes are summarized in Table 12.1.

Table 12.1 *Two regimes of cooperation*

The traditional cooperation regime	*The "new, improved" cooperation regime*
Each country uses its own "traditional" investigative means	Introduction of various modern investigative means
Each country carries out its own criminal investigation	The possibility of joint investigations
Limited scope of offenses; lists of offenses	Broad scope of offenses; no offense lists
Limited scope of mutual assistance available	Many possible forms of mutual assistance available
No provisions on confiscation of the proceeds of crime	Such provisions are included, as are provisions on mutual assistance related to confiscation
Use of diplomatic channels in requesting and giving assistance	Use of a Central Authority, and the possibility of direct contacts between lower level authorities
Bureaucratic	"Good practice" standards followed; e.g. the possibility of consultation before possible refusal
Requested State applies solely its own laws in granting assistance	Procedures requested by the requesting State can be applied if these are not contrary to the laws of the requested State
Extradition of nationals not possible	Nationals can be extradited, although conditions may be imposed

Introduction of new investigative means. Because of the diversity of legal systems, investigative techniques that have proven useful in one country may not be allowed in another. This applies, for example, to such techniques as electronic surveillance, controlled delivery, undercover operations, the promising of immunity from prosecution or a reduced sentence in return for cooperation in investigations, and the use of anonymous witnesses. If an investigative technique is legal in one country (A) but not legal in another (B), this may result in at least two types of problems. The first is that A will be frustrated by the inability of the law enforcement authorities of B to use what A regards as an effective tool. The second is that the judicial authorities of B may not allow the use of any evidence that has been gathered through the use of what, for B, are illegal techniques, even if the evidence has been obtained in a jurisdiction where the evidence was acquired legally.

In response to this problem, the UN instruments encourage State parties to allow the use of certain special investigative techniques. The 1988 Convention introduced controlled delivery (article 11). Article 20 of UNTOC and Article 50 of UNCAC refer not only to controlled delivery, but also to electronic and other forms of surveillance and undercover operations. These techniques are especially useful in dealing with sophisticated organized criminal groups because of the dangers and difficulties inherent in gaining access to their operations and gathering information and evidence for use in domestic prosecutions or in other State parties in the context of mutual legal assistance schemes.[10]

Possibility of joint investigations. A number of provisions in the UN instruments focus on overcoming problems that result when each country carries out their own criminal investigations. Among the innovations are the possibility of the establishment of joint investigation teams,[11] cooperation in the protection of witnesses,[12] the establishment of formal channels for the exchange of operational and general information between police agencies,[13] and the possibility of appointing liaison officers.[14]

Broad scope of offenses. The earliest treaties were based on lists of offenses. If an offense was not included in the list, a country would not provide mutual legal assistance or grant. The reason for this was that countries traditionally wanted to specify in respect of what offenses they would consider providing assistance. This led to several difficulties, including the technical ones that arise due to differences in definitions of even the most basic offenses, such as assault or robbery. The 1988 Convention stipulated that cooperation should be provided in respect of all the offenses defined in it. UNTOC went further, and essentially provided a generic definition of "transnational organized crime," in respect of which cooperation could and should be provided.

Broader range of forms of assistance. As noted above, the earliest agreements on mutual legal assistance treaties concerned merely the service of summons. Over time, the range of measures has gradually widened. For example, the 1988 Convention (article 8), UNTOC (article 21) and UNCAC (article 47) include specific provisions on the transfer of criminal proceedings, whereby if a person is suspected of having committed an offense under the law of one State party, that country may request another country to take action on its behalf in accordance with the Convention, and the latter would prosecute the alleged offender under its own law (Gardocki, 1992, p. 318).

It has only been relatively recently that international agreements began to contain provisions on assistance in identifying, tracing and freezing, or seizing proceeds of crime for the purpose of eventual confiscation (which can be regarded as a special form of mutual legal assistance). The need to come to grips with the profit motive behind the rapid growth of drug crime led the drafters of the 1988 Convention to require that State parties criminalize money laundering. The 1988 Convention also requires State parties to create domestic mechanisms for the tracing, restraint, and confiscation of the proceeds of drug-related crime. International cooperation was recognized in that State parties are also required to be able to respond to requests presented by other States for the tracing, restraint, and confiscation of the proceeds of drug offenses. The 1988 Convention was the primary point of reference in the formulation of the respective provisions in UNTOC (articles 12 and 13) and UNCAC (chapter V).[15]

UNTOC and UNCAC allow several forms of assistance that were not envisaged under earlier international instruments. One example is the result of developments in telecommunications: the use of video conferences, for example for the hearing of witnesses in another State (article 18(18) UNTOC and article. 32(2) UNCAC). A second example is what is known as the "spontaneous transmission of information" (article 18(4) and (5) UNTOC and article 46(4) UNCAC) according to which an authority in one State can send information to the competent authorities of another State even if there has not been a request to do so.

Use of a central authority. Traditional mutual legal assistance treaties required that requests be sent through diplomatic channels. For example, if the prosecutor in State A wants to request evidence from his or her colleague in State B, the request would first go to the competent national court in State A for authentication. It would then be sent to the State Department (or equivalent) in the capital city. The State Department would send it to the local embassy of State B. The embassy would forward it to their own State Department, from where it would in time be transmitted to the competent court, and finally to the competent prosecutor. Assuming that the request has been fulfilled, the resulting documentation would then be transmitted back through the same chain.[16]

The 1988 Convention introduced a significant innovation, the concept of a "Central Authority" (article 7(8)), a concept that was then incorporated into UNTOC (article 18(13) and UNCAC (article 46(13)).[17] Although each State party may continue to insist on diplomatic channels, the 1988 Convention requires that they identify an authority – in practice, often the Ministry of Justice, although also for example Supreme Courts have been designated as such – to specialize in the transmission of international requests, and to provide guidance for practitioners. This has tended to shorten the chain of authorities involved, and accordingly has speeded up the process of obtaining assistance.[18]

Adoption of "good practice" standards. It is commonly assumed by the public that mutual legal assistance is a simple matter of transmitting requests, which would then be speedily executed. Regrettably, getting a request fulfilled may take months or even years, and in fact many requests remain completely unanswered. As a result, suspects must often be freed due to absence of evidence. There may be political reasons for this slowness or lack of reply, but more commonly the reason is more prosaic: incomplete forms, ambiguous requests, a lack of competent staff, language difficulties, overly complex procedures, and so on. Following the model of international business correspondence, "good practice" in mutual legal assistance is evolving towards an assumption that the request is executed as soon as possible. This trend towards good practice was not evident in the 1988 Convention, which did not explicitly require the requested State to be prompt in its reply. UNTOC, however, contains two separate provisions on promptness. According to article 18(13) of the UNTOC Convention, the central authority should ensure speedy and prompt execution or, if it transmits the request for example to the competent court, encourage this court to execute the request speedily and properly. Article 18(24) provides that the request is to be executed "as soon as possible" and that the requested State is to take "as full account as possible of any deadlines suggested by the requesting State Party and for which reasons are given."[19]

Difficulties may also arise due to different legal standards. An example of this is the concept of "prima facie evidence of guilt" which some countries require as a condition for extradition. Since different countries apply differing rules of evidence, it may be difficult for a practitioner in one country to know what evidence should be provided. Both UNTOC (article 16(8)) and UNCAC (article 44(9)) call upon State parties to simplify their evidentiary requirements in this respect.[20]

Possibility to apply the law and procedures of the requesting State. Since the procedural laws of States differ considerably, the requesting State may require special procedures (such as notarized affidavits) that are not recognized under the law of the requested State. Traditionally, the almost immutable principle has been that the requested State should follow its own procedural law. This principle has led to difficulties, in particular when the requesting and the requested State represent different legal traditions. For example, the evidence transmitted from the requested State may be in the form prescribed by the laws of this State, but such evidence may be unacceptable under the procedural law of the requesting State.

The modern trend is to allow more flexibility in respect of procedures. According to article 7(12) of the 1988 Convention, a request shall be executed in accordance with the domestic law of the requested State. However, the article goes on to say that, to the extent not contrary to the domestic law of the requested State and where possible, the request shall be executed in accordance with the procedures specified in the request. Thus, although the 1988 Convention does not go so far as to require that the requested State comply with the procedural form required by the requesting State, it does clearly exhort the requested State to do so. This same provision was taken verbatim into article 18(17) of UNTOC and article 46(17) of UNCAC.

Extradition of nationals. In traditional extradition law, States have refused to extradite their own nationals and will, at most, undertake to bring them to trial in their own courts. Today, more and more States allow their own nationals to be extradited. However, this is usually subjected to conditions, such as the condition that if the national is convicted, he or she should be returned to his or her own country to serve the sentence. UNTOC (article 16(11)) and UNCAC (article 44(12)) incorporate provisions that reflects this development, by allowing for the possibility of "temporary surrender" of the fugitive on the condition that this person will be returned to the requested State party for the purpose of serving any sentence imposed. In cases where the requested State refuses to extradite a fugitive on the grounds that the fugitive is its own national, the State is often seen to have an obligation to bring the person to trial. Where extradition is requested for the purpose of enforcing a sentence, the requested State may also enforce the sentence that has been imposed in accordance with the requirements of its domestic law.[21]

Conclusions

With the increase in international travel, the improvement in technology and communications, the greater likelihood that a crime can have an impact beyond national borders, as well as the increased profits that can be made from organized crime, the need to obtain assistance from other States in bringing offenders to justice, gathering necessary evidence, or confiscating the proceeds of crime has expanded rapidly. The basic modalities of international cooperation that can be used as a response – in particular extradition and mutual legal assistance in criminal matters – continue to evolve, often struggling to keep pace with developments in crime.

Increased efforts have been made over the last years to expand and deepen international cooperation as a response to transnational organized crime through the conclusion of multilateral instruments. The pace of development has clearly quickened during the 1990s and the beginning of the new millennium. The 1988 Convention, UNTOC, and UNCAC are clear signs that multilateral instruments are assuming increasing importance. All these multilateral instruments call upon State parties to seek to conclude bilateral and multilateral agreements or arrangements to enhance the effectiveness of extradition and mutual legal assistance mechanisms and promote the cooperation between law enforcement agencies. Consequently, States will presumably continue to expand their treaty network in the field of international cooperation by entering into bilateral agreements or arrangements with other countries with which they share particular concerns and interests.

The growing number of bilateral and multilateral instruments and, thus, the availability of multiple provisions on international cooperation is not a cure-all for overcoming problems and difficulties encountered in daily practice. These international instruments may provide a satisfactory or even an autonomous and self-contained legal basis for cooperation, given that the recent UN instruments lay down a quite detailed and well-articulated framework for such cooperation. However, their provisions should be applied in a way that avoids piecemeal solutions and takes into account the need to ensure the proper administration of justice. It is therefore important to adopt and follow a holistic and flexible approach that renders the different modalities of international cooperation complementary to each other for the purpose of promoting co-operation among States and avoiding loopholes of impunity. In that sense, prosecution on the basis of the principle "aut dedere aut judicare" where, for example, extradition is denied on the grounds of nationality could only be effective if mutual legal assistance or transfer of criminal proceedings mechanisms are, at the same time, available and used properly. Countries should therefore envisage adopting and implementing the appropriate legal framework that will facilitate and promote the use of the full array of available forms of cooperation.

The 1988 Convention, UNTOC, and UNCAC reflect in many ways the "state of the art" of international cooperation in criminal justice. In particular, they include many provisions that are new for practitioners in many countries, and may well improve the day-to-day practice of international cooperation.

Negotiation of the Conventions, however, is only the first stage. The Conventions must be ratified and the investigators, the prosecutors, and the judges must be given the tools they need to complete the job.

Future research questions

1. Identify the factors that motivated Italy, specifically, to lobby for an international convention on transnational organized crime. Are these factors universal for other countries to agree on the need for such a convention? More generically, are these factors present prior to the development of other conventions?
2. What factors during the 1980s led to the growth in interest in preventing and responding to money laundering? In addition to the conventions mentioned in this chapter, what types of international action developed? What needs to be developed to reduce money laundering?
3. Maritime piracy has a long history. The United Nations Convention on the Law of the Seas from 1982 updated the international definition of the crime of piracy. What factors have contributed to resurgence of maritime piracy, and why does the 1982 Convention appear to have had only limited impact on this? How should both the national and the international response be strengthened?
4. What measures are used by State parties to conventions to ensure that other State parties are implementing them in the proper manner? Would other measures be more effective?
5. Global conventions have been and are being negotiated on drugs, transnational organized crime, corruption, and terrorism. Are further global conventions needed, and if so, on what types of crimes?

Notes

1 The term "transnational crime" is coming into general usage to refer to an offense with a point of contact in two or more countries. For example, an offender may cross a border in order to commit a crime (as with drug trafficking, smuggling, or trafficking in persons) or to flee justice. Another example is where an offender commits an offense in one country that has an effect in another country (such as is often the case with cybercrime and money laundering).

The term has been developed primarily to maintain a distinction with international crimes, which are widely understood to be offenses that are so serious that most if not all countries agree on measures for their prevention and for bringing the offenders to justice. Prime examples are war crimes, genocide, and crimes against humanity.

2 As a general rule, the major powers (such as the United States and the Russian Federation) have preferred bilateral agreements over multilateral agreements. It may be noted that it is easier for a major power to secure its own interests when negotiating a bilateral agreement, as opposed to a multilateral agreement. Smaller States prefer multilateral conventions because this simplifies the negotiation and application of the provisions. The present tendency (also for the major powers) appears to be towards wider use of multilateral conventions.

3 Bassiouni estimates that if each Member State of the United Nations entered into a bilateral treaty with the other Member States, then there would be some 20,000 treaties among these States. The United States alone has such treaties with over 110 states. See Bassiouni, 2002, p. 46. See also Kavass and Sprudzs, 2001.

4 This has subsequently been replaced by the 1981 Inter-American Convention on Extradition.

5 There are several reasons why the first important multinational agreements appeared within the context of the Council of Europe. Among these were the close professional and political ties among the Council of Europe Member States. The constant expansion in the ease with which people could go from one Council of Europe Member State to another meant that there was also a constant increase in the number of criminal cases with transnational connections.

6 The 1925 Convention has subsequently been amended several times with protocols. Following the Second World War, this series was extended in 1953 by the Protocol Limiting and Regulating the Cultivation of the Poppy Plant, the Production of, International and Wholesale Trade in, and Use of Opium.

7 Beginning during the 1970s, a second significant exception is the conventions on terrorism. The first such UN convention was the 1973 Convention on the Prevention and Punishment of Crimes against Internationally Protected Persons, including Diplomatic Agents. However, their emergence (and the negotiating difficulties involved) was due to a very specific set of circumstances: the politicization of terrorism. For this reason, they are not considered in this chapter.

8 General Assembly resolution 51/120 of 12 December 1996.

9 Once again, the United States seems to have been a primary initiator in the evolution of international cooperation. During the early 1990s, some rather prominent corruption cases in Latin America drew the attention of the United States to the need for regional cooperation, as one way of mobilizing political pressure on individual countries.

10 See UNODC, 2004, p. 183, para. 384.

11 See article 9 para. 1 (c) of the 1988 Convention, article 19 of UNTOC and article 49 of UNCAC. Joint investigation teams can be set up when a criminal investigation requires close cooperation among two or more States. They consist of representatives of law enforcement agencies or other competent authorities of the States in question. The members of the team carry out their operations in accordance with the law of the host State.

12 See article 24 of UNTOC and articles 32 and 33 of UNCAC.

13 For example, article 27 of UNTOC encourages State parties to cooperate closely with one another by enhancing and, where necessary, establishing channels of communication between their competent authorities, agencies and services in order to facilitate the secure and rapid exchange of information concerning all aspects of the offenses covered by the Convention, strengthen the cooperation in conducting inquiries, provide items for analytical and investigative purposes, exchange information on offenders' modus operandi or exchange personnel, including the posting of liaison officers. See also article 9 of the 1988 Convention and article 48 of UNCAC.

14 Liaison officers provide a point of direct contact with the law enforcement and government authorities of the host State, develop professional relationships, and foster mutual trust and confidence between the

law enforcement agencies of the two States. Although liaison officers do not have any law enforcement powers in the host State, they can nonetheless use their contacts to gather information that may be of benefit in preventing and detecting cross-border offenses, and in identifying the offenders responsible and bringing them to justice.

15 Another strand in this development was the United Nations Convention for the Suppression of the Financing of Terrorism, which was negotiated in the aftermath of the terrorist attacks in the United States in September 2001. This Convention requires that State parties take measures for the identification, detection, freezing, and confiscation of funds used or allocated for the purpose of committing the terrorist acts that States are required to criminalize under the Convention (article 8). See, inter alia, IMF, 2003, p. 56.

16 Legal scholars in this field have already pointed out that one of the main disadvantages of letters rogatory is their inefficient, costly, and time-consuming transmission. See Bassiouni and Gualtieri, 1999, p. 682.

17 This concept was originally developed in civil law, and introduced in the 1965 Hague Convention on the Service Abroad of Judicial and Extrajudicial Documents in Civil or Commercial Matters.

18 Article 7(8) of the 1988 Convention, article 18(13) of UNTOC and article 46(13) of UNCAC also allow for the possibility that, in urgent cases and when the countries in question agree, the request can be made through the International Criminal Police Organization, if possible.

19 Other elements of "good practice" in mutual legal assistance have also worked their way into UNTOC and UNCAC, making the life of the practitioner easier than under, for example, the 1988 Convention. According to article 18(24) of UNTOC and article 46(24) of UNCAC, the requested state should respond to reasonable requests by the requesting state for information on progress of its handling of the request, and the requesting state should promptly inform the requested state when the assistance sought is no longer required.

20 See also the Report of the Informal Expert Working Group on Effective Extradition Casework Practice (Vienna, 12–16 July 2004), paras. 41–3 and 46.

21 Art 6(10) of the 1988 Convention, article 16(12) of UNTOC and article 44(13) of UNCAC.

References

Andreas, P. and Nadelmann, E. (2006). *Policing the globe: criminalization and crime control in international relations*. New York: Oxford University Press.

Bassiouni, C. (2002) *International extradition: United States law and practice*. 4th edn. New York: Oxford University Press.

Bassiouni, C. and Gualtieri, D.S. (1997) International and national responses to the globalization of money laundering. In E. U. Savona (Ed.) *Responding to money laundering: an international perspective*. Amsterdam: Harwood.

—— (1999) International and national responses to the globalization of money laundering. In C. Bassiouni (ed.), *International criminal law. Procedural and enforcement mechanisms*. 2nd edition. Dobb's Ferry, NY: Transnational Publications.

Bernasconi, P. (1995) *New judicial instruments against international business crimes*. La Città Del Sole, Italy: Instit. Italiano per gli Studi Filosofici.

Clark, R. (1994) *The United Nations Crime prevention and criminal justice program. Formulation of standards and efforts at their implementation*. Philadelphia: University of Pennsylvania Press.

Gardocki, L. (1992) Transfer of proceedings and transfer of prisoners as new forms of international co-operation. In A. Eser and O. Lagodny (Eds.), *Principles and procedures for a new transnational criminal law*. Freiburg im Breisgau: Max Planck Institute.

Gilmore, W.C. (1993). *Dirty money: the evolution of money laundering counter-measures*. Council of Europe.

International Monetary Fund (IMF). (2003). *Suppressing the financing of terrorism. A handbook for legislative drafting*. Legal Department. Online at http://www.imf.org/external/pubs/nft/2003/SFTH/ (accessed November 23, 2010).

Kavass, I. I. and Sprudzs, A. (2001) *Extradition laws and treaties*, 1 and 2. Buffalo, NY: W. S. Hein.

Savona, E. U. (Ed.) (1997). *Responding to money laundering: an international perspective*. Amsterdam: Harwood.

United Nations Office on Drugs and Crime (UNODC) (2004) Legislative guides for the implementation of the United Nations Convention against Transnational Organized Crime and the protocols thereto. New York: UNODC.

13

The United Nations and criminology[1]

Sławomir Marek Redo

Introduction

The United Nations (UN) plays an active role in countering drugs and crime in the world. The history started 165 years ago with international crime control (International Congress of Penitentiary Sciences, Frankfurt am Mein, 1846), and 100 years ago with intergovernmental drug control (the Opium Commission, Shanghai 1909; the International Opium Convention, 1912). Since 2003, drug and crime-fighting functions within the UN have been consolidated into the current United Nations Office on Drugs and Crime (UNODC), which is located in Vienna, Austria.

United Nations and academic criminology

Criminological research at the UN is largely shaped by its 192 Member States. Unlike in the self-governing academe where research is mostly driven by conceptual, theoretical, and methodological considerations (Bassiouni, 2003, p. 5), the UN "governance" dictates its criminological work.

Because of the UN governance and its membership, criminological research by nature is always global. First of all, crime research is driven by Member States' funding, through regular and/or extra-budgetary contributions. Second, research agendas are also driven by non-governmental organizations (NGOs) and private entities although the funding is, by comparison, limited from these sources. Through these two funding mechanisms, criminological research at the UN comprises the:

> collective efforts to identify, understand, or address worldwide problems that go beyond the capacity of individual states to solve. Global governance reflects the capacity of the international system at any moment to provide government-like services in the absence of a world government – the capacity, in short, for collective problem-solving to bring more orderly and reliable responses to international social and political problems than would occur naturally . . . Thus global governance consists of the complex of formal and informal institutions, mechanisms, relationships, and [legislative and other] processes, between and among states, markets, citizens, and organizations through which collective international interests

are *occasionally* articulated, collective international rights and obligations are *occasionally* established, collective international differences are *occasionally* mediated, and collective international problems are occasionally solved."

(Weiss, 2008, p. 219–22)

Early history of UN criminology

The origin of the UN drugs and crime program came from the framework of its antidrugs and anticrime work.[2] In both cases, it is a continuation of the work started by the League of Nations. Originally, the program focused particularly on narcotic drugs, in line with the Treaty of Versailles (1919). In 1920 the Opium Advisory Committee was established to oversee the implementation of the Opium Convention, the forerunner of the UN Commission on Narcotic Drugs (1946–), a 53-Member State functional commission of the Economic and Social Council (ECOSOC), a 54-Member State body. Separately, in 1929–39, the League of Nations started developing the recommendations for a minimum prison code, an inquiry on prison population, and the publication of a set of rules for the treatment of witnesses and persons accused, but had no special intergovernmental crime commission.

Internationalization of UN drugs and crime mandate

The establishment of the antidrug program increased multilateralism in their efforts to control opium cultivation, production, use, and abuse. The anticrime program focused on the social objectives of the UN Charter, spelled out its faith in fundamental human rights, in the dignity and worth of the human person, in social progress and better standards of living, and in the promotion of equality without distinction as to race, sex, language, or religion.

From its very beginning, the UN antidrug program emphasized treaty implementation, while the UN anticrime program started by assisting in domestic criminal justice reform through legal and other advice.[3] The anticrime program initiated a national survey for planning its effort in combating the trafficking in persons and suppressing the prostitution of others, and in promoting criminological research on juvenile justice and delinquency, comparative work on domestic criminal statistics, and probation (IRCP, 1952). Later, it advocated for the humane treatment of offenders, international expert networking, and the legal regulations treating crime and punishment as an internal matter of Member States (1955–2009).

It was not until 1992 that the above founding crime mandate found its home in the intergovernmental Commission on Crime Prevention and Criminal Justice, a 40-Member State functional commission of the Economic and Social Council (ECOSOC). From that time forward, the mandate has developed and combined various social and international elements of crime into the program of its prevention and control, initially domestic then international. The first international virtual elements of criminal justice reform in that program emerged with the adoption of the Model Agreement on the Transfer of Foreign Prisoners (1985),[4] followed by the Model Treaty for the Prevention of Crimes that Infringe on the Cultural Heritage in the Form of Movable Property, another one on extradition, plus a number of others (1990). In 2000, that mandate crime became solidly an international matter, when the General Assembly (GA) approved the UN Convention against Transnational Organized Crime (resolution 55/25, Annex) with its two protocols against trafficking in human beings and migrants, and one protocol of 2001 regulating firearms manufacturing.

Legal resource base of UN criminology

In addition to that treaty instrument and the UN Convention against Corruption (2003), four other such instruments presently create the legally binding framework for the UN drugs and crime mandate: the Single Convention on Narcotic Drugs (1961) prohibiting production and supply of specific (nominally narcotic) drugs and of drugs with similar effects except under license for specific purposes; the Protocol amending the Single Convention (1972), which highlighted the need for treatment and rehabilitation of drug addicts, instructing parties to take all practicable measures for the prevention of abuse of psychotropic substances and for the early identification, treatment, education, after-care, rehabilitation, and social reintegration of the persons involved; the Convention on Psychotropic Substances (1971), which established an international control system for psychotropic substances; and the UN Convention Against Illicit Traffic in Narcotic Drugs and Psychotropic Substances (1988), which provides additional legal mechanisms for enforcing the 1961 Single Convention on Narcotic Drugs and the 1971 Convention on Psychotropic Substances.

Moreover, there are now about 60 "soft law" (non-treaty, but legally relevant, see Clark, 1994, Ch. 5) instruments adopted by Member States, starting from the landmark *Standard Minimum Rules for the Treatment of Prisoners* (SMRs; 1955) through the UN *Guidelines for the Administration of Juvenile Justice* (1990) and the UN *Standard Minimum Rules for Non-custodial Measures* (1995), to the more recent *Guidelines for the Prevention of Crime* (2002), the *Principles on the Strengthening Basic Principles of Judicial Conduct* (2006), and the UN *Rules for the Treatment of Women Prisoners* ("Bangkok Rules," 2010). Finally, there are 16 universal legal instruments against terrorism, in whose implementation the UNODC assists. In sum, they all contain, roughly, about 2,000 substantive anti-drugs, -crime and -terrorism provisions, applicable to 192 Member States. Altogether they constitute the legislative mandate from which UN criminology draws its sustenance.

Particular features of UN criminology and its publications

Two features of UN criminology should especially be noted. First, UN criminology does not consider itself bound by the legal definition of "crime." Second, UN criminology has a great transformative power. UN criminology has grown over the years. The First UN Congress on the Prevention of Crime and the Treatment of Offenders (Geneva, 1955) which adopted SMRs, started a series of quinquennial congresses (Alper and Boren, 1972). They not only continued with other standards and norms, but also provide a unique channel of communication with academic criminology. Unlike official world UN drugs and crime meetings, which are limited to Member States and NGOs in consultative status with the ECOSOC or associated status with the Department of Public Information of the UN Secretariat, the rules of procedure of these global events, such as the latest Twelfth Congress (Salvador da Bahia, Brazil, 2010) provide opportunities for individual experts to participate and submit their work. Although Member States ultimately decide what recommendations to adopt, individual experts and the NGOs may interact with Member States and make their own presentations that may influence the outcome of the congresses.

Because of treaty obligations, the antidrug program has produced much impact on global criminology, both through commentaries on the drug conventions as well as statistical reports on drug seizures. It has also provided technical assistance to Member States.

The UN world drug reports (1997–2009)[4] provide comprehensive information on the illicit drug situation. In recognition of the importance of factual and objective information on international drug control, these reports are now issued on an annual basis. First published by Oxford University Press (OUP), these reports inform about detailed estimates and trends on production, trafficking and consumption of opium/heroin, coca/cocaine, cannabis, and amphetamine-type stimulants markets. In 2009, for the first time, the World Drug Report features sections on the quality of drug data available to the UNODC, trends in drug use among young people, and police-recorded drug offences. It also discusses the unintended consequences of drug control – the black market for drugs – and how the international community can best tackle it.

Since the mid-1970s, the UN has conducted regular surveys of crime trends and operations of criminal justice systems (1970–2008), which are now in their eleventh round. Based, inter alia, on them, in 1999 the UN crime program managed to match the world drug report with the OUP-published Global report on crime and justice. For a long time, no follow-up has been published, despite an excellent and ever-growing UN time-series of cross-national data, and qualitative information. Because of the fear that their presentation may heighten the international debate on the effectiveness of various penal and penitentiary measures and lead to politically motivated charges, Member States have been reluctant to mandate the next publication of these otherwise readily available statistics (via the UNODC home page).

In 2005 a global report on *Trends in crime and justice* was prepared by UNODC and the United Nations Interregional Crime and Justice Institute (UNICRI) and distributed to the participants of the Eleventh Congress as "work in progress." HEUNI, the European Institute for Crime Prevention and Control, affiliated with the United Nations, has periodically published reports on crime and criminal justice in Europe and Northern America. HEUNI and UNODC published a new global statistical crime trends report in 2010.

Because the staffing is limited in the UNODC, and the need for research is so great, the work agenda of the UN Crime Prevention and Criminal Justice Programme (CPCJP) is supported by, a network of 16 "institutes," nicknamed "PNIs" (Programme Network Institutes). In the strictest legal sense, there is only one institute which is a fully-fledged UN body: UNICRI (originally United Nations Social Defense Research Institute, established in 1968 in Rome), currently located in Turin, Italy. The institute has published numerous UN research publications and one recurrent *A world directory of criminological institutes and of crime and justice institutions*. Other PNIs have either been "affiliated," "associated," or otherwise incorporated through a memoranda of understanding with the UNODC. They all contribute to the implementation of the UN drugs and crime mandate. Their UN status is not formalized in that strictest sense, and their staff are not international civil servants. But, like UNICRI, they have their own governance bodies and budgets. They contribute to the implementation of the UN crime program, hence to UN criminology. A few of the institutes are described here, but the full list can be accessed via the web (http://www.unodc.org).

The oldest institute, the UN Far East and Asia Institute on Crime Prevention and the Treatment of Offenders (1962, Fuchu, Tokyo), has significantly contributed to the criminological training of regional and other criminal justice staff (about 130 training courses for participants from some 120 Member States of approximately 3,500 officials). Its *Resource materials* contain comparative information and data (also on regional crime trends). The US National Institute of Justice (1995) has made numerous substantive inputs to PNI work agenda, especially in the field of the prevention and control of transnational organized crime. The International Centre for Criminal Law Reform and Criminal Justice Policy (1991, Vancouver, Canada) has also focused on it, but has gone into other criminological fields as well (e.g. violence against women, prison overcrowding, identity theft). The Korean Institute of Criminology (Seoul, The Republic of Korea) and the Institute for Security Studies (Pretoria, The Republic of South Africa) joined as PNIs in 2004. The former has been best known for its spearheading contributions to distance learning (KIC/UNODC Virtual Anti-Cybercrime Forum), and the latter for its African outreach, followed by the UN African Regional Institute (1989, Kampala, Uganda). Likewise spearheading is the global crime prevention work of the International Centre for the Prevention of Crime (2005, Montreal, Canada), and, in its own continental terms, such work by the Australian Institute of Criminology (1988, Canberra). The most known for its work on the implementation of the Standard Minimum Rules is the Latin American Institute on the Prevention of Crime and the Treatment of Offenders (1975, San José, Costa Rica). The most pronounced human rights contributions originate from the Raoul Wallenberg Institute (1996, Lund, Sweden).

Of the over 2,000 NGOs in consultative status with the ECOSOC, each having a place in the criminological interactions with the UN drugs and crime mandate, a few are very active, some are intermittently active, and some are observers. Each of these roles is important to ensure the work of the UNODC is accomplished and transparency is maintained under the watchful eye of civil society. A small sample of NGOs is presented here.

The International Association of Penal Law, the International Society for Criminology, the International Society for Social Defence, and the International Penal and Penitentiary Foundation are known as the "Big Four" group of NGOs because of their founding roles in the UN CPCJP. The Howard League for Penal Reform was added to this group in the early days.

Depending on the entry point into the UN Programme (whether via the UN Secretariat or the UN policy-making bodies), the level of interest and degree of cooperation, their substantive role has differed. Some NGOs have been or/and are making substantive contributions to the Programme via helping it in its clearing-house functions (e.g. the American Society of Criminology has contributed by digitalizing 50 years of UN crime congress documentation; https://www.asc41.com/undocs.htm). Others, such as Asia Crime Prevention Foundation, the Academic Council on the United Nations System, the Penal Reform International, the International Commission for Catholic Prison Pastoral Care, and Amnesty International, have assisted in capacity-building by organizing or/and supporting training courses, symposia, seminars, and other conferences at the national and regional level, as well as held public lectures and other initiatives designed to upgrade the knowledge and know-how of policy makers, administrators, and other professionals concerned with the prevention of crime, administration of justice, and the treatment of offenders and victims. Still others, such as the American Correctional Association, the International Law Association, Pax Romana, Soroptimists International, the International Police Association, the Academy of Criminal Justice Sciences, and the Open Society Institute, are less involved in the proceedings and/or observe the Programme, but inform their constituencies for knowledge and action outside the UN structure. Finally, some NGOs have more specific mandates and enter the discussion when those issues arise, such as Friends World Committee for Consultation (Quakers), Prison Fellowship International, and the World Society of Victimology.

Some of these NGOs and other entities are also involved in the UN's drugs mandate. But there are many more specifically involved in that field only (see, for example, African Action on AIDS, Canadian Centre on Substance Abuse, Centro de Información y Educación para la Prevención del Abuso de Drogas, and Centro Italiano di Solidarieta). Through epidemiological studies, evaluation research, and other methods and findings concerning the addictive potential of marijuana, and by addressing the question of HIV and AIDS prevention and care among injecting drug users and in prison settings, they seek to influence the UN drugs mandate. As opposed to most of the NGOs involved in the crime mandate, "criminology" as a discipline-by-name guiding their contributions to the UN is not in their call. But, in fact, their contributions, whether a part of social welfare assistance, health promotion, or otherwise mandated, are genuinely relevant to its drugs mandate and overlap with criminological perspectives.

Towards operationalization of criminological ideas and a common language of justice

Since the time when the UN operated separate mandates on drugs and crime, the exchange of ideas between the academic world and the UN criminology has been prolific. The role of academic criminology in the UN work has remained prominent. Criminological contributions of the classical and positivist schools, of the social defense movement, and those stemming from the modernization theory have been influential in the UN's development of soft and treaty instruments, intergovernmental recommendations, and the UN's own field-project experience.

While much of the early program was driven by academic ideas, current drugs and crime mandates have become atheoretical and practical, with an orientation towards technical assistance, especially to the developing world.

The UN world has injected into drugs and crime counterefforts its own ideas of human and urban security. The UN's overarching framework in its counteracting efforts is the promotion of social progress and better living standards. Alternative development replacing illicit drug cultivation, and sustainable development have become an UN focus in response to the globalization of crime.

The essential condition for global coordinated crime-fighting efforts is a peaceful political environment. Military conflicts or civil wars render any crime fighting efforts futile because individuals and communities are forced into various forms of organized crime to make a living. In such countries there is no sustainable livelihood and people are forced to take up arms to fight injustice. Assisting these failed states thus becomes an expensive international endeavor. These failed states are often used as transit areas for drug trafficking and human trafficking. Such States have been the target of transnational organized crime groups. They corrupt its officials and gradually take control of their governance. The UN and others are actively involved in providing technical assistance to such countries. International criminologists should vigorously back their service. Among approximately 500 institutes, including academic institutions, governmental institutes, NGOs, private institutes, and international organizations in almost half of the UN membership, listed in *A world directory of criminological institutes and of crime and justice institutions*, there are indications that such a desired field-orientated "international criminology" contribution to that service emerges in the programmes of domestic-level entities (UNICRI, 2009, pp. 157, 169, 195).

In this technical assistance/governance context, there is some incompatibility of methods and concepts between academic and intergovernmental criminology. But there is also some incompatibility of concepts between criminology as a whole and other disciplines.

This is also the case with different understanding of certain concepts between criminology and economics, and political science. In effect, the UN interdisciplinary drugs and crime mandate juggles various concepts with different scope, precision, and levels of complementarities. For a criminal lawyer all this is particularly challenging, because in criminal law its own concepts are far more rigorously defined than in any of the above-named disciplines.

In 2004, the UN Secretary-General in his landmark report to the Security Council wrote that:

> concepts such as justice, the rule of law, and transitional justice are essential to understanding the international community's efforts to enhance human rights, protect persons from fear and want, address property disputes, encourage economic development, promote accountable governance and peacefully resolve conflict. They serve both to define our goals and to determine our methods. Yet, there is a multiplicity of definitions and understandings of such

> concepts, even among our closest partners in the field. At an operational level, there is, for some, a fair amount of overlap with other related concepts, such as security sector reform, judicial sector reform and governance reform. To work together effectively in this field, a common understanding of key concepts is essential.
>
> *(S/2004/616, para. 5)*

In short, a "common language of justice" is needed.

UN Criminal Justice Studies

The UN Criminal Justice Studies, a new discipline, reflect on the still and ever evolving UN drugs and crime mandate, and influence UN-sponsored training activities across the world. With about 2,000 UN substantive standards and norms in crime prevention and criminal justice, multiplied by 192 Member States which either created or/and are the addressees of those provisions, they should respond to different political, cultural, and socio-economic realities. Non-dogmatic practical analyses of crime and its prevention and control in Africa, the Balkans, the Caribbean, Central America, and Western Africa are further strengthened by accompanying handbooks facilitating technical assistance.

The UNODC typically does not engage in empirical research. More often than not UN staff, including hired consultants, base their project activities on existing knowledge. They teach and train the target audiences in what they know from their education and experience instead of what is encapsulated in the UN crime prevention and criminal justice standards and norms. This is a more elaborate version of the "in my country" statement, showing that delivering the UN rule-of-law message which has defined values and is poised for implementing is, in this sense, shallow.

Even if these values can be fully embraced, their effective pedagogy (i.e. teaching and training methods) remains a challenge and requires nuanced attentiveness to cultural differences.

Conclusion

These cross-cutting and interdisciplinary studies on the ideas, program, and practical activities of this great world organization, the United Nations, need more than autonomous academic consideration, and even more than a limited "country" knowledge. No single domestic legal system and no particular school of thought can accommodate the emerging UN criminal justice mandate. It requires a supranational process combining various approaches, theoretical and practical.

For the first time, at the Twelfth Congress workshop entitled "International criminal justice education for the rule of law", the UN in its own "language" and terms had on its agenda the vast, complex, and expanding topic of UN Criminal Justice Studies as a part of an academic curriculum. This process is the logical consequence of the need to develop a "common language of justice." With this new topic the UN CPCJP has once again taken the lead in promoting the rule of law, human rights, and development. Although there are still incompatible elements in this movement, the effort to promote a global platform for crime control and the rule of law remains promising.

Future research questions

1. How can "justice" be defined, incorporating the intent of the UN's 192 Members?
2. Does UN criminology have an ideology?
3. Which criminogenic socio-economic condition is most often emphasized in the UN criminology and why?
4. What is the contemporary understanding of sustainable development and livelihood for counteracting crime more effectively?
5. What legal instruments and common and overlapping interdisciplinary terms in the international and UN criminology contribute to UN criminal justice studies?

Notes

1 Dr hab. (Law/Criminology, Poland). The views expressed in this article are not necessarily those of the UN Secretariat in which its author is employed.

2 The evolution of the UN crime program mandate has not begun with the implementation of the UN Charter that in its preamble and articles 1(1) and 2(3) alluded to achieving "justice," which "means something different from international law . . . and . . . refers to natural law" (Simma *et al.*, 2002, vol. 1: 36). In the UN crime program specifically, "justice," qualified either as "criminal" or "juvenile," has really been only a gradually and constantly developing concept, driven and shaped by various orientations regarding its meaning and scope, as stipulated in its international *criminal* law and other legal instruments.

3 This broad UN definition of "justice" is legally and diplomatically a very subtle matter. It should be embedded in even a broader concept of justice. Over decades of development of that concept it had gone through diffused and often incoherent paths. It has started evolving from the first half of the nineteenth century at the onset of modernization. Then the idea of universalizing of certain concepts across the world, such as expanding "formal" (classical) to "social" justice, had its beginning in Europe (Kennedy, 2003, p. 646).

Unlike the UN drugs mandate, the UN crime mandate has not started from taking over the "legal control" responsibilities from the League of Nations on the implementation of the two international conventions on the suppression of trafficking in women and children (1921) and on the circulation of obscene publications (1933), nor from implementing the Convention for the Suppression of the Traffic in Persons and of the Exploitation of the Prostitution of Others (1950). Likewise, the UN crime program has not been mandated to deal with the implementation of the two first legal instruments against human trafficking – the International Agreement (1904) and the International Convention for the Suppression of White Slave Traffic (1910) – and of one instrument against pornography: the International Agreement for the Suppression of Obscene Publications (1910). It was France that was entrusted to deal with the three of them before the birth of the UN. Taking over, in 1948, France's functions, the UN has administered all the above international instruments, and several subsequent ones, through its Legal Office. Since 1948, with the gradual development of the UN Bill of Human Rights (1948/1966) and subsequent international legal instruments, a considerable portion of criminological work has also been carried out in the UN Secretariat by the Office of the Higher Commissioner on Human Rights (Geneva, Switzerland). The Division for the Advancement of Women, another entity of the Secretariat (New York, USA), after the adoption of the Convention on the Elimination of All Forms of Discrimination against Women (1979), often described as an international bill of women rights, has been carrying out considerable criminological work on violence against women. Outside the Secretariat, several agencies in the UN system, including the UN Development Programme; the UN Educational, Social and Cultural Organization; the United Nations Children's Fund; the World Bank; the World Health Organization; and the UN-Habitat deal with various criminological topics and projects.

4 All these reports and other UNODC publications referred to in this chapter can be accessed through its home page http:// www.unodc.org.

References

Alper, B. S. and Boren, J. F. (1972). *Crime: international agenda, concern and action in the prevention of crime and treatment of offenders, 1846–1972*, New York: Lexington Books.

Bassiouni, C. M. (2003). *Introduction to international criminal law.* Ardsley, New York: Transnational Publishers.

Bruni, F. (1991). *Prevention compendium, training for prevention*, vols 1 and 2. United Nations International Crime and Justice Research Institute.

Clark, R. S. (1994). *The United Nations Crime Prevention and Criminal Justice Program. Formulation of standards and their implementation*, Philadelphia: University of Pennsylvania Press.

International Review of Criminal Policy (IRCP) (1952). *The work of the United Nations in the field of the prevention of crime and the treatment of offenders.* Prepared by the Secretariat, pp. 3–27.

Kennedy, D. (2003). The methods and the politics. In P. Legrand and R. Munday (Eds.) *Comparative legal studies: traditions and transitions.* Cambridge: Cambridge University Press, pp. 345–436.

Simma, B., Paulus, A., and Chatodou (Eds.) in collaboration with H. Mosler, A. Radelzhofer, C. H. Tomuschat, and R. Wolfrum (2002). *The charter of the United Nations. A commentary.* Oxford and New York: Oxford University Press.

United Nations Interregional Crime and Justice Research Institute (2009). *A world directory of criminological institutes and of crime and justice institutions.* 7th edn. Turin.

United Nations Secretariat (1947). *Preliminary report on the prevention of crime and treatment of offenders*, E/CN 5/30, Rev.1, 11 December.

United Nations Secretary-General (2004). *Report of the Secretary-General on the rule of law and transitional justice in conflict and post-conflict societies.* S/616/2004.

Weiss, T. (2008). *What's wrong with the United Nations, and how to fix it?* Cambridge, UK; Malden, MA: Polity.

14
International criminal courts

Harry M. Rhea

Introduction

There are four theaters of tribunals that prosecute international crimes, which are crimes that are so heinous they victimize the international community. These crimes contemporarily include genocide, crimes against humanity, and war crimes. With the exception of piracy, war crimes are the oldest international crime. In the 6th century BC the Chinese warrior Sun Tzu drafted *The art of war*, which attempted to set humanitarian limits to conduct within armed conflict (McCormack, 1997). The four theaters of tribunals that prosecute international crimes include national (i.e. domestic) criminal courts, multinational criminal courts, internationalized (i.e. hybrid) criminal courts, and international criminal courts.

Historically, serious violations of international humanitarian law (i.e. law of war) were prosecuted in national criminal courts (McCormack 1997). There are several examples of national prosecutions for war crimes or inhumane conduct during armed conflict, according to Bassiouni and Blakesley (1992) and McCormack (1997). The practice of national prosecutions for international crimes lasted well into the twentieth century.

There is consensus that the first international prosecution occurred in 1474 when Peter von Hagenbach was prosecuted by an international criminal tribunal for violations of the "laws of God and man" (Schwarzenberger, 1968; Bassiouni, 1991; Bassiouni and Blakesley, 1992; McCormack, 1997; Schabas, 2007). Hagenbach was judged by twenty-seven judges representing the Holy Roman Empire for allowing his troops to rape and kill innocent civilians as well as destroy their properties (Schwarzenberger, 1968; Bassiouni, 1991).

There have been questions regarding the international nature of Hagenbach's prosecution by allied States of the Holy Roman Empire (McCormack, 1997). The Holy Roman Empire was one entity, but Schwarzenberger (1968) describes it as "degenerated" by the time of the trial to the extent that states were acting as "subjects of international law" (Schwarzenberger, 1968, p. 465; McCormack, 1997, p. 38). If this is accurate, then Hagenbach's trial was multinational rather than "international."

Multinational criminal courts include two or more states together prosecuting defendants in the same trial. With the exception of the Hagenbach trial, the first modern multinational criminal court was adopted on paper in article 227 of the Treaty of Versailles, signed on 28 June 1919. The Allied powers arraigned Germany's ex-Kaiser, Wilhelm II of Hohenzollern, "for a supreme offence against international morality and the sanctity of treaties" (Treaty of Versailles, 1919, Article 227). Article 227 further stated:

> A special tribunal will be constituted to try the accused, thereby assuring him the guarantees essential to the right of defence. It will be composed of five judges, one appointed by each of the following Powers: namely, the United States of America, Great Britain, France, Italy and Japan.

The tribunal adopted in article 227 of the Treaty of Versailles envisioned five states together judging the accused. The tribunal never became reality, since Wilhelm II fled to the Netherlands, which offered him sanctuary. Other German war criminals were prosecuted by a German national criminal court in Leipzig.

As World War II was concluding, there were many calls for the prosecution of higher-ranked Nazi war criminals. Germany surrendered on 8 May 1945. In the following month, the United Kingdom invited the United States, the Soviet Union, and France to London to discuss post-war prosecutions of Nazi war criminals (Aide-Mémoire, 1945). The London Conference lasted until 8 August 1945, on which day the Allied victors adopted the Charter of the International Military Tribunal.

The International Military Tribunal prosecuted 21 Nazi war criminals, including Herman Göring and Rudolf Hess. Crimes within the jurisdiction of the tribunal included crimes against the peace, war crimes, and crimes against humanity. In 1993, the Security Council established the International Criminal Tribunal for the former Yugoslavia. The following year, the Security Council established the International Criminal Tribunal for Rwanda. Crimes included in the jurisdictions of these two tribunals were similar to those at the International Military Tribunal.

International criminal courts as a concept or philosophy have been around for at least 100 years (see, for example, Bass, 2000; Ferencz, 1980). However, its implementation was only in the past 20 years or so, beginning with the International Criminal Tribunal for the former Yugoslavia in 1993. This chapter provides a general overview of international and multinational criminal courts, particularly the history and goals of such courts as well as their substantive and procedural law.

The early years

During The Hague Peace Conferences of 1899 and 1907, there was much diplomatic debate concerning international tribunals to resolve disputes between states peacefully without reverting to war (International Convention, 1899). There were few references to establishing an international court with the jurisdiction to criminally prosecute individuals. It was the norm that national courts prosecuted individual criminal behavior, regardless of severity.

As World War I came to an end, the road to international justice was only beginning. When the Paris Peace Conference commenced on 18 January 1919, the issue of war crimes was one of the first questions on the agenda (Rhea, 2011; see also Willis, 1982). On 25 January 1919, the "Great Powers" created a commission to inquire into crimes committed by Germany and Turkey during World War I and whether an international criminal tribunal should prosecute such crimes (Carnegie Endowment for Peace, 1919; see also Bassiouni and Blakesley, 1992; Cryer, 2005; Maogoto, 2004). Its title was the Commission on the Responsibility of the Authors of War and on Enforcement of Penalties (Carnegie Endowment of Peace, 1919).

States could not agree on the establishment of an international criminal court; yet, the Treaty of Peace between Germany and the Allied powers included the right of the Allies to create a multinational criminal tribunal, which would include judges from the Allied states, as follows:

> The Allied and Associated Powers publicly arraign William II of Hohenzollern, formerly German Emperor, for a supreme offence against international morality and the sanctity of treaties.
>
> A special tribunal will be constituted to try the accused, thereby assuring him the guarantees essential to the right of defense. It will be composed of five judges, one appointed by each of the following Powers: namely, the United States of America, Great Britain, France, Italy and Japan.
>
> *(Treaty of Peace, 1919, Article 227)*

It was ultimately decided by the Allied powers that Germany should hold the Leipzig Trials and Turkey should hold the Constantinople Trials as national prosecutions (Willis, 1982; Bass, 2000). Both were ineffective and have been accepted as farces by nearly all scholars in the field of international criminal justice. Bassiouni (1997) has written that the trials did serve a purpose of how not to handle post-conflict justice and that states cannot always be trusted to legitimately prosecute their nationals.

The Treaty of Peace also included the creation of a new non-criminal international court, the Permanent Court of International Justice, within the Charter of the League of Nations (Treaty of Peace, 1919, Article 14). The Permanent Court of International Justice was the predecessor of the current International Court of Justice under the United Nations. Creating the Permanent Court of International Justice was an attempt to establish a more powerful judicial system without the flaws of the Permanent Court of Arbitration established by the First Convention of The Hague Peace Conference of 1899.

Nuremberg and Tokyo

World War II officially began on 1 September 1939, when Germany invaded Poland. Adolf Hitler and the Nazis, however, had taken steps to initiate World War II within Germany beginning in 1937 (Charter of the IMT, 1945, Article 6(c)). The League of Nations and the Permanent Court of International Justice dissolved, because they were ineffective in preventing another world war.

Prior prosecutorial declarations were followed by simultaneous declarations on 7 October 1942, from the United States and United Kingdom, that a United Nations War Crimes Commission would be created to investigate and hold "ringleaders" responsible for the organization and implementation of war crimes (United Nations War Crimes Commission, 1948; see also Harris, 1999; Maguire, 2000; Taylor, 1992). This was the first reference that the Nazi hierarchy would be prosecuted rather than the lower ranked soldier.

The United Nations War Crimes Commission was established on 20 October 1943. Its purpose was to "collect, investigate, and record evidence of war crimes, and to report to the governments concerned all instances in which a prima facie case existed" (Tutorow, 1986, p. 4). The Commission immediately began planning for post-war trials to prosecute war criminals (ibid.).

The United Nations War Crimes Commission's plans to establish a United Nations War Crimes Tribunal were short lived. Twelve days after its creation, President Roosevelt, Prime

Minister Churchill, and Joseph Stalin met in Moscow and declared that Nazi war criminals would be "punished by a joint decision of the Governments of the Allies" (Tripartite Conference in Moscow, 1943, pp. 310–11). The Moscow Declaration, in a sense, would have primacy over the United Nations War Crimes Commission. The decision of the Allied governments, particularly the United States, the United Kingdom, and the Soviet Union, on how to hold war criminals accountable superseded the Commission's jurisdiction over war criminals (Taylor, 1992).

The United Nations War Crimes Commission remained a valuable organization for its investigations and recommendations. In early 1945, the Commission recommended the following regarding prosecuting war criminals:

> It has recommended (1) that, generally speaking, the cases should be tried in the national courts of the countries against which the crimes have been committed; (2) that a convention be concluded providing for the establishment of a United Nations court to pass upon such cases as are referred to it by the Governments; and (3) that pending the establishment of such a court there be established mixed military tribunals to function also in addition to the United Nations court when the latter is established.
>
> *(Secretary of State to the President, 1945, p. 401)*

After World War II, the Allied powers, including France, the Soviet Union, the United Kingdom, and the United States, agreed to create the International Military Tribunal (Agreement, 1945). The International Military Tribunal was created to prosecute major Nazi war criminals (Charter of the IMT, 1945). The word "international" in its title was, and remains, misleading. The International Military Tribunal was not an international tribunal, but rather a multinational military tribunal similar to the tribunal included in Article 227 of the Treaty of Peace with Germany in 1919.

The "Big Four" each appointed a prosecutor and decided which defendants would be charged with what crimes (Harris, 1999). Crimes within the jurisdiction of the International Military Tribunal were crimes against the peace, war crimes, and crimes against humanity (Charter of the IMT, 1945: Article 6 (a), (b), and (c)).

The International Military Tribunal's sister tribunal, the International Military Tribunal for the Far East, was established by an executive decree of General MacArthur on 16 January 1946 (Horwitz, 1950; see also Röling and Cassese, 1994), as a consequence of Japan's surrender on 2 September 1945. Japan signed the Instrument of Surrender, which stipulated that the Allied victors would hold Japanese war criminals to a "stern justice." This "stern justice" was achieved through criminal prosecutions.

The International Military Tribunal for the Far East was created to prosecute Japanese war criminals for their atrocities during World War II. Excluding the formation of the judges and prosecutors, its Charter was very similar to the Charter of the International Military Tribunal. The criminal jurisdiction included crimes against the peace, war crimes, and crimes against humanity (Charter of the IMTFE, 1946; Article 5 (a), (b), and (c)).

Shortly after the International Military Tribunal completed its trial, the United Nations considered the question of establishing a permanent international criminal court. The Convention on the Prevention and Punishment of the Crime of Genocide was adopted on 9 December 1948. Article 6 of the Genocide Convention referred to an international penal tribunal to prosecute accused *genocidaires* (Convention, 1948: Article 6), but the tribunal would only be applied to states that ratified or agreed to its jurisdiction (ibid.; see also LeBlanc, 1991; Schabas, 2009).

The United Nations General Assembly had also established a committee composed of 17 states to draft a statute of an international criminal court. The committee submitted its report and draft statute in 1952. The International Law Commission submitted its report in 1953. After the request of revisions, the final report was submitted the following year. Never before had the world seen such growth in international criminal law defining limitations of conduct by states against their nationals during war and peace. However, in 1954, the United Nations General Assembly decided to postpone consideration of the question of creating an international criminal court (GA Res 898 IX 1954).

Post Cold War

As a result of states declaring their independence from Yugoslavia in the early 1990s, extreme beliefs of cultural identity resulted in crimes against humanity, more specifically referred to as "ethnic cleansing." Orthodox and Catholic Serbs began rounding up and deporting their neighbor Muslims. The former Yugoslavia was an area in turmoil. As a result of modern media technology, for example the Internet and international cable news networks, the turmoil became known to the international community through computers and televisions. As many as 20,000 Muslim women were systematically raped by Bosnian Serb forces as a means of ethnic cleansing to produce Serbian offspring. Not since the Holocaust had the world actually seen such brutal systematic attacks on civilians, including women and children.

The United Nations Charter came into force on 24 October 1945. The purpose of the United Nations is "to maintain international peace and security" (Charter of the UN, 1945, Article 1). Chapter 7 of the United Nations Charter authorizes the Security Council to determine threats to international peace and security and to take any action as it deems necessary to maintain or restore international peace and security (ibid., Chapter 7).

On 13 July 1992, the Security Council passed a resolution warning that individual perpetrators who violated international humanitarian law in the former Yugoslavia would be held accountable (UN Doc. S/RES/764 1992). On 22 February 1993, the Security Council adopted Resolution 808 deciding that it would establish an international criminal tribunal "for the prosecution of persons responsible for serious violations of international humanitarian law committed in the territory of the former Yugoslavia since 1991" (UN Doc. S/RES/808 1993). The Security Council unanimously passed Resolution 827 on 25 May 1993, officially creating the International Criminal Tribunal for the former Yugoslavia (Statute of the International Criminal Tribunal for the Former Yugoslavia,1993). The purpose of the International Criminal Tribunal was to bring to justice "persons responsible for serious violations of international humanitarian law committed in the territory of the former Yugoslavia since 1991" (Statute of ICTY, 1993, Article 1).

The following year genocide occurred in Rwanda. The Security Council, again using its Chapter 7 authority, responded by creating the International Criminal Tribunal for Rwanda "to bring peace and reconciliation in Rwanda" (Statute for the ICTR, 1994) and "to prosecute persons responsible for serious violations of international humanitarian law committed in the territory of Rwanda . . ., between 1 January 1994 and 31 December 1994" (ibid.). For 50 years, the Security Council had not created one tribunal under its Chapter 7 powers, and now in less than two years it had created two international criminal tribunals. At this point, the Security Council was suffering from "tribunal fatigue" (D. Scheffer, personal communication 24 June 2008). Perhaps the time had come for a permanent international criminal court (Bassiouni, 1991).

International Criminal Court

In 1989, the General Assembly urged consideration of establishing an international criminal court (Bassiouni and Blakesley, 1992). In early summer of 1998, the United Nations Preparatory

Commission convened a conference in Rome, Italy, to adopt the treaty for the permanent International Criminal Court. On 17 July 1998, states voted on the treaty, officially titled the Rome Statute; 120 states voted in favor, 21 abstained, and 7 voted against (Schabas, 2007), indicating the world was ready to make the ICC a reality once 60 states ratified the Statute. On 11 April 2002, the Rome Statute received the necessary sixtieth ratification, and on 1 July 2002, the International Criminal Court was born.

The International Criminal Court has jurisdiction over four crimes: genocide, crimes against humanity, war crimes, and the crime of aggression. Currently, the International Criminal Court is investigating five situations: Uganda; Democratic Republic of Congo; Darfur, Sudan; the Central African Republic; and the Republic of Kenya. On 4 March 2009, the president of Sudan, Omar Hassan Ahmad Al Bashir, was indicted and a pre-trial chamber of the International Criminal Court issued an arrest warrant charging him with crimes against humanity and war crimes (*Prosecutor* v. *Omar Hassan Ahmad Al Bashir*). The effectiveness of the International Criminal Court has yet to be determined, but it has demonstrated great potential.

Issues and challenges

The greatest concern states have with international criminal courts is that they tend to infringe on state sovereignty. The International Military Tribunal at Nuremberg and the International Military Tribunal for the Far East were coercive on the states that the defendants were nationals (Slye and van Schaack, 2009). Germany or Japan never consented to the tribunals that prosecuted their nationals. The winners simply prosecuted the losers of World War II, which has now plagued the tribunals as theaters for "victors' justice."

The International Criminal Tribunals for the former Yugoslavia and Rwanda were also coercive over the states which defendants are nationals (ibid.). The Security Council's Chapter 7 powers authorized them to establish ad hoc tribunals which were not only coercive, but had primacy over national tribunals. This means that the ad hoc tribunals' jurisdiction trumped national jurisdiction and could authorize individuals being prosecuted in national tribunals to be extradited to the international criminal tribunals.

The International Criminal Court has corrected this issue. The International Criminal Court is not a creature of the Security Council like its predecessors. A treaty adopted at an international conference in Rome, Italy, in 1998, established the Court. Prior to 1 July 2002, states consented to the jurisdiction of the International Criminal Court by signing and ratifying the Rome Statute. Thereafter, states acceded to the Rome Statute. States may choose not to allow the International Criminal Court to have jurisdiction over its territory or nationals. The only exception is if a national from a non-state party commits one of the crimes within the jurisdiction of the International Criminal Court on the territory of a state party of the Rome Statute (Rome Statute, 1998, Article 12).

Internationalized criminal courts, which are commonly referred to as hybrid or mixed criminal courts, have also attempted to resolve the issue of coercion. Internationalized criminal courts share participants and jurisdiction. For example, often the court is on the territory of the concerned state and judges and prosecutors are from the state and international community. This allows for more national participation, since states often are willing, but unable, to prosecute individuals accused of committing international crimes.

Conclusion

As the previous pages have demonstrated, there are four traditional methods used to prosecute those responsible for committing international crimes. These methods are driven by international criminal law. The purpose of international criminal law is to prosecute those who would otherwise not be prosecuted in national courts. Quite often these include political and state officials.

Ideally, perpetrators of international crimes should also be prosecuted in national tribunals. A recent example of a national tribunal prosecuting its leaders for committing international crimes, including genocide and crimes against humanity, was the Iraqi High Tribunal, which prosecuted Saddam Hussein in 2006 (Iraqi High Criminal Court Law, 2005). However, states often are either unable or unwilling to prosecute state officials.

If a state is willing but unable to prosecute, the best option may be contracting with an international organization, for example the United Nations, and creating an internationalized criminal court. There are many benefits to this method, particularly state consent and justice for the local community. An example of an internationalized criminal court is the Special Court for Sierra Leone, which was established with an agreement with Sierra Leone and the United Nations (Schabas, 2006).

The International Criminal Court is the last resort. Its jurisdiction is complementary, which means that it does not have primacy over national courts. It complements national courts. Therefore, states have the ability to prosecute the accused in their national courts or request external assistance. However, if the state is unwilling to prosecute, the International Criminal Court's jurisdiction may be activated. This is important since international crimes are so horrific and perpetrators of such crimes must be prosecuted on behalf of the international community.

Future research questions

1. Which form of court is most appropriate for the prosecution of international crimes?
2. Why are certain states that have supported past international criminal courts (i.e. United States) suspicious of the International Criminal Court?
3. Under Article 5 of the Rome Statute, the International Criminal Court has jurisdiction to prosecute genocide, crimes against humanity, war crimes, and the crime of aggression. Should the International Criminal Court have jurisdiction of more crimes (e.g. international drug trafficking)?
4. Is the International Criminal Court a sign that international society is becoming borderless? If so, how will this affect national criminal justice systems?
5. How closely should criminologists watch prosecutions of international crimes? Should they be developing case studies of each prosecution?

References

Agreement for the Prosecution and Punishment of Major War Criminals of the European Axis (1945), 8 August. Reprinted in *Department of State Bulletin* 13 (320), 12 August 1945, p. 222.

Aide-Mémoire from the United Kingdom (1945) *Report of Robert H. Jackson United States Representative to the International Conference on Military Trials*. 3 June. Reprinted in 1949. Washington DC: United States Government Printing Office. p. 41.

Bass, G. J. (2000). *Stay the hand of vengeance: the politics of war crimes tribunals*. Princeton, NJ: Princeton University Press.

Bassiouni, M. C. (1991). The time has come for an international criminal court. *Indiana International and Comparative Law Review*, 1: 1–43.

—— (1997). From Versailles to Rwanda in seventy-five years: the need to establish a permanent international criminal court. *Harvard Human Rights Journal*, 10: 11–62.

Bassiouni, M. C. and Blakesley, C. L. (1992). The need for an international criminal court in the new world order. *Vanderbilt Journal of Transnational Law*, 25(2): 151–82.

Carnegie Endowment for International Peace (1919) *Violations of the laws and customs of war: report of the Commission on the Responsibilities of the Authors of the War and on Enforcement of Penalties*. Division of International Law, Pamphlet No. 32. Oxford: Clarendon Press.

Charter of the International Military Tribunal (1945). 8 August. Reprinted in *Department of State Bulletin,* XIII (320), 12 August 1945, pp. 223–6.

Charter of the International Military Tribunal for the Far East (1946). 10 March. *Department of State Bulletin* XIV (349): 361–4.

Charter of the United Nations (1945). Reprinted in *Yearbook of the United Nations* (1975): Appendix II, 1043–52.

Convention on the Prevention and Punishment of the Crime of Genocide (1948). 9 December. Reprinted (1948–9) in *International Law Quarterly*, 2(4): 722–6.

Cryer, R. (2005). *Prosecuting international crimes: selectivity and the international criminal regime*. Cambridge: Cambridge University Press.

Ferencz, B. B. (1980). *An international criminal court: a step toward world peace*. New York: Oceana Publications.

Harris, W. R. (1999) *Tyranny on trial: the trial of the major German war criminals at the end of World War II at Nuremberg, Germany, 1945–1946*. Dallas, TX: First Southern University Press.

Horwitz, S. (1950). The Tokyo Trial. *International Conciliation,* 465: 480. International Convention for the Pacific Settlement of International Disputes (1899) (Hague Convention I) adopted at The Hague Peace Conference, 29 July.

Iraqi High Criminal Court Law (2005), Resolution No. 10. *Al-Waqa'I Al-Iraqiya: official gazette of the Republic of Iraq* 4006. 18 October.

LeBlanc, L. J. (1991). *The United States and the genocide convention*. Durham, NC: Duke University Press.

McCormack, T. L. H. (1997) From Sun Tzu to the sixth committee: the evolution of an international criminal law regime. In T. L. H. McCormack and G. J. Simpson (Eds.) *The law of war crimes: national and international approaches*. Cambridge, MA: Kluwer, p. 31–63.

Prosecutor v. *Omar Hassan Ahmad Al Bashir* (ICC-02/05–01/09) Available at http://www.sc-sl.org/DOCUMENTS/tabid/176/Default.aspx (accessed 30 September 2009).

Maguire, P. (2000). *Law and war: an American story*. New York: Columbia University Press.

Maogoto, J. N. (2004). War crimes and realpolitik: international justice from World War I to the 21st Century. Boulder, CO.: Lynne Rienner Publishers.

Rhea, H. (2011). *The United States and international criminal tribunals: an introduction*. Belgium: Intersentia.

Röling, B. V. A. and Cassese, A. (1994). *The Tokyo trial and beyond*. Cambridge: Polity Press.

Rome Statute of the International Criminal Court (1998), UN Doc. A/CONF.183/9. Washington DC: United States Government Printing Office.

Schabas, W. A. (2006). *The UN international criminal tribunals: former Yugoslavia, Rwanda and Sierra Leone*. New York: Cambridge University Press.

—— (2007). *An introduction to the international criminal court*. 3rd edn. New York: Cambridge University Press.

—— (2009). *Genocide in international law*. 2nd edn. New York: Cambridge University Press.

Schwarzenberger, G. (1968) *International law as applied by international courts and tribunals: the law of armed conflict*. Vol. 2. London: Stevens & Sons Limited.

Secretary of State to the President (1945). 6 January. In United States Department of State, *Foreign Relations of the United States: conferences at Malta and Yalta, 1945* (1955), p. 401. Washington DC: United States Government Printing Office.

Slye, R. C. and van Schaack, B. (2009) *Essentials: international criminal law*. New York: Aspen Publishers.

Statute for the International Criminal Tribunal for the Former Yugoslavia (1993) UN Doc. S/RES/827.

Statute for the International Criminal Tribunal for Rwanda (1994) UN Doc. S/RES/955.

Taylor, T. (1992). *The Anatomy of the Nuremberg Trials: A Personal Memoir*. New York: Alfred A. Knopf.

Treaty of Peace between the Allied and Associated Powers and Germany (1919). 18 June. Reprinted in *International Conciliation* 142 (September 1919).

Tripartite Conference in Moscow (1943). *Department of State Bulletin,* 9(228), 6 November, p. 307–11.

Tutorow, N. E. (Ed.) (1986). *War crimes, war criminals, and war crimes trials: an annotated bibliography and source book*. Westport, CT: Greenwood Press.

United Nations War Crimes Commission (1948) *History of the United Nations War Crimes Commission and the development of the laws of war*. London: H.M. Stationary Office.

Willis, J. F. (1982). *Prologue to Nuremberg: the politics and diplomacy of punishing war criminals of the First World War*. Westport, CN: Greenwood Press.

15

International identity crime[1]

Russell G. Smith

Introduction

In the 21st century, one of the most pressing international crime problems that confronts developed societies is the creation and use of misleading and deceptive identities. Identity-related crime has been greatly facilitated with the advent of information and communications technologies which enable crimes of this nature to be committed with ease across jurisdictional boundaries. Computers and the internet have provided a rich source of personal information to steal, and technologies with which to fabricate documentary evidence of identity.

Identity-related crime is a compound concept used to refer to a range of methods used to commit specific forms of deception and fraud. The creation and misuse of identification evidence lies at the heart of the concept, but the crimes involved invariably entail fraud or obtaining a financial advantage by deception – rather than crimes that proscribe the misuse of personal information itself. Traditionally, identity thieves were usually charged with counterfeiting, obtaining unauthorized access to a computer, or opening a bank account in a false name, rather than making use of another person's name or other personal information without their permission. This is beginning to change in recent years as new and specific offenses of identity-related crime are being enacted in a range of countries. These tend to proscribe the creation, use, supply or possession of so-called identification information with intent that it be used in the commission of a serious criminal offense (see Standing Committee of Attorneys-General, 2008).

A variety of terms have been used in connection with the misappropriation of personal information. These include: identity crime, identity theft, identity fraud, identity fabrication, identity manipulation, lent identities and various other identity-related concepts. It is suggested that 'identity crime' be used as the generic crime category, with the other terms used as specific descriptors of the ways in which such crimes can be committed.

International identity crime methods

To commit identity crime, personal information needs to be obtained. The internet provides a comprehensive, quick and cheap tool for this that is accessible to everyone who has a telephone connection, personal computer and service provider. Extensive amounts of personal information are now held on computer networks and shared, intentionally and unintentionally, with others across the globe. Having autobiographical information available online has made the work of identity thieves that much easier, as, in the past, identity thieves were required to obtain personal information by sifting through rubbish (e.g. dumpster diving), or by tricking unsuspecting individuals into disclosing their details in person, by mail or by telephone.

With the development of the internet as a means of transacting business and engaging with government, it has become important to identify those involved in online transactions. This has led to an unfortunate consequence of crime control owing to the fact that techniques of identification, such as online registration requirements, have meant that individuals now supply vast amounts of personal information online – simply in order to obtain a password or other access key that can be used to facilitate 'secure transactions' with financial institutions or government agencies.

The types of personal information at risk of misuse by identity criminals fall into two categories: life history information, and financial information. Examples of the former include details of a person's name, sex, age, address and a variety of numbers used as identifiers when dealing with government agencies and businesses. Examples of the latter include bank account information such as account names, numbers, commencement and expiry dates, and secure numbers and passwords used to conduct secure electronic transactions. In addition, biometric data such as that obtained from fingerprint or facial scanning is a form of personal information that can be misused for the commission of identity crime.

Personal identification information can be obtained from a variety of sources including accidental data leakage from government or business networks, deliberate harvesting of data through the use of computer hacking or by gathering documents that contain personal information, or by social engineering in which individuals are persuaded or tricked into disclosing personal information to individuals for use in criminal activities.

Recently, cases of accidental or negligent data leakage provide a rich source of personal information available for potential misuse by criminals continue to be disclosed. The precise extent to which data leakage is correlated positively with the commission of identity crime is unknown – although the risk of abuse is clearly apparent. Levi (2009) argues that in none of these cases was a large proportion of the 'stolen' data *actually* used to commit fraud subsequently. Bearing this limitation in mind, some of the more prominent examples of data leakage include the following.

Over a two-year period and in March 2008, a company TJ Maxx lost details of approximately 90 million customers, while in 2008, the HSBC banking group lost a computer disk containing the details (including names and dates of birth) of 370,000 customers (BBC, 2008). In the United States in May 2005, the processor of payment card data, CardSystems Solutions Inc, had its database breached and credit card account information including magnetic stripe data and cardholder names relating to over 40 million accounts were stolen (Krim and Barbaro, 2005). More recently, in late 2007, HM Revenue and Customs lost in the ordinary mail unencrypted CDs containing the financial details of 25 million people (one-third of the United Kingdom population) drawing family benefit (Levi, 2009, p. 55; Information Commissioner's Office, 2007).

In the first half of 2007, Symantec (2007) reported that the primary cause of data breaches that could facilitate identity theft was the theft or loss of a computer or other medium on which data were stored or transmitted such as a USB key or a back-up device. It was found that the loss of such devices comprised 46 percent of all data breaches reported. A range of high-risk activities are engaged in by users of social networking sites with one study finding that 44 percent of adults who had a profile allowed their profile to be seen by anyone and that 25 percent of registered social networking users had posted personal data about themselves on their profiles including their telephone number, home address or email address (Ofcom, 2008). The European

Network and Information Security Agency (2007) has also identified the danger of phishing (see below) offenders making use of information obtained from social networking sites.

Those seeking personal information online are also beginning to make use of an ever-expanding digital underground economy. In North America, Operation Firewall, for example, in 2004 culminated in the arrest of 28 people from six countries for offenses including the buying and selling of 1.7 million credit card numbers (McAfee, 2005). The digital underground economy is expanding and becoming a lucrative source of income for organized criminals.

Arguably the most successful means of dishonestly obtaining personal information online is through the range of activities known as phishing. Phishing involves the use of technological means coupled with social engineering designed to trick unsuspecting users of the internet into disclosing personal information in response to an unsolicited request, usually received by email. Once this information has been obtained, criminals may sell it to another person or use it to commit identity fraud.

The success of phishing was demonstrated in a study by Dhamija *et al.* (2006) in which 20 websites, 7 of which were legitimate, and 13 of which were fabricated, were presented to participants for examination. The study involved 22 university-based participants who examined the 20 sites to determine their authenticity. It was found that 90 percent of participants were deceived by good-quality phishing sites, 23 percent relied only on content to determine authenticity (i.e. without examining browser address bars, status bars or security indictors), and 68 percent ignored pop-up warnings as to content risk. Neither education, age, sex, previous experience, nor hours of computer use showed any significant correlation with phishing risks.

The growth in the number of phishing attacks has been exponential until recently, although now seems to be declining slightly. The actual number of phishing sites is, however, still substantial. The Anti-Phishing Working Group (APWG), which is an industry association formed in 2003 to eliminate identity theft and fraud that results from phishing and email spoofing, received 23,187 unique email phishing reports in the month of December 2008. In addition to these phishing emails reported, the APWG itself detected a further 15,709 sites in December 2008. The United States remained the top country hosting phishing sites, although in the month of September 2008, Sweden became the leading country hosting 63 percent of phishing sites. Another important trend has been an increase in rogue anti-malware programs that can be used for phishing, extortion or the sale of worthless anti-virus products. Such detected programs increased 225 percent from 2,850 in July 2008 to 9,287 in December 2008 (APWG, 2009).

Types of international identity crime

Armed with personal information obtained from data leaked publicly, or extracted from online databases or from users by sophisticated social engineering and other technological means, criminals have been able to commit a wide range of criminal activities. The following examples represent some of the most recent and productive ways in which personal information has been misused for financial gain internationally.

Electronic financial transactions

In the past, identity thieves were required to counterfeit or alter checks in order to commit transaction-based identity fraud. Now, all that is required is the ability to gain access to a network using a stolen logon and password and funds can be transferred seamlessly and instantaneously. In terms of international identity fraud, so-called 'card-not-present' transactions represent the greatest area of risk. These use account information including pseudo-account information without the physical card being involved, via the telephone, mail, internet etc. without the authority of the cardholder (APCA, 2009).

A recent example of a large-scale card-not-present fraud in Australia, that resulted in arrests in March 2009, concerned a syndicate of individuals based in New South Wales who were alleged to have purchased more than A$4.5m in goods using credit cards bearing bank account details 'skimmed' or stolen from legitimate card-holders. The goods, including brand new LCD televisions, laptop computers, cameras, power tools, GPS systems and iPods, were then allegedly sold on various online auction sites at reduced prices, allowing the syndicate to launder the profits. The syndicate had been in operation for some time and had allegedly sold 6,000 items for A$1.3 million (New South Wales Police Force, 2009).

In March 2008, the Association of Payment Clearing Services, now the UK Payments Administration Ltd (APACS, 2008) reported that there had been a 25 percent rise in the fraudulent use of United Kingdom credit and debit cards in 2007, with losses amounting to £535m. Some £290.5m of this took place on the internet, via phone or mail order, where the credit or debit card holder was not present, a year-on-year rise of 37 percent. APACS indicated that the first rise in three years of overall card fraud was mainly due to stolen and counterfeit cards used abroad. Card fraud overseas rose by 77 percent in 2008 to £208m and accounted for 39 percent of the total (ibid.).

The recent introduction of Chip and PIN cards in the United Kingdom and certain other countries has made it more difficult to commit fraud, although evidence has emerged of the ability to compromise even the more secure Chip and PIN reader technologies (Drimer, Murdoch and Anderson, 2008). Concerns of displacement are also evident, for although incidents of payment card fraud may be decreasing in the United Kingdom, there has been a increase in overseas fraud involving British victims as data from stolen Chip and PIN cards is transferred to magnetic stripe cards and used in jurisdictions that have not yet integrated Chip and PIN technologies (APACS, 2008).

Mobile and wireless transactions

Identity crime facilitated through the internet is also beginning to be perpetrated through wireless communication systems, some of which have less robust security measures in place. Mobile and wireless devices, such as third-generation (3G) and fourth-generation (4G) mobile phones and PDAs equipped with global system for mobile communications/general packet radio service (GSM/GPRS), will become increasingly important tools for assessing information when personal (desktop) computers are no longer the main means of computing. Mobile devices and networks will continue to become more capable and better able to support a wide range of communication and collaboration functions (Jones, 2006).

Wireless networks create a number of risks of relevance to identity crime. Of particular concern is the potential for users who have created an insecure and unencrypted network to have their network used by nearby users within wireless range of the available computer. This, itself, is a form of identity theft as the individual who makes use of an unsecured network is pretending to be the person who created that network and the person who is paying the ISP for the service provided. In one survey conducted by AusCERT of the security measures used by a sample of 1,001 adult home computer users with internet access in Australia, it was found that 16 percent of those surveyed used insecure wireless networks, and 5 percent of those surveyed admitted to using a neighbour's wireless connection (AusCERT, 2008).

Consumer scams

The development of the internet has been identified as a key factor in the expansion of consumer fraud (Choo *et al.*, 2007) as large numbers of potential victims can be located easily and unsolicited invitations can be sent without disclosing the true identity of the fraudsters. The principal technology used involves 'spamming' in which scam invitations are able to be sent in bulk by email to countless recipients at once, in any location in the world. The use of networks of millions of compromised computers known as botnets has created the opportunity to target an ever-increasing pool of potential victims and greater opportunities for organization and networking between groups and perpetrators of fraud.

Criminal misuse of identity lies at the heart of most consumer scams, with offenders pretending to be other people or businesses in order to trick the victim into participating in the scam, while at the same time making their own identity hard for police to discover. A good example of this concerns the various advance fee frauds perpetrated by a group of West Africans and others since the 1980s globally. Various offenders began working from Nigeria targeting victims across the globe. Email has proved to be an effective way of disseminating advance fee letters as the true identity of the sender is easy to disguise and original supporting documentation unable to be checked for authenticity.

The extent of the problem

Determining the size of the problem of identity crime can be approached from a number of perspectives, each of which has its own problems and limitations. Some of the main impediments to the effective quantification of the extent of the problem of identity crime are as follows. First, as already noted, the concept of identity crime is far from settled, making categorization for the purpose of counting crimes and offenders in official statistics problematic. Secondly, the units of measurement are often not clearly delineated, varying from exposure to risks, through participation in criminal conduct, to actual victimization and financial loss. Survey research also presents problems in this area, although the difficulties of conducting large scale, costly surveys, achieving meaningful response rates and representative results are by no means unique to the field of identity crime. Further, because many identity criminals implicate victims in the criminal enterprise, official reporting rates tend to be low as victims may be fearful of official action being taken against them for participating in a criminal activity. Victims are also often unwilling to publicly describe the details of their sometimes less than cautious conduct in sharing passwords or failing to secure personal information. Bearing these limitations in mind, the following data have been collected concerning identity crime incidence and cost.

In Australia, the Australian Bureau of Statistics (ABS, 2008) undertook a study on personal fraud in 2007 in which over 14,000 participants aged 15 years and over were asked about all fraud incidents that they had experienced in the previous 12 months. It was found that a total of 806,000 Australians aged 15 and over had been victims of personal fraud in the preceding 12 months. This equated to approximately 5 percent of the Australian population. Of these, over 450,000 victims lost money as a result of the fraud. Of this 5 percent, identity fraud accounted for 499,500 victims in Australia or 3 percent of the population. Of the 499,500 victims of identity fraud, the majority (383,300 or 77 percent) were a victim of credit or bank card fraud. This equated to a victimization rate of 2.4 percent. These victims experienced at least one unauthorized, fraudulent transaction using their cards or account details. Identity theft accounted for 124,000 victims of identity fraud.

In the United States, Javelin Strategy and Research (2008) conducted a survey of 5,075 consumers, representative of the United States population, to determine the manner in which identity theft occurred. Some 445 (8.8 percent) of those interviewed were victims of identity fraud. Contrary to popular belief, in cases where victims knew how their data had been stolen, online identity theft methods (phishing, hacking and spyware) only constituted 12 percent of fraud cases. The vast majority of known cases occurred through traditional methods (79 percent), when a criminal made direct contact with the consumer's personal identification. These instances include stolen and lost wallets, checkbooks or credit cards, 'shoulder surfing' (when someone looks over your shoulder at an ATM or cash register) and stolen mail from unlocked letter boxes. So-called 'friendly theft' was reported by 17 percent of victims, such as when friends, family or in-home employees took private data for their personal gain (ibid., pp. 5–6).

In the United Kingdom, 150 online merchants and 1,000 online shoppers were surveyed in 2008 (CyberSource, 2009, p. 9). It was found that online fraud had increased since the 2007 survey, and that fraud losses in 2008 consumed more than 1 percent of revenue for 37 percent of United Kingdom online merchants. Some 13 percent lost more than 5 percent of their revenue and 54 percent of merchants indicated that theft of customer data was their greatest business threat, followed by 52 percent who identified online fraud as the greatest threat. Merchants also identified as the two most common methods used by fraudsters, making multiple orders with similar identity data but different card numbers (38 percent) and using multiple identities using the same card number (34 percent) – both examples of online identity crime (ibid.).

CyberSource also interviewed 1,000 adults in the United Kingdom, aged 16 years or more, during the weekend of the 17 to 19 October 2008. The survey group was designed to be nationally representative of adults throughout the United Kingdom, and weighting was applied to the results to bring the data in line with national profiles. It was found that 66 percent of those who responded indicated that that they were concerned about the level of risk when shopping online. Over one in three claimed to have been a victim of online credit card fraud, or to have known someone who was (ibid., p. 16).

The cost of identity crime

Attempts to quantify the overall cost of identity crime have faced a range of challenges as official crime statistics rarely include a discrete category of identity crime, or identity fraud, while surveys have often been small in scale and insufficiently specific to permit accurate costing of identity crime categories. The most recent available evidence is as follows.

In the United Kingdom, identity fraud was estimated to cost £1.3 billion involving 80,000 victims in 2005 (Levi *et al.*, 2007). Another survey by CIFAS (2006), the United Kingdom's Fraud Prevention Service, found the number of victims of impersonation to be more than 67,000, with total cases of identity fraud reported at over 80,000.

In Australia, the Securities Industry Research Centre of Asia–Pacific (SIRCA) in 2003 claimed that identity fraud cost Australian large business A$1.1 billion in the year 2001–2 (Cuganesan and Lacey, 2003). As we have seen, victims of personal fraud in Australia reported losses of A$977 million in 2007. Some 16.3 percent of respondents said that in respect of the most recent incident of identity theft, they had incurred a financial loss, with 8.0 percent losing A$500 or less and a further 8.2 percent losing more than A$501 (ABS, 2008, p. 15).

In the United States, the Javelin Strategy and Research survey found that 445 (8.8 percent) of those interviewed reported being victims of identity theft. Between 2007 and 2008, 8.1 million Americans (4 percent of the adult population) reported being victimized by identity fraud, losing an estimated US$45 billion. Over the preceding four years, both the total number of victims and the overall monetary losses have steadily decreased. However, the time spent by victims in resolving identity fraud cases increased (Javelin Strategy and Research, 2008, pp. 5–6).

Also in the United States, between January and December 2005, Consumer Sentinel, the complaint database developed and maintained by the Federal Trade Commission, received over 685,000 consumer fraud and identity theft complaints, 37 percent of which concerned identity theft. Consumers reported losses from fraud of more than US$680 million in 2005 (Federal Trade Commission, 2006).

In Canada, a national survey of 1,000 Canadians, aged 18 years and older, conducted in mid-March 2005, found that 20 percent had been victims of identity theft, an increase of 5 percent on the corresponding figure in the 2003 survey (Canadian Competition Bureau, 2005). In 2002, Public Safety and Emergency Preparedness Canada (2004) estimated that total losses due to identity theft were approximately Can$2.5 billion.

Responses

A wide range of measures have been developed to deal with identity crime, many of which are described in the extensive compendia produced by the United States President's Taskforce on Identity Fraud (2008) and in reports on identity crime to the United Nations Commission on Crime Prevention and Criminal Justice (United Nations, 2007). White and Fisher (2008), in the United States, and Smith (2003), in Australia, have also provided full reviews of the specific measures designed to reduce identity crime committed in the transnational online environment. The most frequently adopted responses to identity crime risks relate to legislative reform, improvement of identification procedures, user education and victim support.

Legislative reform

The legislative responses to identity crime generally fall within four areas: amendments to laws that proscribe financial crime and fraud; laws which proscribe the criminal misuse of computers and computer networks; laws which provide for the introduction and use of identity cards and other types of identifiers; and laws which proscribe identity crime specifically. Legislative reform to deal with identity-related crime is one of the specific measures identified at the Eighteenth Session of the United Nations Commission on Crime Prevention and Criminal Justice that will contribute to the delineation of a guidance framework on the most appropriate initiatives to be prioritized and pursued in the future (United Nations, 2009).

In the United States, specific legislation was introduced to deal with identity-related crime some time ago. The Federal Identity Theft and Assumption Deterrence Act 1998 (18 USC 1028), which became effective on 30 October 1998, made identity theft a crime with maximum penalties of up to 15 years' imprisonment and a maximum fine of US$250,000. It established that the person whose identity has been stolen is a victim who is able to seek restitution following a conviction. It also gives the Federal Trade Commission power to act as a clearing house for complaints, referrals and resources for assistance for victims of identity theft.

In Australia, three states, South Australia, Queensland and Victoria, currently have specific identity fraud legislation. The Victorian Crimes Amendment (Identity Crime) Act 2009 created new offences of assuming a false identity with intent to commit a serious offence; making, using or supplying identification information with intent to commit an indictable offence (which carries a maximum penalty of five years' imprisonment); possessing identification information with intent to commit an indictable offence (which carries a maximum penalty of three years' imprisonment); and possessing equipment capable of making identification information with intention to use in the commission of an indictable offence (which also carries a maximum penalty of five years' imprisonment). The legislation does not apply to using one's own identification information and it is not a defense to a charge that the victim consented to the use of the victim's personal information. Attempting to commit these offences is also not a separate criminal offence and the law applies even if the commission of the indictable offence is impossible. The Victorian law also applies to deceased persons' identities that have been misused and to entirely fictitious identities. Finally, the legislation gives power to courts to issue an identity crime certificate to victims to verify the fact of their victimization. This can be used to assist victims in re-establishing their stolen identities and in ensuring that they are not liable for crimes committed in their name. The certificate is, however, not a remedy in that it does not compel others to take restorative action – for example, it does not compel financial institutions to reinstate a person's credit rating. Rather, the certificate provides a means to present the outcome of a court's decision in a way that may be readily used by the victim to ensure the outcome of the legal proceeding (Standing Committee of Attorneys-General, 2008).

In the United Kingdom, the Identity Cards Act 2006 (Eng.) prohibits the use of all false identity documents. This is supported by a range of new measures to respond to identity crime which are coordinated by an Identity Crime Task Force, chaired by the National Fraud Authority. This Task Force is acting to implement a 28-point action plan to combat identity crimes throughout the United Kingdom (National Fraud Authority, 2010, p. 35).

Identification procedures

A range of policy reforms have also been devised to improve identification procedures used by government and business and, importantly, to enable agencies to verify documents and information tendered as evidence of identity with issuing agencies. In many countries, documents used to establish identity are issued by a number of government agencies including passport offices, birth registries and drivers' license issuing agencies. Cross-validation enables inconsistencies to be ascertained and identity-related fraud minimized. The solutions to the problem lie not so much in increasing the number of proof of identity documents required, but in improving the security features of documents, enabling staff who inspect documents for authenticity to be able to detect counterfeits and to verify the information contained on documents with the issuing source, and for alternative means of identification to be used, such as interviews, or biometrics.

In the United Kingdom, efforts have been made to address the creation of false documents, the use of specialist printing equipment by criminals, fraudsters obtaining genuine identity credentials and websites that sell false identities (National Fraud Authority, 2010, p. 35). In addition, in November 2009, the Identity and Passport Service began to issue identity cards on a voluntary basis to British citizens aged 16 and over, resident or working in Greater Manchester. Identity cards were also offered to British and European Economic Area nationals working at Manchester and London City airports, as well as people in the North West region, those aged 16 to 24 in London and those who had registered an interest (ibid.).

Biometric identification systems are also attracting great interest for the apparently higher level of integrity that they offer in comparison to the standard knowledge-based and token-based systems of identification (see Smith, 2003). There is a wide variety of such systems being used which make use of an individual's unique physical properties. Common biometric identifiers today include fingerprints, voice patterns, typing patterns, retinal images, facial or hand geometry, and even the identification of a person's subcutaneous vein structures or body odors. Although such systems achieve much higher levels of security than those which rely upon passwords, they are expensive to introduce and raise potential problems in terms of privacy and confidentiality of the personal data stored on computer networks (see Smith, 2003).

User education and victim support

Considerable effort is made each year by government and private sector organizations in seeking to educate consumers as to the risks of identity crime, especially those forms which occur online. Targeted education campaigns are conducted each year by members of the International Consumer Protection and Enforcement Network (ICPEN).

In the United States, the Identity Theft and Assumption Deterrence Act 1998 created a centralized victim assistance, complaint and consumer education service for victims of identity theft. This means that victims need not contact each of the relevant agencies separately. Instead, there is a 'joint fraud alert' that the three major credit reporting agencies administer. Victims can access assistance in the absence of a conviction for identity theft. The Fair and Accurate Credit Transactions Act 2003 also introduced a series of protections for consumers. Consumers are able to obtain a free credit report on request, to help them monitor their financial information and provide an early alert of unlawful activity. Consumers can also place a fraud alert on their account. Once the alert has been placed on the account, credit reporting agencies must block potentially fraudulent information on consumer credit reports from being released. In Britain, similar support services for victims are being introduced as part of the National Fraud Strategy (National Fraud Authority, 2010).

Conclusion

This chapter has outlined various identity crime risks that have arisen internationally in recent times, and identified some of the key issues to be addressed in responding to the problem. It is clear that there is not a single solution to identity crime and that a range of measures will need to be adopted that will involve both government agencies as well as organizations in the private sector all working cooperatively across the globe. Technology will provide some solutions, such as the development of biometric identification systems, but these will not solve all of the problems as technological solutions, no matter how sophisticated, are able to be circumvented by those with the necessary skills and resources.

Adopting a range of identification strategies is likely to be the most effective response coupled with appropriate and secure sharing of information across agencies. At the same time, privacy considerations need to be taken into account and legislation reviewed to keep pace with technological developments.

Future research questions

1. In what ways can various biometric systems be compromised by criminals and what risk management strategies can be devised to deal with these?
2. In what ways can crime displacement effects arise following the implementation of identity crime prevention measures, and how can these be addressed?
3. To what extent has the introduction of computer chip payment cards used in conjunction with Personal Identification Numbers been effective in reducing plastic card fraud? One possible project could examine this by comparing rates of plastic card fraud in the United States with those in the United Kingdom.
4. How do computer users manage passwords? What are the associated risks? What is the extent of misuse and compromise of passwords? And how these can be addressed? One possible method would be to survey a sample of members of the public.
5. What legislative and evidentiary problems have arisen in trials? How can they be addressed? One way is to analyze a sample of completed prosecution files concerning criminal misuse of identity.

Note

1 This chapter is a condensed and revised version of the author's chapter 'Identity fraud and theft,' published in Yvonne Jewkes and Majid Yar (Eds.) *Handbook of internet crime* (Willan Publishing: Cullompton, 2010) and is reproduced with the permission of Willan Publishing.

References

Association of Payment Clearing Services (APACS) (2008). *Fraud: the facts 2008*. London: APACS.

AusCERT (2008). *Home Users Computer Security Survey*. Brisbane: AusCERT. See http://www.auscert.org.au.

Australian Bureau of Statistics (2008). *Personal fraud 2007*. Cat no 4528.0. Melbourne: Australian Bureau of Statistics.

Australian Payments Clearing Association (APCA) (2009). *Fraud Perpetrated on Cheques and Plastic Cards*. Sydney: Australian Payments Clearing Association. See http://www.apca.com.au.

Anti-Phishing Working Group (2009). *Phishing activity trends report – July to December 2008*. San Francisco: Anti-Phishing Working Group. Online at http://www.antiphishing.org (accessed November 20, 2010).

British Broadcasting Corporation (BBC) (2008) HSBC loses customers' data disc, 7 April. Online at http://news.bbc.co.uk/1/hi/business/7334249.stm (accessed November 20, 2010).

Canadian Competition Bureau (2005). *Findings from the 2005 Fraud Awareness Tracking Study*. Ottawa: Canadian Competition Bureau.

Choo, K-K. R., Smith, R. G. and McCusker, R. (2007). *Future directions in technology-enabled crime*. Research and Public Policy Series no 78. Canberra: Australian Institute of Criminology.

CIFAS (2006). *Online fraud trends*. London: CIFAS. Online at http://www.cifas.org.uk/press_20070130.asp (accessed November 20, 2010).

Cuganesan, S. and Lacey, D. (2003). *Identity fraud in Australia: an evaluation of its nature, cost and extent*. Sydney: SIRCA.

CyberSource (2009). *Fifth annual UK online fraud report*. Reading: CyberSource.

Dhamija, R., Tygar, J. D., and Hearst, M. (2006). Why phishing works. CHI 2006, April 22–7. Montreal: CHI.

Drimer, S., Murdoch, S. J., and Anderson R. (2008). Thinking inside the box: system-level failures of tamper proofing. Paper presented at the IEEE Symposium on Security and Privacy, May, Oakland, California.

European Network and Information Security Agency (2007). *Security issues and recommendations for online social networks*. ENISA Position Paper no. 1. Heraklion: European Network and Information Security Agency.

Federal Trade Commission (2006). *Consumer fraud in the United States: an FTC survey*. Washington: Federal Trade Commission.

Information Commissioner's Office (2007). Confidential details lost by revenue and customs. 20 November. London: Information Commissioner's Office. Online at http://www.ico.gov.uk/upload/documents/pressreleases/2007/personal_details_lost_by_hmrc_201107003.pdf (accessed November 20, 2010).

Javelin Strategy and Research (2008). 2008 identity fraud survey report: consumer version. Pleasanton CA: Javelin Strategy and Research.

Jones, N. (2006) *Europeans expect mobile technology to facilitate collaboration in 2009*. Stamford CT: Gartner.

Krim, J. and Barbaro, M. (2005). 40 million credit card numbers hacked. *Washington Post*, 18 June. Online at http://www.washingtonpost.com/wp-dyn/content/article/2005/06/17/AR2005061701031_2.html (accessed November 20, 2010).

Levi, M. (2009). Suite revenge? The shaping of folk devils and moral panics about white-collar crimes. *The British Journal of Criminology*, 49(1): 48–67.

Levi, M., Burrows, J., Fleming, M. H., Hopkins, M., and Matthews, K. (2007). *The nature, extent and economic impact of fraud in the UK: report for the Association of Chief Police Officers Economic Crime Portfolio*. London: Association of Chief Police Officers.

McAfee (2005). *McAfee virtual criminology report*. Santa Clara: McAfee.

National Fraud Authority (2010). *A Fresh Approach to Combating Fraud in the Public Sector: The Report of the Smarter Government Public Sector Fraud Taskforce*. London: National Fraud Authority. Online at http://www.attorneygeneral.gov.uk/nfa/WhatAreWeSaying/Documents/Smarter%20Government%20Public%20Sector%20Fraud%20Taskforce.pdf (accessed November 20, 2010).

New South Wales Police Force (2009). Police and eBay smash multi-million dollar fraud syndicate. *Media Release.* 10 March. Sydney: New South Wales Police Force.

Ofcom. (2008). *Social networking: a quantitative and qualitative research report into attitudes, behaviours and use.* London: Office of Communications. Online at http://stakeholders.ofcom.org.uk/binaries/research/media-literacy/report1.pdf (accessed November 20, 2010).

Public Safety and Emergency Preparedness Canada (2004). *Report on identity theft.* Ottawa: Public Safety and Emergency Preparedness Canada.

Smith, R. G. (2003). Travelling in cyberspace on a false passport: controlling transnational identity-related crime. In R. Tarling (Ed.) *The British Criminology Conference: Selected Proceedings,* vol 5. Papers from the British Society of Criminology Conference, Keele, British Society of Criminology. Online at http://www.britsoccrim.org/volume5/004.pdf (accessed November 20, 2010).

Standing Committee of Attorneys-General (2008). *Final report: identity crime.* Canberra: Model Criminal Law Officers' Committee of the Standing Committee of Attorneys-General.

Symantec (2007). *Internet security threat report.* Cupertino: Symantec.

United Nations (2007). *Results of the second meeting of the intergovernmental expert group to prepare a study on fraud and the criminal misuse and falsification of identity.* Report of the Secretary-General, E/CN.15/2007/1. Vienna: Commission on Crime Prevention and Criminal Justice Sixteenth Session.

United Nations (2009). *International cooperation in the prevention, investigation, prosecution and punishment of economic fraud and identity-related crime.* Report of the Secretary-General, E/CN.15/2009/1. Vienna: Commission on Crime Prevention and Criminal Justice Eighteenth Session.

United States President's Taskforce on Identity Theft (2008). *President's Identity Theft Taskforce report.* Washington: United States President's Taskforce on Identity Theft.

White, M. D and Fisher, C. (2008). Assessing our knowledge of identity theft: the challenges to effective prevention and control efforts. *Criminal Justice Policy Review,* 19(1): 3–24.

16

Cybercrime and online safety in cyberspace

Roderic Broadhurst and Kim-Kwang Raymond Choo

Introduction

Information and communications technologies (ICT) have become a crucial element in our day-to-day activities. This is hardly surprising as the proliferation of ICT and connectivity of the Internet in today's information age open the door to increased productivity, faster communication capabilities, and immeasurable convenience. Unfortunately, our increased dependence on ICT and the pervasive interconnectivity of our ICT infrastructure also expose us to an evolving spectrum of cyber-threats.

Cybercrime is essentially a transnational crime with a "modus operandi" that exploits inter-state differences in the capacity to respond to such crime, and appears in the same company as such powerful global concerns as civil war, genocide, and poverty (United Nations, 2004). This transnational characteristic provides cybercriminals, especially organized crime, with the ability to avoid countermeasures even when implemented by capable actors (Brenner, 2002, 2006; Council of Europe, 2004). Although some have questioned the existence of organized criminal activities in cyberspace, several studies have noted the potential and actual synergy between organized crime and cyberspace in recent years. McCusker (2006, p. 257), for example, suggested that "cybercrime has become an integral part of the transnational threat landscape, and conjures up pressing images of nefarious and increasingly complex online activity."

Choo (2008) outlined three categories of organized groups in cyberspace:

1. Traditional organized crime groups which make use of ICT to enhance their terrestrial criminal activities;
2. Organized cybercriminal groups which operate exclusively online; and
3. Organized groups of ideologically and politically motivated individuals who make use of ICT to facilitate their criminal conduct.

These forms of organized crime look to exploit cyberspace in a number of different ways by committing a wide range of crimes that may be conducted or enhanced by computer and digital devices.

Cybercrime offenses

Although there is no definitive list of what constitutes cybercrime or computer-related crime, the following presents the typical scope of offenses that occur in cyberspace.

1. Telecommunications theft and illegal interception
2. Piracy copyright theft
3. Cyber stalking
4. Electronic money laundering and tax evasion
5. Electronic vandalism, cyber-terrorism, denial of service, extortion
6. Sales and investment fraud, forgery (classic pyramid schemes)
7. Electronic funds transfer fraud and counterfeiting (carding, identity theft and misrepresentation)
8. Content crime – offensive materials
9. Espionage
10. Resource theft – illegal use of personal computers (PCs) or other digital devices

Cybercrime ranges across a wide spectrum of activities and behaviors: at one end are crimes that involve fundamental breaches of personal or corporate privacy, such as assaults on the integrity of information held in digital depositories, identity theft, and the use of illegally obtained digital information to blackmail a firm or individual. Midway along the spectrum are transaction-based crimes such as fraud, trafficking in child pornography, digital piracy, money laundering, and counterfeiting. These are specific crimes with specific victims, but the offender hides in the relative anonymity provided by the Internet. Another aspect of this type of crime involves those that deliberately alter data for either profit, or personal or political objectives. At the other end of the spectrum are those crimes that involve attempts to disrupt the actual workings of the Internet. These include spamming, hacking, and denial of service attacks against specific sites to acts of cyber-terrorism by non-state actors – that is, the use of the Internet to affect a nation's economic and technological infrastructure and cause public disorder or disturbances and even death (Broadhurst and Chantler, 2006).

The threat environment

Cyberspace provides criminal actors a safe haven that enhances their organizational and operational capabilities. Information security and associated laws and policy are also less well developed in emerging economies, thus providing an environment in which criminal activities can be conducted at lower risk but still have an impact on advanced economies (Choo *et al.*, 2007). Such threats are increasingly important and strategically relevant (Rudd, 2008). For example, a 2008 report of the Centre for Strategic and International Studies (CSIS) Commission on Cybersecurity for the 44th Presidency began with a central finding: "The United States must treat cyber-security as one of most important national security challenges it faces" (CSIS, 2008). A 2009 Australian Defence white paper also voiced similar concerns.

ICT advances have undeniably changed the way criminals conduct their activities, and policing also needs to adapt enforcement strategies that reflect changes in society. With the increasing digitalization of information, "policing will be carried out over a borderless community, rather than within the confines of national boundaries" (Sim, 2000, p. 116).

Data breaches

Almost every business in developed economies makes use of the Internet. As businesses continue to engage in electronic commerce, they will become increasingly globalized and interconnected and the level of data being created by society is set to increase. In terms of the future threat landscape, it is argued that the increased variety and volume of attacks are inevitable given transnational crime networks' desire to obtain personal and confidential information. Not all criminal misuse of computers or digital devices involves hacking, since passwords, PIN (personal identification numbers), and other protective codes can be obtained by "social engineering"[1] to gain access then erase, modify, or copy the information to suit the needs of their attack (Guenther, 2001). Non-physical data breaches (e.g. due to computer or network intrusions) are a cause for concern. According to the data breach investigations conducted by Verizon Business from 2004 to 2008, for example, only 9 percent of the 90 data breaches (involving 285 million compromised records) were attributed to physical attacks. In the Verizon investigations, hacking is one of the leading causes of data breaches (64 percent of cases) and reportedly a favored technique of cybercriminals, and "unauthorized access via default, shared, or stolen credentials constituted more than a third of the entire Hacking category and over half of all compromised records" (Verizon, 2009, p. 16).

The involvement of organized crime groups in computer or network intrusions such as hacking and unauthorized access to obtain sensitive information now emphasizes the importance of large-scale profit-driven incentives. As noted by Peretti (2009, p. 379), a Senior Counsel with the United States Department of Justice's Computer Crime and Intellectual Property Section, "compromise of credit and debit card account information most often results in the type of identity theft referred to as 'account takeover,' which involves fraud on existing financial accounts.". For example in a recent case in the United States, two accused persons were indicted on charges of "unlawfully, intentionally, and knowingly, acting in interstate and foreign commerce," via access of a computer and "thereby obtaining information from a protected computer for the purposes of commercial advantage and private financial gain." According to court documents, both accused persons (and others known and unknown) "allegedly participated in a scheme to steal funds from bank and brokerage accounts by hacking into those accounts through the Internet, using personal financial information obtained through computer viruses" (*United States of America* v. *Alexander Bobnev and Alexey Mineev*).[2] The accused persons subsequently sent a portion of the stolen funds to their associates in Russia using money-remitting services after keeping a portion of the fraud proceeds for themselves.

Internet frauds, scams, and phishing

In online or Internet scams, cybercriminals approach potential victims across the globe by sending unsolicited messages purporting to originate from legitimate organizations in order to deceive individuals or organizations into disclosing their financial and/or personal identity information. Information obtained from "phishing"[3] and other illegal means is often for the purpose of using it to commit or facilitate crimes such as financial fraud and identity theft. A 2008 Gartner survey of 4,988 American adults, for example, indicated that top causes for financial fraud against consumers and payment card frauds are data breaches at a retailer, government agency or other, and third party phishing (Litan, 2009). The biennial KPMG fraud survey of 420 organizations in Australia and New Zealand reported similar findings. Within the financial services sector, credit card fraud accounted for 39 percent of the value of fraud attributable to external parties. Fraudulent access to financial services' accounts (by adopting the identity of the account holder by "phishing" or "Trojan horse" attacks over the Internet) amounted to 31 percent of the total value attributable to external parties (KPMG Forensic, 2009, p. 13). Several researchers and security practitioners have also suggested the involvement of organized crime groups in phishing scams and messages are increasingly targeting top company executives – also known as "spear phishing" or "whaling" in reference to bigger "fish" (Choo and Smith, 2008).

Organized crime groups have also been known to use identity fraud to either conceal their identities to evade detection and protect their assets from confiscation or as an enabler to commit various frauds and other crimes. Internet frauds and scams include "advance fee" frauds (also known as "419" cases named after the relevant section of the Nigerian Criminal Code), online auction frauds, and identity and payment card frauds. These take many forms but include enticements to use your bank account to deposit the plunder of a former despot in Africa, administrative fees to transfer a huge lottery pay-out (for which you strangely cannot remember buying a ticket), or the bond money and advance rent for a non-existent but reasonably priced apartment suitable for an international student, and so on. Out of 275,284 complaints to the Internet Crime Complaint Centre in 2008, 26.5 percent or 72,940 cases were reported to US law enforcement: online auction fraud accounted for 25.5 percent of the reported cases and 16.3 percent of the total loss; payment card fraud accounted for 9 percent of cases and 4.7 percent of the total loss; and Nigerian advance fee scam accounted for 2.8 percent of cases and 5.2 percent of the total loss. The total monetary loss from all *reported* cases of Internet fraud and scams to United States law enforcement agencies in 2008 was $264.6 million USD – an increase of 10 percent from 2007(NW3C, 2009).

Malware creation and dissemination

McAfee (2008)'s virtual crime report indicated that cybercriminals are increasingly exploiting vulnerabilities in software and applying social engineering to spawn a broad range of threats including spyware, phishing, adware, rootkits,[4] and botnets. In 2008, Symantec (2009, p. 15) reported that new malicious code had increased by 265 percent since 2007 and 60 percent of all current malicious code was detected in 2008.

Malware[5] is software designed to infiltrate, compromise security, or damage a computer system, without the owner's informed consent and includes viruses, worms,[6] backdoors, keyloggers, and trojans. The 2008 UK Threat Assessment report observed that "most new malware is designed to steal financial data (such as credit card details, bank account details, passwords, and PINs) as a precursor to various frauds and other deceptions" (SOCA, 2008, p. 9). An example of information stealing malware is keylogging programs that are designed to monitor user activity including keystrokes. This can then be used by cybercriminals to steal passwords or credit card details, which can then be used for malicious purposes such as identity/online fraud. An example of a "keylogger" case was the attempted theft of more than £229m from Sumitomo Matsui Banking Corporation in London. Three individuals were extradited to the UK from Belgium and Spain and £1.5m in assets was (reportedly) restrained (SOCA, 2009).

McAfee (2005) estimated that the number of potentially malicious threats emerging each month increased from roughly 300 to 2,000 between 2003 and 2005, largely due to the growth of bot-malware.[7] Sophos (2006), an IT security company, noted that an unpatched computer without antivirus protection or a firewall would have a 50 percent chance of becoming a zombie within 30 minutes of being connected to the Internet. Bot malware are often surreptitiously forwarded to victims by various means, such as via email attachments, peer-to-peer (P2P) networks, and visits to an infected website. Building botnets requires minimal levels of expertise

(Ianelli and Hackworth, 2005; Choo, 2007). Bot malware typically takes advantage of system vulnerabilities and software bugs or hacker-installed backdoors that allow malicious code to be installed on computers without the owners' consent or knowledge.

Compromised computers (also known as bots) are then turned into zombies. The shift in motivation from curiosity and fame seeking to illicit financial gain has been marked by a growing sophistication in the evolution of bot malware, as illustrated by recent examples of detected bot malware such as Conficker. Conficker has received a considerable amount of media attention, and has been reported to have successfully infiltrated government networks, home PCs, critical infrastructure, and universities (Porras *et al.*, 2009). According to analysis of the Conficker and its variants (Conficker B and C) by Sophos and the Malware Threat Centre at SRI International, Conficker was designed to provide a secure binary updating service that effectively allows the bot malware designer instant control of millions of PCs. The design included sophisticated defensive mechanisms such as binary encryption methods and compiler-level code obfuscation to hinder detection by anti-malware software. Reverse engineering was made more difficult for investigators analyzing the malware (Porras *et al.*, 2009; Fitzgibbon and Wood, 2009)

Compromised computers – zombies – can then be used as remote attack tools or to form part of a botnet under the control of the botnet controller. According to Symantec (2009), bot networks accounted approximately 90 percent of all spam email in 2008. A 2008 report by McAfee also stated that:

> the number of compromised zombie PCs in botnets has quadrupled in the last quarter alone and that these are capable of flooding the Internet with more than 100 billion spam messages per day . . . [and] are increasingly switching to phishing, distributed denial of service (DDoS) and website attacks which are capable of causing a huge amount of damage and are a growing threat to the security of nations, the national information infrastructure, and the economy
>
> *(McAfee, 2008, p. 5)*

Although malware are still disseminated using conventional tools such as email, cybercriminals have turned recently to exploiting browser plug-in and webserver vulnerabilities. A large number of commercial, government, university, and other high-profile and high-traffic websites worldwide apparently may have been successfully compromised to allow "infection" of unwitting visitors with malware. For example in May 2009, the UK regional director of Finjan, an IT provider of secure web gateway solutions, noted that a botnet discovered by the company in February 2009 contained 1.9 million infected computers including 73 government domains (Raywood, 2009). Similarly in the first quarter of 2009, McAfee (2009, p. 3) reported an increase in the number of malicious websites created and "sites that host malware– with thousands of new sites appearing daily." They also discovered a search-engine-optimization ring that targeted the top Google search terms to enable the installation of anti-virus software. Business, government, and individual householders need to be aware of risk mitigation strategies and implement and update them because search engine optimization will continue to be one of the most sought after attack vectors by criminals.

Responses and countermeasures

The threat of cybercrime has given rise to a demand for strategies for prevention and control, particularly in the area of organized crime in cyberspace. Some of the key approaches reduce opportunities for the commission of cybercrime, making such activities more difficult to commit, increasing the risks of detection, enhancing the level and certainty of sanctions, and reducing the benefits likely to be derived from committing such crimes. For example in the context of keeping children safe online, international treaties such as the Council of Europe (CoE) Convention on the Protection of Children against Sexual Exploitation have been introduced to deal with child sex offenses. A recent report, for example, pointed out that countries, particularly common law jurisdictions such as Australia, Canada, Singapore, United States and United Kingdom, have introduced online child grooming offenses and laws that regulate the behavior of sexual offenders on release from custody, such as sex offender registration and community notification (Choo, 2009).

Anticipating the likely actions of transnational criminals and terrorists is a key role of law enforcement agencies. The effectiveness of these responses is debatable given the hierarchical nature of law enforcement agencies, inter-agency rivalry, and organizational pathology deemed to exist within some intelligence systems (see, for example, Sheptycki, 2004; Walker *et al.*, 2006). In our increasingly interconnected world, threats to national security can come from unexpected sources and directions.

Organized crime and cybercrime appear to have grown in volume and impact, and both will increasingly affect the financial security of online business in addition to continuing to cause social harm to individuals and social cohesion (Morris, 2004; Broadhurst and Grabosky, 2005; Choo and Smith, 2008). The widespread incidence of identity theft, including online theft of virtual identities, for example, is a major challenge since such theft is a common precursor offense that requires a broad-based prevention effort (White and Fisher, 2008). Furthermore, the potential for mitigation of transnational cybercrime lies in effective public–private partnerships. The role of public policing agencies will be a necessary but only one part of the overall response to cybercrime (Wall, 2007). Convincing relevant private sector actors of the need to cooperate in crime prevention, and forging regional multi-lateral cooperation between jurisdictions in partnership with the public sector, are key challenges (Choo *et al.*, 2007). The "securitization" process evokes a crisis-like security context in order to permit extra-ordinary measures to reduce risk. How this may occur in a multi-lateral context, where harmonization of response to non-traditional security threats is relatively novel, is the immediate challenge for effective control of cybercrime "anarchy" (Thomas, 2009). Greater knowledge, and the recognition of a sense of "shared fate" in cyberspace, will quicken the development of multilateral responses and the capability for transnational crime control.

Organized crime and terrorist groups have also recognized the value of leveraging information and ICT to facilitate, or enhance the commission, of crimes and are dynamic in identifying new opportunities and ways to overcome countermeasures. Extraterritoriality, the notion that cyberspace has no geographic boundaries has driven the e-commerce revolution, but organized crime also operates online under the same free market principles. The emergence of an underground economy as the source/provider of illicit information may now indicate the level of professionalism and commercialization present in the transnational crime sector. The illicit enterprise nature of the current digital underground market is an example. Organized crime activities in cyberspace have serious implications for national security, and trends in cybercrime have shown that attacks are increasingly originating from regions where sanctions are often non-existent or operate as "on-costs," and enforcement is less robust. The need for greater uniformity/harmonization of cybercrime legislation within Australia and across the region will become more pronounced as the number of cybercrime cases increases as forecast (Grabosky and Broadhurst, 2005; McAfee, 2007; Choo *et al.*, 2007). Existing legislative regimes, despite attempts at "technical neutrality," remain vulnerable in the context of rapidly emerging, new generation technologies to commit crimes (Grabosky, 2007). In addition, existing offense definitions, although technically adequate, may be impossible to apply in practice (Brenner and Frederiksen, 2002). For example, in the case of the prosecution of "botnet" intrusions, evidence would need to be obtained concerning each of the thousands of computers that have been compromised – a gargantuan task. Thus a new offense category, such as creating a network for illegal purposes and selling/renting established botnets (networks of compromised computers) to commit or facilitate criminal activities, could be developed to deal with these threats.

The true impact of cybercrime is unknown due to poor detection and under-reporting, but cybercrime prosecutions involving multiple jurisdictions will be an essential response (Broadhurst and Grabosky, 2005; Choo *et al.*, 2007). Because online offending easily transcends borders, numerous territories can simultaneously assert jurisdiction, particularly when an attack transits multiple jurisdictions with different regimes for preserving evidence. Timely access to evidence located in one or more foreign jurisdictions may be difficult or impossible, as it would normally require the assistance of authorities in the foreign jurisdiction(s), who may be unwilling or unable to assist. When the suspect is located abroad, these difficulties are compounded. Countering the risks of cybercrime is a multi-dimensional challenge and requires effective coordination and collaborative efforts on the part of a wide range of government and private sector entities. Achieving some uniformity will be an essential strategy to minimize the risk of so-called safe havens and "jurisdiction shopping," in which offenders seek out countries from which to base their activities that have the least severe punishments or which have currently no extradition treaties.

A recent report by the Commission of the European Communities (2008), for example, highlighted the need to enhance cross-border law enforcement and judicial cooperation in the fight against transnational payment fraud, and improve the response of the UN, INTERPOL, and other international agencies efforts (Dandurand *et al.*, 2007). Nevertheless a review by Microsoft of the criminalization of cybercrime in several Asian jurisdictions[8] showed that serious gaps continue to exist in the "seamless web" of cyber laws needed to counter cybercrime (Microsoft, 2007). The review applied the CoE Cybercrime Convention bench-mark adopted by Japan and the Philippines and also influential in the development of laws in Thailand and Indonesia (Broadhurst, 2006b). The review noted the poor compliance with model privacy laws. Even for core offenses such as the criminalization of unauthorized access to computers, systems, programs and data some Asian countries had yet to enact laws or provide for civil remedy. Despite widespread public alarm only one jurisdiction met the model laws for online child safety and six countries did not have adequate laws.

Theoretical problems

The absence of settled theory about the interaction of organized crime with cyberspace is an impediment to the development of sound countermeasures. At present, crime prevention practices based on actor choice (cf. neo-classical deterrence theory) are usually applied with variable effect (Grabosky *et al.*, 2001; Newman and Clarke, 2003). Routine activity theory draws on rational exploitation of "opportunity" in the context of the regularity of human conduct (Felson, 1998; Yar, 2005) to design prevention strategies, especially where terrestrial interventions are possible – for example in the transit of goods. This approach assumes criminals are rational and appropriately resourced actors that operate in the context of high-value, attractive targets protected by weak guardians (e.g. ill-managed ISPs and jurisdictions with weak legal enforcement of the Internet). An assumption is that organized crime consists of profit-focused enterprises that seek out opportunities provided by cyberspace, and acquire the necessary resources for cybercrime by (inter alia) using delinquent IT professionals and targeting weakly protected computers/ networks or other digital devices. Consequently, deterrence (increased penalties and detection) is the preferred policy response enhanced by appropriately trained police (capable guardians) and target "hardening."

The myriad motivations of offenders requires no elaboration in the rational-choice model, and prevention strategies should be as effective against terrorists using the Internet as they would be for individual "hackers" seeking reputation, or organized crime seeking illicit gain. However, such an assumption in respect to some forms of cybercrime may be misplaced. There is an absence of evidence-based research about offender behavior and recruitment in cyberspace, although learning and imitation play important roles (Broadhurst, 2005). Hence, organized crime groups cannot be understood from just their illicit activities alone, that is – as rational profit-driven networks of criminal actors, since socio-cultural forces play an important role in the genesis and sustainability of such groups.

Alternative theoretical approaches that posit particular offender motives or pathologies, or the role of social conflict, have not featured widely in explanations of cybercrime. Early accounts of "hackers" emphasized individuality and a non-profit orientation, but also observed the likely shift to profit-oriented misuse as the Internet developed (Chantler, 1996). Indeed the role of social learning and offender pathology has been neglected but may play a significant role in predisposing some actors to criminal activity and risk-taking in cyberspace, where anonymity reduces social surveillance and self-control (Jayawardena and Broadhurst, 2007; Jones, 2007). Hate and so-called "content" crimes perpetrated via the Internet may reflect social or individual pathologies, and less the exercise of rational choice – although it may be "rational" to adopt Internet strategies of dissemination (Broadhurst, 2006a).

Functionalist approaches assume crime is a normal adaptation to change, and indeed represents a creative response to adversity (usually experienced as different forms of social exclusion) – cybercrime in this sense is normal, although novel in its form. Thus, the cost of suppression of cybercrime may only be achieved by curtailment of the Internet's natural advantages, such as low-cost connectivity. Another approach is to see the rise of certain forms of crime as a result of conflict within society and disputes about what constitutes "real" crime: here, the criminalization of an act represents the exercise of power by elites. Thus, defining behavior as deviant or criminal may represent only sectional interests with little real community support. For example, the practice of illegally copying digital media without paying the copyright holders has only been recently "criminalized," with attendant changes to community attitudes, opportunities for criminals, and policing practice.

Wikström and Treiber (2007, p. 244) noted that in order "to advance criminological theory we need a developed theory of action through which we can address causal mechanisms." Functionalist, learning, and conflict explanations, as well as choice theories, are often applied to explain organized crime. In the context of cyberspace, we have limited understanding and empirical sources about these "causes" with respect to profit and content forms (e.g. hate crime, child pornography, etc.) of cybercrime. We therefore propose the following:

1. The extent of profit-oriented cybercrime will index organized crime activity in cyberspace, and the more lucrative, the more likely organized crime rather than individual offenders will dominate, and – the corollary that – content-related cybercrime will reflect "pathology" and be dominated by individuals rather than organized crime.
2. Criminal networks operating in cyberspace will tend to be new forms of organized crime rather than traditional "mafia"-like groups. Traditional organized crime will have limited operations and focus on precursor offenses such as identity theft or money laundering.
3. Organized crime operating in cyberspace will trade primarily in the protection of illicit data and information (e.g. compromised credit card and identity details) and will be less likely to be engaged in systematic fraud/deception-related cybercrimes.

These propositions offer challenging research questions and are conditioned by the way we see cybercrime evolving with the advent of technological and behavioral changes among those who use the Internet.

Future trends

The use of "bots" is expected to increase in the near future. Botnets are expected to become involved in more sophisticated, targeted attacks and reflect a general trend toward more focused hacker attacks (Choo, 2007). While "syntactic" attacks such as worms and viruses were previously spread to cause disruption and inconvenience, the use of "semantic" or social-engineering methods such as "pharming"[9] are used to steal personal information that may be used to access bank accounts (Choo *et al.*, 2007). Therefore organized crime is expected to adopt this activity and take a more active role in future cyber crime. There will be a shift in targets from desktop computers to smart devices (i.e. cellular phones, Blackberrys) and other such Internet-linked personal organizers partly due to the ordinary user's inclination to store confidential information such as bank PINs on such devices. These are expected to become the next prime target for attacks (Chantler and Broadhurst, 2008; Choo *et al.*, 2007).

The introduction of commercial appliances linked to the Internet (e.g. vending machines, gas pumps, ATMs) and the increased usage of mobile phones to pay for such products suggests that this will be the target of malware in the future. Other non-PC devices will also be targeted. This includes routers, switches and backup devices. Furthermore, real-time programs such as IM (Instant Messaging) are likely to be increasingly targeted in the near future and are rapidly becoming a major risk vector (Choo *et al.* 2007). There appears to be a trend towards a greater emphasis on the development of semantic/human intelligence methods rather than the syntactic measures. This is due to semantic methods placing value on particular types of information (i.e. credit card information) rather than the use of syntactic methods to release viruses and denial-of-service attacks. Human-based social engineering is able to obtain information in many cases that technological methods are unable to. This further illustrates the changing trend towards profit-motivated attacks and the involvement of organized crime (Chantler and Broadhurst, 2008; Choo, 2008).

Research agenda

A 2007 inquiry into the future impact of serious and organized crime on Australian society raised concerns about "the increasing use of technology, transnational connections and fluidity of organized crime groups [that] will make law enforcement's task of policing organized crime's illicit activities more difficult" (PJCACC, 2007, p. 28). In the inquiry, the Australian Crime Commission "called for a greater involvement and contribution by academia to the body of research informing Australia's policy and operational choices in fighting organized crime" (PJCACC, 2007, p. 78).

The importance of looking ahead to future offending in the online environment was highlighted by Smith *et al.* (2004, p. 156) who, only seven years ago, noted that crime in the digital environment was prone to rapid change and "those who fail to anticipate the future are in for a rude shock when it arrives." An urgent research project would be to launch region-wide studies of the cybercrime threat environment that aim to address the impact of organized crime involvement in cybercrime, the nature of new variants of cybercrime and the response of regulators. Such research would need to entail an extensive multi-method approach to data collection designed to address the future research questions identified in the next section. Such an agenda would help fill gaps in the knowledge base about cybercrime, and provide a vital *regional* perspective. In addition, the research enhances greater collaboration within the international community that will allow law enforcement agencies, policy makers, and other key stakeholders to better understand and manage potential cybercrime threats in their jurisdictions, regions and globally.

Future research questions

1. What are the current trends and emerging challenges that impact on cyber-security, specifically the use of new and emerging technology to facilitate and/or commit cybercrime?
2. What is the extent of the shift toward organized crime cybercriminal activities and what are the characteristics of organized crime online activities?
3. What are the best practices in responses to cybercrime and the best ways regulatory agencies can minimize the risks of cybercrime?
4. What are the challenges for law enforcement agencies in detecting and prosecuting cybercriminal activities and what new technologies are needed to combat cybercrime?
5. What prevention strategies best help individuals and corporations avoid cybercrime risks?

Notes

1 The term used to describe the use of psychological tricks and the manipulation of behavior often by means of deception, by cyber-criminals on unsuspecting users to gain "access information" in order to commit crime.

2 See http://www.wired.com/images_blogs/threatlevel/files/alexander_bobnev_indictment.pdf.

3 Phishing: online or Internet scams that frequently use unsolicited messages purporting to originate from legitimate organizations in order to deceive the recipient into disclosing their financial and/or personal identity information.

4 Rootkits are cloaking technologies usually employed by other malware programs to abuse compromised systems by hiding files, registry keys and other operating system objects from diagnostic, antivirus, and security programs (AIC, 2006a; AIC, 2006b).

5 Malware, also known as malicious software, includes trojans, viruses, and worms.

6 A worm is similar to a virus by design, and is considered to be a sub-class of a virus. Worms spread from computer to computer, but unlike a virus, have the ability to travel without any help from a person. The danger with a worm is its ability to replicate itself on your system, so rather than your computer sending out a single worm, it could send out hundreds or thousands of copies of itself, creating a huge and devastating effect.

7 A botnet is a network of individual computers infected with bot malware. These compromised computers are also known as zombies or zombie computers. The zombies, part of a botnet under the control of the botnet controller, can then be used as remote attack tools to facilitate the sending of spam, hosting of phishing websites, distribution of malware, and mounting denial of service attacks. Among the three botnet communication typologies identified are centralized, distributed P2P and random – the most commonly used are centralized and P2P modes (Cooke *et al.*, 2005).

8 That is: Australia, Hong Kong, New Zealand, India, Taiwan, China, Japan, Vietnam, Malaysia, South Korea, Philippines, Indonesia, Thailand, and Singapore.

9 An attack aimed at redirecting a user to a bogus website where personal details may be stolen or "farmed" as in phished.

References

Australian Institute of Criminology (AIC). (2006a). High tech crime tools. *High Tech Crime Brief* no. 12. Online at http://www.aic.gov.au/publications/current%20series/rpp/100-120/rpp103.aspx/htcb/1-20/htcb012.aspx (accessed July 31, 2009).

—— (2006b). Acquiring high tech crime tools. *High Tech Crime Brief* no. 13. Online at http://www.aic.gov.au/en/publications/current%20series/htcb/1–20/htcb013.aspx (accessed July 31, 2009).

Brenner, S. W. (2002) Organized cybercrime? How cyberspace may affect the structure of criminal relationships. *North Carolina Journal of Law & Technology*, 4(1): 1–50.

—— (2006). Cybercrime jurisdiction. *Crime, Law and Social Change*, 46: 189–206.

Brenner, S. W. and Frederiksen, B. A. (2002). Computer searches and seizures: some unresolved issues. *Michigan Telecommunications & Technology Law Review*, 8: 39–114.

Broadhurst, R. G. (2005). International cooperation in cyber-crime research. Paper presented at the 11th UN Congress on Crime Prevention and Criminal Justice, Workshop 6: Measures to Combat Computer Related Crime, Bangkok, April.

—— (2006a). Content cybercrimes: criminality and censorship in Asia. *Indian Journal of Criminology*, 34(1&2): 11–30.

—— (2006b). Developments in the global law enforcement of cyber-crime. *Policing: An International Journal of Police Strategies and Management*, 29(3): 408–33.

Broadhurst, R. G. and Grabosky, P. (2005). Computer-related crime in Asia: emergent issues. In R. Broadhurst and P. Grabosky (Eds.), *Cybercrime: the challenge in Asia*, pp. 347–60. Hong Kong: University of Hong Kong Press.

Broadhurst, R. G. and Chantler, A. (2006). Cybercrime update: trends and developments. In *Expert Group Meeting on the development of virtual forum against cybercrime report,* June 28–30, 2006, Seoul Korea, KICJP and UNODC, pp. 21–56.

Center for Strategic and International Studies (CSIS). (2008) *Securing cyberspace for the 44th presidency*. Washington, DC: Center for Strategic and International Studies.

Chantler A. (1996). *Risks, the profile of computer hackers*. PhD thesis. Curtin University, unpublished.

Chantler A. N. and Broadhurst, R. (2008). Social engineering and crime prevention in cyberspace. Paper presented to the Korean Institute of Criminology, October 30, Seoul.

Choo, K. K. R. (2007). Zombies and botnets. *Trends & Issues in Crime and Criminal Justice*, 333. Canberra: Australian Institute of Criminology. Online at http://www.aic.gov.au/publications/current%20series/tandi/321-340/tandi333.aspx (accessed July 31, 2009).

—— (2008). Organized crime groups in cyberspace: a typology. *Trends in Organized Crime*, 11(3): 270–95.

—— (2009). *Online child grooming: a literature review on the misuse of social networking sites for grooming children for sexual offences*. Research and public policy series no. 103. Canberra: Australian Institute of Criminology. Online at http://www.aic.gov.au/en/publications/current%20series/rpp/101–20/rpp103.aspx (accessed July 31, 2009).

Choo, K. K. R. and Smith, R. G. (2008). Criminal exploitation of online systems by organized crime groups. *Asian Journal of Criminology*, 3(1): 37–59.

Choo, K. R. R., Smith, R. G., and McCusker, R. (2007). *Future directions in technology-enabled crime: 2007–09*. Research and public policy series no. 78. Canberra: Australian Institute of Criminology. Online at http://www.aic.gov.au/publications/current%20series/rpp/61–80/rpp78.aspx (accessed July 31, 2009).

Cooke, E., Jahanian, F., and McPherson, D. (2005). The zombie roundup: understanding, detecting, and disrupting botnets. In *SRUTI'05 Workshop Proceedings*, pp. 35–44. Berkeley CA: USENIX Association.

Council of Europe. (2004). Summary of the organized crime situation report: focus on cybercrime. Octopus Interface conference: challenge of cybercrime, September 15–17, Strasbourg.

Dandurand, Y., Colombo, G., and Passas, N. (2007). Measures and mechanisms to strengthen international cooperation among prosecution services. *Crime, Law and Social Change*, 47(4–5): 261–89.

Felson, M. (1998). *Crime and everyday life*. New York: Pine Forge Press.

Fitzgibbon N. and Wood, M. (2009). *Conficker C: a technical analysis*. Online at http://www.sophos.com/sophos/docs/eng/marketing_material/conficker-analysis.pdf (accessed July 31, 2009).

Grabosky P. (2007). Requirements of prosecution services to deal with cyber crime. *Crime, Law and Social Change*, 47(4–5): 201–23.

Grabosky, P. and Broadhurst, R. G. (2005). The future of cyber-crime in Asia. in R. G. Broadhurst and P. Grabosky (Eds.), *Cybercrime: the challenge in Asia*, pp. 347–60. Hong Kong: University of Hong Kong Press.

Grabosky, P., Smith, R. G., and Dempsey, G. (2001). *Electronic theft: unlawful theft in cyberspace*. Melbourne: Cambridge University Press.

Guenther, M. (2001). Social engineering – security awareness series. UK: Information Warfare Site. Online at http://www.iwar.org.uk/comsec/resources/sa-tools/Social-Engineering.pdf (accessed December 20, 2006).

Ianelli, N. and Hackworth, A. (2005). *Botnets as a vehicle for online crime*. Pittsburgh: CERT Coordination Center.

Jayawardena, K. and Broadhurst, R. (2007). Online child sex solicitation: exploring the feasibility of a research "sting." *International Journal of Cyber Criminology*, 1(2), pp. 228–48.

Jones, B. (2007). Comment: virtual neighborhood watch: open source software and community policing against cybercrime. *Journal of Criminal Law & Criminology*, 97(2), 601–29.

KPMG Forensic. (2009). *Fraud survey 2008*. Australia: KPMG.

Litan, A. (2009). *2008 data breaches and financial crimes scare consumers away*. Stamford: Gartner.

McAfee (2005). *McAfee virtual criminology report*. Santa Clara: McAfee.

—— (2007). *Cybercrime: the next wave*. Santa Clara: McAfee.

—— (2008). *McAfee virtual criminology report: cybercrime versus cyberlaw*. Santa Clara: McAfee.

—— (2009). *McAfee threats report: first quarter 2009*. Santa Clara: McAfee.

McCusker, R. (2006) Transnational organized cyber crime: distinguishing threat from reality. *Crime, Law and Social Change*, 46(4–5): 257–73.

Microsoft (2007). Asia Pacific legislative analysis: current and pending online safety and cybercrime laws. A study by Microsoft, November. Online at http://www.itu.int/ITU- D/cyb/cybersecurity/docs/microsoft_asia_pacific_legislative_analysis.pdf (accessed July 31, 2009).

Morris, S. (2004). The future of netcrime now: part 1 – threats and challenges. UK: Home Office. Online at http://www.homeoffice.gov.uk/rds/pdfs04/rdsolr6204.pdf (accessed July 31, 2009).

National White Collar Crime Center (NW3C). (2009). *2008 Internet crime report*. Online at http://www.nw3c.org/downloads/2008_IC3_Annual%20Report_3_27_09_small.pdf (accessed July 31, 2009).

Newman, G. and Clarke, R. (2003). *Superhighway robbery: preventing e-commerce crime*. Devon: Willan Publishing.

Parliamentary Joint Committee on the Australian Crime Commission (PJCACC). (2007). *Inquiry into the future impact of serious and organized crime on Australian society*. Canberra: Parliament House.

Peretti, K. K. (2009). Data breaches: what the underground world of "carding" reveals. *Santa Clara Computer and High Technology Law Journal*, 25(2): 375–414.

Porras, P., Saidi, H., and Yegneswaran, V. (2009). *An analysis of Conficker C*. Online at http://mtc.sri.com/Conficker/addendumC/ (accessed July 31, 2009).

Raywood, D. (2009). Botnet discovered by Finjan contained 73 government domains. Online at http://www.scmagazineuk.com (Accessed 31 July, 2009).

Rudd, K. (2008). Address by the Prime Minister of Australia The Hon. Kevin Rudd MP, 4 December.

Serious Organized Crime Agency (SOCA). (2008). *The United Kingdom threat assessment of serious organized crime*. Online at http://www.soca.gov.uk/assessPublications/downloads/UKTA2008–9NPM.pdf (accessed July 31, 2009).

—— (2009). *Serious organized crime. Agency annual report 2008/9*. Online at http://www.soca.gov.uk/assess Publications/downloads/SOCA_AR_2009.pdf (accessed July 31, 2009).

Sim, S. H. (2000). Effective countermeasures against economic crime and computer crime. Resource material series no. 55. Tokyo, Japan: United Nations Asia and Far East Institute for the Prevention of Crime and the Treatment of Offenders. pp: 103–16.

Sheptycki, J. (2004). Organizational pathologies in police intelligence systems: some contributions to the lexicon of intelligence-led policing. *European Journal of Criminology*, 1(3): 307–32.

Smith, R. G., Grabosky, P., and Urbas, G. (2004). *Cyber criminals on trial*. Cambridge: Cambridge University Press.

Sophos. (2006). *Stopping zombies, botnets, and other email-borne threats*. Abingdon: Sophos.

Symantec. (2009). *Symantec global Internet security threat report trends for 2008*. Vol. XIV. Mountain View, CA: Symantec.

Thomas, N. (2009). Cyber security in East Asia: governing anarchy. *Asian Security*, 5: 1–23.

Raywood. (2009). Botnet discovered by Finjan contained 73 government domains. *SC Magazine*, 1 May. Online at http://www.scmagazineuk.com/botnet-discovered-by-finjan-contained-73-government-domains/article/135953 (accessed July 31, 2009).

United Nations (2004). A more secure world: our shared responsibility: report of the high-level panel on threats, challenges and change. Online at http://www.un.org/secureworld/report2.pdf (accessed July 31, 2009).

Verizon. (2009). *2009 data breach investigations report*. Online at http://www.verizonbusiness.com/resources/security/reports/2009_databreach_rp.pdf (accessed July 31, 2009).

Walker, D., Brock, D., and Stuart, T. (2006). Faceless-oriented policing: traditional policing theories are not adequate in a cyber world. *The Police Journal*, 79(2): 169–76.

Wall, D. (2007). Policing cybercrimes: situating the public police in networks of security within cyberspace. *Police Practice and Research: An International Journal*, 8(2): 183–205.

White, M. and Fisher, C. (2008). Assessing our knowledge of identity theft: the challenges to effective prevention and control efforts. *Criminal Justice Policy Review*, 19(1): 3–24.

Wikström, P. and Treiber, K. (2007). The role of self-control in crime causation. *European Journal of Criminology*, 4(2): 237–64.

Yar. M. (2005). The novelty of "cybercrime": an assessment in light of routine activity theory. *European Journal of Criminology*, 2(4): 407–27.

17

Immigration and criminology

William F. McDonald

The discipline of criminology has come a long way since 1934, when Edwin Sutherland first marked its territory as the scientific study of crime including the processes of making laws, of breaking laws and of reacting to breaking laws. While those divisions continue to capture the horizontal scope of the field, new theoretical, methodological and geopolitical perspectives have grown the discipline vertically. Today, criminologists are concerned with the transnational and global dimensions of law making, law breaking and reactions to the breaking. Remarkably, a large part of this history can be traced by pursuing the links from one node in the web of knowledge, namely the immigration and crime nexus. A focus on immigration and crime involves examining the interconnection of global, transnational and domestic phenomena.

Background

Modernity, migration and crime

The processes of globalization, modernization and migration are intertwined (Melossi, 2003). Their roots can be traced back to the late Middle Ages. The replacement of the feudal world by the modern one was accompanied by a universal migratory movement, that from rural to urban locations. From the beginning these migrants were labeled "criminals." As Marx observed:

> The proletariat created by the breaking up of the bands of feudal retainers and by the forcible expropriation of the people from the soil, this "free" proletariat could not possibly be absorbed by the nascent manufacturers as fast as it was thrown upon the world. On the other hand, these men, suddenly dragged from their wonted mode of life, could not as suddenly adapt themselves to the discipline of their new condition. They were turned *en masse* into beggars, robbers, vagabonds, partly from inclination, in most cases from stress of circumstances. Hence at the end of the fifteenth century and during the whole of the sixteenth century throughout Western Europe experienced a bloody legislation against vagabondage.
>
> *(ibid., p. 371)*

Freedom of movement was restricted under feudalism. Serfs were tied to the land of their lords by feudal obligations. If they wanted to travel they needed the permission of their masters. As feudalism declined and increasing numbers of individuals were no longer attached to any feudal superior, states asserted increasing control over restrictions on who could move about and under what conditions. These "masterless" people came to be referred to as the "dangerous classes." States tried to control their movements by vagrancy and poor laws.

Under eighteenth- and nineteenth-century American law the poor did not have a right to geographic mobility. The poor laws inherited from England made the relief of the poor the responsibility of the community in which they were legally "settled." The law gave localities the right to prevent the settlement of people who might become financial burdens and to "remove" them to the place where they were legally settled (Neuman, 1993, p. 1,846).

In eighteenth-century France commoners on the move within the territory were required to carry either a passport issued by the town hall of the traveler's home village or an *aveu*, a testament of good character from local religious authorities. People could not leave the territory of France without permission. These restrictions on movement were abolished by the French revolutionaries in the name of liberty. Today, the freedom to move about within a country and to leave a country are hallmarks of free societies.

On the other hand, the freedom to enter a country is not a principle of liberty. States have the sovereign right to decide who shall be admitted to their territories. With the threat of international terrorism, states are redoubling their means of controlling their borders. Advocates of open borders who regard such restrictions as illiberal should consider the experience of the liberty-loving French revolutionaries. They abolished passport controls in the name of liberty but found that without border controls their liberty was at risk from reactionaries and hostile external and internal forces. They restored border controls in the name of liberty (Torpey, 2000, p. 21).

Before criminology

Even before there was criminology, there were studies of the connection between immigration and crime. In the middle of the nineteenth century several government reports documented the large and often disproportionate number of foreigners filling American lunatic asylums, jails and reform schools (Abbott, 1969 [1926]). In the eighteenth and nineteenth centuries globalizing processes involved the international transfer of crime problems. European governments emptied their jails and poor houses by shipping their convicts and vagrants to the new world. The American colonies and later the states resisted the transportation of felons by repeated protests and later by legislation (Neuman, 1993, p. 1,842)

The process of shipping criminals to other countries continues today. The United States and other advanced countries are destabilizing small countries in Central America and elsewhere by deporting to them thousands of "criminal aliens," legal and illegal immigrants who have committed crimes. Ironically, not only does this politically popular (at home) immigrant control policy give the receiving countries new crime problems – such as drive-by shootings and gang violence – but it also fosters a new crime problem for the sending countries as well. Deported criminals travel back and forth linking gang activities between countries forming transnational gangs, such as Mara Salvatrucha, or MS-13 – the so-called "biggest gang in the world" (Ling, 2007).

The transporting of criminals to foreign lands is a penal practice with ancient roots. Primitive peoples commonly sent unwanted persons into exile, a punishment often tantamount to death. In England the first law authorizing the "banishing from the realm and beyond the dominions" was enacted in 1597 (Francis, 1981, p. 6). Transportation became an alternative to capital punishment and a means of obtaining a pardon. By 1776 an estimated 15,000 to 100,000 criminals and debtors were shipped to the American colonies. Australia was founded as a penal colony. Between 1788 and 1867 a total of 123,000 men and 25,000 women were transported there.

Also before criminology, there were international gatherings convened by activists intent on stopping what is known today as the trafficking in human beings for sexual exploitation. All the hype in December 2000 associated with the opening for signing of the United Nations Convention against Transnational Organized Crime with its Protocol to Prevent, Suppress and Punish Trafficking in Persons, Especially Women and Children failed to mention that the crusade was over a century old and notably unsuccessful. Nineteenth-century reformers convened meetings of government and police leaders who enacted legislation and established specialized units to fight "white slavery" – a phrase used to distinguish their campaign from the earlier and notably successful campaign to end black slavery (McDonald, 2004). Today criminologists are just beginning to evaluate the efficacy of the newly energized and heavily funded initiatives to combat this old problem. While the verdict is still out, early studies suggest that the new campaign is far less effective than one might hope.

The criminalization of immigration

We are living in an "age of migration." International population movements are at an all time high. In 2005, according to UN estimates, more than 3.3 percent of the world's population were migrants. This amounts to between 190–200 million people, up from a mere 62 million in 1960 (International Organization for Migration, 2005, p. 379). The majority of today's migrants are concentrated in a relatively small number of advanced industrial countries. Almost half are women (49 percent in 2000). The fastest growing single form of migration in the past decade is illegal migration, estimated at between 15 and 20 percent of the world's immigrant stock (between 30 and 40 million immigrants) (Papademetriou, 2005). Not surprisingly, these days in many countries xenophobia is on the rise. Anti-immigrant sentiment is most intense when it comes to the matter of illegal immigration.

For many people, illegal immigration is the quintessential transnational/cross-border crime. For some countries this belief is not correct; for others it is correct. Illegal presence in the United States, for example, makes a person deportable but not criminal. It is a civil violation, not a crime. Illegal entry is a misdemeanor; but it is not a continuing offense. It ends as soon as the alien reaches a safe place (Reyna Yanez and Soto, 1994). In March 2006, when Congress proposed to make illegal presence a felony, hundreds of students walked out of their schools and joined three-quarters of a million protestors in major cities across the country to demonstrate against the legislation (Suarez and Kennedy, 2006). The proposal failed.

In Germany, however, illegal residence is a crime punishable with fines and imprisonment of up to one year.[1] The German police are required to investigate all crimes that come to their attention including illegal residence. A large proportion of what is referred to as "foreigners' criminality" consists of crimes that only foreigners can commit (i.e. violations of laws concerning the status of the foreigner) (Schneider, 1995).

For the entire nineteenth century there was no such thing as illegal immigration to the United States. Indeed, illegal entry was not a misdemeanor until 1929. However, the reentry of a previously deported alien was made a felony.[2] Immigration was regulated by the states until 1870 when the federal government finally got directly involved by prohibiting for the first time the entry of undesirable immigrants. Specifically, criminals and prostitutes were excluded; and a form of human trafficking was made a felony, namely the bringing in of "Oriental persons without their free and voluntary consent," a practice known as "contracting to supply 'coolie' labor."[3]

The criminalization of immigration has occurred ever since. While illegal presence has not been criminalized in the United States, criminality of even the most petty degree has been used to expand the list of reasons for excluding and deporting people. In this era of political correctness, the "criminal alien" has become a safe scapegoat for the politician seeking to look tough on immigration without alienating ethnic voting blocks.

Immigration law versus criminal law

Liberal societies do not control immigration with criminal law. They use immigration law. They do not "punish" immigrants. They exclude or deport them. Criminologists may find the operation of immigration law harsh, unfair or unjust. Immigration law has not had the benefit of Enlightenment-inspired reformers like Cesare Beccaria or Jeremy Bentham. Deportation, for instance, often entails tremendous hardships as, for example, when an adult who was brought to the country illegally as a child is separated from his/her family and repatriated to his native land where he/she does not speak the language or have any resources. No matter how severe the consequences, however, deportation is not considered for legal purposes as a "punishment." Rather it represents the sovereign right of the government to refuse to harbor persons it does not want.

Principles dear to criminologists – such as statutes of limitations, the prohibition against retroactive laws, penalties proportionate to the crimes, returning to the community after serving one's sentence – do not govern American immigration law. An immigrant who, for example, served a sentence 20 years earlier for a minor crime and who has since stayed out of trouble, raised a family and operated a successful business can be deported when identified at the custom's inspection upon returning from a vacation abroad.

Public opinion and immigration

Public opinion about immigrants waxes and wanes with the economy. Immigrants are looked upon favorably when times are good and unfavorably when times are bad. Distaste for foreigners (xenophobia) often has a racist character and frequently involves the belief that immigrants are criminally inclined. Local, national, regional and world public opinion surveys indicate that whereas publics vary greatly in the extent to which they believe that immigrants cause crime and in the extent to which they mistrust strangers, they are virtually unanimous that illegal immigration must be stopped.

Until the second half of the twentieth century in advanced countries it was socially acceptable to discriminate against people based upon race, ethnicity and religion and to openly express virulent bigotry. For example, in 1916 Park Avenue socialite Madison Grant put the case in favor of restricting immigration this way:

> We should have learned from our experiences with the Negro problem that you cannot expect inferior people to make good citizens. The immigrants from Southern and Eastern Europe are far below the average intelligence of the Nordics [in the United States]. If we continue to let these people come in the numbers that they have been, the American people will be mongrelized by these alien hordes and the average intelligence of the country will be steadily reduced by newcomers.
>
> *(Simon, 1985, p. 75)*

These days law and culture have changed. Discrimination is unlawful. The expression of extreme bigotry happens only among small, radical groups. Tolerance is a value that is now widely supported in Western culture. It is enforced by formal and informal means (Nevitte, 1996; Inglehart, 2000). But, there is a tolerance paradox. The defense of tolerance requires a certain degree of intolerance (Sullivan *et al.*, 1982, p. 9). While tolerance is generally endorsed, it is also recognized that there are proper limits regarding what should be tolerated. Deciding precisely what those limits should be, however, remains problematic.

In contravention of the traditional jurisprudential principle that motivation is not a legal element of a crime, a wide range of acts from homicide to making threats and vandalism have been outlawed as "hate crimes" if motivated by intolerance. The expression of intolerant points of view – such as those of white supremacists, extreme right-wing groups, skinheads and neo-Nazis – has not been criminalized (with certain exceptions such as denying the Holocaust in Germany).

In liberal societies the expression of intolerant views is generally protected as a form of free speech. However, individuals and groups expressing such views are often tracked and denounced by liberal minded organizations such as the Southern Poverty Law Center and the American Civil Liberties Union whose mission is to promote tolerance and to prevent harm to people of minority status. Also, the informal enforcement of the norm against intolerance and the expression of a long list of socially unapproved words and ideas are routinely done in face-to-face interactions. People are expected to observe political correctness or risk the censure of their audience.

Immigration is a key focal point in this dialectic. The politics can be intense. Discussions are polarized. One is either pro- or anti-immigrant. Merely discussing the link between immigration and crime can be tarred as being anti-immigrant or racist xenophobic. Just being in favor of stronger borders or better control of immigration can be cast as anti-immigrant.

Organizations that promote the latter goals range from extreme right-wing groups, to conservative political parties with anti-immigrant agendas to more moderate advocacy groups who publish essays and studies documenting the negative consequences of immigration, to proactive groups such as the pejoratively labeled "border vigilantes" who patrol the border and the interior helping law enforcement catch illegal immigrants.

The management of public opinion about immigrants has been identified as an important factor in controlling the outbreak of xenophobic violence. Analyses of the emergence of right-wing anti-foreigner violence in Germany in the early 1990s identified means by which public opinion was influenced in ways to support and encourage anti-foreigner acts: the failure of authorities to adequately condemn the violence; the rise of anti-immigrant political parties; and the activities of anti-racist organizations (Bjorgo and Witte, 1993; Willems, 1995).

Definitions

Research on the criminality of as well as the criminal victimization of immigrants suffers from a serious problem of definition. The concept "immigrant" has never been carefully or uniformly defined. It is used loosely as synonymous with terms such as "foreigner," "foreign born," "nationality," "tourist" and "alien." It is also used to describe the children of immigrants ("second generation immigrants"). It does not correspond to the term in immigration law.

The concept of immigrant over-aggregates. It lumps together under one label people from dramatically different cultural origins. A review of the literature from 30 countries in Europe, North America and Australia concluded that there is no uniformity in counting foreigners (Mukherjee, 2002, p. 188). Since the 1960s some researchers have stopped using the term and have substituted the use of race, ethnicity and national origin instead. Nevertheless, the term continues to command attention. Immigration played a major role in the history of American criminological thought and today it is the rubric that is commonly used in public discourse to identify one of the pressing concerns on the international agenda.

The criminality of immigrants

Public criminology

The century-long stream of research addressing the criminality of immigrants has two notable features. First, there is a remarkable degree of agreement among studies done at different times in several countries (especially the US, Canada and Australia) using a variety of methods applied to diverse samples. They have often found that – contrary to popular belief – first-generation immigrants tend to be less criminally inclined than the native-born people of the host countries. There are, of course, exceptions and qualifications to this general finding particularly found in European studies. Nevertheless the degree of agreement is worth special note. It at least supports the conclusion that immigrants are not always and everywhere more criminally involved than natives.

The second notable feature of this long line of research is that it appears to have had little, if any, effect on public opinion. Despite the frequent negative findings, publics generally believe that immigrants are criminally inclined. This discrepancy between the research findings and what the public believes bears some analysis.

The discrepancy undoubtedly reflects the gap between researchers and the general public regarding what is meant by the answer to their question about immigrant criminality. Like Quixote and Panza, they are talking about different things. For researchers the question is answered by determining whether immigrants are *more* criminally involved than native born people. For the general public, the question is about whether immigrants are involved in *any* criminality.

The unstated logic of the latter view is that the crimes of an immigrant could have been avoided if the immigrant had not been admitted to the country. This logic is vehemently asserted in the case of crimes committed by illegal immigrants. In both the public mind and in law, immigrants are held to a higher moral standard than natives. Immigration law provides for the deportation of lawfully admitted immigrants who commit crimes. The possibility of rehabilitation is not a consideration.

Methodological issues

The critical methodological problem in determining whether immigrants are more or less criminally inclined than natives has been to obtain valid and reliable measures of criminality and of immigrant/foreign-born status and to be able to make comparisons after controlling for the age and gender of individuals and adjusting for the age and gender distributions of the immigrant-born and native-born populations being compared. In addition, the urban–rural distribution of the population should be controlled. Immigrants tend to disproportionately locate in urban areas. Urbanization is a known correlate of criminality and, hence, would artificially make the rate for immigrants higher than that for natives.

Crime statistics have well-known limitations. Official statistics understate the true amount of crime and often overstate the criminality of immigrants and other minorities due to racial discrimination or structural biases such as detaining immigrants pre-trial due to the possibility of flight. Victim surveys and self-reported crime questionnaires were invented to get around the limitations of official statistics. They too have their limitations. Since every method and every measure has its weaknesses, it is essential to use multiple methods. If the findings converge, credibility increases.

The findings: first-generation criminality

An ideal way to answer the question of whether immigrants are more criminally inclined than natives would be to compare the average number of crimes (controlling by crime type) committed per year by immigrants and natives of the same ages and gender; in short, their age and sex adjusted lambdas (λ's) (Blumstein *et al.*, 1986). This gold standard has not yet been achieved regarding immigrants. But, the finding that first generation immigrants are less involved in crime than natives has been supported by many, although not all, studies.

United States

Beginning with the first major study of immigration and crime, the study by the US Commission on Immigration, virtually the same conclusion has been found repeatedly in the US and elsewhere. The Commission concluded:

> No satisfactory evidence has yet been produced to show that immigration has resulted in an increase in crime disproportionate to the increase in adult population. Such comparable statistics of crime and population as it has been possible to obtain indicate that immigrants are less prone to commit crime than are native Americans.
>
> *(US Immigration Commission, 1911, p. 1)*

Twenty years later the Wickersham Commission reached the same conclusion (US National Commission on Law Observance and Enforcement, 1931, p. 195). The finding that "immigrants in general contribute less than their quota to the criminal population of the United States when correction is made for variations in the age composition of the immigrant population" (Sutherland, 1947 [1939], p. 123) became a staple in textbooks from the 1930s to the 1980s when the immigration and crime nexus temporarily disappeared from the radar of American criminologists.

By the beginning of the twenty-first century, immigration was again a hot political issue; and criminologists were using more sophisticated research tools. Again, they found that immigrants are not just less criminally inclined than natives but that they appear to revitalize neighborhoods and to reduce crime (Sampson, 2008; Lee and Martinez, 2009). Meanwhile, research on immigration and crime had emerged in other countries. It did not always confirm what had been found in the US.

Australia

Between 1952 and 1990 studies of immigrant crime in Australia generally reinforced the conclusion that immigrants are less criminal than natives.[4] This pattern was challenged by a study in 1999 which found that immigrants from eight countries had higher arrest rates than native-born Australians. The results, however, were less than convincing due to the inability to control for age structures (Mukherjee, 1999).

Canada

Beginning in 1957 several studies of migrant crime in Canada confirmed the conclusion that immigrants are generally less crime prone than natives. But there were important exceptions to the rule, usually linked to the cultural heritage of the immigrants. The conviction rates of Asians and Italians, for example, were higher than natives for gambling and lottery offenses. One study concluded that the foreign born were "very significantly under-represented among those incarcerated for serious crimes in Canada in both 1989 and in 1991" (Thomas, 1992, p. 10). Yet, immigrants were found to be over-represented for narcotics offenses.

United Kingdom

The pattern of under-representation of immigrants in crime compared to natives has been challenged by the findings of studies in the United Kingdom. Irish immigrants as well as immigrants from the Commonwealth and other countries have been shown to be more criminally active than native-born British (see, for example, McClintock and Gibson, 1961). However, there are some studies that suggest that certain immigrant groups are less criminally involved than natives.

Continental Europe and Australia

The challenge to the proposition that immigrants are less criminal than natives also comes from studies in Australia (Mukherjee, 1999), France (Tarde, 1895, p. 541), Germany (Schneider, 1995), Switzerland (Killias, 2009), Sweden (von Hofer *et al.*, 1997, p. 80), the Netherlands (de Haan, 1997), and Italy (Barbagli, 2002, p. 118). In that literature the results are mixed. Several studies show higher rates for immigrants by type of crime and by nationality. A few suggest lower rates for immigrants. The more complex pattern of results one finds from these studies are more in keeping with what one might expect: differences among groups and among host settings that cannot be reduced to one size fits all.

The findings: second-generation criminality

The pattern of relatively lower criminality rates among first-generation immigrants has not been found frequently for the children of immigrants, the so-called "second generation" immigrants. Indeed the opposite finding has been more common – leading to the conventional wisdom that the greater the acculturation to the host society, the more the immigrant's criminality resembles that of the native born. To the extent that this conclusion is correct, it points to a dilemma for immigration policymakers. The preferred policy is to promote the integration of immigrants into their new societies. But that may unwittingly increase their criminality.

A key point about the children of immigrants is that they often suffer the greatest degree of adjustment problems. They are caught between the expectations of the culture of their parents and that of the host society. This heightens their experience of culture conflict and anomie and distances them from the control of the parents. Brown captures this problem as follows:

> The immigrant of the first generation is struggling to maintain his old life organization and to preserve the culture he acquired, over a period of half his life, against great odds, the greatest of which is the effort on the part of his children to become American and thus get out of the culture that is sacred to their parents.
>
> The immigrant of the second generation has to play roles and pose because he has to behave in several cultures. He is too American to be appreciated at home, and too Italian, too Polish, or too Jewish to be accepted away from home
>
> *(Brown, 1969 [1933], pp. 253–4)*

The findings: illegal immigrants and crime

Although illegal immigration is one of the hottest topics in the public mind, almost no systematic criminological research has addressed it. One 1993 study in San Diego County (CA) indicated that illegal immigrants were over-represented among arrestees. It estimated the illegal population in the county at 7.9 percent of the county's total population and reported that approximately 22 percent of felony arrestees were illegal immigrants (Parker and Rea, 1993).

In 1997 Minister of the Interior, Georgio Napolitano, claimed that 83 percent of the extracommunitari detained in the five major Italian prisons were illegal immigrants. Therefore, he reasoned, most of the deviance done by foreigners in Italy was due to illegal immigrants. His claim was refuted with data by Barbagli (2002).

Immigrants as victims of crime

Immigrants are the victims of every imaginable crime. The victimization begins in their home countries, continues through the countries of transit and flourishes in the countries of destination. Their vulnerability is writ large by many factors: their lack of language skills and knowledge of how things work in their foreign countries, their lack of resources, their own cultural prohibitions against seeking help from outsiders, their distrust of government particularly the police; their isolation and detachment from social support networks; the prejudices against them; and their obviously foreign appearance that invites many otherwise law-abiding people to take advantage of them.

Systematic research on the victimization of immigrants has been hampered by the lack of reliable data about immigrant status of victims. What is known about the problem is based on a few studies using limited official government statistics, victimization surveys and news reports. The findings are mixed. A few suggest that immigrants are less often than natives to be the victims of ordinary personal and property crime (Makkai and Taylor, 2009). But more commonly immigrants have been found to suffer higher rates. For instance, immigrants have been found to be at greater risk than natives for homicide and other forms of violence including domestic violence in the United States, the United Kingdom, Germany, Italy, Sweden, the Netherlands and Switzerland (Sorenson and Shen, 1996; McDonald, 2009). Also, several studies have found that immigrants are more frequently the victims of certain property crimes including burglary and theft, particularly theft of wages.

Two patterns that have often been found are: immigrants are most likely to be victimized by other immigrants, particularly for crimes of violence but also for some property crimes such as theft; and when immigrants live in enclaves they are less likely to be the victims of inter-group crime but they are still subject to intra-group victimization and they are more likely to engage in criminal behavior resulting from participating in activities traditional for their home cultures but criminal in their new home.

Correlation, causation and theory

When examining the correlation or non-correlation between immigration and criminal behavior or victimization, it is important to remember a crucial principle of statistical analysis. Correlation is not causation. Being an immigrant is one of many factors that can influence the probability of committing crime or being victimized – just as other factors such as age, gender, urban location, and family stability, to name a few. Being an immigrant does not "explain" the criminality or the victimization. It is only in the political realm that nothing more is needed to explain why an immigrant commits a crime. Scientific explanations require more. They need a set of concepts, definitions and propositions which taken together provide a logical account of past findings and a testable prediction of future findings.

With regard to both the criminality and the victimization of immigrants no one general theory prevails. Instead a mix of theories has developed. Theories of culture conflict, social disorganization, anomie and opportunity all provide partial explanations. For some dimensions of the subject these explanations are quite efficient. For instance, the high rates of certain types of crimes related to traditional cultural practices which had been acceptable and expected in the homeland of some immigrants groups certainly are well accounted for by culture conflict. The theory has the utility of pointing to the kind of research that would predict the decline of that particular type of criminality among those immigrants. Specifically it suggests that as immigrants move away from their identity with their culture they would be less likely to commit that type of crime. Such a systematic analysis is well demonstrated by Ribordy (1980) who found that as immigrants moved away literally and mentally from their Italian heritage they were less likely to be involved in crimes related to traditional Italian cultural practices such as gambling.

Opportunity theory certainly makes sense of the empirical findings that immigrants tend to be victimized by their own kind; that they are less vulnerable to inter-group victimization when living in enclaves; and that they are more likely to commit crimes typical of their cultural heritage when their lives are spent mostly with members of their immigrant group.

Although correlations are not explanations, they can be powerfully subversive of explanations. The biological theory of crime favored by a long line of race supremacists from Madison Grant to today's neo-Nazis and others have a hard time explaining why immigrants are less criminally involved than natives.

Conclusion

Criminologists' interest in international, comparative and global crime that has emerged since the 1990s is not as novel as it may seem. It is not the subject matter but the research that has changed. From before criminology became a discipline and throughout its growing years, concern about the criminality of immigrants has sparked research and debate. Immigration is an international process. Thus, from the beginning criminology has had an international dimension. Over time the research tools became more sophisticated and the discipline grew to include concern for victims. Today as criminologists pursue research on so many topics related to immigrants they are discovering the international roots of their discipline and that their work on this issue is not finished.

Future research questions

1. What impact on immigrant crime and victimization rates do differences among countries in their policies for receiving and integrating immigrants have? What are the best practices?
2. What are the criminogenic consequences of the deportation of criminal aliens both for the home countries and for the phenomenon of transnational crime?
3. What explains the differences among national/cultural groups of immigrants in their criminal and victimological adjustments to their new societies?
4. What theories best account for the empirical data regarding the criminality and victimization of immigrants?
5. To what extent and in what ways do ideological biases of the researchers distort/influence the findings of research on immigration and crime?

Notes

1 Section 95, Residence Law.
2 45 Statutes-at-Large 1551.
3 18 Statutes-at-Large 477.
4 For these and other pre-1996 studies of immigration and crime alluded to but not cited see (Yeager, 1996).

References

Abbott, E. (Ed.) (1969 [1926]). *Historical aspects of the immigration problem: select documents*. The American Immigration Collection. New York: Arno Press and *The New York Times*.

Barbagli, M. (2002). *Immigrazione e reati in Italia*. Bologna: Il Mulino.

Bjorgo, T. and Witte, R. (Eds.). (1993). *Racist violence in Europe*. New York: Macmillan Press.

Blumstein, A., Cohen, J., Roth, J. A., and Visher, C. A. (Eds.). (1986). *Criminal careers and "career criminals."* Washington, DC: National Academy Press.

Brown, L. G. (1969 [1933]). Immigration: cultural conflicts and social adjustments. In *The American immigration collection*. New York: Arno Press and *The New York Times*.

de Haan, W. (1997). Minorities, crime, and criminal justice in the Netherlands. In I. H. Marshall Minorities, migrants and crime, pp. 198–223. Thousand Oaks, CA: Sage.

Francis, R. D. (1981). *Migrant crime in Australia*. St. Lucia, Queensland: University of Queensland Press.

von Hofer, Hanns; Sarnecki, Jerzy; Tham, H. (1997). Minorities, crime, and criminal justice in Sweden. In Ineke Haen Marshall (Ed.). *Minorities, migrants, and crime: diversity and similarity across Europe and the United States*, pp. 62–85. Thousand Oakes, CA: Sage Publications.

Inglehart, R. (2000). Globalization and postmodern values. *The Washington Quarterly*, 23(1; winter): 215–28.

International Organization for Migration. (2005). World migration: costs and benefits of international migration: 2005. Geneva: International Organization for Migration.

Killias, M. (2009). Paradise lost? New trends in crime and migration in Switzerland. In W. F. McDonald, Immigration, Crime and Justice, , pp. 33–45. Bingley, UK: Emerald/JAI Press.

Lee, M. T. and Martinez, J. R. (2009). Immigration reduces crime: an emerging scholarly consensus. In W. F. McDonald (Ed). Immigration, Crime and Justice, pp. 3–16. *Sociology of Crime, Law and Deviance*, vol. 13. Bingley, UK: Emerald/JAI Press.

Ling, L. (2007). World's most dangerous gang. February 12. National Geographic Channel (National Geographic). Washington, DC: National Geographic.

McClintock, F. H. and Gibson, E. (1961). *Robbery in London*. London: Macmillan.

McDonald, W. F. (2004). Traffick counts, symbols and agendas: a critique of the campaign against trafficking of human beings. *International Review of Victimology*, 11(1): 143–76.

—— (Ed.) (2009). Immigration, crime and justice. *Sociology of Crime, Law and Deviance*, vol. 13. Bingley, UK: Emerald/JAI Press.

Makkai, T. and Taylor, N. (2009). Immigrants as victims of crime: the Australian experience. In W. F. McDonald (Ed). Immigration, crime and justice, pp. 95–105. *Sociology of Crime, Law and Deviance*, vol. 13. Bingley, UK: Emerald/JAI Press.

Melossi, D. (2003). "In a peaceful life": migration and the crime of modernity in Europe/Italy. *Punishment and Society*, 5(4): 371–97.

Mukherjee, S. (1999). Ethnicity and crime. *Trends and Issues in Crime and Criminal Justice*, 117, May. Australian Institute of Criminology..

—— (2002). Crime and victimisation of migrants in Australia: a socio-demographic view. In J. D. Freilich, G. Newman, S. G. Shoham, and M. Addad (Eds.) *Migration, culture conflict and crime*, pp. 187–209. Dartmouth: Ashgate.

Neuman, G. L. (1993.). The lost century of American immigration law (1776–1875). *Columbia Law Review*, 93 (Dec.): 1833–901.

Nevitte, N. (1996). Tolerance and intolerance in advanced industrial states: the cross-time evidence. In L. Halman and N. Nevitte (Eds). *Political value changes in Western democracies*, pp. 59–79. Tilburg, The Netherlands: Tilburg University Press.

Papademetriou, D. G. (2005). The global struggle with illegal migration: no end in sight. In *Migration information source*, September 1. Washington, DC: Migration Policy Institute.

Parker, R. A. and Rea, L. M. (1993). Illegal immigration in San Diego County: an analysis of costs and revenues. Sacramento, California: Senate, Special Committee on Border Issues.

Reyna Yanez, L. and Soto, A. (1994). Local police involvement in the enforcement of immigration law. *Texas Hispanic Journal of Law & Policy*, 1(9): 11–50.

Ribordy, F. (1980). Culture conflict and crime among Italian immigrants. In R. A. Silverman and J. J. Teevan (Eds). *Crime in Canadian society*. Chap. 11, 2nd edn., pp. 190–202. Toronto: Butterworths.

Sampson, R. J. (2008). Rethinking crime and immigration, *Contexts*, 7(1, winter): 28–33.

Schneider, H. J. (1995). Foreigners as perpetrators and as victims in Germany. *Eurocriminology*, 8–9: 95–108.

Simon, R. J. (1985). *Public opinion and the immigrant: print media coverage*. Lexington, MA: Lexington Books. pp. 1,880–1,980.

Sorenson, S. B. and Shen, H. (1996, Jan.). Homicide risk among immigrants in California, 1970 through 1992. *American Journal of Public Health*, 86(1): 97–101.

Suarez, K.-A. and Kennedy, J. M. (2006). L.A.'s top officers vow crackdown on students, *The Los Angeles Times*, March 29.

Sullivan, J. l., Piereson, J. and Marcus, G. (1982). *Political tolerance and American democracy*. Chicago and London: University of Chicago Press.

Sutherland, E. H. (1947 [1939]). *Principles of criminology*. Philadelphia: J.B. Lippincott.

Tarde, G. (1895). *Philosophie pénale*. 4th edn. Paris.

Thomas, D. (1992, April). Criminality among the foreign born: an analysis of the federal prison population. Unpublished paper on file with National Criminal Justice Reference Service, NCJRS # 143344 (Strategic Planning, Immigration Policy Branch, EIC).

Torpey, J. C. (2000). *The invention of the passport: surveillance, citizenship, and the state*. Cambridge studies in law and society. Cambridge: Cambridge University Press.

US Immigration Commission (1911). Immigration and crime. Senate. 61st Congress, 3rd Ses. Doc. # 750. Reports of the US Immigration Commission, vol. 36. Washington, DC: Government Printing Office.

US National Commission on Law Observance and Enforcement (1931) Report on crime and the foreign born. No. 10. Washington, DC: Government Printing Office.

Willems, H. (1995, Spring). Development, patterns and causes of violence against foreigners in Germany: social and biographical characteristics of perpetrators and the process of escalation. *Terrorism & Political Violence*, 7(1): 162–82.

Yeager, M. G. (1996). Immigrants and criminality: a meta survey. Ottawa, Canada: Ministry of Citizenship and Immigration.

18

Trafficking in persons

Kristiina Kangaspunta

A brief article in a Finnish newspaper tells the story of three East European students who were recruited in their home countries to come to Finland to work in the fields picking berries. They soon found out that their salary was only one third of the promised one. They were forced to sleep in a small room with ten other workers without running water. The same kind of story is repeated over and over again in several parts of the world; instead of berries it could be tomatoes or some other kind of fruit or vegetable, and deceived workers come from different countries around the globe. Are these people victims of trafficking?

Defining trafficking in persons

In many countries, cases involving poor salaries, substandard working and living conditions and other irregularities related to the job are dealt with by labor inspectors or labor unions. When does a bad job then become a case of trafficking for forced labor? Often, the line is not clear even though there is an internationally accepted definition of trafficking in persons in the Protocol to Prevent Suppress and Punish Trafficking in Persons, especially Women and Children, which supplements the United Nations Convention against Transnational Organized:[1]

> "Trafficking in persons" shall mean the recruitment, transportation, transfer, harbouring or receipt of persons, by means of the threat or use of force or other forms of coercion, of abduction, of fraud, of deception, of the abuse of power or of a position of vulnerability or of the giving or receiving of payments or benefits to achieve the consent of a person having control over another person, for the purpose of exploitation. Exploitation shall include, at a minimum, the exploitation of the prostitution of others or other forms of sexual exploitation, forced labor or services, slavery or practices similar to slavery, servitude or the removal of organs.
>
> *(United Nations, 2000, article 3(a) Protocol)*

The main differences between the definition of trafficking in persons and smuggling of migrants are:

1. Consent. Smuggled migrants generally consent to being smuggled. Victims of trafficking have either never consented or, if they had initially consented, their consent has been rendered meaningless by the traffickers' actions.

2. Transnationality: Smuggling facilitates the illegal border crossing of persons and entry into another country. Trafficking in persons need not involve the crossing of any border and where it does, the legality or illegality of the border crossing is irrelevant.
3. Exploitation: The relationship between the smuggler and the smuggled migrant usually ends after crossing the border and the smuggler has no intention of exploiting the smuggled persons after their arrival. Trafficking involves the ongoing exploitation of the victims in some manner that will generate illicit profits for the traffickers. The traffickers' intention is to continue the exploitative relationship with the trafficked person after arriving at their final destination.
4. Source of profit: Smugglers generate their profits from fees exacted to move people across borders. Traffickers make most of their profits by exploiting their victims.

Even though in reality it might be difficult to draw a line between trafficking in persons and smuggling of migrants, the consequences of mistakenly identifying a trafficking victim as a smuggled migrant can seriously prevent the trafficked person from being treated in a way which respects the victim's rights to support and protection.

The trafficking process

The trafficking process usually starts with the recruitment of the trafficked person in the country of origin. For this to work, traffickers must either force or convince the trafficked person to leave their familiar surroundings. This can be achieved in different ways. The basic means for recruitment include deception by promising a job, marriage or education in the country of destination, selling a person, usually a child, or kidnapping the victim, which is the rarest method of recruitment.

For trafficked persons, most cases start as a migration process with people seeking a better life abroad. For many people, it is difficult to migrate: restricted possibilities of leaving their homeland or entering the destination country or lack of resources to organize the travel can all hinder their migration process. This gives a possibility for criminals to "offer their service" for those planning to migrate. This might involve corrupting officials, arranging forged documents or some other illegal measures to facilitate the travel. Contact with the criminal in the beginning of the migration process often leads those desiring to move abroad in the hands of traffickers.

The recruitment is followed by transportation. The journey can take place by aircraft, boat, rail, ferry, road or foot, and the final destination can be reached directly or by passing through transit countries. Borders may also be crossed illegally when trafficked persons are smuggled in the country in vehicles, containers, ferries or using other methods to cover up the entry. Illegal border crossing can also be done by using stolen or forged documents that provide a right to enter the country or bona fide documents providing false visa entitlements. In trafficking cases, border crossing can also be fully legitimate.

Once the destination country is reached, traffickers use different methods to control their victims in order to exploit them for profit. These methods include debt bondage, physical, linguistic and social isolation, confiscation of travel documents, physical and psychological violence and threats, reprisal against the victim's family and the use of magical beliefs and practices. For many years, trafficking for sexual exploitation has dominated the debate on human trafficking, while other forms of trafficking have received less attention.[2] Victims can also be exploited through forced labor, removal of organs or other body parts, criminal activities, begging, forced marriages, illegal adoptions and even armed conflicts. When examining sexual and labor exploitation, several studies show that about 70–80 percent of reported cases are related to sexual exploitation and roughly 20–30 percent involve labor exploitation (UNODC, 2006a, p. 33;

UNODC, 2009a, p. 57; IOM, 2009). However, these numbers should be read with caution because of the reasons explained in the following section on victims of trafficking.

In the destination country, trafficked persons may be identified as victims, they may be rescued and they may receive protection and support. Often, victims return to their origin country either after being repatriated or deported. This usually occurs when trafficking victims fail to be identified as such and they are instead treated as being illegal migrants in the country of destination. Sometimes, victims also can be relocated to a third country.

The geography of human trafficking

Human trafficking cases can be found in all parts of the world.[3] The report issued by UNODC (2006a, pp. 17, 58) documents trafficking in persons originating from 127 countries and destined to be exploited in 137 countries. In total, reported trafficking cases were found in 161 countries. According to the International Labor Organization (2005, p. 17), forced labor as a form of human trafficking is present in all regions of the world and in all kinds of economies. In general, human trafficking routes go from poorer countries to more affluent ones. However, the picture is not always that clear. Main countries of origin, transit and destination are identified based on the number of documented incidences in those countries as presented in Table 18.1.

As Table 18.1 illustrates, the origin countries appear to be mainly located in Eastern Europe, CIS (Commonwealth of Independent States), Asia and Africa. On the other hand, destination countries are mainly found among Western Europe and North America. There are several difficulties encountered in reporting and comparing trafficking in persons in different countries,[4] including so-called horizontal trafficking in which people are trafficked between countries with similar human development levels and which is often not recognized as trafficking. For example, in Africa several neighboring countries are involved in trafficking in both directions across common borders. In these cases trafficking often occurs in different and separate markets so that children may be trafficked from one country to the neighboring one for forced labor. On the other hand, women might be trafficked for sexual exploitation from that neighboring country to the first one (UNICEF, 2005, pp. 12–13).

Table 18.1 *Incidence of origin, transit and destination country, alphabetical order*

Very high origin	*Very high transit*	*Very high destination*
Albania	Albania	Belgium
Belarus	Bulgaria	Germany
Bulgaria	Hungary	Greece
China	Italy	Israel
Lithuania	Poland	Italy
Nigeria	Thailand	Japan
Republic of Moldova		Netherlands
Romania		Thailand
Russian Federation		Turkey
Thailand		United States of America
Ukraine		

Source: UNODC, 2006, pp.18–20.

The severity of human trafficking

Assessments on the severity of human trafficking are based on several estimates. However, broad agreement has not been reached regarding which method or standardized instruments should be used to calculate such estimates. As a result, quoted figures often contradict each other.

As of today, data on the severity of the phenomenon of trafficking in persons can be found only from a few regions, even though some initiatives have been started to improve the situation (Bosco *et al.*, forthcoming; UNIAP, 2009). In South-Eastern Europe an effort to systematically measure the severity of trafficking was started in the beginning of 2000. Between 2000 and 2004, the total number of assisted victims in South-Eastern Europe residing in the region was approximately 5,800 persons. However, the research methods consider only victims who were assisted, because theirs were the only verifiable numbers available on trafficking. Nevertheless, it is well known that assisted victims represent only a portion of all trafficking victims, as many victims are never identified or assisted. Information drawn from victims, governments, and non-governmental and international organizations has made it clear that the actual number of trafficking victims is significantly higher than the number of assisted victims (Surtees, 2005, pp. 31–2).

At the country level, there are several efforts to assess the severity of human trafficking; however, the same problems in measuring the number of victims or cases are present in these studies. The following are some examples of these efforts. In the Netherlands, data on trafficking cases have been collected since 2002 and show that the number of trafficking victims has grown annually. In 2004 a total of 403 victims were registered, in 2005 the number was 424 and in 2006 it was 579. However, not all victims were identified, and of the victims who had been identified, not all of them were reported (Dettmeijer-Vermeulen *et al.*, 2008, p. 7). In Nigeria, there are studies collecting the number of rescued victims. The analysis shows that around 400 victims were rescued by the national anti-trafficking agency in 2004–5. The number of rescued victims increased to nearly 1,300 in 2006–7 (NAPTIP, 2009). These data probably provide more information on the successful rescue operations than on the severity of the problem in Nigeria. In the USA, data based on alleged human trafficking incidents show that in 2007–8 there were nearly 1,230 incidents involving a total of 1,442 victims. However, also in this case, the data include incidents from selected areas covering only 25 percent of the nation's resident population (Kyckelhahn *et al.*, 2009, p. 8).

The severity of human trafficking can also be measured by the profits made from the exploitation of trafficked persons. At the global and regional level the annual profits are estimated to be (in $US billions):

- 31.7 at global level;
- 15.5 for industrialized economies;
- 3.4 for transition economies;
- 9.7 for Asia and the Pacific;
- 1.3 for Latin America and the Caribbean;
- 1.6 for Sub-Saharan Africa;
- 1.5 for the Middle East and North America.

(ILO, 2005, p. 55)

In an attempt to compare the value of human trafficking with other illicit markets originated from or trafficked to West Africa, the UN has taken into consideration the estimated values of cocaine trafficked through West Africa, stolen oil from Nigeria, illicit cigarettes to West and North Africa, counterfeit medicines to West Africa, victims of trafficking for sexual exploitation from West Africa, small arms to West Africa, toxic waste to West Africa and smuggled migrants from West Africa. As shown in Figure 18.1, the values generated from human trafficking are higher than those of smuggled migrants, toxic waste and arms trafficking, but lower than profits made from counterfeit medicines, illicit cigarettes, trafficking in cocaine and stolen oil (UNODC, 2009b, p. 75).

As shown above, severity of trafficking remains difficult to measure. Some innovative efforts have been started and there are hopes that in the future there will be possibilities to measure human-trafficking severity in a more reliable and comparative way.

Root causes, vulnerability and market demands

While root causes are not identical to vulnerability, they can nonetheless have a great impact on vulnerabilities as well as on the markets demanding trafficked persons. Root causes are determined by domestic policy decisions and social, cultural and religious practices; they may include the following phenomena (UNODC, 2008, p. 19):

- Gender-based violence;
- Discriminatory labor practices;
- Patriarchal social structures;
- Breakdown of family networks;
- Ethnic, racial and religious marginalization;
- Failed and corrupt governments;
- Women's role in the family and in the labor markets;
- Power, hierarchy and social order;
- Children's roles and responsibilities;
- Historical precedents of bonded labor;
- Early marriage and forced marriage;

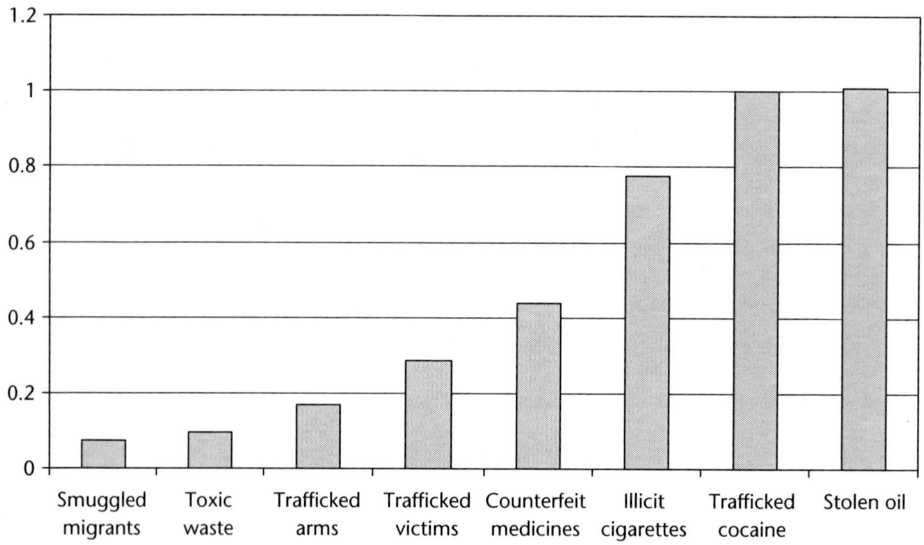

Figure 18.1 Values of selected trafficking flows in West Africa (US$ billions)

- High rates of divorce and social stigma;
- Disruption to personal development;
- Limited educational achievement;
- Limited economic opportunities;
- High presence of organized crime;
- Immigration and labor policies.

A review of studies conducted on the matter, however, reveals some of the contributing factors, while also showing how little we know about the relationship between root causes, vulnerability and human trafficking. Potential and actual victims can be vulnerable to victimization throughout the whole trafficking process.

The link between poverty and human trafficking is a very complex issue. Poor people are vulnerable to trafficking by virtue of having few options to earn income and being unable to challenge social superiors in relation to migrant contracts and work conditions. However, it is not necessarily the "poorest of the poor" who become victims of trafficking. When the main reported countries of origin and destination are compared with the United Nations Human Development Index (UNDP, 2009) it can be seen that, while the top destination countries are at the high end of human development, most of the top origin countries are at the middle human development level. Thus, it can be concluded that people need to have at least some resources to leave their countries.

Moving from one country to another, or even moving within a country, often makes people vulnerable. During the transportation process many potential victims run the risk of being abused and exploited because of their legal status, or their relationship with those responsible for their transportation. Sometimes, asylum seekers also risk falling in the trafficking trap with other victims. There have been cases when the traffickers were literally standing outside of asylum centers waiting to recruit the asylum seekers.[5]

The actual exploitation takes place in the countries of destination. The vulnerabilities are related to physical and mental control, social isolation and, again, irregular status. Victims can be menaced by direct violence or by threatening harm to their families. They are excluded from any health or social services; moreover, without knowing the language spoken in the destination country and without the support of a social network it is difficult for the victim to seek help. Confiscating their travel documents and making the victims believe that they are in the country illegally prevents them from turning to authorities for help. Even when the help of officials could be received, trafficking victims may be seen as illegal immigrants who should be deported. Sometimes service providers may increase the vulnerability for re-trafficking when treatment is poor, support is conditional or when the victim's rights are not respected. This may lead victims to decide not to use the services. There are reported cases when the victims received assistance only after they converted to a certain religion or attended regular religious practices (Surtees, 2007, p. 228). In several countries, access to support and protection for trafficked persons has been made conditional on their agreeing to cooperate with the police and prosecutors. Victims are forced to give evidence or testify against the traffickers to access assistance. This might result in a lack of trust towards criminal justice practitioners, hindering the victim from testifying and thus preventing the trafficker from being convicted (Dottridge, 2007, p. 14; Kangaspunta, 2001, pp. 159–60).

While vulnerabilities are often connected to the supply side of human trafficking in origin countries, market demands represent the factors affecting people's desire to seek a better life in destination countries. The demand has often been discussed in the context of the commercial sex industry, where the demand is driven by those controlling and using those markets.[6] Labor markets have gained much less attention, even though the demands related to them can be connected to the everyday life of many citizens. The demand for ever-cheaper products reverberates in cuts in production and distribution costs. One efficient way of doing that is to use forced and child labor. Buying the products produced by trafficking victims contributes to financing criminal activities involved not only in human trafficking, but also in drug and arms trafficking, counterfeiting of products and other forms of organized crime.

Creating a positive demand for ethically produced goods and services that ensures that no exploited labor force was used also will prevent human trafficking. Some examples already exist. Efforts have been made to establish a certification process for the chocolate industry to make sure that no form of child labor exploitation was involved in the production process. The use of trafficked children in cocoa production is a well-documented problem in West Africa, which supplies nearly 80 percent of the world's cocoa (ILO, 2007). Another example illustrates the efforts to stop the use of child victims of trafficking in the production of carpets in India. In European countries and in North America, a labeling plan has been developed to guarantee that hand-woven carpets from India are not made by child labor.

Victims

Human trafficking victims can be women, men, girls and boys. Several studies show that the majority of the victims are adult women, followed by children. In addition, according to these studies, the majority of the victims are trafficked for sexual exploitation.[7] The small number of men among victims and forced labor can be a reflection of a bias based on several reasons. Until recently, in many countries the legislation on trafficking in persons has covered only trafficking in women and children for sexual exploitation. This has excluded male victims from the official records. Often, service providers offering support and protection to victims limit their services to women and/or children, resulting in a lack of knowledge of male victims needing assistance. However, there are some interesting exceptions in the general trend. For example, in Côte d'Ivoire, of all the trafficking victims identified in 2005 and in 2006, respectively 69 percent and 86 percent were boys. Nearly all the victims were trafficked for forced labor. In Mali the majority of the victims trafficked between 2003 and 2006 were also boys. In Argentina, the majority of the victims in 2006 and 2007 were women, but the main form of trafficking was labor exploitation.

Traffickers

Based on the IOM (2009) Counter Trafficking Database which includes information collected from victims assisted by IOM projects around the world, over 50 percent of recruitments in origin countries were done through personal contacts. In some cases, newspaper, internet and television advertisements also led to trafficking. Around 4 percent of assisted victims were sold by their families and fewer than 1 percent were kidnapped. Of those cases where the recruiter's gender is known, 51 percent were men, 42 percent were women and in 7 percent of cases the recruitment was done by both men and women. Around half of the recruiters were previously known to the victims; in 21 percent of cases the recruiter was a friend. Other recruiters include relatives, acquaintances, business contacts, partners and pimps. Most of the victims were promised a job before leaving their countries, some were also promised marriage or study opportunities and some thought they were going on a holiday trip. The majority of the jobs offered to the victims were in domestic work, or as a waitress, as a dancer or entertainer, in agricultural work, or in the selling business. Only 8 percent of the victims were directly offered a job in the sex industry. It should be kept in mind that the work intentions and experiences in the origin country do not have any impact on the victim's status and on the rights of a person who has been trafficked.

Even though human trafficking often contains transnational elements, in many countries the majority of offenders are nationals of the countries where the trafficking case was identified (UNODC, 2009a, p. 45). In Germany, almost half of the suspects were German nationals, of which 20 percent had a non-German place of birth (BKA, 2007, p. 7). In the Netherlands, again the Dutch nationals formed the majority of convicted traffickers (Dettmeijer-Vermeulen *et al.*, 2008, p. 22). In Belarus, 93 persons prosecuted for trafficking in persons were nationals of Belarus. In Western and Central Europe and in the Middle East, foreign offenders had a more significant role in trafficking cases than in other regions. In the United Arab Emirates, the majority of convicted offenders come from South Asia, from Eastern Europe and Central Asia. In Italy, the majority of the convicted offenders are from South East Europe, followed by Italians and then West African offenders. (UNODC, 2009c, pp. 45, 211).

The question of gender

Traffickers can be men and women. They can work alone, with partners, as part of a family business or as a member of an organized crime group. Even though the majority of traffickers are men, women offenders are also being investigated, prosecuted and convicted in several countries, particularly in Eastern Europe and Central Asia. In general, women are found to play a more prominent role in the crime of human trafficking than in other types of crimes. In the USA, 26 percent of the suspects in confirmed trafficking incidents were women. When looking at labor exploitation, women constituted 46 percent of the suspects, while in sexual exploitation cases women represented 20 percent of suspects (Kyckelhahn *et al.*, 2009, p. 6).

There are also cases of female victims becoming offenders. Often they have started as victims and are then promoted to the next step at the bottom of the criminal hierarchy. They are usually involved in tasks which are the most visible and dangerous in regard to being exposed to the police. It also should be remembered that even though these former victims have some new victims to control, they are also controlled by people who are above them in the hierarchy. In Italian crime groups the main activities carried out by women included recruitment of victims as well as controlling and cashing in on them, as shown in Figure 18.2 (Ciconte, 2005).

When victims are trafficked for domestic work, in many cases the exploiter is a woman. Several reports refer to cases where these victims are subject to physical and psychological violence and their living conditions are inhumane (Moniaga, 2008).

Organized crime's involvement in human trafficking

The question of "How organized is trafficking in persons?" has frequently been asked when trying to determine the extent of organized crime's involvement in the trafficking phenomenon. Some studies have attempted to illustrate the involvement of organized crime in human trafficking. When human trafficking was studied in the Czech Republic, out of 15 criminal procedure case files from the period between 1996 and 2001, 8 cases of trafficking were carried out by an individual, 3 cases were committed by a married couple and 3 cases included perpetrators that were involved in the sex industry either abroad or in the Czech Republic. In two cases, however, the trafficking crime had an organized character. The first case involved a loose network of perpetrators who were acquaintances. The second group was more organized, as it involved six offenders and a clear leadership. In both cases all offenders were Czech nationals

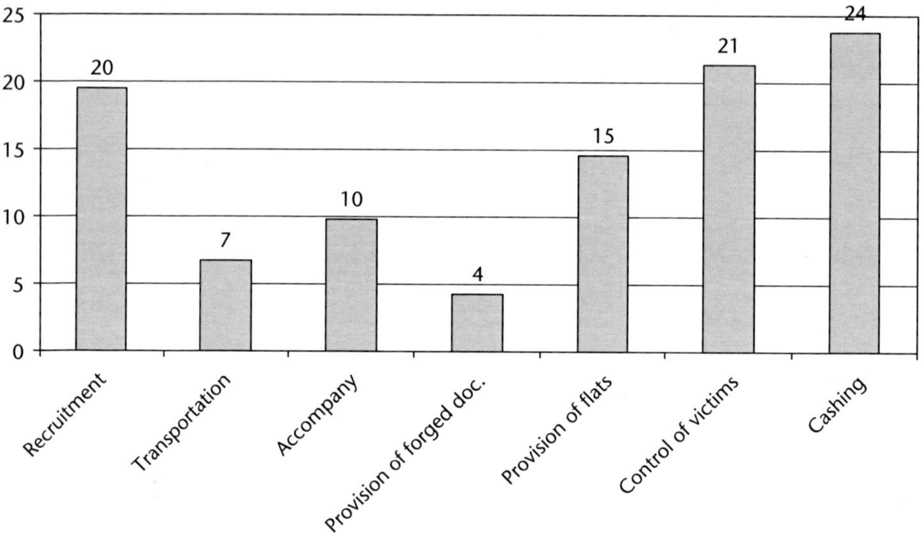

Figure 18.2 Activities of women in crime groups, Italy, 1996–2003

(Trávníčková, 2004, p. 84, 85). A study on trafficking in women from Nigeria to Italy found that over 65 percent of Nigerian law enforcement officials perceived that human trafficking is in the hands of organized criminal groups with a predominantly loose structure. On the other hand some trafficking groups in Nigeria are well organized and based on ethnic affiliations (UNICRI, 2004, p. 95).

There are mainly three types of organized crime groups involved in human trafficking. Mafia-type groups using standard hierarchy are characterized by a single leader and a relatively clearly defined hierarchy. Strong social or ethnic identities can be present. There is a moderately clear division of labor and there is often an internal code of conduct. A standard hierarchical criminal group has a name by which it is known, both to its members and to outsiders. In most cases the size of such groups is between 10 and 50 people.

The so-called Core groups consist of a relatively small number of individuals forming a tight and structured group to conduct criminal business. The Core group is surrounded by a wider circle of people who are used for corruption, document forgery and other criminal activities. They have little or no social identity or name and often include several nationalities.

The third type often connected to human trafficking is a criminal network, which is defined by the activities of key individuals who engage in illicit activity in often-changing partnerships. Even though such groups may not be regarded as a criminal group by outsiders, they join forces around a series of criminal projects. These criminal networks usually do not carry any name reflecting their shifting and fluid nature (UNODC, 2002, pp. 39–42).

Human trafficking groups have also been categorized as different business types or criminal enterprises. Five types were identifying and associated with national crime groups and market forces that drive the trafficking phenomenon, as presented in Box 18.1 (Shelley, 2003).

The question remains, how organized is human trafficking? Traffickers can be individuals, couples, loose networks and more organized groups and it is difficult to say which form is predominant. However, because of its rather complex nature, trafficking is a crime that must be somehow organized at least to a certain extent (Finckenauer, 2007, pp. 155–7).

Box 18.1. Categorization of trafficking groups as business types and criminal groups

1) Natural resource model: post-Soviet organized crime
   - Focus on short-term profits from trafficking in women who are sold as if they were a readily available natural resource such as timber or furs
   - Women are sold to the most proximate crime group, who deliver them to the markets
   - Profits are not maximized or used for long-term investment but are used through conspicuous consumption, or are sometimes used to purchase another commodity with a rapid turnover such as rubber boots for sale or cars for sale
   - Significant violations of human rights because the traffickers have no long-term interest in long-term profits from victims and have no connections to their families
2) Trade and development model: Chinese traffickers
   - Operate as integrated business which controls the trafficking process from start to finish
   - High long-term profits resulting in significant investment capital
   - Assets are returned through underground banking such as gold shops
   - Less significant violations of human rights because the traffickers have long-term interest in long-term profits from victims and often have connections to their families
3) Supermarket model: low cost and high volume: low-cost and high-volume US–Mexican trade
   - Maximize profits by moving large number of people with low individual fee
   - Exploitation of vulnerable groups such as deaf persons who are forced to peddle drugs or young girls who are forced into sex work
   - Presence of corruption with significant profit sharing with local border officials
   - Millions of dollars of profits are returned and invested in land and farms
   - Significant violations of human rights and even fatalities because there is little profit to be gained from each individual
4) Violent entrepreneur model: Balkan crime groups
   - Trafficking in large number of women who are controlled from recruitment to exploitation
   - Opportunistic using the instability and civil conflict in the origin countries
   - Significant use of corruption
   - Very high levels of profits which are used to finance other illicit activities or are invested in property and trade businesses
   - Extreme violations of human rights and brutal violence against victims
5) Traditional slavery with modern technology: trafficking from Nigeria and West Africa
   - Multi-tasked crime groups, trafficking in persons being one part of their criminal profile
   - Combining modern transport links with traditional practices for mental and physical control
   - High profits but only small amounts are returned to the local operations of the crime groups and occasionally to family members of victims
   - Much of the profits flow to other illicit activities and are laundered
   - Significant human rights violations involving victims who are exploited in the most physically dangerous conditions

Responses

Responses to human trafficking are often sought in three different fields: prosecution, protection, prevention and cooperation.

Prosecution

In 2008, around 20 percent of UN Member States[8] did not have in their legislations a specific offence on trafficking in persons. Even though many countries have sufficient legal frameworks against trafficking in persons, there are still very few prosecutions and convictions of traffickers. Between 2003 and 2007, 32 percent of the UN Member States recorded no prosecutions and 40 percent recorded no convictions. Out of those states that had a specific offence on trafficking in persons, 20 countries recorded no convictions during 2003–7. Around 30 percent of countries recorded ten or more convictions per year, most of the convictions being recorded in Western and Central Europe, in Eastern Europe and Central Asia and in South Asia. In order to improve the law enforcement, 40 Member States have established a special antihuman trafficking police unit or a similar body that was actively functioning in 2008 (UNODC, 2009a, pp. 39–40). Moreover, in many countries sentences of trafficking crimes are very mild, making trafficking a high-profit, low-risk crime.

Protection

Protection, and support of victims and their rights, is one of the cornerstones of the work against human trafficking. There are several international guidelines on how trafficked persons should be protected and assisted.[9] Non-governmental organizations as well as public institutions provide services to victims in different countries including housing, medical and psychological care, material assistance, employment and education opportunities, and legal assistance. In addition, the physical safety, privacy and identity of the victims should be protected as well as their right to participate in the court proceedings and the possibility of obtaining compensation (UNODC, 2009d). The main problem in victim protection is that most of the victims go through the entire trafficking process without ever being identified. Unidentified or wrongly identified victims are usually regarded as illegal migrants instead of being supported. They are sent back to their country of origin, where they sometimes face stigma, or with sexually transmitted diseases and physical or mental trauma, a condition which might lead them to being re-trafficked. Even though the estimated number of unidentified victims remains high and unsubstantiated, there have been some improvements in the overall identification trends. The global number of identified victims has increased by 27 percent between 2003 and 2006 (UNODC, 2009a, p. 48). It is difficult to find systematically collected information on the numbers of assisted victims or service providers. One of the few sources for this type information is the IOM Counter Trafficking Database. The analysis of their data show that the number of those victims who were assisted has been decreasing since 2005 (IOM, 2009).

Prevention

Prevention efforts often focus on addressing the root causes in the origin countries, such as eradicating poverty, increasing employment and education opportunities, securing social services and child protection, promoting equality and reducing marginalization. Awareness campaigns to increase knowledge about human trafficking are used both in origin and destination countries.

The problem with many efforts is that many of them lack evidence-based research and planning, and the impact of these efforts is often not evaluated. In addition to these traditional prevention measures, it should be considered whether migration policies and employment laws could be used to prevent human trafficking. Strict migration policies intended to stop unwanted migrations might make it so that those who wish to migrate, or have already migrated, will try to contact organized criminals to arrange their entry or stay in the destination country. Irregular status and contact with criminals create vulnerabilities that might easily lead the person into the hands of traffickers. In addition, efforts to prevent and redirect criminal careers should be developed also in connection to trafficking crimes.

Cooperation

At the national level, cooperation and coordination is needed to develop comprehensive policies against human trafficking and to avoid duplication in different sectors. National task forces, national rapporteurs, referral mechanisms and national action plans are those tools used in trying to ensure coordination and cooperation between all stakeholders, including officials, international and non-profit organizations, academia and the private sector. Before the end of 2008, 76 UN Member States had adopted a specific national plan of action against trafficking in persons (UNODC, 2009a).

At the international level, there are both bilateral and multilateral cooperation agreements and practices aiming to ensure the exchange of information, mutual legal assistance and joint investigations, as well as risk assessments, when victims are returned to their home countries. Furthermore, there are also initiatives to ensure cooperation and division of labor among international organizations. These initiatives are much needed, as shown by an unpublished study that was carried out following a request by the UN System Chief Executives Board for Coordination concerning the activities of different UN bodies and other international organizations against human trafficking. The result was that, regardless of their mandates, everybody is doing a bit of everything.

A question was raised in the beginning of this chapter on whether those people presented in exploitation cases were trafficking victims. Based on the definition of the UN Trafficking Protocol, the answer is: yes, they can all be perceived as victims of human trafficking.

Future research questions

1. How is corruption linked to trafficking in persons at the different phases of the trafficking process?
2. What is the severity of human trafficking at national, regional and global level? How can it be measured and which indicators could be used?
3. Economy of human trafficking. How big are the profits? How are they laundered and used?
4. What is the connection between migration, smuggling of migrants and trafficking in persons?
5. Map the situation of trafficking in persons for the removal of organs and body parts. Where does it happen? How acute is the problem? Who are the traffickers and the victims?

Notes

1 The Organized Crime Convention was adopted by the General Assembly in its resolution 55/25 of 15 November 2000 and entered into force on 29 September 2003. The ratification status of the Convention can be consulted at http://www.unodc.org/unodc/en/treaties/CTOC/signatures.html.

2 On under-reporting of trafficking for forced labor, see Kangaspunta, 2007, pp. 30–1.

3 For the history of human trafficking, see Kangaspunta, 2008.
4 See Kangaspunta, 2004, p. 83–7.
5 Oral information given by NGO representatives working at the refugee centers and dealing with potential and actual trafficking victims in Slovenia, Croatia and Bosnia Herzegovina. See also Uherek *et al.*, 2001.
6 See for example Di Nicola *et al.*, 2009.
7 See for example ILO, 2005; UNODC, 2006; US State Department, 2008; UNODC, 2009a.
8 One hundred and fifty-five countries were included in the study.
9 See for example UNHCHR, 2002; UNICEF, 2003; UNHCR, 2006.

References

Bundes Kriminal Amt (BKA). (2007). Human trafficking national situation report 2007. Wiesbaden: Bundeskriminalamt.

Bosco, F., Luda di Cortemiglia, V., and Serojitdinov, A. (forthcoming). Human trafficking patterns. In Friesendorf, C. (Ed.) *Strategies against human trafficking. The role of the security sector.* Geneva: Centre for the Democratic Control of Armed Forces (DCAF).

Ciconte, E. (2005). The trafficking flows and routes of Eastern Europe. WEST Project ref. N. 2A071. Bologna: WEST.

Dettmeijer-Vermeulen, C. E., Boot-Matthijssen, M., van Dijk, E. M. H., de Jonge van Ellemeet, H., and Smit, M. (2008). *Trafficking in human beings, supplementary figures.* 6th report of the Dutch National Rapporteur. The Hague: Bureau of the Dutch National Rapporteur on THB.

Di Nicola, A., Cauduro, A., Lombardi, M., and Ruspini, P. (Eds.) (2009). *Prostitution and human trafficking, focus on clients.* New York: Springer.

Dottridge, M. (2007). Introduction. In *Collateral damage: the impact of anti-trafficking measures on human rights around the world.* Bangkok: Global Alliance Against Traffic in Women (GAATW).

Finckenauer, J. O. (2007). *Mafia and organized crime: a beginner's guide.* Oxford: Oneworld Publications.

International Labor Organization (2005). A global alliance against forced labour. Global Report under the Follow-up to the ILO Declaration of Fundamental Principles and Rights at Work. Report of the Director General. International Labour Conference, 93rd Session. Report I (B). Geneva: International Labour Organization.

—— (2007) *Rooting out child labour from cocoa farms.* Paper No. 4. Child labour monitoring – a partnership of communities and government. Geneva: International Labour Organization.

International Organization for Migration (IOM) (2009) IOM counter trafficking database. Counter Trafficking (CTM) – Return and assistance. Unpublished material.

Kangaspunta, K.(2001). Losing control: trafficking in women. In A. Gaudreault and I. Waller, *Selected symposium proceedings.* X International Symposium of Victimology. Quebec: Bibliothèque nationale de Québec.

—— (2004). Mapping the inhuman trade: preliminary findings of the database on trafficking in human beings. *Forum on Crime and Society*, Vol 3, Nos 1 and 2: 81–103. New York: United Nations.

—— (2007). Collecting data on human trafficking: availability, reliability and comparability of trafficking data. In E. U. Savona and S. Stefanizzi, *Measuring human trafficking. Complexities and pitfalls.* New York: Springer.

—— (2008). Trafficking in persons: a brief history. *Freedom from Fear.* Issue 1: 38–41. Turin: UNICRI.

Kyckelhahn, T., Beck, A. J., and Cohen, T. H. (2009). *Characteristics of suspected human trafficking incidents, 2007–8.* Bureau of Justice Statistics, Special Report. US Department of Justice, Office of Justice Programs. Online at http://bjs.ojp.usdoj.gov/index.cfm?ty=pbdetail&iid=550 (accessed November 24, 2010).

Moniaga, R. (2008). Indonesian migrant domestic workers: an analysis on human rights, gender and migration. The New School Graduate Program in International Affairs (GPIA).

NAPTIP. (2009). Database analysis. National Agency for Prohibition of Traffic in Persons and other related Matters. Online at http://naptip.gov.ng/index.php?option = com_frontpage&Itemid = 1 (accessed November 24, 2010).

Shelley, L. I. (2003). Trafficking in women: the business model approach. *Brown Journal of International Affairs*, Vol. X(I): 119–31.

Surtees, R. (2005). Second annual report on victims of trafficking in South-Eastern Europe 2005.Geneva: IOM.

—— (2007) *Listening to victims, experiences of identification, return and assistance in South-Eastern Europe*. Vienna: International Centre for Migration Policy Development (ICMPD).

Trávníčková, I. (2004). *Trafficking in women: the Czech Republic perspective*. Prague: Institute for Criminology and Social Prevention (IKSP).

Uherek, Z., Skřivánková, K., and Weinerová, R. (2001) Women asylum seekers and trafficking. Research report for the United Nations High Commissioner for Refugees. Branch Office Prague, Czech Republic. Prague: Institute of Ethnology of the Academy of Sciences of the Czech Republic Department of Ethnic Studies.

United Nations (2000). United Nations convention against transnational organized crime and its protocols. Online at http://www.unodc.org/unodc/en/treaties/CTOC/index.html#Fulltext (accessed November 24, 2010).

United Nations Children's Fund (UNICEF) (2003). Guidelines on the protection of child victims of trafficking. Online at http://www.unicef.org/ceecis/0610-Unicef_Victims_Guidelines_en.pdf (accessed December 7, 2010).

—— (2005). Trafficking in human beings, especially women and children in Africa. Innocenti Research Centre, Innocenti Insight, Second Edition. New York: UNICEF.

United Nations Development Programme (UNDP) (2009). Human development report. Overcoming barriers: Human mobility and development. New York: UNDP. Online at http://hdr.undp.org (accessed November 24, 2010).

United Nations High Commissioner for Human Rights (UNHCHR) (2002). Recommended principles and guidelines on human rights and human trafficking. Report of the United Nations High Commissioner for Human Rights to the Economic and Social Council. E/2002/68/Add.1.

—— (2006). Guidelines on international protection: the application of Article 1A(2) of the 1951 Convention and/or 1967 Protocol relating to the status of refugees to victims of trafficking and persons at risk of being trafficked. Online at http://www.unhcr.org/cgi-bin/texis/vtx/refworld/rwmain?docid=443679fa4&page=search (accessed December 7, 2010).

United Nations Inter-Agency Project on Human Trafficking (UNIAP) (2009). SIREN report. Strategic Information Response Network,

United Nations. Online at http://www.no-trafficking.org/siren.html (accessed November 24, 2010).

United Nations Interregional Crime and Justice Research Institute (UNICRI) (2004). Trafficking of Nigerian girls to Italy. Turin: UNICRI.

United Nations Office on Drugs and Crime (UNODC). (2002). Results of a pilot survey of 40 selected organized criminal groups in 16 countries. Vienna: UNODC.

—— (2006a). Trafficking in persons, global patterns. Vienna: UNODC.

—— (2008). Human trafficking: an overview. Vienna: UNODC.

—— (2009a). Global Report on Trafficking in Persons. Vienna: UNODC.

—— (2009b). Transnational Trafficking and the rule of law in West Africa: a threat assessment. Vienna: UNODC.

—— (2009c). Combating trafficking in persons in accordance with the principles of Islamic law. The Protection Project and Naif Arab Security for security Sciences. Vienna: UNODC. Available at http://www.unodc.org/documents/human-trafficking/Islamic_Law_TIP_E_ebook_18_March_2010_V0985841.pdf (accessed November 24, 2010).

—— (2009d). International framework for action: to implement the Trafficking in Persons Protocol. Vienna: UNODC.

United States State Department (2008). Trafficking in persons report. US Department of State Publication 11407. Washington DC: US Department of State.

19

Trafficking in antiquities

Blythe Bowman Proulx

Looting at archaeological sites and the trade in illicitly obtained antiquities represent serious threats to the preservation of cultural heritage (see glossary, p. 197 for definitions of "antiquity" and "loot"). As part of the archaeological landscape, antiquities are some of the few objects from the human cultural past that survive today. Antiquities are both irreplaceable and finite; once they are gone, they are gone forever. Gone too is valuable information about the human past: objects ripped from archaeological sites to be traded as commercial commodities cannot contribute much to human history and cultural heritage.

Possibly one of the largest illicit businesses around the globe,[1] the antiquities trade involves local, small-scale thieves, larger groups of looters, and international connections with auction houses, galleries, museums, dealers, and collectors. With the help of middlemen, antiquities looted from archaeological sites are generally smuggled transnationally, laundered, and end up in the open, legal antiquities market. Despite efforts to curb the looting problem and thus eliminate supply to satisfy international demand,[2] the global situation does not appear to be improving (Bowman, 2008). Improvements in the means, ease, and speed of travel and communications, for example, have opened regions of the world that used to be unreachable (Brodie, 2002). Archaeological sites once buried deep in the jungles, deserts, and mountains of the world, for example, are no longer so inaccessible. Advancements in technology also have yielded machinery with unprecedented destructive capabilities (Atwood, 2004; Brodie, 2002). Many looters are now equipped with mechanical digging and drilling equipment, bulldozers, metal detectors, and in some cases even aerial maps of the archaeologically rich countryside (Brodie, 2002; Conklin, 1994). The technology available to aid in the looters' quest for saleable treasure has made illegal digging all the more devastating, and archaeological sites are scavenged at an increasingly accelerated pace (Bowman, 2008).

Licit and illicit elements of the antiquities trade

The illicit antiquities trade is an example of a transnational "gray" market – that is, a market with both licit and illicit elements. While the means and ways in which antiquities are obtained may be illegal,[3] it must be emphasized that, on the demand end of the market, trading in antiquities is altogether perfectly legal (Alder and Polk, 2002). Unlike drugs, arms, or other illicit items, antiquities are sold out in the open often in upscale, sophisticated art galleries and auction houses

(Alder and Polk, 2005). The antiquities market is thus unlike other illicit markets because it is not wholly illegal from source to demand. As Alder and Polk (2005) note, "this is not a trade, like drugs, where the ultimate market activity is as illicit and hidden as the production and transport processes of the material being sold" (p. 101). Owning an antiquity becomes illegal only when it has been illicitly exported, stolen, smuggled, or forged (Tijhuis, 2006). Unlike other forms of trafficking, the illicit ways that the licit antiquities trade is supplied must be disguised in order to be profitable (Tijhuis, 2006). It is this illegal–legal transformation that most clearly distinguishes the illicit antiquities trade other forms of trafficking. Moreover, the existence of legally obtained antiquities existing side by side on the market with illegally obtained antiquities turns the issue from one of black and white to an ambiguous shade of gray.[4]

A second element that distinguishes the trade in illicit antiquities from other international markets is that objects for sale on the licit antiquities market can yield staggeringly high prices (Massy, 2001). In December 2007, for example, Sotheby's auction house set a new world record for the highest price for any antiquity with the sale of the Guennol Lioness, which sold for upwards of $57.1 million USD, more than tripling its high pre-sale estimate of $18 million USD (Artdaily, 2007; New York AFP, 2007). Moreover, items on the antiquities market often accumulate astronomical value as a tradable commodity relatively quickly. The collection of Morgantina silver from Sicily, for example, was illegally excavated in 1979, sold to middlemen for just over $1,000 USD and less than a year later sold to a private collector for more than $1 million USD (Brodie, 1998, p. 7).

Very little of this profit, however, ever filters down to the original digger. On the contrary, a number of studies have shown that original diggers consistently receive less than 1 percent of an antiquity's final sale price (Brodie *et al.*, 2000; Brodie, 1998; Boylan, 1995). The Morgantina silver collection, for example, which initially sold for $1,100 USD and re-sold for $1 million USD, was ultimately sold to the Metropolitan Museum of Art in New York ("the Met") for upwards of $2.5 million USD. The middlemen received nearly 100 percent of the final price (Brodie *et al.*, 2000).

These are just a few examples of the large sums of money that circulate in the antiquities market, which further distinguishes it from other markets. It is the middlemen, however, who profit from the trade – not the impoverished looters. The trifling reward a looter receives for his/her find may be immediately significant, but as Brodie (1998) observes, it is a short-term economic gain. When the antiquity becomes a tradable commodity on the international market and acquires monetary value through circulation, both original diggers and the country of origin are deprived of long-range economic gain, and original diggers are ultimately twice-swindled: "first out of the initial monetary value of their find, and then out of its long-term economic potential" (Brodie, 1998, p. 15). This point is critical because many dealers and collectors who favor an open, free trade in antiquities have argued that it is economically beneficial to archaeologically rich but economically underdeveloped nations (Brodie, 2002). There is substantial evidence to suggest otherwise.

Since there are tremendous amounts of money that change hands in the antiquities market, it is no surprise that a final defining characteristic of the antiquities trade is its socioeconomically prominent clientele (Alder and Polk, 2002). In many cases, collectors, dealers, and museums are not only financially prosperous but are also often highly esteemed members of the community (Alder and Polk, 2005). Indeed, as Meyer (1973) has noted, the illicit antiquities trade is unique in that it comprises a broad social spectrum of actors "extending from illiterate peasants to cultivated and wealthy collectors; one can sensibly speak of the trade as a democratic demimonde, since rich and poor, highborn and lowborn, are all citizens within it" (p. 156).

Archaeological site looting: is it really a problem?

The antiquities trade is largely fed by the looting of archaeological sites, but it is difficult to assess the true scope and frequency of archaeological site looting around the world. For one thing, looting is necessarily a clandestine activity, making it difficult to document the scope of looting activity. For another, the damage caused by looting is that it can involve two types of archaeological sites – sites that are known to archaeologists and sites that have not yet been discovered (Conklin, 1994). Turkey, for example, is teeming with a rich archaeological heritage – the whole of the country is littered with archaeologically significant structures both known and as of yet undiscovered. The vast size of the country and sheer volume of archaeological sites, both excavated and undetected, make estimation of looting damage a formidable task.

Despite these difficulties, there is a substantial body of research that paints a dismal picture of the scale of on-the-ground damage around the world through archaeological field surveys (c.f., for example, Brodie *et al.*, 2006; Luke and Henderson, 2006; Roosevelt and Luke, 2006; Brodie and Tubb, 2002; Gilgan, 2001; Paredes Maury, 1999; Gutchen, 1983; Coggins, 1969) and photographic testimony (c.f., for example, Toner, 2002; Schick, 1999). In a recent study, Bowman (2008) surveyed over 2,300 archaeologists working throughout the world about their personal experiences with site looting. Since archaeologists work regularly at the very sites of interest to looters, it is not all that surprising that 98 percent of the study participants reported that looting was happening in some capacity in the area where they conducted archaeological research. The majority (68 percent) of respondents also reported having personally encountered evidence of looting activity on site (holes, pits, stolen excavation equipment, stashes of artifacts hidden elsewhere for later removal), and 24 percent reported having encountered looting in progress (Bowman, 2008). When asked to estimate whether they perceived looting to be getting worse, better, or remaining constant where they work, one third of the respondents felt that it was fluctuating; that is, some years were worse than others. Only 7 percent of responding archaeologists felt that the site looting where they work was decreasing. Indeed, if archaeologists' assessments of the presence and magnitude of looting is any indication of the true scope of the problem, then the damage is as pervasive as it is devastating. The scope of the looting problem is a reflection of the size of demand for antiquities, and it is likely that, as Bator (1982) remarks, "so long as there is a world market for beautiful objects, a substantial amount of looting will persist no matter what regulatory system is installed" (p. 49).

The gray market in antiquities

Because there is nothing illegal per se about owning antiquities, whether an antiquity is legal depends primarily on how it has been acquired or moved. (See glossary, p. 197, for definition of "gray" market.) Illicit antiquities are illicit in that they have been illegally removed from somewhere, meaning that they have been looted from some place, smuggled (Mackenzie, 2005), and laundered (Tijhuis, 2006). Illegal excavations yield never-before-seen undocumented antiquities that cannot be identified and therefore cannot be legally construed as stolen or illegally exported (Brodie, 2006). Even if a country recognizes an antiquity and attempts to claim ownership over it, there is little chance that the country will be able to prove that the object was looted, or was exported after its national cultural heritage laws were enacted (Brodie, 2002).

Antiquities obtained from illegal excavations also make their way onto the legal market because of differences in countries' property laws. Following the Anglo-American *nemo dat*[5] rule, for example, a thief can neither convey good title nor can someone claim good title through a thief, even if the property is transferred to a good faith purchaser (Gerstenblith, 2004). Unlike common law countries such as the United States, good title to a stolen object can be conveyed in the bulk of European continental civil law countries if the object was purchased in "good faith." This means that even if an antiquity was looted and illegally exported from its country of origin, if it was subsequently purchased in good faith in a civil country, then the good faith purchase is favored and the object is no longer legally construed as stolen (Brodie, 2002). Civil countries – most famously, Switzerland – become transit ports in which antiquities change hands and title is obtained. With "good" title secured, an antiquity can now obtain legal export documentation, be legally imported elsewhere, and thus begin to circulate freely and legally on the antiquities market (Alder and Polk, 2005, 2002). Many buyers are unaware of the criminal elements that brought the object onto the market, but many more are simply willing to turn a blind eye to such matters (McCalister, 2005; Brodie, 2002; Conklin, 1994).

Where crime and archaeology meet

The existence of a gray antiquities market facilitated by legal loopholes and fed by theft from archaeological sites has led a number of scholars to conclude that the looting situation has reached epidemic proportions, and that the world's archaeological resources are vanishing at an alarming rate (Hoffman, 2006; McCalister, 2005; Brodie, 2002, *et al.* 2000). Numerous reports surfacing in recent years have documented the connection between antiquities trafficking and other transnational crimes (McManamon and Morton, 2007; see glossary, p. 197, for definition of "transnational crime"). There is some evidence to suggest that organized criminal groups are now smuggling not only illicit drugs and arms, but are also dealing in looted antiquities (Hanley, 1999; Bernick, 1998). Looted antiquities are reportedly being uncovered during drug raids with increasing regularity. In 1999, Spanish police thwarted efforts of an international smuggling ring to trade stolen art and antiquities for cocaine (Brodie *et al.*, 2000, p. 16). Among the objects seized were pre-Columbian antiquities (Reuters, 1999). In 1985, US Customs tracked a smuggler's plane from Mexico to Colorado, whose cargo included not only thousands of dollars worth of marijuana but also priceless pre-Columbian antiquities from western Mexico (McManamon and Morton, 2000). Some of the world's greatest archaeological sites are reportedly now the nuclei of flourishing drug industries (McCalister, 2005).

Illicit antiquities must move transnationally to meet international demand, and their status must be transformed from illicit to licit in order to be sold (Alder and Polk, 2005). The ability to move illicit antiquities from one country to another makes two things necessary: first, a network of smugglers who are skilled in moving illicit goods transnationally; and second, some corruption on the part of customs inspectors, border patrol agents, or law enforcement in order to facilitate cross-border movement or acquisition of forged ownership and export documentation (Alder and Polk, 2005; McCalister, 2005; Conklin, 1994). Italy's Cultural Patrimony Protection (TPC) squad, for example, recently exposed an international antiquities smuggling network that, stretching across Western Europe, involved government officials, teachers, gallery owners, dealers, and even an Italian *carabiniere* (see glossary, p. 197). In a similar corruptive vein, numerous reports from around the world have also surfaced on antiquities secreted across borders in diplomatic bags (Brodie *et al.*, 2001). Protected by the 1961 Vienna Convention on Diplomatic Relations, diplomatic bags are allegedly one of the safest ways to move antiquities transnationally (Bailey, 2007).

Smuggling of looted antiquities has also been connected to terrorism. Hijacker Mohamed Atta, for example, attempted to peddle stolen antiquities in order to help finance the terrorist attacks of September 11, 2001 (de la Torre, 2006). Similarly in Afghanistan, British officials reported that antiquities were being looted and sold in order to fund resistance to the Taliban regime (Fidler, 2003). In a similar vein, Al Qaeda is reported to have smuggled Afghan antiquities to fund its jihadist activities (Kaplan, 2005).

Looting can also turn violent. In 1998, for example, two guards at archaeological sites in Guatemala were killed while on duty (Honan, 1995). In the early 1990s, a guard was murdered while looking after an antiquities storehouse in Angkor, Cambodia (Brodie *et al.*, 2000, p. 16). In 2002, the investigation of an Oregon looter convicted of possessing stolen property and destruction of archaeological resources revealed that he had also been planning the murder of several people: "his ex-wife, two former business partners, the Oregon State Police sergeant who headed the original investigation into the looting case, and the judge who presided at the 1996 trial" (Powell, 2003). According to Kaylan (1987), Turkish authorities have concluded that more deaths have occurred as a result of competition within the illicit antiquities trade than in disputes that arose during the heroin trade when it was at its height in the 1960s (Conklin, 1994, p. 161).

The transnational links between archaeology and crime can be traced throughout the entire journey of an antiquity from the ground to the market: acquisition via illegal digging, movement, export, distribution, and sale (McCalister, 2005). Clearly, the mechanisms of looting and smuggling coupled with colossal sums of money to be made on the legal market have made antiquities trafficking a profitable transnational crime. Perhaps even more tragically, however, the dramatic market values of antiquities have meant economic prosperity only for the criminal middlemen, not for the original finders, who are often as much victims of such exploitation as the denuded archaeological landscapes themselves. The uneven economic rewards for looting are noteworthy because many advocates in favor of a free, open trade in antiquities insist that illicit digging provides economic plentitude for developing source nations (Brodie, 2002).

Conclusion

The world's archaeological resources are disappearing at an alarming rate. While there is some debate over the extent to which organized criminal and/or terrorist groups are involved in looting antiquities trafficking, there is no question that the illicit antiquities trade is fueled by archaeological site looting and the antiquities market operates under the cloud of a criminal dynamic (Bowman, 2008). In light of these criminal undertones, criminology has much to contribute to the study of the illicit traffic in antiquities. What follows are some questions for future criminological research consideration.

Future research questions

1. What is the size of the illegal market, in terms of either volume of artifacts or monetary value? Of the overall antiquities trade, what proportion of it is, in other words, illicit?
2. The ability to move illicit antiquities transnationally presumably requires smuggling networks and some corruption. But how exactly do objects travel from the ground in source countries to market nations? Who is involved, and how do networks form, collaborate, and bond? What is the nature of the inner-workings of markets and trafficking patterns?
3. Is there a profile of a criminal or smuggler who deals in antiquities?
4. To what extent is antiquities trafficking connected to other forms of illegal activity, such as organized crime, drug trafficking, and terrorism? Do the same people do both? Are the same criminal networks and smuggling routes used?
5. How open are dealers and collectors to criminal deterrence? Would restorative (non-punitive) responses be an effective supplement to extant criminal sanctions?

Glossary

Antiquity: Objects of sociocultural or historical significance more than 100 years old and, in this case, refers to materials from archaeological sites.

Carabiniere (carabinieri, plural): Italian military police officer.

Gray market: A market that is neither definitively "black" nor "white" in terms of its legality. Gray markets instead exhibit dynamics of both the licit and the illicit.

Loot: To remove culturally significant material from archaeological sites for commercial gain, the act of which destroys archaeological context or evidence needed to learn from the site.

Transnational crime: Crime that somehow exerts an influence on more than one country either directly or indirectly, in terms of its commission, planning, preparation, perpetrators, or effects.

Notes

1 Estimates of economic losses and commercial gains due to transnational criminal activity vary wildly, and the illicit antiquities trade is no exception. This is not all that surprising given that no one really knows exactly how much illicit money is actually earned, saved, moved, and laundered around the world precisely because it is earned, saved, moved, and laundered illicitly (Naylor, 2002). Establishing the economic losses and gains associated with looted antiquities is further complicated in that there exists a legal and thriving international market for antiquities. Since both licit and illicit antiquities end up side by side on the legal market, it is impossible to distinguish which commercial transactions have involved antiquities that are incontrovertibly legal or illegal. Crimes involving plundered archaeological resources are more commonly subsumed under the rubric of cultural property or art crimes with annual estimated losses as high as $6 billion USD (FBI, 2007).

2 Legislative attempts to curb antiquities trafficking have in general identified the issue as one of theft or illicit export; that is, the enactment of national laws that vest ownership over antiquities to the state, in which case the removal of such objects constitutes theft; or, laws that attempt to prohibit exportation of such objects from national borders (Alder and Polk, 2002). The salient difference between these two legislative efforts concerns its enforceability – market nations that top the list of antiquities importers have been reluctant to enforce other nations' export laws, and source nations are more successful in pursuing legal recourse when such items are legally construed as stolen (Alder and Polk, 2002).

3 Illegal acquisition of antiquities at archaeological sites is not limited to theft. These activities can also include breaking and entering, vandalism, trespassing, human burial disturbance, violation of protected historic or religious sites, permit violations, and even violation of wildlife protection laws (Hicks, 2006).

4 Legal trade in antiquities is subject to the laws of the country in which the objects originate, as well as international regulations and agreements. These regulations govern everything from how antiquities may be excavated to whether and how they may leave the country of origin. Nations' laws governing antiquities and other cultural property differ, and many nations have entered into bilateral agreements with one another in a mutual effort to protect cultural heritage.

5 The *nemo dat quod non habet* ("no one can give what one does not have") expression captures the Anglo-American common law conceptualization of property (Clarke and Kohler, 2005).

References

Agence France-Presse (AFP) New York (2007). Mesopotamian sculpture sells for record 57 million dollars. December 5. Online at http://afp.google.com/article/ALeqM5gMfDoQ_vX7HpjKjVVxJK7NwsMfIw (accessed January 23, 2008).

Alder, C. and Polk, K. (2002). Stopping this awful business: the illicit traffic in antiquities examined as a criminal market. *Art, Antiquity, & Law*, 7(1): 35–53.

—— (2005). The illicit traffic in plundered antiquities. In P. Reichel (Ed.), *Handbook of Transnational Crime and Justice*, pp. 98–113. Thousand Oaks: Sage Publications.

Artdaily (2007). Guennol Lioness sells For $57.2 Million. *Artnews*, December 6. Online at http://files.shareholder.com/downloads/BID/0x0x149024/4befa6c0-fa94-45fc-98c7-246f3cfd2b7e/149024.pdf (accessed January 23, 2008)

Atwood, R. (2004). *Stealing history: tomb raiders, smugglers, and the looting of the ancient world.* New York: St Martin's Press.

Bailey, M. (2007). Diplomatic licence: an unpublished report claims that antiquities are being smuggled by embassy staff. *Art Newspaper,* 176, January.

Bator, P. (1982). An essay on the international trade in art. *Stanford Law Review,* 34(2): 275–384.

Bernick, L. (1998). Art and antiquities theft. *Transnational Organized Crime,* 4(2): 91–116.

Bowman, B. (2008). *Transnational crimes against culture: looting at archaeological sites and the gray market in antiquities.* Dissertation. *Abstracts International,* 69(11A): 4,517.

Boylan, P. (1995). Illicit trade in antiquities and museum ethics. In K. Tubb (Ed.), *Antiquities trade betrayed: legal, ethical, and conservation issues,* pp. 94–104. London: Archetype/UICIC.

Brodie, N. (1998). Pity the poor middlemen. *Culture Without Context,* 3 (autumn): 7–9. Online at http://www.mcdonald.cam.ac.uk/projects/iarc/culturewithoutcontext/issue3/brodie.htm (accessed December 21, 2007).

—— (2002). Introduction. In N. Brodie and K. Tubb (Eds), *Illicit antiquities: the theft of culture and the extinction of archaeology,* pp. 1–22. London: Routledge.

—— (2006). An archaeologist's view of the trade in unprovenanced antiquities. In B. T. Hoffman (Ed.), *Art and cultural heritage: law, policy, and practice,* pp. 52–63. Cambridge: Cambridge University Press.

Brodie, N. and Tubb, K. (Eds) (2002). *Illicit antiquities: the theft of culture and the extinction of archaeology.* London: Routledge.

Brodie, N., Doole, J., and Watson, P. (2000). *Stealing history: the illicit trade in cultural material.* Cambridge: The McDonald Institute for Archaeological Research.

Brodie, N., Doole, J., and Renfrew, C. (Eds.) (2001). *Trade in illicit antiquities: the destruction of the world's archaeological heritage.* Cambridge: McDonald Institute for Archaeological Research.

Brodie, N., Kersel, M., Luke, C., and Tubb, K. (Eds.). (2006). *Archaeology, cultural heritage, and the antiquities trade.* Gainesville, FL: University Press of Florida.

Coggins, C. (1969). Illicit traffic in pre-Colombian antiquities. *Art Journal,* 29(1): 94–8.

Conklin, J. (1994). *Art crime.* Westport CT: Praeger.

Clarke, A. and Kohler, P. (2005). *Property law: commentary and materials.* Cambridge: Cambridge University Press.

de la Torre, L. (2006). Terrorists raise cash by selling antiquities. *Government Security News,* 4(3), February 20. Online at http://www.savingantiquities.org/pdf/GSNarticle.pdf (accessed November 15, 2006).

Fidler, S. (2003). A black art: how the trade in stolen artifacts aids money laundering, organized crime, and terrorism. *Financial Times,* May 24.

Gerstenblith, P. (2004). *Art, cultural heritage, and the law: cases and materials.* Durham, NC: Carolina Academic Press.

Gilgan, E. (2001). Looting and the market for Maya objects: a Belizean perspective. In N. Brodie, J. Doole, and C. Renfrew (Eds.), *Trade in illicit antiquities: the destruction of the world's archaeological heritage,* pp. 73–88. Cambridge: McDonald Institute for Archaeological Research.

Gutchen, M. (1983). The destruction of archaeological resources in Belize, Central America. *Journal of Field Archaeology,* 10(2): 217–27.

Hanley, B. (1999). Law enforcement issues in art theft. Conference paper presented at Art crime: protecting art, protecting artists, and protecting consumers. Landmark Parkroyal, Sydney, 2–3 December. Online at http://www.aic.gov.au/events/aic%20upcoming%20events/1999/~/media/conferences/artcrime/hanleyle.ashx (accessed December 21, 2007).

Hicks, R. (2006). A model investigative protocol for looting and anti-looting educational program. In N. Brodie, M. Kersel, C. Luke, and K. Tubb (Eds.), *Archaeology, cultural heritage, and the antiquities trade,* pp. 133–46. Gainesville, FL: University Press of Florida.

Hoffman, B. (2006). Introduction to parts II and III: cultural rights, cultural property, and international trade. In B. Hoffman (Ed.), *Art and cultural heritage: law, policy and practice,* pp. 89–93. Cambridge: Cambridge University Press.

Honan, W. (1995). Art for whose sake? Trading in antiquities; rare pre-Columbian relics, at any cost. *New York Times,* July 31.

Kaplan, D. (2005). How jihadist groups are using organized-crime tactics – and profits – to finance attacks on targets around the globe. *US News & World Report,* November 27. Online at http://www.usnews.com/usnews/news/articles/051205/5terror_4.htm (accessed February 5, 2008).

Kaylan, M. (1987). Who stole the Lydian hoard? *Connoisseur*, July 217: 66–73.

Luke, C. and Henderson, J. (2006). The plunder of the Ulua Valley, Honduras, and a market analysis for its antiquities. In N. Brodie, M. Kersel, C. Luke, and K. Tubb (Eds.), *Archaeology, Cultural Heritage, and the Antiquities Trade,* pp. 147–72. Gainesville, FL: University Press of Florida.

McCalister, A. (2005). Organized crime and the theft of Iraqi antiquities. *Trends in Organized Crime*, 9(1): 24–37.

Mackenzie, S. R. M. (2005). *Going, going, gone: regulating the market in illicit antiquities.* Leicester, UK: Institute of Art and Law.

McManamon, F. and Morton, S. (2007). Reducing illegal trafficking in antiquities. In F. McManamon and A. Hatton (Eds.), *Cultural resource management in contemporary society: perspectives on managing and presenting the past*, pp. 247–75. London: Routledge.

Massy, L. (2001). *Le vol d'oeuvres d'art: une criminalité méconnue.* Bruxelles: Bruylant.

Meyer, K. (1973). *The plundered past.* New York: Atheneum.

Naylor, R. (2002). *Wages of crime: Black markets, illegal finance, and the underworld economy*. Ithaca, NY: Cornell University Press.

Paredes Maury, S. (1999). Surviving in the rainforest: the realities of looting in the rural villages of el Peten, Guatemala. Foundation for the Advancement of Meso-American Studies (FAMSI). Online at http://www.famsi.org/reports/95096/index.html (accessed December 20, 2007).

Powell, E. (2003). Cave looter solicits murder. *Archaeology*, January 27 Online at http://www.archaeology.org/online/features/nevadacave/index.html (accessed February 8, 2008).

Reuters (1999). International art-theft ring busted in Spain. *Reuters*, January 16. Online at http://www.museum-security.org/reports/000899.html (accessed December 19, 2007).

Roosevelt, C. and Luke, C. (2006). Looting Lydia: the destruction of an archaeological landscape in Western Turkey. In N. Brodie, M. Kersel., C. Luke, and K. Tubb (Eds.), *Archaeology, cultural heritage, and the antiquities trade,* pp. 173–87. Gainesville, FL: University Press of Florida.

Schick, J. (1999). *The gods are leaving the country*. Bangkok: White Orchid.

Tijhuis, E. (2006). *Transnational crime and the interface between legal and illegal factors: the case of the illicit art and antiquities trade.* Nijmegen: Wolf Legal Publishers.

Toner, M. (2002). *The past in peril.* Tallahassee, FL: Southeast Archeological Center, National Park Service.

20

Trafficking of "conflict diamonds"

Dina Siegel

Introduction

Millions of people are involved in the diamond industry – from digging in Africa to selling jewels in the shops of Antwerp, Dubai, New York, or Moscow. The diamond industry includes specialists, such as geologists, geophysicists, and chemists. It includes businesspeople, such as mine owners, bankers, investors, dealers, and brokers. It includes diamond workers, from diggers to cleavers, cutters, and butters. It includes government officials, security, customs, and police. And it includes smugglers, illegal traders, and underground bankers. Today the organization of the diamond industry is presented as a diamond pipeline, the continuous process from the production countries to retail and jewelry shops.

Throughout history, diamonds were mined from the gravel and sand around rivers. The first riverbed (alluvial) diamonds were discovered in India in approximately 800 BC. The Indians were also the first to use diamonds in exchange for goods and services. Diamonds were traded between India and Babylon, Israel, Egypt, Syria, Mesopotamia, and Ceylon. The earliest European diamond trade center was Venice, where the diamond-cutting industry started sometime after 1330. The Flemish town of Brugge later became a trade center in diamonds in the Western world, famous for its canals and relatively large community of Italian traders, who transported diamonds to Brugge for cutting. The legendary Lodewyk van Bercken from Brugge was the inventor of the scaife, a polishing wheel with a mixture of olive oil and diamond dust (Legrand, 1985, p. 38; Seidler, 1964, p. 14). In the fifteenth century Antwerp grew as an international trade market and has remained the capital of the diamond world until today. Sea adventurers brought to the port of Antwerp first Indian diamonds and, since 1725, also Brazilian diamonds. The peak Brazilian mines production was reached in the mid-nineteenth century. In addition to the legal production of diamonds with the Portuguese license, the Brazilian period is characterized by different waves of adventurers, the so-called *garimpeiros* and later *feitores* (clandestine wholesale buyers). In 1869 after the first important discoveries of diamonds in South Africa, diamonds were found also in Congo, Angola, Ghana, Sierra Leone and Russian Siberia, and lately in Australia, United States, and Canada (Legrand, 1985; Dickinson, 1965; Epstein, 1982).

Diamond pipeline – organization and criminal acquisitions of diamonds

The diamond pipeline depicts the movements of diamonds from the mine to the shops. The company De Beers and its Central Selling Organization (CSO) have dominated the international diamond trade for more than 70 years in all phases – sorting, evaluation, and selling – remaining the biggest diamond concern in the world, which is continuously modernizing the whole chain, from mine exploitation to the jewelry shops. World production of rough diamonds in 2005 has been estimated at 160 million carats (valued at $13.4 billion USD). Diamonds are mined today in more than 25 countries, while diamond working takes place in 30 countries worldwide. To produce a single 1-carat diamond, about 250 tons of earth is mined. The greatest quantities of diamonds are mined today in Botswana, South Africa, Angola, Namibia, Congo, Russia, and Australia. To a smaller extent diamonds are produced in Brazil, Venezuela, Sierra Leone, Ghana, Central African Republic, China, India, and a few other countries.

Several attempts were made to identify the vulnerability of the diamond industry to illicit activities. There are many weak points on the diamond pipeline and plenty of possibilities to steal, hide, and transport rough diamonds (Tamm, 2002, pp. 6–7; Vander Beken *et al.*, 2004; Siegel and van de Bunt, 2009). These possibilities vary from individual smuggling of small amounts directly to Europe, which involves little risk, but also little profit for criminals, to sophisticated networks, which include various players: diggers, couriers, brokers, local dealers and their international contacts, and huge amounts of money. The situation and settings vary from one country to another and on different phases of the diamond pipeline.

Diamond-related crimes may be either local or transnational, varying from spectacular robberies from the big museums and exhibitions to smuggling through complex schemes from Africa to Europe and the United States. Since the beginning of the 1990s, the diamond sector in different countries in the West has been confronted with the rising interest of criminal groups in diamonds in the context of smuggling, organized robberies, money laundering and fraud activities. Although there are different criminal organizations involved in illicit diamond activities, this chapter focuses only on trafficking of the so-called "conflict" or "blood diamonds" from some African states to Europe. In official reports, conflict diamonds play an important role in the financing of civil wars and in the abuse and exploitation of innocent people. Various rebel groups smuggle these diamonds to the West (Belgische Senaat, 2001). The question is what are the so-called "conflict diamonds," how and by whom are they smuggled from their countries, and how do they end up in the legal circuit?

Conflict diamonds

The term "conflict diamonds" was introduced by several non-governmental organizations (NGOs). It refers to rough diamonds obtained from areas under the control of rebel groups in some African countries in the second part of the 1990s. This concerns only 3–4 percent of the total production of all mined rough diamonds (Tamm, 2002). The concept was so attractive that very quickly it was adopted by the media, and later also used by politicians, governmental and law officials, representatives of diamond industry, and even filmmakers.

Most of the world's diamonds are mined in the peace regions, such as Australia, Canada, South Africa, or Russia. However, these regions usually are not discussed in the media. The picture that emerged since the end of 1990s is that the "real" diamond trade comes from the countries and regions, controlled by rebel movements in Sierra Leone, Angola, Liberia, and the Democratic Republic of the Congo.

At the end of the 1990s, dramatic reports came from Sierra Leone about rebels cutting off limbs and torturing powerless civilians who dared to oppose them. Other horrific stories about military commanders, deportations, killings, and confiscations of land and property came from Angola and Liberia. One of the first NGO actions was the publication of the Global Witness report in 1998, which accused the De Beers firm of purchasing diamonds from the Angolan rebel movement UNITA (National Union for the Total Independence of Angola) (Global Witness, 1998). The report was followed by the Fatal Transactions Campaign, a cooperative alliance by a number of human rights organizations. Two years later the Partnership Africa Canada produced another report about the conflict in Sierra Leone, which described the way in which the rebels from the Revolutionary United Front exchanged diamonds for drugs and weapons via neighboring Liberia (Smile *et al.*, 2000). In 2001, no less than 73 American NGOs joined forces to launch the Campaign to Eliminate Conflict Diamonds.

Detailed reports about raped victims and traumatized civilians appeared in the media and caused public concern all over the world. They described the atrocities not only as war horrors, but also as part of the problem of "conflict diamonds." Diamonds slowly became associated with bloody conflicts. Rivalry over the control of diamond mining was viewed as one of the sources of the violence. Moreover, the proceeds of the diamond trade were allegedly fueling the civil wars. The image of the diamond as a peaceful symbol of love was damaged as diamonds became associated with war and misery.

To talk about the "conflict diamonds" is already to assume the character of the phenomenon. "Conflict diamonds" or "blood diamonds" conjure up dramatic images. To understand the meaning of conflict diamonds, a wider context must be considered, which includes wars, poverty, local interrelationships, and natural resources. Diamonds and "conflict diamonds" themselves are not wrong or just, good or bad. The existence of the "conflict diamonds" is a result of a procedure by which the war, casualties, and diamonds have been construed as a problem of societal concern.

Violent conflicts in Africa existed for centuries. Social science literature is full with small and large-scale intertribal and international quarrels, conflicts, coups, and wars. The roots of these wars, as presented in the literature, are to be found in the "political misrule and economic decline of the post independence era" (Adebajo, 2002, p. 103), in "autocratic rule" and "rulers' manipulative skills aided by infusion of foreign aid driven by the imperatives of the Cold War" (Dunn, 1999, p. 98), in poverty, and in ethnic factors (Copson, 1994, pp. 78–9). But when the concept "conflict diamonds" was invented, it was precisely this phenomenon which became considered as a number one cause of the wars and conflicts.

The escalation of the "conflict diamonds" problem peaked in 2001–2. A local African problem now became a problem for the Western world. Buying diamonds originating from conflict regions meant (unwillingly) facilitating and supporting civil wars.

Kimberley process

In a short period of time the NGOs succeeded in placing the topic of "conflict diamonds" high on the international political agenda. The UN has adopted a number of resolutions to bring a halt to the illegal trading of diamonds in the African countries in question. In 2001, representatives of the most important diamond producing countries and NGOs met in the South African city of Kimberley to develop a system to regulate the import and export of rough diamonds (namely the Kimberley Process). One of the most important decisions, adopted by 52 nations on November 2002, was that of certification of diamonds – the Kimberley Process Certification Scheme (KPCS). Various diamond organizations, such as the Hoge Raad voor Diamant (HRD, the Diamond High Council), an umbrella organization of Antwerp diamond dealers, and De Beers, the largest multinational, participated in and supported the KPCS.

Some of the main points of the KPCS were: 1) government officials in each producing country must seal rough diamond exports in tamperproof security containers; 2) each such container has to be provided with a special certificate that identifies the shipment and registration of characteristics of the diamonds; 3) such a certificate is allowed to be issued only if an export country can prove that the diamonds originate from legal mines and; 4) the importing country must confirm the arrival of shipment to reduce the risk of fraud (Weyzig, 2004). Moreover, trading in rough diamonds is only permitted between countries that participate in the KPCS for rough diamonds.

Up until now, this certification process appeared to be a success: both NGOs and governments as well as the representatives of the diamond industry were working together to exclude diamonds from areas of conflict in Africa. However, almost since the start of the Kimberley process, various evaluation reports on the Kimberley-regulation raise doubts about the success of the Kimberley process and about the effectiveness of the certificates.

Critics on Kimberley Process

The US General Accounting Office (GAO) (2002) was the first to draw the conclusion that the KPCS did not work. Criticism has also been expressed in other reports and publications (e.g. Peleman, 2002).

After the KPCS was accepted, it became obligatory for all participant countries involved with production, processing or import of diamonds to have a "non-conflict" certificate. This transformation of the local African situation into a worldwide problem is usually considered as one of the consequences of the globalization process. The rebels in Sierra Leone, Angola, Liberia and the Democratic Republic of Congo controlled only between 3 and 4 percent of the world's total rough diamond supply (Tamm, 2002), yet Russia, Australia and many other countries are obliged to produce certificates, indicating the "non-conflict" origin of diamonds. In addition, many non-producing countries in the world, which are the majority of the Kimberley Process participants, are also involved in a complex, non-effective, and simply unnecessary control in the form of certificates, increasing bureaucracy and costs for the diamond traders.

By accepting the KPCS, the idea was to establish control on mining diamonds, without differentiating between countries. However, the issue of the inner control remained out of the competence and knowledge of the NGOs. The GAO (2002) charged that the plan did not propose the necessary oversight of the transport from a diamond's mine or alluvial field to its point of first export where "conflict diamonds" could enter the legitimate trade. Most of the countries where diamonds are mined lack law enforcement to prevent diamonds from being smuggled. Inner loyalties and interrelationships are crucial in most African countries. It is therefore almost impossible to have special units or organizations to effectively control the certification process in these countries, including conflict areas.

Another main criticism of the GAO is on the identification of the origin of rough diamonds. Determining the origins of rough diamonds based on physical inspection is almost impossible. Compared with other types of gems, high-quality diamonds are very similar, but variations can turn up within a single mine. There are no unique Australian or Angolan diamonds. In order to be able to determine whether certain characteristics are typical of diamonds from a specific geographic area, one would need first to create a database from a sufficient number of diamonds known to be from a particular area. There are 26 countries currently producing diamonds, with 500 kimberlitic deposits, of which 50 are being mined (15 large mines, not to underestimate alluvial diamond occurrences; about 4,000). Creation of a database, therefore, could take many years and millions of dollars. Even then, there is still a possibility that diamonds from some deposits may not have characteristics of their geographic source.

While geologists and mineralogists try to find ways to identify diamond's origin, the diamonds from the conflict areas are simply being transported across the border and mixed with clean "non-conflict" diamonds.

Smuggling of conflict diamonds

The most serious problem, one that the Kimberley agreement cannot solve, is smuggling of rough diamonds from the conflict areas to Europe (Belgische Senaat, 2001). The Kimberley Process does not examine the mechanism of the illegal trade in diamonds. According to Peleman, unregistered, smuggled diamonds "are by definition not covered by the Kimberley agreements" (Belgische Senaat, 2001). One of the weakest points in implementing the KPCS is that rough diamonds may come from unregistered stock and therefore cannot be verified, or that the diamonds are easy to enter into Europe through overseas territories.

One of the strategies in laundering conflict diamonds is to smuggle them into the markets of the Kimberley Process participant countries and mixing them with the local diamonds. Although there is some control in conflict countries, there is almost no control in the neighboring countries, such as Tanzania or Central African Republic, through which the diamonds are being smuggled. Another option is smuggling directly to either one of the cutting countries, or into a country that is not a participant in the Kimberley Process. Rough diamonds are smuggled out of the conflict countries without little difficulty and bought by dealers who sell them on to international trading centers in London, Antwerp, or Tel Aviv.

Three main characteristics are associated with the diamond smuggling business. Firstly, *smuggling for survival*, when extreme poverty pushes miners and diggers to steal diamonds from the mines and sell them to the local dealers. Secondly, *smuggling by organized crime groups*, when false certificates are used so that the origin of diamonds is provided with a "legal" cover. Thirdly, the *diamonds laundry*, where diamonds from conflict regions are smuggled to neighboring non-conflict countries to enter the legal trade. The difficulty in verifying the origin of rough diamonds on the basis of mineralogical analysis and the weak state control make diamond smuggling an easy activity.

Smuggling for survival

The phenomenon of smuggling from the diamond mines can perhaps be explained by the extreme poverty and few economic opportunities for the local population. Diamond diggers are mostly unskilled laborers with a shovel or a sieve. Their pay is about 1 USD per day or a few cups of rice and other goods. There are no written contracts. Witchcraft and sorcery are employed before and during digging by diggers to increase their luck or to ward off various evils.

In some African countries the so-called "casino economy" takes place. Most of those involved are actually gambling to find a large diamond and refer to money they earn as "winnings" rather than salaries and profits. This gambling is based on pure luck, when the wish and dream of every digger is to get in his hands this one special, large diamond, which is similar to the first prize or winning in lottery or casino and will transform him into a millionaire and will totally change his life. It is precisely the reason why so much control is exercised, since no one wants to become a "loser," to miss the happy moment of transformation.

Diamond mines are usually located many kilometers outside the villages or small towns, often in impenetrable jungles. In general "diamond searchers" can be divided in two categories: (1) those who receive a license from the local authorities to dig or working for another licensee; and (2) those who have no official permits to dig, the so-called "illegal miners." Officially, all miners must have licenses. However, in many countries illicit mining is a regular phenomenon. In Congo, for example, less than 10 percent of miners are officially registered (*Diamond Industry Annual Review*, 2004).

In Africa, each of the many small mines is controlled by licensees, who in turn often work for investors. These investors supply the equipment and other facilities. Looking for diamonds under water, for example, depends on good equipment. Workers can stay under water up to two to three hours, using the air, which comes from a diesel oxygen compressor. The life of the divers is difficult as they suffer various chronic diseases and injuries in addition to alcoholism and drugs addiction. Most divers and/or diggers who work for licensees do not get salaries; but they are fed, better or worse, varying from place to place. When a diamond is found, its value is evaluated on the spot and everybody get his/her share. The more people work at the mine, the less money each gets to earn. Under such conditions, it is tempting to hide one's find. If a diamond can be hidden, the digger can sell to a local trader in the village. Mutual suspicion is prevalent because everyone realizes the difference in value, when the earnings of a diamond are divided among the 10 to even 50 workers or being smuggled and sold direct to a local trader. When individuals smuggle diamonds found in a mine, they hope to improve their personal situation or that of their families. Smuggling can also be viewed as an economic guarantee or investment, when people migrate from one country to another.

In addition to the inner control of the co-diggers, there is also external control by the licensee. This control varies from watching that nothing is hidden in the mouth, nose, or clothes of the workers at the end of the day to armed men keeping a close watch during the whole process of digging. Many miners feel unprotected and unsafe. Local conflicts between different ethnic groups or between individuals are frequent. In Angola, for example, the local *garimpeiros* believe that Congolese miners, who are illegally looking for diamonds, have "magic powers." They steal luck from Angolans with the help of snakes, witchcraft, and curses. In 2004, the Angolan government decided to expel about 100,000 illegal Congolese migrants from Angola who were accused of stealing diamonds from the local mines.

Smuggling by organized crime groups

There is another kind of smuggling. Couriers who work for large crime groups, or individual smugglers who work independently, are often arrested in different European sea- and airports. The methods of smuggling vary from sticking stones to different parts of the body, to swallowing them, or hiding them in double-bottom suitcases. Smugglers usually arrive legally in Europe, with tourist or business visas. However, they stay much longer than legally allowed. A few hotels in the diamond neighborhood of Antwerp have become a typical meeting place for these couriers, who often know each other, or who make their first contacts with their "friends of friends."

There are various criminal organizations involved in illicit diamond activities. Since the beginning of the 1990s, the diamond sector in Antwerp has attracted rising interest of organized crime groups specialized in smuggling, money laundering, organized robberies and fraud activities. The main criminal groups are Russian and Georgian Jews, Israelis, Italians, Nigerians, and Ghanaians (Siegel, 2009). Since the Kimberley Process was initiated, the smuggling of diamonds increased from the areas in which civil wars took place in the late 1990s. Some scholars even called the introduction of the Kimberley certificates a perfect system to launder conflict diamonds. Very often rough diamonds from Sierra Leone, Angola, and other "problematic" countries simply appear at the diamond market in Europe. The Kimberley Process did not study the mechanism of illegal diamond trade. The non-registered smuggled diamonds were not even mentioned as a possibility and therefore did not appear in the Kimberley agreement. The diamond smuggling networks from Angola are mentioned in different reports. There are informal contacts between the officially registered diamond traders and the so-called pseudo-diamantairs (i.e. self-appointed), despite the assertive statement of many diamantairs that the sector is hermetically closed to any dubious figures. Business remains business and brokers connect not only among the respectable diamond dealers, but also among the diamantairs and those who offer a good price for good stones. The certificate of origin, unable to prevent smuggling, thus creates an illusion that the consumer will not buy the "blood diamond."

The role of Antwerp is important in this context as a meeting place for divergent criminal entrepreneurs. Criminals from different countries come to Antwerp to meet in anonymity to make agreements and plan future activities, including smuggling diamonds from areas of conflict. According to a report issued by the Belgian Military Intelligence, there are networks in Antwerp that specialize in smuggling diamonds from Angola (cited in Vander Beken *et al.*, 2004, p. 275). Some diamond companies supply false declarations of origin, for example from Zambia, a country without conflicts where absolutely no diamonds can be found (UN Security Council, 2002). There are also known cases of diamond dealers who import diamonds directly from Africa for their own use (Belgische Senaat, 2000). There are regular reports in the media about arrests of smugglers at customs controls at Zaventem airport.

Diamond whitewashing

All countries require that all diamond shipments from Angola, Sierra Leone, and Liberia have a certificate of origin. However, determining the original source of rough diamonds based on physical inspection is almost impossible. Geologists and mineralogists have always had an interest in studying the formation process of diamonds. The "conflict diamonds" issue has heightened their professional interest. Politicians and commercial-diamond experts always ask scientists how to identify the origin of "conflict diamonds." Many years of studying polished diamonds in gemological laboratories have led to the conclusion that diamonds cannot be distinguished according to their particular geographical areas. This scientific discovery is very useful for criminal groups involved in smuggling rough diamonds.

The impossibility of determining the origin of rough diamond and the lack of control of transport of diamonds inside and out of the conflict areas to neighbouring countries make smuggling relatively easy. In the non-conflict countries, rough diamonds are mixed with the local "innocent" diamonds and also get the legal certificate of origin from the non-conflict area. According to Peleman, the certificate of origin threatens "to become the ultimate whitewash system for conflict diamonds" (Belgische Senaat, 2001).

Diamond smuggling and financing terrorism

Two Antwerp diamond dealers, Aziz Nassour from Lebanon and Samih Ossaily from Sierra Leone, were convicted of fraud and leading a criminal organisation in the Antwerp criminal court in 2000 for importing diamonds from Sierra Leone and the Democratic Republic of Congo. The suspected connection between terrorism and "blood diamonds" was highly important for the Kimberley Process activists to make their point even stronger, namely that diamonds not only contribute to regional conflicts but also jeopardize the security of the United States and Europe. The issue appeared in a convenient context: the events of 9/11 affected the global security agenda and shifted attention of decision-makers from war-related issues to terrorism. Diamond smuggling suites this agenda. Reports that al-Qaeda converted about $20 million USD into conflict diamonds before the attacks in New York City and the continuous ties between

Osama Bin Laden and the sale of Sierra Leone conflict diamonds provided further support to the NGOs' anti-blood diamond mission (Global Witness, 2003).

According to NGO reports, members of al Qaeda established trading companies in Kenya and Tanzania to raise funds for terrorist attacks. In addition, the governments of Liberia and Burkina Faso were implicated by media reports for allegedly facilitating al Qaeda diamonds through West Africa around the 9/11 attacks. The Liberian president, Charles Taylor, was suspected of receiving a huge sum ($1 million USD) to harbor al-Qaeda members after the 9/11 attacks (Global Witness, 2003).

Subsequent research has challenged the link between terrorism and diamond smuggling, citing a lack of empirical evidence. The final report issued by the Commission on the 9/11 attacks states that its investigation of the media claims found "no persuasive evidence that al-Qaeda funded itself by trading in African conflict diamonds" (National Commission on Terrorist attacks upon the United States, 2004, p. 171).

Smuggling and corruption

Diamond smuggling is often associated with corruption. In many countries, access to scarce and demanded resources, in this case the Kimberley certificates, becomes a commodity for sale. Corruption, which in the Western world is commonly considered an abuse of public office for private gains, has elusive meanings in the non-Western world and it is often difficult to achieve moral clarity. Corruption there can mean gift-giving, solidarity, predatory authority, and negotiation process. The Western concept presumes a separation between the public and the private and ignores the reality of face-to-face communities that are based on exchange of gifts, patronage, and strong kinship links. Such societies and social relations have been well documented in scientific literature. What in the Western world is considered corrupt and illegal may be viewed as moral and normal in some social contexts.

The control system in the production countries presents the weakest point in diamond production, because there is a competition-based diamond buying system participated by individuals of varied backgrounds. In such a system no central registration and monitor is possible. The major actors are diamond middlemen who buy diamonds from diggers, miners, and *garimpeiros*. With the right connections and good gifts, it is not difficult to avoid the bureaucratic procedures and to transfer diamonds to Europe. These gifts include TV or DVD players, mobile telephones, and sometimes cars. The moral dilemma reflects two socio-cultural logics: what is considered corrupt in Europe is not necessarily so in Africa. In societies where familial obligations form the basis of the predominant social moral principles, one cannot expect public employees to uphold their official duties ahead of their own claim's requests. As some authors argue, "centuries-old and widely accepted social norms will often prove more powerful as guides to behavior than new and often imported rules based on arm's length, impersonal, and universal principles" (Tanzi, 1995, p. 25). In other words, when discussing the problem of corruption in some of the diamond producing, mainly African, countries, generalizations and superficial conclusions must be avoided. Tradition, cultural codes and existing relationships and networks must be carefully analyzed to avoid irresponsible blaming and moral clichés. Patronage and clientelism have their own morality, at least in the eyes of the local people.

Combating trafficking of conflict diamonds

As discussed, the KPCS cannot effectively control the trafficking of rough diamonds from the conflict areas to Europe. But how can this illegal trade and smuggling be combated, if at all?

Diamond traders have always been aware of the dangers in their business and have used various means to limit or minimize the risk. Monitoring mechanisms at the diamond mines and the use of private security have been around for a long time. As early as in the 1950s, De Beers realized that it needed to invest in surveillance and security, which resulted in the formation of the Diamond Protection Force. It used the latest technology, including light planes and helicopters, radio communication, and other sophisticated methods. Since then the security measures during the different phases of the diamond pipeline have been continuously improved.

Advanced technology is in use in the first phase of the diamond pipeline, mainly to control the flow of rough diamonds from the mines. In large mines diggers are regularly scanned by X-ray. Because of the health danger of frequent exposure to radiation, such scans are only applied randomly. De Beers, in their attempt to stop the mass smuggling from mines, developed "a low-dose x ray called Scannex, which allowed the security staff to use the x rays more frequently" (Hart, 2003, pp. 169, 170).

De Beers and other large companies employ private security intelligence teams, which are chiefly engaged in collecting information to help develop new preventive measures (Vander Beken *et al.*, 2004, p. 127).

The control of diamond smuggling involves targets at the individual diggers, who steal from mines and sell the stones to local small dealers and potential competitors for De Beers' control of supply. Mines are robbed everywhere, from Botswana by South African criminal groups to Australia by organized gangs. In 1995 a large number of deals between illicit diamantaires and workers in alluvial fields in Sierra Leone were discovered by De Beers. De Beers is interested in criminalizing these persons and their activities, for example by promoting anti-smuggling campaigns, or even assisting local authorities in catching the thieves. The elimination of competition means the avoidance of uncertainty and the minimization of risks.

The diamond trade has certain characteristics, which make it difficult for external monitoring agencies to get a clear view of the flow of money and goods. During the transformation from rough to processed diamonds, the stock constantly changes in size, value, and destination. As a result of these circumstances and the changing prices caused by fluctuations in the market, diamond transactions are often nontransparent to outsiders and difficult to audit (GAO, 2002; Vander Beken *et al.*, 2004, p. 261). This situation creates opportunities for diamond dealers to evade taxes, to sell illegal diamonds, or to keep certain transactions out of the records. Preventive measures in the diamond industry devised to protect the sector against the outside world may unintentionally bring the threat of organized crime closer to home. Diamond traders are slowly becoming aware of this threat. They realize that "only a compliant and fiscally transparent diamond business can survive in the global world of the twenty-first century" (Meeus, 2006).

In addition, the diamond trade is sensitive to its image, and for that reason keen to address alleged abuses (e.g. conflict diamonds). This explains the willingness of the diamond industry to invest in security and to deal with events that could tarnish its image. The association between diamonds and the arms trade or drug money is disastrous for the image of the diamond as a jewel of love. The awareness that risks should be tackled by an alliance of the diamond business and public agencies is also growing at the local level. In Antwerp, the Belgian police and the HRD are now cooperating in the fight against organized crime, including fake and stolen jewels and money laundering. The diamond business has tried to distance itself from these groups, and does not allow the dubious African dealers to become members of an official diamond bourse. They have also joined forces with the Belgian police to "fight organized crime."

Conclusion

As we have discussed thus far, diamonds are not safe in the production countries, on mines, nor are they safe crossing the borders. International diamond trade is based on the free movement from one place to another, as from mines to local trade centers, and from there to the capitals in African countries. In some African countries, numerous reports link diamonds with arms, smuggled by international networks of arm traffickers and brokers from the USA, Great Britain, Israel, and Russia, and especially for supplying weapons to the conflict African countries. Important weapon traffickers such as Leonid Minin or Victor Bout are almost always presented in the media as being "paid in diamonds." There is, however, no evidence of their direct involvement in exchange of trafficked arms for diamonds in the conflict areas. Other criminal activities which are almost automatically pronounced in the context of diamond-related crimes are money laundering, fraud, and tax evasion. The diamond industry has always been aware of external threats and has tried to protect itself by strong internal cohesion and by shielding itself from the outside world. In the last decades, these traditional lines of defense have been increasingly affected by external factors. Professional criminals and organized crime groups have discovered the value of diamonds. Over the last few years, a series of criminal events have brought to light the vulnerability of the diamond business. The changing economic reality and the introduction of the phenomenon of "conflict diamonds" have led to the appearance of new players on the global market. One of the most important consequences is that globalization has had an impact on transnational organized crime. As a result of growing mobility and increase in international flows of goods and money, the opportunities for crime have increased as well.

Whether there are "conflict," or "peacefully" smuggled or stolen diamonds, criminals make huge profits on these small stones.

Future research questions

1. How was the concept "conflict diamonds" constructed? How does it vary across regions?
2. What were the reasons for establishing the Kimberley Process? Is it effective? How can it be improved?
3. What are the main characteristics of the diamond smuggling business? How do these correlate with policing practices?
4. Why is the smuggling of conflict diamonds difficult to control?
5. What processes or procedures are most effective against conflict diamond smuggling?

References

Adebajo, D. (2002). *Building peace in West Africa. Liberia, Sierra Leone, and Guinea-Bissau.* Boulder, London: Lynne Rienner Publishers.

Belgische Senaat (2000). *De Georganiseerde criminaliteit in Belgie: eerste tussentijds verslag namens de Opvolgingscommissies inzake de Georganiseerde criminaliteit,* zitting 2000–1, nr.2–425/1.

—— (2001). Parlementaire onderzoekscommissie 'Grote Meren', Hoorzittingen, *Verslag,* September 7, gr. 4.

Copson, R. (1994). *Africa's wars and prospects for peace.* New York: M. E. Sharpe.

Dickinson, J. Y. (1965). *The book of diamonds. Their history and romance from ancient India to modern times.* New York: Avenel Books.

Dunn, D. (1999). The civil war in Liberia. In T. Ali and R. Matthews (Eds.) *Civil wars in Africa. Roots and resolutions,* pp. 89–121. Montreal, Kingston, London, Ithaca: McGill-Queen's University Press.

Epstein, E. J. (1982). *The rise and fall of diamonds.* New York: Simon & Schuster; and *The Diamond Invention* online at http://www.edwardjayepstein.com/diamond/htm (accessed November 23, 2010).

General Accounting Office (GAO) (2002). *International trade. Critical issues remain in deterring conflict diamond trade.* Report on Congressional Requesters. June.

Global Witness (1998). *Rough trade: the role of companies and governments in the Angolan conflict*. December.
—— (2003).
—— For a few dollars more: how al Qaeda moved into the diamond trade. A report by Global Witness. Online at (pp. 1–50) http://www.globalwitness.org/sites/default/files/import/Few%20Dollars%20More%200-50.pdf; (pp. 50–96) http://www.globalwitness.org/sites/default/files/import/Few%20Dollars%20More%2051-98.pdf (accessed December 10, 2010).
Hart, M. (2003). *Diamond. The history of a cold-blooded love affair*. London: Fourth Estate.
Legrand, J. (1985). *Diamant: mythe, magie en werkelijkheid*. Brussel/Amsterdam: Elsevier.
Meeus, P. (2006) *Rapaport News*. Managing director of the HRD speaks; 7 February. Online at http://www.diamonds.net (accessed November 23, 2010).
National Commission on Terrorist attacks upon the United States (2004). The 9/11 Commission report. Online at http://govinfo.library.unt.edu/911/report/911Report.pdf (accessed December 10, 2010).
Peleman, J. (2002). Conflictdiamanten – gezien vanuit Afrika. In *Tijdschrift voor Criminologie*, nr. 4, jaargang 44, pp. 358–66.
Seidler, N. (1964). *Gems and jewelry*. New York: The Odyssey Press.
Siegel, D. (2009). *The mazzel ritual. Culture, customs and crime in diamond industry*. Dordrecht, New York: Springer.
Siegel, D. and van de Bunt, H. (2009). Case study: the diamond industry. In *Organized crime in the EU. A methodology for risk assessment*. EU: IKOC Project; Milan: Universita Cattolica del Sacro Cuore.
Smile, I., Gberie, L., and Hazleton, R. (2000). *The heart of the matter: Sierra Leone, diamonds and human security*. Partnership Africa Canada. January.
Tamm, I. (2002). *Diamonds in peace and war: severing the conflict-diamond connection*. World Peace Foundation: WPF Reports, number 30.
Tanzi, V. (1995). Corruption, governmental activities, and markets. *Finance and Development*, 32(4): 24–6.
UN Security Council (2002). Additional report of the monitoring mechanism on sanctions against UNITA, 26 April.
Vander Beken, T., Cuyvers, L., De Ruyver, B., Defruytier, M., and Hansens, J. (2004). *Kwetsbaarheid voor georganiseerde criminaliteit. Een gevalstudie van de diamantsector*. Gent: Academia Press.
Weyzig, F. (2004). *The Kimberly Process Certification Scheme one year after: state of affairs in the European Union.*, SOMO, NIZA: Fatal Transactions.

21

Conceptualizing and studying organized crime in a global context

Possible? indispensable? superfluous?

Jana Arsovska

Introduction

From the mid-1990s onwards, governments worldwide have regarded organized crime as a major policy issue. At the 2002 London Conference on EU Security, Javier Solana, the EU High Representative for the Common Foreign and Security Policy, stated: "[t]he challenge is vast and our enemies are resourceful. The battle will only be won if we are determined and united. It [organized crime] is an enemy we must defeat, or it will defeat us" (Solana, 2002, p. 3). The topic of organized crime has attracted enormous attention from the media and academia, too. Author Claire Sterling (1994) popularized the notion of "Pax Mafiosa," arguing that in the post-Cold War era, international organized crime groups are working together efficiently in an effort to divide the globe between them. These groups underwent a major transformation and expanded their criminal activities far beyond gambling, racketeering, sex, narcotics and stolen property.

During the last two decades, the predominant view has been that the globalization of the legal economy has globalized the criminal underworld (van Duyne, 1993; Williams, 1994; Galeotti, 2005). Today, organized crime is no longer seen as an American or Italian phenomenon only. Despite much talk, however, a clear understanding of the phenomenon is still lacking, particularly among policy makers. Governments, without having a clear vision of *what* constitutes "organized crime" and *how much* "organized crime" is out there, have deeply engaged in "the fight" against it. Yet, solutions only have meaning if one has a firm grip of the problems being addressed.

Unlike politicians who tend to shift away from scientific definitions, criminologists must first rigorously define the concepts they study. This chapter provides a critical and chronological analysis of the main paradigms on organized crime with the aim to conceptualize the term as accurately as possible. It also discusses the context in which main international definitions and anti-organized crime policies developed, pinpointing the controversial and political nature of organized crime. Finally, it discusses the important, but challenging, role of researchers in studying and measuring organized crime in a global context.

Conceptualizing organized crime: mainstream paradigms

Models of organized crime

There is no doubt that organized crime is a concept difficult to define and conceptualize. As Wright (2006, p. 2) explains, organized crime does not simply mean crime that is organized. In reality many types of crime require organization, but are not labeled as organized crime. The literature sets out almost as many conceptualizations and definitions as there are people with interest in the subject (see Box 21.1).

The extensive debate on the meaning of organized crime has resulted in different models of organized crime often linked to the classification proposed by Jay Albanese (1994), who distinguishes between a "hierarchical model," a "patron-client model" and an "enterprise model" of organized crime. Some models, however, go beyond the underlying conception of the nature of organized crime. They consider the social conditions responsible for the emergence of organized crime (Halstead, 1998). Others examine the social consequences of the different forms of organized crime. Some study the structure and coordination mechanisms of the criminal groups; whereas others explore the patterns of behavior. Certain models are considered definitional ones, while others, normative. All this makes the study of organized crime hard to comprehend.

Early efforts

The first major attempt to provide official definition was made by US Federal Commission (Wickersham Commission) set up by President Herbert Hoover in 1929. The members of the Wickersham Commission – originally established to address the prohibition of alcohol – provided the first insight into what they understood organized crime to be. The significance of their report was that: (1) it laid blame on various actors in the US, including police, judges and politicians, and (2) it put together crimes of legitimate business, commercialized fraud and racketeering under the heading "organized crime." The report provided the basis for the depiction of "organized crime as a business." Dwight Smith (1991, p. 137) explains: "If business men and gangsters behave like each other, what is the sense of having two categories that, by definition, are not mutually exclusive?"

The Wickersham Commission argued that one of the reasons why Americans do not abide by Federal laws lies in the *legal* and *political* foundations of the country. It noted that organized crime is an outcome of the US's contradictory laws. The critical findings of the Commission, however, were largely ignored by US policy makers. Soon after, the US government and the newly formed Federal Bureau of Investigation (FBI) set about improving the image of the police by *externalizing* the problem of "organized crime." This was achieved via media propaganda that glorified police officers and politicians and downplayed their involvement in racketeering, making way for a new description of organized crime.

Formal, hierarchical bureaucracies: the conspiratorial view

From the mid-1940s onward, an increasingly popular theory was that the criminal underworld in the US was centrally organized by a ruthless Italian organization known as the "Mafia," originating in Sicily. In the 1950s, Estes Kefauver, a US senator who conducted hearings on the subject of organized crime, first argued that the "Mafia" is a well-structured, sinister organization – an import of secret criminal societies rooted in foreign cultures. Although this view was subject

Box 21.1 Conceptualizing organized crime. What does it mean?

German criminologist Klaus von Lampe made an impressive collection of more than 100 definitions of organized crime. Grouping the definitions according to similarities, von Lampe came up with several categories of "organized crime," showing how organized crime has been depicted by scholars and governmental institutions worldwide.

"Intelligent individuals"
"While the majority of crimes are poorly planned, frequently violent and generally not enormously financially rewarding, organized crime, committed by rational and intelligent individuals, is well planned and always aimed at an immense financial gain." (Kelland, 1987, p. 356)

"Series of illegal transactions"
"Organized crime consists of a series of illegal transactions between multiple offenders, some of whom employ specialized skills, over a continuous period of time, for purposes of economic advantage, and political power when necessary to gain economic advantage. Normally, but not always, techniques of bribery, intimidation, and violence are used and hegemony over services sought." (Rhodes, 1984, p. 4)

"Illegal activities"
"Organized crime means: the illegal activities carried out by structured groups of three or more persons existing for a prolonged period of time and having the aim of committing serious crimes through concerted action by using intimidation, violence, corruption or other means in order to obtain, directly or indirectly, a financial or other material benefit" (Council of Europe, 2002, p. 6).

"Non-ideological enterprise"
"Organized crime is a non-ideological enterprise involving a number of persons in close social interaction, organized on a hierarchical basis, with at least three levels/ranks, for the purpose of securing profit and power by engaging in illegal and legal activities." (Abadinsky, 1994, p. 6)

"Group"
Any group having some manner of a formalized structure and whose primary objective is to obtain money through illegal activities. (FBI, n.d.)

"A social system"
"(O)rganized crime is both a social system and a social world. The system is composed of relationships binding professional criminals, politicians, law enforcers, and various entrepreneurs." (Block, 1983, p. vii)

Visit http://www.organized-crime.de/OCDEF1.htm for the complete list of definitions.

to criticism years later (Box 21.2), in 1967, the President's Commission on Law Enforcement and Administration of Justice confirmed the conspiratorial nature of organized crime by arguing that it is "a society that seeks to operate outside the control of the American people and their governments."

The testimony of the first "insider" of organized crime (Kefauver, 1950s and McClellan, 1960s Committees), Joseph Valachi, was the basis for the hierarchical model of organized crime.[1] Valachi argued that the criminal organization's name is La Cosa Nostra and not Mafia, and described it as a family structure with graded ranks of authority (Cressey, 1969; Albanese, 2000). Territory and criminal enterprises were divided among "families" of men of Italian descent. In 1967, although Valachi's flawed testimony has been disproved many times, the conspiracy model was given a degree of academic legitimacy. Criminologist Donald Cressey (1969), a member of the

Box 21.2 Alien conspiracy theory

Throughout the years, critical criminologists have argued that politicians and law enforcement agencies were greatest promoters of alien conspiracy theory, to secure greater enforcement resources and to advance their careers. Criminologist William Chambliss in his book *Power, Politics and Crime* writes that US President Nixon focused on organized crime to keep crime at the forefront of the political agenda and thus to provide a smoke screen for an assault on civil liberties. In his April 23, 1969, message to Congress, Nixon warned of the dangers of organized crime: "It is vitally important that Americans see this alien organization for what it really is – a totalitarian and closed society operating within an open and democratic one. It has succeeded so far because an apathetic public is not aware of the threat it poses to American life" (Chambliss, 1999, p. 21). Chambliss argues that the outcome of such speeches resulted in authorized widespread wiretapping of suspected organized crime figures, establishment of 20 Federal racketeering field offices, the approval of $300 million appropriation in the 1970 budget for the Law Enforcement Assistance Administration, and change in legislation (Chambliss, 1999).

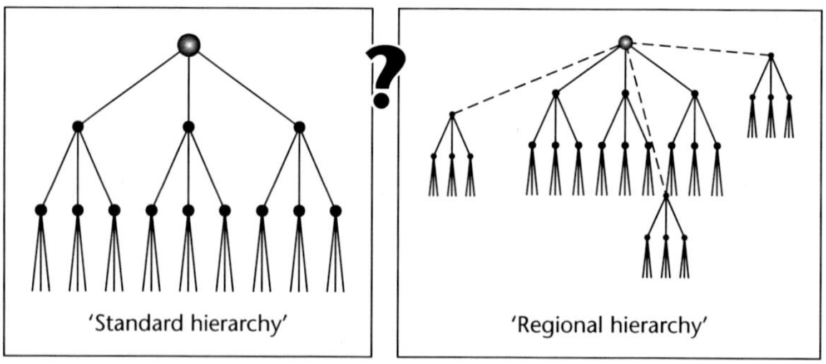

Figure 1 Hierarchically structured alien organization

Source: Typology based on 2002 UNODC Pilot Survey of 40 organized crime groups; http://www.unodc.org/pdf/crime/publications/Pilot_survey.pdf.

1967 Presidential Task Force, claimed that organized crime in the US comprised a nationwide alliance of 24 tightly knit criminal "Mafia families." These families were hierarchically structured (bosses, captains, "buffers," "soldiers" and "buttonmen") and comprised a well-defined criminal organization (Cressey, 1969).

Mario Puzo's *The Godfather* (1969) had also its part in shaping the mystifying image of the Mafia as a criminal conspiracy and hierarchy. As Paoli (2003, p. 3) rightly argues, hardly any phenomenon since the Second World War has fascinated the American public more than the Italian Mafia as presented in *The Godfather*.

Ethnic ties and patron–client relations: the socio-cultural view

The 1970s witnessed a growing body of scholarly research on organized crime, examining the organizational, institutional, commercial and behavioural aspects of organized crime. Sociologist Joseph Albini (1971), anthropologists Francis Ianni and Elizabeth Reuss-Ianni (1972), and others were unable to find connections between the criminal groups they studied and a well-structured hierarchy. The researchers found that friendships based on cultural, ethnic (e.g. Italian links) and economic ties formed the basis for organized crime activities. Albini (1971) claimed that organized crime consisted of networks of patrons and clients, rather than rational hierarchies. He viewed a criminal group as a system of loosely structured relationships where every participant is interested in maximizing their own profits. Ianni and Reuss-Ianni (1972) argued that kinship groups are the basis of organized crime.

Prominent sociological theories from this period also tackled the root causes of organized crime in the US. Donald Bell's (1953) ethnic succession or "queer ladder" thesis and Robert K. Merton's (1938) anomie and social strain theory argued that immigrant groups experience strains in North American society (e.g. discrimination, poverty and unemployment). They react to blocked opportunities by becoming involved in (organized) criminal activities to achieve economic success. When the strain subsides, the ethnic group relies less on crime to subsist, and moves into mainstream society. This creates an opportunity for succeeding (immigrant) groups to fill the criminal void (Bell, 1953; Ianni and Reuss-Ianni, 1972). Other scholars, however, have concluded that Italians were not giving up crime, but were only withdrawing from frontline operations (Lupsha, 1981). Despite slight disagreements between scholars, the paradigm prevalent until the early 1980s presented the "Mafia" as a *cultural attitude* and *social system* responsive to culture, excluding any corporate dimension (Block, 1978).

Rational, illicit enterprises: the economic view

In the 1980s judicial investigations in Italy started to provide proof of the existence of well-structured Mafia groups. This resulted in a shift of scholars' attention towards *entrepreneurial features* of organized crime actors. Organized crime groups, including the Mafia, were conceptualized as an *enterprise* and their *economic activities* became the focus of academic analysis (Smith, 1978, 1991; Reuter, 1983; Arlacchi, 1986). Pino Arlacchi (1986) argued that the Mafiosi in Italy underwent an entrepreneurial transformation, abandoning the traditional roles of mediators. He maintained that only by shifting the attention from the more strictly sociological understanding of organized crime to the concept of enterprise is an understanding of the modern Mafia possible.

According to the economic view, organized crime groups form and thrive in the same way legitimate businesses do: they respond to the needs and demands of suppliers, customers, regulators and competitors. Criminal actions are motivated by expected economic gains; hence, committing crime is based on a rational evaluation of the expected benefits of the crime compared to the expected costs and risks involved. This model argues that regardless of ethnicity or hierarchy the *economic* concerns and *market* forces are the primary cause of criminal behavior.

Similar to sociological theories, economic approaches also situate the cause of organized crime within the societies in which it exists; organized crime is a part of society's (underground) markets. Criminal organizations exist to supply goods and services demanded by the public, but declared illegal by the state. In this view, prohibition of goods and services drives the trade underground, where it is monopolized by criminal entrepreneurs.

An extensive focus on entrepreneurship in the study of organized crime, however, has led to what Fijnaut and Paoli (2004) describe as a simple reduction of contemporary "Mafia" groups to business enterprises; thus, denying them any other goal but profit. An integrative approach to the study of organized crime is hence necessary.

The "battle" against the "enemy": global efforts

Defining organized crime: international perspectives

The expansion of organized crime and its global dimension have led various international and governmental agencies to develop their own definitions of organized crime in order to improve the "fight" against it. These definitions, although seen as more "practical," are rooted in existing theoretical frameworks, such as those discussed earlier.

From the mid-1970s, the UN gradually started to seek a universal definition of organized crime that would serve as a basis for policy makers and law enforcement officials worldwide. It was not, however, until 1994, when the World Ministerial Conference on Organized Transnational Crime – held in Naples and attended by governmental representatives from 142 countries – officially baptized the term "transnational organized crime."

Six years later in Palermo, the UN developed its first legally binding instrument in the field of crime: the UN Convention on Transnational Organized Crime (Palermo Convention, 2000).[2] By introducing the Palermo Convention the UN tried to provide a universal definition of organized crime (Box 21.3). After several days of negotiations between delegates from various countries, the Convention was ratified by more than 120 countries. This was a great step forward in the fight against transnational organized crime. Unfortunately and unsurprisingly, however, the painstaking process gave rise to a broad definition of organized crime – the result of the political process of developing one unique instrument to be applied in 192 different political and legal structures.

As Levi (2002) rightly points out, in national and international definitions (EU, UN), which bind together countries to action, there is frequently a tension between (a) those who want the legislation to cover a wide set of circumstances to avoid the risk that any major criminal might "get away with it"; and (b) those who want the law to be tightly drawn to avoid the overreach of powers which might otherwise criminalize groups who are only a modest threat.

One debatable issue is the UN definition of "structured group." It is formulated in broad terms, so as to include both groups with hierarchical or other structures, and non-hierarchical groups where the roles of the members of the groups need not be formally defined (Levi, 2002, p. 884). Again, as a result of the political process of developing a global instrument, the UN definition makes no clear distinction between "organized crime group" and "organized crime," implicitly treated as synonyms. Some have also questioned the "duration" condition (extending over a "prolonged" period of time). Criminologist Michael Levi (2002, p. 884) has noted that by these criteria a group of Chinese or East European origins, which engages in "skimming" credit card details with an inexpensive piece of software, and re-encoding them onto plastic cards to be used in another country, qualifies as a transnational organized crime group.

Box 21.3 UN definition of organized crime

Article 2 of the Convention:

(a) "Organized criminal" group shall mean a structured group of three or more persons, existing for a period of time and acting in concert with the aim of committing one or more serious crimes or offences established pursuant to this Convention, in order to obtain, directly, or indirectly, a financial or other material benefit;

(b) "Serious crime" shall mean conduct constituting an offence punishable by a maximum deprivation of liberty of at least four years or more serious penalty;

(c) "Structured group" shall mean a group that is not randomly formed for the immediate commission of an offence and that does not need to have formally defined roles for its members, continuity of its membership or a developed structure.

Transnationality of offence: Article 3.2 of the UN Convention

Office is transnational in nature if:

(a) It is committed in more than one state;

(b) It is committed in one state but a substantial part of its perpetration, planning direction or control takes place in another state;

(c) It is committed in one state but involves an organized criminal group that engages in criminal activities in more than one state; or

(d) It is committed in one state but has substantial effects in another state.

(Source: Council of the EU, 2001)

Moreover, at the beginning of the twenty-first century, the concept of organized crime has also gained almost absolute legitimacy in Europe as well. This is shown by the fact that most European governments have issued laws and strategies targeting organized crime. In 1998, the EU set out a definition of organized crime in order to consolidate policy on the subject, and to make it a criminal offence to participate in criminal organization in the member states of the EU. In 2001, the European Commission and Europol tried to operationalize this broad definition in order to ensure more coherent action among Europe's law enforcement agents. They developed a working definition of organized crime according to which 11 characteristics of criminal organizations are associated with the label of organized crime. The EU definition (Box 21.4) requires the presence of a minimum of six characteristics: four core/mandatory criteria and two optional to be drawn from a list of criteria.

As in the case of the UN definition, the EU definition has also been criticized because of its vagueness. For example, Levi (2002) claims that the optional criteria are easy to satisfy: major profitable crimes always entail money laundering; a degree of specialization always exists to some extent between participants; and the criteria of "duration" is very vague. He argues that the EU definition includes anything from a major Italian syndicates to three menacing burglars with a window cleaning business who have divided among themselves the criminal tasks.

Criticizing is easy, but an important question still remains: What *should be done,* at both national and international levels, to improve existing definitions and anti-organized crime policies, and what *can we, as criminologists, do* to contribute towards a better understanding of the phenomenon

Box 21.4 EU definition of organized crime

Four mandatory:
(1) Collaboration among more than two people;
(2) Extending over a prolonged or indefinite period (referring to stability and [potential] durability);
(3) Suspected of committing serious criminal offences, punishable by imprisonment for at least four years or a more serious penalty; and
(4) The central goal of profit and/or power.

Two optional:
(5) Specialised division of labour among participants;
(6) Exercising measures of discipline and control;
(7) Employing violence or other means of intimidation;
(8) Employing commercial business-like structures;
(9) Participating in money-laundering;
(10) Operational across national borders;
(11) Exerting influence over legitimate social institutions (polity, government, justice, economy).

of organized crime? This chapter does not provide a solution to a global problem; however, it identifies areas where future research is certainly needed.

Gaps, problems and policy recommendations

Organized crime: nature and political biases

Not an alien conspiracy . . . In the new century, it seems that the alien conspiracy theories of organized crime have been officially ousted. In reality, however, many of those who favor the inclusive UN or EU definitions still remain captivated by the notion of organized crime as a criminal entity that poses existential threat to "civil society" and is rooted in foreign cultures. For instance, the UN Convention (2000) focused on the need to regulate organized crime as a global threat; however, the insertion of the word "transnational" in the definition enabled more powerful countries to externalize their domestic crime problems to foreign regions. One can, nevertheless, easily turn the argument around and claim that Western "civilized" societies pose a threat to "third world countries" or "states with weak laws" precisely because the demand for various illicit products and services often comes from the West. It is this demand that drives illegal markets and enables organized crime groups to flourish. Thus instead of focusing extensively on the supply side, should one not first try to understand why people in Western countries demand narcotics, prostitutes, cheap labor, guns, children for sexual purposes and other "forbidden goods"? One thing is certainly clear: Politicians must be reminded over and over again that organized crime is *not* a problem that should be externalized to foreign countries or uncivilized societies.

. . . But part of the social fabric: Organized crime in its different forms has been part of the social fabric of every society, no matter whether a "Western democracy" or a "third world country." Common people, taxi drivers, police officers, politicians, street criminals, Russian nationals,

indigenous criminal groups, Western diplomats, US citizens, businessmen and other actors have been all involved in criminal activities labeled "organized crime." As French sociologist Emile Durkheim (1965) argued, human appetites are unlimited, and crime is a normal phenomenon. All segments of every society might engage in profit-oriented crimes as long as there is, for example, a demand for the illegal product and enormous emphasis placed on materialistic values by society. Peter Lupsha (1981) analyzed available data on the date and place of birth and year of arrival in the US of major organized crime leaders and their associates. He found that the overwhelming majority were American born or raised – not foreigners.

Also, throughout the years, conventional criminologists have been fixated on a narrow idea of crime as something that low-income people do. This idea is unfortunate because the scale and the scope of crimes committed by powerful companies, high-income professionals and state officials are staggering (Watts *et al.*, 2008). As members of the Wickersham Commission argued, blame should be laid also on police, judges, politicians and businesspeople (Box 21.5).

Box 21.5 Criminal–political–business ties

The case of SHQIPONIJA

During the UN embargo on Yugoslavia (1992–5), the Albanian state set up a firm called SHQIPONIJA. The firm was a property of the Democratic Party. It developed a monopoly in the transport of oil and violated the UN embargo for three years. Police cars escorted the trucks loaded with oil. Under the pressure of the International Community, SHQIPONIJA was closed down. Its financial statements were never found. (Based on internal intelligence report.)

The case of "South 1"

In November 2006, the Macedonian court sentenced 28 people for smuggling 44 Albanian migrants and luxurious cars from Macedonia to Greece. The transport from Albania to Macedonia was organized by Albanian nationals for a price of 1,500 Euros per person. At the border, taxi drivers took the migrants and drove them to the mountain pass Pletvar where a truck was waiting. Among the convicted people were several Bulgarian nationals, a police officer and the head of the border police station, responsible for trafficking stolen cars from Bulgaria to Macedonia (Arsovska, 2008).

Agim Haxhiu, diplomat – drug trafficker?

In May 2009, Agim Haxhiu, the second secretary of the Albanian embassy in Macedonia, was detained in Turkey on charges of drug trafficking. He was arrested while carrying 65 kilograms (143 pounds) of heroin with a street value of 2.5 million Euros in Italy or Greece. This was Albania's second recent diplomatic drug embarrassment after an embassy driver was arrested in Italy with a kilogram of cocaine in 2008 (World News, 2009).

Police evidence room robbed

In January 2009, the evidence room at the Kosovo Police headquarters in Pristina has been broken into, and a substantial amount of narcotics and money was reported stolen. Five policemen, including the Deputy Colonel and Director of the Directorate against Organized Crime and his deputy, were suspended in relation to the theft of drugs and foreign currency.

Corrupt officials

Case G-V (2001–2) concerns an international criminal network composed of Italian, Bulgarian, Albanian and Greek traffickers corrupting police officials, and a disciplinary inquiry regarding seven Belgian police officers. A Belgian ex-prostitute accused two of those agents of corruption. The policemen regularly visited prostitution bars to control prostitutes. The exploiter told the police that she received protection from Bulgarian and Albanian criminals but also from police officials (Arsovska and Janssens, 2009).

Visa fraud in Western Europe

A Belgian civil servant employed in the protocol service of the Belgian Ministry of Foreign Affairs arranged the distribution of diplomatic passports in the 1990s. He admitted to having sold at least 300 residence permits to people associated with the Russian Mafia and people known for espionage. Four Filipino girls received illegal diplomatic passports. Three of them had jobs as domestic servants. One of the accomplices in this case was an important figure in a large Russian company. The company was also laundering dirty money. Five diplomatic passports were given to this company illegally. The Belgian civil servant was trailed and convicted of forgery (Arsovska and Janssens, 2009).

The Thalidomide case

In the 1950s the major German pharmaceutical company Grunenthal produced a drug called Thalidomide, developed as a tranquillizer. The drug was advertised as safe, non-poisonous and non-toxic. It was marketed as being safe to be taken by pregnant women. In the 1960s evidence began to emerge of birth defects associated with the use of the drug by pregnant women. Babies were born without legs and arms. In 1968 a civil case was brought against the company, and after two and a half years of legal argument the company agreed to settle out of court and escaped criminal prosecution (Watts *et al.*, 2008).

Activities, structures and operational methods

Not necessarily violent and hierarchical . . . Organized crime encompasses a wide range of activities from racketeering, extortion and gambling to commercial fraud, fraudulent acquisition of state funds, money laundering and smuggling of people, drugs and other commodities.

Organized crime activities are performed by groups with different structures; some closely knit and hierarchical, while others fluid, international and heterogeneous. Some groups use sophisticated business methods for achieving their goals, while others rely on violence. For some subcultural codes are important, while for others – which are more business-oriented and rational (in the economic sense) – such codes might be superfluous. It is difficult to describe accurately these different markets, groups, structures and cultures by referring to one model of organized crime (Box 21.6).

. . . But diverse and ill-defined: As Albanese (2000, p. 87) rightly claims, there is evidence to support the applicability of all models of organized crime to any given group. Organized crime groups can be simultaneously hierarchical, ethnically bound and also maintained by market forces. Seeing the different models as incompatible is what causes confusion in the literature on organized crime. Thus, integrated, interdisciplinary and cross-national studies of organized crime are needed

Box 21.6 The different faces of organized crime

Activities (diversity)

Examples:

Organized theft

Racketeering and extortion

Trafficking of persons

Business fraud and money laundering

Smuggling of arms and drug trafficking

Structures (diversity)

Examples:

1. Networks: human trafficking

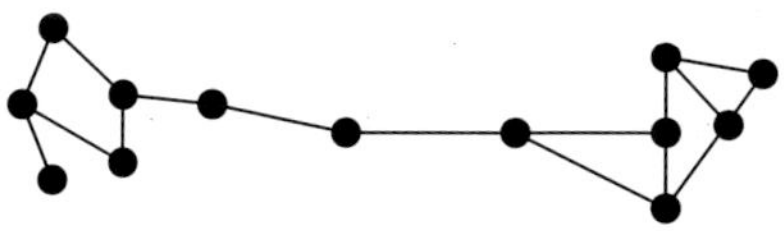

2. Networks: car theft

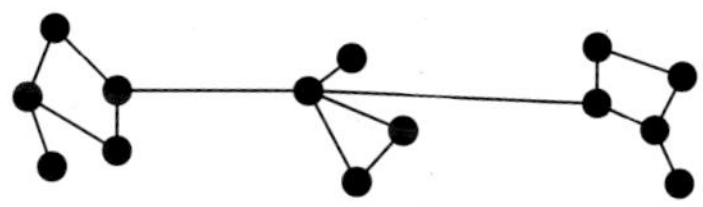

3. Networks: cocaine trafficking

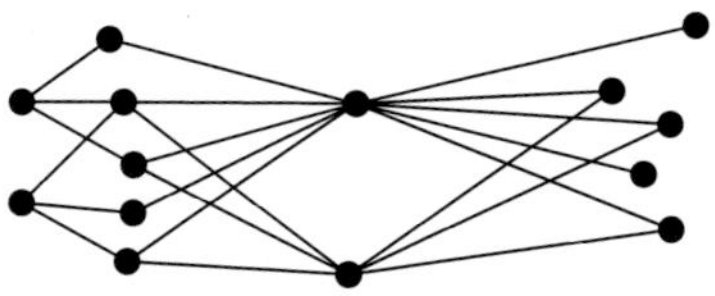

4. Cell structure

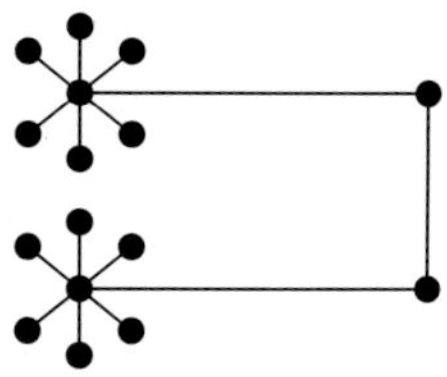

5. Networks: the jelly fish

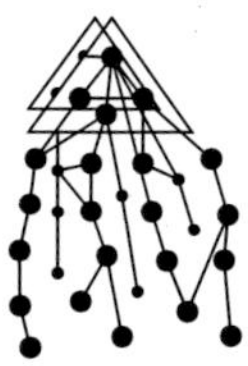

6. Networks: the bridge builder

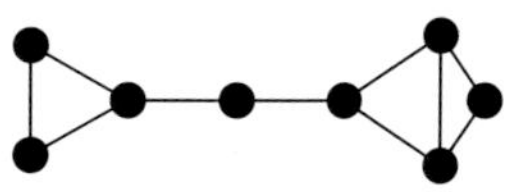

Ties and bonds of trust (diversity)
Examples:
Friendship ties
Business relation and reputation-based ties
Ethnicity, kinship and family ties
Locality-based ties
Criminal–political ties

Methods, culture and internal dynamics (diversity)
Examples:
Violence and threats
Secrecy and loyalty; exclusive membership
Corruption
Specialization/division of labor
Use of legitimate companies and sophisticated business methods

(Source: Most of these models are based on various studies. The models were presented by Dr. Peter Klerks from the Dutch Police Academy during a summer school on organized crime in Catania, Italy (June 2009).)

to make sense of the phenomenon. These studies, however, should first provide a clear distinction between the different forms of "organized crime."

Before defining organized crime, it is important to ask the right questions: Do we want to understand the illegal market dynamics, the group structures, the nature of the ties that bond criminals together, or their culture, methods and internal dynamics? Answers to such questions will lead to a better understanding of the activities labeled "organized crime" and the people involved in these activities. Knowing *what* or *who* should criminal policies target is indispensable.

It is not wrong to argue that crime is a social construction, and thus it is not so important which approach one will take, as long the various concepts are meticulously defined, widely applied and ideally depoliticized and unbiased.

The future of criminological research: challenges, prospects and limitations

The role of organized crime researchers is crucial; they serve as critical voices in this understudied field, reminding policy makers of their biases. It is important to note that the concept of organized crime is not only difficult to define, but also to study and measure. Many have argued that organized crime is a topic beyond objective measure because doing reliable empirical research on the topic seems problematic. It is not easy for law enforcement officers and researchers to investigate organized crime groups properly. Even if it were possible to interview offenders, one should remain skeptical as to the reliability and validity of the collected data. Many have argued that accounts of informers are unreliable too since, as collaborators of justice, informants are often entitled to police protection, living allowances and a reduction in their prison terms (Potter, 1994; Salerno and Tompkins, 1969).

Thus, social scientists are often forced to rely on accounts given by police, judicial authorities and the media and on reports of key witnesses. Getting access to police files and interviewing victims or witnesses, however, is far from a simple task. Also, reliance on police sources and the media is not unconditional. Galliher and Cain (1974) explain that scholarly literature on organized crime relies profoundly on sensational journalistic accounts or highly politicized government documents. Furthermore, collecting scientific data on organized crime in a variety of jurisdictions is also difficult because of definitional problems, methods of recording and collecting data, and language barriers. A series of factors constitute sources of distortion of cross-national comparison of reordered crimes and must be controlled by the researchers.

Obviously, the "reality of organized crime" is not easy to discover. On the other hand, organized crime as a research topic offers an exceptional opportunity to utilize a truly interdisciplinary research method. By combining multiple observers, theories, methods and empirical materials, criminologists can hope to overcome the intrinsic biases linked to single method studies. Most importantly the link between theory, empirical studies and policy should become stronger and scholars should not be discouraged or negatively influenced by "practical people." There should be no impatience with theory from those wanting simply to get on with the job of "fighting" crime. This impatience can be costly and short-term policies are often ineffective. Thus scholars and policy makers must work hand in hand in order to develop most effective, multi-faceted, anti-crime policies.

Future research questions

1. What are the main three paradigms of organized crime and how do they differ between them? Are they mutually exclusive?
2. What are some problems with the UN and EU definitions on organized crime and why is it difficult to develop a global definition of organized crime?
3. What are some reasons countries tend to externalize and securitize the problem of "organized crime?"
4. What are some methodological challenges researchers face when studying organized crime?
5. Conduct an additional research and find existing definitions of the following crime categories: "organized crime," "professional crime," "white-collar crime," "corporate crime," "transnational crime," "occupational crime," "serious crime" and "predatory crime." Are these definitions mutually exclusive? Are there overlaps?

Notes

1 Authors over the years have termed this the "bureaucratic model," "national conspiracy" or "corporate model" of organized crime.

2 This convention spells out how countries can improve cooperation on matters as extradition, mutual legal assistance, transfer of proceedings and joint investigations. There are two optional protocols on combating the smuggling of migrants and the buying and selling of women and children for sexual exploitation. A third protocol on arms dealing is under negotiation. See http://www.uncjin.org/Documents/Conventions/dcatoc/final_documents_2/convention_eng.pdf.

References

Abadinsky, H. (1994). *Organized crime*. 4th edn. Chicago: Nelson-Hall.

Albanese, J. (1994). Models of organised crime. In R. J. Kelly, K. Chin, and R. Schatzberg (Eds.) *Handbook of organized crime in the United States*, pp.77–89. USA: Greenwood Press.

—— (2000). The causes of organised crime. *Journal of Contemporary Justice*, 16(4): 409–23.

Albini, J.L. (1971). *The American Mafia: genesis of a legend.* New York: Irvington.
Arlacchi, P. (1986) *Mafia businesses: the Mafia and the spirit of capitalism.* London: Verso.
Arsovska, J. (2008). Countering criminals, Macedonia's fight against organised crime. *Jane's Intelligence Review*, 20(1): 44–7.
Arsovska, J. and Janssens, S. (2009). Human trafficking and the police: good and bad practices. In Cornelius Friesendorf (Ed.), *Strategies against human trafficking: the role of the security sector.* Geneva: DCAF.
Bell, D. (1953). Crime as an American way of life. *The Antioch Review*, 13: 131–54.
Block, A. (1978). History and the study of organized crime. *Urban Life*, 6: 455–74.
Chambliss, W. (1999). *Power, politics and crime.* Colorado: Westview.
Council of Europe (2001), Recommendation REC(2001)11 of the Committee of Ministers concerning guiding principles on the fight against organized crime, September 19, 765th meeting.
—— (2002). Crime analysis: organised crime – best practice survey no. 4. Strasbourg, France.
Council of the EU (2001). Conclusions adopted by the Council (Justice and Home Affairs). Brussels, 20 September, doc. SN 3926/6/01 REV 6.
Cressey, D. R. (1969). *Theft of the nation: the structure and operations of organized crime in America.* New York: Harper & Row.
Durkheim, E. (1965). The normal and the pathological. In George E. G. Catlin (Ed.) *The rules of the sociological method*, translated by Sarah A. Solovay and John H. Muller, pp.65–73. New York: Free University Press.
Federal Bureau of Investigation (FBI) (n.d.) Organized crime. Online at http://www2.fbi.gov/hq/cid/orgcrime/glossary.htm (accessed December 9, 2010).
Fijnaut, C. and Paoli, L. (Eds.) (2004). *Organised crime in Europe: concepts, patterns and control policies in the European Union and beyond.* The Netherlands: Springer.
Galeotti, M. (Ed.) (2005). *Global crime today. The changing face of organised crime.* London: Routledge.
Galliher J. F. and Cain J. A. (1974). Citation support for the Mafia myth in criminology textbooks. *American Sociologist*, 9: 68–74.
Halstead, B. (1998). The use of models in the analysis of organized crime and development of policy. *Transnational Organised Crime*, 4(1):1–24.
Ianni, F. A. J. and Reuss–Ianni, E. (1972). *A family business.* New York: Russell Sage.
Kelland, G. (1987). Crime in London: from postwar Soho to present-day "supergrasses." London: Grafton.
Levi, M. (2002). The organization of serious crimes. In M. Maguire, R. Morgan, and R. Reiner (Eds.) *The Oxford handbook of criminology*, pp. 878–938. Oxford: Oxford University Press.
Lupsha, P. A. (1981). Organised crime in the United States. In R. J. Kelly (Ed.), *Organised crime: cross-cultural studies*, pp. 32–57. Totowa, NJ: Rowman & Littlefield.
Merton R. K. (1938). Social structure and anomie. *American Sociological Review*, 3(5): 672–82.
Paoli, L. (2003). *Mafia brotherhoods. Organized crime: Italian style.* New York: Oxford University Press.
Potter, G. W. (1994). *Criminal organisations: vice, racketeering, and politics in an American city.* Prospect Heights, Ill: Waveland.
President's Commission on Law Enforcement and Administration of Justice (1967). *The challenge of crime in a free society.* Washington.
Puzo, M. 1969. *The Godfather.* New York: G. P. Putnam's Sons.
Reuter, P. (1983), *Disorganized crime: the economics of the visible hand.* London: MIT Press.
Rhodes, R. (1984). Organized crime: crime control vs. civil liberties. New York: Random House.
Salerno, R. and Tompkins, J. S. (1969). *The crime confederation: Cosa Nostra and allied operations in organized crime.* New York: Doubleday.
Solana, J. (2002). Intervention by Javier Solana, EU High Representative for the Common Foreign and Security Policy. London Conference on Organized Crime, November 25. Online at http://www.consilium.europa.eu/uedocs/cmsUpload/London%20Conference.pdf (accessed November 24, 2010).
Smith, Dwight C. (1978). Organized crime and entrepreneurship. *International Journal of Criminology and Penology*, 6: 161–77.
—— (1991). Wickersham to Sutherland to Katzenbach: Evolving an "official" definition for organized crime. *Crime, Law and Social Change*, 16: 135–54.
Sterling, C. (1994). *Thieves' world: the threat of the new global network of organized crime.* New York: Simon & Schuster.
United Nations (UN) (2000). UN Convention against Transnational Organized Crime. Online at http://www.uncjin.org/Documents/Conventions/dcatoc/final_documents_2/convention_eng.pdf (accessed December 9, 2010).

van Duyne, P. (1993). Implications of cross-border crime and risks in an open Europe. *Crime, Law and Social Change*, 20: 99–111.

Watts, R., Bessant, J., and Hill, R. (2008). *International criminology: a critical introduction*. London: Routledge.

Williams, P. (1994). Transnational criminal organisations and international security. *Survival*, 36(1): 96–113.

Wright, A. (2006). *Organized crime*. Cullompton: Willan.

World News (2009). Turkey holds Albanian diplomat in heroin bust. *World News*, May 8. Online at http://www.javno.com/en-world/turkey-holds-albanian-diplomat-in-heroin-bust_256666 (accessed November 24, 2010).

22
Hong Kong triads

Yiu Kong Chu

The triad society

According to legend, the triad society was founded by monks of the Shaolin Temple in 1674 in China with the specific aim of overthrowing the alien Qing dynasty and restoring the native Chinese Ming dynasty. The original Chinese name of the triad society is *Sahehui* (i.e. Three United Society). The modern explanation is that the society name came from the combination of the three primary forces of the universe: Heaven, Earth, and Man. The English word *triad* was coined to describe these three forces of the society. After the Qing dynasty was overthrown in 1911, triad societies degenerated into purely criminal organizations. As Chinese migrants continued to move to Hong Kong, Southeast Asia, North America, and Europe, the triads emerged in Chinese communities all over the world (Morgan, 1960).

This popular view has been challenged by recent historians who discovered that the original name of the triad society was the *Tiandihui* (the Heaven and Earth Society), founded by the monk Hung Erh at the Guanyin Temple in Gaoxi Village, Zhangpu County, in Zhangzhou Prefecture of Fujian Province in 1761 (Murray and Qin, 1994). The main purpose of the Tiandihui was to create pseudo-familial networks for unacquainted people through the rituals of sworn brotherhood so that members could offer mutual protection to each other. The expansion of the Tiandihui was directly linked to the socio-economic circumstances and migration patterns of the lower classes in southeast China.

Hong Kong triads

Although the triads in Hong Kong had some indirect links with those in China, the beginning of Hong Kong triads was a direct response to the conflicts between different migratory dialect groups for job opportunities in the labor market by the turn of the twentieth century. According to the record of the Hong Kong police, there were more than 300 triad societies in the region, most of which were established between 1914 and 1939.

Nowadays, around 50 triad societies still exist in Hong Kong, about 15 of which regularly come to police attention. The most active triad societies are Sun Yee On, 14K Hau Group, 14K Tak Group, 14K Ngai Group, Wo Shing Wo, Wo Hop To, Wo On Lok (Shui Fong), and Luen Ying Sh'e. While Sun Yee On was believed to be the most powerful triad society in Hong Kong in the 1990s, the Hong Kong police have paid more attention to the Wo Shing Wo triad society since 1997. In terms of membership, 14K is believed to be the largest triad society in Hong Kong (Chu, 2005).

Triads as loose cartels

Hong Kong triads do not possess a central organization with a Godfather at the top directing their local and overseas branches to organize a variety of criminal activities. They are loose cartels consisting of a number of independent societies which adopt a similar organizational structure and ritual to bind their members together. Although various societies are symbolically under the same roof of the triad family, they are decentralized to a certain extent, in that no one single central body unites different societies and gives universal commands.

A well-organized triad society may have a central committee at the top to coordinate many autonomous gangs under its name. The Chairman, Treasurer, and other committee members are elected by various area bosses who physically control a particular territory with their own followers. A fragmented triad society such as the 14K has no central committee, but consists of various independent gangs headed by different area bosses. They only cooperate on an ad hoc basis. Therefore, triads are neither a highly centralized nor a totally disorganized organization. They are not a single big pyramid with a Godfather at the top controlling the whole organization, but have many small hierarchical pyramids led by area bosses at the district level.

Although the triads are still secret societies, their organizational control is no longer strict. The so-called triad members always put personal benefits before organizational interests. It is now not uncommon that different triad gangs in the same society constantly fight against one another for the control of profitable businesses. On the other hand, former rival triad groups are increasingly looking for ways to collaborate to make money.

Since triads are decentralized and each group operates separately and independently, it is not likely that Hong Kong is the world's triad headquarters, deliberately exporting their members abroad to expand its territory or influence. Although there are some links between Hong Kong and overseas triads, these links are weak and through informal networks. The emergence of triad societies in Western countries is largely due to the local environment being conducive to the development of Chinese secret societies like triads.

Ranks and rituals

Most of the triad societies in Hong Kong were established between 1914 and 1939. Triad societies during that period were divided into eight major groups: the Wo, T'ung, Tung, Chuen, Shing, Fuk Yee Hing, Yee On, and Luen. The eight triad groups established their spheres of influence in different parts of Hong Kong. Each of these main groups consisted of a headquarters and a number of branch societies operating in their respective areas. The organization was managed by a group of triad officials (Morgan, 1960). The rank structure during that period was as follows:

Ranks	Code No.
1. Shan Chu (Mountain Master)	489
2. Fu Shan Chu (Deputy Mountain Master)	438
3. Heung Chu (Incense Master)	438
4. Sin Fung (Vanguard)	438
5. Hung Kwan (Red Pole)	426
6. Pak Tsz Sin (White Paper Fan)	415
7. Cho Hai (Straw Sandal)	432
8. 49 Chai (Ordinary Members)	49

In a traditional ceremony the new recruit was taught the mythical history of the society, its rules and punishment, hand signs, and identification verses, and avowed total loyalty to the society. In the legend of the foundation of the triad society, the First Five Ancestors were said to have experienced a number of heroic and miraculous events during their flight from the Shaolin Temple to safety. Some of the more significant of these "happenings" were honored in the ceremonial rites of the movement (Morgan, 1960). Through the ceremonies, the members were socialized into the triad world. The initiation ceremony can be summarized by 18 steps (Chu, 2000: 32):

1. Tapping the new recruit's left shoulder
2. Dashing the joss stick
3. Covering the yellow gauge quilt
4. Passing through the Heaven and Earth ring
5. Passing through the fiery pit
6. Passing the two plank bridge
7. Eating the five seasonal fruit
8. Drinking the three river water
9. Smashing the bowl
10. Chopping the chicken's head
11. Pricking the middle finger on the left hand
12. Drinking the Red Flower wine
13. Eight-step worshipping in front of the altar
14. Old and new members bowing to each other
15. Washing the face of new recruits
16. Teaching triad hand signs
17. Blowing to the office-bearers
18. Giving lucky money to protectors

Today the organizational structure of the triad society in Hong Kong has become flexible. The traditional rank system has largely reduced to mainly three ranks, i.e. 426 Red Pole, 49 ordinary member, and "hanging the blue lantern." The simplified initiation ceremony and the method of "hanging the blue lantern" based on oral agreement are widely practiced to recruit new members (Chu, 2000).

It is no longer possible for many triad societies to enforce strict discipline over their members. Membership transfer can be done quite easily. Triad Big Brothers have no obligation to look after their followers when they encounter problems. In addition, triads are still a male-dominated secret society. Triads may allow other races who live in Hong Kong to join their societies. Nevertheless, very few females can join a triad society through the formal initiation ceremony (Chu, 2000).

Triad activities in Hong Kong

There is no doubt that triads are a menace in Hong Kong. They drive public fear through their mystery and intimidation. In reality, not all organized crime is done by triads. According to the Hong Kong police, in the last 15 years approximately 3–4 percent of crime cases were related to triads (Chu, 2005).

Although triads are known to have long been involved in illegal businesses, the illegal market is not monopolized by triads with a Godfather-like figure at the top to control his members for the production of illegal goods and services. For instance, there is no sufficient evidence to show that the triads are dominant in the businesses of smuggling, counterfeiting, swindles, organized illegal immigration, and money laundering. Illegal operations can be headed or run by persons without a triad background.

Triad participation in illegal businesses varies from one to another, or even within the same business. Even if triad members are involved in a specific illegal operation, it is not a society business. Instead, it is strictly a private investment. Profits will remain in the hands of the individual members and do not channel up to the triad hierarchy. Moreover, triad members are free to seek business partners from their own circle, other societies, or people who are not triads.

Hong Kong triads have become adept at adjusting themselves in a changing environment. There are three general trends of triad activities in Hong Kong. First, triad members from various societies tend to group together to run profitable criminal projects. A typical example is the operation of underground casinos. As underground casinos need to float from one place to another to avoid police detection, the operation does not rely on triad territorial basis for protection against extortionists or fellow competitors. Consequently, underground casinos tend to be operated in the form of a joint venture (Chu, 2005).

Second, they tend to team up with legitimate entrepreneurs to monopolize a newly developed market. In Hong Kong it has long been known that unlicensed hawkers pay protection fees to local triads to secure their hawking positions from other competitors. Triads are brought in by minibus operators to protect their lucrative routes by limiting the entry of other drivers. Fish buyers in the wholesale market employ triad members to manipulate the auction process by deterring other would-be buyers from bidding the fish lots which they have "pre-selected." Compared with traditional triads, modern triads are more flexible in providing strong-arm services to the business community. Their recent entry to interior decoration, the selling of new residential flats, and their use of intimidation to force popular actors to make films, demonstrates that they are now able to team up with business entrepreneurs to run big-time projects when a lucrative market emerges (Chu, 2005).

Lastly, triad members increasingly invest in legitimate businesses. Compared to traditional triads, modern triad bosses are more keen on using their established power to invest in legitimate businesses. For instance, triads have not only come to sell protection services to entertainment establishments, but have also persuaded the owners to employ their members to operate the car jockey services. Triads are also found to heavily invest in the entertainment industry such as bars, night-clubs, restaurants, dance halls, and the film industry. However, it is not clear to what extent the triad is involved in these legitimate businesses (Chu, 2005).

Hong Kong triads and 1997

Since the Italian Mafia is no longer the dominant force of the international underworld, Western law enforcers are quite concerned that Hong Kong triads – the so-called "Chinese Mafia" – will replace the Italian Mafia to be the most powerful criminal organization in the twenty-first century. They predicted that a number of triad members would emigrate to their countries before Hong Kong reverted to Chinese control on 1 July 1997 (Black, 1991).

This view has a historical basis. After the Communist Party came to power in China in 1949, it took tough measures to combat organized crime problems. After a few years nearly all organized crime groups which existed before 1949 were destroyed. Since China has a successful record in dealing with criminal organizations, it was believed that that Chinese government would suppress Hong Kong triads right after 1997.

After the Joint Declaration signed by the Chinese and British governments in 1984, the Chinese government guaranteed that Hong Kong's existing system would remain after 1997.

Some Hong Kong citizens – especially the rich, the professionals, and the people whose earlier generations were persecuted by the Chinese Communist Party – did not trust the Chinese government and they left Hong Kong before 1997. Triad members might also think that it was far safer to obtain foreign citizenship. However, there was no indication that mass triad migration happened before 1997.

It should be understood that emigration was not easy for triad members. The vast majority of junior triad members were poorly educated and many had criminal records. The selection procedures of most Western countries such as the USA, Canada, Australia, and Western European countries tended to reject them. As a result, most of them will remain in Hong Kong, although some triad criminals might use illegal means to gain entry into Western societies and some senior triad members were able to use their money and influence to emigrate to Western countries.

Hong Kong has reverted to mainland China's control for 12 years. According to the Hong Kong police, to date, their major triad targets have no intention of leaving Hong Kong for Western countries. By contrast, it is now quite clear that many Hong Kong triads have moved into China to set up illegal, legal, and international businesses.

Three major triad societies in Hong Kong

Sun Yee On, Wo Shing Wo, and 14K are believed to be three most influential triad societies in Hong Kong. They are selected here to illustrate the latest development of triad societies in Hong Kong (Chu, 2005).

Sun Yee On

Sun Yee On was originally formed by a Chinese minority native group called Chiu Chau in Hong Kong. Nowadays, members of Sun Yee On come from different ethnic Chinese groups. A small number of locally born Indians and Pakistanis are also recruited to the Society as junior members.

Traditionally the Sun Yee On triad society liked to conduct the full initiation ceremony for their newly recruited members. To avoid being detected by the police, however, Sun Yee On hesitated to arrange the formal initiation ceremony for their new members in the last decade. Compared with other triad groups, senior Sun Yee On members are relatively interconnected. They may offer assistance to each other, especially when their members are in legal trouble.

There is evidence that Sun Yee On members are found in the USA, Canada, the UK and Australia. In the United States, some individual members may have connections with the Fuk Ching Gangs. However, it should be noted that this is not an organized movement launched by Sun Yee On in Hong Kong. No mass triad migration to Western countries has occurred before or after 1997. Their connections with overseas criminal organizations are largely based on personal networks and probably has nothing to do with the Society.

Individual Sun Yee On members may get involved in drugs, street-level selling of pirated VCDs/DVDs, speculative activities in the stock market, money laundering, vehicle theft and smuggling, prostitution, extortion, loan sharking, illegal gambling, and so on. These are their private investments. They are not required to get permission from the Society to conduct these businesses.

In the past Sun Yee On members were known to be active in international drug trafficking, especially the import of heroin from Thailand to Hong Kong and some of the drugs were smuggled to Western countries. Although individual Sun Yee On members are still engaging in the drug business, there is insufficient evidence to support the conclusion that Sun Yee On members play a significant role in the trade. In fact, members of other triad groups and non-triad people can get involved in this international business if they have the capital, connections, and skills to do it.

Although individual Sun Yee On members may have been involved in some specific legitimate businesses such as the catering business, the film industry, or even in the stock market, their roles in the legitimate economy are unclear. For instance, it is difficult to confirm whether they are simply legal entrepreneurs, using their triad reputation to monopolize the business, or laundering their money through investing in legitimate businesses. Compared with other triad groups, it is quite clear that Sun Yee On members tend to participate in more non-violent crime, such as black market crime and economic crime. In addition, they have more connections with legitimate business entrepreneurs and professionals, such as lawyers and accountants.

Before 1997, journalists reported that senior Sun Yee On members had connections with some high-ranking Chinese government officials. In the last few years, we have seldom heard these kinds of reports. In short, Sun Yee On has kept a very low profile since 1997.

Wo Shing Wo

Wo Shing Wo was originally an offshoot society of the Wo Hop To triad society which was established in 1908. Wo Shing Wo broke away from Wo Hop To in 1930 and then became an independent triad society. Members of Wo Shing Wo come from different walks of life including a small number of local born Indians and Pakistanis.

Wo Shing Wo has a Central Committee composed of a body of influential and senior officials. The Chairman and Treasurer, now known locally as *Cho Kun* and *Cha So*, are often elected from this Central Committee at an annual or bi-annual meeting. The leadership in the Central Committee may help to settle internal and external disputes, but they are unable to dictate to their members participation in any specific criminal activities

It is evident that Wo Shing Wo members are also found in the UK, Canada and the USA. According to Hong Kong police, some individual members may have connections with the Big Circle Gangs in Holland. However, it should be noted that their contacts with overseas criminal organizations are largely based on personal networks and are likely to have nothing to do with the society. There are no indicators that mass Wo Shing Wo triad migration to Western countries took place either before or after 1997.

Individual Wo Shing Wo members may get involved in drugs, street-level selling of pirated VCDs/DVDs, London Gold scams, money laundering, vehicle theft and smuggling, prostitution, extortion, loan sharking, illegal gambling, and so on. These are their personal investments. They will not transfer part of their profits to the Society.

According to police sources, Wo Shing Wo members have their strengths in the pirated VCD/DVD industry. They not only are involved in street-level distribution, but they also are involved in the manufacturing of pirated VCDs/DVDs. Compared with other triad groups, Wo Shing Wo members participated in more violent crime and tried to be dominant in street-level organized crime over the last few years. Some journalists reported that Wo Shing Wo has become the most influential triad society in Hong Kong. Although individual Wo Shing Wo members have been involved in some specific legitimate businesses, such as the catering and entertainment business, their roles in the legitimate economy are not clear.

14k

14K was formed in Hong Kong in the early 1950s by a group of triad members with a Nationalist Party background in Guangdong Province in China. Compared with other triad groups, 14K is relatively disorganized. It has different sub-groups and each sub-group has developed into a separate triad society in its own right. Gang fights among different sub-groups are not uncommon.

It is evident that 14K members are found in the UK, Holland, USA, Canada, and Australia. According to police sources, some individual members may have connections with the Big Circle Gangs in Holland, Yakuza in Japan, and the United Bamboo Gangs in Taiwan.

Individual 14K members may get involved in drugs, street-level selling of pirated VCDs/DVDs, London Gold scams, money laundering, vehicle theft and smuggling, prostitution, extortion, loan sharking, illegal gambling, and so on. Again, these are their private businesses and all profits will remain in individual hands.

According to police sources, 14K members have their strengths in organizing illegal gambling, including underground casinos and illegal bookmaking. In addition, many detected London Gold scams revealed that 14K members were the organizers and operators. Compared with other triad groups, 14K members tend to participate in traditional street-level organized crime.

It is true that some 14K members in Hong Kong had a close relationship with senior Nationalist Party members in Taiwan in the 1960s and 1970s. Today, however, 14K members in Hong Kong no longer appear to be interested in political movements.

Triads in China after its economic reforms

Opposed to the popular view that Hong Kong triad members would emigrate to Western countries, in the last two decades Hong Kong triad members were found increasingly to be entering the Chinese market. The main reason for entering this market was the huge potential to make fast money in both legal and illegal businesses since China's introduction of its Economic Reforms in the late 1970s. By contrast, the Hong Kong market was saturated and there is no big money to be made.

It is reported that all major triad societies in Hong Kong, such as Sun Yee On, 14K, Wo Shing Wo, Wo Hap To, and Wo On Lok (Shui Fong), have established power bases in China, especially in Guangdong province, where the shared Cantonese dialect makes the business of extending their influence easy. Although it is clear that Hong Kong triads have increased their activities in China, particularly in Guangdong Province, we cannot jump to the conclusion that Hong Kong triads have systematically branched out on the mainland. In many cases, it is individual triad members who take the initiative to enter the Chinese market, and their purposes vary (Chu, 2002).

Triad members may enter China for specific criminal projects. Individual Hong Kong triad members may move into China to set up their power base by recruiting native Chinese into their gangs in Guangzhou and other booming towns in the Pearl River regions. Their aim is to facilitate their cross-border smuggling activities, such as highly prized consumer goods, illegal immigrants, prostitutes, stolen vehicles, counterfeiting currency, weapons and drugs, or looking for mainland Chinese to carry out dangerous jobs, such as armed robbery in Hong Kong.

There has been a trend that Hong Kong triad members increasingly invest in the entertainment industry in China, especially in dance halls and karaoke lounges. Some members use their entertainment establishments as fronts to operate prostitution and underground casinos. It should be noted that triad members will not run the business alone. It is operated by partnerships, usually involving three groups of people. Individual triad members are the main organizers, Hong Kong businessmen who can contribute capital and business resources form the second group, and local powerful people who have strong connections with government officials and law enforcers, as well as local gangs, form the third group. Without the collaboration of these three groups, it is difficult to run this lucrative but vulnerable business in mainland China (Chu, 2002).

Some Hong Kong triad members, originally emigrating from China, return to their home towns to organize their own triad gangs. In some cases triad criminals chased by the Hong Kong police take refuge in China. These groups of gangsters have triad links in Hong Kong and local connections in mainland China. They are quite resourceful people who can manage various criminal projects at local, regional, or international levels.

It should be noted that it is not true that Hong Kong triads are taking over China's underworld. China is a large country with a long tradition of secret societies and organized criminality before the Chinese Communist Party came to power in 1949. Many gangs based on traditional secret society rituals, or simply on their ethnic and dialect connections, have emerged in mainland China in response to the market economy. If these gangs are protected by corrupt government officials, they are powerful enough to fight with imported triads and other overseas gangs. Therefore, it seems impossible for Hong Kong triads to play a leading role in the Chinese criminal market.

Like their Hong Kong counterparts, Taiwanese gangs, such as the United Bamboo gang, Four Sea gang, and Tian Dao Mun, also have moved into mainland China. Taiwanese criminals are mainly active in Fujian, which is the nearest province from Taiwan. They team with local gangsters to commit different kinds of crime. They particularly get involved in the manufacture and smuggling of illegal drugs. In addition, Japanese Yakuza members are reported to be found in mainland China. A police source claims that Taiwanese gang members arrange for mainland Chinese to produce amphetamine in China and then smuggle drugs to Japan. Hong Kong triads assist Yakuza members in investing in real estate in Shenzhen (Chu, 2002).

Because China has a huge market for illegal activities – a major transit country for heroin produced in the Golden Triangle region, a great demand for stolen cars, availability of cheap weapons, a shelter for criminals, a market for illegal emigration – which have created a favorable environment for the growth of local gangs and attracted overseas criminals to flock into China, it is expected that Hong Kong criminals, including triads, and other overseas Chinese gang members will continuously move into China to team with local Chinese criminals for illegal as well as legal businesses.

Globalization and ethnic Chinese organized crime

Because the Italian Mafia is no longer the dominant power of the international underworld and the Chinese have recently been active in heroin trafficking, human smuggling, and credit card fraud, some people foresee Hong Kong triads replacing the Mafia in global organized crime in the near future. Western governments are particularly concerned that Hong Kong triads are going through the process of globalization and posing a serious threat to their societies.

Traditionally, any overseas Chinese found committing a crime, whether drug smuggling or petty theft, is usually automatically labeled a triad member by the police of the country involved. In reality, not all Chinese organized crime is committed by Hong Kong triads. Other ethnic Chinese gangs from Malaysia, Singapore, Vietnam, Cambodia, Thailand, Taiwan, Macau, and recently mainland China are also involved in various types of Chinese organized crime.

In Europe, Chinese communities were relatively homogenous in previous years. Apart from a group of Chinese from Zhejiang and Guangdong provinces in China who came to continental Europe to be seamen before the Second World War, most Chinese came from Hong Kong during the 1960s and 1970s and they spoke the same Chinese dialect: "Cantonese." In the last two decades, however, Chinese communities in Europe have become increasingly diverse, including ethnic Chinese from Vietnam, Cambodia, Indonesia, Singapore, Malaysia, Taiwan, and Thailand. After China opened its doors in the late 1970s, many Chinese, especially those from Zhejiang and Guangdong provinces, emigrated to mainland Europe to join their families. Since Western European governments adopted a liberal approach to granting Chinese immigrants asylum after the 1989 Tiananmen Square incident, this has attracted mass Chinese illegal immigration to Europe during the 1990s (Chu, 2002).

In the UK, four main Hong Kong triad societies, Wo Shing Wo, 14K, Wo On Lok (Shui Fong), and Sun Yee On, have been identified by the police. During the 1990s, the British police were not only confronted by these four Hong Kong triad groups, but also by the Vietnamese gangs. In the early stage, ethnic Chinese-Vietnamese were recruited by the triads as enforcers. Later they were increasingly involved in the operation of Asian vice establishments, particularly in the business of illegal gambling. In addition, they were found to engage in cross-border robberies between Britain and other European countries by exchanging intelligence of the targets (Chu, 2002).

In the last 15 years, a large number of Chinese from the Fujian province arrived in the UK illegally to seek political asylum. Because some Fujianese immigrants were unable to pay their "traveling" fee, they were kidnapped by their snake-heads (human smugglers) to extort money from their relatives in China. Although there is no sufficient evidence that Fujianese immigrants are currently committing serious and organized crime in the UK, some may resort to crime if they fail to find legitimate jobs to support their living expenses.

By contrast, the 14K has greater influence in continental Europe. Nevertheless, it is quite likely that Hong Kong triads are losing their power in continental Europe as other ethnic Chinese gangs emerge as influential crime groups. For example, the 14K members played a significant role in the European heroin market and had a solid base in Amsterdam during the early 1970s. Nevertheless, the 14K was forced out of Amsterdam after 1975 when its leader was shot dead by a powerful Singapore gang known as "Ah Kong." They were actively involved in smuggling heroin from the Golden Triangle region of Southeast Asia into Amsterdam and then exporting it to other cities of Europe. In the mid-1980s, a group of the Big Circle Boys, originally from the Guangzhou, the capital city of Guangdong Province of China, who illegally emigrated to Hong Kong in the late 1970s, moved into the Netherlands from Hong Kong. They operated in Amsterdam, Paris, Frankfurt, and Antwerp and became the main suppliers of heroin from the Golden Triangle in Southeast Asia (Chu, 2002).

Because the mainland Chinese population, mainly from the Zhejiang province, has increased significantly in continental Europe in the last two decades, it is speculated that the mainland Chinese gangs may pose a serious threat to European law enforcers in the future. In the Netherlands, most illegal Chinese immigrants are believed to come from Wenzhow city and Ging Tian county of the Zhejiang province. In Italy, the police have identified three Chinese crime groups: Tiger Head, Bird of Paradise, and Oriental Alliance of Ging Tian. It should be noted that these three crime groups are organized by Wenzhowese from China and they are not Hong Kong triads. Because Chinese illegal immigrants spent a huge sum of money through snake-heads to emigrate to Europe, some of them may be forced to undertake illegal activities for survival (Chu, 2002).

In fact, Chinese criminal gangs organized by new immigrants from China have emerged as a major challenger in North America. The Fuk Ching gangs (organized by young immigrants from the Fujian Province of China), after the Vietnamese gangs, have become another powerful Asian crime group in the underworld. They have accumulated considerable power and capital through smuggling Chinese citizens from China to North America. It is also evident that they are expanding their businesses of international heroin trafficking and credit card fraud (Chu, 2002).

It is undeniable that in the last two decades Hong Kong Chinese have been found to be increasingly involved in international organized crime, including drug trafficking, human smuggling, and economic organized crime, such as credit card fraud, counterfeiting, and money laundering. Nevertheless, Hong Kong triads are not likely to be the background organizers. In fact, international Chinese organized crime is committed by different ethnic Chinese crime groups. Apart from Hong Kong Chinese, Singapore and Malaysia ethnic Chinese, Vietnamese Chinese, Taiwanese Chinese, and recently mainland Chinese are also involved in international organized crime.

Even if international crime is organized by Hong Kong Chinese, in many cases, they are not triads. International criminal projects normally involve a large sum of capital, specialist techniques, extensive business connections, and high level managerial skills. A group of people, whether they are triads or not, can team to organize the business if they possess the required resources. Ironically, triad members normally are short of such business assets, they have no competitive advantages in running these international criminal projects. International business entrepreneurs are usually the persons behind the curtain. Therefore, we should not jump to the conclusion that triad members are lurking, waiting, and capable of entering any lucrative markets in which fast big money can be made.

It is also important to note that in the international crime scene, members from various ethnic Chinese criminal organizations may collaborate to run business projects. Their cooperation is largely based on family and kinship ties, ethnic and dialect links, personal connections, and mutual business interests. Triad membership is unlikely to be an important factor for the collaboration of an international criminal project. As international organized crime has no gang boundary, it has attracted non-gang members to be the background organizers or financiers of these criminal projects.

Because Western law enforcers are not simply dealing with Hong Kong triads, but mainly ethnic Chinese organized crime, more attention should be given to the new dynamics of the local Chinese criminal community and their worldwide criminal networks. To combat various ethnic Chinese organized crime, Western law enforcers may set up a national Chinese intelligence unit to collect, analyze, and disseminate the information about Chinese organized crime. As global organized crime cannot be controlled without international police cooperation, it is important for law enforcers in the North America, Europe, and Australia to share their intelligence about Chinese organized crime. Finally, Western law enforcers may consider taking further steps to liaise with their colleagues in Hong Kong, Singapore, Malaysia, Vietnam, Taiwan, Macau, Cambodia, Thailand, and mainland China.

Future research questions

1. Are young people forced to join a triad society? If they voluntarily join a triad society, do they join it for curiosity, material gains, or protection?
2. To what extent is the portrayal of the Big Brothers in the Hong Kong Gang Movies true?
3. Do Hong Kong triads mainly practice extortion, provide illegal goods and services, or sell private protection?
4. Can Hong Kong triads be exported easily to other countries?
5. If international police cooperation is an effective way to combat transnational Chinese organized crime, what are the major obstacles to implementing it?

References

Black, D. (1991). *Triad takeover; a terrifying account of the spread of triad crime in the West.* London: Sidgwick & Jackson.

Chu, Y. K. (2000). *The triads as business.* London and New York: Routledge.

—— (2002). Global triads: myth or reality? In M. R. Berdal and M. Serrano (Eds.) *Transnational organized crime and international security: business as usual*, pp. 183–93. Boulder Colo. and London: Lynne Rienner.

—— (2005). Hong Kong triads after 1997. *Trends in Organized Crime*, 8(3): 5–12.

Morgan, W. P. (1960). *Triad societies in Hong Kong*. Hong Kong: Government Printer.

Murray, D. H. and Qin, B. (1994). *The origins of the Tiandihui: the Chinese triads in legend and history*. Stanford: Stanford University Press.

Zhang, S. (2008). *Chinese human smuggling organizations: families, social networks, and cultural imperatives*. Stanford, Calif.: Stanford University Press.

23

Ants moving houses

Cross-border drug trafficking in the Golden Triangle[1]

Sheldon X. Zhang and Ko-lin Chin

Background

One of the world's major opium-cultivation and heroin-producing areas is the Golden Triangle, a 150,000-square-mile, mountainous area located where the borders of Myanmar, Laos, and Thailand meet (McCoy, 1992; United Nations International Drug Control Program, 1997). Although there is a geographical region promoted by the tourism industry as the Golden Triangle, where the Mekong River flows through the three countries, when it comes to drug production and trafficking activities, the territory covers a much larger area, including most border regions between Thailand and Myanmar and between China and Myanmar.

The Golden Triangle has long fascinated researchers and anti-narcotics agencies around the world. The major opium-growing and heroin-producing area in Myanmar (formerly known as Burma) is located in the Shan state (McCoy, 1972; Renard, 1996), which is occupied by various ethnic armed groups (Smith, 1999). The Shan state was the base of the Burmese Communist Party, which collapsed in 1989 and its followers splintered into different armed groups occupying territories of various sizes mostly along the Sino–Myanmar border regions. Under a ceasefire agreement, these warlord armies promised not to launch military attacks against the government, and in return, the Myanmar authorities allowed these ethnic groups to keep their armed forces while turning a blind eye to their involvement in the opium trade (Lintner, 1991; Albor, 1992; Takano, 2002). US sources estimated that Myanmar's opium production rose from 1,250 metric tons in 1988 to 2,450 metric tons in 1989 and continued to increase thereafter to 2,600 metric tons in 1997 (Lintner, 1998). It was the bread basket of the world's illicit opium trade before Afghanistan's ascent to prominence in the last decade.

For many decades, the majority of the heroin produced in the Golden Triangle had been smuggled into Thailand overland and then to Hong Kong onboard Thai fishing trawlers (Belanger, 1989; Dobinson, 1993; McCoy, 1999; Chalk, 2000). Hong Kong has long been the organizational and financial center for the region's heroin trade (Gaylord, 1997). China in recent decades has become a major market for drug consumption as well as a trafficking transit country. There are several reasons for the rise of China in the world's illicit drug trade. First, the economic reform in China has opened its domestic and international commercial activities. The economic growth also brought about demand for illicit goods and services. By the mid-1980s, drug consumption was no longer confined to the border areas in Yunnan Province adjacent to the

Golden Triangle. Drug addicts were found in all parts of China. The Chinese government openly acknowledged about ten years ago that people in every province and all major urban areas had drug addiction problems (China State Department, 2000). The country was no longer just a transit country as the government had long maintained. Although limited in number, studies on drug use in China found that the majority of addicts were male, young to middle aged (20–40 years), unemployed, and with a middle school education; and heroin was the predominant drug used by addicts (Hao *et al.*, 2002; Liu *et al.*, 2002).

Second, the Myanmar government, after reaching peace agreements with various warlords, managed to concentrate its resources on subduing Khun Sa, the King of Heroin who led the Mong Tai Army (MTA) in direct confrontation with the government forces. After the surrender of Khun Sa to the Myanmar government in 1996, the MTA collapsed and the drug trade through Thailand was seriously disrupted. As a result, drug producers and traffickers in the region were in need of alternative routes. China became an obvious choice because of its geographical adjacency.

Finally, the growing economy in China significantly improved the standing of its currency (i.e. yuan or renminbi) in cross-border trading activities. Meanwhile, both the Thai baht and Myanmar kyat were depreciated amidst international financial problems in the late 1990s. Drug traffickers came to believe that the Chinese yuan was more desirable for trading purposes (Wang and Liang, 1999). As a result of these fortuitous events, China quickly became a major transit and consumption country in the world drug trade. Despite the fact that thousands of drug traffickers and dealers have been executed in recent decades under China's draconian justice system, Chinese authorities cannot help but admit that they are not gaining an upper hand in the war against drugs.

This chapter presents some of the findings from a two-year study in and around the Golden Triangle. There are two main questions about drug trafficking activities in this region: Who are the traffickers? And: How do they organize themselves in the business? The data came from both primary and secondary sources. Data sources include interviews with government and law enforcement officials, community leaders, street drug dealers, drug addicts, convicted drug traffickers, and field observations in and around major drug trading and distributing areas in southern China, Myanmar, Hong Kong, and Thailand.

Conceptual orientation

This study was primarily guided by two theoretical paradigms in the analysis of drug trafficking activities: 1) the traditional corporate model, against which many contemporary organized crime theories have been proposed (McIllwain, 2003); and 2) the enterprise model, which for the past two decades has been used to explain many variations of criminal groups engaged in illicit business activities (Zhang and Chin, 2002). Under the traditional corporate model, criminal organizations possess a clear division of labor and chain of command. Tasks and responsibilities are assigned according to members' skills and abilities. Rules and regulations govern members' activities. Examples of these corporate-like crime syndicates include the Italian Mafia and Japanese Yakuza. Such structured organizations are thought to fulfill certain social functions, such as inefficiencies in government services, demand for fringe goods and services (e.g. gambling, prostitution, and controlled substance), and cultural tolerance of informal business dealings and unconventional solutions to personal problems unique to different countries. Despite their shady reputations, many criminal organizations nonetheless have existed in some societies for centuries, if not longer, and are believed to fulfill some "useful" functions to their host societies. In these criminal organizations, membership is restricted and criminal entities are often visible in the community.

The same cannot be said of the enterprise model, which suggests flexible and adaptive networks that expand and contract to deal with the uncertainties inherent in an illicit marketplace. These organizations are made up of loosely affiliated individuals who come to know each other through their social and business networks. They are more disorganized than organized from an organizational perspective (Reuter, 1983). These entrepreneurs are organized only to the extent that they can effectively carry out business transactions. There is no clear hierarchy and no formal recognition of membership.

Both paradigms have been used in studies of various criminal enterprising activities, such as transnational human smuggling and cross-border drug trafficking activities. Complex relationships have been found among enterprising individuals involved in various emerging transnational criminal activities (Zhang and Chin, 2003; Zhang, 2008). Many of these relationships represent largely free associations of individuals for whom the only qualification for entering the business is some valuable contribution, such as money or connection. Others occasionally possess a few rudimentary hierarchical features, in which some individuals have more say than their partners in how and when a smuggling operation is to be executed. In these organizational features, the hierarchical structure and horizontal differentiation (i.e. division of labor) do not evolve in the same direction (i.e. the greater the hierarchical differentiation, the greater the division of labor). The relationship between hierarchy and division of labor in many criminal organizations is diagonal rather than a continuum or parallel. Such a diagonal relationship may better explain criminal organizations when they adopt various forms in response to the constraints of market conditions (Zhang and Chin, 2002). The study employs this perspective to examine the features of drug trafficking organizations in the Golden Triangle, such as their hierarchical arrangement, division of labor, risk management strategies, and business practices.

Analysis and findings

China and Myanmar share more than 2,000 kilometers of common land borders, porous and loosely guarded. For centuries local people have traversed back and forth without much regard to which country they happen to step on. Farmers cultivate lands that straddle both countries, while local women rummage through thick vegetations that blanket rolling hills in search of edible fungi and medicinal herbs.

The region along the border between Yunnan and Myanmar has a long history of opium cultivation which the local people use for medicinal as well as recreational purposes. During the first few decades after the communists took control of China in 1949, opium cultivation was largely wiped out. Now, Yunnan has become an engine driving the economic growth and commerce in and around the Golden Triangle region, the so-called Mekong River sub-region. For instance, the trade between Yunnan Province and Myanmar represents about half of all Sino–Myanmar commercial exchanges (Myanmar Information Committee, 2005).

Major trafficking routes in China

As reported by other researchers (Lintner, 1994; Ma, 1994; Chalk, 2000), China has become a country with high levels of heroin importation for transshipment purposes and for a booming domestic addict population. For obvious geographical reasons, most of the heroin trafficking activities take place along the porous Yunnan–Myanmar borders. Once inside China, traffickers employ three main routes to forward their drugs into the interior of the country: one to the north through Sichuan Province, one through Guizhou Province towards the heart of the interior, and one through Guangxi and then Guangdong along the southern coastline heading towards Hong Kong for export to the international market.

Traffickers and their social organizations

Individuals of diverse backgrounds participate in cross-border trafficking activities. These traffickers range from illiterate peasants to college professors, from entrepreneurs to government officials, and from street vendors to ranking police officers (on many occasions anti-narcotic police officers). By and large, the vast majority of traffickers tend to be poorly educated and have no regular employment (i.e. salaried jobs) and whose livelihood involves a constant search of money-making opportunities. Both men and women participate in drug trafficking activities, although women in most cases play subordinate roles or act simply as carriers (or mules). Despite the fact that drug users are mostly young (particularly among those using methamphetamine), most drug traffickers were married and in their 30s and 40s.

Drug traffickers often came from the same village or belong to the same ethnic or linguistic group. They were often migrants from one specific region, such as Weishan County in the north part of Yunnan Province, Putian County in costal Fujian Province, and Wuhan City in Hubei Province. The stories reported by the traffickers often shared similar themes. It typically started when a few people in the village became rich quickly. Soon, other villagers found out how the wealth was accumulated and explored ways to emulate these successful stories.

Presumably, people of the same hometown, once established in the drug trade, are likely to bring out others from the same village when additional hands are needed. As a result, from time to time anti-narcotics officials notice sharp increases in the arrests of individuals from specific geographic regions. Once traffickers from one region begin attracting police attention, all people from the region become suspect whenever they are stopped along well known trafficking routes in China. Intensified police efforts soon disrupt the movement by these region-specific traffickers. Traffickers from other regions soon fill in the supply lines vacated by these targeted groups. As one ranking police official at a border town in Yunnan observed, "in the old time, many of the traffickers were Hui minority people in Yunnan. Now there are few of them. Most traffickers now are from Hubei, Sichuan, and Hunan." Such observations also seem to coincide with that reported by the incarcerated traffickers themselves. One incarcerated trafficker, who spent more than 14 years in a large provincial prison, concurred that traffickers (especially the mules) come from specific geographical regions. He stated:

> Many of the inmates here come from Liangshan Prefecture (in Sichuan Province) and Mengcheng in Anhui Province. Most of them were "mules" from the same villages. There is this domino effect in these cases. After a few villagers returned home with handsome profits from the drug trade, others wanted to follow suit. They either ask to join these successful individuals or explore their own ways. Then a few more successful traffickers return home. Soon, more and more villagers start looking for similar opportunities. Death penalty and imprisonment do not deter these people. To these people, the drug trade offers the only chance they know that will allow them to make enough money to bring about fundamental changes to their life.

Data gathered from interviews and field observations seemed to suggest that the social organization of the drug trade in the Golden Triangle were singularly linked social networks, in which individuals gathered in various small social settings at various stages. In an attempt to examine the structure of drug trafficking organizations in the Golden Triangle and the Yunnan

Province of China, this study focused on key players and their roles within trafficking activities, together with their socio-economic backgrounds and styles of transactions during the trafficking process. Drug trafficking groups were found to be small in general, with just a few people either blood-related or familiar with one another in their previous social transactions. Because the drug trade is highly secretive and traffickers risk the death penalty or certain long prison sentences, traffickers always deal with one another on a one-on-one basis, with no redundancies and no backups. Restricted communication serves to maintain secrecy and minimize their exposure. Close interpersonal interactions also seem to build and sustain trust and confidence in a relatively short period of time.

The rise of entrepreneurs and the business of drug trafficking

After decades of relentless crackdowns by governments in the Golden Triangle, large scale drug manufacturing and trafficking activities in the Golden Triangle region have largely disappeared. Warlords who previously engaged in open production and transportation of illicit drugs are now seeking political legitimacy and refrain from direct involvement in the drug trade. Armed patrols along miles of opium transportation caravans have faded into folklore. However, the demand for illicit drugs remains.

Small-time entrepreneurs instead have risen to meet the market demand. The drug trade and distribution system appear to take the shape of a fan, with a geographically concentrated location for drug production (i.e. northern Myanmar) branching out through increasing numbers of small groups of entrepreneurs forwarding the drugs from one stage to the next before reaching the street level vendors. Chinese nationals appear to be the most active players in the trafficking and distribution of heroin and other illicit drugs in Southeast Asia.

Multiple groups of individuals are involved in multiple stages of the drug trade. For obvious safety reasons, transactions in the drug trade were almost always carried out on a one-on-one basis at any particular stage. Even when seizures of large amounts of heroin were announced by law enforcement agencies, they were mostly caught at some particular stages along the trafficking routes. Thus far no claims, news stories, or government reports have been found in this study that are capable of demonstrating the transactions or transportation process from the point of manufacturing to the street vendors.

The drug market appears to be dominated by loosely affiliated enterprising agents, who typically specialize in moving limited amounts of drugs through personal networks. As one ranking police official described the current drug trafficking business:

> Large drug consignments are becoming rarer these days. Drug traffickers realize the penalty for small drug carriers is less severe and the potential loss is also small. So they take the approach of ants moving their house, small pieces by small pieces. They hire "mules" to pick up and deliver drugs at predetermined locations within specified time frame, and their only connection is a mobile phone number. We have captured many of these "mules" but rarely can we reach the organizers behind them. As soon as an arrest is made and the delivery is disrupted, the mobile phone number becomes invalid. These organizers are watching the mules from a distance.

This finding led us to believe that the drug trade as a whole is a fragmented marketplace, with numerous segments of direct transactions. Individual shipments may vary in the distance between two points within a transaction, for instance from Kunming to Guangzhou by airfreight or long-haul trucking. But all transactions appeared to commence and terminate between two points by any trafficking group. In other words, the activity of moving drugs from the production region in northern Myanmar into interior China resembled a series of independent or even disjointed relays with each successive stage involving one or two people who only knew where to receive and deliver the merchandise. As shown in Figure 23.1, such disconnected and mutually independent trafficking entities seemed well suited to carry out one lap and to pass the baton to the next stage. Because all parties involved in moving a drug consignment must minimize their exposure to possible law enforcement detection and safeguard their own financial interests, each stage represents a complete business transaction. The individuals inside one trafficking group would not have any idea nor do they care where their consignment would travel in the next stage. Despite such restricted communication process and lack of collective actions among trafficking groups, the drug market as a whole manages to function effectively with drugs flowing from the manufacturers into the hands of the users continuously.

Similar business practices have been found in other studies in transnational human smuggling activities (Zhang and Chin, 2002). The *dyadic cart wheel network* (Zhang and Chin, 2002) has been observed at work in this study to map out the social network of drug traffickers (i.e. their primary as well as secondary contacts in the business). The one-on-one transactions again seemed most

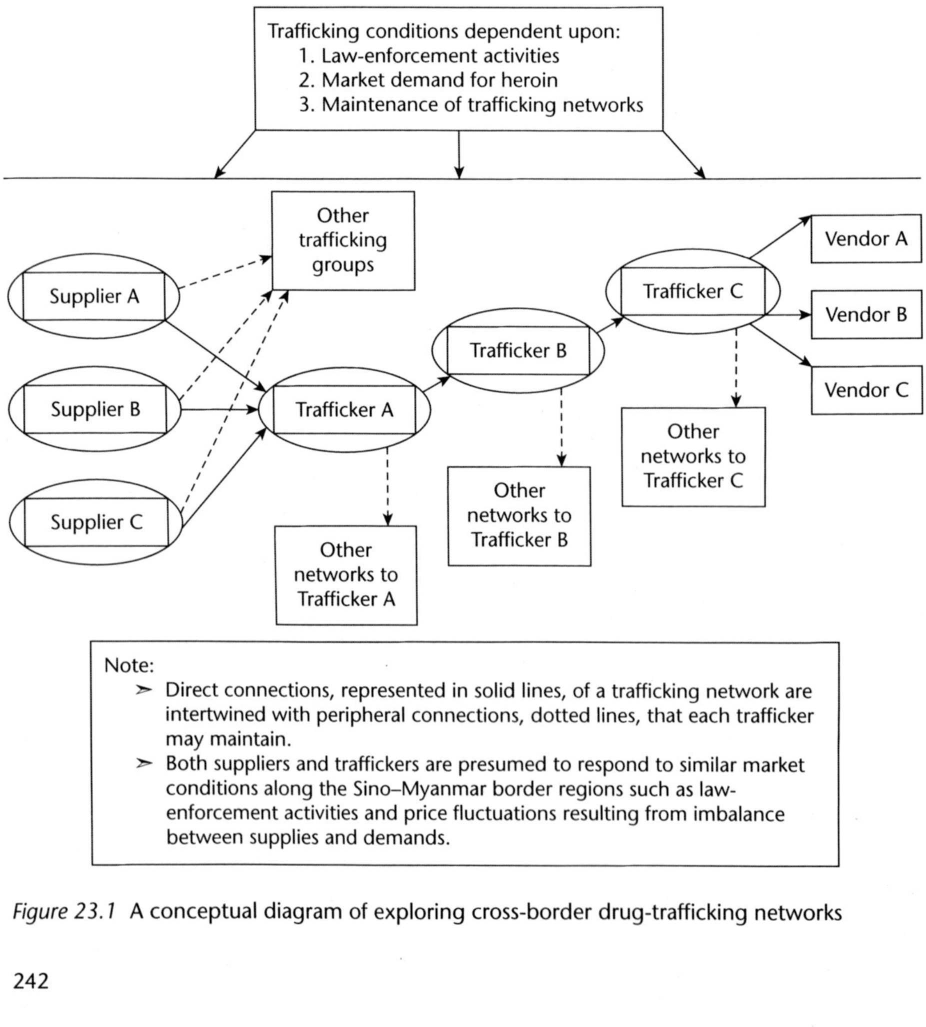

Figure 23.1 A conceptual diagram of exploring cross-border drug-trafficking networks

optimal and effective in fulfilling the fundamental requisites of this illicit enterprise – risk management and profit maximization.

Traditional Chinese criminal organizations and drug trafficking groups

US authorities have long asserted that US-based tongs and gangs are actively involved in the transportation of Southeast Asian heroin into the United States. Over the years, a number of tong[2] and gang leaders in San Francisco, Chicago, Boston, and New York have been convicted of heroin trafficking (Chin, 1996). However, there have been no known studies that examined how US tongs and gangs are linked to drug producers and traffickers in China and Southeast Asia. This study attempts to uncover the nexus between drug trafficking and traditional Chinese criminal organizations, such as those based in Taiwan, Hong Kong, China, and the United States, and tried to understand whether traditional criminal organizations actively participate in the drug trade, at what stage, and how important their influence is in these transnational activities.

After two years of field work, data gathered in this study were not able to substantiate any clear linkage between transnational drug trafficking and any traditional Chinese criminal organizations anywhere in the world. This observation does not suggest that no individual members of these criminal organizations ever took part in a trafficking business. There is simply neither evidence nor rational explanations in believing that triad societies in Hong Kong or tongs in the US are significant players in transnational drug trafficking activities. Representatives of law enforcement agencies and government officials in China and Southeast Asian countries agreed with this assessment when probed.

Despite its tremendous profits, transnational drug trade as a business does not fit well with the primary organizational requisites of the traditional criminal underworld. Zhang and Chin (2003) argued that most illicit transnational activities are fraught with risks and uncertainties that offer poor prospects for long-term and stable income (Zhang and Chin, 2003). Fluidity in transactions and unpredictable outcomes, not to mention likely exposure to law enforcement activities, are among the elements that deter established criminal organizations from entering into transnational enterprising activities. For these established crime families, the lure of enormous profits is not enough to outweigh the organizational tendency towards sustainable and predictable profitability. On the contrary, individual entrepreneurs have no such organizational baggage and are willing to confront the adverse conditions in the marketplace.

Findings in mainland China remained the same. Criminal organizations, or the so-called "dark societies," are a recent development in China. Although China's one-party political system does not tolerate any criminal organizations, their existence has been acknowledged for years by law enforcement officials as well as academics. The Chinese government refuses to acknowledge that the country has any organized crime, as is perceived in the West. However, it does acknowledge there are organizations with "dark society characteristics" (Chin and Godson, 2006). This study, however, has not found evidence that substantiate any connection between organized crime entities and drug traffickers. Even in Guangdong Province (next to Hong Kong), where anything goes, criminal organizations are not known for their involvement in the drug trade. According to the interviews with government and law enforcement representatives in mainland China, several factors seemed to hinder the convergence of these two groups of players. First drug trafficking and consumption still provoke strong negative emotions in a country that fought wars and lost dearly over drugs (i.e. the two Opium Wars in the nineteenth century). Second, any criminal organizations that rely on bribery to facilitate their racketeering activities will lose their protection from government or police officials if they deal into illicit drugs. As one ranking

Chinese police official proclaimed, "no one can save you if you are caught dealing drugs. Corruption exists in many parts of the society, but not in the drug business."

This is found to be true in the study's review of the press stories in China on official corruption and drug seizures. Stories about government anti-corruption efforts typically produce a laundry list of charges against arrested officials and criminal organization figures, such as operating gambling dens, extorting local businesses (or collecting protection fees), controlling restaurant and entertainment businesses, and conspiracy in collective bidding for government projects. Not drug trafficking. There were government officials and even police officers who were arrested on drug trafficking charges. But they were always acting on their own in the drug trade. Rarely were there any reported implications on political corruption.

The future of drug trafficking in the Golden Triangle

China has been accused of being ineffective in curbing many transnational crimes, such as human smuggling and piracy of intellectual property; but China's efforts in combating transnational drug trafficking and substance abuse have been unequivocally aggressive and forceful. During this two-year study, scores of interviews were conducted with law enforcement officials along most major trafficking routes and at different levels from Beijing to remote outfits in rural Yunnan along the border regions. Despite their meager budgets and poor equipment, the Chinese law enforcement agencies have done a remarkable job in gaining the upper hand in their war against drugs. Although drug addiction has become a widespread problem in many urban centers, the government has remained committed to fighting drugs.

China's relationship with countries around the Golden Triangle remains a sensitive one. On the one hand, Chinese authorities have for years been providing workshops and training conferences to law enforcement representatives of neighboring countries to improve their working relationships and effectiveness in the investigation of drug production and trafficking activities. On the other hand, China also applies pressure on its neighbors to step up on their efforts to eliminate opium cultivation and trafficking of heroin and other drugs through China. Such pressure is sometimes perceived as hegemonic and provokes resistance.

The warlords in the opium cultivation regions also fear direct confrontations with China. Although their influence remains substantial in the clandestine drug cultivation and transportation (Chin, 2009), these warlords have for years evaded direct accusations and challenges from Chinese authorities. In recent years, the warlords have grown even more cognizant of the fact that their political legitimacy and economic survival depend more on their relationship with China than with their own government. All warlord governments in northern Myanmar, despite their differences, have publicly vowed to eradicate opium cultivation and ban production of any illicit drugs in their jurisdictions.

Myanmar, in an effort to maintain economic ties and avoid complete international isolation, has maintained a cordial relationship with China and responded to its requests for various collaborations. For instance, when Chinese dissident Peng Ming was conducting anti-Beijing activities in Myanmar, the Chinese government pressured the Myanmar government to arrest him on charges of possessing fake Chinese money and they turned him over to China in May 2004 (Associated Press, 2005). Peng was later convicted of leading a terrorist group and kidnapping and sentenced to life in China. For years, China has relied on the Myanmar government to capture all its high-profile political or criminal fugitives.

This two-year field study has also identified two divergent trends in the drug trade in the region: (1) the heroin traffickers tended to be older and married; and (2) the methamphetamine traffickers were much younger. Poly drug traffickers as well as users were not common. Heroin addiction has over the years become stigmatized to the point that its users were commonly referred to as losers or "social garbage." On the other hand, methamphetamine and ecstasy users were not so stigmatized and were even considered hip among the youth culture. Years of public education and cultural taboo associated with heroin use appeared to have gained some momentum in China. Sources in both public and private sectors informed us that the size of the heroin addict population in China was on steady decline. Instead, the so-called "new drugs" (i.e. methamphetamine, ecstasy, and ketamine) were becoming popular in recent years in China. These drugs were thought to be non-habit forming and more "fun" to use, particularly at KTV bars and dance clubs.

Changes in the consumer market also brought about changes in the drug trade. As one drug dealer serving a life sentence noted:

> I can tell you the changes in drug traffickers just by looking at the kind of people coming here over the years. I have been here a long time. I'd say 90 percent of new prisoners these days are from the rural areas. Most of them are laborers and peasants from some of the poorest regions in China: Ningxia, Xinjiang, Guizhou, and Yunnan. Very few of them are from the cities. Almost all of them are "mules," carrying drugs for people they don't even know. Many of these couriers (mules) are also addicts. There are many willing addicts who want to participate in the trafficking business. They are easy targets for recruiters. In my days, we were far more diverse and mostly from urban areas. There were businessmen, government officials, teachers, and all kinds of people.

Recent development in the drug trade into China and Southeast Asia

The United States claims that with the decline of the Golden Triangle as the main source of opium supply, there have been increased activities in the border regions along China, Pakistan, and Afghanistan (US Department of State, 2009). Arrests for trafficking Afghan heroin to China have increased. Much of the trafficking is carried out by West African criminal networks; some of them have set up locations in Guangdong Province, managing drug traffic in Southeast Asia. One ranking police official in Guangdong Province explained that the increasing presence of drug traffickers from African countries was mostly due to the lack of hard currency in these countries for buying and importing Chinese merchandise. This police official noted:

> Because Guangdong is the backbone of China manufacturing business, many countries have set up companies here buying and exporting Chinese merchandise. African countries need Chinese products but lack the necessary hard currency. Many entrepreneurs from Africa turn to the drug trade for quick cash to enable them to buy Chinese products.

Drug traffickers are adept at dealing with the pressure from international cooperative efforts. Entrepreneurs develop specialty in the business and focus on different aspects of the illicit drug business, such as supplying chemical precursors. For a long time, drug traffickers have been exploiting the loophole of legitimate chemicals used in pharmaceutical products, such as ephedrine. The Chinese law enforcement has increased its efforts in regulating so-called dual-use chemicals. According to the US intelligence community, China's strong response to controlling dual-use chemicals has forced drug traffickers to explore new transshipment routes through Southeast Asia and Africa, particularly India (US Department of State, 2009).

The future of drug trafficking in China is juxtaposed between two conflicting forces. On the one hand, China's booming economy and frenzy to get rich will undoubtedly encourage entrepreneurship among its populous. Drug trafficking, with its immense profit potential, will continue to lure risk takers whose opportunities in life are otherwise few. On the other hand, strong social stigma surrounding illicit drugs and related drug trafficking activities, coupling with a draconian penal system and a totalitarian government, will restrain the growth of daring entrepreneurs. Unlike other illicit enterprises, particularly the so-called victimless crimes (e.g. gambling, prostitution, and financial malfeasance), there is little moral ambiguity on drug trafficking. Drug trafficking is among the few offenses that easily qualify for the death penalty.

As a result, the drug trade must rely on highly secretive networks of individuals who are mutually independent. Such a restricted trafficking and distribution environment likely hinders the expansion of any particular trafficking group. Although modern communication technologies may expedite transactions, the inherent uncertainties of the market and distrust among traffickers will hamper the growth of the business.

In the 1990s, China was also used as a transit country for traffickers to ship drugs through the southern route to Hong Kong for distribution to other parts of Southeast Asia. It is not clear as to what extent China continues to serve as a transit. One thing is clear: China's large population base will likely absorb most illicit drugs that manage to get into the marketplace, leaving few for export purposes. Despite high profit potentials for consignment orders from overseas, the fundamentals of illicit enterprises remain the same; that is, drug traffickers will choose the shortest distance and least risky venue to unload their illicit cargoes and realize profits. The role of China as a transit country, particularly for such a long distance from Yunnan to coastal Guangdong, will likely remain limited. The future of the drug trade in Southeast Asia appears to remain in China's domestic market.

Future research questions

1. How did Chinese nationals manage to command a prominent role in the drug trade in the Golden Triangle?
2. What will the Golden Triangle be in global drug trade when 95 percent of the opium poppies are now produced in Afghanistan?
3. What organizational structures seem most appropriate for cross-border drug trafficking missions?
4. Will amphetamine-type stimulants replace heroin and give the Golden Triangle a new lease of life?
5. Where do you think the drug trade is heading in the Golden Triangle?

Notes

1 This study was supported by a grant (#2004-IJ-CX-0023) from the National Institute of Justice, Office of Justice Programs, US Department of Justice. Points of views in this chapter are solely those of the authors.

2 Tongs are Chinatown-based associations in the US whose members typically belong to the same ancestral lineage or come from the same villages. Tongs are often believed by US law enforcement to participate in illicit activities either benefiting their members or vying for control of the underground economy.

References

Albor, T. (1992). Myanmar's heroin trade picks up despite US isolation policy. *The Christian Science Monitor*, 29: 6.

Associated Press (2005). Dissident's life sentence upheld. *The Honolulu Advertiser*, sec. A8.

Belanger, F. (1989). *Drugs, the US, and Khun Sa*. Bangkok: Editions Duang Kamol.

Chalk, P. (2000). Southeast Asia and the Golden Triangle's heroin trade: threat and response. *Studies in Conflict & Terrorism*, 23: 89–106.

Chin, K. (1996). *Chinatown gangs: extortion, enterprise, and ethnicity*. New York: Oxford University Press.

—— (2009). *The Golden Triangle – inside Southeast Asia's drug trade*. Ithaca, NY: Cornell University Press.

Chin, K. and Godson, R. (2006). Organized crime and the political–criminal nexus in China. *Trends in Organized Crime*, 9(3), 5–44.

China State Department. (2000) (in Chinese). *Drug prohibition in China – a White Paper*. Online at http://www.mps.gov.cn (accessed November 24, 2010).

Dobinson, I. (1993). Pinning a tail on the dragon: the Chinese and the international heroin trade. *Crime & Delinquency*, 39(3), 373–84.

Gaylord, M. (1997). City of secrets: drugs, money and the law in Hong Kong. *Crime, Law & Social Change*, 28: 91–110.

Hao, W., Xiao, S., Liu, T., Young, D., Chen, S., Zhang, D., Li, C., Chen. G., and Yang, K. (2002). The second national epidemiological survey on illicit drug use at six high-prevalence areas in China: prevalence rates and use patterns. *Addiction*, 97: 1,305–15.

Lintner, B. (1991). *Cross-border drug trade in the Golden Triangle (S.E. Asia)*. Durham, UK: Boundaries Research Press.

—— (1994). The volatile Yunnan frontier. *Jane's Intelligence Review*, February: 84–92.

—— (1998). Drugs and economic growth: ethnicity and exports. In Robert Rotberg (Ed.) *Myanmar: prospects for a democratic future*. Washington, DC: Brookings Institution Press.

Liu, Z., Lu, X., Mu, Y., Lian, Z., and Zhou, W.H. (2002) (in Chinese). Epidemiological survey for drug abusers in China. *Chinese Journal of Drug Abuse Prevention*, 40: 27–30.

Ma, M. (1994) (in Chinese). *Drugs in China*. Taipei: Kenin Publishing.

McCoy, A. (1972). *The politics of heroin in Southeast Asia*. New York: Harper & Row.

—— (1992). Heroin as a global commodity: a history of Southeast Asia's opium trade. In A. McCoy and A. Block (Eds.) *War on drugs: studies in the failure of US Narcotics Policy*. Boulder, CO: Westview Press.

—— (1999). Requiem for a drug lord: state and commodity in the career of Khun Sa. In J. Heyman (Ed.) *States and illegal practices*. Oxford, UK: Berg. pp. 129–67.

McIllwain, J. (2003). *Organizing crime in Chinatown: race and racketeering in New York, 1890–1910*. Jefferson, NC: McFarland & Company Publishers.

Myanmar Information Committee (Yangon). (2005). Information sheet, July 7. Online at http://www.myanmar-information.net/infosheet/2005/050707.htm (accessed August 15, 2009).

Renard, R. (1996). *The Burmese connection: illegal drugs and the making of the Golden Triangle*. Boulder, CO: Lynne Rienner Publishers.

Reuter, P. (1983). *Disorganized crime: the economics of the visible hand*. Cambridge, MA: MIT Press.

Smith, M. (1999). *Myanmar: insurgency and the politics of ethnicity* (revised and updated edition). London: Zed Books.

Takano, H. (2002). *The shore beyond good and evil: a report from inside Myanmar's opium kingdom*. Reno, NV: Kotan Publishing.

United Nations International Drug Control Programme. (1997). World drug report. New York: Oxford University Press.

US Department of State. (2009). International narcotics control strategy report, 2008. Washington, DC.

Wang, Y. and Liang, J. (1999) (in Chinese). The drug problem in Lincang and its drug control strategies. In B. Luo and J. Liang (Eds.) *Essays on the suppression of drug in Yunnan*. Beijing: Qunzhong Publication.

Zhang, S. X. (2008). *Chinese human smuggling organizations – families, social networks, and cultural imperatives*. Palo Alto, CA: Stanford University Press.

Zhang, S. and Chin, K. (2002). Enter the dragon – inside Chinese human smuggling organizations. *Criminology*, 40(4): 737–68.

—— (2003). The declining significance of triad societies in transnational illegal activities – a structural deficiency perspective. *British Journal of Criminology*, 43(3): 469–88.

24

The production of ecstasy in the Netherlands

Melvin R. J. Soudijn and Matthijs F. J. Vijlbrief

Introduction

Organized crime in the Netherlands can be characterized as cross-border crime. Criminal groups are primarily involved in illegal international trade, using the same opportunity structure that facilitates legal economic activities. For this reason, it is interesting to note that the Netherlands also acts as a major *production* country for the synthetic drug ecstasy. In 2008, the UN reported that 42 percent of the ecstasy seized worldwide originated in the Netherlands (UNODC, 2008, p. 135). The US Drug Enforcement Administration (DEA) also recognized that seized batches were primary produced in clandestine laboratories in the Netherlands and Belgium (see DEA website; details on p. 259).

Because the Netherlands is considered a source country, the Dutch government has taken an active role in detecting production sites and devising countermeasures. Using organized crime theory, this chapter examines three policy options to curtail the production of ecstasy. These are judicial interventions based on organized crime as a hierarchical entity, judicial interventions based on organized crime as networks, and opportunities for situational crime prevention. To understand the choices involved, the chapter begins with a short historical background of ecstasy, continues with a description of the ecstasy production process, and ends with an examination of the logistics of production (including the flow of goods, information, and money) and, most importantly, of the people involved.

History

Ecstasy is a synthetic drug with Methylenedioxymethylamphetamine (MDMA) as its active psychotropic ingredient. MDMA was first synthesized in 1889. In 1912, the German pharmaceutical company Merck applied for a patent on the drug. Merck was considering putting it on the market as an appetite suppressant, but there was insufficient demand for it. At the beginning of the Cold War, the US army became interested in MDMA's potential for use as a truth serum, a use for which it later turned out to be unsuitable (Huisman, 2005).

In the early 1970s, some members of the US psychiatric community made use of MDMA. Dr. Alexander Shulgin, famous author of *PiHKAL*,[1] heard from the young chemistry student Merrie Kleinman that MDMA had interesting psychoactive effects. After performing a number of experiments on himself, he introduced psychotherapist Leo Zeff to the drug's effects. Zeff was so taken by the effects of MDMA that he postponed his retirement to travel around the US promoting its therapeutic use to colleagues (POD, 2008).

MDMA was first used recreationally in the early 1980s, and pills containing MDMA were given the name ecstasy because of the euphoria they caused. By 1984, MDMA was widely used as a recreational drug (Shulgin and Shulgin, 1991). In 1985, MDMA was outlawed in the US and placed on Schedule I of the Controlled Substances Act.[2] As a result, the drug went underground and prices skyrocketed.

About one year after ecstasy was outlawed in the US, it surfaced in Europe and became popular on the party scene. In 1988, ecstasy was added to List I of the Dutch Opium Act. The increase in ecstasy use went hand in hand with the growing popularity of huge raves, techno parties, and dance parties in the UK, Belgium, and later in the Netherlands.

In the years following its emergence in the Netherlands, ecstasy was still imported from the US. The illegal production of ecstasy in Western Europe first appeared in amateur labs in the Netherlands (Husken and Vuijst, 2002). In addition to MDMA, these labs manufactured a variety of related chemical compounds, referred to as designer drugs or research chemicals (RCs). Many RCs were not yet covered by the Opium Act, and so it was not illegal to produce or sell them. Over the years, experimenting with RCs decreased and MDMA held its ground as the most used synthetic drug, apparently because it produced the most desirable effects for users.[3]

Ecstasy in the Netherlands

Although MDMA has been included in the Dutch Opium Act since 1988, the need to address the synthetic drug problem has only been acknowledged since 1997 (Schoenmakers, 2005). In that year, the report *Ecstasy in Nederland* (Ministerie van Volksgezondheid, 1997) was sent to the Dutch House of Representatives. This report made clear that ecstasy was the most used hard drug in the Netherlands, in part due to its association with the popular dance culture. But it was not only in the Netherlands that people were eager to get their hands on ecstasy. A number of criminal entrepreneurs exported the drug to other countries. Worldwide, a substantial increase was seen in the counts of seized synthetic drugs which had some connection with the Netherlands (Schoenmakers, 2005). Various countries, including the US, confronted the Netherlands with this issue. In 2001, partly as a response to international pressure, the Dutch Justice Department released a memorandum (Ministerie van Justitie, 2001) in which synthetic drugs were made a distinct priority among Dutch investigative authorities, a situation that continues to this day (Vijlbrief, 2009). But how did the Netherlands manage to become a major producer of ecstasy when the drug had its origins in the US? Most likely, a number of unique circumstances regarding supply and demand for this drug lay at the root of this development (Blickman, 2004).

The demand for ecstasy increased quickly. Korf (2003) attempted to explain the success of ecstasy by looking at the characteristics of its users, the social and cultural environment in which the drug was used, and the drug itself. He found that ecstasy was primarily used in the party scene starting in the mid-1980s. Teenagers and young adults attended techno parties that quickly gained in popularity. Through their ecstasy use, people experienced these parties as intimate, blissful, and pleasurable gatherings of a large group of friends. In addition, ecstasy was relatively cheap, easy to take, and had a party reputation. Ecstasy spread quickly to other countries, due to increased mobility and cheaper means of travel to clubs in tourist destinations (Huisman, 2005). The market for ecstasy was flexible and ever-changing, with new pill logos and colors appearing in quick succession.

An important factor in the supply side of ecstasy is the fact that the infrastructure required for the production and trade in MDMA was already largely in place in the Netherlands. After all, the Dutch played a leading role in illicit alcohol distillation and the production of amphetamine since the 1970s. Both production processes are suitable for the production of ecstasy. In this respect, one can speak of "routine socio-economic activities" (Blickman, 2004). Criminal organizations then only have to switch over to another product line, so to speak, in order to manufacture the new drug. Examples of this type of shift in production have indeed been encountered. A number of individuals suspected of manufacturing MDMA were already known to the police, for instance, from their past involvement in the illegal distillation of alcohol. The laboratory experience required for ecstasy production, as well as the contacts needed to obtain the necessary equipment and chemicals, was already in place. In the 1970s, Dutch amphetamine manufacturers already had good contacts and large supply markets in Germany and Scandinavia (Huisman, 2005). Moreover, their existing partnerships allowed them to swiftly move in to serve the British market for ecstasy. Through the years, a certain division of labor emerged within the Netherlands: ecstasy was primarily manufactured in the south, while traffickers with international contacts were concentrated in and around Amsterdam.

The number of current ecstasy users[4] in the Netherlands was estimated at 40,000 in 2005. Although ecstasy use declined between 1996 and 2003, especially among school-aged youth (from 2.3 percent to 1.2 percent), ecstasy remains the second most used drug in the Netherlands, after cannabis. In Western Europe, Central Europe, and North America, current ecstasy use is just under 1 percent, while in Australia and neighboring countries, it stands at 3 percent. Current use in East Asia and Southeast Asia is still low at 0.1 percent, but the user population is growing fast (Huisman and Smits, 2008).

Ecstasy produced in the Netherlands is largely for export. Only a small portion is for domestic consumption.[5] This can be easily explained by the considerably larger profit margins to be had in other countries, especially those outside Europe. Since Dutch ecstasy producers have a high level of expertise which results in high-quality products, their pills are in demand. The average production cost of a single ecstasy tablet amounts to €0.15 – €0.20, while individual tablets fetch an average price of €3.49 each on the street in the Netherlands. The street value is far higher in many major North American cities (€20–€30), Australia and New Zealand (about €30), and Japan (€25–€50). These price differences illustrate the motive for cross-border crime: export and transit can produce significant profits.

Production process of MDMA

To give a better understanding of the logistical steps a criminal organization must take in manufacturing ecstasy and trafficking in it, the production process is further discussed below. The process requires experienced lab technicians. In practice, some lab technicians have limited knowledge and experience, but work with a recipe from a "cookbook." They are most likely directed by people who do have a good understanding of the synthesis process. There are eight main steps in the production of ecstasy. The description below is given in non-specialist language, without details of the specific chemical processes involved.

Synthesis

The actual synthesis takes place in this phase and requires the precursor Piperonyl Methyl Keton (PMK). PMK is primarily produced in China. The main legal application of PMK is as an ingredient in perfumes and cleaning agents. However, the quantity required for these uses is limited in comparison with that used in the production of MDMA. Obtaining PMK is one of the greatest challenges in MDMA production. Unlike other ingredients in MDMA, there are no good alternatives for PMK. So to a large degree, PMK suppliers determine the production of MDMA.

In addition to PMK, other chemicals are needed to make MDMA; for instance, monomethylamine, methanol, platinum oxide, acetone, and hydrochloric acid. Although most of these ingredients have legal applications, using them for the production of synthetic drugs is a criminal offense.[6]

Required hardware includes a pressure tank with pressure gauge, a temperature gauge, tap, propulsion engine, mixing mechanism, and vacuum pump, and sometimes an industrial freezer. In one method of production, all ingredients are put into the pressure tank, and synthesis takes place in about four hours. The yield depends largely on the amount of PMK available, which, after synthesis, is roughly one-third of the volume of the pressure tank. One of the largest tanks encountered in a laboratory had a volume of 500 liters (see Plate 24.1). In theory, this allows for batches of 170 liters of MDMA oil at a time. Synthesis is a complex and dangerous process, but it is also crucial for the quality of the final product.

Distillation

In this phase of the process, various fluids are separated from one another using their difference in boiling points. Hardware needed for this phase include heating mantles, gas burners, 20-liter round-bottomed flasks with cooling units, a vacuum pump, temperature gauge, or a distillation unit with collection tank. This phase takes several hours. Synthesis and distillation can both be carried out within a period of ten hours.

Crystallization

During this phase, MDMA oil is transformed into a solid form which can be readily absorbed by the human body. Acetone and hydrochloric acid are used as solvent and acid. The actual crystallization can take place in a plain plastic tub, a crystallization tank, or a deep freezer, and is a time-consuming process. It takes at least 24 hours, and the mixture must be stirred continually. The resulting crystals are occasionally sold as a final product, though generally not in the Netherlands. In other countries, MDMA sometimes appears in the form of these coarse crystals. By and large, MDMA is first made into tablet form, for which a number of further steps are needed.

Filtration

In the filtration phase, superfluous fluid is removed from the wet MDMA. Common household materials are often used in this process. The wet MDMA may be placed in a pillowcase and then spun in a spin-drier or filtered using a homemade filtration device. A vacuum pump and Büchner funnel are also needed. Following filtration, the MDMA must be dried.

Drying

Unlike amphetamine, MDMA is generally consumed in pill form. To make tablets, MDMA powder must be completely dry. The presence of even the smallest amount of moisture will cause the pills to fall apart. All kinds of equipment is used to dry MDMA power, from industrial drying cabinets to ovens to hair dryers. The powder can also be spread out on a tarpaulin and dried using fans.

Plate 24.1 Industrial-size pressure reaction vessel, seized in a clandestine lab in the south of the Netherlands. This vessel has a potential capacity of producing 400 liters of MDMA oil per batch, which equals approximately 480 kilos of MDMA powder or 5 million ecstasy tablets.

Pulverizing

The dried MDMA powder is still relatively coarse. To make pills, the powder must first be made very fine. To do so, an industrial pulverizer can be used, as well as mixers, meat grinders, and other common kitchen equipment. Professional equipment is often used due to the frequently large quantities of MDMA powder to be processed.

Mixing and coloring

In this phase, the fine MDMA powder is mixed and dyed, to the specifications of the buyer. MDMA powder is mixed with a variety of other substances that serve as fillers and make it easier to produce a smooth tablet, such as microcellulose, lactose, talcum powder, magnesium powder, starch, and caffeine. Any sort of dye may be used. The mixing phase is often carried out using a drum mixer, food processor, or cement mixer, and weighing equipment. At the completion of this phase, the MDMA powder is ready for tabletting.

Tabletting

Ecstasy is nearly exclusively sold and used in the form of pills with logos. In most cases, tabletting takes place in a different location than the MDMA synthesis. This may have to do with attempts to spread the risk, as well as the fact that different people with distinct expertise are involved in this phase. To produce the pills, a tabletting machine and the associated logo-stamps are needed. There are all kinds of tabletting machines around, from relatively small pieces of equipment, with a capacity of fewer than 5,000 pills an hour, to large industrial machines with a capacity of more than 15,000. Criminal organizations obtain tabletting machines second-hand, on the internet, or by buying up the assets of bankrupt companies. Pill-stamps are used to print logos on the pills. In practice, there are countless different sizes and types of pills, but they almost always have a certain logo, for example, a well-known brand of automobile or exclusive clothing line, or a popular cartoon character. These stamps must be made of a special reinforced steel because they are often used thousands of times. If one were to use regular steel, the stamp would wear down too quickly and the imprint would no longer be clear. Making these stamps is the work of specialized professionals, who supply these high-quality stamps to various tabletters. After the pills are made, they are weighed and packed, and the production process is complete.

The above description makes clear that a number of links are essential in the production of MDMA and ultimately ecstasy tablets: laboratory technicians, suppliers of PMK and other ingredients necessary for the synthesis, and producers of pill-stamps and necessary hardware. The next section goes into these issues further.

The criminal business process

The synthetic drug production process carries with it an inherent division of duties which greatly influences the structure of the criminal organization (Kleemans *et al.*, 2002). Spapens (2006) uses a model devised in the field of business administration to describe the criminal business process, whereby logistical processes are divided into the flow of goods, information, and money.

Flow of goods

The flow of goods is defined as the chain in which illegal goods or services are produced or provided, including both real estate and moveable goods, both legal and illegal. The flow of goods in relation to the criminal business process for synthetic drugs is as follows:

1. Obtaining a production location and production resources:
   a. Obtaining the production space
   b. Obtaining standard equipment and legal raw materials
   c. Obtaining specialized equipment and illegal materials
2. Setting up the laboratory:
   a. Ensuring transport of equipment and materials
   b. Installing the equipment
3. Carrying out the production process:
   a. Performing the various steps of production
   b. Disposing of waste
4. Trafficking in the final product, in consumer or wholesale quantities
5. Transport and distribution of the final product, in consumer or wholesale quantities

Flow of information

The second component of the criminal business process is the flow of information exchanged among members of the criminal organization as a function of the business process, and includes content-related, organizational, and social information.

Flow of content-related information

This comprises all information that has to do with the flow of goods or money. The flow of information must be concealed because it can lead directly to criminal acts or products. For this reason, such information is exchanged as much as possible during face-to-face meetings.

Flow of organizational information

This information has to do with meetings to be arranged, or conversations to direct one another to certain locations, etc. This information is largely communicated by phone or cell phone.

Flow of social information

This exchange of information is not directly functional for carrying out the illegal activities at hand but involves the social context in which the producers operate.

Flow of money

This comprises all financial transactions, be they cash or check, money transfers, or payment in kind.

Organization

Various roles can be differentiated on the basis of the above breakdown of the production process and business transactions. An organizer, for example, can be identified for each production process. The organizer oversees the logistics from a higher managerial position. In addition, they often finance the operation, or make use of investors who are willing to fund part of the operation in exchange for a share of the profits. These organizers shield themselves as much as possible from the actual operation by creating intermediary layers of personnel, or assistants. For a set fee, assistants perform work like processing or moving goods. The description of the business process showed that specialized expertise was also necessary. This is rendered by service providers. Service providers are paid per job, and do not share in the profits of the criminal business process. But service providers have specific knowledge or skills at their disposal, which makes them scarcer than assistants. Service providers often only come to the fore briefly in investigations, because their contributions frequently just involve single transactions. Moreover, they often work for more than one organizer, sometimes at the same time. Five important categories of service providers follow:

The first important group of service providers specializes in supplying illegal materials. The precursor most used in the production of MDMA is PMK, which turns out to be primarily manufactured and sold in China (Huisman and Smits, 2008; Soudijn and Kleemans, 2009).

The second important group of service providers is hardware manufacturers and suppliers. The hardware required for the production of synthetic drugs includes pressure tanks, heating mantles, 20-liter round-bottomed flasks, and reactors. Most of these items are not themselves illegal, but they are difficult to obtain through regular channels or have few legal applications. Moreover, most of the hardware must first be adapted or customized in some way by individuals with the expertise, skills, and tools to do so.

A third important group of service providers are the laboratory technicians. They are responsible for actually carrying out the synthesis and/or tabletting. Only a few lab technicians are trained chemists. The vast majority learn on the job (Spapens, 2006, p. 187).

Transport personnel can be considered a fourth category of service providers. They are responsible for transporting various legal and illegal goods from one location to another. Transporters often work for more than one criminal organization.

The fifth category of service providers in the world of synthetic drugs deal with financial matters and include lawyers and accountants.

Finally, there is the type of service provider whose "profession" is to facilitate identity-shielding for the members of a criminal organization. These providers often lease cars from mala fide companies, and arrange discreet means of communication and rental properties.

Theoretical implications and debate

There is a lively academic debate on the type of cooperation among people involved in the production of synthetic drugs. The two most prominent theories deal with people cooperating as hierarchical organizations or as fluid networks. Another approach is a situational crime perspective. These three types are explained below.

At one end of the spectrum, one finds the view of organized crime as a bureaucratic hierarchy. This (traditional) view of organized crime is often traced back to the findings from several American congressional committees on organized crime, such as Cressey's report for the 1967 Task Force on Organized Crime for the President's Crime Commission (Cressey, 1967). In this model, large-scale, ethnically homogeneous, hierarchical entities participate in various highly lucrative criminal activities in a systematic (i.e. bureaucratic) way. Based on this view, the judicial authorities should focus on the prosecution of the organizers, without whom the criminal enterprise would collapse. This leads to long-term investigations that take at least several months or years.

In the 1970s, this view of organized crime as hierarchical organizations shifted to criminal networks (Albini, 1971; Ianni, 1974). These days, crimes that are well organized are often regarded as having network characteristics. This entails people working less in accordance with hierarchy or continuity, but rather taking advantage of criminal opportunities (Reuter, 1983;

Kleemans *et al.*, 1998; Van de Bunt and Kleemans, 2007). Social capital and social network theories are used as the primary tools for analyzing criminal partnerships. For example, people who are able to bridge social and geographic gaps are very important in a network. Following on from Burt, such nodes in criminal networks can be referred to as "structural holes" (Burt, 1992). With this network template, the judicial authorities can target specific people to disturb the production and logistical process. For instance, it may be effective just to tackle the financial service providers of criminal networks. Few people in a criminal network have the necessary skills to carry out money laundering schemes. This makes them of great value to criminal entrepreneurs. As such, financial advisers often provide their services for different criminals and illegal enterprises. By the same logic, lab technicians are also crucial in the production chain. The necessary skills are hard to find, and here too it has been observed that the technicians render their services to various criminal entrepreneurs. Suppliers of PMK are another important link in the chain. They are vital in providing access to the key ingredient in the production process. On the other hand, targeting international transporters is a less fruitful approach for an investigation. They are easily replaceable and have less specialized skills than financial advisers or lab technicians.

In many ways, the network model seems the best fit when it comes to studying the synthetic drugs sector. Organizers make use of many different couriers, transport personnel, lab technicians, and errand boys and are not particularly committed to sustaining a working relationship with any of them. However, the current view of organized crime as being comprised of fluid criminal networks – with few sustained or hierarchical relationships and characterized instead by dynamism, flexibility, and member turnover – does need to be qualified. This is especially true of organized crime operating in the synthetic drugs sector (Vijlbrief, 2009). First, there is often a group of core members within networks who take the initiative, while co-perpetrators and contractors are then approached on a more ad hoc basis (Klerks and Kop, 2004; Soudijn, 2006). For this reason, it is still useful to identify and try to tackle the organizers.

Secondly, there are no hard-and-fast rules that organized crime will always follow a given pattern. Apart from flexible networks, there are also strongly cohesive or hybrid networks (Rogovin and Martens, 1997; Williams, 2001). Examples include ethnically homogeneous groups with affective (family) relationships (Bruinsma and Bernasco, 2004). It is precisely because they are not purely instrumental that these latter networks are durable.

Lastly, networks are often difficult to define. What counts as a network and what does not? For example, the essential precursor PMK is often imported from China. Several police investigations have revealed a pattern of Chinese criminals bringing PMK into the Netherlands and selling it to Dutch producers of ecstasy (Huisman and Smits, 2008; Soudijn and Kleemans, 2009). Due to language barriers and the scarcity of the product, the import side has become the exclusive domain of Chinese criminals. One could argue that they make up part of the network of the Dutch synthetic drug producers. But one could also argue that the Chinese and Dutch criminals constitute two separate networks that work together. The illegal importation of PMK itself constitutes a separate criminal process.

In contrast to the views based on hierarchical or network models, the theory of situational crime prevention bypasses discussions about the nature of organized crime. Studies using this approach focus on how situational crime analysis may help identify both the circumstances that facilitate crime, and viable measures for reducing the opportunities to commit crime (for examples, Felson and Clarke, 1998; Cornish and Clarke, 2002). If the aim is to implement effective crime prevention measures, the question of whether or not criminal groups are, strictly speaking, "organized" is not always relevant.

From a situational perspective, the production of ecstasy leads to some opportunities for intervention. A classic example is subjecting certain precursors to strict international monitoring.

In the Dutch case, it is clear that without PMK, the production of MDMA will be severely hampered. New legislation in China means that as of 2008, the production of PMK is being more closely monitored. As a result, ecstasy producers in the Netherlands are rumored to be having more difficulty obtaining this precursor. For the moment, drug experts have observed that less ecstasy is being confiscated worldwide.[7]

However, several other, more small-scale (local) opportunities for intervention also present themselves. The production of synthetic drugs requires not only specific chemicals, but also specialized equipment, such as flasks and glass mantles. Of course, it is not illegal to buy or sell glasswork. Yet most glassblowers are unaware that their equipment may be being used for the production of ecstasy. For this reason, the police launched an initiative to raise awareness among glassblowers. This turned out to be extremely effective. In the wake of the campaign, it was observed that ecstasy producers had great difficulty in obtaining special flasks. What we should learn here is that this sort of campaign was not focused on a particular criminal organization or transnational network.

However, the use of situational crime prevention comes with one important caveat. A local approach is only possible on the basis of knowledge attained from the thorough analysis of the criminal operations of large-scale producers and traffickers. It is precisely those "old-fashioned" police investigations focusing on the organizers that produce insight into the crucial bottlenecks encountered by ecstasy producers. Without these investigations, many options for situational measures may never enter the policy arena.

Future research questions

1. How does the business process of ecstasy compare to the process of another criminal activity?
2. Compare a situational crime prevention measure discussed in this chapter to one that has not been referred to in this chapter.
3. Is the risk of displacement a fundamental flaw in situational crime prevention?
4. Sometimes it is advocated to have an 'ecstasy test team' on the premises of major parties. Such a team would test designer drugs on proper ingredients. Buyers could test their pills and discard dangerous ones. What are the implications of such measures?
5. What conditions must be satisfied in order to compare seizures of ecstasy pills worldwide? Consider differences in definitions, levels of purity, time spans, etc.

Notes

1 *PiHKAL* stands for "Phenethylamines I Have Known and Loved." Shulgin devoted nearly 30 years of his life to synthesizing, using, and evaluating almost 200 types of chemical substances. He also tested new substances on his wife and close friends. They describe their findings and experiences in *PiHKAL* (Shulgin and Shulgin, 1991).

2 Schedule I drugs are deemed too dangerous to have any accepted medical or therapeutic purposes. MDMA is listed along with LSD and MDA.

3 For more information on the harmful effects of all kinds of drugs, see also http://www.emcdda.europa.eu/publications (Risk assessments).

4 "Current use" means use by a person in the past month (Huisman and Smits, 2008).

5 An extensive study in 2003 concluded that an estimated 78 to 131 million pills of ecstasy are manufactured per year in the Netherlands. Of these, 7 to 13 million are for the domestic market, 43 to 73 for the EU market, and 28–48 for the rest of the world. This means that the Netherlands is responsible for supplying a total of 32–42% of the total global demand for ecstasy pills (Blickman, 2004).

6 Article 10a of the Dutch Opium Act was formulated for this purpose: it criminalizes certain actions as preparatory acts. This makes it a criminal offence, even in the case of raw materials that are not in themselves illegal, to acquire, possess, or sell them with the intent of using them for illegal purposes.

7 Pills often include a mixture of MDMA and other substances or MDMA substitutes. However, limited forensic capacity often leads to confusion about the actual content of tablets believed to be "ecstasy" (MDMA) (WDR, 2009, p. 115).

References

Albini, J. L. (1971). *The American mafia: genesis of a legend.* New York: Appleton, Crofts.

Blickman, T. (2004). The ecstasy industry: exploring the global market. Transnational Institute. (TNI) Briefing Series, No 2004/9. Amsterdam.

Bruinsma, G. and Bernasco, W. (2004). Criminal groups and transnational illegal markets: a more detailed examination on the basis of Social Network Theory. *Crime, Law & Social Change*, 41: 79–94.

Burt, R. (1992). *Structural holes.* Cambridge, MA: Harvard University Press.

Cornish, D. B. and Clarke, R. V. (2002). Analyzing organized crimes. In A. Piquero and S. G. Tibbetts (Eds.) *Rational choice and criminal behavior: recent research and future challenges*, pp. 41–62. New York: Garland.

Cressey, D. R. (1967). The functions and structure of criminal syndicates. President's Commission on Law Enforcement and Administration of Justice: Task Force report: organized crime. Washington, DC: Government Printing Office.

Felson, M. and Clarke, R. V. (1998). Opportunity makes the thief: practical theory for crime prevention. London: Police Research Series.

Huisman, S. (2005). Crime pattern analysis synthetic drugs 2002–4. Driebergen: Netherlands Police Agency.

Huisman, S. and Smits, E. M. (2008). Synthetische drugs en precursoren. Deelrapport Criminaliteitsbeeldanalyse 2007. Driebergen: Netherlands Police Agency.

Husken, M and F. Vuijst (2002). Ecstasy smokkel. Amsterdam: Uitgeverij M.

Ianni, F.J. (1974). Black mafia: ethnic succession in organized crime. New York: Simon and Schuster.

Kleemans, E. R., van den Berg, E. A. I. M., and van de Bunt, H. G. (1998). Georganiseerde criminaliteit in Nederland, Rapportage op basis van de Monitor Georganiseerde Criminaliteit. The Hague: WODC, Onderzoek en Beleid.

Kleemans, E. R., Brienen, M. E. L. and van de Bunt, H. G. (2002). Georganiseerde criminaliteit in Nederland, Tweede rapportage op basis van de Monitor Georganiseerde Criminaliteit. The Hague: WODC, Onderzoek en Beleid.

Kleemans, E. R., Soudijn, M. R. J. and Weenink, A. W. (2010). Situational crime prevention and cross-border crime. In Bullock, K., Clarke, R. V. and Tilley, N. (Eds.). *Situational prevention of organised crimes* (Crime Science Series). Abingdon: Willan Publishing, pp. 17–34.

Klerks, P. P. H. M. and Kop, N. (2004). De analyse van criminele infrastructuren, verslag van een pilotproject. Onderzoeksgroep Politieacademie.

Korf, D. J. (2003). What makes ecstasy so successful? International Synthetic Drug Conference. The Hague, 8–9 October.

Ministerie van Justitie (2001). Samenspannen tegen ecstasy. Een plan van aanpak ter intensivering van het Nederlandse beleid inzake synthetische drugs.

—— (2002). Plan van aanpak drugssmokkel Schiphol. Tweede Kamer, vergaderjaar 2001–2, 28 192, nr. 1.

Ministerie van Volksgezondheid Ruimtelijke Ordening en Milieu. (1997). Ecstasy in Nederland. Ingezonden rapport aan de Tweede kamer als onderdeel van jaarlijkse voortgangsrapportage Drugsbeleid.

Programmatorische Federale Overheidsdienst (POD) Wetenschapsbeleid. (2008). Chemische profilering van afvalstoffen uit de clandestiene productie van drugs. Louvain: KUL.

Reuter, P. (1983). *Disorganized crime: illegal markets and the Mafia.* Cambridge, MA: MIT Press.

Rogovin, C. H. and Martens, F. T. (1997). The evil that men do. In P. J. Ryan and G.E. Rush (Eds.). *Understanding organized crime in global perspective, a reader*, pp. 26–36. Thousand Oaks, CA: Sage Publications.

Schoenmakers, J. J. A. (2005). De korte klap als strategie in de strijd tegen de synthetische drugscriminaliteit. Kernopgave 53.3.08, Wetenschappelijke expertise en opsporing, Helmond (unpublished).

Shulgin A. and Shulgin, A. (1991). *PHIKAL, a chemical love story.* Berkeley, CA: Transform Press.

Soudijn, M. R. J. (2006). Chinese human smuggling in transit. The Hague: Boom.

Soudijn, M. R. J. and Kleemans, E. R. (2009). Chinese organized crime and situational context: a comparison of human smuggling and synthetic drugs trafficking. *Crime, Law and Social Change*, 52(5): 457–74.

Spapens, A. C. M. (2006). Interactie tussen criminaliteit en opsporing, De gevolgen van opsporingsactiviteiten voor de organisatie en afscherming van XTC-productie en-handel in Nederland. Antwerp–Oxford: Intersentia.

United Nations Office on Drugs and Crime (UNODC) (2008). World Drug Report 2008. Vienna: UNODC.

—— (2009). World drug report. Vienna: UNODC. Online at http://www.unodc.org/documents/wdr/WDR_2009/WDR2009_eng_web.pdf (Accessed December 3, 2010).

Van de Bunt, H. G. and Kleemans, E. R. (2007). Georganiseerde criminaliteit in Nederland, Derde rapportage op basis van de Monitor Georganiseerde Criminaliteit. The Hague: WODC.

Vijlbrief, M. F. J. (2009). Traditie of Innovatie? Een verkennend onderzoek naar de relatie tussen kenmerken van georganiseerde misdaad en de inzet van opsporingsstrategieën in onderzoeken van de unit Zuid-Nederland van de dienst Nationale Recherche. Erasmus Universiteit Rotterdam.

Williams, P. (2001). Transnational criminal networks. In J. Arquila and D. Ronfeldt (Eds.) *Networks and netwars: the future of terror, crime and militancy*, pp. 61–97. Santa Monica, CA: Rand Corporation.

Relevant websites

DEA website on MDMA: http://www.justice.gov/dea/concern/mdma.html

United Nations Office on Drugs and Crime (UNODC): http://www.unodc.org/unodc/en/data-and-analysis/index.html

Australian Crime Commission: http://www.crimecommission.gov.au/

Royal Canadian Mounted Police (RCMP): http://www.rcmp-grc.gc.ca/drugs-drogues/poster-affiche/index-eng.htm

Bureau for International Narcotics and Law Enforcement Affairs: http://www.state.gov/p/inl/rls/nrcrpt/2010/vol1/137193.htm

International Narcotics Control Strategy Report (INCSR): http://www.state.gov/p/inl/rls/nrcrpt/

SOCA (Serious Organised Crime Agency): http://www.soca.gov.uk/threats/drugs

National Drug Intelligence Center: http://www.usdoj.gov/ndic/

25
Drug violence in Colombia

Gipsy Escobar

Introduction

During the past four decades, Colombia has faced a number of challenges that have had detrimental consequences for the quality of life and safety of its citizens. Since the mid-1960s the country has been thrown into continuous internal conflicts involving the government, left-wing guerrillas, and right-wing paramilitary groups. Thousands have been killed and more than a million civilians displaced. The emergence of violent drug cartels in the 1970s, and their consolidation in the 1980s, added an extra layer of complexity to the conflict, as drug lords got involved in the financing of paramilitary groups and engaged in a terrorist campaign against the government and society at large. Following the demise of the big drug cartels in the mid-1990s, the guerrilla and paramilitary groups became more active in the illicit drugs market as a way of financing their terrorist activities and gaining control over parts of the Colombian territory.

By the mid-1990s the criminal ethos and the techniques and technologies used by these organized groups had permeated some sections of Colombian society, increasing the levels of criminal activity in the streets and corruption inside government agencies. This chapter will examine the evolution of drug crime in Colombia, its social and political implications, and its links to violent crime.

Evolution of drug crime in Colombia

The evolution of drug crime in Colombia is closely tied to the evolution of America's war on drugs. Indeed, during the 1960s and 1970s the great majority of marijuana entering the United States originated from Mexico and the Caribbean. However, after the governments of Lyndon B. Johnson and Richard Nixon pressured Mexico and Jamaica into curtailing the cropping and distribution of marijuana, the production of the psychotropic was displaced to the North Coast of Colombia, where the tropical climate, the location on the Caribbean Sea, and the pre-existence of criminal organizations dedicated to smuggling legal and illegal products provided a natural haven for its production and trafficking. The marijuana boom in Colombia reached its highest point in 1975 when the country became the largest world producer of *cannabis sativa* (Pardo, 1996). In the 1980s a US "Congressional committee estimated that between 15 and 60 thousand tons of marijuana were exported from that country to the United States each year" (President's

Commission on Organized Crime 1986,p. 137). The American war on drugs now turned its eye to the Colombian territory, providing aid to the local authorities to launch interdictions and to reduce the production of marijuana through aerial spraying (Pardo, 1996). As a result of these policies, the Colombian share of the marijuana market in the United States started to decline sharply in the mid-1980s to the point that by the of end the 1990s this country supplied only about 40 percent of the *cannabis sativa* consumed in the US (Bagley, 2001; President's Commission on Organized Crime, 1986). Today, the American marijuana market is primarily supplied by domestic and Mexican producers.

Nonetheless, the money, know-how, transportation routes, and contacts in the US (primarily in South Florida and the East Coast) developed during the marijuana boom allowed traffickers to get involved in the more profitable cocaine business, as demand for the stimulant increased in the United States. Colombia's involvement in the world cocaine trade started in the late 1970s when individual drug entrepreneurs imported the coca base from Peru and Bolivia, processed it into cocaine in Colombia, and exported it to the United States. According to Pardo (1996), the complexities involved in the processing and trafficking of cocaine required that drug traffickers became more organized in the 1980s. Indeed, the centralization and monopolization of the business was achieved by eliminating or subsuming independent distributors into the new powerful organizations managed primarily from Medellín and Cali, thus giving rise to the so-called drug cartels. By the mid-1980s Colombia had become the largest cocaine processing country in the world, supplying 90 percent of the cocaine consumed in the United States. In fact, conservative estimates calculate that, at the height of their operations, the Medellín and Cali cartels produced between $2 and $5 billion USD in annual revenues (Thoumi, 1995).

The downfall of the big drug cartels started in the late 1980s after the Colombian government began using more aggressive legal practices against drug lords. The main strategy involved the extradition treaty with the United States put to full use in the mid-1980s in response to the dramatic increase in drug-related violence and the assassinations of several political and social leaders by the Medellín cartel. The first drug traffickers were delivered to the American justice in 1985. In reaction, a clandestine organization calling themselves *Los Extraditables*, composed of drug traffickers led by the Medellín cartel, appeared in late 1986 publicly demanding the elimination of this legal tool or else. The ensuing wave of violence and terrorism turned into a national security issue, which led the Colombian and US governments to strengthen efforts to pursue the drug cartels. The subsequent deaths of Medellín cartel drug lords Gonzalo Rodriguez Gacha (1989) and Pablo Escobar (1993), both gunned down by the police, a wave of arrests and extraditions of mid- and high-level members of the organization, and the taking over of business by the Cali cartel brought about the demise of the Medellín cartel.

In turn, the Cali cartel established a less violent and more efficient control over the business, using corruption as their most important weapon. The Cali group was able to infiltrate all levels of government, so much so that the 1994 presidential elections were tainted by the discovery that members of the cartel had contributed a large amount of money to the campaign of Ernesto Samper, the winning candidate. This scandal, known as the *8000 Process* for its docket number, generated a crisis of legitimacy for the Colombian government, and although Samper was never impeached, some of his close collaborators landed in prison. At the same time, the United States government, while refusing to cooperate with a corrupt government, still needed to find a trustworthy partner to continue with the war against the Cali cartel. This condition was met by the then Director of the National Police, Rosso José Serrano, who became the United States' best ally in the war on drugs in Colombia. Through this collaboration it was possible to capture and imprison the Rodriguez Orejuela brothers, founders of the Cali cartel, in 1995. In Serrano's words:

> The Colombian National Police dismantled the Cali cartel through the development of a new style of intelligence, the assiduous use of informants, the employment of modern technology, and zero tolerance of corruption within the [police] force . . . US assistance also contributed to the success of [the] overall operation
>
> *(Serrano, 2003, p. 43).*

However, this did not end with the illegal drugs industry in Colombia. On the contrary, the vacuum left by the big cartels was quickly filled by smaller, lower profile criminal organizations (many of which involved former members of the Medellín and Cali cartels) on the one hand, and by guerrilla and paramilitary groups on the other. In fact, drug crimes known to the police experienced considerable growth in the 2000s (see Figure 25.1).

Furthermore, successful government policies in Peru and Bolivia, aimed at eradicating coca leaf crops using aerial spraying and at disrupting the traffic of coca base to Colombia using an effective air interdiction strategy by the local and American military, displaced coca cultivation to the remote southern areas of the Colombian Amazon basin. According to Pardo (2004), coca crops in Colombia increased from just about 20,000 hectares in 1994 to over 100,000 in 1996. By 1998 Colombia had surpassed the combined extension of land dedicated to coca cultivation in Peru and Bolivia (see Figure 25.2).

Today, Colombia continues to receive support from the United States' government to fight the supply of drugs. In fact, through the Andean Counterdrug Initiative, the US provided upwards of $6 billion USD between 1999 and 2009 in technical (includes military and police training) and financial support to the war on drugs in Colombia (Kushner, 2009). The main strategies of the anti-drug policy continue to include the elimination of crops using aerial spraying and manual eradication; interdiction tactics aimed at both stopping the influx of chemicals used in the processing of cocaine and seizing the drugs before they reach the United States; and the arrest and extradition of drug traffickers wanted by the American government. Although the area cultivated with coca has decreased since 2001, the production of cocaine has remained practically unaffected for most of the decade (see Figure 25.3), and Colombia continues to be the largest cocaine supplier in the world.

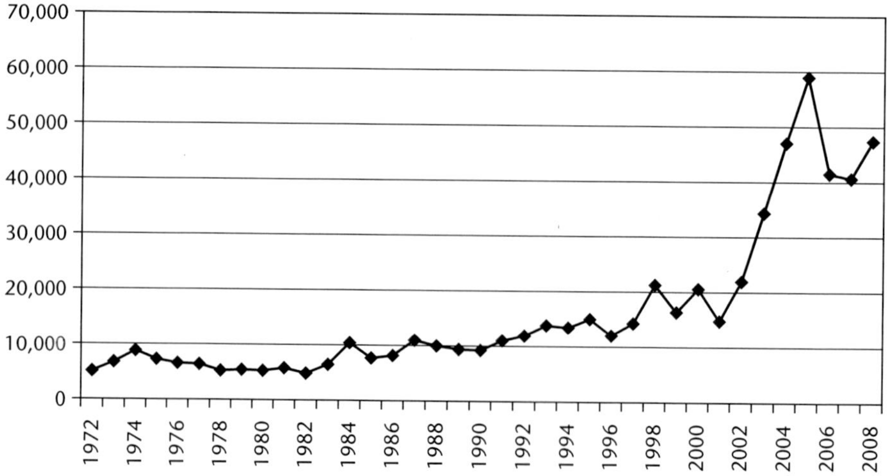

Figure 25.1 Drug crimes known to the police, 1972–2008

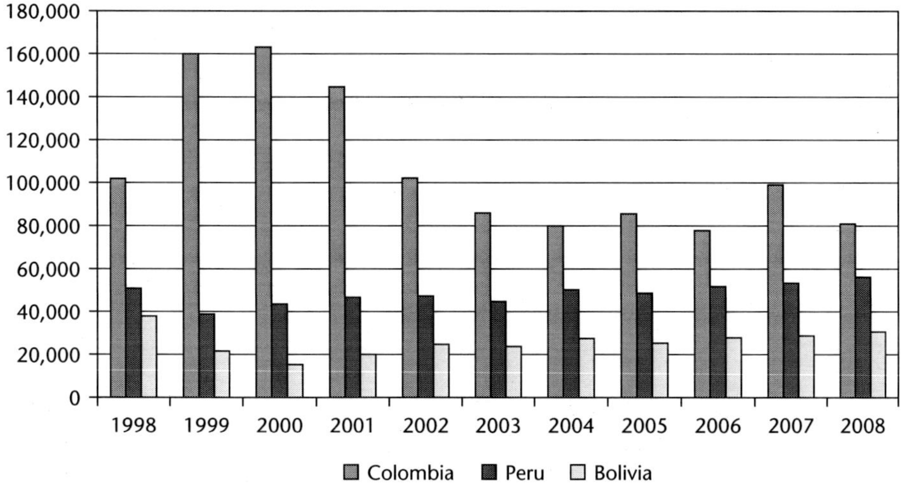

Figure 25.2 Coca cultivation (hectares) in Colombia, Peru, and Bolivia, 1998–2008

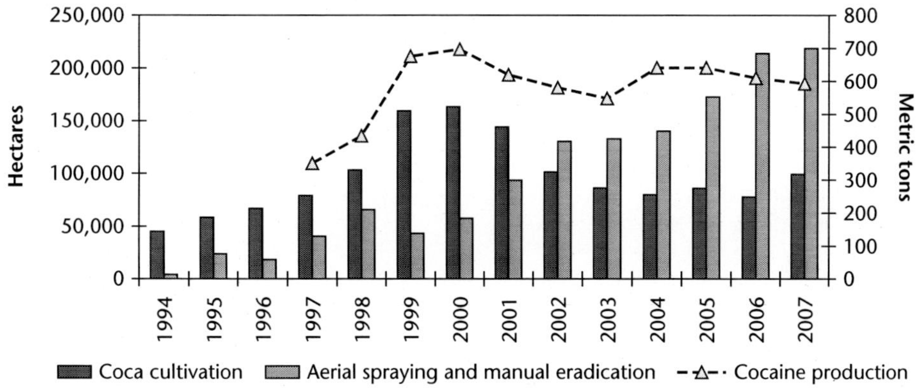

Figure 25.3 Coca cultivation (hectares), aerial spraying and manual eradication (hectares), and cocaine production (metric tons), 1994–2007

Violent crime and drug violence

During the last four decades, violent crimes have consistently represented a large proportion (about one third and sometimes more) of all crimes in Colombia (see Chapter 34 in this volume). The behavior of the homicide and assault rates is particularly interesting. During the 1970s both crime rates were moving upwards, and the assault rate was not only growing faster than the homicide rate, but it was also about six times greater in size (see Figure 25.4). This trend, although indicative of a gradual increase in violence, can be expected in societies with relatively low levels of violence. For instance, in the United States the assault rate is several times larger than the homicide rate, and both moved in the same direction (up between 1988 and 1991, and down since 1992) during the past two decades.

However, between 1985 and 1993 the homicide rate in Colombia experienced a steep increase, while the assault rate exhibited an uneven, but continuous decline, to the point that in

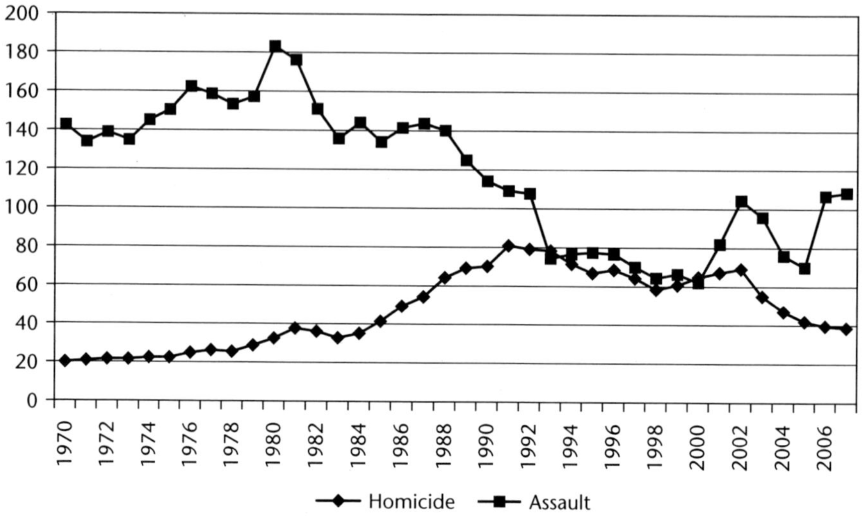

Figure 25.4 Evolution of the homicide and assault rates per 100,000 population in Colombia, 1970–2007

1993 the homicide rate was slightly greater (78) than the assault rate (75). These trends show that there was an increase in the lethality and intentionality of the violence in Colombia during the 1990s, reaching a point observed only in nations at war.

As noted above, the criminal organizations involved in the drug economy have relied heavily on the threat and use of violence as a means to regulate each stage of the process from cropping to processing to trafficking. This section will examine the links between the evolution of violent crime in Colombia and the illegal drug economy.

The marijuana mafias: violence and corruption in the North Coast region

During the marijuana boom smugglers used violence to ensure compliance with the rules of the business, to avoid infiltration by outsiders, to protect properties and bosses from threats made by their own partners as well as by their rivals, and to intimidate and avoid the authorities. Although the levels of violence and corruption increased in the North Coast region, the marijuana mafias did not engage in widespread violence against the government and social institutions. The violence tended to be framed more within a context of vendettas amongst the different players than as a real threat to national security (Pardo, 1996).

Still, homicide rates escalated in the region in the mid 1970s, surpassing the national rate practically until the marijuana boom ended in the mid 1980s (see Figure 25.5). Once the marijuana mafias were dismantled, those who did not make it into the cocaine trade were absorbed by the societies of the North Coast. This brought about a reduction in the levels of violence but, at the same time, led to the acceptance or normalization of mafiosi values by the middle class in that region, also having a long term effect on its levels of political corruption.

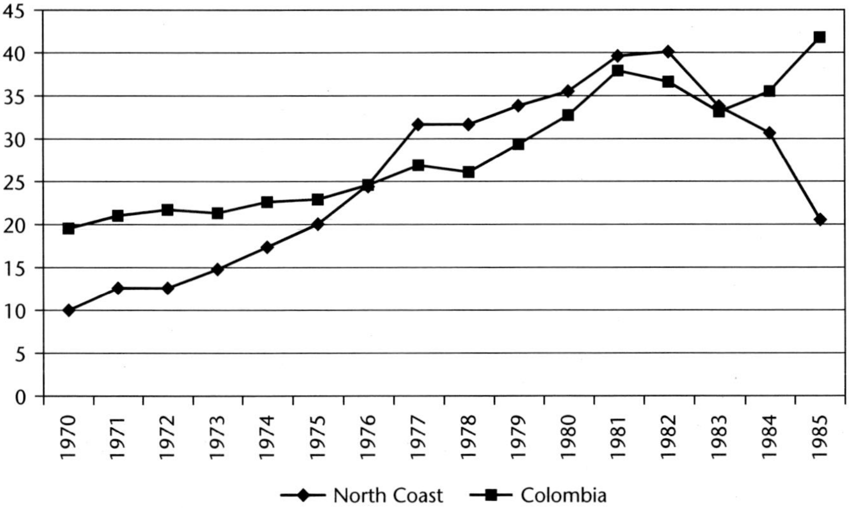

Figure 25.5 Evolution of homicide rates in the North Coast departments involved in marijuana trade, 1970–1985

The cocaine cartels: narcoterrorism and dirty war

According to Vargas Meza (1999), the cocaine cartels utilized two types of violence in Colombia. On the one hand, during the late 1980s and 1990s, the Medellín cartel declared war against the government in a desperate attempt to stop extradition to the US. During this period, the cartel ordered the assassination of politicians (including three candidates to the 1990 presidential elections), journalists, judges, prosecutors, and police officers who overtly opposed to the mafia counterculture and supported extradition. In addition, terrorism was used as a way to force the public to pressure politicians to make extradition unconstitutional. Some of the most egregious terrorist acts included the siege of the Supreme Court of Justice in November of 1985 by the guerrilla group M-19 at the behest of the Medellín cartel, aimed at destroying extradition documents, and which ended with the deaths of 55 people (including 11 magistrates) and the disappearance of 10 more; the detonation of several car bombs in Medellín and Bogotá between 1989 and 1993 killing hundreds and injuring over 1,000 civilians; and the explosion of Avianca flight 203 over Bogotá in 1989 killing all 107 people on board. This type of violence was aimed at gaining, by force, a social and political acceptance by the Colombian establishment.

On the other hand, the drug cartels waged a dirty war against small land owners in different zones of the country aimed at gaining control over territory not only to produce drugs but also for recreational purposes, making a symbolic show of social power and sending a strong message to the establishment that drug lords would get the privileges traditionally possessed by the oligarchy one way or another. In order to achieve this goal, drug cartels formed strategic alliances with large-scale land owners and some sectors of the military to form paramilitary groups with the intention of confronting the communist guerrillas. However, the paramilitary strategy included very little armed confrontation with the guerrillas and a heavy emphasis on terrorizing the population of areas allegedly controlled by guerrilla groups. According to estimates made using newspaper and human rights reports by the author of this chapter, between 1982 and 2005 there were 4,376 civilian victims and 511 cases of massacres conducted by paramilitary groups (see Figure 25.6). However, these figures underestimated those cases that were not known to

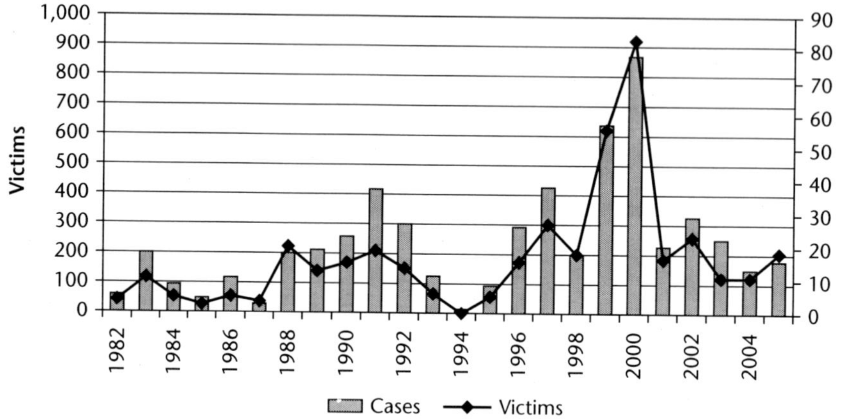

Figure 25.6 Victims and cases of massacres by paramilitaries, 1982–2005

the press or non-governmental organizations. In fact, the recent demobilization process of paramilitary groups required that high ranking and mid-level former paramilitary leaders revealed the location of mass graves so they could get judicial benefits. According to the National Reparation and Reconciliation Commission (Munoz, 2009), over 1,300 mass graves have been located and about 6,000 homicides have been solved through the ex-paramilitaries' statements to the justice.

In addition, the consolidation of the Medellín and Cali cartels was tied to an increase in the homicide rates in those two cities, which in fact exceeded the national rate for most of the 1990–2005 period (see Figure 25.7).

The extent of the violence produced by these criminal organizations was amplified by their recruiting and training of young men in the slums of Medellín and Cali, a phenomenon that has

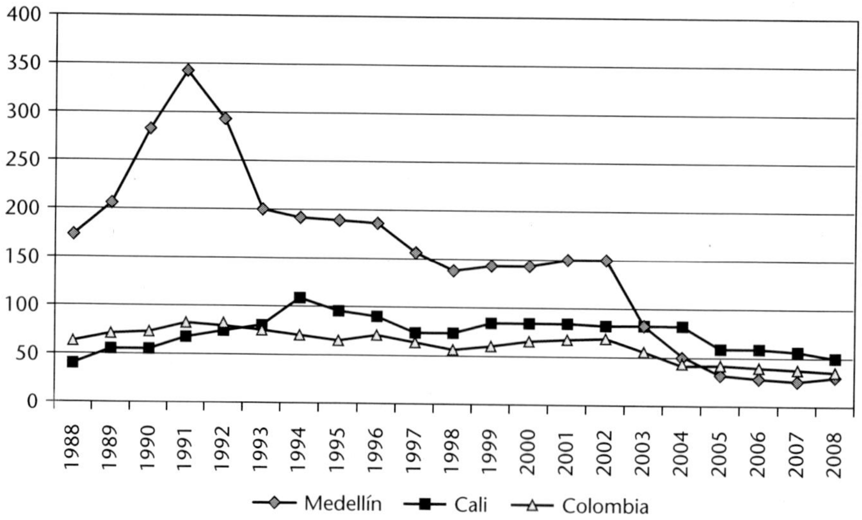

Figure 25.7 Comparison of the Medellín, Cali, and Colombia homicide rate per 100,000, 1988–2008

played a key role in the reproduction of violence in future years. For instance, the groundbreaking work of the journalist – and current mayor of Medellín – Alonso Salazar (1993), revealed important aspects of the culture and way of thinking of young people involved with gangs at the service of the Medellín cartel during the late 1980s. Through personal interviews with young *sicarios* (i.e. assassins by hire) used by the cartel to conduct their violent deeds, Salazar showed a daunting landscape in the slums of Medellín, where youth lived fast and died young in the pursuit of excitement and material success.

The FARC: armed conflict and illicit drugs

The displacement of coca crops to the south of the country in the mid-1990s allowed the Revolutionary Armed Forces of Colombia (FARC, for its acronym in Spanish), that traditionally had an important presence in this area of the country, to gain control over the cultivation and processing of cocaine in Colombia. A 2005 intelligence document estimated that the FARC controlled about 70 percent of coca crops in its area of influence, while the remaining 30 percent was cropped by small-scale peasants who agreed to operate within the business terms established by the FARC. In addition, the guerrilla group taxed the activities of third parties involved in the drug economy, including charging "security" taxes to independent croppers and processing labs, and steep fees for the use of their clandestine landing runways. In all, it is estimated that in 2003 the FARC derived about 46 percent of their income from the production of cocaine (Junta de Inteligencia Conjunta, 2005).

The resources obtained from the coca business allowed the FARC to grow both in terms of manpower (see Figure 25.8) and military strength, as they were now able to obtain more sophisticated armament. Between 1996 and 1998, the FARC engaged in much more aggressive military operations launching attacks against military bases and police stations in the southeast of the country. In addition, they increased their terrorist attacks against the electric, oil, and highway infrastructures, in an attempt to destabilize the government in Bogotá (see Figure 25.9).

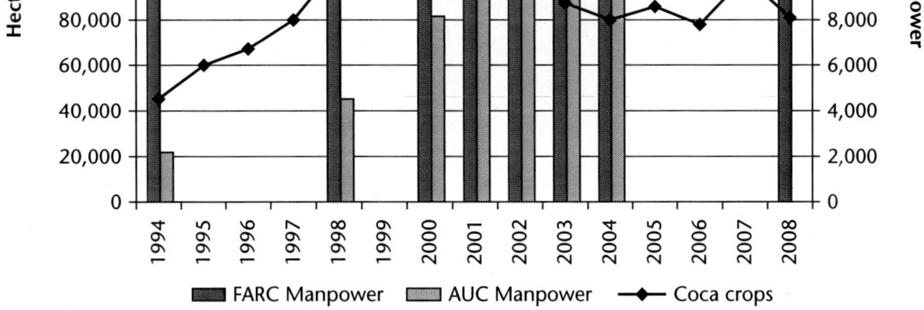

Figure 25.8 Evolution of the extension of coca crops (hectares), FARC and AUC manpower, 1994–2008

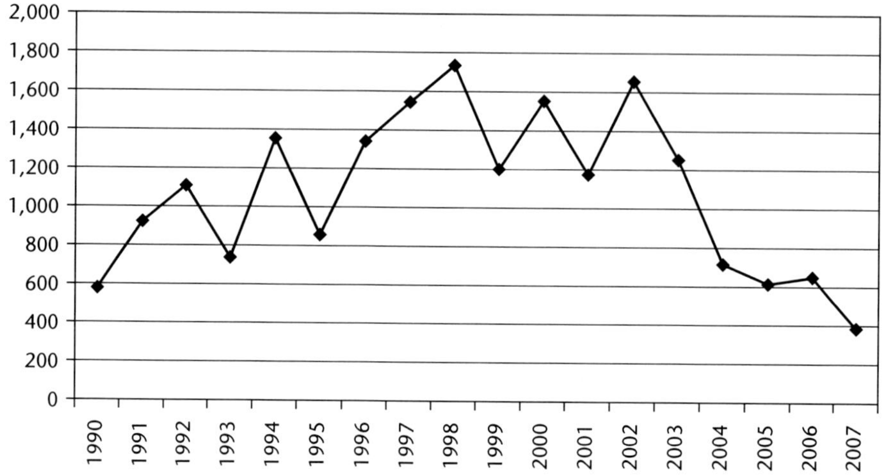

Figure 25.9 Terrorist acts in Colombia, 1990–2007

In 1998 the newly elected president, Andres Pastrana, proposed a peace negotiation to the FARC. The guerrilla group accepted under the condition that the government demilitarized the Caguan region[1] in the southeast of the country. However, during the three years (1999–2002) of bumpy negotiations, the FARC continued engaging in criminal activities – including kidnapping, extortion, cropping of coca leaf and production of cocaine – from the demilitarized zone, and kept on engaging in military operations against the government forces.

This period coincided with a spike in the homicide rate (see Figure 25.10). The United Self-Defense Groups of Colombia (AUC, for its acronym in Spanish) – an organization founded in 1997 to centralize the command of formerly dispersed paramilitary groups – are largely responsible for the resurgence in violence. In 1998, the AUC began expanding their operations to the coca cropping areas controlled by the FARC, escalating their violence against civilians in an attempt

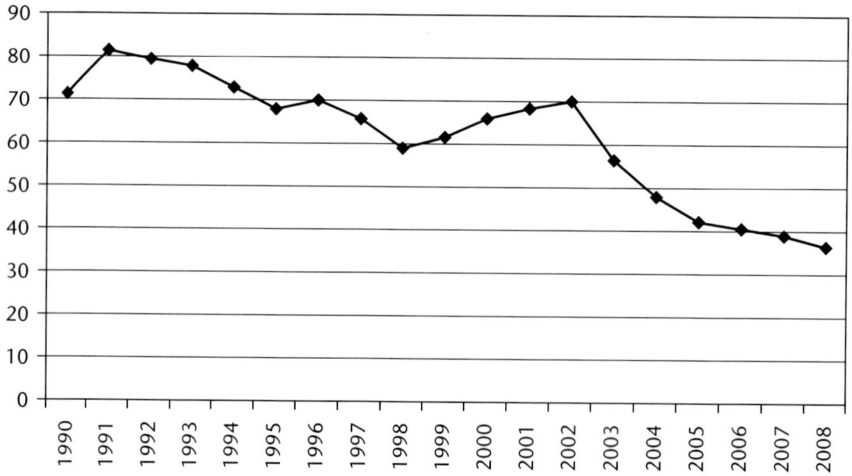

Figure 25.10 Colombia homicide rate, 1990–2008

to weaken the FARC's "social support" and gain control over the business (Pardo, 2004). In the process, they were able to contest the FARC's quasi-monopoly of the coca market, which also allowed them to grow in numbers and technology (see Figure 25.8).

Drug violence in the 2000s: Democratic Security and new criminal networks

The failed peace process between the Pastrana administration and the FARC radicalized Colombians who, frustrated with the escalation of kidnappings (see Figure 25.11) and other criminal activities committed by this group while engaged in negotiations with the government, wanted a more hard-handed approach to the internal armed conflict. This radicalization was evident in the 2002 presidential elections when right-wing candidate Alvaro Uribe obtained a sweeping victory (53 percent of votes) on a tough-on-crime, tough-on-the-FARC platform.

The core of Uribe's government was the Democratic Security program whose main objectives included: (1) consolidation of state presence across all of the national territory; (2) protection of the population against terrorist organizations and reincorporation into civilian life of those who deposed their arms; (3) elimination of the illicit drugs trade; (4) strengthening of border protection; and (5) improving government efficiency, transparency, and accountability (Presidencia de la Republica, 2003).

During the Uribe administration the combined military and police budgets went from representing 2.9 percent of the GDP in 2002 to 3.2 percent in 2008. In addition, the manpower of both institutions grew 40 and 46 percent respectively during the same period (see Figure 25.12).

Uribe's commitment to increasing investment in the recovery of public order was accompanied by a reincorporation policy aimed at encouraging members of illegal armed groups to depose their arms and return to civility. The most publicized component of this policy was the negotiation of the demobilization of the AUC in exchange for limited financial aid and judicial benefits to those paramilitaries who disclosed to the authorities information on crimes – including crimes against humanity and drug trafficking – committed by their organization. Between 2003

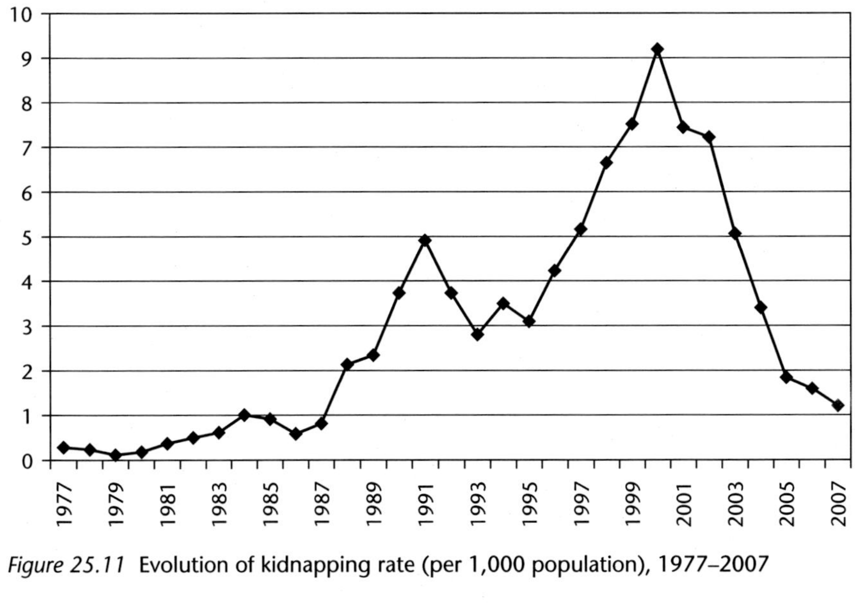

Figure 25.11 Evolution of kidnapping rate (per 1,000 population), 1977–2007

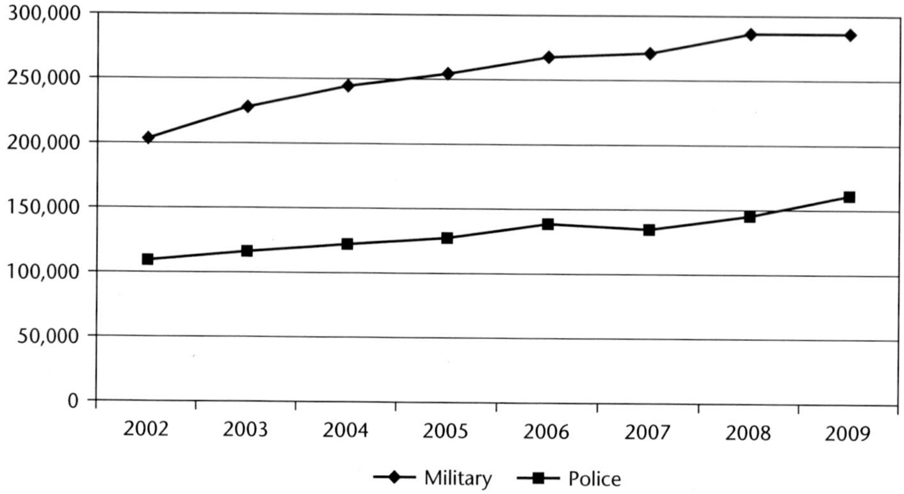

Figure 25.12 Growth of military and police manpower during Uribe's administration, 2002–9

and 2006 – amidst reports that the AUC were paying young men to pass themselves as members of their organization so real long-term combatants could remain at war – 35,281 alleged AUC members were demobilized. In addition, in response to the military pressure applied by the government, thousands of FARC combatants took advantage of the demobilization policy as well. In all, between 2002 and 2009, 51,992 combatants belonging to the AUC (68 percent), the FARC (27 percent), and other groups (5 percent) have been reincorporated to civil life.

In addition, between August 2002 and February 2010, as part of the anti-narcotics strategy, the Uribe government extradited 873 individuals (some of whom were former paramilitaries) on drug trafficking charges and 95 on money laundering charges to the United States.

Although the Democratic Security policy has significantly reduced terrorist acts (see Figure 25.9), homicides (see Figure 25.10), kidnappings (see Figure 25.11), the forced displacement of civilians (see Figure 25.13), and commercial cargo theft in the highway system[2] (see Figure 25.14), the policy has been criticized for being just a bandaid and not a long term solution to drug violence in Colombia. Indeed, Wills (2009) argues that the demobilization of the AUC and the extradition to the US of those paramilitary leaders accused of trafficking narcotics provoked a reconfiguration of criminal networks in Colombia through which mid-level and high-ranking paramilitaries who did not demobilize took advantage of the weakening of the FARC and sought to gain control over areas key to the trafficking of drugs and weapons. In this process, these new warlords eliminated the competition and ensured control of strategic areas by taking over marginal communities, particularly where victims of forced displacement reside, recruiting unemployed young men, and assassinating the opposition (e.g. left-wing community leaders, and members of victims and human rights organizations).

In addition, the National Reparation and Reconciliation Commission (Munoz, 2009) reported that about 8 percent of paramilitaries who demobilized during the Uribe administration have reorganized in 22 criminal groups dedicated to drug trafficking. According to the director of the Commission, the problem was caused by the meager financial benefits offered by the government which could not compete with the profits produced by the trafficking of narcotics.

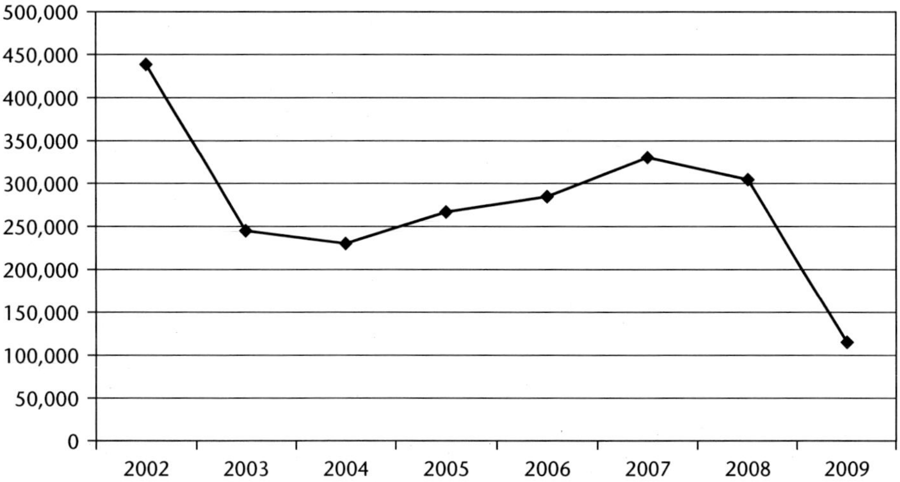

Figure 25.13 Individuals forcibly displaced by armed groups, 2002–9

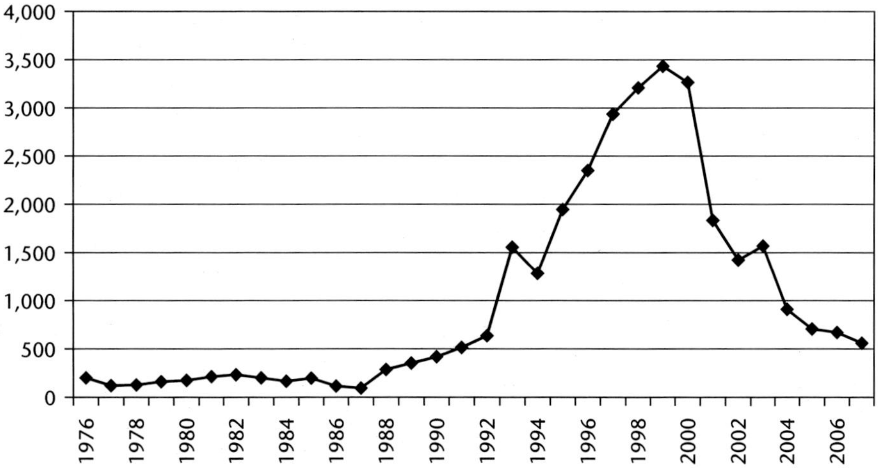

Figure 25.14 Evolution of commercial cargo theft on the roads of Colombia, 1977–2007

Conclusion

In short, violent crime in Colombia is greatly influenced by the illicit drug trade and the intertwining armed conflict. Aside from the loss of human lives, drug violence debilitates the sovereignty of the Colombian state, encourages the reproduction of mafiosi values at different societal levels, and increases political corruption and social intolerance. Different governments, always with the support of the United States, have attempted a number of strategies to tackle drug violence without complete success. The very flexible and adaptable nature of the "business" makes it difficult for the authorities to catch up with those involved in drug crimes. Recent policies have been effective at reducing violence in the short term; however, a long-term solution requires more investment in social justice, particularly in rural areas where peasants cannot find gainful activities other than getting involved in the drug economy, either as croppers, processors, transporters, or combatants of drug-fueled criminal organizations.

Future research questions

1. How do the new criminal networks that emerged after the demobilization of the AUC operate and what is their effect on current violent crime?
2. What is the future of violence in Colombia after the demobilization of the AUC and the military weakening of the FARC?
3. Given the ineffectiveness of the war on drugs in Colombia, what can be done to reduce drug-related violence and terrorism?
4. Given the influence of criminal organizations on the youth residing in urban slums, what can be done to prevent crime and violence in these communities?
5. Is the short-term success of Uribe's Democratic Security policy sustainable?

Notes

1 This region is about the size of Switzerland.

2 One of the main purposes of the Democratic Security program was to increase security throughout the highway system, aimed at reducing illegal roadblocks by the guerrillas, which had become commonplace since the 1990s. These roadblocks were used to extort money and take kidnapping victims amongst passengers and drivers. Increased security in the highway system has also been able to reduce commercial cargo theft in the roads of Colombia.

References

Bagley, B. M. (2001). Narcotráfico, violencia política y política exterior de Estados Unidos hacia Colombia en los Noventa. *Revista Colombia Internacional*, 49/50: 5–38.

Junta de Inteligencia Conjunta (2005). *Estimación de los ingresos y egresos de las FARC durante 2003 basados en información de inteligencia recolectada por las agencias del Estado*. Online at http://www.semana.com/documents/Doc-1760_2008926.pdf (accessed November 23, 2010).

Kushner, A. B. (2009). The truth about Plan Colombia. *Newsweek*, January 12. Online at http://www.newsweek.com/id/ 177681

Llorente, M. V. (2003). *Desmilitarización en tiempos de guerra? La reforma policial en Colombia*. Paper presented in the Panel Police Reform in the Americas. Center for Hemispheric Defense Studies, Santiago de Chile, October 27–30.

Munoz, F. (2009). 2500 paramilitares desmovilizados han regresado a las armas en Colombia. In *Noticias24*, April 27. Online at http://www.noticias24.com/actualidad/noticia/41530/2500-paramilitares-desmovilizados-han-regresado-a-las-armas-en-colombia/ (accessed November 23, 2010).

Pardo, R. (1996). *De primera mano. Colombia 1986–1994: entre conflictos y esperanzas*. Bogotá: CEREC, Grupo Editorial Norma.

—— (2004). *La historia de las guerras*. Bogotá: Ediciones B Colombia S.A.

Presidencia de la Republica (2003). *Política de defensa y seguridad democrática*. Online at http://www.presidencia.gov.co/seguridad_democratica.pdf (accessed November 23, 2010).

President's Commission on Organized Crime (1986). *America's habit: drug use, drug trafficking, and organized crime*. Washington, DC: US Government Printing Office.

Salazar, A. (1993). *No Nacimos Pa' Semilla*. Bogotá: CINEP.

Serrano, R. J. (2003). Capturing the Cali cartel: selections from Jacque Mate. *Crime, Law & Social Change*, 40: 43–59.

Thoumi, F. (1995). *Political Economy and Illegal Drugs in Colombia*. Boulder, CO: Lynne Rienner Publishers, Inc.

United Nations Office on Drugs and Crime (UNODC) (2009a). *Colombia. Coca cultivation survey*. Online at http://www.unodc.org/documents/crop-monitoring/Colombia_coca_survey_2008.pdf (accessed November 23, 2010).

—— (2009b). *Peru. Monitoreo de cultivos de coca.* Online at http://www.unodc.org/documents/crop-monitoring/Peru_monitoreo_cultivos_coca_2008.pdf (accessed November 23, 2010).

—— (2009c). *Plurinational State of Bolivia. Coca cultivation survey.* Online at http://www.unodc.org/documents/crop-monitoring/Bolivia/Bolivia_Coca_Survey_for2008_En.pdf.pdf (accessed November 23, 2010).

Vargas Meza, R. (1999). *Drogas, máscaras y juegos: narcotráfico y conflicto armado en Colombia.* Bogotá: Tercer Mundo Editores.

Wills, M. E. (2009). ¿Seguridad Democrática Selectiva? *El Espectador*, December 28. Online at http://www.elespectador.com/impreso/articuloimpreso179511-seguridad-democratica-selectiva (accessed November 23, 2010).

26

The basics of terrorism and counterterrorism

Mustafa Cosar Unal

As a corrosive form of political violence, terrorism has been prevalent in many regions of the world and has captured the world's attention intermittently since the late nineteenth century. Recently, terrorism became more prominent with the September 11, 2001 attacks in the US and the bombings of the Madrid train station in 2004 and London transit in 2005.

Such massive terrorist attacks reminded us that terrorism poses a major threat to nations around the world. In addition to the damaging effects to the interrelated structures of social (e.g. intimidation), political (e.g. destabilization), and economic (e.g. recession and instability) contexts of a country at the state level, it establishes a sphere of anxiety, causes fear, and invokes defiance in the social context at the individual and society levels (Crenshaw, 1995; Netanyahu, 1995). No country is immune from terrorism because the contemporary form of terrorism is considered to be an effective tool to swing social and political structures to reach a specific political end (Crenshaw, 1995). The effectiveness is embedded in the discrepancy between the input and output; that is, a high impact with few resources has made terrorism far more attractive compared with other means of political activism (Crenshaw, 1995).

Definition of terrorism

Terrorism is one of the most controversial terms to be defined (Ramraj *et al.*, 2005) because it is subjective rather than objective (Crenshaw, 1995). The grounds for defining terrorism are ideological rather than intellectual or analytical, based on the lack of common understanding and perception of ethics, history, and politics (Ramraj *et al.*, 2005). In addition to the perception and subjectivity-driven differences, there have been varying perspectives from different disciplines. Legal approaches for defining terrorism focus on the criminal aspect, while political science emphasizes governmental concerns (i.e. military and political response). A psychological definition of terrorism, on the other hand, stresses the motivation and impact from the individual and the group perspectives (Donohue, 2000).

The main purpose of terror actions is to draw public attention to a specific issue to gain support and to create fear, intimidation, and anxiety in the public sphere. Terrorism in general shares two characteristics: 1) it involves premeditated violence (Sandler and Enders, 2007), and 2) such violence is mostly targeted at noncombatants (Lal, 1999), for their symbolic values rather than directly or indirectly targeting the political cause or social grievance (Crenshaw, 1995). However, without deontological considerations, these characteristics can be applied to many violent actions against a government so that the ruling regimes can gain legitimacy over whatever violent and suppressive measure it may take, against the oppositional movement. This is why a uniform definition of terrorism has not yet been reached.

From a deontological perspective, legitimacy is the main element to be considered in defining terrorism. For example, political violence organized by an opposition group to resist or overthrow a state's illegitimate suppression of a specific social group can be considered a legitimate social reaction and a way of communication (the voice of unheard and politically suppressed) – not terrorism. In many cases, labeling political violence as terrorism represents a deliberate effort by the government to ostracize or stigmatize certain activities or groups to make the group appear illegitimate and, in turn, the potential national and international support toward the oppositional group would be decreased.

Terrorism is not the only type of political violence (e.g. ethnic, revolutionary insurgencies). Also, there are different levels of political violence; that is, an individual can commit a violent crime with a political motive (e.g. anti-abortion protests). A group can use violence either toward the government forces or symbolic targets including noncombatants. Yet, a state can foster and/or sponsor a group to use violence in a third country for a political end. The nature of the violence (i.e. form, purpose, and the way of production), on the other hand, can be grouped in such categories as civil wars, ethnic conflicts, and genocide.

The conception of terrorism and counterterrorism

The conception of counterterrorism is strongly related to the perception of terrorism and in particular to the perception of the cause of terrorism (Omelicheva, 2007). The "cause" of terrorism is conceptualized differently by various people. Some (Shultz, 1979; Netanyahu, 1989; Will, 1989) tend to believe that the cause of terrorism is a sole political one, wherein terrorism is used as a tool to reach specific political objectives and therefore hard-line containment strategies and repressive counterterrorism measures are suggested. Others (Cluskey, 1989; Wilkinson, 1999; Frey, 2004) point to social and economic dynamics, wherein disparities and grievances create a fertile breeding ground for violent discontent. The latter approach suggests soft-line and reformative counterterrorism measures that are more accommodative in nature.

"What causes terrorism" does not have a normative and an analytically useful answer, because terrorism is a multi-faceted phenomenon. Social, economic, and psychological factors exert various influences over individuals who engage in terrorism. The cause and consequence of terrorism can only be conceptualized as an interaction between the ruling regime and the opposing political movement (Landes, 1978; Sandler and Enders, 2004). It is therefore difficult to conceptualize a theory about certain conditions that lead to terrorism (Crenshaw, 1995).

Generic characteristics of terrorism and counterterrorism literature

Literature on terrorism has been growing rapidly, which has also led to concomitant increase in interests on counterterrorism (Mentan, 2004; Sandler, 2005). Of particular reason, the recognition of the nexus between terrorism and counterterrorism has made the counterterrorism studies vastly important (Omelicheva, 2007).

There are several approaches to the study of terrorism and counterterrorism. Each approach draws perspectives and concepts from different disciplines such as economics, political science, history, political economy, sociology, and psychology. Although some studies are heavily quantitative, the bulk of the counterterrorism literature has been qualitative, predominantly descriptive and exploratory in the form of case studies. Each perspective has its own weaknesses and strengths.

Some scholars have applied economic analyses techniques (e.g. Landes, 1978; Hewitt, 1984; Enders and Sandler, 1993; Arce and Sandler, 2005; Sandler and Enders, 2007) and claim that economic concepts are well suited for analyzing terrorism and provide analytical findings on structural interactions between terrorist groups and targeted governments (Landes, 1978; Sandler and Enders, 2004). Other scholars (e.g. Crenshaw, 1995) argue that an economic-only approach may result in misleading findings because it neglects the underpinnings of the social and political context that are specific to each case of terrorism. Many scholars have conducted qualitative research mostly using case studies (e.g. Wilkinson, 1977; Levitt 1988; Crenshaw 1995; Netanyahu 1995; Alexander, 2002; Mead, 2004).

Definition and typology of counterterrorism policies

Counterterrorism can be broadly defined as all of the domestic and foreign government policies and actions devised to curb terrorism to protect the public and to restore and uphold some social order (Omelicheva, 2007). According to Smith (1990, p. 31), anti-terrorism policy is "fundamentally an aim, intention or expectation, which may be expressed in a variety of ways and means." Mentan (2004) defined counterterrorism measures as identifiable government interventions undertaken in response to terrorist activities.

Countermeasures of terrorism span across numerous policy areas and may involve almost every governmental agency (e.g. commercial aviation control unit, education, institutions responsible for social and economic development) beside security forces, intelligence functions, and law enforcement agencies. Therefore, counterterrorism encompasses a wide variety of direct and indirect governmental interventions ranging from tactical changes in law enforcement activities to social reforms (Hewitt, 1984; Omelicheva, 2007). Hence, not surprisingly, terrorism and counterterrorism shares the inseparable nexus in complexity. This complexity around the conceptualization of counterterrorism has been based heavily on the wide range of state responses. Because of the wide spectrum, counterterrorism policies reflect multiple aspects in their nature, aim, scope, targeted population, and directness, which constitute a foundation for policies' theoretical frameworks and their expected impact. Hewitt (1984) recognized the varying implications of different counterterrorism policies originating from the differences in these aspects. He based his impact analysis of different countermeasures on whether the counterterrorism policy was directed at the terrorists (e.g. use of security forces) or against their supporters (e.g. social reforms).

States' responses to terrorism are therefore classified as soft-line and hard-line measures. The category of "soft-line" policies involves social reforms, use of intelligence, diplomacy, and negotiation. The category of "hard-line" policies embraces repressive means of legal and criminal sanctions, use of military force, and economic sanctions (Omelicheva, 2007). Hewitt (1984) classified counterterrorism policies based upon their scope and breadth as "macro" and "micro," where the former refers to policies with wide application to or of a general dimension, such as making reforms, proclamation of emergency law, and repressive policies of security force use, and the latter stands for narrow involvements of government strategies on a tactical level, such as hostage negotiations and surveillance techniques.

There are other ways to classify counterterrorism measures. Crenshaw (1999) grouped countermeasures into four strategies reflecting different concepts from a governmental perspective: deterrence (i.e. use of government coercive power), criminal justice (i.e. use of civilian law), enhanced defense (i.e. target hardening), and negotiation policies. However, Arce and Sandler (2005), and Netanyahu (1995) grouped countermeasures as either passive (defensive) or active (proactive). Counterterrorism strategies are also classified as "criminal justice" and "warfare," where the former has police responsible under the civilian rule of law while the latter relies on military forces (Omelicheva, 2007).

Principal theories and related research

There are major theoretical models upon which most of the research on counterterrorism has been developed and government polices formulated, such as deterrence, defiance, and desistance models.

Deterrence

The theoretical premise of the deterrence notion is founded on rational choice theory, which assumes that individuals act in their own self-interest (Moran, 1996; Frey, 2004). Individuals are dissuaded from engaging in a criminal activity when the cost of committing that particular crime is raised. When applied to terrorism (e.g. Landes, 1978; Sandler et al., 1983), individuals conduct rational cost–benefit analysis and choose between terrorist and non-terrorist activities based on their expected benefits. Appropriate policies can exert a deterrent effect on terrorist activities by imposing constraint on the expected utility of engaging in terrorist activities (Landes, 1978; Frey and Luechinger, 2002). In other words, when the cost of a terrorist act exceeds the benefits, individuals are more likely to be dissuaded from the act. In this context, the commodity produced by the terrorist attack is the establishment of fear, chaos, and anxiety aimed at forcing a government to concede to a political demand.

Raising the cost of terrorist activity has several aspects. These include raising the certainty and severity of the punishment, increasing logistical complexity for terrorist attacks by tightening security around potential targets, and increasing the threat of injury and death by conducting military operations (Enders and Sandler, 1999; Kenney, 2003).

Counterterrorism policies that are based on the rational choice perspective must focus on either raising the cost or reducing the benefit of any terrorist act (Enders and Sandler, 1993). However, most governments, confronted with a terrorism problem, have exclusively relied on raising the cost (e.g. rewarding the benefit of non-terrorist activity/raising the opportunity cost) rather than reducing the benefit of terrorist activities (Frey and Luechinger, 2002). This is because of the uncertainty and unpredictability of benefits of terrorism as well as the complexity of reducing the terrorists' perceived benefit from terrorism (Kenney, 2003; Mendes, 2004).

Counterterrorism policies can be categorized as defensive, preemptive, and proactive. Some researchers view deterrence as more of a defensive measure, intelligence as a preemptive measure, and the use of military force as a proactive policy (for example, see Arce and Sandler, 2005; Sandler, 2005). However, proactive measures (e.g. military operations), preemptive measures (e.g. intelligence gatherings), and defensive measures (e.g. target hardening and increasing criminal sanctions) all increase costs for terrorists. Therefore, all three categories are considered part of the deterrence perspective.

The main difference between the defensive and proactive policies is the directness of the measures to curb the terrorist incidents. In defensive measures, governments erect greater barriers and obstacles to reduce the risk exposure of potential targets. In proactive measures, government forces, either military or police, go directly at terrorists as opposed to merely tightening the security measures (Netanyahu 1995). Proactive measures reduce the level of terrorist resources and assets and their ability to conduct future attacks (Enders and Sandler, 1993; Kutan and Drakos, 2003).

The use of intelligence is considered a preemptive and preventive measure in countering terrorists' attacks and activities. Intelligence gathering on terrorism activities is one of the essential tools and strategies for most countries facing terrorist threats (Hewitt, 1984; Netanyahu, 1989; Vigna, 1989). In a narrow sense, intelligence is used to anticipate and to figure out the operational and structural dynamics (e.g. decision-making processes) of a terrorist group so the government can take the necessary action to prevent terrorist attacks (Crenshaw, 1999; Faria, 2006). In a broader sense, intelligence is used to understand the grievance of the terrorist organization and how the terrorist group is interpreting and labeling that grievance so the government can adjust or reform its social policies (Crenshaw, 1999; Faria, 2006).

Deterrence-based governmental policies

Many counterterrorism policies fall under the deterrence category. These include declaring emergency rule, establishing collective punishment, enlisting international cooperation, putting pressure on terrorism supporting countries, disintegrating the terrorist group, eliminating the leadership cadre, and incapacitating terrorists.

Granting excessive power through the proclamation of a state of emergency and passing anti-terrorism laws are commonly used in counterterrorism efforts by countries facing terrorist activities. Particularly in ethno-terrorism, and in some cases in religion-abusing terrorism, where a sizeable population supports a core terrorist group and where certain ethnic population predominantly lives in a specific geographical region, emergency powers and collective punishment are used to deter terrorist activities (Hewitt, 1984).

There are differences in the policies of emergency laws versus collective punishment. In collective punishment, the civilian population living in certain area is held responsible for the terrorist activity and subjected to certain sanctions. These sanctions may include levying fines, closing some businesses in the area, seizing property, and closing and evacuating one or more houses (Hewitt, 1984). The state of emergency, however, typically suspends certain fundamental human rights and the supremacy of civilian rule in certain areas in the name of public or state safety and security. Security forces under emergency powers can arrest and question people without charge, impose curfews, and conduct house searches (Ramraj, 2006). Special courts are created to deal with terrorism cases without following the ordinary procedures of the civilian law, which include pre-trial detentions, admission into courts of evidence gathered from secret interrogations, and violations of due process on the grounds of public safety. In most cases emergency laws are supplemented with extended anti-terrorism legislation to impose extra penalties (i.e. increased cost of engaging in terrorist activity) on people convicted of terrorism. In addition, some of the political rights, such as freedom of speech or right of assembly, are curtailed and censorship over the media and press are used by the states (Wilkinson, 1977; Hewitt, 1984).

Collective punishments and emergency powers have been found to have unintended negative consequences over the civilian population in the form of "minority alienation" (Ramraj, 2006). In ethnic-based terrorism, the public sentiment is often shared among societies of the same ethnicity (Crenshaw, 1995; Crenshaw, 1999; Ramraj, 2006). Negative effects include defiance against the government and increased sympathy and support for the terrorist group. Such sentiments in most cases beget further violence (Byman, 1998; Braithwaite, 2002).

Deterrence-based policies include international policies, as well as domestic policies to counter terrorism. Terrorism cannot be curbed solely by domestic policies (Crenshaw, 1999, 1995; Vigna, 1989). Even if a terrorist organization carries out violent attacks in a concentrated geographical area, it may develop support structures and front activities within another country to finance and wage its terror campaign. These support structures can be logistical and financial such as fund-raising, arms procurement, and recruitment (Vigna, 1989; Netanyahu, 1995). Therefore, effective international cooperation can reduce logistical and financial support and eliminate safe havens for terrorist groups in the international arena (Crenshaw, 1999).

Another policy to thwart terrorist violence is to put pressure on states that are either sponsoring or sympathetic to terrorist organizations, thereby avoiding taking necessary steps against terrorist groups (Crenshaw, 1999). The logistics of terrorism (e.g. money and weapons) flow easily across the borders. Therefore, putting pressure on these states to cease the support and to expel terrorist groups can help eliminate terrorist safe havens. This, in turn, can increase financial pressure and logistical difficulties for terrorist groups (Shultz, 1986). However in many cases, putting pressure on foreign countries is not easy because there is no consensus over the definition of terrorism in the international arena.

Most of the proactive approaches in counterterrorism effort aim to prevent and/or reduce future terrorist incidents. This has been the core notion behind the US anti-terrorism programs (Langdon et al., 2004). The most visible strategy focuses on incapacitating the terrorist leadership (Langdon *et al.*, 2004). In this regard, the US military launches missile strikes on suspected Al-Qaeda leaders in Yemen or Pakistan. However, Langdon *et al.* (2004) found that the incapacitating strategy may not be effective. Killing a terrorist group leader generally will not make a big impact on the path where the radicalized movement is already heading because replacement is easy with new recruits among sympathizers. Different counterterrorism policies that aim at incapacitating terrorists have different unintended consequences. Policies that are perceived illegitimate and unfair by society are likely to increase anti-government sentiment and result in more support for the terrorists (Crenshaw, 1999; Kim and Yun, 2008).

Research on deterrence-based policies

There have been many studies (e.g. Landes, 1978; Lichbach, 1987; Enders *et al.*, 1990; Enders and Sandler, 1999; Frey, 2004; Arce and Sandler, 2005) on deterrence-based counterterrorism measures. The results are mixed. While some studies found support for deterrence (e.g. Landes, 1978; Prunckun and Mohr, 1997), others suspected that deterrence might be counterproductive (Turk, 2002; Frey, 2004; Schnellenbach, 2006).

Enders and Sandler (1999) conducted a time-series analysis of transnational terrorist incidents and found that the decrease in transnational terrorist attacks after the Cold War was partly due to the countermeasures including deterrence policies (i.e. implementation of metal detectors, extra anti-terrorism legislations) taken by the industrialized states towards terrorism. Landes (1978) also conducted an economic analysis of aircraft hijackings in the US, irrespective of terrorist or non-terrorist related, and found that increased apprehension and conviction through tighter security checks and metal detectors had a deterrent effect on skyjackings.

Hewitt (1984) in his analysis of five terrorist cases in different countries (EOKA, Cyprus; IRA, Britain; ETA, Spain; Tupamaros, Uruguay; and Red Brigades, Italy) found no support for the use of military forces on the level of violent incidents. He further analyzed the collective effect of multiple counterterrorism policies and concluded that there was a positive correlation between the use of military force and terrorist attacks, meaning the greater the crackdown, the more attacks. On the other hand, some studies (Cauley and Im, 1988; Enders and Sandler, 1993) found that deterrence-based countermeasures had a substitution effect. If the countermeasures focus on one type of target, then terrorists will choose to attack less guarded targets with different tactics. Therefore, there will be no significant deterrent effect on the overall terror incidents.

In summary, studies on the effectiveness of deterrence policies showed contradictory findings. The mixed findings are partly due to the different analytical approaches. Most of the studies that support deterrence are based on the evaluation of a single mode of terrorist attack and a specific government intervention. The most popular example of this is the implementation of metal detectors and tighter security checks in airports and their effect on skyjacking. While the findings are robust in these studies, a macro analysis of overall terrorism revealed that such a deterrent effect on a single mode of attack does not necessarily mean a deterrent effect on the entirety of terrorist incidents. That is because when governments impose deterrence-based policies terrorists are apt to select other targets to continue their campaigns. As a result, deterrence-based policies are found to have a counterproductive impact in the long run.

Defiance theory and desistance model

The notion of defiance implies a different policy approach to countering terrorism. Defiance (a.k.a. legitimacy) theory focuses on how the audiences of terrorism perceive and respond to terrorists and terrorists actions. It suggests that government anti-terrorism policies are more effective if they are perceived as legitimate and procedurally fair by both the terrorists and the society (Sherman, 1993; Braithwaite, 2002).

Defiance theory takes its roots from the literature of psychology, particularly from the criminal psychology (Braithwaite, 2002). Many studies revealed that perceived justice is a great determinant of people's feelings and actions in social interactions. When people are satisfied and when they feel that they are treated fairly, justly, and legitimately, they are more willing to accept and also tend to abide by the rules (Tyler *et al.*, 1996; Tyler, 2000).

In the field of terrorism, the intended cost imposition by deterrence-based repressive policies, either defensive or proactive, might not be perceived by the target population in the same way as they are by the implementers (Crenshaw, 1995). Raising the severity and intensity of sanctions and increasing the threat of death or injury might create mythologies of martyrdom, strengthen group solidarity and loyalty, and invoke revenge, rage, and vengeance (Crenshaw, 1995; Wilkinson, 1996)

The desistance model focuses on cutting off or reducing the public support towards the core terrorist group from the sympathizers (i.e. supporting militia in ethnic-based terrorism) to diminish terrorist activity (Crenshaw, 1999; Kim and Yun, 2008). In this regard, public opinion is considered an important element in counterterrorism because terrorist groups strive to seek support for their ideologies (Crenshaw, 1999; Whittaker, 2003). Therefore, Crenshaw (1983, 1995, 1999) sees underscores public support and sentiment as the most crucial elements in anti-terrorism policies aiming to reduce terrorist violence, especially in the case of ethnic-based terrorism.

The emphasis of the desistance model is the psychological bond and [passive] support between the supporters and the terrorist group (Crenshaw, 1999). Psychological and physical/logistical supports are strongly interrelated with where mostly the former leads leading to the latter (Kim and Yun, 2008). In this regard, policies intended to cut off logistical support may include the evacuation of villages, establishment of volunteer guard villagers, and proclamation of emergency rules in the region. Policies intended to cut off the psychological support from the sympathizers may include social reforms to raise government legitimacy.

Repressive measures taken by the government (e.g. military strikes, martial law, state of emergency) can decrease the government's legitimacy and thus increase the psychological and logistical support for terrorists, especially in ethnic based terrorism (Byman, 1998). In this context, military force used to retaliate against terrorist attacks might yield unintended consequences and have a counterproductive effect (Wilkinson, 2001; Frey, 2004; Martin, 2006).

Shultz (1979) and Crenshaw (1995) argue that intense emotion and ideological motivation can alter terrorists' perceptions of cost or benefits. Benefits drawn from terrorist activities in terms of ideological satisfaction and self-actualization are intangible and all embedded in the terrorists' decision-making process. That is to say, a terrorist's response to an imposed cost might be irrational in order to reach his or her goals, which he or she is presumably highly committed to do; meaning that his or her willingness to bear the imposed cost might exceed the rationality line.

The desistance model can complement the defiance perspective. The desistance model underlines the importance of public support, while the defiance perspective focuses on the perception of government policies to that specific public (i.e. increasing government legitimacy will decrease the social support to terrorists).

Defiance and desistance-based governmental policies

Many government policies may fall into the anti-defiance (i.e. defiance and desistance) policy category. These include reforms (e.g. social, political, and economic), accommodative policies of repentance and amnesty law, truce and ceasefires, negotiation, and so forth. In ethnic terrorism and insurgency, terrorist organizations enjoy the logical and psychological support of their sympathizers (Byman, 1998).

The concept of reform is very broad. Any macro-level policy that is designed to remove certain grievances from the social, political, and economic areas can be considered reform policy in the context of counterterrorism. One of the anti-defiance government policies is offering repentance to the terrorists (Crenshaw, 1999).

Ceasefires are also fairly common in counterterrorism, resulting in a reduced level of violent incidents. However, Hewitt (1984) argued that discussions between governments and terrorist groups rarely resolve the conflict when terrorist demands threaten the sovereignty and regime of the state. In addition, terrorists in most cases would not settle with less than their original end goals. Because governments often cannot accept terrorists' full demands, ceasefires are difficult to sustain. In the meantime, ceasefires give terrorists the opportunity to rebuild their strength and even enhance their public image (Crenshaw, 1995). Hewitt (1984) and Crenshaw (1995) concluded that calling a truce with terrorists or declaring a ceasefire are short-sighted policies and do not lead to conflict resolution.

Negotiating is another option for the governments to end terrorist violence (Segaller, 1987). The decision for negotiating is and has been difficult for governments confronting terrorism, because of political competition related to reelection concerns. Even though the ruling government sincerely aims to reduce violent terror incidents, its opponents would label it as rewarding or giving in to terrorism to gain more votes in the next election (Crenshaw, 1995).

In the counterterrorism literature, negotiating with terrorist group is found to be helpful in reducing and/or stopping violence if the leadership of the terrorist group is totally convinced that they cannot go any further by terrorizing (Perez, 1989), and if the timing of negotiation is right (Crenshaw, 1995) (i.e. when the terrorist group is going through a self-evaluation process).

Research through the lens of defiance and desistance

Many studies found support for the defiance theory. Nevin (2003) analyzed seven different terrorist cases from several countries and found that intensity of terrorist attacks immediately after the retaliatory military strikes increased the intensity of retaliation in six of the seven selected cases. Yet, he concluded that Al-Qaeda attacks were not reduced before and after retaliatory military strikes carried out by the US in Afghanistan and Iraq. Turk (2002) also found that the use of force in the form of military strikes were always perceived as bullying and produced negative sentiments in the public against the government.

Turk (2002) drew our attention to the dilemma of the use of criminal law and military tribunals in handling terrorists and how they will be received by society, supporting population, and terrorist groups. If regular procedure and criminal law are pursued in terrorism, the accused terrorists may go free. If military tribunals are used to handle terrorist suspects, then it will be perceived as a departure from the "rule of law," hence unjust and illegitimate.

Wilkinson (1999, 2001) argued that the criminal justice system and law enforcement should be used to reduce terrorism rather than military force. The emphasis is using democratic processes to cure the underlying social reasoning for terrorist strikes. Fundamental human rights must be guaranteed regardless of the terrorist provocation. For example, in the case of ETA (i.e. Euskadi Ta Askatasuna, or Basque Fatherland and Liberty) terror in Spain, the government granted autonomy for the Basque regions, which dramatically reduced public support for terrorist activities. Reinares (2000) argued that the democratic avenues for legal expression are far more effective than authoritarian rule and deterrence-based policies. In conclusion, in either domestic or international terrorism, resorting to military force makes the situation extremely sensitive when the states are determined to thwart terrorism through a democratic process and rule of law (Crenshaw, 1995; Wilkinson, 2001; Nevin, 2003).

In summary, contrary to the main philosophy of deterrence policies (i.e. rational choice principle based on utility maximization), many scholars argue that terrorists are irrational rather than rational. Terrorism is not a simple rational decision; rather it is a reactance to the grievance buried in the social, economic, and political contexts. A government that reduces grievances among the politically disenfranchised will restrict the fertile ground for terrorism. Contrary to the anti-defiance policies, deterrence policies, in most cases, produce collateral damages on the civilians. They are not only ineffective but also counterproductive to the social psychological dynamics of the terrorists groups and their sympathizers. Anti-defiance (i.e. soft-line accommodative) policies are found to be more effective in curing terrorism because they increase government legitimacy in the eyes of the public and in turn are effective in reducing terrorism.

Philosophical approach to terrorism

As mentioned in the previous paragraphs, the concept of terrorism is highly embedded in the perception of the terrorism itself. Some believe that the sole rationale of terrorism is to reach a specific political end (Netanyahu, 1986, 1995; Mead, 2004). Others, on the other hand, tend to recognize that the cause of terrorism is more of a *consequence* caused by desperations, deprivations, and deficiencies in the social, economic, and political contexts (Braithwaite, 2002; Frey, 2004).

Those who view terrorism as solely a political act tend to adopt a "get tough" approach and seek to incapacitate terrorists and their leaders by retaliatory strikes through force. Their target population in counterterrorism, in most cases, is the terrorists and their close supporters. They tend to focus on a normative definition of terrorism, such as a political (ideological) goal, and premeditated use of violence against non-combatant individuals. This view neither considers the social and economic dynamics behind the opposition, nor questions the moral dimensions of the social upheaval. Terrorism is viewed as an act of war and terrorists must be punished. Counter-terrorism efforts of this approach revolve around incapacitation of terrorists and their sympathizers (by relying upon the *deterrence-based* policies) and containment of their ideology.

Those who view terrorism as a consequence of deprivations in society are likely to suggest more accommodative policies. They see terrorism beyond the core terrorist group to include the social, economic, and political dynamics. They are more likely to consider policies directed at the social context and perceived grievance rather than the mere terrorist group. In this approach, policies that punish terrorist groups by imposing unjustifiably high costs may increase anti-government sentiment and further alienating the oppositional population (Ramraj, 2006). Instead, they seek to improve the bond between the society and the terrorist group (Crenshaw, 1999). The main responsibility is granted to civilian law enforcement (e.g. police forces) to deal with terrorists, particularly in democratic countries because this type of approach bears minimal collateral damage compared to emergency law or military force.

Most states confronting terrorism wind up relying on "get tough" policies (Frey and Luechinger, 2002). This is because of the dynamics of politics and political institutions (Crenshaw, 2001). Politicians are primarily concerned about their ballot box. Moreover, governments must react immediately to national security threats or risk political backlash from the populace. Particularly in ethnicity or religion based terrorism, patriotic fervor often drowns out efforts to address the root causes of the grievances. But ethnically based terrorist activities are difficult to eliminate because it is difficult to separate civilians from the core terrorist group (Byman, 1998; Crenshaw, 2001; Kim and Yun, 2008).

In contrast, social policies that address terrorism-inducing grievances can reach out to the sympathizers through dialogs and may split the pragmatists from radical rejectionists (Crenshaw, 1999). The focus here is on winning the hearts and minds by recognizing that they have suffered deprivation of rights or benefits (Crenshaw, 1983; Hewitt, 1984). Most importantly, one should see that reducing terrorism (measured by violent terror incidents) does not mean solving the problem of terrorism. The best solution in countering terrorism is to identify the grievances or deprivations before they radicalize a social opposition.

Future research questions

1. What are the determinants of perceived legitimacy for the governments' counterterrorism policies?
2. What are the likely unintended consequences of different counterterrorism policies on dimensions of terrorists, sympathizers, neutrals, and antagonists?
3. What are the determinant factors of emergence of terrorism in different administrative regimes?
4. What factors are to be taken into consideration to measure the level of terrorism in a particular terrorism case?
5. What factors play the premium role in determining the psychological bond and group solidarity between the terrorist group and sympathizers in the context of an ethno-terrorism case?

References

Alexander, Y. (Ed.). (2002). *Combating terrorism: strategies of ten countries*. Ann Arbor, MI: University of Michigan Press.

Arce, D. and Sandler, T. (2005). Counterterrorism: a game-theoretic analysis. *Journal of Conflict Resolution*, 49(2): 183–200.

Braithwaite, J. (2002). Thinking critically about the war model and the criminal justice model for combating terrorism. Law and Society Association Meeting Panel on "Finding ground between traditional adversaries." Vancouver, Canada.

Byman, D. (1998). The logic of ethnic terrorism. *Studies in Conflict & Terrorism*, 21(2): 149–69.

Cauley, J. and Im, E. (1988). Intervention policy analysis of skyjackings and other terrorist incidents. *American Economic Review*, 78(2): 27–31.

Cluskey, F. (1989). The Irish response. In B. Netanyahu (Ed.) *International terrorism, challenge and response: proceedings of the Jerusalem Conference on International Terrorism*, pp. 180–6. Jerusalem: Jonathan Institute.

Crenshaw, M. (Ed.) (1983). *Terrorism, legitimacy, and power: the consequences of political violence: essays*. Middletown, CT and Scranton, PA: Wesleyan University Press.
—— (Ed.). (1995). *Terrorism in context*. University Park, PA: Pennsylvania State University Press.
—— (1999). Martha Crenshaw on how terrorism ends. In J. B. Alterman, *How terrorism ends*. Washington, DC: United States Institute of Peace. pp. 2–4.
—— (2001). Counterterrorism policy and the political process. *Studies in Conflict & Terrorism*, 24(5): 329–37.
Donohue, L. (2000). Civil liberties, terrorism, and liberal democracy: lessons from the United Kingdom. BCSIA Discussion Paper 2000–5, ESDP Discussion Paper ESDP-2000-01, John F. Kennedy School of Government, Harvard University (August).
Enders, W. and Sandler, T. (1993). The effectiveness of antiterrorism policies: a vector-autoregression-intervention analysis. *American Political Science Review*, 87(4): 829–44.
—— (1999). Transnational terrorism in the post-Cold War era. *International Studies Quarterly*, 43(1): 145–67.
Enders, W., Sandler, T., and Cauley, J. (1990). UN conventions, technology and retaliation in the fight against terrorism: an econometric evaluation. *Terrorism and Political Violence*, 2(1): 83–105.
Faria, J. (2006). Terrorist innovations and anti-terrorist policies. *Terrorism and Political Violence*, 18(1): 47–56.
Frey, B. S. (2004). *Dealing with terrorism: stick or carrot?* Cheltenham, UK and Northampton, MA: Edward Elgar.
Frey, B. S. and Luechinger, S. (2002). How to fight terrorism: alternatives to deterrence. pp. 1–35.
Hewitt, C. (1984). *The effectiveness of anti-terrorist policies*. Lanham, MD: University Press of America.
Kenney, M. (2003). From Pablo to Osama: counter-terrorism lessons from the war on drugs. *Survival*, 45(3): 187–206.
Kim, E. and Yun, M. (2008). What works? Countermeasures to terrorism: a case study of PKK. *International Journal of Comparative and Applied Criminal Justice*, 32(1): 24.
Kutan, A. and Drakos, K. (2003). Regional effects of terrorism on tourism. *Journal of Conflict Resolution*, 47(5): 621–41.
Lal, C. (1999). Terrorism and insurgency. A symposium on the role of the police in our society. New Delhi.
Landes, W. (1978). An economic study of US aircraft hijacking, 1961–76. *Journal of Law and Economics*, 21: 1–32.
Langdon, L., Sarapu, A. J., and Wells, M. (2004). Targeting the leadership of terrorist and insurgent movements: historical lessons for contemporary policy makers. *Journal of Public and International Affairs*, 15: 59–78.
Levitt, G. M. (1988). *Democracies against terror: the Western response to state-supported terrorism*. New York: Praeger.
Lichbach, M. (1987). Deterrence or escalation? The puzzle of aggregate studies of repression and dissent. *Journal of Conflict Resolution*, 31(2): 266–97.
Martin, B. (2006). Instead of repression. *Social Alternatives*, 25(1): 62–84.
Mead, W. R. (2004). *Power, terror, peace, and war: America's grand strategy in a world at risk*. New York: Knopf.
Mendes, S. (2004). Certainty, severity, and their relative deterrent effects: questioning the implications of the role of risk in criminal deterrence policy. *Policy Studies Journal*, 32(1): 59–74.
Mentan, T. (2004). *Dilemmas of weak states: Africa and transnational terrorism in the twenty-first century*. Aldershot and Burlington, VT: Ashgate.
Moran, R. (1996). Bringing rational choice theory back to reality. *Journal of Criminal Law and Criminology*, 86: 1,147–60.
Netanyahu, B. (1986). *Terrorism: how the West can win*. New York: Jonathan Institute.
—— (Ed). (1989). *International terrorism, challenge and response: proceedings of the Jerusalem Conference on International Terrorism*. Jerusalem: Jonathan Institute.
—— (Ed.). (1995). *Fighting terrorism: how democracies can defeat domestic and international terrorism*. New York: Farrar, Straus and Giroux.
Nevin, J. (2003). Retaliating against terrorists. *Behavior and Social Issues*, 12(2): 109–28.
Omelicheva, M. Y. (2007). Combating terrorism in Central Asia: explaining differences in states' responses to terror. *Terrorism and Political Violence*, 19(3): 369–93.
Perez, S. (1989). The threat and the response. In B. Netanyahu (Ed.) *International terrorism, challenge and response: proceedings of the Jerusalem Conference on International Terrorism*, pp. 8–11. Jerusalem, Jonathan Institute.
Prunckun, H. and P. Mohr (1997). Military deterrence of international terrorism: an evaluation of operation El Dorado Canyon. *Studies in Conflict & Terrorism*, 20(3): 267–80.
Ramraj, V. (2006). Counter-terrorism policy and minority alienation: some lessons from Northern Ireland. *Singapore Journal of Legal Studies*, pp. 385–404.

Ramraj, V., Hor, M., and Roach, K. (Eds.) (2005). *Global anti-terrorism law and policy*. Cambridge: Cambridge University Press.
Reinares, F. (2000). *European democracies against terrorism: governmental policies and intergovernmental cooperation*. Aldershot, UK and Brookfield, VT: Ashgate.
Sandler, T. (2005). Collective versus unilateral responses to terrorism. *Public Choice*, 124(1): 75–93.
Sandler, T. and Enders, W. (2004). An economic perspective on transnational terrorism. *European Journal of Political Economy*, 20(2): 301–16.
—— (2007). Applying analytical methods to study terrorism. *International Studies Perspectives*, 8(3): 287–302.
Sandler, T., Tschirhart, J., and Cauley, J. (1983). A theoretical analysis of transnational terrorism. *American Political Science Review*, 77(1): 36–54.
Schnellenbach, J. (2006). Appeasing nihilists? Some economic thoughts on reducing terrorist activity. *Public Choice*, 129(3): 301–13.
Segaller, S. (1987). *Invisible armies*. Orlando; Florida: Harcourt Brace Jovanovich Publishers.
Sherman, L. (1993). Defiance, deterrence, and irrelevance: a theory of the criminal sanction. *Journal of Research in Crime and Delinquency*, 30(4): 445.
Shultz, G. P. (1986). The challenge to the democracies. In B. Netanyahu (Ed.) *Terrorism: how the West can win*. New York, Jonathan Institute. pp. 16–24.
Shultz, R. (1979). Coercive force and military strategy: deterrence logic and the cost–benefit model of counterinsurgency warfare. *Political Research Quarterly*, 32(4): 444–66.
Smith, G. D. (1990). *Combating terrorism*. London and New York: Routledge.
Turk, A. (2002). Confronting enemies foreign and domestic: an American dilemma? *Criminology & Public Policy*, 1(3): 345–50.
Tyler, T. (2000). Multiculturalism and the willingness of citizens to defer to law and to legal authorities. *Law & Social Inquiry*, 25(4): 983–1,019.
Tyler, T. R., Degoey, P., and Smith, H. (1996). Understanding why the justice of group procedures matters: a test of the psychological dynamics of the group-value model. *Journal of Personality and Social Psychology*, 70(5): 913–30.
Vigna, P. L. (1989). The Italian response. In B. Netanyahu (Ed.) *International terrorism, challenge and response: proceedings of the Jerusalem Conference on International Terrorism*, pp. 196–200. Jerusalem: Jonathan Institute.
Whittaker, D. J. (2003). *The terrorism reader*. London, New York: Routledge.
Wilkinson, P. (1977). *Terrorism and the liberal state*. London: Macmillan.
—— (1996). The role of the military in combating terrorism in a democratic society. *Terrorism and Political Violence*, 8(3): 1–11.
—— (1999). Paul Wilkinson on the IRA. In J. B. Alterman, *How terrorism ends*. Washington, DC: United States Institute of Peace. pp. 4–6.
—— (2001). *Terrorism versus democracy: the liberal state response*. London & Portland, OR: Frank Cass.
Will, G. (1989). Calculating the public interest. In B. Netanyahu (Ed.) *International terrorism, challenge and response: proceedings of the Jerusalem Conference on International Terrorism*, pp. 208–13. Jerusalem: Jonathan Institute.

27

The ambivalent role of Italian prosecutors and their resistance to 'moral panics' about crime

Riccardo Montana and David Nelken

Introduction

The following study is intended to illustrate the value of empirically informed approaches to comparative criminal justice – requiring close analysis of rules, roles and procedures – as a way of throwing light on central criminological topics (Nelken, 2000, 2010a). The issue considered here has to do with the rise of 'punitiveness' internationally and the part played by criminal justice actors in this process. On the basis of empirical research in Italy this chapter shall be focusing on the role of prosecutors in responding to political and public calls for more severity against crimes by illegal immigrants. After first providing a historical and theoretical context for our research we shall analyze the ambivalent role of Italian prosecutors and then go on to explain how this affects the part they play in the way the criminal justice system responds to such crimes.

Like many other countries, Italy is facing the problems of risk and insecurity that late modernity brings in its wake. In Italy public discussion of these problems emerged later than in some other Western countries (in the second half of the 1990s). This is seen, for example, in the fact that until quite recently, everyday crime in Italy was referred to as 'micro-criminality' – thus distinguishing it from the objectively greater threats to the state posed by terrorism, organized crime and political corruption. Although these major problems have by no means disappeared, worries about security reported in the media are increasingly linked to illegal immigration (or even immigration as such). Illegal immigrants are said to be disproportionately involved in so-called street or diffuse crimes such as mugging, drug pushing and burglary.

The center-right and the center-left political coalitions propose different solutions to these crime problems. The former are more focused on repression, the latter point more to the underlying social conditions that create social conflicts. But even the mass media that are ideologically on the center-left, and normally criticize law and order campaigns, do acknowledge that there is an issue of crime and security, and center-left administrations use rhetoric that is increasingly indistinguishable from their political opponents. Public opinion surveys also suggest high rates of public concern.[1] In addition, citizen committees have been elected in the districts of many cities and towns so as to report and discuss problems concerning crime and deviance within their areas. Their efforts are not only directed against specific crime problems, but incivilities, deviance, immigration, and disorder in general appear to be crucial issues as well.

All this means that there is the potential in Italy as elsewhere for an explosion in prison numbers. And, in fact, the number of immigrants in prison has gone up exponentially since they started arriving in the 1990s (and this does not include those being held in special prisons that until recently were called places of temporary permanence). This is because illegal or irregular immigrants now provide the workforce for crimes such as drug pushing that, if associated with recidivism, are often punished with a custodial sentence. However, despite legislative measures that are clearly designed to tackle street crime and illegal immigration, overall numbers in prison in Italy (around 100 per 100,000 of the population) remain within the average range of what leading comparative penologists have dubbed the 'Continental Corporatist' societies (Cavadino and Dignan, 2006). By comparison 'neo-liberal' societies such as the U.S.A. (700 per 100,000), or even the U.K. (150 per 100,000) show much higher rates of incarceration.

Southern European countries generally have higher rates of immigrants in prison than do neo-liberal societies (Solivitti 2010). What needs to be understood is why numbers in prison have not risen even higher in places such as Italy. For many authors (e.g. Cavadino and Dignan, 2006; Wacquant, 2009a, 2009b; and, with more nuance, Lacey, 2008) differences in the organization of politics and the economy are the crucial explanatory variables. However, this ignores a crucial intermediate variable that affects how many people actually end up in prison – the operation of the criminal justice system. This requires giving close attention to the roles of legal actors, such as prosecutors, and the types of criminal procedure that shapes their roles (Nelken, 2009, 2010).

The significance of differences in the role of prosecutors in continental and common law systems was at the center of the classical debate in comparative criminal procedure between Goldstein and Marcus (1977) and Langbein and Weinreb (1978). But this concerned the extent to which prosecutors and judges in France, Germany and Italy really exercised control over how police conducted their investigations. However, the parties to the controversy may have been largely speaking past each other. If the question was how Continental methods of control over the police would work in the U.S.A., then Goldstein and Marcus were right that such methods would be insufficient to avoid potential misbehavior by the police. But, insofar as the issue was trying to understand what other places were actually trying to do – and sometimes succeeding in doing – *in the context of their own structures and expectations*, then Langbein and Weinreb had the better of the argument.

The research presented here has to do with trying to characterize these (changing) structures and expectations as they currently apply to prosecutors in Italy. But the issue addressed is not the traditional one, their role in supervising the police. Rather it is the less discussed question of whether, when, where, why and how prosecutors in continental legal systems exercise their powers so as to blunt trends towards increasing punitiveness of the weak and marginal sectors of the society. Taking Italian prosecutors as a case study is particularly interesting and instructive for this purpose as for the past 20 years their status is supposed to have been made more like that of prosecutors in the common law world. The findings come from 54 semi-structured interviews that were conducted between April and October 2006.[2] Five consultants, two prosecutors, one police officer and two lawyers were first interviewed as informants. Then, the actual interviews were carried out with 27 prosecutors, 11 police officers and 11 lawyers. These interviews were conducted in 10 prosecution offices (and with lawyers and police officers working in the same area) of various sizes located mainly in the north, but also in the center and in the south of Italy.

The ambivalent role of prosecutors in Italy

The 1989 reform of the Italian Code of Criminal Procedure famously sought to reshape a mainly inquisitorial system into an accusatorial one.[3] The trial stage became central to the determination of guilt, and defense lawyers saw their role increased and were given the power to gather their own evidence. Most important for our purposes, the reform also changed the prosecutors' institutional role from being quasi-judicial figures to state accusers. In practice, however, the Italian criminal justice system is still in many respects embedded in the continental inquisitorial tradition. For example, judges have the power to request further investigation basically at every stage of the criminal process. Constitutional Court decisions (in a context in which organized crime made it dangerous for witnesses to rely only on evidence that comes out in trial) and various legislative reforms have reaffirmed the probative value of the preliminary investigation at trial.

In many Italian textbooks the traditional interpretation that depicts prosecutors as responsible for the correct application of the law as neutral quasi-judicial figures is still well entrenched. And it is crucial too that, institutionally and organizationally, judges and prosecutors are both part of the judiciary. They share the same career path and can – subject to certain conditions – switch functions as their careers develop. Prosecutors, like judges, are also fully independent of any other constitutional powers including the government. They are subject to the legality principle – the obligation to prosecute where evidence is available is a constitutional principle that cannot be compromised even for supposed reasons of 'public interest'.

But, after the 1989 reform reconfigured the role of prosecutors as responsible for constructing a case that will stand scrutiny at trial, the continued accuracy and validity of this traditional inquisitorial model of the quasi-judicial role for prosecutors has been widely criticized both by academic commentators and – for their own reasons – by politicians. Prosecutors have been accused many times over the last twenty years-often misleadingly – of going out of their way to use their powers to attack members of some political parties, as well as Premier Berlusconi. However, in a country such as Italy, where there is considerable suspicion of political corruption it has so far not been possible for politicians to deny that placing prosecutors under government control would lead to (even greater) abuse of their powers.

At the very least it can be said that prosecutors now occupy an especially ambivalent role, still possessing many of the attributes of quasi-judicial actors searching for the truth whilst being inserted in a new legal architecture intended to cast them on one side of a contest over the guilt of the accused. Surprisingly, there has been little research into this ambivalence. The only large-scale empirical study of prosecutors in Italy is that conducted by Di Federico and Sapignoli (2002). But their concern – part of a larger agenda that considered judges and prosecutors too willing to interfere in politics – was that prosecutors did not in practice respect the legality principle and that obligatory prosecution was in practice no more than a myth. In their views prosecutors can and do choose, sometimes on politically influenced criteria, which matters to prosecute. Thus they see prosecutors as effective crime fighters – targeting politically relevant cases. Our study, which focuses more on their de-prioritizing of a large number of normal cases, also shows that prosecutors have their own priorities about what gets dealt with as crime. But we see this not so much as a matter of them exercising political preferences and more as a result of them continuing to see their role in a traditional way. Even though prosecutors cannot formally decide which cases deserve to be prosecuted in a regime where prosecution is obligatory, choosing which cases to handle first is an indirect way of achieving the same result because after a certain point the case becomes time-bound – what Italians describe as 'prescrizione'[4] (Nelken and Zanier, 2006).

It could be said that, in general, all prosecutors occupy an ambivalent position with respect to the different value systems that compete in criminal justice systems, as set out in Packer's famous distinction between crime control and due process (Packer, 1968). Administrative fact-finding serves the aims of crime control values. So, repression of criminal conduct is the most important function performed by the criminal process. As a consequence, this must be efficient and facts must be established as quickly as possible with routine procedures which do not rely on a formal process of examination. Adjudicative fact-finding, by contrast, is more linked to due process values. Almost all criminal justice systems have features that belong to both of these models, although the mix of the elements varies. What makes the Italian case special, however, is the superimposition of a model with a mix more favorable to crime control values over a previous one with, formally speaking, much more bias towards due process values – and the way these two models continue to co-exist.

For Italian prosecutors, this superimposition heightens their ambivalent status between the role of crime fighters and judicial figures. Whereas crime fighters are clearly linked with the concept of crime control related to efficiency, high rate of conviction, and administrative fact-finding model, the judicial task is related to the concept of due process involving legal controls, the primacy of the individual, adjudicative fact-finding model and so on. When asked about their views, a large majority of the Italian prosecutors interviewed insisted that their professional values have nothing in common with that of the crime fighter. Twenty-two prosecutors said that they did not act like crime fighters. One did not answer clearly. Four said that they did act like crime fighters. They explained that they looked for both inculpatory and exculpatory evidence so as to establish the legal and factual truth while, in their opinion, crime fighters search only for a conviction. By contrast, they share the same professional culture as judges. As a number of prosecutors put it: 'it is the law that fights the crime.'

Functionally it is clear that there are important differences in the tasks of prosecutors and judges in Italy. When prosecutors receive a report, they have to determine if a crime has been committed and if the evidence collected is capable to stand scrutiny at trial. This phase continues during the investigation when more evidence is collected by the police and prosecutors directly and it terminates when prosecutors decide to refer the case to trial or to drop the file. As with all prosecutors, they have to filter out reports that do not actually include a crime as defined by the law, and evidence that has not been legally obtained and 'predict' whether there is a 'realistic likelihood' of conviction. Such legal filtering then enables judges to make decisions on legally relevant evidence. This means that they deal with cases before judges do, have direct contact with the police and have to build up a case that will then be presented at trial. Unlike judges, prosecutors are inevitably influenced by information that will never reach the trial stage and rely on police reports that often include the police officers' perceptions and considerations about a specific crime.

Sometimes an official report is not even necessary and there are informal communications between prosecutors and the police that then lead to an investigation. When prosecutors deal with cases, they participate in the investigation and interact with the police and so – to some extent – have to recognize what are priorities for them (Montana, 2009). One prosecutor gave this as an example:

> The police tell me the cases which look particularly serious [. . .] For example, I recently had a case of robbers operating in a small village [. . .] These are bullies who have crossed the line: they go to bars and they do not pay, they require their families to give them money, they blackmail friends and acquaintances and they become violent etc. This case was indicated to me by the chief of the police in that village. So, in three days, I have to say that I had no other urgent matters, I prepared the documents applying [to the judge] for pre-trial custody and the judge decided [agreed with the request] in 15 days [. . .] Anyway, I have to say that, in general, I always intervene when the police report to me that a case is serious.

The role of prosecutors as intermediaries between the police and the courts means that they see much that is prejudicial, irrelevant or partially irrelevant and emotionally charged. The overall goal of the criminal justice process is to render the judge impartial, not the prosecutor. Judges, by contrast, only evaluate the evidence. Although, in Italy, they can still order new investigations, they do not actually direct the police or directly carry out investigation activities. So, compared to judges, prosecutors search for the truth under different conditions. Some admit this. Five prosecutors emphasized in various words that the judges 'cannot see very much'. Judges do not understand the practical difficulties of carrying out an investigation and they only have a partial idea of the factual scenario. This is partially connected to the difficulties created by the ambiguous legal rules that shape prosecutors' and police's investigative powers, not to mention the backlog of cases and the financial and organizational problems. But there is another reason. Prosecutors have a different knowledge of the case because they have a different and more direct contact with the social reality in which a crime has been perpetrated.

The various types of information that prosecutors collect and receive during the investigation contribute to create their own image of a crime. Their close contact with social reality reduces the degree of 'detachment' that, in prosecutors' view, judicial culture guarantees. They present evidence to the judge to convince him or her that their interpretation of events is correct: they are thus functionally a party to proceedings. In the end, the prosecutors' search for the truth takes place in a different context: that of an awareness of a wider range of information, some of it illegally or unfairly obtained, some of it prejudicial or emotionally charged but not formally legally relevant or of doubtful or limited relevance, most of it untested by informed dialogue between parties.

Nonetheless, these functional differences do not seem to affect prosecutors' image of themselves as quasi-judges. On the one hand prosecutors try to assess and increase the possibilities to obtain a conviction for utilitarian reasons – because it is a waste of time to put cases before judges to have them rejected. They have to evaluate the evidence with enough judicial distance to anticipate a judge's reaction. As one prosecutor explained (but many others concurred): 'So, in general, when I decide to begin a prosecution, I try to think like a judge and to decide according to the evidence that the judge will probably have. This is because it is useless to begin a prosecution which will end with an acquittal [. . .] I always try to foresee what can happen.' But Italian prosecutors go beyond this in claiming to have a similar duty of neutrality and impartiality to judge. They value due process and legal values in themselves and place more faith in criminal procedure than administrative fact-finding.

Even in common law regimes public prosecutors in theory are required to do more than partisanly present the prosecution case before the court (Jackson, 2004, p. 112). But, for Italian prosecutors, impartiality is what defines their cultural proximity to judges. Despite the 1989 reform, prosecutors still act in some ways as if they were fulfilling the role of examining magistrates in the inquisitorial tradition. As three of the interviewees saw it, the 'prosecutors' aim is to transfer as many documents as possible from their *dossier* to the judge's *dossier*'. This emphasis on prosecutors' sense of themselves as guardians of the law, their independence and discretionary powers help to distance prosecutors from the pressure of political and popular definitions of the crime problem.

Prosecutors' 'resistance' to the fight against illegal immigration

Over the last 15 years different governments have taken a number of steps to tackle street crime and illegal immigration and reassure the public that they are protecting their security. Arguably, the most draconian of the measures taken to tackle illegal immigration is the Bossi-Fini Act, which was passed in 2002 by the then center-right government. It sets out that a non-Italian national who does not comply with a deportation order shall be arrested and immediately sent for trial. In these cases the punishments range from a minimum of six months' to a maximum of four years' imprisonment, excluding mitigating and/or aggravating circumstances. In theory, prosecutors cannot postpone dealing with these cases. The code of criminal procedure requires that the prosecutor is immediately informed when an arrest has been carried out by the police. The prosecutor then has to review the arrest procedure in order to decide if the arrested person(s) must be set free immediately or the arrest is lawful.

If the arrest is validated, the Bossi-Fini Act requires the trial thus follows a procedure called *direttissima*, that circumvents the need for a preliminary hearing. For the vast majority of the crimes a trial needs to be held before the preliminary hearing judge to determine if there is a case that needs be referred to the judge. At this stage new investigations can be ordered, or the case sent on to trial. The *direttissima* trial by contrast, has to take place within 48 hours of the arrest before the same judge who also decides if the arrest is lawful or not. As a result, prosecutors have no choice, they must deal with the Bossi-Fini cases immediately. Arguably, such legislation aims to circumvent the 'legality' principle by which the executive has no legal power to impose priorities to prosecutors. The Bossi-Fini Act tries to force the criminal justice system to treat immigration as a priority. This is because as the minister of justice at the time explained, 'criminality grows around the clandestine immigrants'.[5]

The reality of what prosecutors do, however, is often quite different. The prosecutors interviewed insisted that that they do not consider these crimes as high priorities. In particular, when it comes to the Bossi-Fini Act, prosecutors admit that they are not interested in investigating illegal immigration unless they can spot a link with organized crime. The relatively low priority is clearly illustrated by the way prosecutors deal with incarceration of accused persons and sentences. In general, one of the criteria prosecutors take into consideration to request pre-trial custody is recidivism. But this does not seem to be relevant when it is only linked with violation of a deportation order under the Bossi-Fini Act. The consequence is that prosecutors never ask for pre-trial custody, unless the accused person(s) has committed other crimes. Moreover, during trials, prosecutors are not interested in asking for a severe punishment. If the crime is only related to the Bossi-Fini Act, illegal immigrants are arrested and, normally, sentenced to a few months of imprisonment (some said three months, others six), but the sentence will be suspended. In practice, this means that illegal immigrants will be set free and, given that they normally have neither documents nor any official residence in Italy, they will disappear.

This lack of prioritization may be further illustrated by the way medium or large prosecution offices use specialized units of prosecutors who only deal with certain categories of crime. Such units are created to tackle in a more structured way crimes that are considered more serious and/or more difficult to investigate. In practice, these units increase co-ordination between prosecutors that, in this way, have a better understanding of the crime problem in the geographical area where they work. None of the prosecution offices included in this study had a unit dealing with illegal immigration – or for that matter street crime – though they were found to be dealing with environmental, organized, corruption and white-collar crimes.

That the Bossi-Fini Act has so far failed to impose its priorities on prosecutors becomes even clearer if examining the conditions that the law imposes on the arrest and prosecution of illegal immigrants. Article 5 *ter* states that the crime is committed when the immigrant remains in Italy without having a 'reasonable reason' to do so. If there is such a reason, prosecutors can set the arrested person(s) free. Prosecutors interpret this concept in a wide variety of ways. One interviewee explained that only a pregnant woman has a reason to remain in Italy. But another argued that the accused person's financial situation must be carefully checked to ascertain whether they have enough money to leave the country and one young prosecutor said that every immigrant who does not have a real home has a justification not to leave, because he or she cannot possibly afford it!

It could be argued that what we have here is further evidence of socio-political considerations influencing prosecutors' definition of the crime problem. But this desire to distance themselves from political or public definitions does not only concern illegal immigration: it is linked to any crime policy indication that prosecutors perceive to be influenced by emotional and populist 'moral panics' (Cohen, 1972). Although this term as such is not used by the media, politicians, public or prosecutors, an expression that comes near to it that is used is *allarme sociale*. *Allarme sociale* literally means social alarm and defines the reaction (often disproportionate) that society has to certain crimes and/or certain perpetrators or victims. This reaction may be targeted against a particular group of people, such as immigrants, but can also be spontaneous and linked to moral and political issues. Crime of course is not the only source of social alarm; disorder and incivilities can also influence the public perception of security (Chiesi, 2004).

Italian prosecutors are well aware of public perceptions about the connection between street crime and illegal immigration. But they assume that *allarme sociale* over these matters is in large part a result of media exploitation of public fears. Prosecutors have their own conception of the sort of *allarme sociale* that merits inclusion in their priorities for prosecution. According to the interviewees, these are crimes that are particularly dangerous, that jeopardize people's sense of security in going about their everyday life, that involve certain kinds of victims (e.g. women, children and elderly people) and, in general, that have a great impact on the society. *Allarme sociale* counts only if it is linked with 'the objective seriousness of the case'.

In general, the more the legal punishment is severe, the more the crime is serious. Crimes which threaten life are more important than crimes which threaten property. Finally, the damage suffered by the victim can be a relevant parameter as well. These are some of the 'objective' criteria that determine if a crime is serious and, as a consequence, if it has caused social alarm. Deliberately leaving a case on one side and allowing a case to fall into *prescrizione* can have consequences for a prosecutor's career and can involve ministerial and the Supreme Council of Judges (CSM) disciplinary hearings. Nonetheless there are ways around this. As one prosecutor said: 'The legality principle is a false problem. There are many ways not to apply it. Then you can say you are sorry, there will be disciplinary proceedings, but how do they prove this was intentional? You just made a mistake.'

Italian prosecutors accept that they have a responsibility to assuage public fears, but, at the same time, they believe they have to decide if the supposed crime problem is commensurate with its level of social alarm. As one of the lawyers interviewed put it, *allarme sociale* is a volatile concept that evokes different images for the public and for prosecutors. Prosecutors compare these two images and filter these external influences, which do not disappear, but they are substantially moderated by other internal considerations. The public perception of social alarm is not sufficient to determine priorities. Prosecutors depict the criteria they use as purely legal and objective but, in practice, they are also subjective and intertwined with socio-political considerations about the problem of crime. The clearest example is the Bossi-Fini Act, which, in theory, provides for violators to be punished strictly but which has a low priority for them.

On the other hand, there is a limit to such 'resistance.' Prosecutors admit, as we have seen, that they are inevitably influenced in choosing what to investigate by the crimes that the police report to them. If the police decide to carry out a particular operation, prosecutors have to deal with the legal consequences that this creates (e.g. a large number of arrested persons). Because the police have the right to arrest, this triggers a procedure that binds prosecutors. One of the prosecutors interviewed explained that: 'for arrested persons caught red handed, it depends whether the police decide to focus on areas where there is drug trafficking or prostitution or where there are illegal immigrants. This is how it works.'

The police for their part follow directives on anti-crime policies that come to them from their organizations at the top of which are the Minister of Interior and the Ministry of Defense. Thus, although the government cannot directly influence prosecutors because the legality principle prevents the government from determining any sort of prosecutorial priority, they do have an indirect impact on the prosecutors' job. Prosecutors do not have any real opportunity to discuss the directives or co-ordinate their priorities with police priorities. The importance of police decisions at this stage of the criminal proceedings is heightened by the fact that police officers are evaluated on the basis of quantitative indicators. Amongst the parameters used to make statistical evaluations are arrests, deportations, denunciations and the controls police perform on persons and vehicles. As a result, street crime and illegal immigration cases make up between 50 and 70 percent of the crimes that prosecutors process.

This places a high burden on the criminal justice system not only because of their number but because prosecutors must always discover the official and fixed residence of all the accused persons so as to deliver the necessary legal notifications during the investigation phase. When immigrants are involved this is difficult because often the residence cannot be found. Prosecutors admit that even if street crime and illegal immigration are more priorities for the police than for them they cannot easily stop the constant stream of street crime and illegal immigration cases. And the number of immigrants in prison has increased dramatically.

But we nonetheless disagree with those academic commentators who argue that this means that prosecutors have come to share public concerns about law and order and common sense notions about crime, such as stereotypes of immigrants as criminals (Sarzotti, 2006a; Faiella *et al.*, 2005; Quassoli, 1999). Instead, it may be true at the level of heads of prosecution offices who, in their 'political' role as court spokespersons, have to echo political and public concerns. But this does necessarily affect the views of single prosecutors. Due account, therefore, should also be taken of the way prosecutors try to minimize the impact of moral panics reflected in legislation such as the Bossi-Fini Act.

As far as initiating investigations is concerned, there may not be very much prosecutors can do. But as the criminal proceedings go on, prosecutors can decide how and where to commit resources during the investigation. A Bossi-Fini case or any form of street crime that did not actually cause serious consequences (e.g. injuries) will rarely be given a detailed investigation. In practice, prosecutors do not see illegal immigration (and even the less-serious street crimes) as 'problems' that deserve to be tackled aggressively. Prosecutors seek to preserve the criminal justice system from interference that would stop what they consider more serious crimes from being prosecuted and punished. As in many other continental European countries, Italian prosecutors see themselves as the experts responsible for defining the priorities of the criminal justice system. As a consequence, they try hard to maintain a cultural distance from different forms of external pressure from victims, communities, or politicians, including legislation such as the Bossi-Fini Act. Legal filtering is not confined to the construction of cases that will stand scrutiny at trial. It also may be seen as filtering out certain forms of political pressure and with it certain forms of social anxiety.

Conclusion

This account of how Italian prosecutors respond to moral panics over immigrant crime has shown how legal actors can maintain some separation from dominant political cultures and dominant legal cultures. This form of resistance stems to a large extent from prosecutors' way of thinking of their role. Independence, the legality principle and cultural proximity with judges are the bricks in the wall that prosecutors have constructed to protect their sense of their own neutrality.

Prosecutors certainly also have their own political views about the prosecution (or persecution) of illegal immigrants. But, they do not all think the same way. The findings in this chapter suggest that it is the prosecutors' role in defining substantive priorities that determines their reaction towards this crime problem – political disagreement is more a consequence than a cause.

Despite the 1989 reform of criminal procedure, prosecutors are reluctant to move to an accusatorial conception of their role. They are still attached culturally to the idea of their role as neutral and impartial. Abandoning this conception would also diminish their credibility when they prosecute in politically sensitive cases. Various socio-legal conditions have favored this outcome. Prosecutors' independence is well established in the constitution and, though increasingly under political threat, this provides at least formal protection for prosecutors from suspicions or allegations of prosecuting a case for reasons other than the purely legal. Italian prosecutors are not in a position to halt the evolution (or involution) of contemporary criminal justice. But they certainly try to balance external pressures by mediating, and not simply executing, anti-crime policies that seek to reassure (or excite) public opinion.

On the other hand, a number of issues remain very much still to be clarified. Most important for present purposes, there is insufficient evidence available to show the actual consequences of current prosecutors' resistance to the campaign to prioritize crimes of illegal immigrants. There is an acute shortage in Italy of reliable statistical information on the functioning of criminal justice agencies that goes beyond records of what kinds of crimes are referred by the police or seen by the courts. Though it would be easy to show that there has been a large increase in the processing of illegal immigrants, it would be tricky to say how much higher this could have gone under different circumstances. The research described in this chapter is limited to interviews with prosecutors, although it was supplemented with interviews with others involved in the criminal process, such as lawyers and police. To engage with the 'counterfactual' – of what would have happened if prosecutors indeed had changed their priorities in line with governmental indications – we would need to have examined a large number of case files over time and see what happened to them. Certainly, giving a low priority to such cases should mean that the cases that prosecutors put forward are less strong than they might otherwise be. In addition *de facto* many cases will not make it through the system in time. On the other hand, relative unwillingness to invest time in such matters may also result in such cases going to court quickly and thus not risking prescription – exactly as the governmental legislation intended.

It is also difficult to predict the future. Prosecutors' dislike of the Bossi-Fini Act may be seen as over-determined – and it is not certain how they would react to other kinds of cases. Many have objections to the way governments have chosen to try to condition their actions on this substantive issue, for example including the high penalties that have been attached to the status crime of being an illegal immigrant so as to make it an arrestable offence for which offenders can be kept in custody before trial. But they also disagree in principle with any interference with their autonomy. We also do not know how much what we are describing is a result of the recency of the 1989 reform and the persistence of the earlier inquisitorial legal culture. Certainly changes in their institutional role, as proposed by center-right governments in particular, intended to separate their role from that of judges and bring it more into line with the accusatorial architecture of the 1989 reform, would make such resistance more difficult.

Future research questions

1. What are the actual consequences of current prosecutors' resistance to the campaign to prioritize crimes of illegal immigrants?
2. Why do they give lower priority to the crime of being an illegal immigrant?

3. There is an acute shortage in Italy of reliable statistical information on the functioning of criminal justice agencies that goes beyond records of what kinds of crimes are referred by the police or seen by the courts. What data should be collected to reliably demonstrate that the processing of illegal immigrants has increased at a greater or lesser rate because of the attitudes of the prosecutors?
4. What are the differences between the way that Italian prosecutors and those in common law systems see their role? How does it affect prosecution of immigrants?
5. What influence should political direction or public concern over the crime problem have on choices made within a criminal justice system?

Notes

1 Italian citizens are mainly scared of theft, robberies, drugs and muggings. See Muratore *et al.* (2004)
2 The empirical research was conducted by Riccardo Montana for his doctoral degree at Cardiff University under the supervision of Dr. Stewart Field and Professor David Nelken.
3 For a recent discussion of the effects of introducing the new Italian code of criminal procedure, see Marafioti (2008), pp. 81–99.
4 This legal concept indicates that prosecutors and courts have a time limit to bring an accusation to closure. This is not fixed but depends on the crime that has been committed (the more the crime is serious, the more time is allowed). If cases do not make it in time the accused is not formally innocent (sometimes he or she is clearly guilty) but cannot be prosecuted and/or tried further for that crime.
5 See Biglia (2005).

References

Biglia, A. (2005). Castelli è la prova che i clandestini portano criminalità. *Corriere della Serra.*

Cavadino, M. & Dignan, J. (2006). *Penal systems: A comparative approach*, London, Sage.

Chiesi, L. (2004). *Le inciviltà: Degrado urbano e insicurezza.* In Silmini, R. (Ed.) *La sicurezza urbana.* Bologna: Il Mulino, pp. 129–40.

Cohen, S. (1972). *Folk devils and moral panics.* Harmondsworth, Penguin.

Di Federico, G. (1998). Prosecutorial independence and the democratic requirement of accountability in Italy: Analysis of a deviant case in a comparative perspective. *British Journal of Criminology*, 38(3), 371–87.

Di Federico, G. & Sapignoli, M. (2002). *Processo penale e diritti della difesa.* Rome: Carocci.

Faiella F., Paduanello, M. & Sbraccia, A. (2005). La costruzione dell'identità dell'imputato nel corso della fase dibattimentale. In G. Mosconi and D. Padovan (Eds.), *La fabbrica dei delinquenti. Processo penale e meccanismi di costruzione del condannato* (pp. 58–121). Turin: L'Harmattan Italia.

Garland, D. (2001). *The culture of control: Crime and social order in contemporary society.* Oxford: Oxford University Press.

Goldstein, A.S. & Marcus, M. (1977). The myth of judicial supervision in three "inquisitorial" systems: France, Italy, and Germany. *Yale Law Journal, 87*(1), 240–83.

Grande, E. (2000). Italian criminal justice: Borrowing and resistance. *American Journal of Comparative Law, 48,* 227–60.

Jackson, J. D. (2004). The effect of legal culture and proof in decisions to prosecute. *Law, probability and risk, 3*(2), 109–31.

Lacey, N. (2008). *The prisoners' dilemma: political economy and punishment in contemporary democracies.* Cambridge: Cambridge University Press.

Langbein, J.H. & Weinreb, L. (1978). Continental criminal procedure: myth and reality. *Yale Law Journal, 87*(7), 1549–69.

Marafioti, L. (2008). Italian criminal procedure: A system caught between two traditions. In J. Jackson, M. Langer and P. Tillers (Eds.) *Crime, procedure and evidence in comparative and international context. Essays in honour of Professor Mirjan Damaška* (pp. 81–99). Oxford and Portland: Hart Publishing.

Montana, R. (2009). Paradigms of judicial supervision and co-ordination between police and prosecutors: the Italian case in a comparative perspective. *European Journal of Crime, Criminal Law and Criminal Justice, 17*(4), 309–33.

Muratore, M. G, Tagliacozzo, G. & Federici, A. (Eds.). (2004). *La sicurezza dei cittadini. Reati, vittime, percezione della sicurezza e sistemi di protezione* [Online]. ISTAT informazioni n. 18. Available at: http://www.istat.it/dati/catalogo/20040915_00/La_sicurezza_dei_cittadini.pdf

Nelken, D. (Ed.). (2000). *Contrasting criminal justice*. Aldershot: Ashgate.

—— (2009). Comparing criminal justice: Beyond ethnocentrism and relativism. *European Journal of Criminology, 6*,(4), 291–311.

—— (2010). Making sense of criminal justice. In S. Shoham, P. Knepper and M. Kett (Eds.) *International handbook of criminology* (pp. 60–80). London: Taylor & Francis.

—— (2010a). *Comparative criminal justice: Making sense of difference*. London: Sage.

Nelken, D. & Zanier, L. (2006). Tra norma e prassi: Durata del processo e strategie degli operatori del diritto. *Sociologia del Diritto*, 143–66.

Packer, H. (1968). *The limits of the criminal sanction*. Stanford: Stanford University Press.

Quassoli, F. (1999). Immigrazione uguale criminalità. Rappresentazioni di senso comune e pratiche organizzative degli operatori del diritto. *Rassegna Italiana Di Sociologia, XXX*(1), 43–75.

Sarzotti, C. (2006). *Cultura giuridica e culture della pena*. Turin: L'Harmattan Italia.

—— (2006a). Le procure della Repubblica come attori del campo giuridico-penale. *Studi sulla questione criminale, I*(2), 67–86.

—— (2008). Le procure della Repubblica come attori nel campo penale. In C. Sarzotti (Eds). *Processi di selezione del crimine. Procure della Repubblica e organizzazione giudiziaria* (pp. 1–116). Milan: Giuffrè.

—— (Ed.) (2008a). *Processi di selezione del crimine. Procure della Repubblica e organizzazione giudiziaria*. Milano: Giuffrè.

Solivetti, L. (2010). *Immigration, integration and crime: A cross-national approach*. London: Routledge.

Wacquant, L. (2009a). *Prisons of poverty*. Minneapolis: University of Minnesota Press.

—— (2009b). *Punishing the poor: The neoliberal government of social insecurity*. Durham, NC: Duke University Press.

Part III

Criminology and criminal justice in context

28

Introduction to country assessments

Rosemary Barberet

The purpose of this part of the *Handbook* is to offer detailed case studies of criminology and criminal justice in individual countries from a variety of regions of the world. Native scholars were located to write these chapters and asked to follow a somewhat standard outline. Recognizing that not all information is available for all countries, the authors nevertheless were asked first for thorough background data on each country. This is because the editors believe that research on crime and social control in each country needs to be carefully contextualized. The information requested comprised common national indicators: geographical situation such as size, boundaries, land use, and environmental issues; economic situations such as gross domestic product, poverty, household income, income inequality, and inflation; labor issues such as types of occupations, unemployment, criminal justice budgets, imports, and exports; energy issues; government type and stability including administrative divisions of justice (i.e. executive, legislative, and judicial branches), political groups, participation in international organizations; state of communications (telephones, radios, television, internet); transportation (i.e. railways, highways); and people, including population size, age structure, growth/death rates, migration issues, gender ratios, cultural groups, nationality, ethnicity, religions, languages, and education. Where possible the authors were asked to relate the contextual background information to opportunities or impediments to crime.

The most salient part of each chapter, of course, deals with crime, criminology, and criminal justice. Authors were asked to describe the administration of justice in their country (structural arrangement of police, court system, and correctional system), along with how justice is handled (primary types of justice, major social control strategies, primary strategies in integrating criminal offenders); criminology, including major research topics in the past five years and the influential research figures associated with these research initiatives; major methodological strategies and an assessment of these research methods and their relative dominance in the country's criminology research community; major data sources; key research institutions and responsibilities; and funding sources. Finally, authors were asked to identify five future research questions for students and young scholars to pursue for this country.

The countries selected, presented in the text in alphabetical order, vary by their income (GNI per capita), including those at the high end (e.g. Australia, Canada, Estonia, Great Britain, Hong Kong, Italy, South Korea, Netherlands), middle (e.g. Brazil, Chile, Mexico, Russian Federation, Turkey), and low (e.g. Cambodia, People's Republic of China, Colombia, Ghana, India, Nigeria,

Sierra Leone). Thus, students or scholars can use Part III of the book not only to familiarize themselves with each country as a case study, but to contrast them in a comparative approach. This introduction serves to look at the chapters as a whole in order to identify cross-cutting themes in terms of crime problems, criminal justice dilemmas, or research topics.

First, one notices the interplay between structural conditions of countries and crime opportunities. Borders with other countries, particularly landlocked or conflictive countries, sometimes facilitate transnational and international crime. Thus, Markina notes in Chapter 35 that the organized crime situation in Estonia is mainly due to its proximity to the Russian Federation. Developments in transportation and communication foster opportunities for crime. Soudijn (Chapter 44) notes that the role of the Netherlands as the gateway to Europe facilitates smuggling and trafficking through its large transportation hubs: the port of Rotterdam and Schiphol Airport. Xu (Chapter 38) notes that when China relaxed its policy towards visiting Hong Kong in 2003, illegal immigration decreased, but two different types of cross-border crimes emerged: (1) Hong Kong juveniles traveling to Shenzhen to use drugs, where they are cheaper and easier to obtain; and (2) the influx of mainland Chinese women in the sex industry of Hong Kong. Jang and Choi (Chapter 41) explain that South Korea's geopolitical situation, bordering with China, Russia, and Japan, facilitates transnational crimes such as drug trafficking, illegal migration, and human trafficking.

War, income inequality, ethnic tensions, land ownership patterns, and educational deficits are reasons for out-migration, urban overcrowding, discontent, and youth unemployment; all facilitators for crime. Poornachandra (Chapter 39) notes that extreme poverty in rural India is a factor associated with a number of relatively unique criminal phenomena, including female infanticide, feticide, family suicide, and murder of family members. Warburton (Chapter 47) explains how migration from rural areas to Freetown due to the war has created "a *fait accompli* – unemployment, vagabondry, theft, burglary, prostitution, inadequate social services, and overwhelmed law enforcement agencies" (p. 513).

The level of development of the discipline of criminology varies, of course, across the sample of countries in this section. In some countries (e.g. Britain, Australia, Canada), criminology is well developed both in academia as well as in the governmental sphere, where research and statistics units provide data and disseminate descriptive, explanatory, and evaluative studies. At the other extreme, the discipline of criminology is next to non-existent and virtually no governmental resources are allocated towards data and research on crime or criminal justice. There may only be a handful of criminologists, most of whom have been trained abroad. In these scenarios, research may be conducted by émigrés in the diaspora, by visiting criminologists who study the country on site or from abroad (e.g. Sierra Leone), or by native scholars who are not criminologists but social scientists from other disciplines (e.g. Mexico, Chile). Important exceptions to these scenarios are countries with strong public agencies that dominate criminological research, such as the Korean Institute of Criminology or the Turkish Police Academy.

In several countries, empirical criminology has been subordinate to law. China and Mexico are examples. This relationship has stifled its development. In countries where local funding is scarce or non-existent, funding from development agencies (e.g. USAID, DFID) or intergovernmental organizations (e.g. European Union, World Bank, UNODC) is often crucial in encouraging research, especially in the area of emerging crime threats or the reform of criminal justice administration (e.g. Estonia, Nigeria). Data availability is paramount. For many of the countries featured in this part, chapter authors lament that data about crime and criminal justice are either not available, or there are grave doubts as to their validity and reliability.

The presence and importance of corruption is a more salient theme in this volume than in Elmer Johnson's 1983 edition. But so is its study and denouncement. Certainly, there is an awakening in this volume to the fact that crime must be broadly conceptualized, to encompass corruption (e.g. Russia, Cambodia, Italy), international crime (e.g. Cambodia, Sierra Leone) and also violations of human rights (e.g. Nigeria, Colombia). Thus, many of the chapters access human rights reports as sources of information and research (e.g. Colombia, Cambodia, Nigeria).

The globalization of crime and criminal justice is evidenced by the fact that many chapters in Part III feature very similar crime problems, and the exchange of terms such as restorative justice, community corrections, and community policing (e.g. Britain, Australia, Canada, Estonia, Colombia, Chile, Sierra Leone, Nigeria, Italy, Turkey, China) means that policy transfer between countries, especially in terms of the administration of justice, is becoming more frequent. Certainly, the nexus between research and policy is problematic in most countries. Solecki, Crutcher, and Mihorean (Chapter 31) explain the difficulty of crime policymaking in Canada, where although laws may be uniform across the nation, the combination of a small population over an expansive territory means that crime problems vary enormously throughout Canada. Heskia Tornquist (Chapter 33) notes that despite research input, the change from inquisitorial to adversarial justice in Chile and the implantation of restorative and community-based programs have presented great challenges to the national mindset. Serra (Chapter 40) notes that Italian criminology has focused too much on crime and the offender, and that there is a need for criminologists to supplement that research with empirical research on the criminal justice system. Arroyo Juarez and Martinez Solares (Chapter 42) offer a foreboding conclusion that might well apply to many countries in this part in present or the near future:

> the high politicization of crime and control issues by political parties and victims organizations creates a narrow logic based on the sense of urgency, in which the high level of public visibility and short time gains are more important than evidence-based approaches to crime reduction. (p. 460)

Chukwuma (Chapter 43) ends his chapter offering an optimistic solution for the development of the discipline of criminology in Nigeria, which may also increase the policy impact of criminological findings: collaboration on comparative research projects with criminologists from around the world. It is in this spirit that the reader is encouraged to delve into Part III of our volume, and imagine the future of international criminology.

29

Australia

The state of criminology

Judy Putt and Jade Lindley

Introduction

A relatively safe and affluent country by world standards, Australia has witnessed a decline in property crime in the past decade. Trends in violent crime are less clear cut, with a decline in homicide rates but an increase in reported assault and sexual assault (Bricknell, 2008), and public debate often centers on violence, alcohol, and young people. Some of the trends in recorded crime and perceptions of safety are believed to be influenced by worldwide phenomena, such as globalization and the rapid evolution in information and communication technology (ICT). This has been apparent in the policy attention given to Australia's vulnerability to terrorist attack, cyber-facilitated crime such as fraud and online child exploitation, and transnational and organized crime. It is also expected that crime will be affected by events such as the global financial crisis and the impact, over time, of climate change. This chapter gives a short overview of Australia's unique economic circumstances, socio-demographic character, location, and governance to provide context for the summary of crime and justice research in the past five years, and to help explain areas of future research interest.

Infrastructure

Australia is the world's smallest continent and largest island nation, with a sizeable landmass of 7,692,024 square kilometers and 34,218 kilometers of coastline. It is in the Asia-Pacific region with Indonesia, Papua New Guinea, and New Zealand nearby. More than 85 percent of Australians live in coastal locations and over 70 percent of the population live in major cities (ABS, 2008a), all of which, with the exception of the nation's capital, are located on the coast. In the less populated interior, the land is used for a variety of purposes including farming, mining, and to a lesser extent forestry, with public national parks and reserves making up almost 10 percent of the country (Australian Government Geoscience Australia, 2009).

Australia's real gross domestic product has grown by an annual average of 3.5 percent over the past decade, to an amount of AUD$1,095,370 in 2007/8, although this has slowed with the global financial crisis and its aftermath. The inflation rate, according to the consumer price index increase, is around 3 percent per year. Australia's wealth is largely from its export of mineral resources and agricultural products, with AUD$190.2 billion generated each year in exports to countries such as Japan, China, the United States, and the Republic of Korea (ABS, 2008a; CIA,

2009). It has a small and declining manufacturing sector, and AUD$193.3 billion worth of goods and services are annually imported, primarily from China (CIA, 2009). Australia is a net exporter of energy, and in 2005/6 Australia's total primary energy production was estimated at 16,729 petajoules of which black coal constituted almost one half (49 percent), followed by uranium (28 percent), natural gas (10 percent), and crude oil (5 percent), with total domestic energy consumption accounting for less than a third of this (ABS, 2008a).

Australia has a highly educated, skilled workforce of more than 10 million people, with the majority employed in the services sector (75 percent), and the rest in industry (20 percent), agriculture (4 percent), and mining (1 percent) (ABS, 2008a; CIA, 2009). During the previous decade the unemployment rate declined to 3.9 percent, though since the global financial crisis it has climbed and reached 5.8 percent in October 2009 (ABS, 2009a). Literacy rates among Australians are high (99 percent) and attendance at school is compulsory until at least 15 years of age. School retention rates have increased rapidly since the mid-1960s, to approximately 80 percent (ABS, 2008a).

The majority of Australians enjoy a good standard of living by world standards. In 2005/6 the average household income was AUD$644 per week (ABS, 2008a). However, since the 1980s there has been an increase in income disparity, with the wealthiest 20 percent holding more than two thirds of Australia's wealth, compared to the poorest 20 percent holding only 1 percent of the wealth (ABS, 2005a). The Gini coefficient for 2007/8 was 0.319, up from 0.297 in 2003/4 (ABS, 2009a; ABS, 2008a). There is also a spatial dimension to the distribution of household wealth, with remote and rural locations, and particular suburbs in the city having much lower average household incomes (ABS, 2008a).

Australia is a constitutional democracy with little corruption in government or business; in 2008, Australia ranked ninth in the Transparency International Corruption Perception Index (2008) and tenth in the democracy index by *The Economist* (2008). A former British colony, Australia's political system is influenced by the Westminster model of government and the country has an adversarial system of criminal justice. It is a federation with six states and two territories, and under its constitution specific powers are allocated to the national federal government with all other powers exercised by the state and territory governments. Elections occur every three to four years and voting is compulsory for all enrolled citizens 18 years and over. Australia is a member of many international and regional organizations, and has ratified the main United Nations conventions and protocols relating to crime. Much of its overseas aid, international law enforcement, and legal cooperation concentrate on the Asia-Pacific region.

Trends in communications in Australia in recent times – personal and business use of mobile phones and the internet – mirror those globally. Nowadays around three quarters of the population own the former and a similar proportion are home internet users (ABS, 2007; ABS, 2008b). The mass media comprises a mix of public-funded and commercial television and radio networks. Almost all Australians own at least one television in their homes and a code of practice guides programming in the free-to-air sector. A recent national survey of social attitudes found that the mass media was the most common source of information on crime and justice issues (Roberts and Indermaur, 2009).

Australia has a network of roads and major rail routes and is linked domestically and internationally through air and maritime services. Air transport is preferred over sea or rail for long distances by passengers within Australia (ABS, 2008a), though 97 percent of international trade between Australia and trading partners is by sea (LINC, 2007). Since the 9/11 attacks and Australia's military involvement in Iraq and Afghanistan, all Australian airlines and airports, the shipping industry, and seaports have increased measures to minimize the risk of terrorist attacks and hijacking.

Car ownership has dramatically increased over the past 50 years and more than 75 percent of Australians use a privately owned vehicle as their normal mode of transport, as opposed to public transport (ABS, 2005b). One of Australia's high-volume property crimes – motor vehicle theft – has declined over the past ten years (NMVTRC, 2009). Priorities for national law enforcement cooperation include the cross-jurisdictional re-birthing of stolen cars, and intelligence assessments of vulnerabilities in domestic transport sectors, including the trucking industry.

People

In 2009, Australia had a population of approximately 22 million, with projections that the population will increase to approximately 27 million by 2026 (ABS, 2008c). The 2006 census showed most of the population aged between 15 and 64 years (67.5 percent), and a median age of 36.9 years (ABS, 2008a). The population is ageing and it is predicted that approximately 24 percent will be over 65 by 2056, an increase of more than 11 percent (ABS, 2008c).

Australia's Indigenous people comprise 2.5 percent of the total population. Over half live in cities but compared with non-Indigenous people, they are more likely to live in rural and remote areas. Since colonization over two hundred years ago, there have been major waves of immigration, mainly from Britain. As a result, English is the national and most widely spoken language. After World War Two, there was a significant increase in migrants from European nations and in the past three decades there has been an increase in migrants from the Asia-Pacific region. At the 2006 census, nearly one quarter of the Australian population was born overseas (ABS, 2008a). In 2005/6 Australia had a net migration increase of 134,600; 17.7 percent from the United Kingdom; 14.5 percent from New Zealand; 8.6 percent from India; and 8 percent from China (ibid.). The majority of the population indicate they belong to one of the Christian churches, although nearly one third professed to have no religion or did not adequately respond to the question (ibid.).

With a comprehensive social security system as well as publicly funded health care, Australia's population, in general, enjoys high standards of health care. Life expectancy on average for Australian females is 82.6 years and males 78.7 years, although Indigenous Australian rates are ten years lower than the national average (ABS, 2009b).

Administration of justice

The Australian criminal justice system is primarily the responsibility of the states and territories, and they have the power to enact criminal legislation specific to their jurisdiction. Each state and territory has its own police service, courts, and corrective services, and there is a federal police service that has responsibility to tackle transnational crime and threats to national security. National victim-based crime data show that the most common crime is theft (excluding theft of motor vehicles). With just under half a million victims in 2007, assault is the most common violent crime (AIC, 2008). In 2007/8, the total government expenditure on crime and justice was AUD$10.7 billion, with the bulk spent on police (67 percent), followed by corrections (23 percent) and civil and criminal courts (11 percent). This expenditure is estimated to be less than one fifth of what is spent on health and about one fifth of what is spent on education (AGPC, 2009).

There are three main tiers of courts in each state and territory, with the magistrates' or local court dealing with summary offences and minor civil matters, whilst the district or county courts handle most criminal trials. There are offices of public prosecution in every jurisdiction and at a federal level, and publicly funded legal aid is available for defendants on low incomes. The majority of cases in both local (86 percent) and higher courts (79 percent) result in guilty outcomes and the most common sentence is a fine. Overall, less than one in ten adult and child defendants receive a custodial order as their principal sentence (AIC, 2008). Children, who in all but one state are defined at those aged under 18, are treated separately through children's courts and juvenile detention centers.

The rate of adult imprisonment has increased steadily over the past 25 years, with over 27,000 people imprisoned in 2007, whilst the number of persons on community corrections orders has stayed relatively steady, with a daily average of just over 50,000 (AIC, 2008). Correctional services include a wide array of education, work, and life skill programs, and treatment programs are available in prison and in the community that address violence, sex offending, and substance abuse.

Key policy or theoretical trends in the past 30 years that have directly influenced or complemented the traditional administration of justice in Australia have included restorative justice, therapeutic jurisprudence, rehabilitation through diversion or reintegration, crime prevention, and performance measurement.

Over the past three decades, Australian governments have invested in crime prevention and reduction, with grants programs to foster partnerships between service providers (mostly police), non-government organizations, and local communities. Community grants have targeted interventions based on community and developmental crime prevention principles. Situational crime prevention strategies combined with hot spot or problem-oriented policing have had a marked increase, particularly in relation to the prevention of motor vehicle theft, residential burglaries, and public disorder, including violent behavior associated with alcohol in licensed premises (Graham and Homel, 2008).

The past decade has witnessed a rapid expansion of police and court drug diversion programs, which focused initially on police diversion of people apprehended for minor drug offenses. Over time they have been extended to enable police and court diversion for more serious matters and/or more serious drug users.

An alternative to the traditional court system, group conferencing has become more commonplace, especially in the juvenile justice system, over the past 20 years. Influenced by the parallel trend to recognize victim rights and the need for victim support, conferencing is a form of restorative justice pioneered in Australia during the 1990s that involves the negotiation of a decision to which all parties agree (O'Connell and Hayes, 2009).

The first Australian specialty courts were drug courts, but over time there has been a proliferation specializing in the underlying issues or crimes (family violence, mental health, alcohol) or focused on a particular group (e.g. Indigenous Australians). As yet, the volume of cases dealt with by such courts is only a small fraction of the total volume handled by the mainstream courts (Bartels, 2009).

The increase in private security over the past 20 years has resulted in the number of personnel employed in the sector now outstripping the publicly funded policing services (Prenzler *et al.*, 2009). Over a 30-year period an increasing proportion of prisons have been privatized, with about one-quarter of the 119 prisons across the nation now run by private companies (AGPC, 2009).

Performance measurement and evidence-based accountability have become increasingly important to governments, including the criminal justice policy arena. The Productivity Commission informs policy review and development by providing an annual report on government services, including justice (policing, courts, and corrections). Re-offending is a dominant but often contested measure of performance for the evaluation of criminal justice interventions and is used by the Productivity Commission as one of its performance indicators for corrections (Payne, 2007).

Criminology

The criminology research community is small, comprising key academic departments and government-funded research centers and roughly equally divided between critical and applied criminologists. Most research is influenced by major studies overseas, especially in the United Kingdom and North America, in terms of theoretical frameworks, research questions, and findings. However, there is a recognition that overseas developments may not apply to the Australian context and that it is important to tease out what can be learned from international research but then identify the specific explanations and interpretations relevant to Australia.

In the past five years, research on crime in Australia has focused on the more common types of crime, offending careers, risk factors for victimization, and monitoring trends. A persistent theme underlying many studies has been the influence of socioeconomic disadvantage, through the analysis of the spatial distribution of key crimes, and the risk of offending and victimization amongst socially distinct groups (such as Indigenous Australians, migrants, and unemployed or drug-dependent persons). The range of topics has broadened during this period because of more investment in evaluations of criminal justice reforms and more research on ICT-facilitated and transnational crime.

The decrease in Australia's property crime in the past ten years has lagged behind other major Western industrial countries, and only Britain seems to have a comparable increase in recorded violent crime. An update of a study that estimated the costs of crime in Australia suggested few changes, except for the greater cost of fraud (Rollings 2008). Efforts to model and forecast trends in crime and the implications for the criminal justice system have been limited to a number of exploratory studies to model the criminal justice system to forecast prisoner numbers and to model drug markets.

A number of studies have examined the contribution of various factors to the documented decline in property crime, including an examination of the heroin shortage in Australia since 2000 and its impact on robbery rates (Moffat *et al.*, 2005), and the relationship between rates of unemployment and property crime (Lee and Holoviak, 2006). Although there has been no major research that seeks to explain violent crime trends, various studies and ongoing data collections relate to factors assumed to impact on violence. These include surveys of community attitudes to and experiences of violence and levels of reporting to police, gun control, and drug and alcohol use and dependence. There is a robust interdisciplinary research community involved in research on drug and alcohol issues in Australia, with a significant investment in national data collections including a national drug household survey conducted every three years. The drug and alcohol trends that have been of greatest interest in terms of their impact on criminal activity have been the increased availability and misuse of alcohol, the decline in heroin use, and the growth in the domestic methamphetamine market and its implications for organized crime within Australia.

Geographical information systems using police data have underpinned studies that seek to identify rural or suburban "hotspots" of criminal activity (examples of mapping of crime in local areas can be found at the New South Wales Bureau of Crime Statistics and Research (BOCSAR) and South Australia Office of Crime Statistics and Research (OCSAR) websites) and to assess the efficacy of policing initiatives, especially those that target repeat residential burglaries, and public disorder and violence in and around licensed premises (for example, Donnelly *et al.*, 2006, and papers on burglary research at http://www.law.uwa.edu.au/research/crc).

Research on violence has specifically addressed homicide, sexual assault, violence by young people, armed robbery, and domestic or family violence (see Australian Domestic and Family Violence Clearinghouse at http://www.austdvclearinghouse.unsw.edu.au/). Gender and race are important themes that underlie or inform violence research in Australia, especially given the risk to women and children from domestic and family violence. Although the overrepresentation of Indigenous people as victims and offenders in the criminal justice system has been recognized for several decades, recent government inquiries have focused on violence and child abuse in remote Indigenous communities and alcohol exacerbated violence. However, criminological research has continued to concentrate primarily on documenting and explaining the over-representation and assessing system reforms (for example, Behrendt *et al.* 2009; Blagg 2008) with few ethnographic or in-depth qualitative studies being undertaken in remote or rural Australia.

In terms of offending, key concerns have been whether young people are becoming more violent, whether females are offending more, and whether recent migrants are more likely to be victimized or to engage in criminal activity. Ethnicity has also been the subject of scrutiny because of well-publicized riots in Sydney in 2005 and of fears that members of certain communities will become radicalized to the point of committing terrorist attacks. Australia is generally considered to be a tolerant and culturally diverse society, but highly publicized events, such as the riots which were reported as racially fuelled, and recent assaults on Indian students, have undermined such perceptions. There has been a noticeable increase in research funding for a range of related topics, but little has been published to date.

The implications of the rapidly changing ICT environment, particularly how it facilitates criminal activity, is of major interest (Choo *et al.*, 2007). There has been research into interpersonal violence and exploitation, such as stalking and online child grooming, and on how ICT has changed the commission of fraud and other economic crime against individuals, governments, and business. It is anticipated that the global financial crisis will increase the risk of economic crime resulting in more identity fraud, internet-facilitated consumer fraud, and online gambling, and it is likely that there will be a rise in research on these and related topics.

The detection and prosecution of transnational crimes, including those facilitated through ICT, poses considerable challenges, resulting in a series of studies on international law enforcement (Grabosky, 2009) and in reviews of regional vulnerabilities and responses to transnational crimes, including drug trafficking (McCusker, 2008), people trafficking (Joudo Larsen *et al.*, 2009), money laundering (Stamp and Walker, 2004), and the illegal timber trade (Schloenhardt, 2008).

It has been primarily intelligence agencies that conduct assessments on organized crime network activities and prevalence and these are rarely released into the public domain. However, the national police intelligence agency has released some unclassified information on the estimated 39 active outlaw motorcycle gangs in Australia (ACC, 2009). Other research refers to domestic and international organized crime involvement in the fishing industry (Putt and Anderson, 2007), property crime markets (a strategic intelligence assessment) (CMC, 2009), and drug markets (McKetin *et al.*, 2005). Recent legislative responses to domestic organized crime groups are likely to trigger further research on their impact and will build on past work, such as the review of legislation in the Asia-Pacific region (Schloenhardt, 2009).

Considerable criminological research in Australia has been directed at evaluating the impact and effectiveness of innovations and changes to the criminal justice system. Policing initiatives that have been assessed include hotspot policing, operational performance reviews, responses to domestic violence and sexual assault, and police drug diversion. There have been major commitments to partnership research that involves police and researchers collaborating on better models of community policing (e.g. see the Nexus policing project at http://www.police.vic.gov.au), and on performance measurement of drug law enforcement (Willis *et al.*, 2006). A major program framed by developmental crime prevention principles to tackle disadvantage in an area in Brisbane involved a partnership between academics and a major non-governmental organization (Freiberg *et al*;, 2007), and is a rare example of a long-term evaluation of a community-based crime prevention initiative.

Nearly all forms of specialist, problem-oriented courts have been evaluated over the past decade (Sarre and O'Connell, 2009). Measures have included the timing and level of subsequent reoffending by participants, and, with conferencing, the participants' satisfaction with the process. Another strand of research has examined law reform, such as changes to sentencing options, and the impact of technological change on the court process, including jury understanding of contemporary forensic evidence and the impact on juries of videotaped or CCTV-relayed victim testimony.

Most correctional research has continued to assess rehabilitation programs (for example, Howells *et al.*, 2004), treatment regimes, and risk assessment tools. Increasingly there has been interest in support and supervision of offenders in the community, including throughcare and post release, prompted in part by research showing high returns to prison and poor health outcomes for ex-prisoners. As there has been a sharp increase in the number of adults and juveniles remanded in custody in recent years, various studies have explored the impact of changes to bail and sentencing legislation and practice.

Another area of interest is crime against the environment and/or natural resource crime from a criminological perspective rather than the more traditional accounts of environmental law and regulatory regimes. So far, mainly theoretical work has been published (White, 2009), but there has been a growing awareness of pressures on natural resources caused by overexploitation, drought, and climate change, and the likelihood of increased vulnerability to criminality and the impact of crime as resources become more scarce and valuable.

Australia relies heavily on administrative data from national and state levels, with the Australian Institute of Criminology (AIC) and state-based research agencies undertaking and reporting on additional analysis of their own data. Several university-based research centres have built linked datasets across elements of the criminal justice system that enable tracking across time of offender involvement in the system and contact with service providers. Stand-alone studies of administrative data are typically conducted at a state and territory level, and usually the analysis is *time* based (time series, survival analysis), or *spatially* based, such as the mapping of police-recorded crime.

National population-based surveys are conducted regularly, some part of international surveys such as the International Crime Victimization Survey. The most comprehensive national survey on crime victimization and perceptions of safety is undertaken every three years and several national surveys, such as the national drug household survey and the Australian social attitudes survey, include crime-related questions. Major one-off surveys have examined computer-enabled crime against business, farm crime, and crimes against small business. An important component of much research is surveys or interviews of policy and practitioner stakeholders, and these can vary in scale and scope, with an increasing reliance on online questionnaires to research purposive or random samples. These are often a critical component of process evaluations and reviews. A key feature of much survey analysis is to isolate or predict individual or collective risk factors or to examine correlations between attitudes, experience, and behavior.

Much research relies on small-scale, qualitative studies, especially if the topic relates to sensitive or complex subjects, such as family violence or community safety in a neighborhood or community. Often a mixed method is employed, with surveys and official data complementing in-depth interviews with victims, offenders, and other critical stakeholders. Few studies can be construed as a classic randomized trial; the best known being undertaken in the 1990s and involved a comparison of the traditional court process with the conference process. A number of studies have employed a mock court setting, with actors and volunteers to test out the understanding, attitudes, and decision making of juries. Moreover, several systematic reviews have been undertaken under the aegis of the Crime and Justice Coordinating Group within the Campbell Collaboration (for example, Mazerolle *et al.*, 2007).

National administrative data collections are maintained by the Australian Bureau of Statistics (ABS) on major crime types (victim-based police data), courts, and corrections, and the Productivity Commission uses these and other data sources for its annual reports on government services. The Australian Crime Commission reports annually on police arrests for drug crime and drug seizures, and the Australian Institute of Health and Welfare (AIHW) maintains a national juvenile justice collection and a national data collection on child protection. The AIC maintains nine national data collections that monitor major crime types (homicide, armed robbery, and firearms theft) and aspects of the criminal justice system, including deaths in police and prison custody. Offender-based data are generated through interviews with police detainees, as part of the AIC's Drug Use Monitoring in Australia program, and offender-based administrative data are collected and reported on in a number of jurisdictions. State and territory justice and corrections departments often have internal research units which report on their own data. And there are other state-based agencies, such as sentencing councils, that generate research and statistics. A recent development has been online data analysis (see, for example, the AIC drugs and offending data tool at http://data.aic.gov.au/duma/duma.html and the BOCSAR data tools at http://www.bocsar.nsw.gov.au/lawlink/bocsar/ll_bocsar.nsf/pages/bocsar_onlinequeries).

National population-based survey data are held by the main collecting agency and include data on experiences of crime and perceptions of safety (ABS and AIC), community attitudes to crime and justice and to violence against women (AIC), public confidence in police, and drug use (AIHW). One-off survey data are held in universities and in public research agencies, and except where survey data are stored in the Australian Social Science Data Archives, access to administrative and survey data has to be sought from the relevant agency, university, or researcher.

Government-funded crime and justice research institutes that maintain statistical collections and undertake research include the AIC, BOCSAR, and OCSAR. Crime and justice research centers within the university sector include the Crime Research Centre at the University of Western Australia; the Key Centre for Ethics, Law, Justice, and Governance at Griffith University; the Tasmanian Institute of Law Enforcement Studies at the University of Tasmania; the Centre for Transnational Crime Prevention at Wollongong University; and the Regulatory Institutions Network at the Australian National University. The Centre of Excellence for Policing and Security (CEPS), a major collaboration of researchers based in four Australian universities and funded from 2007 for four years, represents a significant investment in research on policing and security. In addition, there are a number of criminology teaching and research departments or units in the university sector, including University of Sydney, University of Melbourne, James Cook University, Monash University, Flinders University, the University of Queensland, the University of Western Sydney, Charles Sturt University, Murdoch University, Bond University, and Edith Cowan University (see http://www.aic.gov.au/criminal_justice_system/resources/criminologycourses.aspx for a list of courses).

There are three main areas of funding for criminological research in Australia: government, through contracted or in-house research; academic research through the Criminology Research Council (CRC) and the Australian Research Council (ARC); and the private sector. The ARC funds the bulk of academic research in Australia and the proportion awarded to criminology is relatively small. The CRC consists of representatives of the Australian state and territory governments and administers the Criminology Research Fund, which has a total budget of less than AUD$600,000 a year. It has supported a wide range of studies (see http://www.criminologyresearchcouncil.gov.au). Another joint government research fund, the National Drug Law Enforcement Research Fund (NDLERF), has a budget of approximately AUD$1 million a year. Research on policing has received the most funding support over the past five years, including ARC funding for CEPS and grants to university/police partnership projects, and

NDLERF-funded research. The private sector in Australia does not have a strong tradition of funding criminological research, although there are examples of insurance companies, for example, funding studies.

Future research questions

- Post-global financial crisis what kind of crime should Australia address, and how?
- How will the impact of climate change affect the types of crimes, crime hot spots, time of year/day when crimes are commonly committed and by whom?
- Should Australia seek to move into an integrated justice system with one federal set of laws and policing and justice administration?
- Compared with other Western industrial nations, is Australia more or less vulnerable to transnational and organized crime?
- What are the distinct characteristics of Australia that might contribute to what seems to be the relatively high rates of interpersonal violence?

Key websites for research reports and statistical data

Australian Bureau of Statistics: http://www.abs.gov.au
Australian Government Productivity Commission: http://www.pc.gov.au
Australian Institute of Criminology: http://www.aic.gov.au
Crime Research Centre: http://www.law.uwa.edu.au/research/crc
Criminology Research Council: http://www.criminologyresearchcouncil.gov.au
National Drug Law Enforcement Research Fund: http://www.ndlerf.gov.au
New South Wales Bureau of Crime Statistics and Research: http://www.bocsar.nsw.gov.au
South Australia Office of Crime Statistics and Research: http://www.ocsar.sa.gov.au

References

Australian Bureau of Statistics (ABS) (2005a). *Household income and income distribution, Australia, 2003/4.* Canberra, Australia. Online at http://www.abs.gov.au/AUSSTATS/abs@.nsf/ProductsbyReleaseDate/F509E18B84372C25CA25732A00211901?OpenDocument (accessed November 24, 2010).

—— (2005b). *Year Book Australia, 2005:* Use of urban public transport in Australia. Canberra, Australia. Online at http://www.abs.gov.au/Ausstats/ABS@.nsf/Previousproducts/1301.0Feature%20Article292005?opendocument&tabname = Summary&prodno = 1301.0&issue = 2005&num = &view = (accessed November 24, 2010).

—— (2007). *Australian Social Trends, 2007.* Canberra, Australia. Online at http://www.abs.gov.au/AUSSTATS/abs@.nsf/0/0485BB5550FE5799CA25732C00207C77?opendocument (accessed November 24, 2010).

—— (2008a). *Year Book of Australia 2008.* Canberra, Australia. Online at http://www.abs.gov.au/AUSSTATS/abs@.nsf/bb8db737e2af84b8ca2571780015701e/831FDBA1C86119DDCA2573D20010524E?opendocument (accessed November 24, 2010).

—— (2008b). *Household use of information technology, Australia 2007/8.* Released 18 December 2008. Canberra, Australia. Online at http://www.abs.gov.au/AUSSTATS/abs@.nsf/mf/8146.0 (accessed November 24, 2010).

—— (2008c). *Population Projections, Australia, 2006 to 2101.* Canberra, Australia. http://www.abs.gov.au/Ausstats/abs@.nsf/mf/3222.0 (accessed November 24, 2010).

—— (2009a). *Labour force, Australia,* September 2009. Canberra, Australia. Online at http://www.abs.gov.au/AUSSTATS/abs@.nsf/mf/6202.0 (accessed November 24, 2010).

—— (2009b). *Experimental life tables for Aboriginal and Torres Strait Islander Australians, 2005–7.* Canberra, Australia. Online at http://www.abs.gov.au/AUSSTATS/abs@.nsf/Lookup/3302.0.55.003Main+Features12005%E2%80%932007?OpenDocument (accessed November 24, 2010).

Australian Crime Commission (ACC) (2009). High risk crime groups – special investigation: Serious and Organised Crime National Intelligence Task Force. Canberra, Australia. Online at http://www.crimecommission.gov.au/media/faq/org_crime.htm

Australian Government Geoscience Australia 2009. Education: Australian land tenure 2002. Canberra, Australia. http://www.ga.gov.au/education/geoscience-basics/land-tenure.html (accessed November 24, 2010).

Australia Government Productivity Commission (AGPC) (2009). Report on government services 2009. Canberra, Australia. Online at http://www.pc.gov.au/gsp/reports/rogs/2009 (accessed November 24, 2010).

Australian Institute of Criminology (AIC) (2008). *Australian crime: facts and figures 2008*. Canberra, Australia: AIC.

Bartels, L.(2009). Challenges in mainstreaming specialty courts. *Trends and issues in crime and criminal justice*, no. 383. Canberra, Australia: AIC.

Behrendt, L., Cunneen, C., and Libesman, T. (2009). (Eds) *Indigenous legal relations in Australia*. Melbourne, Australia: Oxford University Press.

Blagg, H. (2008). *Crime, Aboriginality and the decolonisation of justice*. Sydney, Australia: Hawkins Press.

Bricknell, S. (2008). Trends in violent crime. *Trends and issues in crime and criminal justice*, no. 359. Canberra, Australia: AIC.

Central Intelligence Agency (CIA) (2009). *Factbook. Australia*. Washington, United States of America.

Choo, K-K. R., Smith, R., and McCusker, R. (2007). *Future directions in technology-enabled crime 2007–9*. Research and public policy series, no. 78. Canberra, Australia: AIC.

Crime and Misconduct Commission (CMC) (2009). Organised property crime markets in Queensland: a strategic assessment. *Crime Bulletin Series* no. 9, June. Online at http://www.cmc.qld.gov.au (accessed November 24, 2010).

Donnelly, N., Poynton, S., Weatherburn, D., Bamford, E., and Nottage, J. (2006). Liquor outlet concentrations and alcohol-related neighbourhood problems. *Alcohol Studies Bulletin*, no. 8, April. Sydney Australia: NSWBCSR and AER.

Grabosky, P. (2009) (Ed). *Community policing and peacekeeping*. Baco Raton, Florida: CRC Press.

Graham, K. and Homel, R. (2008). *Raising the bar: preventing aggression in and around bars, pubs and clubs*. Cullompton, UK: Willan Publishing.

Freiberg, K., Homel, R., and Lamb, C. (2007). The pervasive impact of poverty on children: tackling family adversity and promoting child development through the pathways to prevention project. In A. France and R. Homel (Eds.) *Pathways and crime prevention: theory, policy and practice*, pp. 226–46. Cullompton, UK: Willan Publishing.

Howells, K., Heseltine, K., Sarre, R., Davey, L., and Day, A. (2004). Correctional offender rehabilitation programs: the national picture in Australia (4/02–03). Online at http://www.criminologyresearchcouncil.gov.au (accessed November 24, 2010).

Joudo Larsen, J., Lindley, J., and Putt, J. (2009). *Trafficking in persons report July 2008 – December 2009*. Monitoring report no. 6. Canberra, Australia: AIC.

Lee, D. and Holoviak, S. (2006). Unemployment and crime: an empirical investigation. *Applied Economics Letters 2006*. Department of Economics, Shippensburg University, Shippensburg, USA (13): 805–10.

Logistics Information and Navigation Centre (LINC) 2007. Aviation/air Transportation. Online at http://www.the-linc.com.au/Home/WA/IndustrySectors/MaritimeSeaTransportation/tabid/1085/language/en-US/Default.aspx (accessed November 24, 2010).

McCusker, R. (2008). *The precursor chemical trade environment in Oceania*. Research and public policy series, no. 96. Canberra, Australia: AIC.

McKetin, R., McLaren, J., and Kelly, E. (2005). *The Sydney methamphetamine market: patterns of supply, use, personal harms and social consequences* Monograph 13, National Drug Law Enforcement Research Fund, South Australia.

Mazerolle, L., Soole, D. W., and Rombouts, S. (2007). Street-level drug law enforcement: a meta-analytic review. Campbell Systematic Reviews 2007: 2. Online at http://www.campbellcollaboration.org/library.php (accessed November 24, 2010).

Moffatt, S., Weatherburn, D., and Donnelly, N. (2005). What caused the recent drop in property crime? *Crime and Justice Bulletin*, no. 85. Sydney, Australia: NSW Bureau of Crime Statistics and Research.

National Motor Vehicle Theft Reduction Council Inc (NMVTRC) (2009). Carsafe: quick stats. Melbourne, Australia. Online at http://ncars.on.net/analyse.asp?p=quick (accessed November 24, 2010).

O'Connell, M. and Hayes, H.(2009). Chapter 19: Victims, criminal justice and restorative justice. In H. Hayes and T. Prenzler (eds.) *An introduction to crime and criminology*, 2nd edn. Australia: Pearson Education.

Payne, J. (2007). *Recidivism in Australia: findings and future research.* Research and public policy series, no. 97. Canberra, Australia: AIC.

Prenzler, T., Earle, K., and Sarre, R. (2009). Private security in Australia: trends and key characteristics. *Trends and issues in crime and criminal justice*, no. 374. Canberra, Australia: AIC.

Putt, J. and Anderson, K. (2007). *A national study of crime in the fishing industry.* Research and public policy series, no. 76. Canberra, Australia: AIC.

Roberts, L. and Indermaur, D. (2009). *What Australians think about crime and justice: results from the 2007 survey of social attitudes.* Research and public policy series, no. 101. Canberra, Australia: AIC.

Rollings, K. (2008). Counting the costs of crime in Australia: a 2005 update. Research and public policy series, no. 91. Canberra, Australia: AIC.

Sarre, R. and O'Connell, M. (2009). The criminal courts. In Hayes and Prenzler (Eds) *An introduction to crime and criminology.* 2nd edn. Australia: Pearson Education.

Stamp, J. and Walker, J. (2004). Money laundering in and through Australia. *Trends and issues in crime and criminal justice*, no. 342. Canberra, Australia: AIC.

Schloenhardt, A. (2008). *The illegal trade in timber and timber products in the Asia-Pacific region.* Research and public policy series, no. 89. Canberra, Australia: AIC.

—— (2009). *Palermo on the Pacific Rim: organised crime offences in the Asia Pacific region.* United Nations Office of Drugs and Crime, Regional Centre for East Asia and the Pacific, Bangkok.

The Economist (2008). Economist intelligence unit's index of democracy 2008. Economist Intelligence Unit. Online at http://graphics.eiu.com/PDF/Democracy%20Index%202008.pdf (accessed November 24, 2010).

Transparency International (2008). Corruption Perception Index 2008. Online at http://www.transparency.org/policy_research/surveys_indices/cpi/2008/cpi_2008_table (accessed November 24, 2010).

White, R. (2009). *Environmental crime: a reader.* Cullompton, UK: Willan Publishing.

Willis, K., Homel, P., and Gray, K. (2006). *Developing and implementing a performance measurement framework for drug law enforcement in Australia.* Monograph 18. South Australia: National Drug Law Enforcement Research Fund.

Note

The authors would like to thank the much-missed Janet Smith and the staff at the JV Barry Library at the AIC.

30

Brazil

The state of criminology

Corinne Davis Rodrigues

Introduction

Brazil has undergone a number of transformations since the mid-1980s. In 1986, the most recent period of military dictatorship which began in 1964 came to an end with the election of President Sarney. After the economic impact of the "lost decade" of the 1980s that saw hyperinflation and high unemployment, Brazil's currency stabilized with the *Plano Real* in 1994 and, beginning in 2000, Brazil began to experience continued economic growth.

Most dramatic, however, has been the increase in crime, especially violent crime. Brazil has seen increases in homicide rates since the mid-1980s when the rate per 100,000 inhabitants was 13.88. By 1995, this rate had risen to 24.3. In 2002, the homicide rate was 30.6 per 100,000. This increase in crime over the past 25 years has impacted public and political opinion alike, making crime one of the most important issues today.

Discussions of the causes of crime in Brazil center around the impact of urbanization and inequality, organized crime (i.e. in the form of drug trafficking), police violence and abuse, and the ineffectiveness of the justice system. Brazilian academics from an array of disciplines, such as sociology, anthropology, political science and economics, have begun in the last 25 years to develop a body of research to examine these issues. Brazilian criminology, as a discipline, is still in its initial stages. The object of this chapter is to examine the characteristics of Brazil, its crime and the body of research that has been produced by Brazilian criminologists.

Infrastructure

Brazil ranks fifth in the world both in terms of land mass and population. It occupies 47 percent of the landmass of South America with over 8.5 million square kilometers of territory. Its total population numbers 183,987,291 inhabitants (IBGE, 2007). It shares borders with all but two of the 12 other countries of South America. It has an extensive coastline along the Atlantic Ocean stretching 7,491 kilometers. It is the only Portuguese-speaking country in Latin America.

After many years of hyperinflation and unstable currencies, Brazil in recent years has seen steady economic growth and expansion. Since the implementation of the *Plano Real* fiscal program in 1994, inflation has gone from levels of 45 percent each month in 1994 to a current annual rate of 5.7 percent. Currently Brazil has the tenth largest economy in the world with an estimated GDP of $1.665 trillion USD with a growth rate of 5.66 percent for 2007 and

5.2 percent in 2008. Brazil is regarded as one of the group of four emerging economies known as BRIC (Brazil, Russia, India and China). The per capita GDP is $10,100 USD (IPEA, 2010).

However, this wealth generated by the Brazilian economy has not resulted in improved economic conditions for all. Brazil has one of the highest levels of income inequality of industrialized nations, with a Gini index of 55.33, ranking tenth in the world in income inequality (IPEA, 2010). In 2007, 17 percent of the population was living below the poverty line and the average per capita household income in 2007 was R$390.39 ($195 USD), compared to an average per capita household income of R$4,870.10 (approximately $2,435 USD) for the richest 1 percent of the population (IPEA, 2010). Government income redistribution programs, most notably *Bolsa Família*, have begun to ameliorate some of these inequalities, but the gap between the richest 20 percent and the poorest 20 percent of the population is still striking.

According to 2008 figures, 93.65 million Brazilians are in the labor force, primarily employed in the service sector (66 percent). Employment in agriculture and industry comprised 20 percent and 14 percent of the rest of the economically active population, respectively. Unemployment has shown steady declines since 2000 and based on 2008 data is currently at a rate of 7.9 percent (IPEADATA, 2010 figures). However, as in other Latin American countries, much of the employed work is in the informal economy, without formal employment contracts or benefits provided by law. A recent study by the Organisation for Economic Co-operation and Development estimated that 51 percent of all employees in Brazil are part of the informal economy (Jütting and De Laiglesia, 2009). This corroborates data from the Instituto Brasileiro de Geografia e Estatística (IBGE) in 2003 that estimates that over 10 million businesses in urban Brazil are informal (non-tax paying) (IBGE, 2005).

Given the increasing rates of violence over the past two decades, violence has become one of the most important issues for local, state and the federal government. In the 2009 federal budget, 39.29 billion reais (approximately $23.11 billion USD) were allotted to the Ministry of Justice, responsible for the police, corrections and the public prosecutor's office. Of this amount, 35 percent was allotted to Pronasci, the National Program in Public Security (Programa Nacional de Segurança Pública), a program designed to "articulate criminal justice policy with social action; prioritize prevention and the search for causes of crime, without compromising strategies of social order and public security" (Ministério de Justiça, n.d.). The program currently invests funds in community programs, improving police training and expanding occupancy in the penitentiary system.

Brazil is a federal republic, divided into 26 states and one federal district, Brasília, the location of the federal government. Brazil officially gained its independence from Portugal in 1822. Its current constitution dates from 1988. Like the United States, the federal government is divided into executive, legislative and judicial branches. The head of the executive branch, the President, is elected for a maximum of two consecutive four-year terms. The federal legislative branch is composed of two chambers: the Senate and the Chamber of Deputies. The Senate has 81 members (three from each state and the federal district) who are elected to eight-year terms. The Chamber of Deputies is composed of 513 seats, with members elected by proportional representation to serve four-year terms (Portal Brasil, 2010). The federal judicial branch is composed of the federal court system, including the Supreme Federal Tribunal, the Higher Tribunal of Justice and the Regional Federal Tribunals. All judges in these courts are appointed for life.

There are a total of 20 distinct political parties in Brazil; however, only six of these have more than a million affiliates. In addition to political parties, there are also other political pressure groups. Most notably among these is the Landless Workers' Movement (MST), a group that lobbies for land reform. In addition, labor unions and religious groups (Catholic and Evangelical Protestant) also exert political influence.

Brazil has a substantial presence in the international community with membership in a number of international organizations. Among these are the United Nations, including participation in the United Nations Security Council; the Organization of American States; the G-15, G-20, G-24 and G-77. Brazil is also a member of major financial and trade organizations, including the International Monetary Fund, the World Trade Organization and Mercosul.

Telecommunications in Brazil has improved substantially since the privatization of the state phone companies in the late 1990s. However, the fixed-line coverage, although expanded during the last ten years, is approximately 20 lines per 100 persons. Mobile phone use is currently at around 80 phones per 100 people (CIA, 2009).

Internet was launched in 1988 as a research network for academics in Rio de Janeiro and São Paulo (Carvalho, 2006). Internet development was dependent on government initiatives until 1998, with the privatization of telecommunications. Since then, the internet (in both internet service providers (ISPS) and usage) has grown considerably. Data from 2008 puts the number of ISPs at 9,573 million, a ranking of tenth worldwide. Data from 2007 estimates 50 million internet users, placing Brazil sixth worldwide in internet usage (CIA, 2009).

People

According to current population estimates from the Brazilian Institute of Geography and Statistics (IBGE), Brazil has approximately 191 million inhabitants (IBGE, 2007). Approximately 51 percent of the total population is female. While Brazil, like other countries in Latin America, continues to have a predominantly young population (51.9 percent of the population is under age 30), the elderly population has grown significantly in the last ten years (now approximately 7.3 percent of the population). This aging of the population can be seen in the change in mortality and birth rates from 2000 to 2005. Births per thousand fell from 22 in 2000 to 18 in 2005 and deaths per thousand also fell from 6.9 to 6.3 in 2005. However, greater declines in mortality rates have been seen for infant mortality, whereas the mortality rates for males between 15 and 24 years of age have increased due to the increase in violent deaths attributed to crime (IBGE, 2009).

Brazil is a racially and ethnically diverse nation. Most Brazilians can trace their ancestry back to original Amerindians, African slaves or Portuguese colonial settlers. However, other nationalities, most substantially immigrants from Japan, Italy, Germany and Lebanon, are also present.

In terms of race, the IBGE classifies Brazilians according to five racial and ethnic categories: white, black, brown (mix of black and white), yellow (denoting persons of Asian descent) and indigenous (denoting those of Amerindian decent). According to the latest estimates from the IBGE (IBGE, 2008), 49.2 percent of Brazilians self-identified as white, 7.5 percent as black and 42.5 percent as brown, with the remaining 0.8 percent self-identifying as either yellow or indigenous.

In terms of religion, Brazil, like other countries in Latin America, is predominately Roman Catholic. According to the 2000 Census, 73.6 percent of the population is Roman Catholic, 15.4 percent are Protestant and 7.4 percent claim no religious denomination. The remaining 3.6 percent of the population is divided among various religions, such as Spiritualist and Bantu (IBGE, 2001).

The Brazilian educational system is comprised of fundamental, intermediate and higher education. The fundamental and intermediate levels of education total 11 years (eight years at the fundamental level and three years at the intermediate level). Attendance is compulsory in Brazil only for the fundamental level, specified for children 7 to 14 years of age. The national average of completed education is only 7.2 years. Public schools are maintained on the city, state and federal level. There is also a state and federal public university system. The literacy rate in Brazil is 88 percent, with the youth literacy (ages 15–19) at 93.2 percent.

Administration of justice

Brazil is a federative system of 26 independent states. As such, each state has autonomy in organizing and regulating criminal justice within its borders. Police, courts and corrections are organized at the state level and answer to the state executive branch (the governor's office). Criminal justice proceedings also exist at the federal level.

Policing at the state level is divided into two separate organizations, the Military Police (Polícia Militar) and the Civil Police (Polícia Civil). The Military Police operates as the preventive and repressive arm of the police, responsible for maintaining public order. The Civil Police is the investigative arm of the police, responsible for investigating crimes. In addition to these two police agencies, many municipalities also have Municipal Guards, responsible for maintaining public order.

The Brazilian court system, due to its colonial heritage, follows the civil law tradition. This means that court cases are decided by a judge through an inquisitorial process. There is one criminal code and one criminal processing code used by courts at all levels of the system (state and federal). However, for the crime of homicide, cases are decided by a jury. Judges, prosecutors and public defenders are all government jobs in Brazil. Entrance into these positions is through competitive exams and all positions are tenured.

There are three types of penal sanctions in Brazil: imprisonment, limitation of rights (for example, community service, confiscation of assets and temporary interruption of rights) and fines. The limitation of rights, known as alternative sanctions, is applicable in cases where the penalty is no more than four years' imprisonment.

In addition to the regular criminal courts, in 1995, a special branch of small claims courts, the *Juizado Especial Criminal*, or Special Criminal Court, was created to handle the processing of minor offenses whose maximum sentence is equivalent to one year in prison. These courts handle minor offenses such as simple assault and traffic accidents, offering alternative sanctions to imprisonment (limitation of rights and fines). Rather than adjudicative, these proceedings are mediations between the victim and offender with the aid of a court appointed moderator.

The majority of prisons operates on the state level and are under the jurisdiction of the state governments. The state penitentiary systems operate with three different types of imprisonment: closed, semi-open and open regimes. In addition to the state systems, in 2006, the Federal Penitentiary System was created and today consists of five federal prisons. These prisons are designed to house prisoners (federal or state) that present a public security risk and operate as closed regimes. In addition, the National Penitentiary Fund allocates additional federal resources to the states in order to maintain their prison systems.

According to the latest figures from the Ministry of Justice, there are currently 469,546 prisoners total in both systems, at a rate of incarceration of 247.68 prisoners per 100,000 inhabitants (Ministério da Justiça, 2008). Overcrowding is a serious problem in the Brazilian system. According to the latest statistics, there are only 299,392 prison spaces to house the prison population, resulting in the system operating at approximately one and a half times its capacity (Ministério da Justiça, 2008).

Criminology

The influence of the social sciences over the study of crime has happened relatively late when compared to the United States. Traditionally, the study of crime and criminal justice has been the domain of legal scholars, with social scientists discussing the broader issue of violence generally or political violence specifically. However, the 1980s marked a shift in the study of crime, brought about due to the stark increase in violent crime, most notably in urban areas, beginning in the mid-1980s. Homicide rates for Rio de Janeiro and São Paulo, the country's two largest cities, increased from 36.14 and 20.32 per 100,000 inhabitants, respectively, in 1980, to 66.49 and 48.31 per 100,000 inhabitants, respectively, in 1990. By 2000, homicide rates for Rio de Janeiro had decreased slightly to 62.96. However, the rate for São Paulo continued to rise, reaching 66.54 by 2000 (CRISP, 2004). By 2008, homicide rates in Rio de Janeiro had decreased, reaching 33 per 100,000 inhabitants. São Paulo also saw reductions in its homicide rates. In 2008, the homicide rate was 10.7 per 100,000 inhabitants (Forum Nacional de Segurança Pública, 2009).

It was in this context of rising crime that social scientists in Brazil began to dedicate attention to documenting and understanding crime in Brazil. Initial research on crime in Brazil focused on understanding and explaining the rise in crime. However, in recent years, the study of crime has grown substantially and expanded into other areas.

Currently, there is much research being undertaken to understand not only the crime causation and crime trends in Brazil, but also the criminal justice system as well. Studies focus on specific actors in the criminal justice system, such as police, prosecutors and judges, as well as the workings of the different components of the system. In addition, current research also focuses on specific types of crime, such as drug trafficking, or specific types of victims, such as women and children. Finally, current research also is focused on the development, implementation and evaluation of crime prevention and correction programs and policies.

Current research on crime causation and crime trends has its origins in two specific debates regarding the causes of the initial rise in violent urban crime in the middle of the 1980s. The first of these debates centered on de-bunking common sense perceptions of poverty as the primary cause of crime.

Unlike in the United States, where academic research had supported theories that linked poverty to crime, such as anomie theory and subculture theories of violence, the academic research produced countering the link between poverty and crime was not responding to academic research showing such a link, but to public opinion about causes of crime. Public perceptions of crime in urban Brazil depicted (and still depict) criminals as poor youth from the shantytowns, or *favelas*. Thus, some of this research aimed at demonstrating the bias of the criminal justice system towards repressing crime committed by such youth, although crime was present in all social groups (Zaluar, 1994). Other research sought to dispel this public perception through the analysis of official data, demonstrating the spuriousness of the relationship between poverty and crime (Beato *et al.*, 1998).

The second debate focused on the role of the criminal justice system in contributing to the rise in crime. Authors such as Edmundo Campus Coelho, Antonio Luis Paixão and Claudio Beato pointed to the relationship between the rise of crime and the lack of deterrent capacity of the criminal justice system. These authors began to argue that reforms and improvements in the criminal justice system rather than social policies would have greater impacts on crime rates.

Another group of scholars, primarily based in the University of São Paulo (Sergio Adorno, Nancy Cardia and Teresa Caldeira), explained the rise in crime in the 1980s due to the arbitrary action of the police and its impacts on the legitimacy of the state, both as an entity with the monopoly over the use of force and as a mediator of conflicts. They specifically examined the role of the legacy of Brazil's 20-year dictatorship and its return to democracy in the 1980s as part of the explanation for the arbitrary nature of police behavior and practices.

Current research on crime causation builds upon each of these original debates. Emerging out of the original discussion of poverty and crime is a body of current research re-examining the role of inequality (most specifically income inequality) in the growth of urban crime. Rather than exclusively associating poverty with crime, these scholars examine the impact of inequalities of opportunities in the commission of crime (Beato *et al.*, 2004), as well as explanations for the spatial distribution of violent crime (especially homicide) in poor neighborhoods (Beato *et al.*, 2001; Cardia, 2008). Included here is the work of Brazilian economists, especially in collaboration with the World Bank (Fajnzylber *et al.*, 1998) who examine the links between inequality and crime, as well as others (Andrade and Peixoto, 2008) who have begun to examine the economic costs of crime, both in terms of state expenditures and loss of property and lives.

Unlike the early explanations that focused on direct linkages between poverty and crime, these newer studies incorporate the body of knowledge of crime causation developed by US sociology and criminology. Especially prominent is the testing of theories, such as opportunity theory, social disorganization theory and rational choice models. Recent work by scholars at Federal University of Minas Gerais (UFMG), especially at the Center for Studies in Criminality and Public Safety (CRISP), follows this trend.

Emerging out of the original discussions of the role of the state and the criminal justice system is a body of work that examines the links between crime, citizenship and human rights. Much of this work focuses specifically on the criminal justice system and will be covered more extensively in the next section. The research relating to crime causation following this perspective focuses on the impacts of criminal justice practices (especially authoritarian and arbitrary police practices) on crime causation. Also considered in these explanations is the level of impunity (crimes not prosecuted) of the criminal justice system and the implications of Brazil's democratic transition and their impact of the level of crime. The bulk of this body of research has been carried out at the University of São Paulo at the Nucleus of Violence Studies. Prominent authors within this perspective include Sergio Adorno and Nancy Cardia and Teresa Caldeira.

Research that examines the role of the criminal justice system in deterring (or failing to deter) crime continues to be one of the central topics in criminology in Brazil. In addition to the earlier studies on the general deterrent capacity of the justice system, there is considerable research on the police and policing, as well as more recent research on the workings of the criminal justice system (Misse and Vargas, 2009).

Within the body of research examining the criminal justice system, research on policing has been the most extensive. Some of the first studies of the criminal justice system focused on policing, especially policing and police abuses during Brazil's dictatorship (Paixão, 1982). Others focused on the everyday practices of the police (Mingardi, 1992). Current studies focus on police reform, especially community policing (Leite Marinho, 2002).

Research focused on the criminal justice process has become more prevalent in recent years. Studies have examined the trajectory of criminal cases through the court system, especially cases of sexual violence (Vargas, 2007) and homicide (Ribeiro, 2009). These studies seek to identify factors that determine length of case time and sentencing outcomes. In addition to these studies focused on case processing, other studies have focused on specialized courts, such as the Juizado Especial (De Azevedo, 2001) and domestic violence mediation (Muniz, 1996).

Since the late 1980s, Brazil has seen a rise in organized crime, especially drug trafficking (Zaluar, 1994). Given the concentration of homicide in poor areas also dominated by drug trafficking, many criminologists have linked the rise in violent crime in urban Brazil to the rise in organized drug trafficking (Beato *et al.*, 1998).

Thus, one area of criminological research in Brazil attempts to understand crime by examining the impact of social transformations on interpersonal relations, particularly in the context of high crime areas (most notably the *favelas,* or urban shantytowns) or criminal groups (especially drug trafficking). These analyses attempt to explain the use of violence or the adherence to violent groups, such as drug trafficking gangs.

Within this perspective, the principal research on the social organization of drug trafficking has been done by Alba Zaluar, but also by others (Alvito, 2001; Dowdney, 2003; Mingardi, 1998).

This research attempts to understand the patterns of drug trafficking and the reasons for adherence to drug trafficking gangs. This research draws heavily from theorists examining patterns of social interactions and civility such as Norbert Elias, rather than gang research from the United States.

Other authors within this perspective, such as Luiz Antônio Machado da Silva and Michel Misse, explain crime by examining changes in sociability, especially the creation of a new violent sociability that co-exists with traditional forms of sociability. Misse (1997), for example, argues that the use of violence on the public level (by police officers) sustains the expansion of this new (violent) mode of sociability to the personal level, resulting in an accumulation of violence.

One prominent feature of current Brazilian criminology is the level of involvement of academic scholars in applied research. Most state criminal justice agencies do not have their own research divisions and rely on academics for conducting evaluation research. As a result, all of the major research centers on crime are involved to some degree in policy initiatives in the area of crime. In most cases, involvement is centered on the evaluation of the effectiveness of government policies in criminal justice or crime prevention. In some cases, however, researchers are directly involved in problem diagnostics, design and/or implementation of policy (for an example see the homicide prevention program Fica Vivo in Minas Gerais).

Since the 1980s when criminological research in Brazil began, researchers have relied almost exclusively on two methodological strategies for research. The first has involved the use of quantitative methods using crime statistics. The second and more prominent strategy has involved the use of various qualitative methods, especially ethnographic methods. More recent research in the area of evaluation research has seen the introduction of outcome evaluation methods, usually employing statistical analysis.

The use of quantitative methods in Brazilian criminology dates back to the beginnings of social science research on crime (Campos Coelho, 1978). However, the sophistication of these methods and their widespread use by Brazilian academics have been severely hampered by the lack of reliable data on crime and the lack of training in these methods for most Brazilian social scientists. Most of the use of quantitative methods has been limited to descriptive statistics of official data, mostly police or mortality statistics. Multivariate analysis, usually in the form of linear or logistic regression modeling, has become more common in the past five years, especially with the production of survey-based data by several of the university research centers that focus on studying crime. Recently, other statistical techniques, such as spatial analysis, have also gained popularity. While most current spatial analysis is descriptive, research produced by CRISP is an exception to this with some use of modeling and spatial regression analyses. In all, quantitative methods are becoming more utilized by criminologists, as more reliable data become available.

Research employing qualitative methods has held a prominent place in criminology for two reasons. First, the lack of good official data on crime, especially individual-level data, has led to the collection of primary data, most of which has been qualitative in nature. Second, the emphasis on explanations of crime focusing on social transformations and social interactions (especially when explaining youth crime and organized crime), have led to research questions in need of qualitative data. Ethnographic studies of high crime areas and of criminals are the most prominent of this type of research, although qualitative studies have also examined the social organization of policing. Given the lack of individual-level data on offenders and offending (self-reported delinquency data), qualitative studies tend to focus on individual causes of crime or the meanings of crime and violence. This is a contrast to most of the quantitative studies that focus on defining and explaining trends in the incidence of crime, the criminal justice response to crime and the types of offenders and victims.

Although much research in the area of crime has been done through the analysis of crime data, there is clear consensus among academics that Brazil lacks adequate data to study crime.

Commonly cited are problems with the accuracy, access and usability of official data, the lack of standardized and repeated victimization surveys, and the almost total absence of data on self-reported delinquency. To remedy this situation, considerable efforts have been made in the past ten years to increase and improve the amount of crime data available.

A number of government agencies collect crime data. The accuracy and availability of these data vary by type of agency and also by state. Crime data from official sources is comprised of data available from the police, the courts and corrections, as well as mortality statistics from public health agencies. Given the structure of Brazilian policing, criminal events often are registered by both the military and civil police, or registered by one agency and not the other, leading to errors in the accuracy of official statistics. As a result, the quality and accessibility of data collected by police on crime incidence varies from state to state, although recent efforts have been made at the federal level to improve data collection and reporting to the Ministry of Justice to compile more accurate crime statistics.

Due to the deficiencies in official data as well as the need for data on crime not collected by official sources (such as crimes not reported to the police and fear of crime), Brazilian criminologists began to develop and conduct surveys, beginning in the 1990s. While the majority of these surveys have focused on collecting data on criminal victimization, others have collected data on fear of crime, public perceptions of crime and self-reported delinquency. All of these surveys have been city-wide in scope. National-level survey data on crime is currently limited to a few questions included in the 1988 national household survey. However, a new national-level victimization survey is scheduled to be carried out in 2010, coordinated by the Secretariat of Public Security of the Ministry of Justice.

Most Brazilian crime surveys have been conceived, financed and carried out exclusively by national researchers; however, some Brazilian cities are included in three prominent international crime surveys as well. These are: the International Crime Victimization Survey (ICVS), funded by the United Nations Interregional Crime and Justice Research Institute (UNICRI); the ACTIVA survey, funded by the Pan-American Health Organization; and the World Bank victimization survey project. These three surveys provide data for the cities of Rio de Janeiro (ICVS 1992 and 1996; ACTIVA survey 1996), Salvador (ACTIVA survey 1996) and São Paulo (World Bank victimization project 1999).

With regards to crime surveys produced in Brazil, since the mid-1990s, there have been seven victimization surveys covering primarily Rio de Janeiro (ISER, 1997; ILANUD, 2002; NEPEV, 2005), São Paulo (NEV, 1999; ILANUD, 2002) and Belo Horizonte (NEV, 1997; CRISP, 2001 and 2005), although some surveys (NEV, 1997; ILANUD, 2002; CRISP, 2004), cover other large Brazilian cities as well. In addition to these surveys of criminal victimization, there have been surveys conducted on public attitudes of crime (NEV, 1999; CRISP, 2008) and self-reported delinquency (CRISP, 2005 and 2006).

Access to crime survey data varies considerably. The ICVS and ACTIVA surveys are publicly available through the Interuniversity Consortium of Political and Social Research (ICPSR) housed at the University of Michigan. The World Bank surveys are available directly from the principal investigators. The majority of the surveys conducted by Brazilian research centers are not publicly available, with the exception of the survey on public attitudes on crime (NEV, 1999), and some victimization surveys (ILANUD, 1997) which are available through the Social Information Consortium (Consórcio de Informações Sociais – CIS), a national academic data depository similar in function and purpose to the ICPSR. The remaining survey data are available on a limited basis directly from the research center responsible for the survey based on criteria of use established by each center. The public use data are available in multi-formats (usually SPSS and Excel). The data housed at the ICPSR is available in English. All of the other survey data is in Portuguese.

The most prominent research centers are located in the southeast, in the cities of Rio de Janeiro, Sao Paulo and Belo Horizonte. In Rio de Janeiro, each of the major public universities has a research center: the Nucleus of Research in Violence (NUPEVI) at the State University of Rio de Janeiro, coordinated by Alba Zaluar; the Nucleus of Studies in Citizenship, Conflict and Urban Violence (NECVU), coordinated by Michel Misse at the Federal University of Rio de Janeiro; and the Fluminese Nucleus of Studies and Research (NUFEP), directed by Roberto Kant de Lima at the Fluminese Federal University. In addition to these university centers, research on youth crime and firearms is carried out by the Institute of Religious Studies (ISER).

In São Paulo, the most prominent research institution is the Nucleus of Violence Studies (NEV) at the University of São Paulo, under the coordination of Sergio Adorno. In addition to NEV, another prominent center is the Brazilian branch of the Latin American Institute of the United Nations for the Prevention and Treatment of Delinquents (ILANUD), directed by Túlio Kahn.

In Belo Horizonte, there are two major research institutions on crime. The first is the Center for Studies in Criminality and Public Safety (CRISP), directed by Claudio Beato, at the Federal University of Minas Gerais. The second is the Nucleus of Public Safety Studies at the João Pinheiro Foundation (FJP), under the coordination of Eduardo Batitucci.

Criminology research is traditionally funded through the National Council for Scientific and Technological Development (CNPq), an agency analogous to the US National Science Foundation. While most of the funding available through this agency is non-criminology specific, public security was included among the strategic areas identified as applicable for funding in order to create nationwide Institutes of Science and Technology in 2008 and three such institutes devoted to the study of crime were created. These institutes are coordinated by NUPEVI, NECVU and NEV. In addition to this source of federal funding, each state government has a foundation to support local academic research.

More recently, however, much funding, especially in the area of applied research, has come directly from the secretariats of public security, either on the state or local level. For example, most of the recent surveys conducted by CRISP were financed directly by state government. In 2004, the Ministry of Justice issued an extensive request for proposals (RFP) in 26 different areas of criminal justice, signaling the first time that this agency of the federal government had directly solicited and funded criminal justice research.

Beyond these local and national funding sources, some international funding agencies provide resources for crime research in Brazil. Most notable are the Ford, Tinker and McArthur Foundations.

Future research questions

1. To what extent do current explanations of crime developed mostly in Rio de Janeiro and São Paulo explain crime in other areas of Brazil?
2. How can US-developed theories of crime explain the Brazilian context? How general or how particular is the Brazil crime situation?
3. What is the impact of crime prevention policies on levels of crime? How do different programs and policies currently in place in Brazil impact levels of crime?
4. What are the levels of recidivism in Brazil? What factors explain recidivism?
5. Are police practices changing in Brazil? What is the impact of these changes on levels of crime?

References

Alvito, M. (2001). *As Cores de Acari: uma favela carioca.* Rio de Janeiro: Editora Fundação Getúlio Vargas.

Andrade, M. V. and Peixoto, B. T. (2008). Avaliação econômica de programas de prevenção e controle da criminalidade no Brasil. In C. Beato Filho (Ed.) *Compreendendo e avaliando projetos de segurança pública.* Belo Horizonte: UFMG.

Beato Filho, C. C., Assunção, R., Santos, M. A. C, Santo, L. E. E., Sapori, L. F., and Batitucci, E. (1998). Evolução da criminalidade violenta em Minas Gerais 1985–97. In *XXII Reunião da ANPOCS, 1997, Caxambu. Sessão Violência Justiça e Direitos.* São Paulo: ANPOCS.

Beato Filho, C. C., Assunção, R., Silva, B. F. A., Marinho, F. C., Reis, I. A., and Almeida, M. C. M. (2001). Conglomerados de homicídios e o tráfico de drogas em Belo Horizonte, Minas Gerais, Brasil, de 1995 a 1999. *Cadernos de Saúde Pública.* Rio de Janeiro: FIOCRUZ.

Beato Filho, C. C., Viegas, M., and Peixoto, B. T. (2004). Crime, oportunidade e vitimização. *Revista Brasileira de Ciências Sociais.* São Paulo: ANPOCS.

Campos Coelho, E. (1978). A criminalização da marginalidade e a marginalização da criminalidade. *Revista Brasileira de Administração Pública.* Rio de Janeiro: Fundação Getúlio Vargas.

Cardia, N. G. (2008). Risco de ocorrencias de homicidios dolosos em São Paulo. In Secretaria Municipal de Planejamento; Departamento de Estatísticas e Produção de Informações (Org.) *Olhar São Paulo-Violência e Criminalidade.* São Paulo: Secretaria Municipal de Planejamento.

Carvalho, M. S. R. M. (2006). *A trajetória da internet no Brasil: Do surgimento das redes de computadores à instituição dos mecanismos de governança.* Master's thesis. Rio de Janeiro: Univerisdade Federal do Rio de Janeiro.

Central Intelligence Agency (CIA). (2009). *The World Factbook.* Washington, DC: Central Intelligence Agency. Online at https://www.cia.gov/library/publications/the-world-factbook/index.html (accessed October 1, 2009).

Centro de Estudos de Criminalidade e Segurança Pública (CRISP) (2004). Homicídios no Brasil – Atlas Brasil. Online at http://www.crisp.ufmg.br/pesquisas_projetos/banco_de_dados (accessed October 5, 2009).

De Azevedo, R. G. (2001). Juizados especiais criminais: uma abordagem sociológica sobre a informalização da justiça penal no Brasil. *Revista Brasileira de Ciências Sociais.* São Paulo: ANPOCS.

Dowdney, L. (2003). *As crianças do tráfico: um estudo de caso de crianças em violência armada organizada em Rio de Janeiro.* Rio de Janeiro: 7 Letras.

Fajnzylber, P., Lederman, D., and Loayza, N. (1998). *Determinants of crime rates in Latin America and the world: an empirical assessment.* Washington, DC: World Bank Latin American and Caribbean Studies.

Forum Nacional de Segurança Pública (2009). Anuário do Fórum Brasileiro de Segurança Pública. São Paulo: Fórum Brasileiro de Segurança Pùblica.

Instituto Brasileiro de Geografia e Estatística (IBGE). (2001) *Censo 2000.* Brasília: IBGE. Online at http://www.ibge.gov.br/home/estatistica/populacao/censo2000/default.shtm (accessed October 5, 2009).

—— (2005) *Economia Informal 2003.* Rio de Janeiro: IBGE. Online at http://www.ibge.gov.br/home/estatistica/economia/ecinf/2003/ecinf2003.pdf (accessed October 5, 2009).

—— (2007). *Contagem da população 2007.* Rio de Janeiro: IBGE. Online at http://www.ibge.gov.br/home/estatistica/populacao/contagem2007/contagem.pdf (accessed October 5, 2009).

—— (2008). *Pesquisa Nacional por Amostra de Domicílios 2008 v. 29.* Rio de Janeiro: IBGE. Online at http://www.ibge.gov.br/home/estatistica/populacao/trabalhoerendimento/pnad2008/brasilpnad2008.pdf (accessed October 12, 2009).

—— (2009). *Indicadores sociodemográficos e da saúde no Brasil 2009.* Rio de Janeiro: IBGE. Online at http://www.ibge.gov.br/home/estatistica/populacao/indic_sociosaude/2009/indicsaude.pdf (accessed October 12, 2009).

Instituto de Pesquisa Econômica Aplicada (IPEA) (2010). IPEAdata. Brasília: IPEA. Online at http://www.ipeadata.gov.br/ipeaweb.dll/ipeadata?Tick=116823281 (accessed December 7, 2010).

Jütting, J. and De Laiglesia, J. R. (2009). *Is informal normal? Towards more and better jobs in developing countries.* Paris: OECD Publishing.

Leite Marinho, K. R. (2002). Mudanças organizacionais na implementação do policiamento comunitário. Master's thesis. Belo Horizonte: UFMG.

Mingardi, G. (1992). *Tiras, gansos e trutas, cotidiano e reforma da polícia civil.* São Paulo: Scritta Editorial.

—— (1998). O que é crime organizado: Uma definição das ciências sociais. *Revista do Ilanud.* São Paulo: Ilanud.

Ministério da Justiça (2008). *Departamento Pentitenciário Nacional DEPEN Sistema Nacional de Informação Penitenciária InfoPen Dados Consolidados*. Brasília: Ministério da Justiça. Online at http://www.mj.gov.br/data/Pages/MJD574E9CEITEMIDC37B2AE94C6840068B1624D28407509CPTBRNN.htm (accessed October 10, 2009).

—— (n.d.) Pronasci. Translation by author. Online at http://portal.mj.gov.br/pronasci/data/Pages/MJF4F53AB1PTBRNN.htm (accessed December 7, 2010).

Misse, M. (1997). As ligações perigosas: mercado informal ilegal, narcotráfico e violência no Rio. *Contemporaneidade e Educação*, Rio de Janeiro: FAEEBA.

Misse, M. and Vargas, J. D. (2009). A produção decisória do sistema de justiça criminal no Rio de Janeiro ontem e hoje: um estudo preliminar. *Revista Brasileira de Ciências Criminais*. São Paulo: IBCCRIM.

Muniz, J. (1996). Os direitos dos outros e outros direitos: um estudo sobre a negociação de conflitos nas DEAMs/RJ. In: L. E. Soares (org.) *Violência e política no Rio de Janeiro*. Rio de Janeiro: Relume Dumará.

Paixão, A. L. (1982). A organização policial numa área metropolitana. *Dados*. Rio de Janeiro: IUPERJ.

Portal Brasil (2010). *Congresso Nacional*. Brasília: Governo Federal. Online at http://www.brasil.gov.br/sobre/o-brasil/estrutura/congresso-nacional (accessed November 24, 2010).

Ribeiro, L. (2009). O tempo da justiça criminal: Portugal e Brasil em uma perspectiva comparada. *Revista Crítica de Ciências Sociais*. Coimbra: Centro de Estudos Sociais.

Vargas, J. D. (2007). Análise comparada do fluxo do sistema de justiça para o crime de estupro. *Dados*. Rio de Janeiro: IUPERJ.

Zaluar, A. (1994). *Condomínio do diabo*. Rio de Janeiro: Editora da UFRJ e Revan.

31

Canada

The state of criminology

André Solecki, Nicole Crutcher, and Stephen Mihorean

Introduction

The Canadian population is ageing and becoming increasingly diverse. Immigration patterns are shifting as source countries change. Broad concerns regarding the future health of Canadians, not to mention increasing educational demands and changing family structures, are bringing new challenges and pressures for Canadian society generally and the justice system in particular.

Public opinion polls show that despite changes in crime levels there is always a fear-prone segment in the population. There are many high-level factors that intersect around the issues of demographics, public perceptions, and crime that influence this perception. Not surprisingly, perceptions of crime vary depending on where you live. These results show the extent to which people in larger urban centers are considerably more concerned with crime than in the smaller communities. The level of fear coincides with the size of city – the larger the city, the more fearful Canadians become.

Expectation by its very nature is forward-looking, and the public's expectation is not much grander than making society better. With this in mind, Canada elected a minority Conservative government in 2006 on a very focused five-pillared platform. One of those pillars was tackling crime and keeping Canada safe. This chapter overviews the context and variables within which that criminal justice agenda is being delivered.

Infrastructure

Canada is second only to Russia in territorial size, covering 9.9 million square kilometres (3.8 million square miles). Canada borders three oceans, the Arctic, Atlantic and Pacific; the coastline is 243,791 kilometres (151,473 miles) in length. To the south, Canada borders the United States of America with the longest undefended border in the world: 8.893 kilometres (5,526 miles) in length. Approximately 90 percent of the Canadian population lives within 160 kilometres (100 miles) of the American border. As a result of this close proximity to the United States, there is a great deal of cultural overlap between the two countries. Despite this, crime is much less. For example, the United States has one of the highest incarceration rates in the world at 756 individuals incarcerated per 100,000 population. The comparable Canadian rate is 116 individuals incarcerated per 100,000 population (Walmsley, n.d.).

Presently, the main environmental issues facing Canada include air pollution and resulting acid rain severely affecting lakes and damaging forests, metal smelting, coal-burning utilities, and vehicle emissions impacting on both agricultural and forest productivity.

Leading up to the 2008/9 recession, indicators of economic participation were strong. Canada's gross domestic product (GDP) was $1.287 trillion in 2009. Overall, compared to other countries, Canada has a strong economy, ranking 15th in 2009, but well behind that of other developed countries such as the United States ($14.260 trillion) and the United Kingdom ($2.165 trillion).

In 2008, and for the first time since the 1990–1 recession, Canada's income per capita decreased. In particular, vulnerable groups such as Aboriginal people, recent immigrants, lone-parents, persons with a work-limiting disability, and unattached individuals between 45–64 years of age face challenges. While there is no official definition of poverty, in 2005, there were 10.8 percent of the population living below a measure referred to as the low-income cut-off. Research has shown that those with lower incomes are more likely to be both a victim of a crime and a perpetrator (Bonta, 1997).

There are five main political parties: the Bloc Quebecois, the Conservative Party of Canada, the Green Party, the Liberal Party, and the New Democratic Party. At 59.1 percent of eligible voters, voter turnout in the last general election (2008) was the lowest since Canada's founding in 1867. This is likely due to the fact that Canada has had three federal elections between 2004 and 2008. The lack of stability associated with minority governments, which have been the norm since 2004, has been the reason for the increase in the number of elections.

Executive branch: The Queen of England, Elizabeth II, is the official head of state. Her representative in Canada is the Governor General. The head of government is the Prime Minister. The Cabinet or federal ministry is chosen by the Prime Minister, usually from members of the Prime Minister's own party sitting in Parliament.

Legislative branch: This branch of government is a bicameral Parliament consisting of the Senate and the House of Commons. The Senate has 105 seats and members are appointed by the Governor General on advice from the Prime Minister. There are 308 seats in the House of Commons who are elected directly by members of the public based on popular vote.

Judicial branch: The Supreme Court of Canada is the highest court. Judges are appointed by the Prime Minister through the Governor General. There is also the Federal Court of Canada, Federal Appeal Court and the Provincial Courts (variously named).

People

Canada's population is about 34 million. The majority of Canada's population live in four of the ten provinces: Ontario (38.7 percent), Quebec (23.2 percent), British Columbia (13.2 percent), and Alberta (10.9 percent). Canada's federally administered Northern Territories combined accounted for less than a single percent of the population.

Demographics, particularly the changing number of Canadians between the ages of 15 and 34, correspond closely to the pattern and level of crime reported by police. This age group was in decline but it is projected that the population will begin to rise again slowly every year until 2013. The crime rate trend has closely followed this particular demographic trend and is likely to continue doing so.

The Aboriginal population is the oldest amalgamation of identifiable ethnic groups. As a whole, they represent 3 percent of the Canadian population, but 22 percent of admissions to sentenced custody. Various measures have been put in place to improve this situation, ranging from specialty courts to Aboriginal-oriented correctional facilities; however, their overall effectiveness in reducing Aboriginal involvement in the justice system is not known. It is important to note that the Supreme Court of Canada has acknowledged the importance of taking into account the unique situation of Aboriginal individuals at the sentencing stage of the criminal process (*Gladue* v. *Regina*, 1999, 1 S.C.R. 688). Aboriginal Canadians are found in all provinces and federally administered territories, but the highest percentages are found in Ontario, British Columbia, Alberta, and Manitoba. Aboriginal identities include North American Indian, Métis, and Inuit.

Immigration is necessary for any future population growth. Data from the last census demonstrate that since 2001 the Canadian population has grown by 1.6 million people, or 5.4 percent. Approximately 1.2 million of this growth was due to immigration, with the rest from natural increases in the Canadian population. Between 1956 and 1961 the growth of the Canadian population was three times greater than during the last five years. During this Canadian "baby boom," women gave birth to an average of 3.5 children compared to 1.5 children today. According to Statistics Canada (2005), if the population projections continue in this manner, immigration could become the sole source of Canadian population growth by 2030.

A population fuelled by immigration means that Canada's diverse character and composition is expected to continue evolving well beyond the next decade, with the proportion of visible minorities projected to double by 2016. As of the 2006 census, Canada's five largest visible minority groups were: South Asian (1,262,865), Chinese (1,216,570), Black (783,795), Filipino (410,695), and Latin American (304,245) (Statistics Canada, 2010). The highest visible minority proportions are in major cities including Toronto, Vancouver, Calgary, Montreal, Edmonton, and Winnipeg. The impact of ethnic diversity in the life of the country is complex, ranging from simple values to foundational shifts in organizational behavior.

Canada has two official languages – English and French. Due to current and historical immigration patterns, there are many other languages spoken regularly in Canadian households. English is most predominant, spoken in 66 percent of Canadian households; French is spoken in 21 percent. The remainder speaks other non-official languages.

The free practice of religion adds layers to the dynamics of multiculturalism. The five largest religious groups as of the 2006 census were: Catholic (44 percent), Protestant (29 percent), no religious affiliation (17 percent), Christian (including Orthodox and unaffiliated) 2 percent, and Muslim 2 percent (Statistics Canada, 2001). Ultimately, Canada remains a largely Christian society with a sizeable non-religious segment. With increasing demographic changes, the justice system will have to adapt to serving a much more diverse population.

The education of Canadians is funded by federal, provincial, and municipal/local governments, and is regulated by each individual province as each province sets its own curriculum for children aged 6–18 years old. The proportion of Canadians aged 25 to 64 who have attained upper secondary education is 84 percent, only second to the Czech Republic (OECD, 2006). This trend continues with the enrolment in universities. In 2005/6, over one million Canadians were registered in a college, university, or trade school. Further, females represented 58 percent of registered university students (Statistics Canada, 2008).

Administration of justice

Justice only accounts for 3 percent of all government spending, a small piece of our spending pie. The typical message has been, we need more dollars to do what we have always done using the traditional responses and frameworks (police, courts, corrections). Specifically, the different jurisdictions indicate they need additional funds to administer justice, and over the last decade, justice spending has increased despite the fact that crime rates have dropped and the number of cases going through the courts has also decreased (Beattie, 2009a; Wallace, 2009; Thomas, 2010).

Canada is characterized as having a dual legal system, with both civil and common law traditions. Almost all cases (both civil and criminal) are dealt with in the provincial court system but may be appealed to higher-level courts. According to the Constitution Act of 1867, the federal government has sole responsibility to legislate criminal law but the provinces are responsible for the administration of the criminal law within their territory. The provinces have sole responsibility for the civil justice system. A civil case is a private case or "suit" whereas a criminal case is prosecution of a violation of an offense under the Criminal Code, the Controlled Drugs and Substances Act, or the Competition Act.

There are a wide range of sanctions that judges can impose for someone convicted of a criminal offence. For those offenders who have mental health issues, the options of not criminally responsible and being found unfit to stand trial are available. For all other offenders, judges may impose a fine, probation, conditional sentence, and/or custody. These sentences may be given alone or in combination with others (see p. 331 onwards on corrections).

According to the Canadian constitution, law enforcement is the responsibility of the provinces and territories; however, the Royal Canadian Mounted Police (RCMP) is a federal law enforcement agency which has agreements with most provinces and territories to provide police services, except Quebec, Ontario, and Newfoundland/Labrador which maintain their own provincial police forces.

Generally, the decision of whether to charge an individual is made by the police, Crown prosecutor or discussions between the two parties and only if there are reasonable grounds to believe that the person committed the offence is a charge laid. Once an individual is charged, they may be kept in jail if there are concerns that the individual will commit another crime, attempt to destroy evidence or threaten witnesses. In order to assess this, there may be a bail hearing where the Court will determine whether the individual should be released, and if so, assign conditions and possibly a financial surety to ensure the person abides by the conditions.

If the defendant decides to plead guilty, they will do so before the Court and the judge will determine the appropriate sentence. The sentence may be based on an agreement between the lawyer(s) for the offender and the prosecutor, or each side may submit to the judge a recommendation for sentencing.

If the defendant decides to plead not guilty, a preliminary inquiry may be held to determine whether there is enough evidence to send the case to trial. During the inquiry, key evidence is presented. If the judge determines there is not enough evidence, charges may be dismissed. If the judge determines there is enough evidence, a date for trial is set.

At the trial, each side normally presents evidence and arguments. After all witnesses and evidence has been entered, the judge determines whether the individual is guilty. If the individual is not guilty, the proceedings are over and the individual cannot be charged ever again with that offense pertaining to that incident(s). If the individual is found guilty, the judge determines the sentence. Again, the defense attorney and the prosecutor can either submit sentencing recommendations together or separately.

The following principles of sentencing are codified in section 718 of the *Criminal Code of Canada*:

- To denounce the criminal conduct
- To deter the offender and others
- To separate offenders from society when necessary
- To assist in rehabilitating the offender
- To provide reparation to the victim and the community
- To give a sense of responsibility to the offender

There are a number of sentencing options available to judges, in order of most restrictive to least restrictive. The judge may impose one or a combination of the sentences.

- Imprisonment. If two years or more, served in a federal institution.
- Conditional Sentence. This is a sentence of custody of less than two years that is served in the community unless the offender violates the conditions of the release, in which case he or she can be sent to jail immediately for the remainder of the sentence.
- Intermittent Sentence. For custodial sentences of 90 days or less the judge may allow the offender to serve the sentence on weekends or other blocks of time which allow the offender to work, go to school, or other responsibilities.
- Probation. This is a community sentence for up to three years in length. The judge may impose a number of conditions that the offender must abide by.
- Fines. This is a financial penalty that requires the offender to pay money to the court as punishment for the criminal act.
- Restitution Order. This is a financial penalty that requires the offender to pay money directly to the victim to make up for loss property or damages.
- Suspended Sentence. A judge may decide to put off sentencing for a period of time while the offender abides by conditions in the community for a specified period of time. If the offender is successful in that he or she does not breach any of the conditions, the judge will determine that the sentence has been completed.
- Absolute or Conditional Discharge. The judge may choose to discharge the charges against an individual, leaving that individual with no conviction on record. The conditional discharge differs from an absolute discharge only in that the judge sets conditions the individual must follow if a discharge is the outcome.

Judges have the option to impose a victim surcharge to any sentence. This is paid to a fund which provides services to victims.

There are two other types of sentences available for extremely serious offenders. For offenders who cannot be controlled in the community and who have a long history of violent behaviour there is the Dangerous Offender designation. These offenders are sentenced indeterminately, meaning it is akin to a life sentence.

The second sentence available for serious offenders is a Long-Term Supervision Order (LTSO). These are offenders who, like Dangerous Offenders, have a long history of violent behaviour but there is evidence to suggest that there is the possibility of control in the community. An LTSO is served after the custodial sentence and provides for intensive community supervision for a period of up to ten years which is determined by the judge. All court proceedings are public unless the judge feels that it is absolutely necessary to close the courtroom to the public.

It should be noted that the courts must also consider the mental capacity of individuals accused of crimes. Psychiatric assessments are completed for those whose mental capacity is in question. If the individual cannot understand the proceedings or the consequences of the proceedings they may be found "unfit to stand trial" or "not criminally responsible" for their actions on account of mental of mental disorder. Further information on this issue, as well as on the criminal justice process in general, can be found at http://www.justice.gc.ca/eng/pi/pcvi-cpcv/guide/evaluation.pdf.

Criminology

Police duties vary by region. Most urban areas have regional-municipal police forces responsible for policing services. Larger rural areas are patrolled by the RCMP, or, like in Ontario and Quebec, are patrolled by provincial police services.

Police statistical reporting is one of the primary databases from which Canadian criminal statistics are drawn: the Uniform Crime Reporting Survey (UCR) is a primary example of incidents of crime reported by police services (Wallace, 2009).

A decade-long decline in police reported crime continued in 2008 as Canada reported a crime rate of 6,588 crimes per 100,000 population. There was a 5 percent decline in the overall volume of crime and severity. Canada's crime rate is largely driven by non-violent offences, such as non-motor vehicle theft under $5,000 in value, mischief, breaking and entering, administration of justice offences, traffic violations, and other federal statute violations.

Young offenders and their crimes are regulated by the Youth Criminal Justice Act (Canadian Legal Information Institute, n.d.a), legislation that outlines the specific violations, legal proceedings, and sentences that can be applied in cases involving an offender under the age of 18 years. The overall youth crime rate declined 5 percent in 2008 from the previous year. Youth violent crime also decreased by 3 percent in 2008.

Violent crimes accounted for 20 percent of the crime rate in 2008, amounting to 1,326 violent offences per 100,000 population. Of these violent crimes, 15 percent were serious assaults; serious assaults are categorized as assaults with a weapon, aggravated assaults, and assaults against peace officers. Serious assaults are the few types of police-reported violent crime to have risen over the past decade (Dauvergne, 2009a).

There were 611 homicides in 2008, representing a 2 percent increase in the rate from 2007 (Beattie, 2009b). Firearms and bladed weapons each accounted for 33 percent of all methods of homicide. The rate of firearm homicides increased 5 percent from 2007; 60 percent of all firearms used to commit homicide were handguns. Homicide rates are highest in western Canada and the Territories. Of all solved homicides, 83 percent involved a killer the victim knew.

Gang-related homicide has become more visible over the last decade: it is estimated that gang violence is currently responsible for nearly a quarter of all homicides. Police reported 138 gang-related homicides in 2008, and nearly half of all homicides committed with a firearm were reported to be gang related.

Data are currently available for 2007 with respect to drug offending (Dauvergne, 2009b). Canada prosecutes drug offences as listed in the Controlled Drugs and Substances Act (Canadian Legal Information Institute, n.d.b). There are four primary drug offences which are enforced: possession of substance, trafficking in substance, importation and exportation of substance, and production of substance.

Canada reported a rate of 305 police-reported drug offences per 100,000 population in 2007, accounting for just over 100,000 actual offences. Police reported drug offences have steadily risen since the early 1990s – an increase that generally correlates with a decline in the overall non-drug crime rate.

It is reported that 60 percent of all drug offences involved cannabis. Possession of substance represents the majority of offences reported. Possession and trafficking of cocaine, crystal methamphetamine, and ecstasy (MDMA) account for the remaining 40 percent. A decrease in cannabis offending reflects the presence and popularity of other narcotics within the Canadian illicit narcotics black market.

Half of those convicted for drug trafficking were sentenced to custody and less than a fifth were incarcerated for possession offences. The most common sentence received for a possession of substance conviction was a fine.

Over a million charges in 372,000 cases were dealt with in Canada's adult criminal courts in 2006/7 (Marth, 2007). In all adult criminal cases brought into Canadian courts, 65 percent of cases were found guilty. Probation was the single most common sentence imposed by the courts, representing 43 percent of all sentences. Incarceration and fines followed representing 34 percent and 30 percent of all cases, respectively, in 2006/7.

Of all offences to be dealt with in a criminal court, violent crime represents 25 percent and property crimes 24 percent. Court related administration of justice offences represented 17 percent of cases, while traffic offences, such as impaired driving, accounted for 14 percent of all cases. Other federal statute violations, drug crimes for example, account for 12 percent of cases. The remainder (8 percent) was comprised of specific criminal violations such as weapons violations, prostitution charges, and violations pertaining to disturbing the peace (Marth, 2007, Table 1).

There were 56,463 cases involving young offenders in Canada's youth criminal justice system in 2006/7 (Thomas, 2007). Of all youth cases in the courts, 60 percent resulted in guilt in 2006/2007. Youth are specifically directed to non-custodial sentences wherever possible by the Youth Criminal Justice Act and, as a result, only 17 percent of all guilty cases result in the young offender being incarcerated in youth correctional facilities. Probation accounts for 59 percent of all sentences imposed.

In 2006/7, crimes against property was the most frequent category of violation before the courts involving youth, accounting for 38 percent of youth cases. Violent crime follows, representing 27 percent of cases. Other federal statute offences account for 17 percent of all cases. Court-related administration of justice offences accounted for 9 percent of all cases, and the remaining 8 percent of cases was comprised of other criminal violations such as weapons violations and residual criminal offences (Thomas, 2007, Table 2).

In 2005/6, there was a 4 percent increase in the number of adults admitted to custody from the previous year; this increase was driven primarily by an increase in the remand population. In addition, data demonstrate that accused individuals are spending longer periods in remand.

As mentioned at various points in this chapter, Aboriginal people were over-represented in the correctional system. While Aboriginal people make up 3 percent of the Canadian population, they accounted for 25 percent of all admissions to provincial/territorial corrections, 19 percent of admissions to remand, and 18 percent of admissions to federal corrections.

In 2007/8, the rate of youth admitted to custody decreased by 5 percent from the previous year and 30 percent from 2003/4 – which is the year the Youth Criminal Justice Act was enacted. This decrease was primarily driven by a decrease in the number of youth sentenced to custody for a property offence.

Though efforts are under way to improve Canada's collection and reporting of victimization, Canada does not have an annual victimization survey. At present, only once every five years is a General Social Survey (GSS) cycle devoted to criminal victimization. At time of press, 2004 data are the most current data publicly available. These data have been analyzed in relation to various groups.

Seniors were three times less likely to experience victimization than other Canadians. This corresponds to feelings of safety from crime in that 92 percent of seniors reported being satisfied with their overall safety. When compared to heterosexual individuals, gays, lesbians, and bisexuals reported higher rates of victimization but had similar levels of fear of crime.

There were no differences in reported victimization between visible minorities and non-visible minority groups but immigrants reported a lower rate of victimization compared to the Canadian-born population.

Only 2 percent of the population reported being a victim of more than one crime but this small group reported experiencing 60 percent of all violent victimizations. Aboriginal people and single people as well as those who reported consuming alcohol more often were more likely to have reported multiple victimizations.

Possibly due to the vast area Canada covers, crime rates and crime issues vary widely. In 2007, Canada's largest city, Toronto, reported a crime rate of 4,728 incidents per 100,000 population as compared to a higher crime rate in a relatively small urban centre such as Regina (11,851 incidents per 100,000 population) (Statistics Canada, 2009). Crime rates tend to increase as one moves east to west. As reported by Statistics Canada in 2007, the highest overall crime rates were found in small urban areas with populations less than 100,000 (Statistics Canada, 2007). Violent crimes in small urban and rural areas both accounted for higher rates than the rates reported in large urban areas. However, when looking at property crime rates, small and large urban areas were close to twice the rates of rural areas of the country.

Of the 2,473,087 incidents of crime reported to police in 2008, the five highest rates of crime were reported in the Northwest Territories, Nunavut, Yukon Territory, Saskatchewan, and British Columbia. It is interesting to note that two of the most populated provinces, Ontario and Quebec, reported crime rates lower than the national average (6,588).

The mentally disordered accused population has been growing and is expected to double in size over the next decade. As of 2009, the Correctional Service of Canada indicates that rates of offenders experiencing mental health problems have increased by 61 percent – 12 percent for the male offender population and 21 percent for the female offender population (Correctional Service Canada, n.d.a).

A central issue is the nature of sentences awarded to mentally disordered accused as they are being treated more severely than non-disordered offenders (Correctional Service Canada, n.d.b). The Correctional Service of Canada also reports that mentally disordered offenders serve longer sentences before release and also serve a larger proportion of their sentences prior to release. Further, mentally disordered offenders were more likely to have their early release suspended – 86 percent of mentally disordered offenders were readmitted to a correctional institution while under mandatory supervision as compared to 55 percent of non-disordered offenders who re-offended.

Recent research has given insight into the legal problems experienced by Canadians (Currie, 2008, 2009). The research measured the nature and extent of legal problems experienced by adult Canadians over a three-year period and how people attempted to resolve problems. Building upon previous research, a legal problem was defined as any problem experienced by an individual whether or not the person was aware of the legal nature or used any part of the justice system to resolve it. Respondents were asked whether they had experienced 83 specific problems – each carefully worded to assure a legal aspect to the problem spanning 15 problem types. Therefore, they can be called justiciable problems since they have a potential legal remedy. The data were collected using telephone interviews from a random sample of 6,665 adult Canadians in January to March 2006.

Almost 45 percent of Canadians experienced one or more legal problems, putting Canada in about the mid-range internationally among countries that have reported prevalence rates of between 25 percent and 65 percent. There results point clearly to the ubiquitous character of legal problems experienced by the public. Approximately 40 percent of problems remain unresolved during the reference period of the study. In about 33 percent of resolved problems, respondents felt that the outcome was unfair.

The most common types of problems reported were: consumer problems (i.e. paid for a service that wasn't satisfactory, safety problem with item purchased and seller would not repair or replace), 22 percent; debt (unfairly refused credit because of inaccurate information, need to declare personal bankruptcy), 20 percent; and employment (i.e. health and safety issues at workplace, obtaining employment insurance, harassment at work), 18 percent.

Most people who experience a serious and difficult legal problem make some attempt to resolve it. According to the 2006 survey, about 12 percent obtained legal advice, 22 percent obtained advice or assistance from a variety of non-legal sources, 44 percent attempted to resolve the problem using various self-help strategies, 16 percent took no action because they experienced some barrier to accessing assistance, and 6 percent took no action for other reasons.

There is a momentum to experiencing legal problems. For each successive legal problem experienced by an individual, the probability that the person will experience additional problems increases. Experiencing legal problems is characterized by trigger and cascade effects. About 30 percent of people reported that a legal problem they experienced triggered another one. About 18 percent of respondents experienced multiple problems, defined as three or more in the study. Legal problems also trigger a variety of non-legal problems, such as problems pertaining to physical health, mental health, or extreme stress and strained relationships among family members. About one third of all legal problems were reported to have triggered a social or health-related problem. The occurrence of trigger and cascade effects and the clusters of interdependent problems suggest that experiencing legal problems may be a part of the processes producing social exclusion. Thus providing advice and assistance for legal problems might forestall the development of patterns of social exclusion.

These data are based on self-reported legal problems gathered by a representative sample survey. This approach avoids the accessibility bias inherent in studying only the problems that come to the attention of the courts or tribunals, or attract the attention of lawyers. The survey approach yields a high prevalence of legal problems suggesting that level problems are, indeed, ubiquitous features of modern society. On the other hand, one has to consider whether results obtained by the survey method tend to "over-legalize" everyday life. Are all the problems reported the sorts of troubles for which people should be provided with some level of legal advice or assistance? The dynamics of legal problems: the momentum of legal problems, the trigger and cascade effects and the clustering of problems, all of which occur in connection with a large percentage of the problems experienced by individuals, suggest that minor problems can become major ones and single problems can evolve into Gordian knots of interdependent problems. Frequently these problems relate to debt, social assistance, disability pensions and family law matters, pulling people from self-sufficiency into lives of disadvantage and dependence on social assistance, and away from the mainstream toward social exclusion. Unfortunately, too little is currently known about the production of these patterns and the people who are most vulnerable. The results suggest the need for early intervention to provide assistance for a wide range of problems. The research suggests that providing access to justice requires a network of access to justice services to address the multiple and interrelated problems experienced by so many people. Overall, the results of this and similar research suggests that we have to look at access to justice much more broadly, from the point of view of the people who experience legal problems rather than from the point of view of the traditional, formal justice system. Our concept of the justice system should evolve in the direction of a broader and more varied set of access to justice services; from public legal information, to advice services, to assisted self-help, mediation, and finally full legal representation, arrayed along a "continuum of service" model providing the appropriate assistance for the particular problem, corresponding to a broader and richer understanding of the legal problems experienced by people in everyday life.

For the most part, the Canadian population is dispersed across our very large and equally diverse land mass and geography. The one hallmark of criminological research in Canada is that the criminological problems that face Canadians differ vastly from region to region, even city to city. It would be difficult, if not impossible, in the context of this Handbook to provide a summary that is fair and reflective of the research being conducted. The primary reason for this is that the issues being examined by criminal justice researchers in Canada tend to be very local. For example, a group of researchers has focused on drug offending in Vancouver whereas another has focused on organized crime activity in Montreal. The very nature of crime and the crime situations in these cities is so different that there are almost no nation-wide studies, with the exception of the national data collection efforts being done by the Canadian Centre of Justice Statistics of Statistics Canada. This situation actually highlights some of the major difficulties within criminological research and policy making in that there is very rarely a problem that affects the entire country. Though unlikely to contain results that are generalizable to other areas across the country, Canadian criminal justice research is being conducted in areas common across the international community. The quarterly *Canadian Journal of Criminology and Criminal Justice* is a peer-reviewed journal containing articles based on research and experimentation (http://www.ccja-acjp.ca/en/cjc.html). In general, Canadian criminal justice research is readily accessible.

Funding for criminological research can come from a number of sources. Different levels of government can provide funding to individual researchers based on proposals. For example, for a researcher wanting to examine gangs in Toronto, it would be possible to apply for funding from the Toronto Police, but also the Ministry of Justice for Ontario. In addition, the researcher could apply to various federal government departments, such as the Department of Justice, the Department of Public Safety, and the National Crime Prevention Centre. There is one federal agency that provides funding (grants and fellowships) to researchers within universities for research projects. The agency, Social Sciences and Humanities Research Council, requires that all interested researchers submit an application to be considered. More information on the Council can be found at http://www.sshrc.ca/site/about-crsh/about-crsh-eng.aspx.

Conclusion

Canada is fortunate in that there is one set of criminal laws to govern the entire country, so researchers can examine problems at a national level. However, because it is a large country with a relatively small population, criminological issues are more local and unique to those areas. This creates a problem for criminal justice policy makers as they must make policy for the entire country. It also creates problems for criminological researchers in two ways. The first is that collecting data from each area of the country is difficult because of the vast distances one would have to travel, and secondly, it also raises the question of whether data collected in each location should be grouped in attempts to generalize to the entire country. Canadian researchers will continue to struggle with these issues as well as others in their attempts to understand impacts of legislation and policy changes.

Future research questions

1. With the number of cases going through the justice system decreasing but the average amount of time cases are taking to get through the system increasing, where are the delays occurring? Are they justifiable delays and what measures can be put in place to minimize delays?
2. As Canadian demographics change, what impacts will this have on offending and victimization?
3. What role are criminal organizations and gangs playing in crime? Is the nature of their illegal businesses changing and to what extent are these groups becoming trans-national?
4. With the governmental priority of developing and securing Canada's north, what impacts will this have on the populations that live there with regards to crime, victimization, and justice services?
5. Technological advances, such as DNA and closed-circuit television cameras, will likely have an impact on everything in the justice system, from how police investigate to how courts

prosecute cases. What will be the nature of the impact and how can other new technologies improve justice in Canada?

References

Beattie, S. (2009a) *Police resources in Canada, 2009.* Ottawa, Ont: Statistics Canada. Catalogue no. 85-225-X, vol. 29, no. 4. Online at http://www.statcan.gc.ca/pub/85-225-x/85-225-x2009000-eng.pdf (accessed December 7, 2010).

—— (2009b). Homicide in Canada 2008. *Juristat*: 85-002-X, vol. 29, no. 4. Ottawa, Ont: Statistics Canada. Online at http://www.statcan.gc.ca/pub/85–002-x/2009004/article/10929-eng.pdf (accessed December 7, 2010).

Bonta, J. (1997). Do we need theory for offender risk assessment? *Forum on Corrections*, 9(1).

Canadian Legal Information Institute (n.d.a). Youth Criminal Justice Act, S.C. 2002, c. 1. Online at http://canlii.org/en/ca/laws/stat/sc-2002-c-1/latest/sc-2002-c-1.html (accessed December 7, 2010).

—— (n.d.b). Controlled Drugs and Substances Act, S.C. 1996, c. 19. http://www.canlii.org/en/ca/laws/stat/sc-1996-c-19/latest/sc-1996-c-19.html (accessed December 7, 2010).

Correctional Service Canada (n.d.a). *A program for every inmate: meeting specific needs.* Online at http://www.csc-scc.gc.ca/education/sse1-eng.shtml

—— (n.d.b). Conditional release and offenders with mental disorders. *Forum on Corrections Research*, (5)3. Online at http://www.csc-scc.gc.ca/text/pblct/forum/e053/e053f-eng.shtml

Currie, A. (2008) The legal problems of everyday life: the nature, extent and consequences of civil justice problems experienced by Canadians. Ottawa: Department of Justice.

—— (2009) The legal problems of everyday life. In R. L. Sandefur (Ed.), *The sociology of law, crime and deviance.* Vol. 12. pp. 1–42. Emerald: Access to Justice.

Dauvergne, M. (2009a). Trends in police-reported serious assault. *Juristat*: 85-002-X, vol. 29, no. 4. Ottawa, Ont: Statistics Canada. Online at http://www.statcan.gc.ca/pub/85–002-x/2009004/article/10930-eng.pdf (accessed December 7, 2010).

—— (2009b). Trends in police-reported drug offences in Canada. *Juristat*: 85-002-X, vol. 29, no. 2. Ottawa, Ont: Statistics Canada. Online at http://www.statcan.gc.ca/pub/85-002-x/2009002/article/10847-eng.pdf (accessed December 7, 2010).

Marth, M. (2007). Adult Criminal Court statistics 2006–7. *Juristat*: 85-002-XIE, vol. 28, no. 5. Ottawa, Ont: Statistics Canada. Online at http://www.statcan.gc.ca/pub/85–002-x/85–002-x2008005-eng.pdf (accessed December 7, 2010).

Organisation for Economic Co-operation and Development (OECD) (2006). *Education at a glance 2006.* New Milford, CT. Online at http://www.oecd.org/dataoecd/52/1/37392733.pdf (accessed December 7, 2010).

Statistics Canada (2001). *Population by religion, by province and territory (2001 Census).* Ottawa, Ont. Online at http://www40.statcan.gc.ca/l01/cst01/demo30a-eng.htm (accessed December 7, 2010).

—— (2005). *The Daily – population projections.* December 15. Ottawa, Ont. Online at http://www.statcan.gc.ca/daily-quotidien/051215/dq051215b-eng.htm (accessed December 7, 2010).

—— (2007). *The Daily.* June 28. Ottawa, Ont. Online at http://www.statcan.gc.ca/daily-quotidien/070628/dq070628b-eng.htm (accessed December 7, 2010).

—— (2008). *The Daily.* February 7. Ottawa, Ont. Online at http://www.statcan.gc.ca/daily-quotidien/080207/dq080207a-eng.htm (accessed December 7, 2010).

—— (2009). *The Daily.* April 21. Ottawa, Ont. Online at http://www.statcan.gc.ca/daily-quotidien/090421/t090421b3-eng.htm (accessed December 7, 2010).

—— (2010). *Visible minority groups, 2006 counts, for Canada, provinces and territories.* Ottawa, Ont. Online at http://www12.statcan.ca/census-recensement/2006/dp-pd/hlt/97-562/pages/page.cfm?Lang=E&Geo=PR&Code=01&Table=1&Data=Count&StartRec=1&Sort=2&Display=Page (accessed December 7, 2010).

Thomas, J. (2007). Youth Court statistics 2006–7. *Juristat*: 85-002-XIE, vol. 28, no. 45. Ottawa, Ont: Statistics Canada. Online at http://www.statcan.gc.ca/pub/85-002-x/85-002-x2008004-eng.pdf (accessed December 7, 2010).

—— (2010) Adult Criminal Court statistics 2008/09. *Juristat*: 82-002-X, summer 2010. Ottawa, Ont: Statistics Canada. Online at http://www.statcan.gc.ca/pub/85-002-x/2010002/article/11293-eng.htm (accessed December 7, 2010).

Wallace, M. (2009) Police-reported crime statistics in Canada, 2008. *Juristat*: 82-002-X, July 2009. Ottawa, Ont: Statistics Canada. Online at http://www.statcan.gc.ca/pub/85-002-x/2009003/article/10902-eng.htm (accessed December 7, 2010).

Walmsley, R. (n.d.). *World prison population list.* 8th Edn. London: International Centre for Prison Studies, King's College. Online at http://www.kcl.ac.uk/depsta/law/research/icps/downloads/wppl-8th_41.pdf (accessed December 7, 2010).

Appendix A: major datasets

Uniform Crime Reporting survey and the Incident-Based Uniform Crime Reporting survey

Annual surveys of police reported criminal incidence information, the Uniform Crime Reporting Survey (UCR), and the Uniform Crime Reporting Survey II (UCR2) serve as primary indicators as to "what is going on" in criminal offence incidence rates, victim characteristics, offender characteristics, geography of criminal activity, and police administrative and organization information. The UCR and UCR2 cover approximately 98 percent of all police services.

Adult Criminal Court Survey

The Adult Criminal Court Survey is an annual survey which contains information regarding appearances, charges, cases, and sentencing in the Canadian criminal justice system. Data are collected from 13 Canadian jurisdictions and represent approximately 98 percent of all adult criminal cases. The ACCS is not a freely accessible database, though Statistics Canada provides relevant methodological and statistical information regarding the survey (http://www.statcan.gc.ca/cgi-bin/imdb/p2SV.pl?Function=getSurvey&SDDS=3312&lang=en&db=imdb&adm=8&dis=2).

Youth Court Survey

The Youth Court Survey (YCS) collects data on young persons who have contact with Canada's court system. Youth in the survey are aged between 12 and 17 years of age, and are included in the survey if they violate a federal law. The YCS is designed to target the population of youth in the court system. Although the data are not freely accessible, Statistics Canada provides analysis of the YCS and methodological information on its website (http://www.statcan.gc.ca/cgi-bin/imdb/p2SV.pl?Function = getSurvey&SDDS = 3309&lang = en&db = imdb&adm = 8&dis = 2).

Adult Correctional Services Survey

Adults in Canada's correctional system are surveyed by Statistics Canada's Adult Correctional Services (ACS) survey. Designed to provide indicators as to the nature of Canada's adult correctional population, the survey collects annual data regarding the delivery of correctional programs at both the federal and the provincial/territorial levels. Data are collected regarding all adults in the correctional system, therefore the target of the survey is at the population and not the sample level. Though the data are not freely accessible, more information regarding the method and products of the survey are located at Statistics Canada's website (http://www.statcan.gc.ca/cgi-bin/imdb/p2SV.pl?Function = getSurvey&SDDS = 3306&lang = en&db = imdb&adm = 8&dis = 2).

Youth Custody and Community Services Survey

Similar to the ACS, the Youth Custody and Community Services (YCCS) survey collects data on the population of young persons receiving correctional services. Information regarding the survey and the survey products are freely available from Statistics Canada (http://www.statcan.gc.ca/cgi-bin/imdb/p2SV.pl?Function = getSurvey&SDDS = 3323&lang = en&db = imdb&adm = 8&dis = 2).

General Social Survey

The General Social Survey (GSS) of Canada collects data on Canadian society as perceived by the citizens. The GSS has two primary goals: to gather data on social and civil trends and to provide immediate information on social policy issues. There are many parts to the GSS: health, victimization, education/employment, family, and social engagement, among others. Information regarding the structure of the GSS is publicly available (http://www.statcan.gc.ca/dli-ild/meta/gss-esg/gssoverview-esgapercu-eng.pdf) and much of the information collected can be queried on the Statistics Canada website (http://www.statcan.gc.ca/start-debut-eng.html).

Canadian Addiction Survey

The Canadian Addiction Survey (CAS) is a collaborative initiative sponsored by Health Canada and the Canadian Executive Council on Addictions. The survey queries Canadians about alcohol and drug use, and probes relevant social and cultural variables, creating a detailed and extensive data set useful to health and sociological initiatives. While the data sets are not publicly available, the CAS website provides information on the survey tool, data access methods, and highlights from the last cycle of the CAS survey (http://www.ccsa.ca/Eng/Priorities/Research/CanadianAddiction/Pages/default.aspx).

Appendix B: key research institutions

Research and Statistics Division, Justice Canada

The Research and Statistics Division (RSD – http://www.justice.gc.ca/eng/pi/rs/index.html) of the Department of Justice (http://www.justice.gc.ca/eng/index.html) is the main research branch for justice policy research within the justice bureaucracy. The research teams in RSD continue research in a variety of fields, including drugs, organized crime, impaired driving, high-risk offenders, mental health, sentencing, victim's issues, access to justice, and legal procedure. Its website contains links to past publications and current publications.

Canadian Centre for Justice Statistics

The Canadian Centre for Justice Statistics (CCJS) compiles, maintains, and analyzes all data reported by the UCR, the UCR2, and the ACCS. The CCJS are a division within Statistics Canada solely responsible for all justice related criminological statistics collected at the national level. While it is are responsible for collecting and cleaning criminological data, the CCJS also publishes various criminological reports, entitled "Juristats," on different types of crime and the impact of crime on Canadian society (http://www.statcan.gc.ca/pub/85–002-x/85–002-x2009004-eng.htm).

Correctional Service of Canada

The Correctional Service of Canada produces much research pertaining to convicted offenders serving federal sentences (greater than two years), addictions treatment, and correctional health statistics, amongst others (http://www.csc-scc.gc.ca/text/rsrch-eng.shtml).

National Crime Prevention Centre

The National Crime Prevention Centre is responsible for providing national leadership on effective and cost-effective ways to prevent and reduce crime by intervening on the risk factors before crime happens (http://www.publicsafety.gc.ca/prg/cp/index-eng.aspx).

International Centre for the Prevention of Crime

Drawing from the United Nations Guidelines for the Prevention of Crime, the International Centre for the Prevention of Crime (ICPC) is an international forum for national governments, local authorities, public agencies, specialized institutions, and non-government organizations to exchange experiences, consider emerging knowledge, and improve policies and programmes in crime prevention and community safety (http://www.crime-prevention-intl.org/).

Appendix C: universities

Several select Canadian universities have developed criminology and sociology departments which have produced much published research on criminological phenomena.

Simon Fraser University: http://www.sfu.ca/criminology
University of Toronto: http://criminology.utoronto.ca/
Carleton University: http://www2.carleton.ca/criminology/
University of Ottawa: http://www.socialsciences.uottawa.ca/crm/eng/research.asp
Saint Mary's University: http://www.smu.ca/academic/arts/sociology/research.html
University of Montreal International Centre for Comparative Criminology: http://www.cicc.umontreal.ca/en/
Faculty of Criminology, Justice and Policy Studies, University of Ontario Institute of Technology: http://criminologyandjustice.uoit.ca/EN/main/programs/crimjustice.html

32

Cambodia

A criminal justice system in transition

Roderic Broadhurst and Chenda Keo

Introduction

Cambodia is a small nation in South East Asia that borders Laos, Vietnam, and Thailand. During the last quarter of the twentieth century Cambodians suffered the greatest of all crimes: genocide, civil war, and foreign aggression. This legacy continues to have a profound effect on the criminal justice system. Following the first free and fair elections under United Nations supervision in 1993, Cambodia has been at peace since 1998 with the final demise of the Khmer Rouge (KR) insurgency.

A major characteristic of the growing (1.5 percent per annum) population of 13.38 million people in 2008 is its youthfulness: 60 percent are under 25 and 40 percent are less than 15 years old. Decades of murderous conflicts also took a toll on the male population (NIS, 2008, p. 6). Most (84.3 percent) of the culturally homogeneous population reside in rural areas and 95 percent are Buddhists and ethnic Khmers.

Despite many improvements, Cambodia remains one of the poorest countries in the world, 137th out of 182 countries in 2009 (UNDP, 2009, p. 145). As of 2004, 35 percent of Cambodians were estimated to live under the poverty line measured at a meager $0.45 USD per person per day (The World Bank, n.d.). Since 1991, Cambodia has received an average of $500 million USD a year in foreign aid that funds about half of its annual budget (Kyodo News International, 2002).

Cambodia has a long, volatile history (see Broadhurst, 2002) leading up to 1993, when the UN Transitional Authority in Cambodia oversaw the adoption of the present constitution and implementation of the first free elections. The royalist party (FUNCIPEC) won a majority of votes but, in the hope of preserving a fragile peace between former warring factions, was forced into an inherently unstable governmental alliance (a joint prime ministership) with the Cambodian's People Party (CPP) led by Hun Sen. This precarious peace was indeed seriously threatened by armed clashes between the CPP and royalist forces in 1997 which led to a significant number of casualties and the end of the co-primeministership with the defeat of the royalist's military capability. After the second elections of 1998, the CPP-FUNCINPEC governmental alliance was eventually reinstated, but with a greatly weakened FUNCIPEC. However, this arrangement was accompanied by continued periods of political uncertainty and violence. Remaining pockets of Khmer Rouge resistance ended in 1998, which also coincided with the death of Pol Pot. After four rounds of national elections in 1993, 1998, 2003, and 2008, the CPP has consolidated its dominance over government and Prime Minister Hun Sen has steadily increased his grip on power (Broadhurst and Bouhours, 2009).

Administration of justice

Cambodia's criminal justice system comprises three separate but interlinked institutions: (1) the policing institution; (2) the judicial institution; and (3) the correctional institution. The available literature paints an unpleasant image of the criminal justice system. It is said to be dysfunctional, under strong influence of the executive branch, and subject to endemic corruption (AusAID, 2007, p. 2; Broadhurst and Bouhours, 2009). Fundamental principles of international law and fair trial are often violated in the criminal justice system. Also impunity, torture, forced confessions, illegal arrests, and detention have frequently been reported by the media and human rights non-governmental organizations. The criminal justice system has lacked the essential components for an independent and efficient judiciary (The Asia Human Rights Commission, 2001).

Street crime and homicides have declined substantially since 2001 and generally fear of crime in both urban and rural areas has abated; nevertheless, significant levels of plunder and state crime are evident (Broadhurst and Bouhours, 2009).

Police

The policing institution comprises both the civil police operating under the Ministry of Interior and the military police (the gendarmerie) operating under the Ministry of National Defense. The gendarmerie of about 10,000 officers also has a legal mandate to investigate and take action on criminal cases (Jaleel, 2001). The focus of this section is on the civil police although relations with the gendarmerie are often critical to the success of criminal investigations.

Cambodia's Police Force was first established in 1884 during the French colonial period. However, the National Police Force was only established 61 years later (16 May 1945). During the Khmer Rouge regime between 1975 and 1979, the police force was totally abolished. After the liberation on 7 January 1979 the police force was reborn. It started with a force of 45 officers for the whole country, including only 10 in Phnom Penh (Ministry of Interior, n.d.). As of December 2008, it comprised 55,277 officers (2,325 females) of which 41,015 (1,428 females) were based in 24 municipal/provincial police commissariats (NPC, 2009, p. 14).

The Cambodian police in general do not enjoy a good reputation, although the UN Crime Victim Survey reported that about two thirds of villagers in one rural province reported that local police were helpful and doing a good job (Broadhurst and Bouhours, 2009, p. 184). The policing system is tarnished by allegations of malpractice, corruption, and favoritism (cronyism and nepotism). Instead of being a neutral institution, it is highly politicized through political patronage in its recruitment, appointment, and operation.

The police force is thought to be understaffed, and those in service often underemployed and under-qualified (Jaleel, 2001; Broadhurst, 2002). The widespread practice of "ghost police" contributes to the under-performance of police. Ghost police are those on the payroll, but who do not normally perform their police duty but work elsewhere. They receive part of their salary and the rest goes to their superiors. Another aspect of under-strength force levels is "name-change police" who work under more than one name and whose commanders then draw the additional salaries from the payroll.

However, the establishment of a police academy and national training standards has generally helped improve criminal investigations among judicial police.

The police institution has a reputation of being one of the most corrupt institutions in the country (Calavan *et al.*, 2004). Their operational context encourages corrupt practices. An ordinary officer received a monthly salary of $25 USD in 2002 (Doyle, 2002), but although this had doubled by 2009 pay remained low.[1] Interviews with police officers at the district and commune level revealed that the police also did not have any operational and administrative budget. Their main sources of income are from the donations and contributions of the wealthy in their respective areas. Consequently officers must seek small monetary incentives to cover the costs for their services (e.g. petrol money). Their involvement in extra-judiciary mediation of conflicts or complaints allows them to generate some income. The meager salary, compounded by limited financial resources for police, leaves them little choice but to rent-seek and makes them prone to corruption.

There are also allegations of police involvement in crime including drug trafficking, protection or extortion and robbery. They are also reported to have accepted bribes (ARCPPT, 2003, p. 32). For example, the much-feared former Municipal Police Commissioner, Heng Pov, who was in power between 2004 and 2006, is currently serving a 92-year prison term for crimes ranging from murder and money extortion to kidnapping (Chrann, 2009).

Cambodia's Constitution requires that the Legislative, Executive, and Judicial powers shall be separate (Cambodian National Assembly, 1993, article 51). Ironically, the Legislative and the Judicial branches are regarded by some as the mere apparatus of the Executive (Muddell, 2003, p.3).

Courts

The Cambodian judicial system is composed of courts of first instance, appeal courts, public prosecutors attached to each court, and independent advocates or barristers. The judicial system suffered the same fate of all the government institutions, at the hands of the Khmer Rouge who replaced them with a rule by terror. Although article 9 of the Constitution of Democratic Kampuchea (the Khmer Rouge Government) referred to tribunals and judges, a court system was never created. No written laws or courts operated at that time (Sok and Sarin, 1998, p. 20).

Cambodians with a legal background such as judges and lawyers were targeted by the regime. Approximately 50 to 80 percent of an estimated 400 or 500 lawyers living in Cambodia prior to 1975 perished either because of murder, starvation, or disease (Sok and Sarin, 1998). Following liberation in 1979 there was a severe shortage of legal professionals: only ten legal graduates including five judges were known to remain in the country (Vickery, 1986).

By 2000, there were 117 judges (12 females) and 54 prosecutors (United Nations, 2004, p. 7). The most recent statistics from the Council of Justice Ministry (CJM) show that, as of May 2006, there were 167 judges (22 females) and 72 prosecutors (one female) (CJM, 2006). As of 2006, there were municipal/provincial courts in all provinces except Pailin, Ordor Meanchhey, and Kep. Female judges and prosecutors are in the minority and most judges and prosecutors are over 50 years of age.

Lawyers play an indispensable role in the judicial system. Among the many achievements of the National Assembly after the 1993 general election was the enactment of the Law on Advocates (National Assembly of the Kingdom of Cambodia, 1995) which was promulgated on 22 August 1995 (1995) and gave birth to an independent Bar Association. The Cambodian Bar Association was established on 6 October 1995 by a group of 38 lawyers who were sworn in before the Appellate Court (Sok and Sarin, 1998, p. 151). In 1996, the number of registered lawyers rose to 54, and rapidly rose to 249 in 2002 (Koy, 1998).

Despite these improvements the judicial system has been implicated in rampant corruption and is believed to lack sufficient independence. Traditionally judges were considered an organic part of, and subservient to, the Executive in the old Kingdom. The current judicial system is regarded as dysfunctional and unable to render justice to the people, especially the powerless. It is corrupted by and biased towards the elites. The NGO Cambodian League for the Promotion and Defense of Human Rights (LICADHO, 2007a, p. 1). The main independent advocacy organization Cambodian League for the Promotion and Defense of Human Rights (LICADHO, 2007), p. 1) concluded that the justice system had failed, because the courts persecute opponents of the government, perpetuate impunity for officials, and protect the interests of the economic elite.

The arrival of UNTAC in 1992 brought about a fundamental change to the entire judicial system in Cambodia (The Khmer Institute of Democracy, n.d.) via the 1993 Law on the Organization and Activities of the Adjudicate Courts. From 1979 to 1985, there was only one-tier level of court (the court of first instance). The establishment of the Supreme Court in 1985 resulted in a two-tier court system (Sok and Sarin 1998, pp. 51–2). The 1993 law mandated the establishment of an Appellate Court and thus created a three-tier civil court system: the Municipal/Provincial Courts (otherwise known as the court of first instance or the lower court), the Appellate Court (court of the second instance), and the Supreme Court (court of final instance) (The Khmer Institute of Democracy, n.d.).

Articles 132–134 of the Constitution established the Supreme Council of Magistracy (SCM) to guarantee the independence and efficiency of the judiciary. It has the power to decide and propose to the King the appointment, transfer, secondment, leave of absence, duties, and dismissal of judges and prosecutors (Koy, 1998). In 1994, the law on the organization and functioning of the SCM was promulgated. The law provided that the SCM members are appointed by Royal Decree with a five-year term with the possibility for reappointment for another term, and shall be composed of nine members, the King as the President, and the Minister of Justice, the President of the Supreme Court, the Prosecutor General of the Supreme Court, the President of the Appellate Court, the Prosecutor of the Appellate Court, and three judges (elected by judges) (Sok and Sarin, 1998, pp. 54–5).

The SCM was convened for the first time on 3 December 1997. The SCM has been criticized for failing to fulfil its mandate. Corruption, lack of independence, and politicization were among several problems encountered by the SCM (COHCHR, 2003, p. 5).

There are four different courts in Cambodia: the Lower Court, the Military Court, the Appellate Court, and the Supreme Court. The lower court's jurisdiction covers a particular geographical area (i.e. the province or municipality) and has a legal mandate to adjudicate on civil, criminal, and commercial matters, and to adjudicate litigation of administrative or labour cases (National Assembly of the Kingdom of Cambodia, 1993, article 6). Judges handle both civil and criminal cases.

The Military Court is also regarded as a court of the first instance, but its jurisdiction covers the entire country. There is only one such a court in Phnom Penh and is administratively, financially, and logistically under the Ministry of National Defence (Koy, 1998). Article 9 of the law on the organization and activities of the adjudicate court provides that "the military court shall have competence to adjudicate and shall be subjected to appeals for those cases of military offence" (National Assembly of the Kingdom of Cambodia, 1993, article 9). However, if military personnel commit a criminal offence, s/he will be prosecuted by the lower court (ibid.).

The Appeal Court, located in Phnom Penh, is staffed with 12 judges (two females) and five senior prosecutors (all males). With jurisdiction covering the whole country, it hears cases appealed from all the lower courts, including the military court. Filing an appeal to the Appeal

Court is not bound by any condition because there are no laws or guidelines specifying the grounds required for making an appeal or providing penalties for making unwarranted or vexatious appeals. In this respect, there is no mechanism to filter groundless or unreasonable appeals to the Appeal Court. This provides further means for corruption because parties to a case can always file an appeal. This also increases the workload of the understaffed Appeal Court, which in turn lengthens the detention of defendants who may remain in jail pending the Appeal Court decision.

The Supreme Court, located in Phnom Penh, is the highest court of appeal and is the court of the third and final instance. As of 2006, the Supreme Court was staffed with 12 judges (one female), and four senior prosecutors (all males) (CJM, 2006). Since 1994, the Supreme Court comprises a panel of five judges that adjudicates questions of "law" for cases appealed from the appellate court a further review is then undertaken by a full bench of nine Supreme Court judges that reviews both questions of "law" and "fact." The Supreme Court does not have any power to review legislation, executive regulations or to make case law (The Khmer Institute of Democracy, n.d.).

Judicial independence

The Cambodian judicial system has yet to establish independence and its reputation is tarnished by allegations of corruption. The current organisation of the judicial system creates dependency and corruption among judicial officials. This is because traditional patronage has yielded to the dominance of one political party within the state. The CPP literally runs the country. The Senate has 61 members (9 women) of whom 45 are from the CPP, and the president of the Senate is also the CPP President (Cambodia in Focus, 2006; CPP, n.d.; The Senate, 2008). Following the 27 July 2008 general election, CPP won 90 out of 123 seats at the National Assembly, and has gained the crucial two-thirds majority needed to amend the Constitution. The President of the National Assembly is also the Honorary President of CPP (Inter-Parliamentary Union, n.d.; CPP, n.d.). The current Prime Minister is one of the longest serving in the world, and is also the CPP's Deputy President. All the ministers of the 26 ministries, including the Minister of Justice, are CPP members. The current President of the Supreme Court, Dith Munty, is also a member of the CPP Standing Committee (CPP, n.d.).

The Supreme Council of Magistracy and the Minster of Justice have a major influence on judges at all levels. Their powers to appoint, to discipline, and to instruct judicial officials place judges and prosecutors in a subservient position (Fernando, 1998, p. 20; United Nations, 2004, p. 7). Cambodian courts have a long history of consultation with the Minster of Justice, and until the establishment of the Supreme Court, the Minster of Justice acted as an appeal court. This was partly due to the dearth of human resources able to staff the lower courts. The Supreme Court once established was also under the control of the Minster of Justice. During the State of Cambodia regime, the decisions of the Supreme Court could be appealed to the Legislative Committee of the National Assembly which was chaired by the Vice Minister of the Minster of Justice. These practices created a tradition of judicial subservience to the Minster of Justice – a pattern difficult to change (Fernando, 1998, p. 60).

Apart from political influences that damage the credibility and independence of the judicial system, the judges also face problems. In Cambodia, personal safety cannot be guaranteed, and judges are no exception. Judicial officials can face repercussions concerning personal safety from those in powers or from parties to a case. In April 2003, three court officials were attacked in three separate incidents. A judge and a court clerk were shot by unidentified gunmen and a prosecutor attached to the municipal court was attacked, but managed to escape with minor injuries (International Commission of Jurists, 2003).

As a matter of principle, judges should receive sufficient remuneration to minimize their susceptibility to inducements and to enable them to perform their duty independently and impartially (Linton, 2006, p. 334). In 2003, judges' salaries were significantly increased from \$47.5–\$62.5 USD per month to \$325–625 USD (Khiev, 2004, p. 22; Linton, 2006, p. 334; LICADHO, 2007a, p. 23). LICADHO (2007a, p. 22) is the main indigenous legal defense non-governmental organization and in a review of the courts concluded that the salary increase had little positive effect on reducing irregularities among judges.

There have been substantial allegations that corruption within the Judiciary System is rampant (Linton, 2006, p. 335). It is widely perceived as one of the most corrupt institutions in the country. A survey of 2,000 households across Cambodia in 2005 by the Center for Social Development found that the courts were one of the most corrupt and dishonest institutions in Cambodia in 2006, and the outcome of a survey of 1,200 businesses by the Economic Institute of Cambodia reinforced these findings (LICADHO, 2007a, p. 22; Broadhurst and Bouhours, 2009, p. 184).

Apart from the issues of corruption and lack of independence that may undermine the right to "fair trial," the working conditions of the courts are poor. Buildings are substandard and poorly equipped (no computers or recording systems), and there is insufficient staff leading to case overload and long delays (Khiev, 2004, p. 11). In some criminal cases hearings are short and the judge may spend approximately ten minutes writing his/her decision (Fernando, 1998, p. 85). Trial reports depend on the notes of clerks and are often inaccurate (Khiev, 2004, p. 11).

Originally the new Kingdom of Cambodia's judicial system followed the socialist model in which "socialist" order took precedent over fair trial. Following liberation, Vietnamese experts, trained in East European countries, assisted Cambodia to revive the judicial system after its eradication by the Khmer Rouge. Judges then operated under the socialist government until the arrival of UNTAC and the first election was held in 1993. Many of the laws and procedures established before the establishment of the new Kingdom continued to be in use and created practices and attitudes that proved difficult to change (Fernando, 1998).

Fair trial is embedded in a wide range of procedural rules, including the presumption of innocence, burden of proof, and rules governing the admissibility and exclusion of evidence. The denial of a fair trial to an accused is a ground of miscarriage of justice (Bronitt and McSherry, 2001, p. 96). The defendant's right to a fair trial and the presumption of innocence are apparently often infringed by Cambodian judges. Judges sometimes pre-judge cases and this was a practice admitted by a former Minister of Justice (*The Phnom Penh Post*, 7–20 November 1998, cited in Fernando, 1998, p. 89).

Although improvements in judicial and advocate training have occurred since then, examples of poor procedure and oversight of police continue to occur. Despite clear prohibitions under the Constitution and procedural law, a widespread problem is the acceptance of dubiously obtained confessions extracted from suspects under duress by police. The Constitution strongly prohibits the extraction of involuntary confession in article 38 (National Assembly of the Kingdom of Cambodia,1993) and article 321 (National Assembly of the Kingdom of Cambodia, 2007). But confession made by the accused during interrogation by the police or by the investigative judges has always been seen as the most crucial piece of evidence sufficient to convict.

A report by a non-governmental organization, the Center for Social Development (CSD), that monitored criminal cases between April and June 2007 showed that 124 of 426 defendants complained that they had been coerced into a confession: 100 of the 124 were convicted (CSD, 2007, p. 7). The report also revealed that judicial police officers exploited the permitted 48 hours' detention period in police custody to extort confessions. In most cases, defendants alleged that they were beaten or threatened. Some officers made false promises (e.g. immediate release) in exchange for a confession. In some cases, defendants were forced to place their thumbprint on a blank paper or on a prepared report which they were not permitted to read. During the hearing, judges seldom fully considered defendants' allegations of coercion or the legality of the confession (CSD, 2007, p. 7).

Criminal trials apparently do not adhere to the basic concept of "presumption of innocence." The Constitution, in article 38, provides that: "The accused shall be considered innocent until the court has judged finally on the case" (Cambodian National Assembly, 1993, article 38). In civil cases, all parties to the case are required to present supporting evidence for their claims. However, in criminal cases it is the responsibility of the prosecutor and the investigating judge to prove the guilt of the accused beyond reasonable doubt (Reid, 2006, p. 12). However, the CSD report noted that Cambodian judges frequently reversed the burden of proof, and required the defendants to disprove the allegations against them, even in cases where the prosecution presented no evidence to support the charge. The report also concluded that the presumption of innocence is not being applied in courts, and that some convictions therefore are unsafe and are miscarriages of justice (CSD, 2007, p. 4).

Correctional services

The General Directorate of Prisons is part of the Ministry of Interior and was initially separated from the National Police in 2000 and later from the General Directorate of Administration in 2006 to form its own division (APCCA, 2007, p. 14–16). The Directorate does not have any jurisdiction over military prisons. As of 2008, there were 26 prisons throughout Cambodia (LICADHO, 2008, p. 1). Most were built around 1920, whilst others are converted civilian buildings and are in poor repair. There have been some instances when walls have partially collapsed. Such conditions are conducive to and encourage escape attempts (General Directorate of Prisons, 2003).

The 23 municipal-provincial prisons (LICADHO, 2008, p. 2)[2] and three national prisons have a capacity from 100 detainees to over 1,200 and a staff of about 1,700 (APCCA, n.d.). As of 2008, there were 10,592 prisoners comprised of 9,262 males, 627 females, and 703 juveniles (LICADHO, 2009, p. 13).[3] This is more than a four-fold increase over the past 14 years, from 2,490 in 1995 (see Table 32.1; APCCA, n.d.).

The national prisons (Correctional Center [CC] 1, 2, and 3) are managed by the Directorate while the other 23 are managed by the respective deputy provincial/municipal governors. CC 1 has the biggest prisoner population followed by CC 3 and Battambang prison.

Generally, each prison has a director who functions as the commandant of the prison and three to five deputies in charge of various departments. Each prison has a small clinic staffed with "para-medical" officers who have attended health training programs that enable them to treat minor illness and make referrals to the public hospitals as necessary. No doctors are assigned to prisons. There is limited employment training, education, or rehabilitation services. Prisons are often short of food and conditions are often crowded and unsanitary.

According to the Prison Procedure (General Directorate of Prisons, 2003b),[4] there are a total of 28 offenses that are punishable by a prison term. They include robbery, theft, sexual harassment, human and drug trafficking, deceiving, and others. Gambling is not listed, although the 1996 Law on Suppression of Gambling prohibits all sorts of unauthorized gambling in Cambodia, and those found guilty may be punished by a fine or short prison term. Many prison procedures issued by the General Directorate of Prison in accordance with the UN Standard Minimum Rules for the Treatment of Prisoners are not implemented.

Table 32.1 Prison population, 1995–2008

Year	*Prison population*				*Remandee*		*Total prison staff*
	Male	*Female*	*Juveniles*	*Total (M+F)*	*Remandee*	*% of Remandees*	
1995	2,373[a]	117[a]	N/A	2,490[a]	969[a]	38.9[a]	N/A
1996	2,685[a]	141[a]	N/A	2,826[a]	971[a]	34.4[a]	N/A
1997	2,749[a]	160[a]	N/A	2,909[a]	975[a]	33.5[a]	N/A
1998	3,030[a]	203[a]	N/A	3,233[a]	1,170[a]	36.2[a]	N/A
1999	3,613[j]	219[j]	128[b]	3,832[j]	1,380[a]	36.0[a]	N/A
2000	5,214[k]	288[k]	205[b]	5,502[k]	1,967[a]	35.8[a]	1,124[e]
2001	5,886[a]	293[a]	223[b]	6,179[a]	1,910[a]	30.9[a]	1,431[e]
2002	5,806[a]	322[a]	273[b]	6,128[a]	2,124[a]	34.7[a]	N/A
2003	6,026[a]	320[a]	270[a]/ 292[b]	6,346[a]	1,933[a]	30.5[a]	1,350[f]
2004	5,942[c]	354[c]	328[c]	6,296[c]	2,094[c]	33.3[c]	N/A
2005	N/A	506[b]	447[b]	8,238[b]/ 8,160[i]	N/A	N/A	N/A
2006	7,847[b]	536[b]	452[b]	8,383[b]	N/A	N/A	N/A
2007	9,084[g]	570[g]	622[g]	9,654[g]	N/A	N/A	N/A
2008	9,262[g] 10,574[d]	627[g] 633[d]	703[g]	9,889[g]/ 11,688[h] 11,207[d]	3,043[d]	27.2[d]	1,661[d]

Sources: (a) APCCA, cited in Egger, 2005, pp. 71–4; (b) This statistic is from 18 prisons monitored by LICADHO (2007b, p. 4); (c) This statistic is from 18 prisons monitored by LICADHO (2005, p. 11); (d) Morgan and Morgan, 2008, pp. 144–6; (e) APCCA, n.d.; (f) GDOP, 2003b; (g) 2008 prison population of 18 prisons monitored by LICADHO (2009, p. 13); (h) 11,688 was the 2008 total prison population (26 prisons). This is based on the General Directorate of Prisons 2008 annual report released on 26 February 2009 as cited in LICADHO, 2009, p. 13; (i) By mid-2005 (Walmsley, 2007, p. 4); (j) APCCA, 1999; (k) APCCA, 2000.

Little is known about corruption in Cambodia's correctional institutions. Whilst not all prison officers are corrupt or are in positions to corrupt, an observational study by the second author revealed that corruption was systemic. For example, there are reports that wealthy "magnate" inmates can bribe staff so as to be placed in a better cell with fewer inmates (LICADHO, 2008; Koh Santeapheap, 2009). Officers reported a case in which a prison cell had been renovated for an affluent prisoner. The renovated cell housed the prisoner and a few poor prisoners whose role was to serve the "magnate" prisoner. Bribes by those that can afford them enabled, inter alia, more time out of cells, being placed in a less crowded cell, being excused from labor, consumption of any kind of food and drink, authorization to undertake medical care outside the prison (such a furlough is an opportunity for detainees to enjoy themselves outside for some time), and access to media and entertainment. Although access to the radio/TV is not prohibited under the prison regulations, the prison authorities have been known to manage access as a form of rent-seeking. Occasionally prison officers are implicated in assisting escapes (*Koh Santeapheap*, 2009).

The prison's budget is a function of the number of inmates and the government allocated 1,500R5 ($0.38 USD) per prisoner per day. Although the allocation is barely sufficient, these funds are often manipulated by inflating the number of prisoners, allowing wealthy prisoners to buy their own food or by buying poor-quality rice, and so on. The absence of a system of accountability compounded by the lack of a computerized data management system fuels such practices.

Prisoners are categorized into any of three security classes – low, medium, high. Affluent detainees reportedly pay to be in a low-security class that allows for more freedom in prison. In a prison, there are reports that poor inmates are allowed to have a brief release from cells once a week or a fortnight. Those having $10–20 USD can bribe guards to leave their cell (or the prison) each day to work. Prison rules require the prison director to ensure that all prisoners have at least an hour a day outside of cells (General Directorate of the Prisons, 2003).

A specific day for family visits is not a common practice. Each prison sets its own schedule, but all allow unofficial visits. Although the prisoner has the right to weekly visits by family and friends an official visit costs on average 5,000R to 10,000R ($1.25–2.50 USD) but double or more for an unofficial visit.[6] The charge varies according to venue and the length of a visit. Usually a visit is between 15–20 minutes and if extended a visitor has to pay more (LICADHO, 2008, p. 10; *Koh Santeapheap*, 2009). The income earned by the prison from visits is often not accounted for and audits of prison expenditure and income are unknown. Income may sometimes be earned by the Parole Committee when it conducts regular performance reviews of convicts. A former director confided that a prison director might act as a facilitator of early release, reduction in sentence, or release for those prisoners who can afford bribes.

Prision in Cambodia is more than a place of punishment and rehabilitation. It is a society within a larger society characterized by inequality, unfairness, hierarchy, and many other aspects observed in Cambodian society. Cambodian prisons are full of the poor, powerless, illiterate, and those without patrons.

Conclusion

In summary, a review of police, courts and prisons reveal a dysfunctional criminal justice system. Thus the criminal justice system is captured by elements of the state and real reform is politically and structurally constrained. The stages of the criminal justice process work in the interest of the powerful while compromising access to justice for the powerless. At each stage money can be used to exit or avoid further involvement along the process to prison and thus the elites and wealthy have more opportunities to escape justice. Even when they are in jail, they can contrive better living conditions. The poor are disadvantaged in such a criminal justice system, and became its victims. Despite improvement many challenging tasks lay ahead while good governance has yet to assert its place.

Future research questions

1. What difficulties are encountered in creating the rule of law in a post-conflict society?
2. Are the pay and conditions of officials key drivers of corruption?
3. Why has the prison population in Cambodia grown so rapidly?
4. How independent is the Cambodian criminal justice system?
5. How do political and social constraints need to be changed to improve conditions in the Cambodian police?

Notes

1 Personal communication with police officers in November 2008 and May 2009.
2 According to LICADHO, Odour Meanchey is the only province that does not have a prison (LICADHO, 2009).
3 There were 11,688 prisoners according to the General Directorate of Prisons.
4 Version as of May 2003. It should be noted that the Department is in the process of drafting the prison management law.

5 R stands for Riel. It is Cambodia's currency. Generally 4,000R equals $1 USD.
6 As per Procedure 8, of the prison regulations and officers are prohibited from soliciting money or other items from visitors. Those found guilty will be punished as per article 5 of the Law on the Civil Servant of the Kingdom of Cambodia (General Directorate of the Prisons, 2003).

References

Asian and Pacific Conference of Correctional Administrators (APCCA) (1999) APCCA statistics: correctional statistics for Asia and the Pacific, 1999. Online at http://www.apcca.org/stats/1999/APCCA%20Statistics%201999.htm (accessed 7 December 2010).

—— (2000). APCCA statistics: correctional statistics for Asia and the Pacific, 2000. Online at http://www.apcca.org/stats/2000/APCCA%20Statistics%202000.htm (accessed 7 December 2010).

—— (2007). *A Bi-annual publication*. pp. 14–16.

—— (n.d.). Cambodian prisons. Online at http://www.apcca.org/News&Events/Discussion%20Papers%20-%20agenda%201/Cambodia.htm (accessed 6 February 2008).

Asia Human Rights Commission (2001). Police abuses in Cambodia. Online at http://www.ahrchk.net/pub/mainfile.php/hrviolations/46/ (accessed 25 November 2010).

Asia Regional Cooperation to Prevent People Trafficking (ARCPPT) (2003). *Gender, human trafficking, and the criminal justice system in Cambodia*. Phnom Penh, Cambodia: ARCPPT, ACIL and AusAID. pp. 1–73.

AusAID (2007). *Australia's assistance to criminal justice reform in cambodia: strategic framework document*. Report of the Government of Australia Scoping Mission. Phnom Penh, Cambodia: Australian Government. pp. 1–62.

Broadhurst, R. (2002). Lethal violence and state formation in Cambodia. *Australian and New Zealand Journal of Criminology*, 35: 1–26.

Broadhurst, R. and Bouhours, T. (2009). Policing in Cambodia: legitimacy in the making. *Policing & Society*, 19: 174–90.

Bronitt, S. and McSherry, B. (2001). *Principles of criminal law*. Sydney: LBC Information Service 2001.

Calavan, M. M., Diaz Briquets, S., and O'Brien, J. (2004). *Cambodian corruption assessment*. Phnom Penh, Cambodia: USAID and Casals & Associates.

Cambodian Government (n.d.). Country overview. Online at http://www.cambodia.gov.kh/unisql1/egov/english/country.overview.html (accessed 31 July 2009).

Cambodia in Focus (2006). Cambodian People's Party wins in the senate elections. Online at http://www.embassyofcambodia.org.nz/February06/February7.htm (accessed 31 July 2009).

Cambodian National Assembly (1993). *The Constitution of the Kingdom of Cambodia*. 21 September.

Cambodia Office of the High Commissioner for Human Rights (COHCHR) (2003). *Note on the legal and judicial reform for the mid-term consultative groups of donors meeting*. Phnom Penh, Cambodia: The United Nations. pp. 1–9.

Cambodian People's Party (CPP) (n.d.). CPP Standing Committee. Online at http://www.thecpp.org/page.php?page=standingcommittee.htm&lang=eng (accessed 31 July 2009).

Center for Social Development (2007). *Court watch bulletin*. Cambodia. Year 4, No. 18. pp. 1–14.

Chrann, C. (2009). HENG POV: judges to rule on top cop appeal. Online at http://www.phnompenhpost.com/index.php/2009061226451/National-news/HENG-POV-Judges-to-rule-on-top-cop-appeal.html (accessed 31 July 2009).

Council of Justice Ministry (CJM) (2006). *List of judges and prosecutors all over the country*. Phnom Penh, Cambodia: Department of Staffs and Training. pp. 1–12.

Doyle, K. (2002). *Magic moto: how a moto taxi driver parlayed his easygoing charm and good looks into a role in a Hollywood film. The Cambodia Daily Phnom Penh*, 10–11 May. Cambodia. Online at http://www.camnet.com.kh/cambodia.daily/selected_features/story1.htm (accessed 7 December 2010).

Egger, S. (2005) *An assessment of the situation of children in conflict with the law in the Kingdom of Cambodia*. Phnom Penh: University of Sydney and Unicef.

Fernando, B. (1998). *Problems facing the Cambodian legal system*. Hong Kong SAR, China: Asian Human Rights Commission.

General Directorate of Prisons (GDOP) (2003a). *National Report on contemporary issues in corrections, 23rd Asian and Pacific Conference of Correctional Administrators, Hong Kong*. Hong Kong SAR, China: Ministry of Interior, Royal Government of Cambodia. pp 1–4.

—— (2003b). *Prison procudure*. Hong Kong SAR, China: Ministry of Interior, Royal Government of Cambodia.

International Commission of Jurists (2003). Cambodia: ICJ deplores murder of judge. Press release. Online at http://www.unhcr.org/refworld/publisher,ICJURISTS,,KHM,48a9281cd,0.html (accessed 29 July 2009).

Inter-Parliamentary Union (n.d.). Cambodian National Assembly. Online at http://www.ipu.org/parline/reports/2051_E.htm (accessed 29 July 2009).

Jaleel, M. (2001). Cambodia: who are Cambodian police? Online at http://www.hrsolidarity.net/mainfile.php/1998vol08no10/1820/ (accessed 25 July 2009).

Khiev, S. (2004). *What makes Australia's judicial system first grade? Why not in Cambodia?* Phnom Penh, Cambodia: Center for Democratic Institution. pp. 1–53.

Khmer Institute of Democracy (n.d.). The judicial system of Cambodia. Online at http://www.khmerrough.com/pdf/CriticalThinking-Eng/Part1-CriticalThinking.pdf (accessed 24 July 2009).

Koh Santeapheap (2009). Prison director jailed for conspiracy in allowing the subsequent escape of eight convicts. *Koh Santeapheap Daily*, p. 4.

Koy, N. (1998). The Cambodian judicial system. Online at http://www.bigpond.com.kh/users/kid/pdf/The%20Cambodian%20Judicial%20Process.pdf (accessed 24 July 2009).

Kyodo News International (2002). Cambodia asks foreign donors for $1.4 billion over three years. Online at http://findarticles.com/p/articles/mi_m0WDP/is_2002_June_24/ai_87697060/ (accessed 31 July 2009).

LICADHO (Cambodian League for the Promotion and Defense of Human Rights) (2005). Human rights and Cambodia's prisons: prison conditions 2004. Phnom Penh, Cambodia: LICADHO.

—— (2007a). *Human rights in Cambodia: the charade of justice.* Phnom Penh, Cambodia: LICADHO. pp. 1–30.

—— (2007b). Prison conditions in Cambodia 2005 & 2006: one day in the life. Phnom Penh, Cambodia: LICADHO.

—— (2008). *Prison conditions in Cambodia 2007: the story of a mother and child.* Phnom Penh, Cambodia: LICADHO.

—— (2009). *Prison conditions in 2008: women in prison.* Phnom Penh, Cambodia: LICADHO.

Linton, S. (2006). Safeguarding the independence and impartiality of the Cambodian Extraordinary Chambers. *Journal of International Criminal Justice*, 4: 327–41.

Ministry of the Interior (n.d.). *History of Cambodia's police: part 3.* The Kingdom of Cambodia: Ministry of the Interior. pp. 1–4.

Morgan, N. and Morgan, I. (2008). Conference report: Malaysia 2008. Paper presented at the 28th Asian and Pacific Conference of Correctional Administrators Langkawi, Malaysia.

Muddell, K. (2003). *Transitional justice in Cambodia: challenges and opportunities.* Symposium report. Online at http://www.ictj.org/static/Asia/Cambodia/cambodiasymposium.eng.pdf (accessed 31 July 2009).

National Assembly of the Kingdom of Cambodia (1993). *Law on the Organization and Activities of the Adjudicate Courts.* 8 February.

—— (1995). *Law on the Bar.* 22 August.

—— (2007). *Law on the Criminal Procedure.* 10 August.

National Institute of Statistics (NIS) (2008). *General population census of Cambodia 2008: provisional population totals.* Phnom Penh, Cambodia: NIS, Ministry of Planning, Royal Government of Cambodia. pp. 1–35.

National Police Commissariat (NPC) (2009). *The 2008 report of the National Police.* Phnom Penh, Cambodia: NPC, The Cambodian Ministry of Interior. pp. 1–23.

Reid, S. T. (2006). *Crime and Criminology.* New York: McGraw Hill.

The Senate (2008). The Senate of the Kingdom of Cambodia. Online at http://senate.gov.kh/index_ni2.php (accessed 7 December 2010).

Sok, S. and Sarin D. (1998). *Legal System of Cambodia.* Phnom Penh: The Cambodian Legal Resources Development Center (CLRDC).

United Nations (2004). *Kingdom of Cambodia: public administration country profile.* Phnom Penh, Cambodia. pp. 1–18.

United Nations Development Programme (UNDP) (2009). Human development report 2009. Overcoming barriers: human mobility and development. New York, USA: UNDP.

The World Bank. (n.d.). Poverty in Cambodia. Online at http://web.worldbank.org/WBSITE/EXTERNAL/COUNTRIES/EASTASIAPACIFICEXT/CAMBODIAEXTN/0,,contentMDK:20720197~pagePK:141137~piPK:141127~theSitePK:293856,00.html (accessed 15 July 2009).

—— (n.d.). Poverty in Cambodia. Online at http://webworldbank.org (accessed 15 July, 2009).

Vickery, M. (1986). *Kampuchea: politics, economics and society.* Sydney: Allen & Unwin.

Walmsley, R. (2007). World prison population list. 7th edn. Online at http://www.apcca.org/stats/7th%20Edition%20%282007%29.pdf (accessed 13 October 2010).

33
Chile
A criminological approach

Joanna Heskia

Introduction

The Republic of Chile is a Latin American country located in the southwestern part of South America. It is considered one of the most politically and economically stable countries of the region. In fact, during the last two decades, it has led Latin America in terms of human development, competitiveness, political stability, economic freedom, low perception of corruption, and comparatively low poverty rates.

From 1973 to 1990, it was governed by a military dictatorship, recovering as a democratic government in 1990. From that date onwards, it has been ruled by four consecutive governments of a center-left coalition.

In the last 20 years, authorities and experts began to realize that the administration of justice needed a profound change because judicial proceedings were obsolete, complicated, expensive, and extremely lengthy. Consequently, a series of judicial reforms started to be implemented, beginning with a reform of the criminal justice system in the year 2000, followed by family law proceedings in 2005, juvenile criminal law in 2007, and labor law proceedings in 2008. A new civil procedure code is now being studied, and should be a reality in the next five years.

Infrastructure

Chile is located in South America. It borders Peru to the north, Bolivia to the northeast, the Andes Mountains and Argentina to the east, and the Drake Passage at the south. The Pacific Ocean forms the country's entire western border, with a coastline that stretches over 6,435 kilometers. Chile's territory also includes the overseas territories of Juan Fernandez Islands, the Salas y Gomez islands, and Easter Island located in Polynesia. It has a total of 2,006,626 square kilometers, including the 1,250,000 square kilometers of territory claimed in Antarctica.

Chile is very rich in natural resources. The Atacama Desert contains a variety of minerals, especially copper, nitrates, and saltpeter, with Chile being the main copper producer in the world.

There are approximately nine million hectares of agricultural land in the central area, of which only 40 percent has been cultivated. The main products are fruits, corn, sugar beet, potatoes, wheat, lentils, and vineyards. Chile is the second producer of wine on the American continent. The south is very rich in forests, being the tenth producer in the world of timber and cellulose. The south also has an important salmon and fish industry.

Chile was ranked 30 in the Global Competitiveness Report of 2009–10 by the World Economic Forum, leading all Latin American countries (World Economic Forum, 2010). According to the 2008 the Economic Commission for Latin America and the Caribbean (ECLAC) *Statistical Yearbook for Latin America and the Caribbean* (ECLAC, 2008), Chile in the year 2006 had a per capita gross domestic product (GDP) at current market prices of $9,872 million USD, and the growth rate of the GDP was 3.8. In this sense, its GDP was well above the Latin American region average of $6,425 USD. Despite having good economic and commercial indicators, Chile has a problem with income distribution. According to the same study, the country's GINI index for 2006 was 0.522, where the poorest 20 percent of the population has 1.5 percent of the national income, and the richest 20 percent of the population has 42.2 percent of the national income.

Regarding poverty issues, the ECLAC statistics (ECLAC, 2008) show that 13.7 percent of the population is poor, and 3.2 of the population is in the range of extreme poverty. The poverty and indigence GAP coefficient is 4.4 for poverty, and 1.1 for extreme poverty.

Although unemployment figures for the year 2006 were 7.6 percent overall, and 17.3 percent for people aged 15 to 24 years (ECLAC, 2008), during 2009 the numbers have risen significantly due to the economic crisis, and they have escalated to almost 11 percent overall.

In 2007, Chile had a production of 65,573.2 barrels of oil, and a production of 117,089.1 barrels of oil of secondary energy (ECLAC, 2008). Chile's consumption of primary energy in 2007 was 40,490.7 barrels of oil, and 114,193.8 of secondary energy.

Nowadays, one of the biggest topics regarding the production of energy is the use of Chile's water resources in the building of hydroelectric plants and the installation of nuclear energy, which are opposed by most environmental groups.

Regarding housing and available services for dwellings, Chile had a total of 3,899,448 occupied dwellings in 2002 (ECLAC, 2008). Of these dwellings, 92.9 percent had piped water, 82.5 percent had excreta disposal systems, and 99 percent had electric lighting. In the same line, according to 2006 numbers, 98 percent of the population had access to drinking water, and 94 percent of the population had access to sanitation services (ECLAC, 2008).

Chile has a good level of communication technology. Internet and mobile phones are widely used. Data from the National Institute of Statistics (INE, 2007) indicates that there are 3,264,000 telephone lines, 13,472,000 mobile phone lines, and 25,033,000 internet connections.

There are two types of television channels. Open national television has seven channels; one is state owned, two are owned by universities, and the rest are owned by corporations. There is also an ample selection of cable television from all over the world. Digital television issues are now being debated and should be a reality very soon.

Transportation in Chile is basically done via highways. There are very good and modern highways, both in the cities and between cities, which have been built in the last 20 years by means of concessions to private corporations who charge for their use.

Since Chile is such a long country, most of the transportation to the far north and the far south is done by airplane. There are two main national airlines that cover the country, both operating with very high international standards. In the far south, some of the villages are so isolated that their only means of transportation is either by small planes or by sea.

Although there have been some important problems with the railway system in the last few years, in particular due to bad management, from the data obtained (INE, 2007), there are still 1,897 kilometers of railroads throughout the country.

Inside Santiago, public transportation is basically by means of buses. During 2005 a big change in the public bus system was launched, but it soon became a failure, still requiring a lot of adjustments. Santiago also has a very modern, clean, and safe subway system that covers most of the city. It has five lines, with a total of 92 stations, and it is now being enlarged.

There are 2,762,593 motor vehicles in Chile; 87 percent are private cars, 6 percent public transport, and 7 percent cargo vehicles.

Chile is ruled by a President elected by people who are over 18 years old and have previously registered in the Electoral Service. The President's term lasts four years and he or she cannot serve a consecutive term. Until March 2010, the President of Chile was Michelle Bachelet Jeria, the first female to serve as such. She belongs to the center-left coalition called *Concertacion*, which ruled the country from 1990. The current President is Sebastián Piñera.

Chile's bicameral Congress has a 38-seat Senate and a 120-member Chamber of Deputies. Senators serve for eight years with staggered terms, while Deputies are elected every four years. The Congress is located in the port city of Valparaiso, about 120 kilometers west of Santiago.

Chile has a binomial system that rewards large representations, consisting of two Senate and two Deputy seats apportioned to each electoral district. This being the case, the political parties are forced to form wide coalitions and, historically, the two largest coalitions, *Concertacion* and *Alianza for Chile*, split most of the seats in a district.

On June 26, 1945, Chile participated as a founding member of the United Nations being among 50 countries that signed the covenant. Since its return to democracy in 1990, Chile has been an active participant in the international community. Currently, Jose Miguel Insulza, a prominent Chilean politician, is serving as Secretary General of the Organization of American States (OAS), planning to become reelected in 2010. Chile is also an active member of the UN Agencies and it is currently bidding for a seat on the UN Human Rights Council. Chile hosted the Defense Ministerial of the Americas in 2002 and the APEC summit in 2004. It also hosted the Community of Democracies ministerial in April 2005 and the Ibero-American Summit in November 2007. An associate member of Mercosur and a full member of APEC, Chile has been an important actor on international economic issues and free trade agreements.

Nowadays, Chile is in the process of becoming a member of the Organisation for Economic Co-operation and Development (OECD) and after many years of discussion, in 2009 the Chilean Congress finally ratified the treaty to become part of the International Criminal Court.

People

Chile's last census was in the year 2002, reporting a population of 15,116,435. According to growth rates, the actual population of the country is about 16,267,279. Almost 87 percent of the country's population lives in urban areas, with 40 percent of the entire population living in the capital city of Santiago and its surroundings. The biggest cities after Santiago are Valparaiso with 804,000 and Concepción with 666,000.

The fertility rate is now at 1.93 children per woman. Approximately 26 percent of the population is younger than 15, 66 percent is between 15 and 65, and 8 percent is older than 65.

In Chile there are mainly three big ethnic groups. Although data vary, the proportion is about 40 percent white, 43 percent mestizo, and 8 percent indigenous population. The remaining 9 percent come from other backgrounds. The modern indigenous population is mostly *Mapuche*, about 87 percent (INE, 2002), which come from the south, but also includes other groups, such as the Aymara, the *Atacamenos*, and the *Diaguitas*, from the north, and the Rapa Nui from Eastern Island. The mestizo population was born from the interaction between the colonial Spanish immigrants from Andalusia, Castille, and the Basque region, and the indigenous population.

After the Spanish, Chile had significant immigration from Italy, Germany, Yugoslavia, and Palestine that contributed to the mestizo blood. Immigrants have been very important in the evolution of Chilean society, even though they never surpassed 4 percent of its total population. They came to Chile from the 18th century up to the first half of the 20th century, vitalizing the economy and forming the political and cultural elite that have dominated the country. In the last 20 years, immigration from neighboring countries has been rapidly increasing. Chile's 2002 census counted 184,464 immigrants in the country, 26 percent of whom were from Argentina, 21 percent from Peru, and 6 percent from Bolivia (INE, 2002).

On the contrary, after big waves of emigration of Chileans due to political and economic problems in the early seventies, this emigration has decreased nowadays. Of those living abroad, more than 50 percent live in Argentina.

According to the 2002 census, 70 percent of the population is Roman Catholic and 15.1 percent is evangelical, a term that refers to non-Catholic Christian churches with the exception of the Orthodox Church, Church of Jesus Christ of Latter-day Saints (Mormons), Seventh-day Adventists, and Jehovah's Witnesses (INE, 2002).

Chile's only official language is Spanish. There are also some indigenous languages spoken, such as *Mapudungun*, *Quechua*, and *Rapa Nui*, but they are scarcely used. Nevertheless, in the last few years, there has being a bit of a revival of the use of *Mapuche* language, *Mapudungung*, especially in the Araucania Region where most of the pure *Mapuche* live.

There is still a big gap between public and private school education. As a general rule, private schools are much better than public schools, but they are also quite expensive. There are three types of schools, totaling 11,561: public education which is administered by the city councils (6,098), private schools which are subsidized by the government (4,630), private schools (763), and 70 belong to either corporations or foundations (Ministry of Education, 2009). There is a national average of 26 pupils per teacher in secondary education (ECLAC, 2008).

Regarding higher education, there are 573 educational institutions. Of those, 205 are universities, 170 are professional institutes, and 198 are Technical Formation Centers. Universities created prior to 1981 (66 of them) receive at least some public funding. All the rest of the universities and institutions are 100 percent private (Ministry of Education, 2009).

In Chile, the average educational level in 2002 was 10 years, but this average has been growing rapidly in the last 20 years. According to the census data, 2 percent of the population has no education, 24 percent has less than 8 years, 26 percent has eight years, 34 percent has completed high school, and 13 percent has a higher education degree (INE, 2002).

Administration of justice

In Chile, the administration of justice is the responsibility of the Ministry of Justice. The judiciary, although an independent branch, has a budget that depends on and is negotiated with the Ministry. Except from the public prosecutor's office, which is also an independent branch, all institutions dealing with the administration of justice depend, either directly or indirectly, on the Ministry. These institutions are the Correctional Services (*Gendarmería de Chile*), the Civil Registry, the Legal Medical Service, Child Services, the Public Defender's office, the Bankruptcy Superintendency, and the Judicial Public Assistance.

Since the beginning of the judicial reforms that started in 2000, the total justice budget has been steadily increasing. In 2007, the total budget in Chilean pesos was M$422,823,006, approximately $729,005 million USD, with an increase of 6 percent from 2006. Between the years 2004 and 2005, when the criminal reform was implemented in Santiago, the budget had increased 19 percent (Ministry of Justice, 2007).

Criminal proceedings are basically handled by two institutions, the Public Prosecutor's Office and the Criminal Courts. The Public Prosecutor's Office is a nationwide institution with 18 regional and local offices, which is constitutionally independent both from the Central Government and from the Judiciary. It is headed by the National Public Prosecutor, whose nomination is a result of input from the Congress, the Judiciary, and the President. Constitutionally, it is the sole holder of public accusation interest investigating all crimes committed, leading the police forces in the investigation, and representing the public interest in the Criminal Courts.

The judiciary in Chile is presided over by the Supreme Court. All criminal proceedings before the trial itself are held before the Guarantee Courts. Trials are carried out before a court presided by three bench judges, called the Oral Trial Courts. Appeals, which are very restricted, are resolved by the Appeals Court, and in complex cases, by the Supreme Court.

Defendants are either represented by private attorneys or, in case of indigence, by the Public Defender's Office. As in the majority of Latin American countries, criminal procedure also allows for an active participation of the victim, parallel to that of the public prosecutor, both in the criminal investigation and in the trial. This participation does not necessarily require their attorney's representation; however, it is only by such representation that is it really possible to address victim's needs seriously, especially those dealing with reparation.

This victim's legal representation usually starts through the presentation of a criminal complaint before the Guarantee Court, in which the private accuser requests the prosecutor to perform investigative proceedings deemed necessary to advance the case. In this complaint it is also possible to request the judge to decree precautionary measures over the defendant's assets in order to secure future civil reparations.

The Chilean criminal system also allows for some alternatives to trial. These are the Reparation Agreements and the Conditional Stay of the Proceedings.

Reparation agreements consist of the possibility for a victim of a crime affecting a disposable legally protected interest to arrive at an agreement with the defendant to satisfactorily repair the damage caused by the crime. This agreement must be consented to voluntarily and with full knowledge of the parties and has to be later approved by the Guarantee Judge. The Court must make sure that these requisites are met, and that the crime does not affect the public interest, thus making the agreement socially damaging. If the agreement is approved, the case is irrevocably dismissed, ending the criminal responsibility of the defendant.

The importance of this alternative lies in the fact that the public prosecutor has a legal obligation to further these agreements to get reparation for the victim. So far, this option has been widely used and has obtained high levels of success and satisfaction for the parties involved. This alternative is used worldwide and basically consists of an agreement between the public prosecutor and a defendant of a crime that carries penalties of no more than three years of imprisonment to temporarily stay the criminal proceedings under certain conditions with which the defendant must comply. This alternative also must be approved by the judge who has to make sure that the crime allows this possibility. The victim cannot oppose the conditional stay, but must be heard in the court hearing. Once the conditions are met and the observation time has passed, without further indictments against the defendant, the case is irrevocably dismissed.

Correctional services are handled by a public institution called *Gendarmería de Chile*, which is part of the Ministry of Justice. This institution is divided into two main groups, uniformed staff and professional personnel. Uniformed staff deal with security and the handling and transportation of prisoners. The professional personnel are part of the Technical Unit which is divided into four departments: Planning, Re-adaptation, Alternative Penalties, and Regulation.[1] Their main responsibilities are the classification of inmates and the development and evaluation of programs aimed at the rehabilitation and resocialization of inmates. They are also in charge of executing and evaluating all alternative punishments, such as probation or intensive probation.

Prisons are one of the greatest weaknesses in the criminal justice system, due to huge overcrowding problems, few rehabilitation or training opportunities, lack of security for inmates, and poor training of the prison personnel. In fact, according to research, the overcrowding rate is 50 percent overall, 78 percent in Valparaiso, and 77 percent in Santiago (Hurtado, 2007).

Regarding the rehabilitation and training opportunities, less than 1 percent of the *Gendarmería* budget is allocated to rehabilitation, and 21,000 prisoners don't have access to employment programs. Of those who do have access, 50 percent work in autonomous craftsmanship, and only 4.8 percent have some sort of link with the private industry (Hurtado, 2005).

In terms of drug rehabilitation programs, they number about 275 (Hurtado, 2005), handling about 572 severe drug addicts and 5,613 problematic consumers. There are also important pending issues regarding security and human rights abuses (Diego Portales University, 2008).

Because of all these problems, in 2005 Chile began building ten contracted prisons, which are under mixed administration. As of now, six of these prisons are already under operation. In these prisons, security and transportation of inmates is handled by *Gendarmería*, whereas all services regarding food, lodging, and general housekeeping are in private hands. Most importantly, the private companies have the responsibility to develop training, education, and employment programs (Blanco, 2005). Nowadays, these prisons handle around 25 percent of the imprisoned population (Ministry of Justice, 2007). The building of these contracted prisons has been advantageous because they seem to offer more rehabilitation and training programs and present fewer security issues and less overcrowding because, by contract, they can only handle a maximum number of inmates. If the numbers rise, the Ministry has to pay a fine. Nevertheless, this has also meant that when there is a greater number of inmates, public prisons get even more crowded.

The problem related to this development is that with faster and more efficient criminal procedure, the number of prisoners is growing at a very fast pace. In fact, according to *Gendarmería*, in 1995 there were 22,027 inmates in Chilean prisons, and in 2007, 43,723. At this pace, in two or three years, the prison system will collapse again (Hurtado, 2005).

All prisons, both public and contracted, are subject by law to the supervision of the Ministry of Justice and the Judiciary. Nevertheless, even though criminal law gives the guarantee judge and the courts the responsibility to supervise the execution of punishments,[2] this is not well institutionalized. In most cases, after the sentence is delivered, all responsibilities related to how this is served is de facto given to *Gendarmería*. A new law regulating the execution of penalties is being drafted but is not seen as a priority.

In 2007, Chile reformed its juvenile justice system. Previously, all young offenders (i.e. up until age 16) were subject to a decision about their criminal responsibility. This was very unsatisfactory due to a lack of precise and standardized criteria. If young offenders were determined to be criminally responsible, they entered the adult criminal justice system, with a small reduction in their penalties.

The new juvenile criminal responsibility act[3] lowered the age of responsibility to all those who are 14 or over. It also established a specialized judiciary, with trained judges, district attorneys, and public defenders. The new act also has a whole different set of penalties for juveniles, all of them based on individualized treatment programs aimed at rehabilitation.

Those young offenders who are remanded or sent to prison are now sent to special units managed by Child Services, with only the security issues being handled by *Gendarmería*. Nowadays, there are special units in all the regions of the country; 17 closed centers for remand and adjudicated juveniles and 17 semi-closed units for juveniles in day treatment programs. There are also five clinics for short drug detoxification stays.

This act is still too new to be able to evaluate it, but critics argue that there are still too many juveniles in prison and that these individual programs are not working very well. There is also huge overcrowding and waiting lists for the short-stay clinics.

The dominant approach to justice in Chile is traditional adversarial. As previously mentioned, in 2000, Chile reformed its criminal justice system. Before that date, it had an inquisitorial written criminal justice system, led by a judge who was in charge of investigating, accusing, and sentencing. Criminal proceedings were very slow, often lasting five or more years.

The new system, introduced in the country progressively, is based on the oral accusatory system. Its implementation was costly, entailing a whole new infrastructure and the creation of the Public Prosecutor's Office.

After nine years, despite an overall positive evaluation by the system's actors and criminal justice specialists, some problems linger. Most of them are related to the paradigmatic change in procedure: there are still many legal actors that continue to apply inquisitorial principles. Another problem is the adjustment necessary to the new public prosecutor's office, especially because this institution was created from scratch, with no history or precedent. There is a general feeling the assistant district attorneys are disconnected from the people and are not functioning correctly.

Due to this long tradition of adversarial justice, there is an important lack of knowledge and of properly trained actors in other justice practices, it having been very hard to install non-adversarial justice practices. Nevertheless, there are some manifestations that can be assimilated to restorative and therapeutic justice. Considering that the victim can participate in the proceedings in an active way, some institutions have some restorative justice elements. In this sense, the reparation agreements between victim and offender are sometimes real restorative processes, especially when either the district attorney or the judge has used mediation to reach the agreement.

Another example is the new Juvenile Justice Act. During its debate, many experts wanted to incorporate restorative elements, and even though this was not to be, many of its punishments were based on it. In this sense, most of the alternative penalties, such as caution and community work, are dealt only after the teenager accepts responsibility, and most of the individual programs need to be accepted by the adolescent. The next step is to be able to incorporate mediation as a consistent practice. Nowadays, there are a few pilot experiences with penal mediation in some local public prosecutors' offices.

Regarding therapeutic justice, there are some very new programs in the country. On December 2007, an agreement was signed between the Ministry of Justice, the Judiciary, the District Attorney Office, CONACE (the specialized national office against drug abuse), the National Defender's Office, and the *Paz Ciudadana* foundation to implement Drug Courts. These have specialized judges, district attorneys, and defenders and are used for cases where drug use has been the primary cause for offending. So far, the results in terms of recidivism have been quite encouraging (Fundación Paz Ciudadana, 2010).

Before the return to democracy, the military based their social control actions in the National Security doctrine based in the repression or reduction of all that was considered subversive. After 1990, social control strategies have been based on trial-and-error formulas, which have been redefined after each change of government. There has not been agreement on how and where to intervene in order to achieve results regarding crime prevention, rehabilitation, and resocialization. This has not been an easy task, especially after so many years of intense repression and human rights abuses. There are still steps to be taken to balance the technical need to implement preventive and long-term public policies against the political need to effectively repress crime.

During the first stage of the transition to democracy, preventive social control strategies were based in three different areas: the foundation of an entity within the government in charge of this area, the strengthening and re-legitimation of policing, and the creation of the first community-based prevention programs.

The creation of the *División de Seguridad Ciudadana* (public security division) in the year 2001 was the first step. It was in charge of managing all topics related to the prevention of public security and crime control. Under its supervision, extensive neighborhood programs were developed, including *Comuna Segura* (safe district) and *Barrio Seguro* (safe neighborhood). Both programs were focused programs developed in very unsafe environments. These programs, some more successful than others, were scattered all over the country, without clear public policies behind them. There was no clear knowledge of the objectives to be met, no rigorous evaluation, and their scientific basis was unclear.

Consequently, those who were seriously researching and implementing prevention programs, such as think tanks, universities and NGOs, started to push for a national agenda able to express the principles and values behind the programs, together with clear objectives, both for the short and the long term.

Nevertheless, it was only in the year 2006 that a national public policy was established, called *Estrategia Nacional de Seguridad Pública 2006–2010* (Public Security National Strategy 2006–10). This strategy plans to consolidate scattered programs into an integrated prevention strategy. Plans are under way to create an under-secretariat of public security and reorganize the two existing police forces, currently located in two different ministries (Defense and Interior). This under-secretariat will have an advisory council and will have the responsibility to coordinate actions from the relevant ministries, such as health, education, justice, housing, and labor. Within this new vision, vital importance is given to accountability through constant monitoring and evaluation. Finally, this strategy also acknowledges that there is a need to invite local communities to participate in program development, although this is still undefined.

Some authors (Alarcón, 2007) have pointed out that for this new strategy to work, there is also the need to define first what will be understood as public security. Should it be only prevention/repression of crime? Or should security be understood as the guarantee and satisfaction of all social rights? This is an ongoing debate in Chile.

Although most experts in Chile believe in the importance of the rehabilitation and reintegration of the offender, there is still an enormous gap between what is deemed necessary and what it is really being done. In fact, the next step after the landmark reforms in criminal procedure and juvenile justice should be a reform regarding the execution of punishments. This reform has been contemplated but has stagnated. So Chile presents a paradox: a very modern and efficient criminal justice system, with no real control over the execution of its decisions. Indeed, 1 percent of the total budget of *Gendarmería* is assigned to rehabilitation and reintegration programs (Hurtado, 2005).

Alternative penalties in Chile are regulated in Act 18.216 of 1983, and include three different alternatives, depending on the offender's background and the severity of the crime. The execution of these alternative penalties is under the responsibility of the Community Based Treatment Department (*Departamento de Tratamiento en el Medio Libre*), part of *Gendarmería*. They are not only in charge of supervising the execution of these alternatives but also have to propose and generate policies and programs. At the operational level, these penalties are administered by the Social Reinsertion Centers (*Centros de Reinserción Social*).

The least severe community-based penalty is the conditional remission of the sentence. The offender is obliged to sign a registry monthly for a period of time which ranges from one to three years. It is delivered when the offender has not been sentenced before, if the imposed prison term is three years or less.

The second alternative is night imprisonment, which is used for those offenders who have committed prior minor crimes, and it consists of spending from 10 p.m. to 6 a.m. in a special prison.

The most intense alternative is probation, used for those offenders who have committed a more serious crime for the first time and where the imposed prison term is between three and five years. The offender is obliged to fulfill certain requirements that are imposed by the probation officer for a period of time, ranging from three to six years.

All these alternatives require the offender to remain crime-free while complying with them. Conditional remission and night imprisonment are oriented basically to control and to deter. This was based on the notion that these offenders were not in dire need of more intense intervention. However, in the last few years, it has become apparent that this is not the case, and that many offenders who at first commit minor crimes do have a need for stronger intervention.

Although these community-based penalties are used in 58 percent of the total cases (*Gendarmería*, 2008), it was clear since the very beginning of their implementation, that they were underfunded. But to the contrary, according to Hurtado (2005), *Gendarmería* spends 33 times more money on offenders that are in prison than those who are in the alternative penalties system. Therefore, it would be prudent to more fully fund the alternatives and reduce the prison population.

Some of the most clear problems are related to the lack of probation officers, with an average of 43.5 offenders per officer, versus the international technical standard of 30 (Hurtado, 2005). This is even more severe in some parts of Santiago, where the average is 72 (Hurtado, 2005).

Regarding night imprisonment, 80 percent of offenders go to a normal prison instead of the intended special unit (*Gendarmería*, 2008). Furthermore, alternative penalties such as community service, day fines, electronic monitoring, or economic reparation are lacking. They only exist for specific crimes and in a limited fashion, under the Juvenile Justice Act.

Nevertheless, in the last few years, the Department of Community Based Penalties has developed some programs to support these alternatives such as the job reinsertion program, the mental health program, the drug addiction treatment program, the strengthening and integration of young offenders program, and the gender equity program.

Similarly, and because of the evidence that shows that the offender profile on probation has become more complex, they have also developed a new intervention model for them, not only centered in the individual, but also working within their local communities.

As previously mentioned, prisons in Chile are very overcrowded and underfunded. Because of this, there is no real capacity to undertake rehabilitation and reintegration seriously. Nevertheless, in 1998, through some legislative changes,4 a public policy regarding employment insertion was launched. It was through these changes that for the first time the private sector could participate in some of these programs. All programs are voluntary, but due to their scarcity, priority is given to those near the end of their term, so they can comply with the requirements of parole and other benefits.

Most employment programs work under a CET (Education and Employment Center), which work formally as a normal business. They are funded by the national budget, credits, projects, donations, and by selling their own services (Blanco, 2005). Less common are cases where employment is self-generated or offered by private businesses that work inside prisons.

As previously mentioned, private companies that administer the new contracted prisons have the obligation to offer quality training and employment programs, and they also have the obligation to hire a minimum number of inmates to do productive work.

Criminology

This section discusses the major research topics in the past five years and the influential research figures associated with these research initiatives. Chile does not have a well-known research tradition in criminology. In fact, according to an important bibliographical study (Matus and Carnevali, 2007) covering 54 Chilean journals over a 121-year period, there were only 938 studies or articles published that dealt with either criminal law or criminology. From the 938 publications in these two fields, only 37 percent of them dealt directly with criminology.

Nevertheless, criminal procedure reform brought in an important amount of research, both before and after its implementation. In fact, of the total of 938 articles, 523 were published between 1995 and 2006, and of those, 319 were published between 2000 and 2006. This research was not only about procedural topics, but also about the effects of the reform in public policies regarding security, incarceration, alternatives to traditional justice, police and forensic work, and other related topics.

In order of amount of research, these articles can be classified as follows: penology (122); prisons and prisoners (82); criminal behavior (53); juvenile crime (41); gender, minorities and victimology (24); social systems and criminology (13); and police and security (11) (Matus and Carnevali, 2007).

Most quality criminology research nowadays can be found in a limited number of sources. These include *Gendarmería*'s technical unit's magazine, *Revista de Estudios Criminológicos y Penitenciarios*, and the publications and research done by the *Paz Ciudadana* foundation. Within academia, important journals include the University of Talca's *Política Criminal* journal and *Ius et Praxis*, Alberto Hurtado's *Persona y Sociedad* journal, Diego Portales University's *Cuadernos de Análisis Jurídico*, and Pontifical Catholic University of Valparaiso's *Revista de Derecho*.

It is precisely because of the lack of consolidated research in criminology that it is not possible to identify major methodological strategies and their relative dominance in the country's criminology research community.

The major datasets in the country are available online. The most important are http://www.ine.cl (the National Statistics Institute), http://www.gendarmeria.cl (belonging to Correctional Services), http://www.defensoriapenal.cl/ (Public Defender's Office), http://www.ministeriopublico.cl (Public Prosecutor's Office), http://www.pazciudadana.cl (Paz Ciudadana) and http://www.flacso.cl/publicaciones.php (Latin American Faculty of Social Sciences).

In Chile, funding sources for social sciences research include the National Fund for Scientific and Technological Development, FONDECYT (http://www.fondecyt.cl); the National Commission for Scientific and Technological Research, CONICYT (http://www.conicyt.cl); and the Fund for the Promotion of Technological and Scientific Development, FONDEF (http://www.fondef.cl/). All these web pages are very user friendly and have complete information regarding funds and scholarships. The fourth source is the Ministry of the Interior (http://www.interior.cl), which through its Public Security Division has some discretional funds that are granted for projects related to public security.

Future research questions

1. How should Chile conceptualize public security as a basis for a successful crime prevention strategy?
2. How can the many different scattered prevention programs in the country be scientifically measured and evaluated?
3. How can Chile better implement and develop local and community participation in crime prevention?
4. How would Chile establish quantitative and qualitative objectives for a national crime prevention strategy?
5. How can Chile identify local and regional relevant differences that should be taken into consideration for effective crime prevention intervention?

Notes

1 D.L. 2859 of 1979 and Decree 26, Ministry of Justice, 1983.
2 Article 466, Criminal Procedure Code.
3 Act 20,191. In effect since June 8, 2007.
4 Decree 518 and Resolution 1583, both from 1998.

References

Alarcón, A. (2007). Seguridad pública e intervención estatal: notas sobre la evolución en la construcción y abordaje de la problemática en Chile. *Debates Sociales, Boletín de Asesorías para el Desarrollo*, 3 (October): 8–11. Online at: http://www.asesoriasparaeldesarrollo.cl/docs/654739723.pdf (accessed 31 July 2009).

Alvarez, P., Marangunic, A., and Herrera, R. (2007). Impacto de la reforma procesal penal en la población carcelaria del país. *Estudios Criminológicos y Penitenciarios*, 11: 117–32.

Blanco, J. (2005) Nuevos desafíos penitenciarios: Inserción laboral de los reclusos. Online at http://www.pazciudadana.cl/docs/pub_20090707165126.pdf (accessed 31 July 2009).

De la Puente Lafoy, E. P. and Torres Rojas, E. R. (2000). Seguridad ciudadana y prevención del delito. Un análisis crítico de los modelos y estrategias contra la criminalidad. *Estudios Criminológicos y Penitenciarios*, 1: 15–62.

Gendarmería de Chile (2008). Sistema de medidas alternativas a la reclusión en Chile. Departamento de Tratamiento en el Medio Libre. *Estudios Criminológicos y Penitenciarios*, 12: 52–87.

Diego Portales University (2008) Anuario de derechos humanos. Condiciones carcelarias. Online at http://www.derechoshumanos.udp.cl/wp-content/uploads/2009/07/cond_carcelarias1.pdf (accessed 21 November 2010).

Economic Commission for Latin American and the Caribbean (ECLAC) (2008). *ECLAC statistical yearbook for Latin America and the Caribbean*. ECLAC. Online at http://websie.eclac.cl/anuario_estadistico/anuario_2008/eng/index.asp (accessed 29 July 2009).

Fundación Paz Ciudadana (2010). Areas de trabajo: tribunales de tratamiento de drogas. Online at http://www.pazciudadana.cl/at_just_reinsercion_drogas.html (accessed December 9, 2010).

Instituto Nacional de Estadísticas (INE) (2002). Síntesis de resultados. Online at http://www.ine.cl/cd2002/sintesiscensal.pdf (accessed 22 July 2009).

—— (2007). Transporte y comunicaciones. Informe annual. Online at http://www.ine.cl/canales/chile_estadistico/estadisticas_economicas/transporte_y_comunicaciones/pdf/2009/transporte2007.pdf (accessed 25 July 2009).

Hurtado, P. (2005). Diversificando la respuesta frente al delito. *Persona y Sociedad*. Vol. XIX. 1: 179–98.

—— (2007). Cárceles y política penitenciaria. Fundación Paz Ciudadana. Online at http://www.pazciudadana.cl/docs/pub_20090707110754.pdf (accessed 20 July 2009).

Matus, J. P. and Carnevali, R. (2007). Análisis descriptivo y cuantitativo de los artículos de derecho penal y criminología de autores chilenos en revistas publicadas en Chile (1885–2006). *Política Criminal*, 3: 1–138.

Ministry of Education (2009). Anuario estadístico de los años 2006 y 2007. Online at http://w3ap.mineduc.cl/DedPublico/anuarios_estadisticos (accessed 30 July 2009).

Ministry of Justice (2007). Balance de gestión.

Online at http://www.minjusticia.cl/minjus/balance-de-gesti-n (accessed 30 July 2009).

World Economic Forum (2010). The global competitiveness report 2009–10. Online at http:/www.weforum.org/pdf/GCR09/GCR20092010fullreport.pdf (accessed 19 March 2010).

34

Colombia

Crime trends, criminal justice, and criminology in a society in turmoil

Gipsy Escobar

Introduction

Since the 1980s, Colombia has experienced some of the highest crime rates in the Western hemisphere. The first decade of the twenty-first century has seen a reduction in violence, particularly in the main urban centers, but crime rates are still high and organized crime remains a problem. This chapter will introduce the reader to the social and structural characteristics of Colombia that may be related to crime rates; the organization and philosophy of the administration of justice; the crime trends in the last three decades; and the state of the study of crime.

Infrastructure

Colombia has an area of 440,839 square miles and shares borders with Venezuela and Brazil to the east, Ecuador and Peru to the south, and Panama to the northwest. Colombia is also bordered by the Pacific Ocean to the west and the Caribbean Sea to the north, making it the only country's in South America to have access to both the Atlantic and Pacific Oceans.

Even though only 2 percent of the land is considered suitable for producing crops, the country's mountainous topography and varied climate zones provide ideal conditions for diverse agricultural products. Coffee (Colombia is the second largest producer of coffee in the world), bananas, rice, tobacco, corn, wheat, potatoes, sugarcane, cut flowers, cocoa beans, and oilseed are amongst the primary agricultural products. These crops are produced mostly in the Andean region. In addition, cattle-raising is common in the savanna regions in the northwest and east of the country.

The Amazon basin has been used by "frontier" peasants and drug-trafficking organizations to crop coca leaf. This has become an environmental issue as coca growers contribute to the deforestation of tropical and rainforests and to the contamination of water sources, both of which are already serious problems. Indeed, the United Nations Office on Drugs and Crime reported in 2009 that coca crops could be found in 14 of the 54 national parks protected by environmental laws (United Nations Office on Drugs and Crime, 2009). Moreover, the environmental impact of coca growing is worsened by the government's use of herbicides, such as glyphosate, as part of its illicit crops eradication program. Besides destroying coca crops, glyphosate dramatically reduces the soil's productivity for several years and adds to the contamination of water sources.

Finally, Colombia is also rich in fossil fuels such as petroleum, natural gas, and coal; minerals such as iron, ore, nickel, copper, gold, and emeralds; and hydropower. The oil industry has been the target of terrorist attacks and extortion by left-wing guerrillas since the late 1980s. The pipelines used to transport oil from the exploitation areas to the exportation ports are the main targets of such attacks. The spillages caused by these acts also have been detrimental for the environment as land fields and water sources are contaminated with crude oil. This situation has forced the state to dedicate an important number of military manpower to guard the country's oil infrastructure.

Colombia's economy experienced sustained growth between 2002 and 2007 (see Figure 34.1), mainly as improvements in domestic security and investor-friendly reforms attracted record levels of foreign investment. However, the economy started to decline in 2008 as a result of the world financial crisis and reduced demand for Colombian products. The services sector represented 52.9 percent of the gross domestic product (GDP) in 2008, while industry and agriculture accounted for 38.1 and 9 percent respectively (CIA, 2009). According to the International Monetary Fund (2009), Colombia's GDP per capita in 2008 was 4,989 USD.

Expenditure in defense and security (includes military and police) represented 4.6 percent of the GDP in 2008, while expenditure in the justice sector (including courts, prosecution, and corrections) was only 0.88 percent.

The Republic of Colombia is a constitutional democracy governed by a publicly elected President who serves both as head of state and head of government. The Constitution declares Colombia to be a regime governed by the rule of law; organized as a united, decentralized Republic; with autonomy of its territorial entities; democratic; and participative. An extensive Bill of Rights is also provided.

The executive branch is represented by the President – elected for a maximum of two four-year terms – the Vice President and the Council of Ministers (13 ministries). At the regional and local levels, the executive power is exercised by departmental governors and municipal mayors respectively; both elected to serve four-year terms. According to the principle of decentralization, governors and mayors are autonomous in the administration of their jurisdictions.

The legislative branch consists of the Senate and the House of Representatives, also elected to serve four-year terms. Senators are elected nationally, while Representatives are elected by

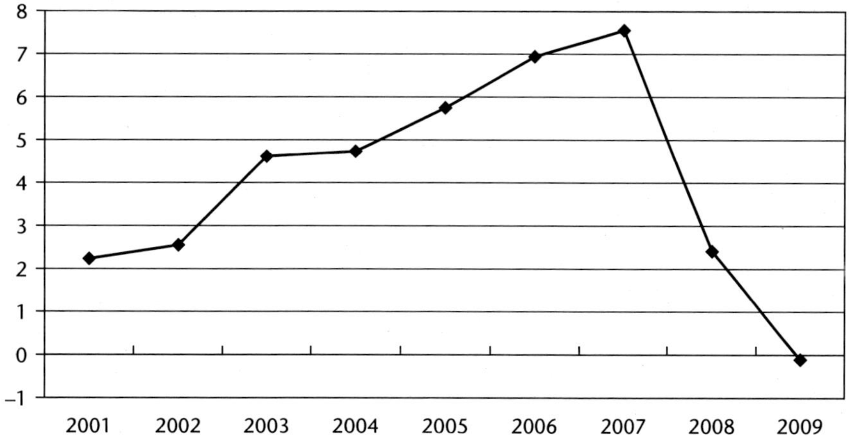

Figure 34.1 Colombia GDP growth rate, 2001–9

the regions. In addition, five seats within the House of Representatives are reserved for the election of ethnic minorities and representatives of Colombians living abroad. Democratically elected departmental assemblies and municipal councils exercise the legislative power at the regional and local levels. All regional elections take place a year after the national elections.

Since 2006, the Colombian Congress has faced a political scandal[1] in which several of its members have been mentioned by demobilized paramilitary leaders in their statements to Colombian and American justice as having received paramilitary support (e.g. coercing votes) during the 2006 elections in exchange for political favors. As of June 2009, 81 members of Congress (almost a third of its membership) were either under investigation or in prison.

Colombia's long history of a two-party system (i.e. the Liberal and Conservative parties) was ended by the 1991 Constitution which favors a pluralistic and multipartisan system, opening the door for new political movements. However, most new parties tend to have brief existences that coincide with electoral periods. For instance, in 2002, there were 64 different parties running for the Senate, but in 2006 only 20 parties did so. Currently, the National Registrar's Office reports 16 registered political parties and movements. In short, although the 1991 Constitution encourages political pluralism, it has also generated an ideological crisis. Many parties are set up to promote particular individuals instead of advocating a particular ideology in governance.

People

According to the 2005 census, Colombia has a population of 42,888,592, with 40 percent being 19 years old or younger. The estimated average population growth between 2005 and 2010 is 1.19 percent, a considerable decline compared to the 2.05 percent average growth of the period 1985–90.

Colombia is divided into 32 departments and one capital district (Bogotá), which is treated administratively as a department. The country has a total of 1,077 municipalities, 54 of which have a population of more than 100,000 inhabitants. The largest urban areas (over one million inhabitants) are Bogotá, Medellín, Cali, and Barranquilla.

Colombia has the third largest Spanish-speaking population in the world after Mexico and the United States. According to the 2005 Census, 84.2 percent of the population does not belong to an ethnic minority[2] (meaning that they are either *mestizo* – mixed Spanish and Amerindian ancestry – or of European ancestry – predominantly Spanish); 3.4 percent are Amerindian; 10.4 percent are of African ancestry; and 0.01 percent self-identify as Romani.[3] The majority of Colombians are Roman Catholics. Other Christian groups include Protestant, Pentecostal, Evangelical, Jehovah Witnesses, and Orthodox Christians. Judaism, Islam, and Buddhism represent a smaller percentage of religious following.

Education levels have slowly improved since the 1990s. Illiteracy among people 15 years old and older declined by 2.6 points between 1992 (9.3 percent) and 2005 (6.7 percent). School drop-out rates have also been reduced from 7.6 percent in 1997 to 6 percent in 2005. Lastly, the average number of years of education has increased by 1.5 years between 1992 (6.4) and 2005 (7.9) (DNP, 2007).

Administration of justice

The judicial branch is divided into five jurisdictions in Colombia:

(1) *Ordinary jurisdiction*. This jurisdiction deals with all civil and criminal matters. It is headed by the Supreme Court, which consists of 23 magistrates serving eight-year terms. The Supreme Court is divided into three chambers: Penal, Civil and Agrarian, and Labor.

(2) *Contentious Administrative jurisdiction.* The Council of State, consisting of 27 judges, deals with disputes that may arise between the state and private individuals, or between two state agencies.
(3) *Constitutional jurisdiction.* This court deals with all constitutional matters. There are nine constitutional magistrates elected for a term of eight years and they cannot be reelected.
(4) *Special jurisdictions.* The Constitution provides for two special jurisdictions of justice. First, it guarantees the right of indigenous communities to have their own system of justice, as long as its norms and proceedings do not violate the Constitution or the law. The second type is the Peace Justice Jurisdiction, which promotes the peaceful resolution of community and private conflicts that do not require a formal process with the Ordinary Justice Jurisdiction. Justices of Peace are independent, autonomous, and are democratically elected at the municipal level to serve five-year terms.
(5) *Military Jurisdiction.* A Military Tribunal deals with all crimes committed in the line of duty by members of the military.

The judicial branch in Colombia also includes the Attorney General Office (AGO) and the Superior Council of the Judiciary. The Attorney General is responsible for representing the state in all criminal investigations and is elected for a four-year term. The Superior Council of the Judiciary is responsible for the management and auditing of all other judicial institutions.

The justice system consists of four main institutions: the National Police, the AGO, the Court System, and the National Institute of Jails and Penitentiaries.

The National Police reports administratively to the Ministry of Defense and has jurisdiction over all the Colombian territory. It is subdivided structurally into 34 departmental commands (32 departments and 2 special regions) and 4 metropolitan commands in the cities of Bogotá, Cali, Cartagena, and Medellín. Governors and mayors are the main police authority at the regional and local levels; therefore, police commanders report to the mayor of the municipality under their jurisdiction, the governor (except for the metropolitan commands), and the Director of the National Police.

The size of the National Police has experienced a sustained growth since 1970 (see Figure 34.2). In 2007, the institution had 134,702 members of which 92 percent were dedicated to

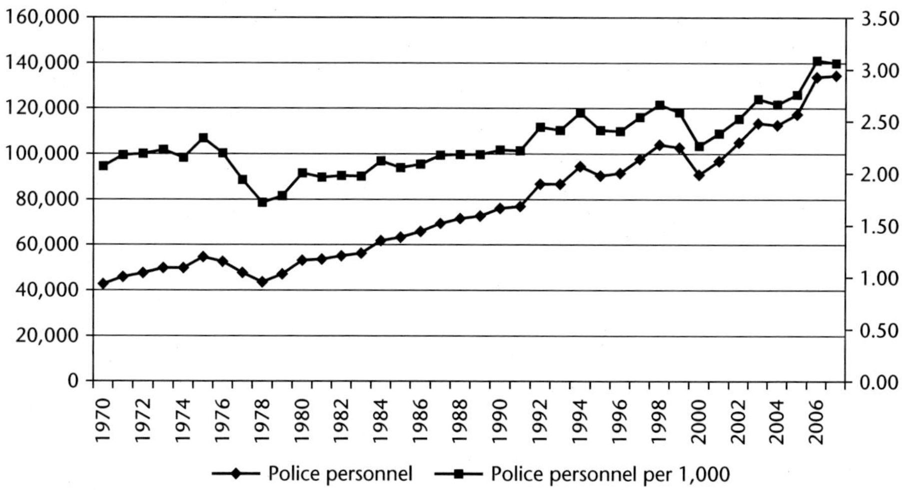

Figure 34.2 Total gross Colombian National Police personnel and rate per 1,000 inhabitants, 1970–2007

providing surveillance services, including responding to calls for service. This is equivalent to a rate of 2.8 police officers per 1,000 inhabitants dedicated to surveillance, crime and traffic control, and crime prevention services.

During the 1990s the National Police were ensnarled in a series of institutional crises. On the one hand, the drug cartels engaged in a terror campaign in the main cities that targeted the police, politicians, economic and social elites, and society in general. Simultaneously, the FARC drew police out of about 15 percent of municipalities in the late 1990s (Llorente, 2003). Today, the government reports that 100 percent of Colombian towns have police presence.

High levels of corruption and low public trust (20 percent in 1993) led to a widespread reform in the 1990s aimed at improving the public image of the institution; creating mechanisms to allow more citizen participation and oversight; increasing police accountability; and restructuring the organization to make it more efficient and horizontal. Moreover, around 10,000 police officers (including high-ranking officials) who were found to be involved in illegal activities were removed from the institution.

As part of the reform process, the National Police adopted the community-oriented policing (COP) model in 1998. COP in Colombia relies on partnerships between the police, the community, and other local authorities and organizations to foster preventive and proactive actions to solve local security problems. The model includes a neighborhood watch program, known as Local Security Fronts, which functions through phone-tree and alarm systems. The COP model also adopted the already existing "security schools" program, where community leaders and residents can get trained on how to organize and mobilize to improve security in their neighborhoods.

COP in Colombia has been criticized for not having had serious support by the police directorate, and for basically adopting police–community strategies that were already being implemented by the institution without producing a structural, functional, and cultural transformation within the organization. Moreover, the program has also been criticized for concentrating efforts in the least problematic urban sectors that may not need the service as desperately as areas with more complex security situations (Llorente, 2006).

Nonetheless, the reform reduced police corruption, improved police coverage and efficiency, and improved police-community relations (68 percent favorable opinion of the police in 2008 [Policía Nacional, 2008]) and trust in the police (46 percent in 2009 [CIMA, 2009]).

The AGO is responsible for representing the state in the investigation and prosecution of all suspected violations of the law. In addition, the institution has complete administrative and budgetary autonomy.

Before 2004, when the penal system in Colombia followed a mixed-inquisitorial model, the AGO had the power to issue search, seizure, and arrest warrants, and had an active role in the imputation and determination of guilt. Currently, after the Congress passed legislation[4] reforming the penal system to adhere to an adversarial model, the AGO cannot issue warrants and plays a more impartial role, leaving the final determination of guilt to the judge.

The clearance rate of cases known to the AGO shows a significant growth during the first years of the reform, increasing from 64 percent in 2003 to an average of 71 percent between 2004 and 2007. However, the clearance rate in 2008 decreased to 60 percent (see Figure 34.3).

The AGO has three directorates. The National Directorate of Public Prosecutors coordinates the administration of justice at the national, district, sectional, and local levels. The National Directorate of Technical Investigation provides support to the prosecution in matters related to the criminal investigation, crime scene investigation, forensic services, and genetics. Finally, the Administrative and Financing Directorate is in charge of managing the human, material, technological, financial, and infrastructure resources of the AGO. In addition, the National

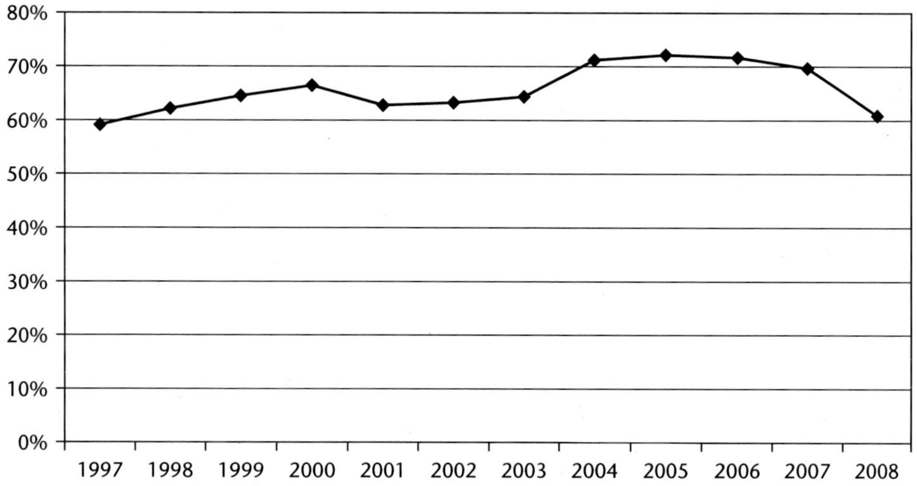

Figure 34.3 Clearance rate of cases known to the Attorney General Office, 1997–2008

Institute of Forensic Medicine (NIFM) is a semi-autonomous institution attached to the AGO whose aim is to provide technical and scientific support to the administration of justice in matters concerning forensic evidence.

The criminal courts system has a stratified structure which distributes responsibilities at the municipal, circuit, district, and national level.

(1) *Municipal Criminal Courts* deal with cases involving violations of the penal law. In addition, municipal judges are responsible for monitoring that due process is guaranteed to the defendant and for the issuing of warrants.
(2) *Circuit Criminal Courts* deal with any appeals to decisions made by municipal judges.
(3) *Circuit Specialized Criminal Courts* are in charge of trying cases involving crimes against humanity such as genocide, aggravated homicide, aggravated assault, violations of international humanitarian laws, aggravated kidnapping, forced disappearance, torture, and terrorism.
(4) *District Superior Courts* decide on appeals to sentences provided by municipal and circuit judges. District judges also deal with crimes committed in the line of duty by agents of the justice system.
(5) The *Supreme Court's Penal Chamber* deals with appeals to decisions made by district superior courts, and with trials of high-ranking government officials such as the President, the magistrates of the Supreme Court, or members of the Congress.

The National Institute of Jails and Penitentiaries (NIJP) is under the Ministry of Interior and Justice and handles 139 national correctional institutions.[5] There are four types of correctional facilities: farming colonies, high and medium security facilities, female facilities, and special imprisonment facilities. The incarceration rate in Colombia in 2009 was 166 per 100,000 residents.

The NIJP provides a number of re-socialization programs in its correctional facilities, including primary and secondary education; financial aid to obtain a technical or professional degree by correspondence to inmates with a record of good behavior; job skills training; child-care facilities for female inmates with children up to three years old; psychological counseling; and strengthening of family bonds. However, the institution lacks a reentry policy.

Following the new adversarial model, the penal process in Colombia takes place in five stages: inquiry, investigation, preliminary hearings, trial, and sentencing or restoration hearings.

(1) *Inquiry.* During the inquiry stage the judicial police collect evidence and prepare a report for the prosecution, determining whether a crime has occurred and identifying the parties involved.
(2) *Investigation.* The prosecution and the judicial police determine whether an arrest or another type of supervisory action is needed, and whether the case can be prosecuted or dropped.
(3) *Preliminary hearings.* During the preliminary hearings the prosecution may request that a due process judge issue arrest and/or search and seizure warrants. The limit for the prosecution to request a preliminary hearing to present charges, make an arraignment, or decline to prosecute a case is 30 business days. If the prosecution is unable to comply with this limit, a new prosecutor is assigned to the case and a new 30-business-days deadline is established.
(4) *Trial.* During the trial stage the prosecution and the defense present their case to the trying judge, who ultimately decides on the guilt or innocence of the accused. This is the equivalent to a *bench trial* in the United States.
(5) *Sentencing hearing.* If the trial judge decides that the defendant is guilty, the case is passed to a sentencing judge who decides on the final sanction the individual will receive.
(6) *Restoration hearing.* Alternatively, and once the trial judge has made a decision of guilt, the victim, the prosecution, or the defense can request a public restoration hearing. During the restoration hearing – which follows restorative justice guidelines – a conciliatory process takes place to determine the damages caused by the crime and to agree on reparations satisfactory to all parties.

The Ministry of Interior and Justice promotes the use of alternative conflict resolution methods at the local and regional levels through the following programs:

(1) *National Program of Houses of Justice.* The main objective of the Houses of Justice is to improve access to justice in disadvantaged communities by housing several justice and social service institutions under the same roof. There are currently 53 Houses of Justice operating in 43 municipalities. There is high demand for the services provided by the Houses of Justice, as shown in Figure 34.4. A large proportion of users are women seeking to solve family conflicts.
(2) *Peaceful Coexistence Centers.* Similar to the Houses of Justice, the Peaceful Coexistence Centers are spaces where disadvantaged communities can have access to a number of institutions and programs that promote civility, peaceful coexistence, and nonviolent resolution of conflicts. There are currently 15 Peaceful Coexistence Centers located in municipalities with high levels of violence related to the internal conflict, primarily in the Andean and eastern regions.
(3) *National Program of Conciliation Centers.* The Conciliation Centers provide a space for the conciliation and arbitration of civil, commercial, family, and criminal conflicts, and can be created by public agencies, non-profit organizations, and law schools. There are currently 310 Conciliation Centers distributed in 71 municipalities.

According to official statistics, between 1970 and 2007 an average of 678 crimes (per 100,000 population) were reported to the police each year, with the lowest rate reported in 1993 (521) and the highest in 2006 (890) (see Figure 34.5).

On the surface, this trend seems to suggest that crime rates were high in the 1970s, decreased in the 1980s and 1990s, and increased again in the 2000s. However, this picture is deceiving, as

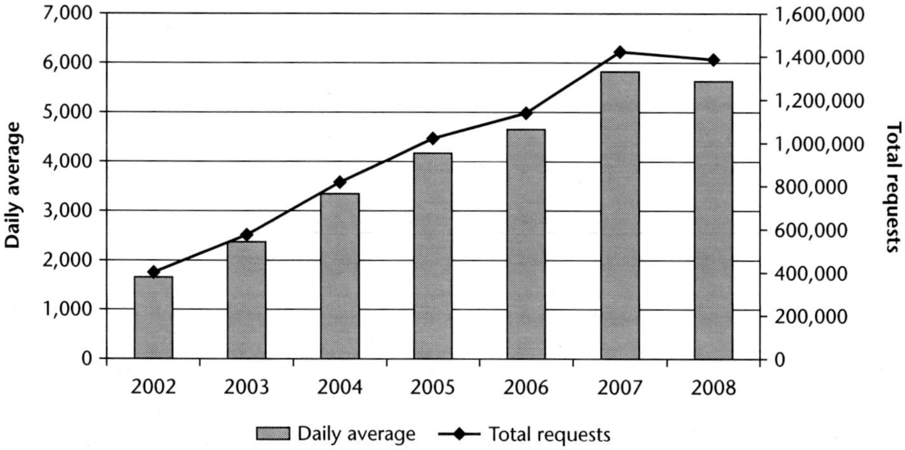

Figure 34.4 Demand for House of Justice services, 2002–8

reforms to the Penal Code implemented in 1980 and 2000 changed the definitions of punishable conducts. Indeed, the Penal Code of 1980 redefined some criminal offenses as violations, accounting for the apparent drop in crime rates in the 1980s, while the Penal Code of 2000 created new criminal offenses, giving the impression of a steep increase in the crime rate in the 2000s.

Figure 34.6 compares the contribution to the general crime rate made by violent crimes (homicide, assault, rape, and robbery), property crimes (theft, motor vehicle theft, and burglary), and other crimes during the same period. Although there are fluctuations, there is a more or less even split among the three groups throughout most of the period. But starting in 2001 the participation of the "other crimes" category grows dramatically, while the contribution of property crimes shrinks considerably and that of violent crimes continues to represent about a third of the total crime rate.

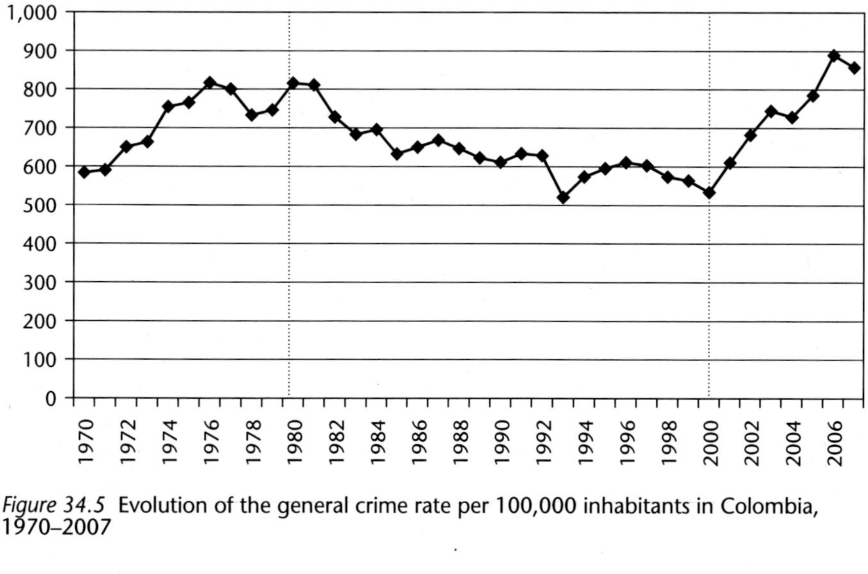

Figure 34.5 Evolution of the general crime rate per 100,000 inhabitants in Colombia, 1970–2007

Furthermore, the rise in the proportion of "other crimes" since 2001 is accounted for by substantial increases in the number of offenses related to domestic violence, sexual abuse of minors, defamation and slander, intellectual property, smuggling, and illicit drugs. This suggests that the rise in the crime rate in the 2000s can be at least partially explained by the introduction of new provisions regarding some of these offenses in the Penal Code of 2000, and not necessarily by actual shifts in criminal activity.

The property crime rate has presented a general downward tendency since 1981 (see Figure 34.7). It is clear that larceny theft is what defines the general trend. However, the proportion of

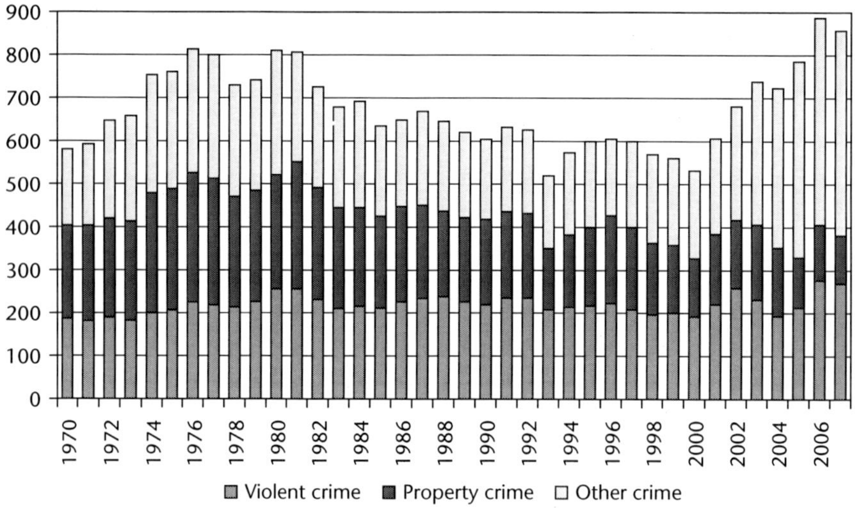

Figure 34.6 Contribution of violent, property, and other crimes to the general crime rate per 100,000 inhabitants in Colombia, 1970–2007

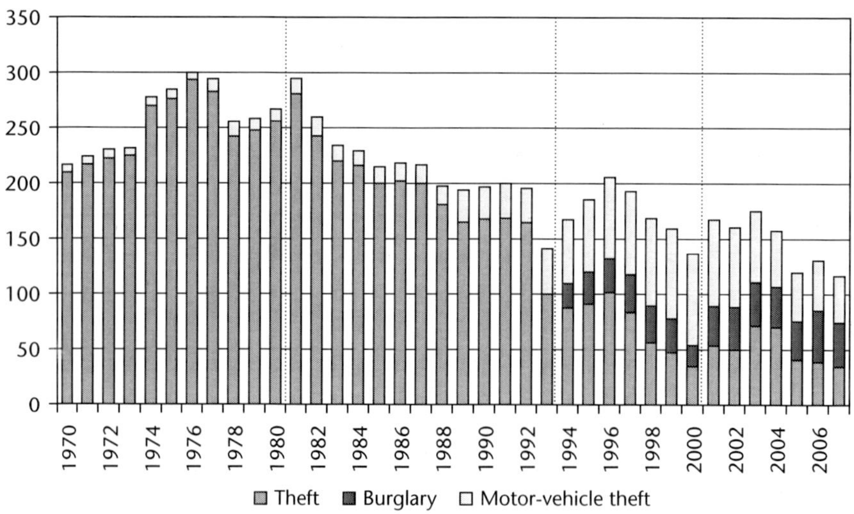

Figure 34.7 Evolution of the property crime rate per 100,000 population and distribution by type of crime in Colombia, 1970–2007

property crimes explained by motor vehicle theft increased markedly during the 1990s, reaching 60 percent in 2000, and averaging 39 percent during the first decade of the twenty-first century. In addition, in property crimes burglaries made up 35 percent in 2007, compared to 13 percent in 1994. Whether these trends are explained by changes in the law, changes in the patterns of reporting to the police, changes in motor vehicles and home appliances markets, or by the implementation of specific criminal justice policies is not clear at this point.

Figure 34.8 shows the evolution of the violent crime rate and the distribution of homicides, assaults, robberies, and rapes within it. On average, between 1970 and 2007, there were 220 violent crimes per 100,000 residents reported to the police in Colombia. However, the trend was driven by different offenses across the period. Indeed, while the behavior of assault defined the fluctuations in the violent crime rate during the 1970s and the first half of the 1980s, high homicide rates seem to explain most of the variation in violent crime between 1985 and 2003. In addition, the contribution of robbery, though initially small, gradually increased from the early 1990s to the point of explaining about 45 percent of violent crimes by the end of the period.

Criminology

In the past decade, economists and epidemiologists have produced the bulk of quantitative research on crime rates, while sociologists and anthropologists have taken a more qualitative approach to the study of different facets of crime. In addition, public agencies at the national and local level have focused on improving their data collection strategies as well as on examining crime trends across time and place, and private organizations – such as the Chambers of Commerce of some major cities – have also looked at the evolution of urban crime rates and its impact on the quality of life of residents. The following presents a summary of major research initiatives of the past decade.

The majority of empirical studies that have analyzed those factors that may explain violent crime rates have focused on the main urban centers, particularly Bogotá and Medellín.

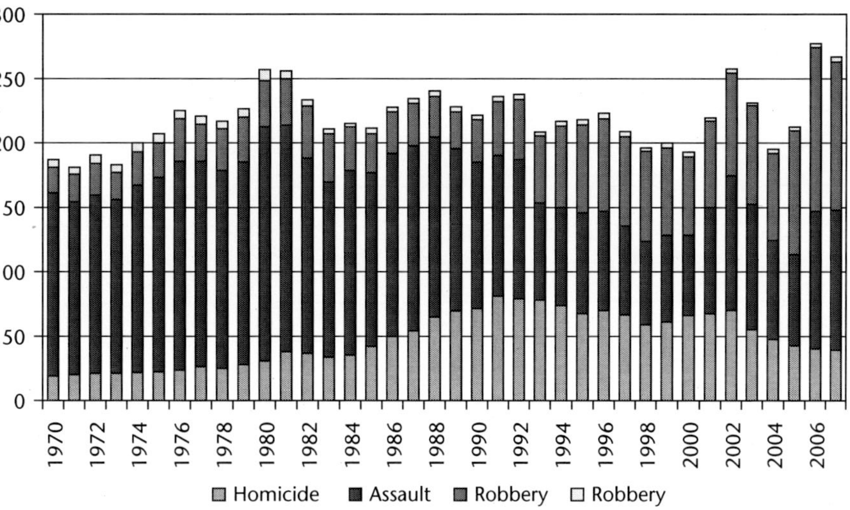

Figure 34.8 Evolution of the violent crime rate per 100,000 population and distribution by type of crime in Colombia, 1970–2007

In the case of Bogotá, the Paz Pública and CEDE research groups at Universidad de Los Andes have conducted the most serious empirical studies on violent crime, using, for the most part, official data sources. The studies on homicide conducted by Paz Pública (Formisano, 2002; Llorente *et al.*, 2001a, 2001b) found that some socio-demographic variables, such as education deficits and proportion of male population, are weakly associated with higher homicide rates, while the presence of bars and liquor stores, criminal structures, and illegal markets have a stronger impact on violence. In addition, they observed that Bogotá localities with higher public expenditure (health, roads, security, education, and recreation) per capita also had higher homicide rates. Nonetheless, another study by CEDE (Sánchez *et al.*, 2007) found the opposite relationship whereby public expenditure in the social sector (health, education, and social development) actually had a negative, but weak, effect on the homicide rate at the locality level in Bogotá. Furthermore, the same study also found that improvements in the efficiency of the Metropolitan Police explained a 53 percent drop in the homicide and a 76 percent decrease in the robbery rates in Bogotá between 1994 and 2002.

Another important source of research on urban violence is the National School of Public Health (NSPH) at Universidad de Antioquia in Medellín. Researchers affiliated to the NSPH have focused on the distribution and characteristics of violent crimes in Medellín, using primarily survey methods. These studies have mainly been descriptive and have relied very little on multivariate statistical techniques. However, their findings are important in understanding the characteristics of violent crime in Medellín. For instance, a survey conducted by NSPH in 2003–4 (N = 2,500) found that 40 percent of respondents reported having been the victims of violent threats, unarmed robbery, and assault with a weapon in the last year; 17 percent said they had assaulted someone else with a weapon in the last year; and 40 percent reported having been the witness to a homicide at least once in their lives. In addition, 75 percent of those who were victimized in the last 12 months said they did not report the crime to the authorities (Duque *et al.*, 2005, p. 1,099).

Domestic violence is also prevalent in Colombia. According to the NIFM, the number of cases known to the authorities increased by 50 percent between 2004 and 2008 (see Figure 34.9). However, it is not clear whether this growth in the trend is due to recent changes in legislation that aim to protect children (Law 1098 of 2006) and women (Law 1257 of 2008) against family violence; to public campaigns promoting the reporting of domestic violence; to better classification techniques by the NIFM; or to an actual increase in the number of cases.

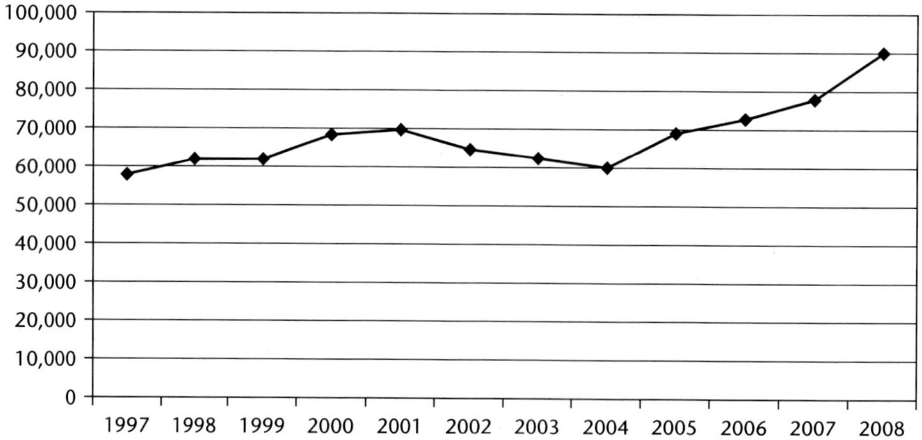

Figure 34.9 Domestic violence cases in Colombia, 1997–2008

Researchers affiliated with CEDE have conducted empirical studies aimed at identifying the determinants, effects, and costs of domestic violence in Colombia, and at understanding its intergenerational transmission. These studies used data collected through a survey administered to a random sample of 2,300 women in three cities (Bogotá, Barranquilla, and Barrancabermeja). These studies found that childhood experience with domestic violence and sharing the household with someone with an alcohol abuse problem were associated with domestic violence victimization. In terms of the costs, the researchers found that domestic violence against women increased their probability of unemployment, decreased their earnings, and had negative effects on their health. In addition, domestic violence against children was detrimental to their health, and it decreased their school attendance and academic attainment. The researchers also estimated that about 4.2 percent of the GDP was lost due to the indirect costs of domestic violence (Ribero and Sánchez, 2005; Salas, 2005, p. 1,100).

The NSPH research group in Medellín and CISALVA housed by Universidad del Valle in Cali have also studied the characteristics of domestic violence in those two cities. However, their approach has been more descriptive than analytic. For instance, between 2003 and 2004, the NSPH conducted a household survey (N = 2,313) in the ten municipalities composing the Metropolitan Area of Medellín, finding that the majority of violence is psychological and verbal (60 percent), while physical violence represents about 18 percent of the cases; and that between 80 and 95 percent of victims of verbal and psychological violence, physical violence without a weapon, and sexual assault do not report the violence to the authorities (Duque and Montoya, 2008, pp. 1,100–1).

Similarly, using reports of domestic violence to different organizations (both official and non-governmental) in Cali during 2008, CISALVA observed that 35 percent of domestic violence in that city can be classified as psychological and verbal, 28 percent as physical, 27 percent as neglect, and 6.5 percent as sexual abuse (81 percent of which is against women). CISALVA also found that in 40 percent of domestic violence cases the perpetrator is a parent (suggesting a large incidence of child abuse), and a current or former intimate partner in 32.9 percent of cases. Finally, domestic violence-related homicides represented 3.7 percent of all homicide cases in Cali in 2008, 81 percent of which were perpetrated by intimate partners.

In sum, domestic violence is an important problem in the main urban centers. The data collection efforts summarized in this section suggest that there is a load of data available to conduct more in-depth analyses on the factors related to family violence, and on the consequences of this conduct on the victims, their children, and society in general.

With a few exceptions, the evaluations of criminal justice policies and programs, particularly those implemented in its main urban centers, have historically lacked sophistication. Indeed, national and local agencies have tended to draw conclusions on the effectiveness of such policies based on simple trends and descriptive statistics, which do not provide enough information to determine whether the policy has been effective or not. Nonetheless, there have been some serious academic efforts to evaluate the effect of public policies on crime rates, especially in Bogotá. For instance, Sánchez and his CEDE colleagues (2007) classified a number of policies and programs implemented by three administrations in Bogotá in the 1994–2002 period into four categories – stick, carrot, carrot–stick, and broken windows – and estimated their effect on the homicide and robbery rates. They found that stick policies (incarceration and police deployment) had the strongest effect on the decrease of both homicide and robbery rates. In comparison, carrot policies (public investment in the social sector) had a weak but significant negative effect on homicides and a strong negative effect on the robbery rate. Carrot–stick programs (aimed at improving civic culture) had a strong negative effect on homicides but no effect on robberies. Broken-windows policies (aimed at recovering public space and social order) had a moderate negative effect on homicides, but a positive effect on robberies. The researchers argue that this last unexpected outcome may be the consequence of an increase in criminal opportunities created by greater commercial and pedestrian activity in the recovered areas.

Moreno and Sánchez (2007) (also from CEDE) evaluated the impact of the Bus Rapid Transit system, *Transmilenio*, on muggings, robberies, burglaries, car thefts, and homicides in Bogotá. The *Transmilenio* project was conceived and developed not only as a solution to the mass transportation problem the city was facing, but also as a strategy to reduce signs of social disorder. To this end, additional police officers were assigned to the system through an agreement between the Metropolitan Police and the Mayor's Office. The researchers focused on the first avenue where the system was implemented, Avenida Caracas, formerly characterized by high levels of traffic congestion, social disorder, and criminal activity. They found that, in general, the participation of the Avenida Caracas area on the overall Bogotá crime rate decreased after *Transmilenio* started operations, with the exception of homicides.

Finally, and with the exception of CISALVA[6] in Cali, evaluation research in other regions of Colombia is still in its infancy. Efforts to measure the impact of specific criminal justice policies and programs require a higher degree of sophistication, including the use of time-series analysis techniques. It is also important to differentiate local from regional and national effects, and to control for the impact of potentially confounding factors related to the war on drugs and the internal armed conflict.

The public can find links to criminal justice statistics on the websites of the Colombian National Police, AGO, NIFM, NIJP, Judicial Branch, and National Department of Statistics. Nevertheless, the user must be aware that official statistics may not provide a true picture of the crime situation in the country and that discrepancies across institutions may be found in the reported number of crimes.

Other problems with these statistics are that in many cases they are only available for a few years, that different data collection criteria may be used across years, and that the data are aggregated at the administrative jurisdictional level utilized by each institution instead of standardized geographic units. These issues are problematic for the researcher who wants to conduct longitudinal and spatial analyses. Legislative changes in criminal laws also make it difficult to compare official statistics across long periods of time. In spite of these shortcomings, these data sources are invaluable resources to the researcher interested in crime and criminal justice in Colombia.

An alternative and more reliable source of crime data are victimization surveys. Unfortunately, with a couple of exceptions, this data collection method is still not widely used. The Bogotá Chamber of Commerce conducts a biannual victimization and perception of safety survey, and the only large effort to administer one simultaneously in the main cities (e.g. Bogotá, Cali, and Medellín) was implemented in 2003 by the National Department of Statistics and the National Department of Planning, and it has not been repeated since.

Table 34.1 summarizes the main public and private sources of data and research on crime and criminal justice in Colombia. The reader should be aware that most websites provide information in Spanish only, although some of them share their reports in English as well. Finally, it is worth mentioning that funding for academic research in Colombia is provided primarily by Colciencias[7] – a public entity in charge of furthering the development of science and technology in the country – through the allocation of competitive grants. Criminal justice agencies and local administrations may also fund research through open solicitations or closed contracts with academic institutions.

Table 34.1 Data and research sources

Institution	*Website*	*Section within website*	*Type of data/research*	*Available years*	*Available in English*
Colombian National Police	http://www.policia.gov.co	Revista Criminalidad	Crimes reported to the police by penal code articles, arrests	1959–2008	Abstracts only
National Institute of Forensic Medicine	http://www.medicinalegal.gov.co	DRIP – Estadisticas: Forensis	Homicides, assaults, domestic violence, sex offenses, suicides, accidental deaths	1999–2008	Abstracts only
Attorney General Office	http://www.fiscalia.gov.co	Gestión: Estadísticas	Cases received, dropped, and prosecuted	2006–2008	No
National Institute of Jails and Penitentiaries	http://www.inpec.gov.co	Estadísticas	Prison population	2007–2009	No
Judicial Branch	http://www.ramajudicial.gov.co	Gestión de la Información de Estadística	Judicial processes	1997–2007	No
National Department of Statistics	http://www.dane.gov.co	Sociales: Seguridad y Justicia	2003 victimization surveys for Bogotá, Cali, and Medellín	2003	No
Observatory of Urban Security, Chamber of Commerce of Bogotá	http://camara.ccb.org.co/contenido/contenido.aspx?catID=126&conID=6573	Bogotá y su Entorno: Seguridad y Convivencia: Observatorio de Seguridad	Victimization and perception of safety surveys	2004–2009	No
Center for Studies in Economic Development (CEDE), Universidad de Los Andes	http://economia.uniandes.edu.co	Documentos CEDE	Research on a variety of social and economic topics, including crime and criminal justice	1999–2010	Some research reports are in English
CISALVA, Universidad del Valle	http://www.cisalva.univalle.edu.co	Publicaciones	Evaluation reports on a variety of violence prevention projects	1998–2010	Some research reports are in English

Future research questions

1. What are the factors associated with the decrease in the violent crime rates in the urban areas of Colombia during the 1990s and 2000s?
2. What explains the reported increase in domestic violence cases in the late 2000s?
3. What has been the effect of the paramilitary demobilization policy on crime rates in urban areas in Colombia?
4. What has been the effect of the transition to the adversarial system on the performance of the criminal justice system in Colombia?
5. Can criminological theories developed in the United States be used to explain criminal activity in Colombia?

Notes

1 Termed by the media as the "parapolitics" or "paragate" scandal.
2 The Colombian census does not collect specific information on race/ethnicity, other than for ethnic minorities. The categories available to respondents are: Amerindian; Romani; Afro-Colombian; and None of the Above.
3 2.08 per cent of respondents did not answer the ethnicity question.
4 Law 906 of 2004.
5 Municipal jails are managed by local mayor's offices and house misdemeanants only.
6 CISALVA has been conducting evaluation research in Cali and other areas of the southwest of the country since the 1990s.
7 http:// www.colciencias.gov.co.

References

Central Intelligence Agency (CIA) (2009). *The World Factbook.* Washington, DC: Central Intelligence Agency. Online at https://www.cia.gov/library/publications/the-world-factbook/geos/co.html (accessed November 25, 2010).

Consorcio Iberoamericano de Investigaciones de Mercados y Asesoramiento (CIMA) (2009). *Barómetro iberoamericano de gobernabilidad 2009.* Online at http://www.cimaiberoamerica.com (accessed November 25, 2010).

Departamento Nacional de Planeación (DNP) (2007). *La educación en cifras.* Online at http://www.dnp.gov.co/PortalWeb/Portals/0/archivos/documentos/DDS/SISD/boletin33.pdf (accessed November 25, 2010).

Duque, L. F. and Montoya, N. E. (2008). La violencia doméstica en Medellín y demás municipios del Valle de Aburrá, 2003–4. *Revista Facultad Nacional de Salud Pública*, 26(1): 27–39.

Duque, L. F., Montoya, N. E., and Restrepo, M. V. (2005). Magnitud y distribución de diferentes formas de violencia en Medellín, 2003–4. *Revista Facultad Nacional de Salud Pública*, 24(2): 61–72.

Formisano, M. (2002). Econometría espacial: Características de la violencia homicida en Bogotá. *Documentos CEDE,* 2002(10). Online at http://economia.uniandes.edu.co/investigaciones_y_publicaciones/CEDE/Publicaciones/documentos_cede/2005/determinants_effects_and_costs_of_domestic_violence (accessed November 25, 2010).

International Monetary Fund (IMF) (2009). World economic outlook database. Online at http://www.imf.org/external/pubs/ft/weo/2009/02/weodata/weoselgr.aspx (accessed November 25, 2010).

Llorente, M. V. (2003). Desmilitarización en tiempos de guerra? La reforma policial en Colombia. Paper presented in the Panel Police Reform in the Americas. Center for Hemispheric Defense Studies, Santiago de Chile, October 27–30, 2003.

—— (2006). Demilitarization in a war zone. In J. Bailey and L. Dammert (Eds.). *Public security and police reform in the Americas.* Pittsburgh: University of Pittsburgh Press, pp. 111–31.

Llorente, M. V., Escobedo, R., Echandia, C. and Rubio, M. (2001a). Violencia homicida en Bogotá: más que intolerancia. In *Documentos CEDE,* 2001(4). Online at http://economia.uniandes.edu.co/investigaciones_

y_publicaciones/CEDE/Publicaciones/documentos_cede/2001/violencia_homicida_en_bogota_mas_que_intolerancia (accessed November 25, 2010).

—— (2001b). Violencia homicida y estructuras criminales en Bogotá. *Paz Pública – Documento de Trabajo No. 20.* Online at http://economia.uniandes.edu.co/investigaciones_y_publicaciones/CEDE/Publicaciones/documentos_cede/documentos_de_paz_publica (accessed November 25, 2010).

Moreno, A. J. and Sánchez, F. (2007). La recuperación del espacio público y su impacto en el crimen: el caso de Transmilenio. In F. Sánchez (Ed.). *Las cuentas de la violencia.* Bogotá, Columbia: Grupo Editorial Normal, pp. 357–92.

Policía Nacional (2008). *Balance de Gestion 2008.* Imprenta Nacional de Colombia.

Ribero, R. and Sánchez, F. (2005). Determinants, effects and costs of domestic violence. *Documentos CEDE,* 2005(38). Online at http://economia.uniandes.edu.co/investigaciones_y_publicaciones/CEDE/publicaciones/documentos_cede/2005/determinants_effects_and_costs_of_domestic_violence (accessed November 25, 2010).

Salas, L. M. (2005). Transmisión intergeneracional de la violencia intrafamiliar: evidencia para las familias colombianas. *Documentos CEDE,* 2005(47). Online at http://economia.uniandes.edu.co/investigaciones_y_publicaciones/CEDE/Publicaciones/documentos_cede/2005/transmision_intergeneracional_de_la_violencia_intrafamiliar_evidencia_para_las_familias_colombianas (accessed November 25, 2010).

Sánchez, F., Espinosa, S., and Rivas, A. (2007). ¿Garrote o zanahoria? Factores asociados a la disminución de la violencia homicida y el crimen en Bogotá 1983–2002. In Sánchez, F. (Ed.). *Las cuentas de la violencia.* Bogotá, Columbia: Grupo Editorial Normal, pp. 301–56.

United Nations Office on Drugs and Crime (2009). Colombia: coca cultivation survey. Online at http://www.unodc.org/documents/crop-monitoring/Colombia_coca_survey_2008.pdf (accessed November 25, 2010).

35

Estonia

Crime, criminal justice, and criminology in a changing socio-economic context

Anna Markina

Introduction

Estonia, one of the three Baltic States, regained its independence in 1991 after the period of Soviet occupation, which lasted for 50 years. Since gaining control over their own country, the people of Estonia have made strenuous efforts to rebuild their democratic institutions and a free market economy.

The first years of independence were characterised by high levels of crime. In 1993, Tallinn was the "world's most violent capital" with the highest homicide rate per capita (Rawlinson, 2003, p.133). Since that time many changes have occurred. The crime rates, especially for violent crimes, have decreased. Citizens' trust in law enforcement agencies increased remarkably, while the level of fear of crime decreased.

The progress made during 18 years is great, but problems remain. The level of prisoners per 100,000 population is the highest among EU member states. The level of alcohol consumption and drug abuse and problems related to it are very high.

This chapter examines various socio-demographic factors that are related to the issues of crime, deviance and social control. Whenever possible, relevant data for criminal justice are presented to demonstrate this relationship.

An important part of this paper is the description of research conducted in the field of criminology. Estonia is a small country with just a dozen or two researchers whose main research interest lies within the field of crime, criminal policy and research. Despite this modest number of scholars, a body of research completed within the last ten years is notable.

Infrastructure

Estonia is the northernmost of three Baltic States, the other two being Latvia and Lithuania. The territory of Estonia covers 45,227 square kilometers. To the north Estonia is bordered by the Gulf of Finland, to the west by the Baltic Sea, to the south by Latvia and to the east by Russia. The eastern border of Estonia is the outer border of the European Union.

The geopolitical situation of Estonia has its potential (e.g. tourism, transit trade) but also a potential for cross-border criminal activities. The Organized Crime Threat Assessment (OCTA) prepared by Europol in 2006 states:

> The organized crime situation in Estonia, Latvia and Lithuania, for instance, is mainly conditioned by its proximity to Russia. The latter is a source for illegal tobacco, alcohol and heroin in transit from Central Asia but also represents a market for stolen vehicles and synthetic drugs.
>
> *(Europol, 2006, p. 7)*

Oil shale is the most important natural resource in Estonia. Over 90 percent of electricity in Estonia is produced on the basis of oil shale. The level of electricity production per inhabitant is 7.5 MWh (megawatt hours), which is the average level of the European Union. To reduce the share of oil shale in the energy production several wind farms were established in recent years. In 2008, the production of wind energy totaled 130 GWh (gigawatt hours) and hydro energy totaled 28 GWh (Statistics Estonia, 2009a). Among other mineral resources extracted in Estonia are peat, phosphorite, amber, clay, limestone and dolomite.

Nearly half (48 percent) of land in Estonia is covered with forests. Swamps cover 5 percent and inland waters 3 percent of the territory. Agricultural land makes up less than one third (30 percent) of the country (Statistics Estonia, 2009a).

The gross domestic product (GDP) at current prices per capita grew rapidly from $2,607 USD in 1995, reaching the level of $17,541 USD per capita in 2008. With the last ten years' average growth rate of over 7 percent, Estonia was one of the fastest growing economies in the European Union. The growth peaked at over 10 percent in real terms in 2006. In 2007, GDP growth decelerated to 6.3 percent compared to the previous year. In 2008 due to the crisis, the economic growth decreased (Statistics Estonia, 2009b).

During the period of rapid economic growth (2003–7) the living standard of Estonian households also grew. The average household income in real prices in 2007 had increased 63 percent compared to 2003 (Tiit, 2006). The overall growth in average household income had not decreased the inequality of income distribution. The central concept to estimate the distribution of income in society is relative poverty. A person is considered to be at risk of poverty if his or her equalized disposable income falls below 60 percent of the national median equalized disposable income. According to the Estonian Social Survey data, in 2007 the relative poverty line was €3,328 per year; nearly 20 percent of households lived below the poverty line. The poverty rate among single parents with dependent children is twice higher – 40 percent of such households lived at risk of poverty in 2007 (Statistics Estonia, n.d.a). Figure 35.1 demonstrates the dynamics of growth of income per household members.

The transition from a socialist to market economy brought about the growth in inequality during the 1990s. While in some countries of the former socialist bloc inequality has grown moderately, in Estonia it has increased considerably. According to the *Estonian human development report* (Vetik, 2003) the Gini coefficient used to estimate the level of inequality in a given country has increased from 27.7 in 1989 to 39.6 in 1994–5. The inequality of income distribution has been decreasing during the last years, reaching the average level for EU countries (see Figure 35.2).

In 2008, 656,000 of the population aged 15–74 were employed, 38,000 were unemployed and 348,000 were economically inactive. The labor force participation rate for the population aged 15–74 was 67 percent in 2008. Starting from 2001 and up to 2008 employment grew on average by 1–2 percent per year, but then slowed to 0.2 percent in 2008 (Statistics Estonia, 2009b). In the beginning of 2009 employment decreased due to the budget cuts and bankruptcies accompanying the economic crisis.

The highest level of unemployment of 13.6 percent was registered in 2000 and the lowest level registered in 2007 was 4.7 percent. Because the economic crisis hit mostly the construction

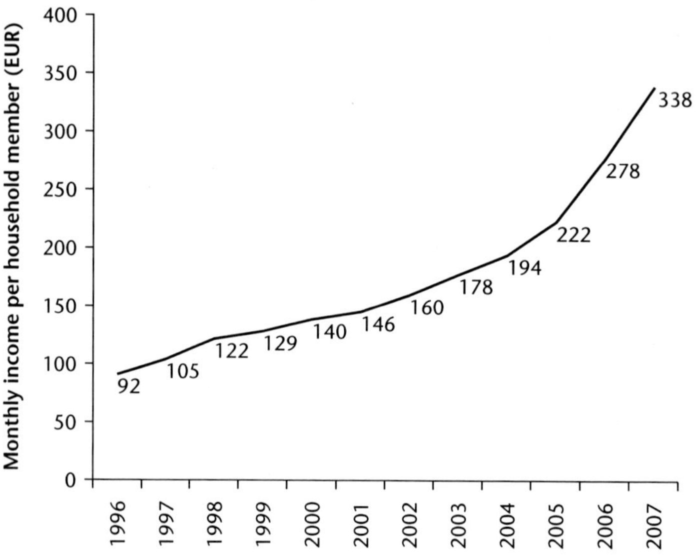

Figure 35.1 Disposable income per household member in a month (euros), 1996–2007

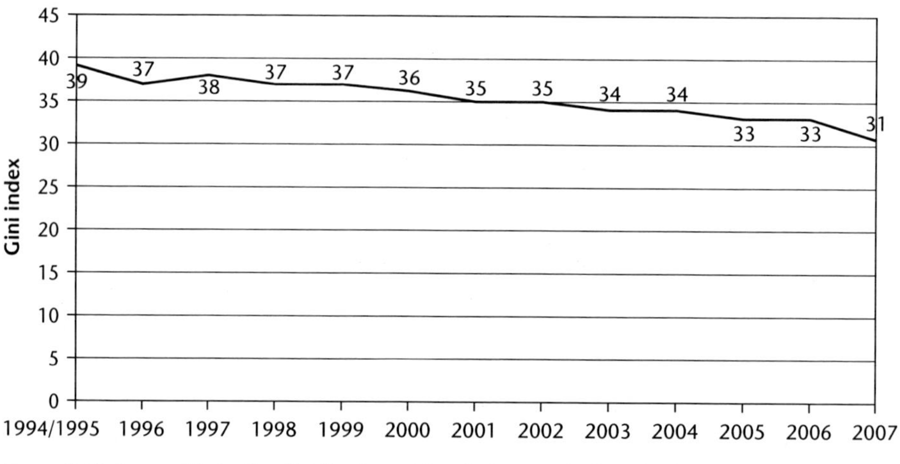

Figure 35.2 Inequality in the distribution of family income in Estonia (Gini index)

and manufacturing sector, unemployment has increased especially among men (Statistics Estonia, 2009b); see Figure 35.3.

The structure of employment has changed since the restoration of independence, with a decrease from 19 percent in 1991 to 4 percent in 2008 of the population employed in the primary sector (e.g. agriculture, hunting, forestry and fishing). Employment in the secondary sector (e.g. mining, manufacturing, electricity, gas and water supply, construction) has not changed in the same way. There was some decrease between 1991 and 2002, but this sector started to grow in 2002, and then declined again during 2008–9 in the economic crisis. The proportion of persons employed in trade and services (tertiary sector) increased remarkably from 44 percent in 1991 to 61 percent in 2008.

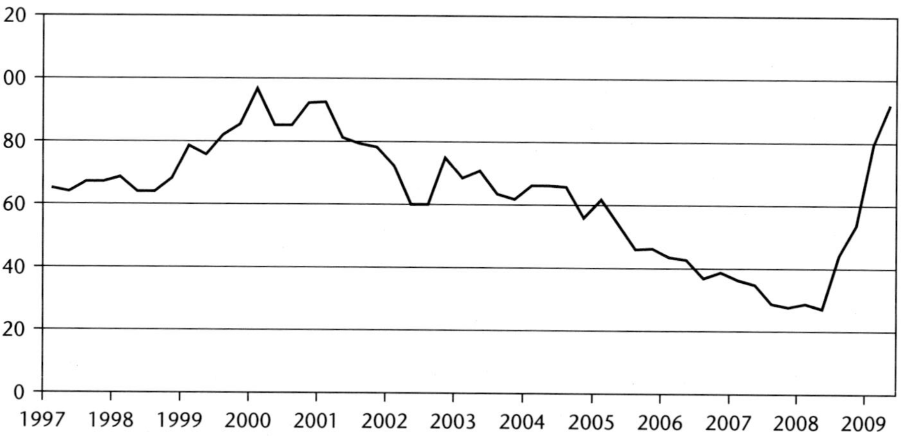

Figure 35.3 Unemployed persons (thousands) by year

Estonia is an independent and sovereign democratic republic. A 101-member Parliament is elected every four years. The Parliament (Riigikogu) chooses a president, who can be in office for a five-year period for a maximum of two terms. The activities of the Parliament, the president, the government and the courts are organized on the principle of separation and balance of powers. Estonia does not have a state church; religious freedom is guaranteed by the constitution.

Estonia has a multi-party system, which leads to the formation of a coalitional government. Similar to other post-communist countries, the Estonian political landscape is characterized by constant fusion of the existing political groups and formation of new ones, weak party identification, low citizen participation in the elections and disappointed voters. The general weakness of left-wing parties and absence of any noteworthy ethnic party are particular characteristics of the Estonian party system in comparison to other former socialist countries (Mikkel, 2006). In the last parliamentary elections that took place in 2007 the participation rate was 61 percent. Of 101 members of Parliament elected, 24 were women and 77 men (Estonian National Electional Committee, n.d.).

The recent 2009 data provided by Internet World Stats (http://www.internetworldstats.com/) show that 68 percent have internet access. The growing use of the internet results in an increase in computer-related offenses. Figure 35.4 demonstrates trends in two computer related crimes: computer fraud and unlawful use of computer system. While the number of unlawful uses of computer systems remained at a low level, the growth in computer fraud is remarkable, from 19 cases in 2003 to 367 cases in 2008.

The International Self-reported Delinquency Study-2 conducted in 2006–7 revealed that 7 percent of adolescents aged 12 to 16 have been engaged in hacking activities in the last 12 months (Markina, 2008). The development of technology not only increases the vulnerability to new types of crime but also provides new opportunities for more effective criminal procedure. E-File has been launched in Estonia recently to provide the parties to criminal, civil, administrative and misdemeanor proceedings with a comprehensive overview of different stages and operations of proceedings, as well as decisions made (http://www.just.ee/e-file).

About 1.9 million passengers were served in Estonian airports in 2008. There are 32 regular lines, mostly international. The main connection with other countries are sea transport, buses and air transport. The railway plays only a marginal role. In 2008, 7.4 million passengers visited Estonian ports in international traffic, with most coming/going to Finland, Sweden and Germany respectively.

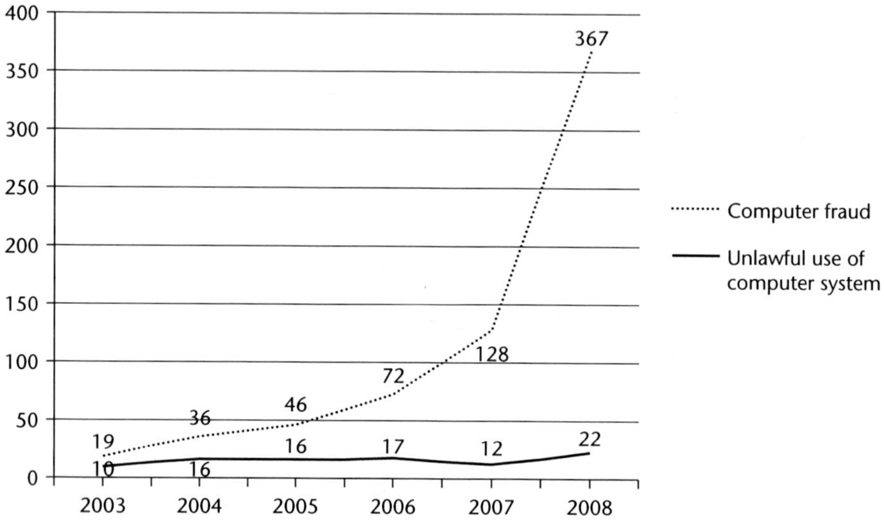

Figure 35.4 Computer-related crimes registered by law enforcement (absolute numbers)

Tourism is a vital part of the Estonian economy. However, it also has a potential for criminal activities, especially related to smuggling of illegal goods and trafficking activities, such as cigarette smuggling. Because of differences in excise tax, cigarette price discrepancies between Estonia and neighboring countries is remarkable. While cigarettes in Estonia are considerably cheaper compared to Scandinavian countries, the prices in Russia are half as much as in Estonia. This makes Estonia attractive not only as a transit country, but also as a destination country for illegal cigarettes.

Estonia became a member of the United Nations on 17 September 1991 and joined the Eastern European Group in May 2004 upon becoming a member of the European Union (EU). Since January 2008 Estonia became a part of the Schengen Area, the European border control-free territory. In March 2004 Estonia become a full member of NATO.

People

The number of people living in Estonia as of 1 January 2009 was 1,340,415 (Statistics Estonia, 2009b). Since 1991, the population in Estonia has been decreasing. According to the 2000 population census data, the population has decreased by 215,985 persons or 14 percent compared to the 1989 census data.

The reasons for this development are twofold. First, the population has decreased due to a considerable number of Russian citizens leaving Estonia after the re-establishment of independence. Second, for several years in the 1990s Estonia had one of the lowest birth rates in the world. From 1991 until now the natural increase rate of population has been negative. The worst year was 1994, when deaths surpassed births by 8,036. In recent years the number of births has been growing and mortality is decreasing, which results in slowing the decrease in population. In 2008, deaths surpassed births by 647.

The majority of the Estonian population (65 percent) live in the cities and 35 percent in the countryside. The biggest city is Tallinn, where 400,000 people or almost one third of the country population lives.

As a result of negative natural increase, the population of Estonia is getting older. In 2009 the proportion of population younger than 15 years old was 15 percent. The proportion of people 65 and above is 17 percent. In 2007 the life expectancy in Estonia was 67.1 years for males and over 78.7 years for females. The proportion of the population in the 20- to 24-year-old category is the largest in the Estonian demographic pyramid.

Estonians represent 69 percent of the population according to 2008 data, with Russians forming 26 percent. The remaining 6 percent are people of various nationalities, including Ukrainians, Byelorussians, Finns and others.

After regaining independence in 1991, Estonia adopted a very strict citizenship policy. Only pre-annexation[1] Estonian citizens and their offspring were acknowledged as legitimate Estonian citizens. All others (mostly those whose native language was Russian) were obliged to either apply for Estonian citizenship by naturalization or apply for a residence permit. Those persons whose citizenship remained unspecified got status of "non-citizens" or "aliens." This problem of a high proportion of permanent residents with the "alien" status is a pending issue.

According to recent data (January 1, 2009), 60 percent of persons serving custodial sentences have Estonian citizenship. The proportion of ethnic Russians in prison population is 52 percent. The possible explanation for the high proportion of Russian-speaking people among prisoners is the difference in the seriousness of the offences they commit. The research shows that non-Estonians commit offences against persons somewhat more frequently, while Estonians commit offences against property and against public order (above all traffic offences) more frequently (Saar *et al.*, 2003). However, it does not provide a sufficient explanation for the large ethnic differentiation in the composition of prisoners.

Administration of justice

The Estonian police is under the supervision of the Ministry of Internal Affairs. There are four territorial police units, called Police Prefectures. There are two national units: the Central Criminal Police and the Central Personal Protection and Law Enforcement Police (Estonian Police Board, n.d.). At the end of 2008 police staff consisted of 3,218 sworn police officers, and 1,015 non-sworn civilian public servants as support staff.

The pre-trial investigation is led by the Prosecutor's Office, a government agency within the Ministry of Justice. The Prosecutor's Office participates in planning surveillance required for the prevention and detection of crimes and represents public prosecution in court. The Prosecutor's Office consists of two levels: the Office of the Prosecutor General as the superior prosecutor's office and four District Prosecutor's Offices (Prosecutor's Office, n.d.).

Estonia has a three-level court system. County and city courts and administrative courts adjudicate matters in the first instance. Appeals against decisions of courts of first instance shall be heard by courts of second instance. Courts of appeal are courts of second instance (sometimes also called circuit courts). The Supreme Court is the court of the highest instance.

Currently, there are five prisons in Estonia with a total capacity of 4,529 inmates. All prisons in Estonia, except the all-female prison of Harku, have maximum-security status. In two prisons there are also open prison wards: for 48 people in Murru Prison and for 75 people in Viru Prison (Estonian Ministry of Justice, 2008).

At the end of 2008 there were 3,656 persons in the Estonian penitentiary institutions: 2,666 prisoners under sentence and 990 (27 percent) were pre-trial prisoners.

Administrative managing and supervision of the prison system is a duty of the Department of Prisons. The department is led by the Deputy Secretary-General for prisons of the Ministry of Justice and is divided into four divisions: sentencing enforcement, rehabilitation, legal and development, and internal control division.

To ensure the accountability of such a closed system and to make visible and understandable for society what is going on in prisons, the Ministry of Justice has convened prison committees of citizens and their associations, such as non-governmental organizations, local governments, and universities.

The Estonian probation supervision system started to function on May 1, 1998. By the end of 2008, there were 8,363 persons on probation, of whom 542 were women and 346 juveniles (Statistics Estonia, 2009b).

The penal policy of a state is characterized by the application of custodial sanctions. Until 2007 the prison population remained on the same level, varying between 4,200 and 4,800. The imprisonment rate over 320 prisoners per 100,000 of population remained among the highest in the Europe. Figure 35.5 demonstrates the dynamic of changes in prison population in 1991–2008.

A noticeable reduction in prison population was made in 2007. The rate dropped from 321 in 2006 to 257 prisoners per 100,000 of population in 2007, due mainly to changes in legislation, such as use of electronic monitoring after an offender serves part of his or her sentence.

Also, changes in the procedure of parole were introduced. Until 2007, inmates had to apply for parole, but post-2007 the prison was obliged to send the prisoner's case to the court once the certain part of prison term was served, resulting in an increase in parolees.

Thirdly, since 2007, due to the changes in the Penal Code, community service or a fine became an option for those committing minor new offenses, rather than automatically returning to prison. This change resulted in fewer returns to prison.

A fourth change in the Penal Code that influenced the number of prisoners regarded the decriminalization of minor thefts. Since March 15, 2007, a theft of property less that $85 USD was reduced to a misdemeanor, resulting in a fine or arrest instead of prison. However, it should be mentioned that decriminalization of minor thefts resulted in a dramatic growth in such offences

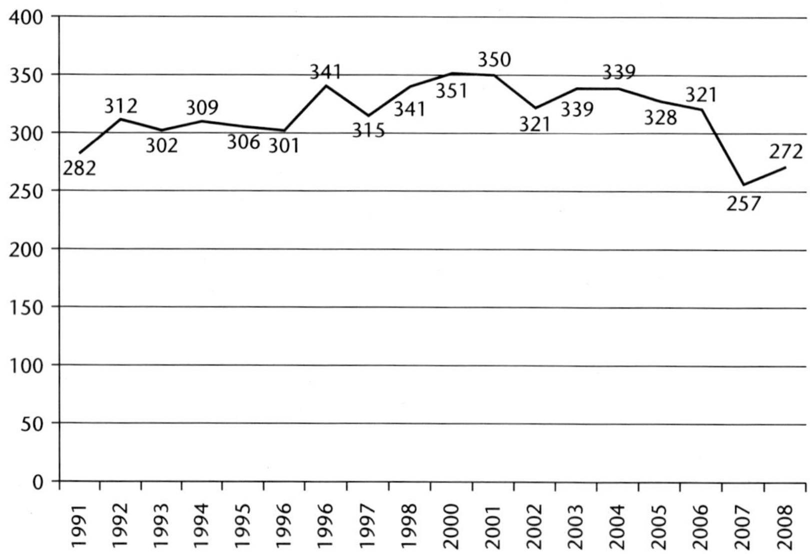

Figure 35.5 Prison population rate per 100,000 in Estonia, 1991–2008

and overcrowding of arrest houses. In 2008, this change in legislation was considered void (Ahven *et al.*, 2010).

Recently, elements of restorative justice have been introduced in Estonia. Mediation in criminal proceedings has been regulated by the Code of Criminal Procedure since spring 2007. The public prosecutor decides whether particular criminal cases may be referred for conciliation, a process led by an independent mediator. The main goal of the conciliation procedure is to secure a better position for victims of crime. It is also aimed at the reintegration of the offender. The possible outcomes of the conciliation procedure may be the waiver of criminal prosecution or, in case of serious crimes, decrease in length of prison sentence (Kruuser *et al.*, 2008). It is too new to have much use, with only 109 criminal cases being sent to conciliation in 2008, with 90 percent of the cases for violent offences (Ahven *et al.*, 2010). This option existed for juveniles previously.

Criminology

Jüri Saar, currently a professor of criminology at the University of Tartu, notes that at the end of the 1990s, Estonian criminology experienced a revival, manifested by an increased volume of research and publications. New textbooks (Raska, 2002; Sootak, 1997), monographs and the journals *Juridica* and *Juridica International* were produced, dealing with both theoretical and policy issues (Saar, 2004). Although there are not too many people involved in the criminological research, the field of interests covered by the research is very broad.

A traditional topic of interest in criminology is research in crime trends. One of the first important publications in this field has been the collective monograph on crime in Estonia from 1991–2001 (Saar *et al.*, 2003). This book, written by the criminology research group led by Jüri Saar, analyzes crime patterns and trends during the first ten years of independence. The book is written in Estonian and supplemented with an extensive summary in English and tables of crime statistics.

Since 2007, the regular analysis of crime trends became a task of Criminal Policy Department at the Ministry of Justice. Three annual reviews, "Crime in Estonia," have been published so far – the analyses for the years 2006 to 2008 (Liiv, 2007; Sööt, 2008; Estonian Ministry of Justice, 2009; Ahven *et al.*, 2010). These analyses contain summaries in English, so the publications may be of interest to foreign specialists. They are available online at the Ministry of Justice home page (http://www.just.ee/30140). In addition to annual analyses the Criminal Policy Department publishes *The Estonian crime barometer* (Estonian Ministry of Justice, n.d.). Andri Ahven from the Ministry of Justice represents Estonia in the European Sourcebook of Crime and Criminal Justice Statistics working group (European Sourcebook of Criminal Justice Statistics, n.d.).

Another topic of research is related to penal policy. The main figure in this field is definitely Professor of Criminal Law at the University of Tartu Jaan Sootak, also one of the authors of the Estonian Penal Code. He has extensively published on the theoretical grounds of Estonian penal reform (e.g. Sootak, 2000). Criminal policy choices is a topic of interest of Professor of Criminology Jaan Ginter (2000).

An important field of criminological research in Estonia is the Crime Victimization Survey. The latest survey conducted in Estonia as a part of International Crime Victim Surveys took place in 2004. The survey has been carried out previously in Estonia in 1993, 1995 and 2000, providing researchers with trend data for the period of nearly ten years. The biggest role in the arrangement of the survey in Estonia belongs to Finnish researcher Kauko Aromaa. In Estonia, from the very first survey Andri Ahven was involved in conducting a survey and analysis of data

(Aromaa and Ahven, 1995, 1993, 1998). In 2004, the data were analyzed by the criminological research group from the University of Tartu (Saar *et al.*, 2005). Since 2009, the crime victim survey has been conducted by the Statistical Office of Estonia.

Juvenile justice is a topic of interest for many Estonian criminologists. Jaan Sootak and Jaan Ginter have studied trends in juvenile offending, mainly concentrating on legal and procedural aspects of juvenile justice in Estonia (Ginter *et al.*, 2000).

In 2003, Jüri Saar defended his doctoral dissertation, which focused on the later criminal careers of former juvenile delinquents and offenders. The dissertation analysis was based on longitudinal research over the period 1985–99 into 317 male respondents who at the beginning of the study were inmates of two special institutions for juveniles in Estonia (Saar, 2003). In 2009, Saar received a four-year grant from the Estonian Science Foundation to continue the longitudinal research.

Interesting research was conducted on residential care for delinquent girls by Judit Strömpl (2002). In her dissertation Strömpl looks at the problem of the residential care of young persons from a new perspective. She analyzes the impact of everyday interactions in a closed institution on the troublesome girls, staff of the institution, and society in general. The uniqueness of this study is that it was based on ethnographic research at the girl's reformatory.

In recent years, Strömpl and her colleagues have been studying juvenile violence. School bullying has been the main topic of research completed in 2007 with the support of the Estonian Ministry of Social Affairs (Strömpl *et al.*, 2007). Based on the analysis of children's stories about school problems, the school comes across as "a multi-layered, hierarchical, differentiating system, in which both students and teachers are competing for their position, everyone using methods of self-assertion that are at hand and within their powers" (ibid., p. 123). The school violence study was followed by the study of peer violence in public space – an international project conducted also in Finland, South Wales in the UK, and Austria (Riepl and Williamson, 2009).

Estonia has participated in the second sweep of the International Self-Reported Delinquency Study (ISRD-2), an international survey conducted in a total of 33 countries. The aim of the study is twofold: first, to compare the level and prevalence of juvenile delinquency in participating countries; and second, to explain juvenile delinquency and test the etiological theories of crime (e.g. social bond theory). Data collection in Estonia was completed in 2006. The research was based on the national sample of all compulsory school students from seventh, eighth and ninth grade aged 12–16 years (except schools for children with special needs). The data have been analyzed for Estonia separately (Markina and Shahverdov-Zharkovski, 2007) and in comparison with five other new EU member states that participated in the study – Cyprus, Czech Republic, Estonia, Lithuania, Poland and Slovenia (Steketee *et al.*, 2008).

The 1990s were characterized by the growing interest toward research in organized crime, especially organized crime in former socialist countries. The first studies on organized crime in Estonia were conducted by colleagues from abroad. Patricia Rawlinson conducted an ESRC project "Crime borders and law enforcement: a European dialogue for improvement of security" aimed at discovering the nature and extent of Russian-speaking organized crime in and across the Baltic States (Rawlinson, 2003). Mika Junninen and Kauko Aromaa from the Helsinki Institute of Crime Prevention and Crime Control affiliated with United Nations (HEUNI) studied the activities of Finnish professional criminals across the Estonian–Finnish border (Junninen and Aromaa, 2000).

Later, Estonian criminologists became part of international research teams. Several co-operative projects were launched. The project "Assessing organized crime: testing the feasibility of a common European approach in a case study of the cigarette black market in the EU" was led by Petrus van Duyne from Tilburg University. This study aimed at developing and testing a cross-national and cross-sectorial method for assessing the nature, social relevance and dynamics of patterns of criminal cooperation, taking the trafficking in untaxed cigarettes in the European Union as an object of study for a first pilot with the intention of improving organized crime research results (Balcaen *et al.*, 2007). In Estonia the project was carried out by Anna Markina from the University of Tartu. One of the outcomes of the project is the analysis of cigarette black market in Estonia (Markina, 2007).

In recent years, three projects in this field have been completed in the field of trafficking in human beings. First, there was a study on trafficking for sexual exploitation supported by the International Organization for Migration (IOM), concentrating on legal regulations, the extent and nature of the problem, general public awareness and attitudes on the trafficking of human beings for sexual exploitation, and media reports on trafficking and major vulnerabilities of risk groups (Saar *et al.* , 2005). Another project was conducted in co-operation with The University of Manchester and HEUNI, concluding that there are many different forms of crime groups operating in the illegal immigration enterprise. The movement destination of illegal immigrants is based on historical associations and connections with family and friends. One of the conclusions of the project is that there is no apparent systematic and organized corruption of public officials in connection with illegal immigration (Spencer *et al.*, 2006). Finally, in 2007–8 a project called "Mapping organized crime; a market perspective on trafficking in persons for the purpose of sexual exploitation" was carried out. The project looked at the organization and structure of criminal networks involved in trafficking for sexual exploitation in Sweden, Finland and Estonia (Englund *et al.*, 2008).

The most prevalent methodological strategy in Estonian criminology is quantitative analysis of, most frequently, official crime data. However, the prevalence of one or another methodological strategy depends on the nature of phenomenon under study, scientific traditions, availability of official crime data, research questions etc.

Trend analysis is the main stress on official statistics. At the beginning of the last decade, two important changes took place that influenced the field of criminology in Estonia: the Ministry of Justice became responsible for collecting, handling, analyzing, and publishing crime statistics; and a new analytical unit, the Criminal Policy Department, was created. The group of researchers employed by the department gained access to major databases on crime, prosecution, penal history and imprisonment. Thus, the growing bulk of research on criminal justice.

Qualitative methods have been used in studies of phenomena, where no statistical data are available. In such projects (e.g. studies on extent and nature of organized criminal activities) the main method of data collection is usually semi-structured interview with experts, victims and perpetrators. Focus groups have been conducted in some cases (Saar *et al.*, 2005).

An ethnographic study was conducted a few years ago (Strömpl, 2002) and a longitudinal study started in 1985 (Saar, 2003) is the exception. Interested persons in crime analysis will find five data sources of interest: 1) statistical database (http://pub.stat.ee/px-web.2001/dialog/stat file1.asp) where the section "Justice and Security" contains numerous data on crime and criminal justice; 2) Crime Victims Survey data are in the possession of the Ministry of Justice, but not available to the general public; 3) ISRD-2 data are the property of the University of Tartu; in 2010 the total dataset will be available for participating institutions and for the general public in 2012; 4) database of court decisions (KOLA) (http://www.kohus.ee/1526) on administrative, misdemeanor, civil and criminal matters after they have entered into force and have some parts available for public use; statistical returns related to judicial proceedings are also accessible to the public, but the database is in Estonian only; and 5) Constitutional judgments (http://www.riigikohus.ee/?id = 823) are available online and in English.

There are two key research institutions in the field of criminology in Estonia: the University of Tartu and the Criminal Policy Department at the Ministry of Justice. The criminological research group is part of the Law Department. However, other departments of the university (e.g. the Department of Social Sciences) are also involved in research on crime and social control.

The main objective of the Criminal Policy Department is to carry out the necessary analyses and research necessary to provide policy makers with knowledge of the effects, the risks of implementation and the costs of criminal policy decisions. The Criminal Policy Department also analyzes the performance of criminal justice institutions. The department carries out research but also co-ordinates research in the field of criminology funded by the Ministry of Justice.

The main funding sources of research are competitive targeted financing by the Minister of Education and Research, following the recommendation of the Estonian Research Council, for the implementation of large-scale scientific projects.

Estonian Science Foundation research competitive grants are applicable for small-scale projects. The purpose is primarily to support high-level initiative research, new ideas and studies. The fifth stage of longitudinal research carried out in 2009–12 by Jüri Saar's research team is financed by this scheme.

Quite often international co-operative research is done with support of EU grants. Run in 2003–6, AGIS was a framework programme aimed to help police, the judiciary and professionals from the EU Member States and candidate countries co-operate in criminal matters and in the fight against crime. Several projects with participation of Estonian researchers were financed within the AGIS scheme (Moving People Across Borders, Mapping Organized Crime). The AGIS programme was closed in 2006 and succeeded by new programmes in the area of internal security and criminal justice: under the framework programme "Security and safeguarding liberties" specific programmes "Prevention, preparedness and consequence management of terrorism and other security-related risks" and "Prevention of and fight against crime" and, under the framework programme "Fundamental rights and justice," the new specific programme "Criminal justice" (European Commission, n.d.a).

The Seventh Framework Programme (FP7) funded by the European Commission bundles all research-related EU initiatives together under one roof. The broad objectives of FP7 have been grouped into four categories: cooperation, ideas, people and capacities (European Commission, n.d.b). For each type of objective, there is a specific programme corresponding to the main areas of EU research policy. All specific programmes work together to promote and encourage the creation of European pools of (scientific) excellence (CORDIS, 2009). The Project "Assessing organized crime" (Assessing Organized Crime Research Consortium, 2007) was funded by the Sixth Framework Programme (FP6).

Conclusion

Estonia has gone through dramatic socio-economic changes, including changes in dynamics and structure of crime as well as constantly reforming the criminal justice system. Some of these processes, such as organized crime, were thoroughly analyzed by criminologists, while investigation of many other processes and phenomena is still pending. The limited number of researchers and often fragmented financing of scientific inquiries in the field of criminology results in most criminologists providing expertise in multiple disciplines, such as juvenile crime and media research. Selection of a research topic is too often related not to the intrinsic interest of a researcher, but to the funding available. As a result, what is still lacking in Estonian criminology is a shaping of one school or development of certain theoretical approaches. But every cloud has a silver lining – the more we participate in various projects, the wider will be our international network and selection of projects to which Estonian criminologists can contribute.

Future research questions

1. How does the geographical situation of Estonia influence the crime situation?
2. How can you explain the relatively high Russian-speaking population among offenders?
3. What can be done to increase the use of the restorative-justice approach in criminal cases?
4. The fear of crime rates, as measured by International Crime Victim Surveys, are higher in post-communist countries compared to old democracies. What are the possible explanations?
5. Will a decrease in prison population result in an increasing crime rate?

Note

1 Annexation of Estonia by Soviet Union in 1940 that lasted until 1991.

References

Ahven, A., Jakobson, J., Klopets, U., Kruusement, A., Leps, A., Rennik, H., Salla, J., Surva, L., Sööt, M-L., and Tamm, K. (2010). Kuritegevus Eestis 2009. (Crime in Estonia 2009.) *Kriminaalpoliitika uuringud*, no. 12. Tallinn: Justiitsministeerium.

Aromaa, K. and Ahven, A. (1993). *Victims of crime in two Baltic Countries: Finnish and Estonian data from the 1992/1993 International Crime Victimization Survey*. Helsinki, Finland: National Research Institute of Legal Policy.

—— (1995). *Victims of crime in a time of change: Estonia 1993 and 1995*. Helsinki: National Research Institute of Legal Policy.

—— (1998). National Report: Estonia. In O. Hatalak, A. Alvazzi Del Frate, and U. Zvekic, *The International Crime Victim Survey in countries in transition*. Rome: UNICRI.

Balcaen, A., van Dijck, M., van Duyne, P. C., Eisenberg, U., Hobbs, R., Hornsby, R., von Lampe, K., Markina, A., Vander Beken, T., and Verpoest, K. (2007). *Assessing organized crime by a new common European approach. Final report*. Project no. CIS8-CT2004-501767. Tilburg, NL: European Commission.

Englund, C., Viuhko, M., Jokinen, A., Aromaa, K., Resetnikova, A., Markina, A., Söderström, U., and Nilsen, M. (2008). *The organisation of human trafficking: a study of criminal involvement in sexual exploitation in Sweden, Finland and Estonia*. Vol. 2008: 21. Stockholm: The Swedish National Council for Crime Prevention.

Estonian Ministry of Justice (2008). Estonian prison system and probation supervision yearbook 2007. Tallinn: Estonian Ministry of Justice.

Estonian Ministry of Justice (2009). Kuritegevus Eestis 2008 (Crime in Estonia 2008). Tallinn: Estonian Ministry of Justice.

—— (n.d.). *Crime barometer*. Online at http://www.just.ee/43479 (accessed November 30, 2010)

Estonian National Electional Committee (n.d.). Election results 2007. Online at http://www.vvk.ee/index.php?id = 11535 (accessed November 30, 2010).

Estonian Police Board (n.d.). Organisatsioonist. Online at http://www.politsei.ee (accesses November 30, 2010).

European Commission (n.d.a). Justice Funding 2003–2007 – AGIS. Online at http://ec.europa.eu/justice/funding/2004_2007/agis/funding_agis_en.htm (accessed November 30, 2010).

European Commission (n.d.b). The main objectives of FP7. Online at http://cordis.europa.eu/fp7/understand_en.html (accessed November 30, 2010).

European Sourcebook of Criminal Justice Statistics (n.d.). *European sourcebook of criminal justice statistics*. Online at http://www.europeansourcebook.org (accessed November 30, 2010).

Europol (2006). *EU organized crime threat assessment*. The Hague: European Police Office.

Eurostat (n.d.). Gini coefficient. Online at http://epp.eurostat.ec.europa.eu/tgm/table.do?tab=table&init=1&language=en&pcode=tessi190&plugin=1 (accessed November 30, 2010).

Ginter, J. (2000). Criminal Policy Choices and the Reform of the Estonian Criminal Law. *Juridica International*, (1): 79–84.

Ginter, J., Saarsoo, H., and Sootak, J. (2000). *Alaealiste õigusrikkumised: kriminaalõiguslik, menetluslik ja kriminoloogiline aspekt*. Tartu: Juura.

Junninen, M. and Aromaa, K. (2000). Professional crime across the Finnish–Estonian border. *Crime, Law and Social Change*, 34 (4): 319–47.

Kruuser, A., Roosaare, J., and Lepik, Õ. (2008) Restorative justice in Estonia. Online at http://www.euforumrj.org/readingroom/Countries/Estonia/Estonia.pdf (accessed November 30, 2010).

Liiv, M.-L. (Ed.) (2007). Kuritegevus Eestis 2006 (Crime in Estonia 2006). Kriminaalpoliitika uuringud, no. 4. Tallinn: Estonian Ministry of Justice.

Markina, A. (2007). Cigarette black market in Estonia. In P. van Duyne, A. Maljevic, M. van Dijck, K. von Lampe, and J. Harvey (Eds.), *Crime business and crime money in Europe: the dirty linen of illegal enterprise*, pp. 195–208. Nijmegen: Wolf Legal Publishers.

—— (2008).Youth delinquency in Estonia. In M. Steketee, M. Moll, and A. Kapardis (Eds.), *Juvenile delinquency in six new EU member states: crime, risky behaviour and victimization in the capital cities of Cyprus, Czech Republic, Estonia, Lithuania, Poland and Slovenia*, pp. 56–61. Utrecht: Verwey-Jonker Instituut.

Markina, A. and Shahverdov-Zharkovski, B. (2007). *Eesti alaealiste hälbiv käitumine*. Tallinn: Tartu University and Estonian Ministry of Justice.

Mikkel, E. (2006). Patterns of party formation in Estonia: consolidation unaccomplished. In S. Jungerstam-Mulders, *Post-Communist EU Member States: parties and party systems*, pp. 23–43. Aldershot: Ashgate.

Prosecutor's Office (n.d.). General introduction. Online at http://www.prokuratuur.ee/6848 (accessed November 30, 2010).

Raska, E. (2002). *Kriminoloogia*. Tallinn: Juura.

Rawlinson, P. (2003). Bad boys in the Baltics. In A. A. Edwards, *Transnational organised crime: perspectives on global security*, pp. 131–42. London: Routledge.

Riepl, B. and Williamson, H. (Eds.) (2009). *Portraits of peer violence in public space: experiences from young people in four localities in Europe*. Vienna: Austrian Institute of Youth Research.

Saar, J. (2003). *Õigusvastane käitumine alaealisena ja kriminaalsed karjäärid (eesti 1985–1999 longituuduurimuse andmetel). Dissertationes Iuridicae Universitatis Tartuensis 9*. Tartu: Tartu University Press.

—— (2004). Crime, crime control and criminology in post-communist Estonia. *European Journal of Criminology*, 1(4): 505–31.

Saar, J., Markina, A., Ahven, A., and Annist, A. G. (2003). *Kuritegevus Eestis 1991–2001. (Crime in Estonia 1991–2001)*. 2nd edn. Tallinn, Estonia: Juura.

Saar, J., Markina, A., Oole, K., and Resetnikova, A. (2005). *Rahvusvaheline kuriteoohvrite uuring Eestis 2004. Kriminaalpoliitika uuringud*. Vol. 1. Tallinn: Ministry of Justice.

Saar, J., Strömpl, J., Markina, A., and Annist, A. (2005). *Trafficking in human beings for sexual exploitation: an analysis of the situation in Estonia*. Helsinki: IOM.

Sööt, M.-L. (Ed.) (2008). Kuritegevus Eestis 2007 (Crime in Estonia 2007). Kriminaalpoliitika uuringud, no. 8. Tallinn: Estonian Ministry of Justice.

Sootak, J. (1997). *Kriminaalpoliitika: Õpik Tartu Ülikooli õigusteaduskonna üliõpilastele*. Tartu: Juura.

—— (2000). Theories of punishment and reform of criminal law (reform as a change of mentality). *Juridica International*, V: 68–78.

Spencer, J., Aromaa, K., Junninen, M., Markina, A., Saar, J., and Vijanen, T. (2006). *Organised crime, corruption and the movement of people across borders in the New Enlarged EU: a case study of Estonia, Finland and the UK*. Helsinki: HEUNI.

Statistics Estonia (2009a). *Minifacts about Estonia*. Tallinn: Statistics Estonia.

——(2009b). *Eesti statistika aastaraamat 2009. Statistical Yearbook of Estonia 2009*. Tallinn. Also available at http://www.stat.ee/31366 (accessed November 30, 2010).

—— (n.d.a). Statistical database. Online at http://pub.stat.ee/px-web.2001/dialog/statfile1.asp (accessed November 30, 2010).

—— (n.d.b). Disposable income per household member in a month. Online at http://pub.stat.ee/px-web.2001/Dialog/varval.asp?ma=HH03&ti=DISPOSABLE+INCOME+PER+HOUSEHOLD+MEMBER+IN+A+MONTH&path=../I_Databas/Social_life/06Households/02Household_budget/04Monthly_income/&lang=1 (accessed November 30, 2010).

—— (n.d.c). Indicators of income inequality of household members by age group and sex. Online at http://pub.stat.ee/px-web.2001/Dialog/varval.asp?ma=HHS07&ti=INDICATORS+OF+INCOME+INEQUALITY+OF+HOUSEHOLD+MEMBERS+BY+AGE+GROUP+AND+SEX&path=../I_Databas/Social_life/13Social_exclusion_Laeken_indicators/&lang=1 (accessed November 30, 2010).

—— (n.d.d). Annual statistics on unemployed persons. Online at http://pub.stat.ee/px-web.2001/I_Databas/Social_life/09Labour_market/12Unemployed_persons/02Annual_statistics/02Annual_statistics.asp (accessed November 30, 2010).

Steketee, M., Moll, M., and Kapardis, A. (2008). *Juvenile delinquency in six new EU member states: crime, risky behaviour and victimization in the capital cities of Cyprus, Czech Republic, Estonia, Lithuania, Poland and Slovenia.* Utrecht: Verwey-Jonker Instituut.

Strömpl, J. (2002). *The K. School. Residential management of troublesome girls in transition-time Estonia.* Academic Dissertation. Tartu: Tartu University Press.

Strömpl, J., Selg, M., Soo, K., and Shahverdov-Zharkovski, B. (2007). *Eesti teismeliste vägivallatõlgendused.* Vol. 3/2007. Tallinn: Proceedings of the Ministry of Social Affairs.

Tiit, E.-M. (2006). *Vaesus ja Selle mõõtmine. Vaesuse suundumused Eestis.* Tallinn: Ministry of Social Affairs.

Turu-uuringute, A. S. (2009). Trust in public institutions. Online at http://www.turu-uuringute.ee (accessed November 30, 2010)

Vetik, R. (Ed.) (2003). *Eesti inimarengu aruanne. Estonian human development report.* Tallinn: International Institute for Social Studies, TPU.

36

Ghana

The state of criminology in a changing society

Obi N. I. Ebbe

Introduction

Ghana has a checkered history having been settled by many European countries. Beginning with the Portuguese, who named the region in West Africa the Gold Coast and spread the news in Western Europe that this region was rich in gold, spices, and "black ivory," other European nations, including the Dutch, French, Swedes, and Danes, sailed to the Gold Coast. The Europeans built forts around their trading coasts. The Ashanti Kingdom was in control of the region at the time.

In 1874, the British conquered the Ashanti and took full administration of the coastal regions by annexing them as the Gold Coast Colony.

In March 1957, after 203 years of British control, Gold Coast became an independent country and changed its name to Ghana, and Dr. Kwame Nkrumah became the first Prime Minister. A year later, Ghana declared itself a Republic, and Dr. Kwame Nkrumah became the first President of Ghana.

Kwame Nkrumah continued to be re-elected until he was overthrown in a military coup d'état, when he was on a state visit to Soviet Union in 1966. After the overthrow of Kwame Nkrumah, there were many coups d'état. The last one was on 31 December 1981, when J. J. Rawlings, an Air Force lieutenant, overthrew a civilian government of Ghana after three previous military governments. Rawlings remained a military Head of Government and Commander in Chief until he decided to return the government to civilians, but he had to contest for the presidency of the civilian administration. In a multi-party general election for the presidency, on 28 April 1992, Rawlings was elected President by 58 percent of the votes. On 4 January 1993, the Fourth Republic was proclaimed and Rawlings was inaugurated as President.

After Rawlings completed two four-year terms as the constitution limited him, he peacefully handed over the office to the next elected President. Since then, Ghana has been the best administered democracy in Africa south of the Sahara.

Infrastructure

The Republic of Ghana is located in West Africa on the Gulf of Guinea and less than 5 degrees north of the Equator with 92,100 square miles (238,538 square kilometers) of land. Most of its area is grassland in the north and rain or mangrove forests in the south. Its 334-mile

(537-kilometer) coastline is mostly low, sandy shore rivers and streams flowing into the Atlantic Ocean. The largest river in Ghana is the Volta River which has a dam that provides hydroelectric power to most of the Ghana population. Ghana is surrounded in the north by Burkina Faso, Ivory Coast in the west, Togo in the east, and the Atlantic Ocean in the south. The land of Ghana is rich in cocoa plantations. There are many minerals in Ghana, including gold, diamond, aluminum and bauxite, manganese, cement, and other small-scale minerals.

Ghana is mainly an agricultural economy, accounting for one-third of the gross domestic product (GDP), and more than 50 percent of the labor force (Coakley, 2002). Formal mining and quarrying account for 25 per cent of the GDP and employs approximately 14,000 workers. In Africa, Ghana ranks second in gold production and third in aluminum and manganese ore production, and has significant diamond and bauxite production. Also, it produces a number of industrial minerals which include dimension stone, limestone, clays, salt, sand and gravel and silica sand (Barning, 1997).

Ghana's GDP in 2007 was $15.2 billion USD, with a growth rate of 6.3 per cent and a per capita GDP of $690 USD. The inflation rate, based on consumer prices on 31 October 2008, was 17.3 per cent (http://www.ghanaweb.com; accessed 19 March 2010).

In agricultural production, the typical products of Ghana are cocoa, coffee, tea, coconuts, pineapples, cashews, spices, grains, and many tuberous crops. Business and industry in Ghana concentrate on mining, lumbering, light manufacturing, fishing, aluminum, tourism, herding in the north, textiles, steel, tires, oil refining, flour milling, beverages, tobacco, simple consumer goods, and car, truck, and bus assembly. The main exports totaling $3.9 billion USD annually include cocoa ($1.26 billion USD), gold, timber, diamonds, and manganese.

Ghana's population below the poverty line was estimated at 31.4 per cent in 1992. Also, in 1999 the population whose earnings are in the lowest 10 percent possesses 2.2 per cent of the wealth and those with income in the highest 10 per cent have 30.1 per cent of the wealth. These figures have not changed much with the lowest 10 per cent at 2.0 per cent and the highest 10 per cent at 32.8 per cent in 2006 (CIA, 2010).

Ghana has a parliamentary system of government with a President who is the head of state and the chief of the Executive branch of the government. The President is elected by the people for four years for a maximum of two terms. The President is the Commander in Chief of the Armed Forces of Ghana. The President operates with a Council of State comprised of prominent citizens of Ghana of proven character as provided by the 1992 Constitution. The members of the Council of State are appointed by and advise the President on national issues. In the traditional system of government, they were known as Council of Elders. According to the Constitution, there are supposed to be 25 members, but in 2008, the President, John Atta Mills, appointed 11.

The government of Ghana is based on a multi-party democratic system. Ghana has a unicameral Parliament of 230 legislators plus the Speaker of the House of Assembly. The members of the legislature are elected to serve for four years.

Ghana is divided into ten administrative regions which report to the central government in Accra. The regions are Northern, Eastern, Western, Central, Upper East, Upper West, Volta, Ashanti, Brong-Ahafor, and Greater Accra.

The three branches of government in Ghana are the Executive, the Legislative, and the Judiciary. The President (Executive) appoints the Attorney-General with the approval of the Legislature. There is independence of the Judiciary in Ghana. The President has veto power in all legislative matters except in cases of emergency.

Ghana is a member of the African Union, the United Nations Organization, the Economic Community of West African States, the Commonwealth of Nations, and a host of other international humanitarian organizations.

The Ghana Broadcasting Corporation (GBC) is a radio and television medium of communication between the government and the people of Ghana and the world. Under the GBC, the "Voice of Ghana" broadcasts in short-wave and can be received in most countries of the world. The GBC television has school programs and a variety of shows daily. Ghana Internet providers include AfricaOnline, Broadband4u from Ghana Telecom, InternetGhana, NCS, Tif-ifa Ghana Ltd; wwwplus, and other ISPs. The number of household users is estimated at 997,000 (CIA, 2010).

Travel in Ghana can be accomplished by road, rail, air, and water. As last measured in 2006, Ghana has a 62,221-kilometer road system with 52,266 kilometers of those unpaved (CIA, 2010). In addition to road travel, Ghana has railway, airway, and water transportation systems. As last measured in 2008, Ghana's 947-kilometer railway system (CIA, 2010) is concentrated in the mineral and cocoa production areas, thus there is no international railway system, although there are future plans for expansion.

Ghana has a government-owned commercial airway system, with the major airport in Kotokar International Airport. There are domestic flight airports at Sekondi-Takoradi, Kumasi, and Tamale. The seaports, which harbor international shipping lines, have weak security, making them vulnerable to piracy and associated crimes. Also, Ghana's busy international airport takes many European, Middle East, and African air carriers, thereby making Ghana a transit for international trafficking in drugs, women, and children (Akyeampong, 2005; Ebbe and Das, 2007, 2009).

People

Ghana has a population of 23 million people. There are 247 persons per square mile. The main ethnic groups are Akan (Ashanti), Ewe, Ga, and Moshi-Dagomba.

English is the language of the formal educational system in Ghana. As a former British colony, Ghana's educational system follows the British system of primary, secondary, and university education with some variation. Very few Ghanaians enter university. It is very competitive based on the senior secondary national final examination (school certificate). Public education is free in Ghana from primary through senior secondary school and private education is for the wealthy. The University of Ghana at Legon is the most popular university, an offspring of the University of London (1946–50).

Like most African countries, Ghana has sanitation problems and health care is very poor, especially in rural towns and villages. The number of well-trained medical doctors compared to the general population is very small. The general hospitals operated by the government are inexpensive, but they are not suitable for serious health problems. The private hospitals and clinics are costly for the average Ghanaian.

Administration of justice

This part of the chapter discusses the structure of the criminal justice system beginning with criminal law, followed by police, the judiciary, and ending with the prisons.

The criminal laws of Ghana today are a combination of English law and the customary conduct norms of the Ghanaian citizens. As a result of 203 years of British domination, the English legal system permeates the social, political, and economic life of the Ghanaian people. Between 1843 and 1925, a British governor and an all-European executive and legislative council made laws for the people of Ghana. During this period, all the laws of Ghana were based on the English legal system and English normative standards (Ebbe, 1989; Abotchie and Ebbe, 2000; Adinkrah, 2008).

When the Gold Coast gained its independence on 6 March 1957, the Independence Constitution created a National Assembly to act as the main law-making body for Ghana, replacing the colonial legislative assembly.

For a bill to become law, it is first introduced to the National Assembly. After the bill has passed three readings on the floor of the National Assembly, it is submitted to the President for his approval. For a bill to become an Act of Parliament, the President's approval is required. The President has the right to veto a bill. Over the years, the Ghana Independence Parliament has amended the colonial laws to suit the norms, beliefs, and standards of the Ghanaian people.

Ghana has a centralized police system, with members recruited from all ten regions of the country. The police districts report directly to the Ghana Police Regional Headquarters, who in turn report to the Ghana Police Services Headquarters in Accra.

The Republican Constitution of 1960 empowered the President to appoint the Chief Executive Officer of the Ghana Police Services (GPS), who has the title of Inspector General of Police. GPS fall under the authority of the Ministry of the Interior.

There are ten police regions, including the GPS Headquarters in Accra. Each police region is administered by an Assistant Commissioner of Police. Each region is divided into divisions, and each division is subdivided into police districts with many police stations and posts operating in each district.

The Inspector General of Police and a Deputy Inspector General are in charge of the Criminal Investigation Department (CID). Another Deputy Inspector General is in charge of the Administration Department. There are five other departments operating under the authority of a separate commissioner or a deputy commissioner. These five departments include the Training Department, Welfare Department, Services Department, Technical Department, and Operations Department.

The police are responsible for the detection of crime, offender apprehension, law and order maintenance, protection of lives and property, motor vehicle licensing and driver licensing, the licensing of hunting guns, inspection of vehicles for road worthiness, escort and body-guard services for ministers and senior government officials, the prosecution of offenders, riot control, collection of certain rates and taxes for the government, traffic control, and the escort of convicted offenders to prisons. Presently there are 23,000 policemen and women in Ghana. There is one police officer for over 1,300 persons.

The Ghana Police Training Center (PTC) in Accra trains recruits for a six-month duration. Individuals aspiring to join the PTC must be between 18 and 35 years old and be at least 5 feet, 8 inches tall. The minimum educational requirement for recruits is a high school diploma. The individual must be free from sight, vocal, and physical impairments (Ebbe, 1995; Quaye, 1993).

The Ghana Police College (GPC) in Accra trains cadets who become police officers. Cadets spend a year at the GPC to become commissioned Assistant Superintendents. Today, individuals with a university degree in the social sciences and other sciences have started joining the police. However, these individuals must also undergo the one-year training at the GPC. Some non-commissioned officers with the rank of Inspector can be promoted to the rank of Assistant Superintendent without undergoing any training at the GPC (Agyapong, 1993).

The police use deadly force only when an offender resists an arrest or is armed and refuses to surrender. Ghana police have wide discretionary powers in the areas of arrest, search and seizure, and determining the cases they will bring to court. An offender reaches a district court or a magistrate's court only if the police decide to take the matter to court. There is nothing like the "District Attorney" in the Ghana Criminal Justice System. The District Public Prosecutor prosecutes all cases in each District. The District Public Prosecutor is not required to have a law degree.

The police are required to obtain a warrant from the District Magistrate before any search and seizure may take place. However, in practice, a warrant is not always obtained. Even if the police engage in a warrantless search and seizure, the case can still be brought to court. Any statement made by a suspect in the absence of a defense attorney can be admitted into evidence.

The Ghana police is a political force and strong ally of the Head of State and top government officials. In effect, the Police Service Commission is powerless to discipline police officers. There is no agency or person responsible for monitoring the police in Ghana.

The defendant has a right to plead guilty before the prosecution presents the case to the court. However, a guilty plea does not automatically result in the magistrate or judge imposing a lesser sentence. The defendant also has the right to introduce witnesses in his/her defense, as well as a right to confront opposing witnesses. If the accused is indigent, the state will provide a public defender for legal representation.

After police arrest a suspect, criminal proceedings are initiated in a District Court or a Circuit Court, with the exception of offenses that require a death sentence or life imprisonment as the maximum penalty. All crimes that require death penalty or a life sentence are first initiated in a High Court. A crime may be tried summarily or by indictment depending on whether the crime is a misdemeanor or a felony (Twumasi, 1985). Generally, most misdemeanors are tried summarily, which does not require going to the High Court. All serious offenses are tried by indictment in a Circuit Court or a High Court. Offenders are tried by a Magistrate in the District Court and by a Circuit Judge in a Circuit Court. There are neither jury trials nor grand juries. Jury trials in Ghana ceased with the end of the colonial administration of justice in 1957.

Police officers who investigate a crime may also appear as crown witnesses. There is no plea bargaining. In certain cases when the offender and victim live in the same locality, the judge may refer the case to the local chief who attempts to settle the matter informally. Cases involving the possibility of a trial often require suspects to be kept in police custody until they are bailed out by a relative, an acceptable friend, or a defense attorney. Only well-known property owners are ever released on their own recognizance. Suspects charged with serious offenses may be granted bail if there is reason to believe they will not abscond. If the offense carries a maximum penalty of life imprisonment or death, suspects are not granted bail. For the years 1989, 1990, and 1991, not more than 36.5 per cent of the cases that were sent to court had suspects incarcerated while awaiting trial.

The judiciary is independent of the executive branch and the National Assembly. The Republican Constitution and the Court Act of 1960 established a dual system of courts, which modified the older colonial judicial system. This dual system of courts consists of superior and inferior courts (Ebbe, 1989, 1995; Twumasi, 1985).

The superior courts handle English laws that are still operative, as well as statutory law, common law, ordinances, and laws that have been promulgated by Ghana post-independence legislatures. Inferior courts decide less serious felonies, misdemeanors, and cases involving customary law violations (Abotchie and Ebbe, 2000; Ebbe, 1995).

There are three levels of superior courts: the Supreme Court, the Court of Appeal, and the High Court. The Supreme Court and the Court of Appeal do not sentence offenders in criminal cases. They review the legal principles applied and direct the lower court from where the appeal came to deliver an appropriate judgment and sentence the offender accordingly. Inferior courts consist of the Circuit Court, the District Court, and all customary courts.

The Supreme Court of Ghana is the highest court of the land, composed of the Chief Justice (the president of the court) and nine other justices. The Court hears all criminal cases referred to it. Supreme Court decisions are final. Appeals from this court to the Privy Council in London are not allowed anymore. The 1992 Constitution provided for not less than ten judges of the Supreme Court, including the Chief Justice.

The Court of Appeal has appellate jurisdiction over all High Court decisions, except in cases where appeals must be brought to the Supreme Court or where appeals are derived from a criminal conviction arising from a summary trial in a Circuit Court (Twumasi, 1985; Abotchie and Ebbe, 2000; Ebbe, 1995).

The High Court hears appeals from Circuit Courts, District Magistrate's Courts, or Juvenile Courts. One to three judges of the Supreme Court or Circuit Court can be requested to hear a case at the High Court. There is a High Court in each of the 10 regions of Ghana and an 11th in the capital city of Accra (Abotchie and Ebbe, 2000; Ebbe, 1995; Twumasi, 1985).

Circuit Courts have original jurisdiction in less serious criminal cases. Appeals from a Circuit Court are brought to the High Court, while indictment decisions made at the trial are specifically brought to the Supreme Court (Abotchie and Ebbe, 2000; Ebbe, 1995; Twumasi, 1985).

District Courts are divided into Grades I and II. A Grade I District Court has greater power than a Grade II District Court. Both have original jurisdiction in criminal matters. District Court judges cannot impose more than one year's imprisonment, and fines cannot exceed 65,000 Cedis ($43,000 USD). Appeals from the District Courts are brought to the High Court that has jurisdiction over the district. The High Court also has authority over all District Court Magistrates in its jurisdiction (Abotchie and Ebbe, 2000; Ebbe, 1995; Twumasi, 1985).

Customary courts are located in rural towns and are loosely regulated. Case decisions are made by a chief or a council of elders. Appeals can be made to the District Court.

The Juvenile Court is made up of four members: a laywoman, a layman, and two magistrates. They hear cases involving juveniles who are 17 years old or under. The court itself is not permanent. It operates on an ad hoc basis because there are long periods of time without juvenile cases to hear. Juvenile Court sessions are usually held only in large city districts. Because most juvenile offenses are handled informally, there are usually a maximum of 20 Juvenile Court sessions held during the year for the entire country (Ebbe, 1995).

The Chief Justice is the head of the Judiciary. The Chief Justice of the Supreme Court and other justices are appointed by the President, with the recommendation of the Ghana Judicial Council. The justices of the Supreme Court serve the Court until the age of 65. The justices of the Court of Appeal, the Circuit Court Judges, the High Court Judges, and District Magistrates are appointed by the President.

All the judges and magistrates of the courts have law degrees either from British universities or Ghanaian universities. To practice law in Ghana, each judge, magistrate, and lawyer must become a member of the Ghana Bar Association, by passing the Ghana Bar Examination. Customary court judges are laypeople without formal legal training. They are appointed by the government either by inherited traditional leadership or other qualifications (Agyapong, 1993).

A District Magistrate, or the judge of a High Court or Circuit Court, can sentence an offender. When a panel of judges hears a case in a High Court, conviction and sentencing decisions must be unanimous. There is no special sentencing hearing, because Ghana has no jury trial system.

Professionals have input into the sentencing process. Psychiatrists may be consulted if insanity is being used as a defense. Social workers acting as probation officers and medical experts may be consulted in sentencing as well.

The penalties imposed include fines, compensation, community services, or probation for less serious offenses (e.g. petty larceny, aggravated assault, strong-arm robbery). Prison sentences range from one year to life without parole. Life sentences are imposed for murder and treason, and can be imposed for armed robbery and counterfeiting or currency offenses. Death sentences are carried out by a firing squad. The number of persons executed over the past five to ten years has not been made public. Most offenders that were executed between 1975–8 were convicted of felony treason and conspiracy to overthrow the government of Ghana.

Pre-colonial Gold Coast (Ghana), like other African societies south of the Sahara, had no idea of the prison system. To sub-Saharan African societies, an offender is a member of the society and must be corrected in the community in which he belongs.

The Ghana penal system is governed by the Prison Ordinance of 1960. The system is a national, centralized system, operating under the authority of the Director of Prisons. Most of the prison officers are trained in Ghana; some are trained in Europe. Some officers also hold university degrees. Depending on the qualifications at the point of entry into the prisons service, training can last from six months to one year. Warden recruits are required to have a First School Leaving Certificate (Elementary School diploma) or a high school diploma. These recruits must complete six months training before they become certified wardens and can be assigned to any correctional facility in the country.

Based on the latest data available (Butler, 1994), the Prison Service Board administers Ghana's 27 prisons, including 6 central prisons for men in Accra (Ussher Fort and James Fort), Sekondi, Kumasi, Tamale, and Nsawam, and 2 prisons for women in Ekuasi near Sekondi and Ho. There are 15 local prisons (minimum and medium security) and 2 open prisons in various parts of the country. Some of the local prisons have annexes for women. About 75 per cent of the commitments are for less than six months. Parole and probation programs are available to non-serious offenders due to overcrowding in the prison facilities.

A convicted offender may be released on probation for six months to three years. Any violation of the probation results in the offender serving the sentence for the original offense. Probation is used for young offenders.

Juveniles appear before a juvenile court only if they have committed a crime. Activities resembling "status offenses" are resolved as family matters.

Because of the few number of prisons and the fact that each prison is capable of holding only up to 500 inmates, there is a tremendous overcrowding problem (Appiahene-Gyamfi, 2008). Today, Ghana prisons are operating at 145.5 per cent above capacity.

The number of inmates in all prisons is estimated at 10,992 (2008 est.). Females constitute 2 per cent of the inmate population. Of the 10,992 prison inmate population, 24.5 per cent are pre-trial detention. Actual or estimated proportions of inmates incarcerated is 52 per 100,000 population.

Each prison has vocational and education programs. It should be noted that the offender's prior criminal record does not affect employment opportunities after release, because potential employers are not allowed to inquire about prior criminal convictions.

Criminology in Ghana

Crimes are classified as serious and non-serious crimes or as felonies and misdemeanors, with the exception of the "all other offenses" category. The most serious felonies are murder, armed robbery, abortion, rape, stealing (grand larceny), unlawful entry (burglary), possession of dangerous drugs, possession of cocaine, possession of heroin, extortion, forgery, smuggling contrabands, and counterfeiting. Misdemeanor offenses include tax evasion or violation of ordinances that can be disposed of by fines instead of imprisonment. Additionally, there are cyber crimes, such as electronic theft, credit card fraud, online auction fraud, pyramid fraud, fraudulent internet banking sites, ATM fraud, cyber terrorism, and lottery scams. The age of criminal responsibility is 18 years old.

The three types of dangerous drugs listed in the Ghana police crime statistics are cocaine, heroin, and Indian hemp. While certain drugs, such as barbiturates, are not illegal, it is illegal to import them for commercial purposes without a license and can result in a criminal charge of smuggling and possessing dangerous drugs.

Crime is predominant in the big cities of Accra, Takoradi, Tamale, Tema, and Sekondi where it is concentrated in poor neighborhoods and congested large business areas. The following crime statistics are provided and recorded by the 1989–1991 Annual Report of the Ghana Police Crime Data Services Bureau. The approximate population of Ghana in 1991 was 14 million. Recent criminological studies in Ghana have shown that murders are mostly vigilante murders, felony murders, and organized crime murders (Adinkrah, 2004, 2005; Appiahene-Gyamfi, 2007).

- Murder: At a rate of 2.01 per 100,000 population, there were a total of 282 (1991), 275 (1990), and 239 (1989) murder cases. Attempts are not included.
- Rape: At a rate of 2.91 per 100,000 population, there were a total of 408 (1991), 375 (1990), and 274 (1989) cases of rape.
- Theft: At a rate of 287.52 per 100,000 population, there were a total of 40,254 (1991), 38,532 (1990), and 41,056 (1989) cases of theft.
- Drug offenses: At a rate of 5.5 per 100,000 population, there were a total of 770 (1991), 737 (1990), and 637 (1989) drug offense cases, including possession of dangerous drugs and marijuana. In the past ten years, drug abuse has permeated low- and middle-class neighborhoods in Ghanaian large cities. In effect, trafficking in drugs and human beings has become one of the most serious crimes in Ghana (Appiahene-Gyamfi, 2003; Ebbe, 2006, 2007; Akyeampong, 2005).
- Crime regions: In the period between 1989 and 1991, the Ashanti and Accra regions had the highest incidence of murder, rape, and armed robbery. They were also the regions with the highest population density and the most commercial enterprise.

As of 2007, crime reports from Ghana show that the rates of murder, rape, theft, drug offenses, fraud, assault, robbery, and burglary have gone up 20 times more than the rates in 1991. For instance, the rate of crime in Accra (population 2.9 million people) has reached the level similar to the level of inner-city crime in the United States (OSAC, 2007). The crimes most often reported in Ghana are burglary, armed and unarmed robberies, purse snatching in streets, mugging in streets, pocket picking in streets, and fraud (e.g. requesting an advance fee to transfer millions into your account).

The modus operandi of the criminals varies. For example, criminals ride on motorcycles and snatch a victim's purse, set fake police roadblocks for robbery, pretend to be beggars, or perpetrate crime in dark areas of a street. Sometimes the robbers use machetes or handguns. Highway robbery is easily carried out, because Ghana's population density is very low (247 per square mile). Also, the crime rate is higher in the southern regions than in the northern regions, because the southern regions are the areas of heavy business districts and very high availability of things to steal and burglarize, and people to rob.

There are no systematic records of the number of victims or their personal characteristics. Ghana does not have victim assistance programs. Victim service agencies are regarded as unnecessary. If the victim observed the crime being committed, s/he may appear as a crown witness in the prosecution. However, the victim has no role in the sentencing process.

Criminological studies of Ghana in the past five to ten years have concentrated in the areas of violent crimes (Appiahene-Gyamfi, 2007; Adinkrah, 2004, 2008; Abotchie, 1997), such as armed and unarmed robbery, rape, burglary, assault, and vandalism (Abotchie and Ebbe, 2000; Ebbe, 1995). Other areas studied include juvenile delinquency (Abotchie and Ebbe, 2000; Ebbe, 1995), trafficking in women and children (Ameh, 2006; Amoakahene, 2004; Ebbe, 1996, 2001, 2006, 2007), corruption in government (Ebbe, 2004), drug smuggling, and piracy (Adu-Mireku, 2002; Abotchie and Ebbe, 2000; Appiahene-Gyamfi, 2003; Ebbe, 2001, 2007).

The problem of criminological studies in Ghana, like in Kenya, Nigeria, Sierra Leone, Uganda, and other developing countries of Africa, is the absence of systematic records of crime statistics. There are no systematic records of arrests, indictments, prosecutions, sentencing, incarceration rates, recidivism rate, number of each type of crime committed, number of inmates incarcerated each year and number released, number of beds in each prison, and number of inmates without beds.

Conclusion

Ghana is the most stable democracy in sub-Saharan Africa. The police are not as corrupt as police in Nigeria and Kenya and other parts of Africa (Ebbe, 2004). The Ghana Judiciary is very strong. The court system in Ghana is designed to take care of custom and tradition. Presently, a Ghanaian trained lawyer, Judge Akua Kuenyenia, is a member of the International Criminal Court (ICC); her term ends in 2015. And the seventh Secretary-General of the United Nations, Kofi Annan, is from Ghana.

The Ghana prison system needs improvement, beginning with caseload reductions (Appiahene-Gyamfi, 2008). On the whole, Ghana has a promising criminological development and effective criminal justice system. Many Ghanaians are now graduating in the fields of criminology, sociology, and criminal justice, more than ever before. Unmistakably, criminological studies by eminent Ghanaian scholars such as Abotchie (1997, 2000), Adinkrah (2004, 2005, 2008), Appiahene-Gyamfi (2003, 2007, 2008), Agyapong (1993), Ameh (2006), and Akyeampong (2005) have provided solid foundation for future studies in Ghanaian criminology.

Future research questions

1. What are the social, economic, and cultural factors in the etiology of violent crimes in Ghana?
2. What are the characteristics of convicted prison inmates in Ghana prisons?
3. What measures should the government and the Ghana Police Service take to reduce street crimes in Ghana?
4. How can the Ghana government safeguard tourists who visit Ghana from criminal victimization?
5. Finally, lack of employment opportunities may explain youth crimes in Ghana; how can the Ghana government increase employment opportunities for high school and university graduates?

References

Abotchie, C. (1997). *Social control in traditional Eweland of Ghana*. Accra: University of Ghana Press.

Abotchie, C. and Ebbe, O. N. I. (2000). Crime and crime control in Ghana: post-traditional and nation-state. In G. Barak (Ed.) *Crime and crime control: a global view*, (pp. 49–63). Westport, CT: Greenwood Press.

Adinkrah, M. (2004). Witchcraft accusations and female homicide victimization in contemporary Ghana. *Violence Against Women*, 10(4): 325–56.

—— (2005). Vigilante homicides in contemporary Ghana. *Journal of Criminal Justice*, 33(5): 413–27.

—— (2008). Criminalizing marital rape: the view of Ghanaian university students. Paper presented at an annual meeting of the American Society of Criminology. St. Louis, MO.

Adu-Mireku, S. (2002). Fear of crime among residents of three communities in Accra, Ghana. *International Journal of Comparative Sociology*, 43(2): 153–68.

Agyapong, O. A. (1993). Personal interview on police, prisons, and crime in Ghana. 6 September.

Akyeampong, E. (2005). Diaspora and drug trafficking in West Africa: a case study of Ghana. *African Affairs*, 104(416): 429–47.

Ameh, R. K. (2006). Uncovering truth: Ghana's National Reconciliation Commission excavation of past human rights abuses. *Contemporary Justice Review: Issues in Criminal, Social and Restorative Justice*, 9(4): 345–68.

Amoakahene, M. I. (2004). Violence against women in Ghana: a look at women's perceptions and review of policy and social responses. *Social Science and Medicine*, 59(11): 2373–85.

Appiahene-Gyamfi, J. (1998). Violent crime in Ghana: the case of robbery in Ghana. *Journal of Criminal Justice*, 26(5): 409–24.

—— (2003). Urban crime trends and patterns in Ghana: the Accra case. *Journal of Criminal Justice*, 31(1): 13–23.

—— (2007). Interpersonal violent crimes in Ghana: the case of assault in Ghana. *Journal of Criminal Justice*, 35(4): 419–31.

—— (2008). Exploration of the prevalence of HIV/AIDS cases in Ghanaian prisons. Paper presented at an annual meeting of the American Society of Criminology. St. Louis, MO.

Barnsing, K. (Ed.) (1997). *Industrial mineral resources of Ghana*. Accra: Ghana Minerals Commission.

Butler, R. (1994). Ghana prison system. Online at http://www.mongabay.com/history/ghana/ghana-prison_system.html. (accessed December 10, 2010).

Central Intelligence Agency (CIA) (2010). *The world factbook*. Washington, DC: Central Intelligence Agency. Online at https://www.cia.gov/library/publications/the-world-factbook/fields/2047.html (accessed December 10, 2010).

Coakley, G. J. (2002). *The mineral industry of Ghana*. Accra: Ghana Minerals Commission.

Ebbe, O. N. I. (1989). The emergence of criminal law in developing countries. Paper presented at an annual meeting of the American Society of Criminology (ASC). Reno, NV.

—— (1994) Crime and victimization in Ghana. Paper presented at the annual meeting of the Academy of Criminal Justice Sciences (ACJS). Chicago, IL.

—— (1995) The juvenile justice system in the Republic of Ghana. Paper presented at an annual meeting of the ACJS. Boston, MA.

—— (1996) Organized crime in Africa. Paper presented at the Third International Police Executive Symposium. Kanagawa University, Yokohama, Japan.

—— (2001) Political corruption in Africa. Paper presented at the Ninth International Police Executive Symposium. Szcztyno, Warsaw, Poland.

—— (2004). Political corruption in Africa. In R. Sarre, D. K. Das, and H. J. Albrecht (Eds.) *Political Corruption: International Perspectives*. Lanham, MD: Lexington Books.

—— (2006) Domestic and international trafficking in human beings: sex and body parts trade. Paper presented at the annual meeting of the ASC. Las Angeles, CA.

—— (2007). Urbanization and security in Africa. Paper presented at the annual meeting of the International Police Executive Symposium. Dubai, United Arab Emirates.

Ebbe, O. N. I and Das, D. K. (Eds.) (2007). *Global trafficking in women and children*. Boca Raton, FL: CRC Press of Taylor & Francis Group.

—— (2009) *Criminal abuse of women and children: an international perspective*. Boca Raton, FL: CRC Press of Taylor & Francis Group. Ghana Police Force Headquarters Annual Reports, 1957–70; 1989–91.

Overseas Security Advisory Council (OSAC). (2007). *Ghana 2007 crime and safety report*. Sub-Saharan Africa, Ghana. January 23.

Quaye, P. (1993). Chief Superintendent, personal interview at Accra. June 10.

Twumasi, K. (1985). *Criminal law in Ghana*. Accra: Ghana Publishing Corporation.

37

Great Britain

Criminology and criminal justice

Anne Brunton

Introduction

This chapter explores "British criminology": both the idea of it and what it might possibly be. The idea of a British *criminology* is problematic because there is some question about whether criminology can make claims to being a separate academic subject in its own right. Rock and Holdaway (1998) refer to criminology as a "rendezvous" discipline, meaning that it is a meeting point for the concerns of many others, such as psychology, law, social work, sociology and social policy. Additionally, in terms of attempting to bound the subject geographically, we must also ask whether one can practice this subject without reference to the work of colleagues producing debate, thoughts and ideas within their own jurisdictions or countries. It can be argued, fairly convincingly, that we are influenced by criminal justice practice and ideas from elsewhere. Finally, there is a question about the contemporary nature of criminology. A cursory examination of its history, within what might be loosely termed "the discipline," and before it in analogous subject areas, will show startling similarities to "modern" thoughts and ideas about those who commit crime. Therefore, British criminology at times draws influences that are historical (things we have done before within our own country) and sometimes what is done in other countries. An example of this geographical eclecticism or "borrowing" in Britain would be restorative justice. Restorative justice is traditionally a practice of New Zealand Maori tribes and yet many of its founding principles have been adopted within youth justice in England and Wales.

This chapter will address some of these issues as well as draw a brief picture of British criminology and its criminal justice system. By doing this we will consider the major functions of criminal justice and our criminological interest in them.

Infrastructure

Britain lies off the coast of mainland Europe. It is made up of a group of islands and one small landmass and has four countries within its boundaries: England, Wales, Scotland and Northern Ireland. Only one of these boundaries abuts another European country (Ireland). In addition, there are the Channel Islands, which lie off the coast of the main landmass, having their own systems of law and criminal justice, but are not covered in this chapter. In this chapter the main concern will be with the jurisdictions of England and Wales although some mention will be made of Northern Ireland and Scotland.

Britain has a long history marked by invasion by its neighbors as early as 43 BC, including the Romans, Angles, Saxons, Jutes and eventually Vikings. This period saw the adoption of a monarchy in a series of kingdoms. Britain has largely remained a monarchy with the exception of a brief period as a republic (1649–60). Therefore, even today British people are subjects of a monarchy and not citizens of a republic. This has ramifications in terms of constitutional rights (Office of National Statistics, 2004).

Britain was eventually united under two "Acts of Union." The first, in 1707, united the parliaments of England and Scotland, and in 1800, Northern Ireland. This situation remained until 1999, when power devolved to Wales, Scotland and Northern Ireland. This is an indicator of the difficult relationship Britain has had with its closest European neighbor – Ireland. "Partition" of Ireland effectively occurred in 1922 when the southern section of the country left Britain. This had been preceded by almost 500 years of complicated and problematic relations including violent and terrorist acts in the northern protestant reaches of Ireland and mainland Britain by the Irish Republican Army (IRA) – a revolutionary armed militia. The peace process mainly concluded this in 1999 although the relationship remains a complicated one (Office of National Statistics, 2004).

This early history informs contemporary understanding of the criminal justice system, particularly the way Great Britain made law, managed "law breakers," protected its boundaries (locally through property and ownership and geographically through international law and treaties), controlled domestic populations when there were periods of unrest and developed systems of justice and accountability.

It can be argued that there is "a" British culture which might be expressed in the following way as food preferences and culinary history – tea, scones, roast beef, or politically as a liberal tradition, or finally as part of the history and development of music and art and culture, for example – "Land of hope and glory." However, largely, these form convenient cultural stereotypes and like all stereotypes are only partly true. This is because Britain has a long history of colonizing other cultures and the taking of cultural practices from elsewhere. This snapshot is a fairly modern, crude and sweeping interpretation of "Britishness." In addition, of course, British culture remains intensely problematic because of the separate identities of the English, Scots, Welsh and Irish. There is a substantial and interesting literature on this (Colls, 2002).

Administration of justice

Globalization is a contested idea and in broad terms may refer to the complications and benefits from the exchange or spread of political, economic or cultural artefacts or ideas. In terms of criminal justice, an example of our global influence is the British police service, which as one of the first police forces was extremely influential on the development of other policing organizations in Europe, Asia and Africa. Indeed the British police service has provided officer training for countries worldwide.

However, the impact of globalization can also have a significant effect on other aspects of the criminal justice system and the patterns and trends of criminal offenses. Significantly, the recent global downturn which was felt throughout 2008 has had a significant impact on Britain with a serious and debilitating decrease in the public sector, productivity, job vacancies and security. There is a possibility that the current social and economic conditions that have arisen now will result in a further "order consensus," the second of which emerged in the 1990s. This is mentioned in further detail later but basically refers to a time when there is general cross-party agreement on "law and order" but that in recent times that consensus has been a punitive one (Newburn, 2007). For example, young people in an economic downturn are always adversely affected (Dorling, 2006).

The British system of government is bicameral, with two legislative Houses. The House of Commons forms the primary legislature. The representatives, called "members of parliament," are elected by the people through a democratic process. The second, "House of Lords," is not elected and members used to be selected through hereditary or life peerage, although now members can also be recommended. The House of Lords remains a "check" on the activity of the House of Commons, but it can be overruled (Budge and McKay, 1993).

The British political system particularly in national elections has been dominated by a two-party system for the past 50 years, the Conservative Party (broadly at the right of the political spectrum) and the Labour Party (broadly at the left of the political spectrum). Politically this is of concern because in the recent past the stance taken on crime has been seen as a "vote winner" or potential loser. The British political system is highly centralized and in recent years there has been less and less to choose from between the two primary political parties on law and order policy (Newburn, 2006).

Although Britain could be called politically liberal, criminal justice has become increasingly thorny over the past 40 years. It is only relatively recently that the use of criminal justice has become a political one. In the 1970s crime was not on the political agenda. There was generally a consensus across all political parties about what was the right approach to take towards crime. This cross-party support ended with the advent of the 1979 election where criminal justice policy took center stage in a general election. The tough stance that was taken by the Conservative Party was crucial in their political campaign and win. It was also apparent that during this period there was a politicization of the police: the police became actively involved in offering support to a "tough on crime" stance (Newburn, 2007).

Britain is a Common Law system, referring to the practice and development of the law. Law is developed through a case-by-case basis and defining judgments in courts and tribunals. This approach allows for flexibility and a pragmatic approach. However, this flexibility also means that there is a degree of discretion in the way in which the law is brought to bear (Rubin, 2007).

The legal system deals with those suspected of committing a criminal offense. It is made up of three stages: the police, the courts and sentences. Underpinning these areas are the laws on which the legal system is built. However, laws are not applied equally to all. In addition, laws are not produced in a social vacuum. They may be in response to mass media campaigns or possibly be politically expedient.

The UK does not have a written constitution; instead, it has various legal principles and conventions that are used to decide how laws can be made and applied (Black, 1976). The most important of these is the rule of law. This sets out two underlying principles: firstly that nobody should be above the law; and secondly that laws cannot be made to fit crimes already committed.

Another convention is that the powers of the legal system *should* be separate. Thus, the making of laws corresponds to Parliament, the interpreting of laws, to magistrates/judges, and the enforcing of laws, to the police (Newburn, 2007).

A key separation is between enforcing the law and the prosecution of those suspected to have broken laws (conducted by the Crown Prosecution Service). However, in Northern Ireland the police not only enforce the law but in some cases have the power to prosecute offenders (as they did in England and Wales until very recently).

Separation of powers is often not so separate in practice, and although the so-called "Westminster System" (a two-tier system of government with an upper and lower house) was used as a blueprint for many other systems of government, it is often criticized for having a weak separation of powers because there is a good deal of overlap (Lijphart, 1999). An example of this constitutional quirk used to be the use of the House of Lords and the law lords as the ultimate court of appeal in Britain. This also changed under the Constitutional Reform Act in 2005 with the creation of the Supreme Court and therefore ended the conflict between the legislative (makers of laws) and the judiciary (interpreters of laws).

When thinking about crime we often come to the orthodox view that a criminal act is the "breaking of laws" (Tappan, 1947). However, examination of the creation of laws reveals that it occurs within a particular social context and the police do not enforce all laws equally. The criminal justice system is often experienced differently by black and multi-ethnic populations, women and the poor.

In the last ten years crime has been falling, although leveling off recently. However, in the previous 50 years crime increased. By 2007, crime was down to roughly the 1982 level. Nevertheless, crime remains much higher than in the 1950s, 1960s or even 1970s (a period of economic upheaval in Britain), but it cannot be assumed that this is simply due to an increase in crime or criminality. Notably, in Britain there have been recent changes in recording practices, which caused an apparently upward swing in crime rates. Also, there has been a concurrent increase in the detection of crime and the reporting of crime by the public, an increase in types of crime and criminal offending (increase in "law making"), and an erosion of the boundary between civil and criminal law, referred to as "net widening" and "mesh thinning" (Cohen, 1979).

As noted by Newburn (2007) and others the important thing to remember about the criminal justice system in Great Britain is that there is not one unified system. It is made up of three distinctive systems in England, Scotland, Wales and Northern Ireland. It is not possible to discuss all three systems in this text. As a result, this section refers most often to England and Wales. In addition, when referring to the "system" this confers upon it an impression of coherency. However, in reality the "system" is a multitude of overlapping agencies with differing histories, cultures and purposes. In response to calls for efficiency, "partnership working" has been seen as a new tool for addressing geographical and systematic inconsistencies in agency outcomes. (See, for example, Hughes (2007: Ch. 8) and Crawford (1997) for more details.)

The police are the first point of contact for members of the public with concerns and apprehended offenders. In 75 percent of these cases, there is either no suspect or a suspect is not identified (Newburn, 2007). However, if an offender is identified, then the police are the starting point for their path through the criminal justice system. The length of the association depends on the discretion exercised, with about 5 percent of cases concluding with a conviction in the Magistrates', Youth or Crown Courts. This process is known as 'attrition'.

The "typical offender" is most likely to be a young, white, male. However, given the relatively low numbers of ethnic minorities in Scotland, England and Wales, and Northern Ireland (e.g. 2.8 percent black and 4.7 percent Asian), a greater proportion of black men end up entwined in the criminal justice system. When reviewing stops and searches for these two groups, it is about 14.1 percent and 7.2 percent respectively and 10.2 percent and 5.4 percent of the prison population (Newburn, 2007). Additionally, the working classes make up about 85 percent of the prison population, but only 54 percent of society (Morgan and Liebling, 2007).

As Bowling and Phillips (2002) note there is no evidence to suggest that the black population of Britain is more criminogenic than the white population although their pattern of offending may be different in some categories. In fact, the Asian population is likely to be less criminogenic, but still remain over-represented in stop and search statistics. Young black men have levels of criminality similar to those of young white men, but also show high levels of fear of crime and victimization, unlike their white counterparts (Home Affairs Committee, 2007).

The typical offender is also likely to have been the victim of bullying, experienced relationship breakdown and be grieving from the death of a friend or family member (including spouse, child or parent). They are likely to have run away from home, experienced homelessness, been expelled from school, be in debt and be jobless. In addition to this, female offenders are likely to have experienced violence in the home and sexual abuse (Office of National Statistics, 1998). Therefore, they usually have low levels of educational attainment and shamefully this group has one of the highest levels of illiteracy in Britain. Indeed if a young person has experienced the "care" system – that is, they have been looked after by the state – then they are almost three times as likely to end up in prison than to end up at university (DFES, 2006; Centre for Social Justice, 2007). They are likely to be victims of crime as well as perpetrators.

Continuing this categorization of the typical offender, is there any evidence that those from the lower orders are more criminogenic than the middle or upper classes? Moreover, is this likely to lead to an increased notice of the police? The argument is fairly complicated but the salient points are about power – as outlined by Taylor and colleagues (1973), visibility and availability. Firstly, as McBarnet (1988) notes and Reiner (2010) explores in his ground-breaking study of the police – the police operate with *discretion*. As such, not every crime they encounter or "police" has to be reported or recorded. Much research has shown that the police respond in particular ways to social interaction which are framed in part by their authority and in part by their status as an institution of the state that can use legitimate force (Reiner, 2010). In addition, the police draw on organizational and occupational culture to aid them in their work. As such, certain groups are perceived as being troublesome or problematic, such as the black population who are subject to a stop and search rate which is six times higher than that of the white population. The populations who are likely to be stopped and searched are those who are more likely to conduct their lives in public spaces. Therefore, those who are poor and live in overcrowded accommodation and have less disposable income to afford leisure pursuits are likely to conduct their social lives on the street (Jefferson, 1993). Talking, drinking, arguing and fighting occur in places where it can be seen because privacy costs. They have high levels of visibility. In addition, the type of crime that is committed is crime that can be seen. Criminal justice response to drug use has caused the criminalization of a vast swathe of young people through use and street dealing.

There is much evidence that the police find policing diversity problematic and this has not eased after the Macpherson Report (1999) found the police institutionally racist. After the Brixton Riots in 1981, the Scarman Report (1983) had not found the police institutionally racist. However, Scarman did note that if practices could be adopted by public bodies which were "unwittingly discriminatory" against black people, then this would deserve "serious consideration, and, where proved a swift remedy" (Scarman, 1983). This debate has continued and a swift remedy has not been found resulting in black people continuing to be overrepresented in the criminal justice system.[1]

In England and Wales once the police have charged the individual in question, the case is passed to the Crown Prosecution Service (CPS). The CPS decides if it is in the public interest to pursue the case. They will advise the police, determine the charge, prepare cases for court and present them. If it seems that there is insufficient evidence to secure a conviction or it is not in the public's best interests on other grounds (usually cost), the CPS can decide not to progress the case any further.

If it is decided to progress the case further, then depending on the seriousness of the offense the case will be sent to either the Magistrates' Court or the Crown Court. In Magistrates' Court the defendant's case will be heard in front of three magistrates. Magistrates are three volunteer members of the community aged between 18–65 who have been selected and trained. In the Crown Court a case is heard by a judge and jury – jurors are randomly selected from people aged 18–70. In addition, there are Youth Courts for most 10- to 17-year-olds, which are similar to Magistrates' Courts, and finally specialist Coroners' Courts when a death is unnatural or unexplained.

Britain uses an adversarial form of justice which in criminal cases is pursued by the Crown. When the British subjects are wronged the Crown (the Queen currently) pursues justice on behalf of her subjects. Hence all criminal cases are *R* (i.e. Latin for queen) v *Defendant.* There are various accounts of the value of the adversarial system of law that is pursued in Britain and America, as well as its impact on victims and offenders. Nader (1991) takes a cross-cultural look at this issue, whilst also taking a critical look at "harmony" or non-adversarial models of law. Rock (1993) considers the adversarial system and what it means in practice – he explores its antagonistic nature – two parties in a "fight." As such, it is not just on the nature of the facts that a case is won or lost, but on the presentation of the evidence by the parties involved. Carlen (1976) notes the theatrical nature of the court process.

What is apparent is that the court system relies on the judgment of people in court, professionals and if a jury is present, then also members of the public. Goffman's (1959) "Presentation of Self" and Garfinkel's (1956) "degradation ceremonies" are helpful in trying to understand the differential outcomes experienced by offenders within systems of codified and case law. As with the police, magistrates and judges have *discretion.* As such they are able to consider the evidence and decide on a sentence once guilt has been found. This now occurs within an increasing framework of guidance to avoid discrepancies across the judicial system. However, it is apparent by considering the disproportionately large numbers of black men in the prison system and the steep rise in the female prison population, as well as the large number of the poor who are imprisoned, that sentencing does not seem to be equitable.

When passing sentence on a convicted offender, judges have, depending on seriousness, a wide raft of sentences to choose from, ranging from discharge through custodial sentences. In between, there are various possibilities with varying degrees of control and use of restraint in the form of conditions and technology. Tagging of offenders in the community has become an increasingly used option as an alternative to custody or for early release of offenders from prison. However, in response to public accusations of leniency there has been an increasing use of custody over the past 20 years, which has caused a sustained ballooning of the prison population.

In an attempt to halt this flow of offenders into prison there has been the introduction of various community programmes and sentencing options, which include Drug Treatment and Training Orders. The way in which probation services are funded has changed to encourage the numbers of offenders put on these orders – this is despite little evidence that enforced treatment programmes work and that breach by the offender leads to incarceration, therefore swelling the numbers in prison. In the case of women offenders, feminist writers such as Heidensohn (1986) Carlen (2004) and Gelsthorpe (2006) suggest that increasing types of sentences only lead to what they term "uptarriffing," the process of applying a sentence or a harsher sentence to an offense that might previously not have attracted one.

Feely and Simon (1992) and Wacquant (2009) suggest that these increasingly large populations that are seen in America and Britain (although not to such extremes) are a strategy that states have developed to manage problematic populations. Wacquant (2009) suggests it is the black poor who fill prisons in the United States and statistical evidence seems to support his critique. Jones and Newburn (2007) considered whether or not Britain was consistently following the United States in terms of criminal justice policy and practice. What they discovered was that the picture varied. Cohen and Gelsthorpe (2009) suggest that the experience of the criminal justice system in Britain is very different than that experienced in America, in that the prison system in Britain is part of the welfare state for the care and control of the subject. Can prison merely be for incarceration and punishment when we seek for it the higher purpose of rehabilitation?

As a reflection of this, when research was conducted with the public Hough and Roberts (2002) found that the public were not as punitive as perceived by judges. Through media exposure to high-profile cases the public perception was of a lenient judiciary. However, when the public were given the facts of the case and a choice over sentencing of the offender, they were less punitive than the judge had been in the case. The lowering of trust in justice seems to be being fueled through misinformation.

England and Wales have 128 prisons which are run by the prison service and 11 are operated by private companies. The Scottish Prison Service has 16 prisons under its authority and Northern Ireland has 3 prisons (Newburn, 2007). There are five types of prison and four categories of security – open prisons, and category a–c depending on seriousness of offence or the vulnerability of the prisoner. England and Wales has the highest rates of incarceration in Western Europe (Newburn, 2007). This is not just about Britain being more punitive like Cohen's idea of net-widening, but it is also the decision to imprison more frequently, for longer and increase capacity in the prison estate – allowing for an ever increasing prison population. Other punitive Western European states have not taken this route – instead they may have waiting lists for prison places and radical early release schemes.

Hearnden and Hough (2004) note that prisons in England and Wales contain, proportionally, four times the number of black to white prisoners. In reality, what the prison system offers is a snapshot of everything that has gone wrong in society up until that point and may continue to do so.

Captivity exacerbates already underlying problems including ongoing social and health-related problems. As such, prison is often a violent, threatening and unpredictable place to live. Edgar *et al.* (2003) found particularly high levels of bullying and violence in young offenders' institutions with many prisoners of both the youth and adult systems being subject to verbal assaults, theft and threats. The rate of suicide was over 2.5 times higher amongst prisoners than the general British population because of the high levels of vulnerability and the high degree of social exclusion and isolation (Liebling, 2007).

In conclusion, it may way well be that the degree of distress that prisoners experience is an inherent but unarticulated part of the punishment regime we wish to inflict upon them. The problems that arise from this assertion is that the degree of distress is felt differentially across the prison population: female offenders, young offenders and those who are mentally ill are likely to experience the burden of the disassociation from the "home world" much more heavily than others. It should be noted that the British abolished capital punishment in 1969; however, it is clear that for the particularly vulnerable prisoners who conclude their life in prison it becomes a death sentence. This has occurred despite increasing regulation and monitoring of prison regimes – the iniquity of the process places a heavy burden on the state, society and the prisoner.

The Probation Service deals with community sentences. These can occur after sentencing as an alternative to discharge or a custodial sentence *or* after a custodial sentence. Therefore, the probation service has two often conflicting purposes, one of monitoring the offender and one of reintegration of the person into the community. Maruna (2001; Maruna and Immarigeon 2004) notes the problems of rehabilitation and reintegration and the lack of any ceremonial nature in this process. The high level of reoffending is indicative of the apparent problems inherent in reincorporating ex-offenders back into society. Currently 65 percent of the prison population has experienced previous periods of incarceration and almost 40 percent of offenders when released from prison reoffend within a year. It is difficult to ascertain the root of this failure. Criminologists, such as Farrington (1996), identify that offenders have certain risk factors in their past, such as low educational attainment or a chaotic family background – however, these are not predictors of future offending.

The probation service has undergone radical changes in its core work during the previous 20 years and has been subject to the tenets of new managerialism (the application of private business principles on public services), value for money and target setting. Its "market" position has moved from being a provider to a commissioner of services, coordinating packages of training and support through the charitable sector.

Criminology

Official crime statistics are gathered through measuring how many people are arrested by each police force and for which offense, and the results show the number of arrests which result in a conviction and what type of sentence. Official crime statistics are now triangulated with a victimization survey – the British Crime Survey (BCS).

Although official statistics are useful, they only include offenses that come to the attention of the police. Attrition results in only a small number of reported offenses being prosecuted. Only 5 percent of offenses are cleared by the police and approximately only 5 percent of those make it through to formal sentencing (Newburn, 2007). However, this may be due to issues, such as lack of evidence or, more importantly, the lack of an offender or the offense failing to be in the public interest to pursue. Therefore, official statistics do not give a realistic view of crime levels in Britain because they leave out so much criminal behavior.

In response to actual and perceived problems with official crime statistics, Britain followed the US in developing victimization surveys, asking a respondent within a household whether they have been the victim of crime in the previous year. The first British Crime Survey was published in 1983 and was conducted by taking a sample of 10,000 households and asking those aged 16 or over their experiences of crime.

Today the BCS is used as a more realistic portrait of crime in Britain, although it still has its limitations. In recent times a degree of triangulation now occurs between the BCS and other statistical sources. Over the years the BCS has changed to incorporate criticisms of its broad-brush approach. For example, it has developed a new survey so those under 16 can participate. In addition, local surveys are conducted so that it is more geographically sensitive. A random sample would not, for example, necessarily reveal a community's problematic relationships with the police.

Problems with the BCS include relying on the testimony of individuals' experiences of crime. A victim's memory may not be accurate, which would place the crime event in the wrong year or level of seriousness, and low reports of sensitive crimes, such as domestic violence and missing the homeless and institutionalized.

Anti-social behaviour (i.e. dancing in public, caring for a friend's child or wearing certain clothing or engaging in eccentric behavior can now all be considered as "law breaking" behavior), broadly defined in the Anti-Social Behaviour Act (2003) as conduct which is capable of causing nuisance or annoyance to any person, has become an increasing political (and perhaps) social concern over the last ten years and emblematic of social disintegration. Mainly the spotlight has fallen on young people and poorer, working-class communities. The effect seems to have been an erosion of traditional strategies for dealing with what is often normal behavior by young people and in addition an erosion of what we might call "intergenerational trust," what older people think about younger people and vice versa.

Social changes that have occurred over the past 50 years that may explain the rise in crime discussed earlier include an increase in property on our person that is visible and easy to steal (i.e. mobile phones, laptops and music players). In addition, items in the home have become easier to remove, such as personal computers, televisions and digital recorders (Cohen and Felson, 1979).

In Britain until relatively recently the most influential arguments remained firmly situated on the social causes of crime. This was particularly driven in the last instance by the New Criminology. *The New Criminology* was not created in a vacuum: it draws on important American and British criminology. Theories which were clearly influential on the authors, were the Chicago School, cultural and sub-cultural theories, interactionism and labelling theory. They reviewed these existing theories and set about creating a new criminology, which was critically and politically engaged. *The New Criminology* draws attention to context and power discrepancies between those who commit crime and those who label behavior as criminal. Because it draws on labeling theory so strongly, it utilizes a culturally subjective position, meaning that it challenges our ideas about right and wrong.

Taylor *et al.* (1973) have been criticized for romanticizing crime and masculinizing it. Crime is seen as a reaction to a capitalist system, which it may be in part for some. By taking this approach it does not then consider the problematic other crimes that are committed, such as crimes of passion, state crimes and white-collar crimes, which do not seem to be reactions against an 'over-bearing' capitalist state. Moreover the theory ignores the crimes of women. As such, *The New Criminology* begins to be representative of only a small proportion of men who commit crime and a disempowering explanation at that. A criticism that was levelled by Taylor *et al.* (1973) was the lack of reference in this theory to the experience of victims of crime. In *The New Criminology* the perpetrator of crimes gains victim status (the victim of the state). As such, there is no room for the victim of the crime. Therefore, *The New Criminology* has left many questions unanswered.

In the past ten years criminology in Britain has been struggling with the questions of how to communicate and influence political and public discourse on crime. Whilst there was a period when criminology was much more influential on criminal justice policy, there has been recently a seeming divergence between findings and reality. This is despite recent Labour governments suggesting that they rely on "evidenced based" policy. Increasingly the evidence that they use has not been gathered by academics, but by contracted out "business" which in the main provides short, directed and targeted commissioned research packages into identified issues. What this research often fails to do is identify the extraneous issues and the problems in infrastructure, the meaning of action and the weight of political expectations. As such, although policy is increasingly "evidenced based," it has moved away from contextualized scientific findings and the link between academia and government has been eroded. Although some research funding does still find its way to academic institutions, it is often to the same few, resulting in maximizing quality, perpetuating poor research or reducing diversity of perspectives.

Garland and Sparks (2000) were at the forefront of trying to unpick this unsatisfactory relationship between government and academia in criminology, followed by Burawoy (2005) in sociology. Becker (1967) had already ascertained that sociological research was inherently partisan (that it involved taking sides) – usually that of the "underdog" and therefore involved a radical critique of established positions. As such, it is clear that the criminologist is best placed to forge this work as the "outsider." For Gouldner (1968) this stance by critical criminology was unhelpful and he accused the work of the new critical criminologists, Becker in America and Taylor *et al.* in Britain, of being the "zoo keepers of deviance." In essence they captured and examined deviance (like a zoo keeper keeps a rare species) but failed to see how this work might inform or change practice.

Recently Loader and Sparks (2010) have attempted to reinvigorate and bring center stage the question of the role and value of criminology in a democratic society in what they term a "hot" political system. They ask how criminology can find a voice in what has become an intensely mediated world in which "crime and punishment loom large in government agendas and public discourses."

Conclusion

Beginning with questioning the ability to identify a discrete "British criminology," this chapter reveals that it is indeed difficult to see the geographical and intellectual boundaries of the discipline. The uniqueness of British criminology become apparent when applied to the criminal justice system, which represents the discrepancies in British society. As the Macpherson Inquiry (1999) noted and academics such as Waddington (1999) have pointed out, an institution such as the police resides within the society which created it. It undoubtedly attracts certain personalities to the work, but they are derived from a society which still has underlying beliefs about the role and nature of ethnic minorities, the young, women and the poor – as such the criminal justice system becomes a reflection of these inadequacies.

Whilst British criminology continues to define its role, the critical questioning still remains important, if only as a reminder of how institutions might look in a (for example) more equal society. Moreover, whilst the relationship with government remains problematic – there still is one. As such it remains the remit of government to manage the pressures and strain of policy making in a hot political and economic climate.

Future research questions

1. Why do the poor end up in prison?
2. Is it vital for a criminal justice system to have an underpinning reason for punishment?
3. Why is police discretion so important?
4. There was a change between the first bi-partisan consensus and the second. How did this impact offenders?
5. What is strictly "British" about the criminological enterprise?

Note

1 See http://www.guardian.co.uk/politics/2009/apr/06/met-police-not-racist-stephen-lawrence (accessed March 20, 2010).

References

Beck, U. (1992). *Risk society: towards a new modernity*. London: Sage.

Becker, H. S. (1967). Whose side are we on? *Social Problems*, 14: 239–47.

Black, D. J. (1976). *The behavior of law*. New York: Academic Press.

Bowling, B. and Phillips, C. (2002). *Racism, crime and justice*. Harlow: Pearson Education.

Budge, I. and McKay, D. (1993). *The developing British political system: the 1990s*. London: Longman.

Burawoy, M. (2005). Presidential address: For public sociology. *American Sociological Review*, 70: 4–28.

Carlen, P. (1976). *Magistrates' justice*. London: Croom Helm.

—— (2004). *Analysing women's imprisonment*. Cullompton, Devon: Willan Publishing.

Centre for Social Justice (2007). *Breakthrough Britain*. London: SFR.

Cohen, L. E. and Felson, M. (1979). Social change and crime rate trends: a routine activity approach. *American Sociological Review*, 44: 588–605.

Cohen, S. (1979). The punitive city: notes on the dispersal of social control. *Contemporary Crises*, 3(4): 341–63.

Cohen, S. and Gelsthorpe, L. (2009). Presentation at Symposium on Neoliberal Penality. Queen Mary's University, London, October.

Colls, R. (2002). *Identity of England*. Oxford: Oxford University Press.

Crawford, A. (1997). *The local governance of crime*. Oxford: Oxford University Press.

Department for Education and Skills (DFES) (2006). Children looked after in England (including adoptions and care leavers), 2005–6. London: The Stationery Office.

Dorling, D. (2006). *Prime suspect: Murder in Britain*. Prison Service Journal 166, 3–10.

Edgar, K., O'Donnell, I., and Martin, C. (2003). *Prison violence: the dynamics of conflict, fear and power*. Devon: Willan Publishing.

Farrington, D. (1996). Understanding and preventing youth crime. York: Joseph Rowntree Foundation. Summary report available at: http://www.jrf.org.uk/knowledge/findings/socialpolicy/sp93.asp (accessed November 25, 2010)

Feeley, M. and Simon, J. (1992). The new penology: notes on the emerging strategy of corrections and its implications. *Criminology*, 30: 449–74.
Garfinkel, H. (1956). Conditions of successful degradation ceremonies. *The American Journal of Sociology*, 61(5): 420–24.
Garland, D. and Sparks, R. (2000). Criminology, social theory and the challenge of our times. *British Journal of Criminology*, 40: 189–204.
Gelsthorpe, L. (2006). COUNTERBLAST: women and criminal justice: saying it again, again and again. *Howard Journal of Criminal Justice*, 45(4), 421–24.
Goffman, E. (1959 [1990]). *The presentation of self in everyday life*. Reprint. London: Penguin Books.
Gouldner, A. W. (1968). The sociologist as partisan: sociology and the welfare state. *The American Sociologist*, 3: 103–16.
Hearnden, I. and Hough, M. (2004). *Race and the criminal justice system: an overview to the complete statistics*. London: Criminal Justice System Race Unit.
Heidensohn, F. (1986). Models of justice: Portia or Persephone? Some thoughts on equality, fairness, and gender in the field of criminal justice. *International Journal of the Sociology of Law*, 14, 287–18.
Home Affairs Committee (2007). *Young black people and the criminal justice system*. London: The Stationery Office.
Hough, M. and Roberts, J. V. (2002). Public knowledge and public opinion of sentencing. In C. Tata and N. Hutton (Eds.) *Sentencing and society: international perspectives*, pp. 157–76. Aldershot: Ashgate.
Hughes, G. (2007). *The politics of crime and community*. Basingstoke: Palgrave/Macmillan.
Jefferson, T. (1993). *The racism of criminalization: police and the reproduction of the criminal other*. In L. R. Gelsthorpe (Ed.), *Minority ethnic groups in the criminal justice system*. Cambridge: The Institute of Criminology, Cambridge University.
Jones, T. and Newburn, T. (2007). *Policy transfer and criminal justice*. Maidenhead: Open University Press
Liebling, A. (2007). Suicide and its prevention. In Y. Jewkes (Ed.), *Handbook on prisons*. Devon: Cullompton: Willan Books.
Lijphart, A. (1999). *Patterns of democracy*. London and Harvard: Yale University Press.
Loader, I. and Sparks, R. (2010). *Public criminology*. London: Routledge.
McBarnet (1988). Law, policy and legal avoidance. *Journal of Law and Society*, 113–21.
Macpherson, Sir W. (1999). *The Stephen Lawrence inquiry: the report of an inquiry*. London: HMSO.
Maruna, S. (2001). *Making good: how ex-convicts reform and rebuild their lives*. Washington, DC: American Psychological Association Books.
Maruna, S. and Immarigeon, R. (Eds.) (2004). *After crime and punishment: pathways to ex-offender reintegration*. Cullompton: Willan Books.
Morgan, R. and Liebling, A. (2007). *Imprisonment: an expanding scene*. In M. Maguire, R. Morgan, and R. Reiner (Eds.), *The Oxford Handbook of Criminology*. 4th Edn. Oxford: Oxford University Press.
Nader, L. (1991). Harmony models and the construction of law. In E. K. Avruch, P. W. Black, and J. A. Scimecca (Eds.) *Conflict resolution: cross cultural perspectives*. Westport, CT: Praeger.
Newburn, T. (2006). Criminal justice policy. In B. G. Peters and J. Pierre (Eds.) *Handbook of Public Policy*. Thousand Oaks, CA: Sage.
—— (2007). *Criminology*. Cullompton: Willan Publishing
Office of National Statistics (1998). *Psychiatric morbidity amongst prisoners in England and Wales*. London: The Stationery Office.
—— (2004) *UK 2005 The Official Yearbook of the United Kingdom of Great Britain and Northern Ireland*. London. The Stationery Office.
Reiner, R. (2010). *Politics of the police*. 4th Edn. Oxford: Oxford University Press.
Rock, P. (1993). *The social world of an English crown court*. Oxford: Clarendon.
Rock, P. and Holdaway, S. (1998). *Thinking about criminology*. London: UCL Press.
Rubin, P. H. (Ed) (2007). *The evolution of efficient common law*. Cheltenham: Elgar.
Scarman, L. G. (1983) *The Scarman report. The Brixton disorders, 10–12 April 1981*. Harmondsworth, Middlesex, England: Penguin Books.
Tappan, P. (1947). Who is the criminal? *American Sociological Review*, 12: 96–102
Taylor, I., Walton, P., and Young, J. (1973). *The new criminology: for a social theory of deviance*. London: Routledge.
Wacquant, L. (2009). *Punishing the poor: the neoliberal government of social insecurity*. Durham, NC: Duke University Press.
Waddington, P. A. J. (1999). Police (canteen) sub-culture. An appreciation. *The British Journal of Criminology*, 39: 287–309.

38
Hong Kong
The state of criminology

Jianhua Xu

Introduction

This chapter explores crime and criminology in one of the safest cities in the developed world, Hong Kong. It examines current research topics in criminology regarding juvenile delinquency, drug abuse, policing, cross-border crime and organized crime. It also points out limitations, challenges and opportunities for criminology research in a society undergoing dramatic political changes towards becoming a democracy.

Infrastructure

Hong Kong, officially the Hong Kong Special Administrative Region (HKSAR) of the People's Republic of China, was a British colony for more than 150 years from 1842 to 1997. It borders Shenzhen in the north and is surrounded by the South China Sea in the east, south and west. As one of the most crowded cities in the world, it only covers a small area of 423 square miles, but it has a population of 7 million according to the 2008 census. The fertility rate of 0.95 children per woman is one of the lowest in the world, but the population continues to grow due to the influx of immigrants from mainland China of approximating 45,000 per year. Around 95 percent of the population is Chinese by ethnicity and the remaining 5 percent is mainly composed of Indians, Pakistanis and British. Most of the British left Hong Kong before the handover in 1997. English and Cantonese are co-official languages while 95 percent of the population uses Cantonese as their first language. According to a 1996 census, English was spoken by around 38 percent of population, of whom 3.1 percent regarded English as their first language.

Religious institutions enjoy a high degree of freedom guaranteed by the Basic Law of Hong Kong Special Administrative Region (Basic Law) and around 90 percent of the population practices Buddhism and Taoism. Around 8 percent of the population is Christian. Hong Kong is a society with a wide wealth gap and social inequality. Its Gini coefficient is fairly high, with a rate of 0.476 (1991), 0.518 (1996) and 0.525 (2001) according to the Hong Kong Census and Statistics Department. Today's Hong Kong is a global metropolis and international financial center with a highly developed capitalist economy.

Crime

Although Hong Kong is one of the most crowded and commercialized cities in the world, it also has a reputation as one of the safest cities of the developed world. Both crime victim surveys and police data depict low crime rates in Hong Kong. According to the tenth United Nations Survey on Crime Trends and the Operations of Criminal Justice System (UNSCTOCJ) (UNODC, 2006) the overall recorded crime rate per 100,000 population in 2006 was 1,222.54, lower than Japan (1,602.81) in Asia and much lower than the United States (3,764.78), Italy (4,715.12), Denmark (6,812.94), Australia (7,078.94), Germany (7,628.46), Canada (8,317.24), Finland (9,825.43), and England and Wales (10399.21) (2005) in Western countries.

Due to the differing definitions for crime and practices in reporting and recording crime, the overall crime rate may not be ideal for international comparison. A relatively more reliable piece of official data for international comparison is the homicide rate. From 2005 to 2008, homicide cases in Hong Kong totaled only 34, 35, 18 and 36 for each respective year, roughly 0.5 per 100,000 annually. The lowest rate in recent years was in 2007, at 0.26 per 100,000. Comparatively, the homicide rate in other industrialized countries is much higher, such as the United States (5.62), Canada (1.86), England and Wales (1.43) (2005), Germany (0.88), Greece (0.94), Italy (1.06) in 2006. The United Nations International Crime Victim Survey (2004/5) also confirmed the low crime rate of Hong Kong and only 7.9 percent of Hong Kong citizens experienced at least one crime in 2005, which ranked Hong Kong as the lowest in all 32 participating cities with a mean victimization rate of 21.7 percent (van Dijk *et al.*, 2008). The same survey also indicated that fear of crime was very low in Hong Kong. More than 90 percent of the residents reported feeling fairly safe or very safe while walking alone in their neighborhoods after dark (Broadhurst *et al.*, 2008, p. 46).

Hong Kong's crime rate has not always been as low as it is currently. There have been several crime waves since the 1960s. In 1963, the official data showed a crime rate of 407 per 100,000. By 1974, the rate rapidly increased to 1,294 per 100,000. It stabilized at a relatively high level from 1975 for 20 years. The year 1983 witnessed the highest officially recorded crime rate in Hong Kong's history: 1,610 per 100,000. For ten years after the handover from the British control to mainland China, the crime rate remained at a low level although 2003 experienced a little rise of 1,229 and it reduced to its new record low of 1,123 in 2008 (Broadhurst *et al.*, 2008, pp. 47–8).

In explaining the currently low crime rate in Hong Kong, Broadhurst *et al.* argued that this might be due to a mixture of factors, including family-oriented Confucian values, a large professionalized and localized police service, strict gun laws, effective suppression of cross-border crime, high level of formal or informal surveillance, ethnic homogeneity, proactive efforts against organized crime and corruption, and severe punishment of the convicted (Broadhurst *et al.*, 2008, p. 63).

Administration of justice

The police, courts and prisons are the main criminal justice organs. Today's Hong Kong Police Force (HKPF) can be regarded as one of the finest police organizations in the world (Jiao, 2007). Several surveys have shown that it is regarded by the public as a force free of serious corruption and one that is professional, efficient and effective in maintaining law and order (Lau, 2008). High-profile policing and community policing are two major characteristics of HKPF. The creation of the Independent Commission Against Corruption in 1974 was one of the most significant changes in Hong Kong's history and had a revolutionary impact on preventing police corruption. Comparatively, Hong Kong has a very large police force per capita. The tenth UNSCTOCJ showed that HKPF employed 431.94 per 100,000 population in 2006, surpassing most industrialized countries, such as England and Wales (264.06), Germany (302.86), Greece (375.23) and the United States (225.66).

Despite the return of sovereignty to China, Hong Kong remains a common law jurisdiction. According to China's "one country, two systems" policy, Hong Kong will retain its capitalist system and way of life for 50 years after 1997. The Basic Law is its mini-constitution and guarantees it executive, legislative and independent judicial power.

Hong Kong's incarceration rate is also fairly high. According to the tenth UNSCTOCJ, Hong Kong's incarceration rate was 168.38 per 100,000 in 2006, higher than Denmark (72.4), Finland (73.20), Greece (92.43), Germany (92.73), Canada (108.82), Italy (104.23), and England and Wales (142.63) (2005). The population of youth and adult prisoners has been on the rise since the turn of the century. The total number of that population has increased from 14,343 in 1996 to 18,513 in 2001 and reached its peak with 27,930 inmates in 2004. The female incarceration rate is also extremely high and female inmates have increased threefold from mid-1990 to the mid-2000s. This is mainly due to the wide use of incarceration of those in the sex industry from mainland China. The Prisons Department was renamed the Correctional Services Department in 1982, which reflects a philosophical change of a punishment form that emphasizes coercive custody to one highlighting rehabilitation and reintegration (Lo, 2008). Due to its high incarceration rates, Hong Kong's correctional institutions have been facing the problem of overcrowding since the 1990s.

Criminology

As some criminologists observe, Hong Kong criminology has a "decidedly administrative character," with a close relationship to social and public policy, pursuing solutions to officially defined problems (Jones and Vagg, 2007, p. 4). In the past five to ten years, the main research topics include issues surrounding juvenile delinquency, drug abuse, policing, cross-border crime and organized crime – namely the Hong Kong triads.

Juvenile delinquency has been a long-lasting topic in Hong Kong, although official data show that the rate has continued to decrease since the 1990s. According to police records, juvenile delinquency rates were at 212 per 100,000 in 1976. The rate increased fourfold to 962 per 100,000 in 1989 and started to decline after that and reached 905 in 2006 (the minimum age of criminal responsibility increased from seven to ten in 2003). After a systematic review of all papers published in English journals about criminal justice and criminology in Hong Kong from 1990 to 2004, Chui (2005) found that among all 274 papers, 53 of them were about juvenile delinquency, accounting for 20 percent of all studies. Another 10 percent of papers were about child abuse. Juvenile delinquency commands the predominant attention of criminologists in Hong Kong.[1]

Using official police data, Wong (2000) argued that although Hong Kong's juvenile delinquency rate was higher than that of China, it was much lower than in Japan and the United States. He also found that juvenile crime accounted for a similar proportion of total crimes in Hong Kong, China and the United States, which are much lower than rates in Japan. Some studies try to explore how restorative justice is used to deal with juvenile delinquency in Hong Kong. With a self-report survey of 2,280 young people aged from 12 to 20, Vagg (1998) argued that although "re-integrative shaming" has been widely accepted within criminology, in Hong Kong, shaming was not regarded as privileged over the assertion or acceptance of guilt, but rather as a method of "disintegrative shaming," with a strong commitment to labeling and exclusion.

Delinquents were punished quickly unless they demonstrated contrition and subservience and a high degree of respect for those who challenged their behaviors.

Among many theories, social control theory was widely used to explore the strategies to prevent juvenile delinquency. The popularity of social control theory might reflect a strong preference for social order in Hong Kong. With data collected from 1,015 secondary school students, Cheung and Cheung (2008) found that low self-control was correlated with delinquency. However, when social variables were controlled, self-control failed to predict delinquency. They argued that it was a combination of self-control and social factors in the prediction of delinquency in Hong Kong. Other studies also explored how social control worked on juveniles differently across different socio-cultural contexts in Chinese society. A survey conducted in Hong Kong, Guangzhou and Shanghai among delinquent youths found that social control by parents exerted more effects in Hong Kong on youths' gang involvement, while social control by teachers were a greater protective factor in mainland China. They argued that this difference might be due to the capitalist-individualist culture in the former and socialist-collectivist context in the latter (Ngai *et al.*, 2007).

From "The Opium War" to "The Sick Man of East Asia," Hong Kong has had a painful experience with drugs. Hong Kong's drug policy has experienced three different stages, namely "Government Opium Monopoly (1841–1945)," "Prohibition Era (1946–60)" and "Enlightened Prohibition (1961–present)." The current drug policy, namely "Enlightened Prohibition," emphasizes both voluntary drug treatment, rehabilitation services and tough law enforcement (Cheung and Ch'ien, 1996). Unlike criminological research in Britain and the United States, where much research is about drugs in relation to crime, in Hong Kong, there is almost no such research. On the contrary, Hong Kong criminologists pay more attention to how drugs are abused, especially among juveniles, and how to rehabilitate drug abusers. A recent contribution in this field is the book *A brighter side: protective and risk factors in the rehabilitation of chronic drug abusers in Hong Kong* (Cheung, 2009). With a two-and-a-half-year longitudinal study of 547 drug abusers who took rehabilitation treatment, Cheung tried to figure out the protective factors for, and risk factors against, maintenance of post-treatment abstinence. He disclosed that self-efficacy, life satisfaction, positive job attitudes, support from non-drug using friends and length of short-term abstinence achieved in past years could all contribute to full recovery from drug abuse. To the contrary, however, association with drug-using friends was the highest risk factor against maintenance of abstinence. He also advocated that while rehabilitation did not preclude the possibility of full recovery, a more realistic goal was to maximize the length of abstinence (Cheung, 2009, p. 127).

As one of the most professional, efficient and clean police forces in the world (Lau, 2008), HKPF has aroused many research interests in criminology. The study of police organization, police history, police corruption, policing strategy and community policing are important topics in this area. The book *The police in Hong Kong: a contemporary view* provides a comprehensive understanding of HKPF (Jiao, 2007). With interview data from over 200 Hong Kong police officers of different ranks as well as observation of police work, Jiao systematically explored the history, structure and operation, learning culture, street officer behavior, corruption, changes and continuity brought about by the 1997 handover to HKPF. Among many other findings, one particularly interesting point was the problems encountered in the transition from a paramilitary force to a service-oriented organization. Jiao argued that although HKPF was successful in suppressing public protests and maintaining public order in colonial times, it failed to gain public confidence due to the lack of legitimacy. In order to get public confidence and support after the handover, the police started to emphasize "quality service." However, there has been great resistance to this transformation, especially from frontline police officers. Many police officers believed that the traditional police duties, such as maintaining public order and crime control, are much more important than service (Jiao, 2007, pp. 5, 44–50).

The Hong Kong triads have long been believed to be involved in many illegal activities such as drug trafficking, gambling, prostitution, loan sharking, debt collecting and smuggling, and extortion from legitimate businesses such as the entertainment industry, street hawkers, wholesale markets, minibus services and the film industry. The book *The triads as business* provides many insights for these groups (Chu, 2000). The book was based on extensive interviews with ex-triad members, victims of triads, police from Hong Kong, mainland China and Europe and documentary studies. Influenced by the economic theory of protection of organized crimes, Chu argued that although triad activities did have their victims, such as unprotected competitors, consumers and rival gangs, they can also provide effective protection services to some businesses against attack by other gangs, to manipulate a market by suppressing competitors and to recover stolen property or debt. In many cases, as Chu argued, they entered a legitimate market by "invitation" rather than on their own initiative (Chu, 2000, p. 124).

Some observers worried that the Hong Kong triads might come into a dominant position in the international underworld and pose a great risk to the Western society after 1997 when China reclaimed its sovereignty over Hong Kong from the British and mass triad emigration might occur. Chu (2002), however, argued that the fears were overblown and the Hong Kong triads cannot "go global." He pointed out that the fears of triad dominance of international crime were based on fundamental misunderstandings of the nature of ethnic Chinese organized crime. Although such crimes did exist in Western countries, not all ethnic Chinese criminals were from Hong Kong and even if they were from Hong Kong, not all of them were triad members.

Chu's observation was also supported by some other studies. Based on evidence collected from several studies about Hong Kong triads from 1984 to 2001, Zhang and Chin (2003) demystified the global threat of the Hong Kong triads by disclosing that the significance of triad society in transnational illegal activities was actually declining. They argued that although Chinese organized crime groups had gained much notoriety in transnational crime activities and had caught the attention of law enforcement and governments in Western countries, these organized Chinese criminals were not associated with triad societies or any other traditional Chinese organized criminals: they were freelancers. They argued that the main reason that the Hong Kong triads did not become a global threat lay in their culture and patterns of organization. Although the triad's entrenched culture and patterns of organization served them well for centuries, they were incompatible with conditions necessary for entering into present-day transnational criminal activities, such as human smuggling and heroin trafficking.

Hong Kong borders mainland China in the north with Shenzhen, a Special Economic Zone and booming city of the Guangdong province. Due to vast social and economic disparity between Hong Kong and mainland China, cross-border crime is very active and types of cross-border crime also vary across time. Illegal immigration, smuggling and armed robbery used to be the main cross-border threats to Hong Kong. After 1997, with the cooperation between police from Hong Kong and mainland China, armed robbery was not a threat to Hong Kong any more. When China relaxed its policy and allowed more people to visit Hong Kong in 2003, illegal immigration also almost diminished. However, some new types of cross-border crimes emerged. One major threat to Hong Kong is that more and more Hong Kong juveniles travel to Shenzhen to use drugs, where the price is much cheaper and they are easier to get.

Another problem that confronts Hong Kong is the influx of mainland Chinese women in the sex industry. While the first problem is still under-explored, the second gets notable attention in criminology. Although working in the sex industry itself is not a crime in Hong Kong, many related activities, such as soliciting for sex, are prohibited. In particular, it is illegal for visitors to work in the sex industry without an employment visa. They will be arrested, prosecuted, fined and imprisoned as they breach their conditions of stay. From 2002 to 2006, more than 10,000 mainland Chinese women were arrested and sentenced to prison for unlawfully working and/or breaching their conditions of stay (Laidler *et al.*, 2007). With the interview of 58 mainland Chinese women who were convicted and incarcerated in Hong Kong, Laidler *et al.* disclosed that although these cases were processed efficiently with a short-term imprisonment (average time 40 days) for a large number of women, the bureaucratic response was expensive and had no deterrent or rehabilitative effect. Based on data of official reports, internal police and Immigration Department statistics and in-depth interviews with criminal justice practitioners, activists in a sex workers' concern group and academic researchers, Lee (2007) argued that the routine use of imprisonment and zero tolerance-style policing against mainland Chinese women working in the sex industry can reflect the Hong Kong government's twin aims of actively seeking the inflow of rich migrants through a liberalization of border controls and keeping out the poor migrants. However, as Lee argued, there was little evidence to suggest that incarceration can provide a solution to the social problem of migratory sex industry workers and socio-economic disparity in mainland China. The imprisonment can only serve the purpose of warehousing the unwanted and undeserving poor and immobilizing the excluded.

In Hong Kong, there are no independent criminology departments in academic institutions similar to those in the United States. Criminological research is mainly undertaken in sociological departments and other social science disciplines. Among all eight universities in Hong Kong, three institutions conduct most of the criminology research. They are the Department of Sociology at the University of Hong Kong, the Department of Sociology at the Chinese University of Hong Kong and the Department of Applied Social Studies at City University of Hong Kong. The University of Hong Kong plays a key role in conducting criminology research and promoting criminological education. It is the only university in Hong Kong to offer a Master of Philosophy and Doctor of Philosophy degree in Criminology. Professor Jon Vagg, Harold Traver and Roderic Broadhurst used to work in this department and Professor Karen Joe Laidler and Borge Bakken have currently taken an active role in promoting criminological research and education. While Professor Laidler's expertise is on criminology in Hong Kong, Professor Bakken is the leading expert studying criminology in China.

The Hong Kong Society of Criminology was founded in 1983 and is currently administered by the Center for Criminology at the University of Hong Kong. Several criminological projects were conducted in this Center, including the Hong Kong International Crime Victim Survey (2005) and International Crime against Business Survey (China) directed by Professor Roderic Broadhurst. The Department of Sociology at the Chinese University of Hong Kong has a long history of conducting research on drug problems and Professor Yuet Wah Cheung is the leading scholar in this field. The Department of Applied Social Studies at the City University of Hong Kong plays an important part in studying juvenile delinquency in Hong Kong, where Professor Tit Wing Lo and Dennis Wong work.

Hong Kong criminological research has been fairly balanced in both quantitative and qualitative methods. On the one hand, Hong Kong, as a former British Colony, has a strong tradition of British criminology using qualitative methods. Several recently published books were based on qualitative research such as *The triads as business* (Chu, 2000), *The police in Hong Kong: a contemporary view* (Jiao, 2007) and *Criminal justice in Hong Kong* (Jones and Vagg, 2007). On the other hand, several other influential studies were conducted with quantitative methods, mainly survey, such as *A brighter side: protective and risk factors in the rehabilitation of chronic drug abusers in Hong Kong* (Cheung, 2009) and *International crime against business survey in People's Republic of China and Hong Kong Special Administrative Region* and *United Nations (Hong Kong) international crime victim survey* directed by Professor Roderic Broadhurst.

In Hong Kong, there are mainly two funding sources for criminology research. One is the Research Grant Council (RGC). The RGC is a non-statutory advisory body responsible for advising the Hong Kong government on the needs of higher education institutions about academic research and distributing funding for academic research projects. Several criminology research projects were funded by RGC in the past several years. Another funding source is directly from the Hong Kong government, through different programs or divisions, such as Beat Drugs Funds and Action Committee Against Narcotics.

Conclusion

Hong Kong, as an international financial center, also enjoys a low crime rate. Its crime experience does not really fit what modernization theory assumes: that with the process of modernization, the violent crime rate will decrease but economic crime will increase (Shelley, 1981). Hong Kong has experienced a decline in both violent and economic crime over a fairly long time. Hong Kong crime and the criminal justice system are quite different from that found in the Western countries, such as low crime rate, high Gini coefficient, high-profile policing and high incarceration rate.

Criminology in Hong Kong is heavily influenced by theories developed in the United Kingdom and the United States and has not yet developed any localized theory to explain Hong Kong's particular situation. The "administrative" character of criminology in Hong Kong is closely associated with social policy, pursing solutions officially defined problems, such as juvenile delinquency (Jones and Vagg, 2007) and drug abuse. Much research is focused on testing the application of Western criminology theories, which are developed in quite a distinctive situation from Hong Kong. Jones and Vagg (2007, p. 12) argued that this might be due to the reliance of Western scholars in the colonial period which makes the universities very slow to localize, and prestige attached to UK and US degrees has led to students pursuing studies overseas and to undue, uncritical reverence for dominant theories in the field.

Another feature of Hong Kong criminological research is the relative lack of interest in critical criminology. Due to its colonial history and a lack of democracy, criminological studies tend to undermine social structural interpretations towards crime. Much criminological research has focused on juveniles and youth, but fails to recognize that juveniles and youth processed by the criminal justice system are typically working class. Generally, it tends to press for social, economic and political contexts, which affect both crimes and government policy towards crimes (Jones and Vagg, 2007, p. 7).

In recent years, Hong Kong is marching towards a democratic society, and the National People's Congress of China confirmed that Hong Kong would be allowed to have universal suffrage in 2017 at the earliest. In the foreseeable future, political changes in Hong Kong might have its impact on the definition of crimes, explanation for crimes and funding for criminology research.

Future research questions

1. What are the main reasons that Hong Kong became one of the safest cities among industrialized countries?
2. Why has juvenile delinquency become the most researched topic in Hong Kong?

3. What strategies are used to solve the problem caused by the influx of mainland Chinese women in the sex industry in Hong Kong? What are the consequences of these strategies?
4. Why have Hong Kong triads not become a global thereat as some observers predicted after the 1997 handover?
5. To what extent will a democratic society in Hong Kong affect its criminology research in the future?

Note

1 The rest of the study touched broad topics, including crime and its control (3 per cent), drug abuse (3 per cent), elder abuse (1.5 per cent), homicide (2 per cent), organized crime (6 per cent), sex crime (8.4 per cent), violent crime against women (7.7 per cent), policing (10.2 per cent), judicial systems (9.9 per cent), sentencing (2.2 per cent) and punishment and corrections (9.5 per cent).

References

Broadhurst, R., Lee, K., and Chan, C. Y. (2008). Crime trends. In W. H. Chui and T. W. Lo (Eds.) *Understanding criminal justice in Hong Kong*, pp. 45–68. Collompton, UK: Willan.

Cheung, N. W. T. and Cheung, Y. W. (2008). Self-control, social factors, and delinquency: a test of the general theory of crime among adolescents in Hong Kong. *Journal of Youth and Adolescence*, 37: 412–30.

Cheung, Y. W. and Ch'ien, J. M. N. (1996). Drug use and drug policy in Hong Kong: Changing patterns and new challenges. *Substance Use and Misuse*, 31: 1573–97.

Cheung, Y. W. (2009). *A brighter side: protective and risk factors in the rehabilitation of chronic drug abusers in Hong Kong*. Hong Kong: Chinese University Press.

Chu, Y. K. (2000). *The triads as business*. London, New York: Routledge.

—— (2002). Global triads: myth or reality? In M. R. Berdal and M. Serrano (Eds.) *Transnational organized crime and international security: business as usual?* pp. 183–93. Boulder, CO.: Lynne Rienner Publishers.

Chui, W. H. (2005). *Criminal justice in Hong Kong and the People's Republic of China: a selected bibliography*. Hong Kong: City University of Hong.

van Dijk, J. V., Van Kesteren, J., and Smith, P. (2008). *Criminal victimisation in international perspective: key findings from the 2004–2005 ICVS and EU ICS*. The Hague: Boom Legal Publishers.

Jiao, A. Y. (2007). *The police in Hong Kong: a contemporary view*. Lanham, MD.: University Press of America.

Jones, C. A. G. and Vagg, J. (2007). *Criminal justice in Hong Kong*. London: Routledge-Cavendish.

Laidler, K. J., Petersen, C., and Emerton, R. (2007). Bureaucratic justice: the incarceration of mainland Chinese women working in Hong Kong's sex industry. *International Journal of Offender Therapy and Comparative Criminology*, 51: 68–83.

Lau, R. W. K. (2008). The police force. In W. H. Chui and T. W. Lo (Eds.) *Understanding criminal justice in Hong Kong*, pp. 93–114. Cullompton, UK: Willan.

Lee, M. (2007). Women's imprisonment as a mechanism of migration control in Hong Kong. *The British Journal of Criminology*, 47: 847–60.

Lo, T. W. (2008). Custodial sentences and correctional services. In W. H. Chui and T. W. Lo (Eds.) *Understanding criminal justice in Hong Kong*. pp. 224–47. Cullompton, UK: Willan.

Ngai, N., Cheung, C., and Ngai, S. (2007). Cognitive and social influences on gang involvement among delinquents in three Chinese cities. *Adolescence*, 42: 381–403.

Shelley, L. I. (1981). *Crime and modernization : the impact of industrialization and urbanization on crime*. Carbondale: Southern Illinois University Press.

United Nation Office on Drugs and Crime (UNODC) (2006). *Tenth United Nations survey on crime trends and the operations of criminal justice systems*. Online at http://www.unodc.org/unodc/en/data-and-analysis/Tenth-CTS-full.html (accessed 1 August 2009).

Vagg, J. (1998). Delinquency and shame. *British Journal of Criminology*, 38: 247–64.

Wong, D. S. W. (2000). Juvenile crime and responses to delinquency in Hong Kong. *International Journal of Offender Therapy and Comparative Criminology*, 44: 279–92.

Zhang, S. and Chin, K. (2003). The declining significance of triad societies in transnational illegal activities. *The British Journal of Criminology*, 43: 469–88.

39

India

The state of criminology in a developing nation

Prasanna Poornachandra

Introduction

This chapter provides an overview of India and its geographical, economic, and social characteristics, all of which have a vital role to play in the dynamics of crime and the structure of the criminal justice system. Also, the chapter offers a brief account of criminology and criminological research in India.

Infrastructure

India is home to one of the oldest cultures in the world and the birthplace of such religions as Hinduism, Buddhism, Sikhism, and Jainism. Contemporary India also has large populations of Muslims and Christians.

India covers nearly 3.3 million square kilometers, including the mountains of the Himalayas in the north and tropical rain forests in the south through the Tropic of Cancer (India.gov, 2010a). Much of the country is in a tropical climate zone. The country is bordered by the Indian Ocean in the south, the Bay of Bengal in the east, and the Arabian Sea on the west coasts. India is bordered from northwest to northeast by Afghanistan, Pakistan, China, Bhutan, and Nepal. Cross-border crimes, such as smuggling of fake currency and trafficking of girls, illegal border crossings and extremist activities, are prevalent on the northern borders of India.

Other than land and forest reserves, India is endowed with rich natural resources, such as water, minerals, natural gas, diamonds, and petroleum. Crimes against the environment have long been a concern for forest and wildlife authorities. Although there are laws to protect natural reserves, crimes such as smuggling of sandalwood, elephant tusks, and tiger skins still exist.

Growth in urbanization and industrialization has led to environmental degradations. Poor agricultural practices, such as soil erosion and improper irrigation, constrain the nation's food production. Industrial waste, offshore drilling, and overfishing continue to undermine the coastlines, wetlands, and lakes.

In recent years, India has made much progress in elevating the nation's per capita income and gross domestic product (GDP), on an average of 9.6 to 6.6 percent between 2006 and 2008 (CSO, 2009). However, 27 percent of the population are still below the poverty line (Ministry of Information and Broadcasting, 2009). India is considered a "low income" country by the

World Bank with a gross national income of $450 USD. Tremendous economic inequalities persist, with about one third of the nation's wealth being controlled by the richest 10 percent of the households (CIA, 2005). The majority of the Indian population resides in rural areas, and 86 percent of them earn less than $2 USD a day. Of these rural residents, 44 percent survive with less than $1 USD per day and 25 percent are unable to secure adequate food supply (CIA, 2003). Such extreme poverty often causes crimes that are unique to the country, such as female infanticide, feticide, family suicide, and murder of family members.

Economic inequality remains stark in India, and the inflation rate remains high (CIA, 2004). The Indian labor force remains largely dichotomous in terms of literacy and employment skills, with large numbers of illiterate workers unaccustomed to machinery or routine at one end, and a sizeable pool of highly educated scientists, technicians, and engineers, capable of working anywhere in the world at the other.[1]

According to the 2001 Census Report, there are a total of 310 million rural workers and 92.3 million urban workers in India. The unemployment rate as per 2008 estimates is 6.8 percent (CIA, 2009).

The National Sample Survey (NSS) (2004–5) indicates that while the unemployment rate is improving, the number of people regularly employed (i.e. with secured jobs) is actually worsening. Self-employment is on a sharp rise, suggesting people at the margins (especially women) must undertake low-skilled, often tenuous avenues of employment that leave them vulnerable to hardship.

In 1994 the government issued its National Telecommunications Policy in recognition of the "urgent need" to provide universal access to basic telecommunications services by 1997 and offered guidelines for entry of the private sector into basic telecommunications services.

According to the Indian Department of Telecommunications, there were 4,414.75 lakh2 phone connections in 2009, of which 4,036.63 lakh were for mobile phones. Urban areas (3,143.30 lakh) had more phone lines than the rural areas (1,271.45 lakhs). All India Radio is a national service, operated by the Prasar Bharati Broadcasting Corporation of India, and serves 99.14 percent of the population in 24 languages and 146 dialects (India.gov, 2010c). There government-owned television channels, such as Doordarshan Channels (DD), throughout India. DD has five national channels including one exclusively for news and one for sports. It has 11 regional language satellite channels and one regional state network. DD also has an international channel, DD India (India.gov, 2010a).

There were 13 internet service providers in 2009 including BSNL, Airtel, Tata Indicom, and MTNL. India has 45.3 million active internet users and 62.5 million claimed internet users in September 2008 (IAMAI, 2008).

Development of infrastructure within the country has progressed at a rapid pace, and today there is a wide variety of modes of transport by land, water, and air. The Indian Railways is organized into 16 zones; its ridership rose from 1,284 million in 1951 to 6,219 million in 2006. Revenue Freight traffic increased from 73.2 million tons in 1951 to 727.75 million tons in 2006. Transport effort measured in terms of net ton kilometers increased from 38 billion in 1951 to 41.0 billion in 2007 (India.gov, 2010b). India has one of the largest road networks in the world, aggregating to about 33 lakh kilometers. The road network consists of national highways, state highways, major/other district roads, and village/rural roads. National highways are 66,590 kilometers long, comprising only 2 percent of the total roads, but carry over 40 percent of the nation's total traffic (www.india.gov.in).

Shipping plays an important role in the transportation sector of India's economy. Approximately 90 percent of the country's trade by volume is moved by sea. It has a 7,517-kilometer-long coastline studded with 13 major ports and 200 non-major ports (http://www.india.gov.in). India has 14,500 kilometers of inland waterways which comprise rivers, canals backwaters, and creeks. About 50 million tons of cargoes were transported in 2006 through these inland waterways (http://www.india.gov.in). Apart from Air India, Indian Airlines, Alliance Air, and Air India Charters Ltd, there are eight private domestic operators. One cargo airline also operates scheduled cargo services in the country.

India's well-developed transportation infrastructure and long coastline have played into the hands of criminal smuggling operations for drugs, gems, and other prized contraband. Inland container depots provide an easy means of smuggling drugs and other contraband from the interior to Indian seaports such as Mumbai, Goa, Chennai (Madras), and Calcutta which handle a large volume of international trade (US Government, 2000).

People

With more than one billion people, India has roughly 16.7 percent of the world population. The age distribution of the Indian population tilts significantly towards high growth, with 31.5 percent between 0–14 years, 63.3 percent between the ages of 15–64 years, and those 65 years and over comprise about 5.2 percent of the population. There are 21.76 births per 1,000 population, but only 6.4 deaths according to 2008 estimates.

The Republic of India is the world's largest democracy and has a parliamentary form of government based on universal adult franchise. The executive authority is accountable to the elected representatives of the people in the Parliament for all its decisions and actions. Sovereignty rests ultimately with the people. There are national level and state level political parties in India. Major national level political parties include the Indian National Congress (INC), the Bharatiya Janata Party (BJP), the Samajwasi Party, the Bahujan Samaj Party, and the Communist Party of India-Marxist (CPI-M).

Executive Branch: The President of India is the Head of the State, while the Prime Minister is the Head of the Government, and runs the office with the support of the Council of Ministers, who form the Cabinet Ministry.

Legislative Branch: The Indian Legislature comprises of the Lok Sabha (House of the People) and the Rajya Sabha (Council of States), forming both the Houses of the Parliament.

Judicial Branch: The Supreme Court of India is the apex body of the Indian judicial system, followed by other High Courts and subordinate Courts.

India has more than 2,000 ethnic groups in different permutations, but there are five major racial types: Australoid, Mongoloid, Europoid, Caucasian, and Negroid. The Indian caste system prescribes social stratification and is generally identified within Hinduism. However, the caste system is also observed in other religions including some groups of Muslims and Christians. The Indian Constitution has outlawed caste-based discrimination, in keeping with the socialist, secular, democratic principles that founded the nation (BBC, 2005).

Hindus are the majority, making up 80.5 percent of the total 1.03 billion Indians, followed by Muslims (13.4 percent), Christians, Sikhs, Buddhists, Jains, and others (Registrar General and Census Commissioner, India, 2001). Twenty-two national languages are recognized by the Constitution of India; Hindi is the Official Union Language. English enjoys associate status but is the most important language for national, political, and commercial communication. There are 844 different dialects that are practiced in various parts of the country.

In India, a person aged seven and above who can read and write with understanding in any language is considered literate. The general literacy rate is 64.84 percent; male literacy is 75.26 percent, and female literacy is 53.67 percent (Registrar General and Census Commissioner, India, 2001).

Administration of justice

The criminal justice system in India is a legacy of the British system. It has four subsystems: Legislature (Parliament), Enforcement (police), Adjudication (courts), and Corrections (prisons, community facilities). The Constitution gives powers and responsibilities of the police, courts, prisons, and other allied institutions to the states.

The Supreme Court of India's administrative expenditure budget for the year 2009–10 is 880.2 million Indian Rupees (about $18.84 million USD). The Central Police budget for 2009–10 is 218,391.8 million Indian Rupees (about $4.674 billion USD). This includes the border security forces, education training and research, criminal investigation and vigilance, special police, modernization of the force, Delhi Police, and other law enforcement services. The Crime Records Bureau has a separate budget of 219.5 million Indian Rupees (about $4.70 million USD) (Ministry of Home Affairs, 2009). The Prison Budget in 2006–7 was 14,450.98 million Indian Rupees (about $309.28 million USD) (NCRB, 2006).

Each state has its own budget for its criminal justice units. For example, within the Tamilnadu State Budget, Law and Order (Police) had 28,550 million Indian Rupees (about $611 million USD) for the year 2008–9, the Judiciary had 3,780 million Indian Rupees (about $80.9 million USD), and Corrections 989 million Indian Rupees (about $21.17 million USD) (Anbazhagan, 2010).

The police are governed by rules and regulations as outlined in the Police Manuals (CHRI, 2001) and under the control of the Ministry of Home Affairs, which also supervises many other agencies operated and administered by the central government. The Central Bureau of Investigation (CBI) inside the Ministry of Personnel, Pension and Public Grievances, is the premier investigating agency in India. It also serves the nodal police agency that coordinates investigation on behalf of the INTERPOL Member countries (CBI, 2007).

The structure and working of the State Police Forces are governed by the Police Act of 1861 that dictates the Indian Penal Code (1890), the Code of Criminal Procedure (1898), and the Indian Evidence Act (1872). The head of the police force in each state is called the Director General of Police (DGP), who reports to the state government. The hierarchical structure of the police in India follows a vertical alignment consisting of senior officers drawn, by and large, from the Indian Police Service (IPS) who do the supervisory work, the "service delivery" officers (inspectors, sub-inspectors, and assistant sub-inspectors) who work generally at the police station level, and the police constabulary who are delegated to patrols, surveillance, guard duties, and law and order work. The constabulary accounts for almost 88 percent of total police force (CHRI, 2001; Raghavan and Natarajan, 1996; Raghavan, 1999).

Some states have Police Ranges, headed by a Deputy Inspector General of Police (DIG) or Additional Commissioner of Police, which control several Police Districts. The Police District is the fulcrum of State Police activity and each Police District is headed by a Senior Assistant Commissioner of Police or Superintendent of Police (SP). The Police District is divided into subdivisions under the command of Assistant Commissioners or Deputy Superintendent of Police (Dy.SP). Each police subdivision may have one or more Police Circles under the command of an Inspector of Police often referred to as the Circle Inspector (CI). Under the Police Circles are the police stations, generally under the control of a Sub-Inspector (SI). According to Indian law, Sub-Inspectors (and above) are the only officers who can file a charge in the court. Officers below this rank do not have much authority. In addition to the state police, major Indian cities have their own police agencies, which follow the Police Commissionerate System. The Chief of Metropolitan Police is the Police Commissioner.[3]

The police station is the basic unit of police administration in a district. Under the Criminal Procedure Code, all crime has to be recorded at the police station and all preventive, investigative and law and order work is done from there. In order to deal with crimes against women, many states have introduced women police stations that are managed exclusively by women police personnel (for more details see Natarajan, 2008). There are 328 stations state wide (NCRB, 2006).

The Judiciary is independent from the Executive and Legislative bodies of the Indian Government. It takes care of maintenance of law and order in the country along with solving problems related to civil and criminal offenses. The judiciary is stratified into various levels. At the top is the Supreme Court, followed by 21 High Courts and their Benches at the state level, District Courts at the district level, and Lok Adalats at the Village and Panchayat Level.

The Supreme Court is the highest court of appeal and the protector of the Constitution in the country. The Chief Justice of India and 25 other judges are directly appointed by the President of India (Judiciary of India, n.d.). There are High Courts in almost all the states of India and Union Territories. They decide on both civil and criminal cases. Most of the cases handled by the High Courts are passed on from the district or lower courts.

The judges of the High Courts are appointed by the President of India, in consultation with the Chief Justice of India and the Governor of the state. The Chief Justice heads each of the High Courts in India. There are also High Courts that serve more than one Indian state or Union Territory. Summons can also be issued by the High Court. Revenue matters are dealt by original jurisdiction, while an eminent jury handles original criminal cases. The District Courts are administratively and judicially controlled by the High Courts of the respective states. There are also secondary courts under the District Courts.

Tribunals are established for matters of grave concern, such as the Income Tax Appellate Tribunal, the Central Administrative Tribunal, the Intellectual Property Appellate Tribunal, Railways Claims Tribunal, the Appellate Tribunal for Electricity, the Debts Recovery Tribunal, and the Central Excise Service Tax Appellate Tribunal and the Debt Recovery Tribunal.

There are nearly 1,400 prisons of different kinds in India: Central Jails, District Jails, Sub Jails, Women's Jails, Juvenile Jails, Open Jails/Camps/Farms, and some specialized institutions (NCRB, 2006; Sanyal, 2007). The Constitution assigns the custody and correction of criminals to the states and territories. Day-to-day administration of the prisons is governed by the Prisons Act of 1894, the Prisoners Act of 1900, and the Transfer of Prisoners Act of 1950. An Additional Director General of Police manages prison affairs in each state and territory, who is assisted by an Inspector General of Prisons and a few Deputy Inspectors-General in different geographical regions of a state (Raghavan, 2002).

Prisoners are classified on the basis of age, sex, mental health, nature of offense (criminal, civil, or security), and prior offense. Prisoners are also categorized into A and B classes based on social status, education, style of living, character, and criminal history. The Central Prisons and the jails have both custodial and treatment staff such as medical doctors, psychologists, welfare officers, social workers, teachers, and vocational instructors. The hierarchy of prison custodial staff is as follows: superintendent, jailer, deputy jailer, assistant jailer, head warders, and warders (Raghavan, 2002).

India retains the system from its colonial period that mandates different treatment for different categories of prisoners. Under this system, foreigners, individuals held for political reasons, and prisoners of high caste are segregated from lower-class prisoners and afforded better incarceration conditions, which may include more cell space, less crowdedness, access to books and newspapers, and more and better food.

India prison system also has a civilian inspector program, whose members are not affiliated with any of the prisons but ensure that rules and regulations are duly enforced. They visit prisons to hear complaints and if necessary look into prison management records.

India has among the lowest rate of incarceration in the world. Its prisons housed 358,368 individuals in 2008, including pre-trail and remand inmates, who constituted 69.7 percent of the prison population. Women accounted for 4 percent of inmates, and juveniles (those under the age of 18) were less than one fifth of 1 percent (Hill, 2008).

The Indian criminal justice system functions primarily to give victims and witnesses the opportunity to participate in court proceedings without fear and to have their rights protected (Pokhariyal, 2008). The criminal justice system also provides safeguards to and confers a set of rights on the accused. However, the justice system does not exhibit equal concern to victims of crime when it comes to compensating for the loss incurred or physical, mental or emotional injury sustained (Vibhute, 2004).

Although there have been some reforms in criminal investigations and prosecution, the sufferings of crime victims have been largely neglected. In many cases, the only assistance victims of crime receive is the services provided by non-governmental organizations and human rights commissions, as in the cases of sensational crimes. The majority of crime victims in India have no venues for redress, although victim assistance is codified in the Indian Constitution stipulating that the state is mandated to secure "the right to public assistance in cases of disablement and in other cases of undeserved want." Under the criminal law, victims receive compensation only in a limited way when the offender is convicted and sentenced (Chockalingam, 2003).

Central and local governments in India are taking steps to combat crimes in general, and violence against women in particular, including dowry harassment, sexual harassment, domestic violence, eve teasing (sexual harassment of women), female infanticide and feticide, and marital rape. Gender violence, especially dowry demand and harassment, is no longer socially sanctioned. Major awareness campaigns and sensitization programs on socialization of men and women and gender equality are playing a role in curbing violence against women.

Other social control strategies at the community level include the Friends of Police (in the city of Tamilnadu), in which police partner with community volunteers to prevent crime. The Samarth Yojna Community Policing (in the city of Coimbatore) forms area committees to curb communal violence. The City Vigilance Committee, also in the city of Coimbatore, was established to fight property crimes. Others programs to prevent and detect crimes through proactive policing include the Students–Police Interface Program and the Slum Adoption Scheme.

The Indian criminal justice system offers parole as a method of rehabilitating and integrating prisoners. Probation is also liberally used in case of adult offenders and juvenile delinquents. Attempts have also been made to establish assistance programs for discharged prisoners in Mumbai, Uttar Pradesh, Calcutta, and Delhi. But because of lack of support, these programs have been dissolved (Sanyal, 2007). According to the Justice Mullah Committee Report, Upneet (2001) the criminal justice system in India has little to offer to a released offender to reintegrate him into the society and to lead a crime-free life. In recent years a few non-governmental organizations are offering support services to released offenders and children of prisoners.

Criminology

Criminology is taught in many universities in India. Four universities offer doctoral degrees in criminology and two additionally offer master's degrees (Natarajan and Poornachandra, 1994). A few more universities have considered criminology as a full-fledged academic department, such as Manonmaniam Sundaranar University in Tirunelveli and Sagar University in Bhopal. Many mainstream colleges in Tamilnadu, affiliated with the University of Madras, are offering graduate courses in criminology and police administration. The University of Madras has a new master's program in Cyber Forensics and Information Security. The Distance Education Department at the National Law Institute University in Bhopal offers a three-year post-graduate course in criminology, criminal law, and forensic science. These emerging criminology departments are undertaking research projects on cyber crime, human rights, and terrorism. Other criminologists in India are actively involved in research on prisoners' rehabilitation, violence against women and children, victimization survey, and juvenile delinquency.

A variety of research methods including survey, field research, evaluations, and case studies are employed by researchers in India. Both quantitative and qualitative data are gathered and most often they are descriptive rather than explanatory.

The National Crime Records Bureau (NCRB) in Delhi compiles the national crime data on a yearly basis and is available for public use. State governments and union territory administrations and law enforcement agencies also gather crime data. The Judgments Information system (JUDIS) provides a database of the judgments of the Supreme Court of India and several High Courts. These official data and occasional crime victimization surveys are the only data sources available for research.

Major criminology research outfits in India are mostly affiliated with universities. Table 39.1 provides a brief overview of the major criminology research organizations, research topics and their publications.

A few central government agencies fund research projects at the state or national level. The Bureau of Police Research and Development accepts proposals for research projects from universities and research institutions. The National Commission for Women (NCW) sponsors studies related to women's issues. The National Human Rights Commission, an independent organization located in the capital, undertakes and supports research related to human rights issues. The Ministry of Social Justice and Women's Empowerment support projects related to the underprivileged and empowerment of women. The Indian Council of Social Science Research (ICSSR) provides grants to scholars to conduct research in various fields of social sciences, including criminology. The University Grants Commission, a union government body that funds universities, also supports large research projects in various fields of work including criminology.

Conclusion

India's unique social and cultural environment casts its mark on the crime problems and societal response. Crimes such as dowry harassment, female infanticide, marital rape, and many forms of child abuse and sexual exploitation owe their unique attributes to the social inequalities in the country. Many topics such as victim assistance and compensation and offender reintegration deserve much more focused attention from both the research community and government agencies. Criminology in India is blossoming as an academic discipline. Greater international collaboration will enhance India's contribution to criminology research of the global community and bring in fresh ideas to improve the delivery of justice.

Future research questions

1. How effective are the existing coastal border security arrangements in India?
2. Is social disorganization at the city level leading to increase in crime rates?
3. Will properly designed and structured aftercare programs reduce prison overcrowding by habitual offenders?
4. Will the centralized policing system have an impact on innovative policing strategies in reducing crime in neighborhoods at the local level?
5. Does social context at the community level (neighborhood, census trends, etc.) play an important role in the victimization of women?

Table 39.1 Key research institutions in India

Name of research institute	*Research topics undertaken*	*Journals*
Department of Criminology, University of Madras	Trafficking of women and children; drug addiction centers; attitude studies on police work	
Department of Criminology and Criminal Justice, Manonmaniam University, Tirunelveli	Cyber bullying; cyber crimes	*International Journal of Criminal Justice Sciences*; *International Journal of Cyber Criminology*
Indian Society of Criminology, University of Madras	The effects of transcendental meditation on prisoners in Tamil Nadu; public perception of crimes; management of three counseling centers for drug and alcohol abusers	*Indian Journal of Criminology*
Indian Society of Victimology, University of Madras	Compensation to victims of crime and the role of insurance agencies; custodial violence and deaths: problems and prevention	
Department of Criminology, Sagar University, Bhopal	Criminology in India in 2000 AD; psycho-socio consequences of victimization in rape; crime reduction through situational crime prevention; reality behind medical termination of pregnancy: female feticide	
Lok Nayak Jayaprakash Narayan National Institute of Criminology and Forensic Science (NICFS), New Delhi	Rights of women prisoners in Indian jails; shortage of manpower in different FSLS in India: causes and solution; techniques for detection of forgery in bank credit cards	
Bureau of Police Research & Development (BPR&D), New Delhi	Police and prison issues	*Police Research and Development Journal*; *Indian Police Journal*; *Hindi Journal*; *Police Vigyan*
Centre for Social Welfare Administration and Justice, Indian Institute of Public Administration, New Delhi	Comparative study of ombudsman in UK and India (Indo-British project); a study of consumer redressal forums and institutions; effective policing of the national capital territory of Delhi and adjoining areas; social justice: socio-political and legal dimensions	*Indian Journal of Public Administration*

Notes

1 More details on India's economy and the composition of its labor force can be found at http://www.photius.com/countries/india/economy/index.html.
2 A lakh is a unit in the Indian numbering system, equal to 100,000.
3 Additional information about the structure and operation of the Indian police can be found at http://en.wikipedia.org/wiki/Law_enforcement_in_India.

References

Anbazhagan, K. (2010). Budget for 2010–2011 presented to the Legislative Assembly on March 19. Online at http://www.tn.gov.in/budget/budgetspeech.htm (accessed December 9, 2010).

British Broadcasting Corporation (BBC) (2005) Religion and ethics – Hinduism. Online at http://www.bbc.co.uk/worldservice/people/features/ihavearightto/four_b/casestudy_art01.shtml (accessed November 25, 2010).

Central Bureau of Investigation (CBI) (2007). CBI and its roles. Online at http://www.cbi.gov.in/aboutus/cbiroles.php (accessed November 25, 2010).

Central Intelligence Agency (CIA) (2003). *The world factbook*. Washington, DC: Central Intelligence Agency. Online at https://www.cia.gov/library/publications/download/download-2003/ (accessed November 25, 2010).

—— (2004). *The world factbook*. Washington, DC: Central Intelligence Agency. Online at https://www.cia.gov/library/publications/download/download-2004/ (accessed November 25, 2010).

—— (2005). *The world factbook*. Washington, DC: Central Intelligence Agency. Online at https://www.cia.gov/library/publications/download/download-2005/ (accessed November 25, 2010).

—— (2009). *The world factbook*. Online at https://www.cia.gov/library/publications/download/download-2009/ (accessed November 25, 2010).

Central Statistical Organisation (CSO) (2009). *Revised estimates of annual national income, 2008–09 and quarterly estimates of gross domestic product, 2008–09*. India: Ministry of Statistics and Programme Implementation. Online at http://mospi.nic.in/pressnote_t4_29may09.pdf (accessed November 25, 2010).

Chockalingam, K. P. (2003). Position of victim support schemes in India. In Tatsuya Ota (Ed.), *Victims and criminal justice: Asian perspective*, pp. 63–82. Tokyo, Hogaku-Kenkyu-Kai: Keio University.

Commonwealth Human Rights Initiative (CHRI) (2001). *Police organisation in India: biennial report on human rights issues*. New Delhi, India.

Hill, G. (2008). Value of open prisons in India. *Corrections compendium*, 33(3): 29, 30, 34.

India.gov (2010a). Know India: physical features. National Informatics Centre (NIC), DIT, MoCIT, Government of India. Online at http://www.india.gov.in/knowindia/physical_features.php (accessed December 9, 2010).

—— (2010b). Know India: television – Doordarshan. NIC, DIT, MoCIT, Government of India. Online at http://india.gov.in/knowindia/television.php accessed December 9, 2010).

—— (2010c). Know India: All India Radio. NIC, DIT, MoCIT, Government of India. Online at http://india.gov.in/knowindia/radio.php. accessed December 9, 2010).

Judiciary of India (n.d.). *Judiciary of India*. Online at http://www.mapsofindia.com/events/republic-day/india-judiciary.html (accessed November 25, 2010).

Ministry of Home Affairs (2009). Demand No. 53, Police budget 2009–10. Government of India. Online at http://indiabudget.nic.in/ub2009-10/eb/sbe53.pdf (accessed November 25, 2010).

Ministry of Information and Broadcasting (2009). India 2009. Publications Division, Government of India. Online at http://www.mib.nic.in/default.aspx (accessed 9 December 2010).

Natarajan, M. and Poornachandra, P. (1994). Recent developments in criminological education in India. Paper presented at the American Society of Criminology Annual Meetings, Miami, FL.

Natarajan, M. (2008). *Women police in a changing society: back door to equality*. Aldershot, UK: Ashgate.

National Crime Records Bureau (NCRB). (2006). Prison statistics in India 2006. Online at http://ncrb.nic.in/PSI2006/prison2006.htm (accessed November 25, 2010).

National Sample Survey (NSS) (2005). *Employment and unemployment situation among social groups in India 2004–5*. Ministry of Statistics and Programme Implementation, Government of India.

Pokhariyal, P (2008). Post UN declaration on victims scenario in India – assessment of victim's position in India. Indlaw (New Delhi) News, 12 January. Online at http://www.indlawnews.com/ (accessed December 9, 2010).

Raghavan, R. K. (1999). Policing a democracy: a comparative study of India and the US. New Delhi: Manohar.

—— (2002). India, world factbook of criminal justice systems. Bureau of Justice Statistics. Grant No. 90-BJ-CX-0002 to the State University of New York at Albany.

Raghavan, R. K. and Natarajan, M. (1996). India. In G. Newman, D. Cohen, and A. C. Bouloukos (Eds). *International factbook of criminal justice systems: Profile of India*. Washington, DC: Bureau of Justice Statistics.

Registrar General and Census Commissioner, India (2001). Census of India. Online at http://www.censusindia.net/ (accessed November 25, 2010).

Sanyal, S. (2007) Community based correctional services: an alternate to imprisonment. *The Indian Journal of Criminology & Criminalistics*, 23(3).

US Government (2000). International crime threat assessment, a report prepared by a US Government interagency working group. Online at http://www.fas.org/irp/threat/pub45270chap3.html (accessed December 9, 2010).

Vibhute, K. (2004). *Criminal justice: a human rights perspective of the criminal justice process in India*. India: Eastern Book Co.

Websites

http://www.india.gov.in
http://indiabudget.nic.in

40

Italy

An overview of criminology

Rosemary Serra

Introduction

Modern criminology originated in Italy. Its origins can be found in the works of Cesare Beccaria, which are regarded as the starting point of modern criminal law, and those of Cesare Lombroso, which were believed to be the origin of positivism in criminology (Sidoti, 2009). Criminology in Italy is configured at present as a discipline with an integrated approach while at the same time remaining autonomous. It draws on a systematic method from different disciplines, overcoming the typical clinical concept that characterizes criminal anthropology, such as biological, psychological, and sociological conceptions (di Martino, 2009).

In recent years, criminology has expanded to take on greater global and transnational dimensions. Organized crime, terrorism, financial crime, and computer fraud are a few such examples that require the expertise of different fields and increased international collaborations. As noted by Marotta (2008, p. 64), "the globalization of organized crime is progressing in parallel with that of the world economy and it extends to new markets. The globalization of good corresponds to the globalization of evil."

Infrastructure

Italy covers a total area of 301,336 square kilometers, divided into 20 administrative regions and about a hundred provinces. Italy is a peninsula. It borders to France to the northwest, to Switzerland and Austria to the north, and to Slovenia to the northeast. There are four geographical areas – the North (Piemonte, Valle d'Aosta, Liguria, Lombardia, Trentino-Alto Adige, Friuli Venezia Giulia, Veneto, and Emilia-Romagna), the Center (Toscana, Lazio, Umbria, and Marche), the South (Abruzzo, Molise, Campania, Basilicata, Puglia, and Calabria), and the Islands (Sicily and Sardinia).

The population numbers 60 million, of which 98 percent are Roman Catholics. Population growth is among the lowest in the Western world. For instance, in 2008 the population growth was at 0.7 percent, all of which was attributed to immigration. Italy's territory is mainly made up of hills and mountains, but about half of Italians live in the regions of the plains. The average national population density is 198 inhabitants per square kilometer. Small towns up to 1,000 hectares have an average population density of 534, which are among the most densely populated areas, especially in South Italy and the Islands. Some of these areas reach 920 inhabitants per square kilometer.

Italy has a diversified economy. The 2008 per capita gross domestic product (GDP) was \$31,000 USD, or 43rd in the world. The North is industrial and dominated by private companies. The South is, instead, agricultural with high unemployment. High-quality consumer goods produced by small- and medium-sized companies drive, in large part, the Italian economy. Other major economic sectors include agriculture, construction, and the service industry.

The 2009 per capita GDP was \$29,900 USD, or 45th in the world.

The Italian government has struggled to limit government spending, but Italy's exceedingly high public debt remains above 115% of GDP, and its fiscal deficit – just 1.5% of GDP in 2007 – exceeded 5% in 2009 as the costs of servicing the country's debt rose.

For some years the schooling rate in Italy stabilized around 100 percent in pre-primary, primary, and lower secondary schools. In upper secondary schools, the schooling rate also rose from 89.8 percent in 2002 to 93 percent in 2008 (ISTAT, 2009).[1] The percentage of people with a professional certification or an upper secondary diploma remains at 32.4 percent, while those with a university degree are at 10.2 percent. Women were more likely than men to pursue their studies after upper secondary education and complete them.

Italy is a democratic republic that replaced the monarchy in 1946. Its constitution was enacted in 1947. Italy has been at the forefront of European economic and political unification, and joined the Economic and Monetary Union in 1999.

The state government has three branches: legislative, executive, and judiciary. Each power is separate and independent from the others through a system of checks and balances. The nation is governed by the executive branch. The executive branch is composed of the Prime Minister (the head of government) and the Cabinet (the Council of Ministers nominated by the Prime Minister and approved by the President). The President of the Republic heads the armed forces and has the powers to veto legislation, disband Parliament, and call elections. He nominates the senior government minister, called the President of the Council (equivalent to the British prime minister).

The Prime Minister is referred to as the President of the Council of Ministers. An electoral college consisting of both houses of Parliament and the 58 regional representatives elect the President of the Republic. His mandate lasts for seven years without a term limit. The Prime Minister is appointed by the President and confirmed by the Parliament.

The Parliament, or the legislative branch, is made up of the Senate and the Chamber of Deputies. The Senate is composed of 315 seats plus 10 seats reserved for "life members," who are past presidents, and their honorary nominees. Its members are elected by proportional vote with the winning coalition in each region receiving 55 percent of the seats from that region. The Chamber of Deputies has 630 seats. The election of the deputies occurs by popular vote. The winning coalition gains 54 percent of the Chamber seats. Both are elected to serve a five-year term. The Parliament is the only body that produces the Penal Law. The general norms of the penal system are prescribed by the Constitution. No law can conflict with the Constitution.

The Bench (judges and prosecutors) is autonomous and independent from any political, legislative, and executive powers. It has the power to administer justice and enforce the law. It is composed of a Constitutional Court, which is the country's highest court. It consists of 15 judges, one third appointed by the President, one third elected by the Parliament, and one third elected by ordinary and administrative courts. The Constitutional Court is in charge of evaluating the conformity of specific rules of the Penal Law to the Constitution. The Constitutional Court is a post-war innovation. Its powers, volume, and frequency of decisions are not as extensive as those of the Supreme Court in the United States. The other senior court is the Court of Cassation, which is the supreme organ of justice that ensures the abidance with and the uniform application of criminal law, and mediates the conflicts within judicial branches.

All decisions by the Bench are permanent under the responsibility to the self-governed elective Board (Consiglio Superiore della Magistratura). Two thirds of this Board is composed by a large majority of judges and prosecutors. The judges are subject only to the authority of the law as established by the Constitution.

Several political parties operate in Italy. Historically there have been more. No one party has ever gained the absolute majority and thus these political parties must work with each other to form coalition governments. However, since the 2008 general election, only five major parties are represented in Parliament. On one side, the center-right People of Freedom (PdL) and Lega Nord (LN), and on the other side there is the center-left opposition composed of the Democratic Party (PD), the Italian Radicals, and Italy of Values. The Union of the Center (UdC) is the only party outside the two big coalitions represented in Parliament. Other minor regional parties are also represented in the Parliament, notably the Movement for Autonomy (MpA), the South Tyrolean People's Party, and the Valdotanian Union, while many other parties are active or represented at the regional level.

Administration of justice

The legal system is based on a civil law system. The penal law defines what specific behavior is criminal and what the minimum and maximum penalty is for each crime. The basic principles of no penalty without a law (*nulla poena sine lege*) and no crime without a law (*nullum crimen sine lege*) are stated in the Penal Code and in the Constitution.

The Penal Code and many others statutes contain criminal laws. In 1989 the promulgation of the new Code of Penal Procedure made the most significant legislative changes in the criminal justice system. The new legislation introduced a very important innovation: the admission of evidence that, as a rule, can be obtained only during the course of an oral and public trial, in front of the judge on the basis of witnesses' cross-examination and other kinds of proof legally presented in the Court. The prosecution and defense conduct the trial as equal opposing sides.

Although the new Italian Code of Penal Procedure is similar to the adversarial English and American systems, its system of written laws still retains important differences when compared to the Anglo-American system, such as the obligatory nature of penal action (Marongiu and Biddau, 2002). The Constitution sanctions the obligatory nature of penal action. According to this provision, the Public Prosecutor (Pubblico Ministero), when informed of the commission of a crime, is legally bound to start an investigation. The Public Prosecutor takes penal action against the alleged offender if there is enough circumstantial evidence. An Italian prosecutor is therefore without discretionary power to withhold prosecution. Prosecution is not simply a right, but a duty of the Italian Public Prosecutor.

The criminal justice system operates all over the national territory through districts and other minor territorial jurisdictions. Although each district has the power to make laws, only the State has jurisdiction over substantive and procedural penal law.

The criminal justice system in Italy consists of the following organs: the Justice of the Peace (Giudice di Pace), the Court (Tribunale), the Court of Appeal (Corte d'Appello), the Court of Cassation (Corte di Cassazione), and the Public Prosecutor (Pubblico Ministero). Criminal cases are subjected to the various courts of justice depending on their seriousness.

The Justice of the Peace reviews the majority of criminal cases. The Court of Appeal decides on appeals against the verdict by the defendant or the acquittal by the Court in a hearing. It also has the authority over sentences, preliminary investigations, and preliminary hearing. The Court of Cassation ensures the correct abidance and the uniform application of criminal law, the unity of the objective law, and regulates the conflicts within or competence of judiciary officials. The

Public Prosecutor (Pubblico Ministero or PM) supervises and conducts the preliminary investigations and initiates the prosecution. The action of the PM is subjected to the control of the judge for preliminary inquiries (Giudice per le indagini preliminari or GIP), to whom the PM himself forms a request for the dismissal or committal for trial at the end of the investigation phase.

There are three main state police agencies in Italy: the Finance Police (Guardia di Finanza), the State Police (Polizia di Stato), and the Carabinieri. The Finance Police is under the Ministry of Finance, with boats, ships, and aircraft that are responsible, among other things, for patrolling Italy's territorial waters. The Carabinieri are under the Ministry of Defense and police both the military and civilian populations. Both Carabinieri and Finance Police are mainly responsible for the investigation of financial crimes.

The Ministry of the Interior controls the State Police, whose functions are the prevention, detection, and the investigation of crime, as well as the apprehension of alleged offenders (Law n.121/1981, article 24). In addition to the State Police, there are also a few other local or specialized police forces, such as the railway police, the city police, the traffic police, and the rangers. Police officers carry out criminal investigations under the direction of their judicial authority. All of the police criminal investigation activities are coordinated by the Central Operating Service (Servizio Centrale Operativo). This service functions under the authority of the Ministry of the Interior and the Chief of Police.

The Italian prison system is seriously overcrowded. According to the prisoner rights group Associazione Antigone (2009), the number of prisoners has reached 63,460, more than the regulatory capacity of 20,000, and since 2009 has increased by about 1,000 per month. About 40 percent of the prisoners and half of foreign offenders are in prison for drug offenses.

The court system is crowded with pending cases and appeals. More than half of the convicted offenders had previous offenses and two thirds of convicted offenders were sent to prison.

Similar to other countries, rehabilitative efforts in Italy for convicted offenders have thus far been mostly ineffective. The sub-cultural effects and the deprivation of the detention, and the inconsistency of the results of the various treatment strategies and re-socializing programs in the reduction of recidivism have pushed researchers and policy makers to seek alternative solutions to prison (di Martino, 2009).

The Italian Constitution stipulates that "the penalties may not consist of treatment contrary to a sense of humanity and must aim to rehabilitate the convicted." For decades, Italy provided individualized rehabilitation treatment inside prisons (Fanchiotti, 2002). The introduction of alternative measures to imprisonment represented a significant innovation in Italian offender rehabilitation. The power to decide an offender's rehabilitation is handled by a new judicial body, the Court of Surveillance. Established in 1986, this court consists of two magistrates and two experts in psycho-social disciplines.

Three alternatives are available in lieu of detention: probation (affidamento in prova al servizio sociale), semi-liberty (semilibertà), and early release (liberazione anticipata). The first solution is an alternative to detention in the true sense, during which the offender can work, go to school, or take vocational training. This community-based corrections approach has been refined and expanded over the years to include additional conditions under supervision and house arrest (detenzione domiciliare). Many types of offenders are now eligible for these community-based alternatives, such as those with health problems, mothers with young children, pregnant women, minors, and those older than 60 years old. It should be noted that in the current criminal system juvenile offenders receive special treatment services. Their detention is no different from residential facilities of boarding schools. The goal of the system is to reintegrate juvenile offenders back into their families or communities.

In the Italian Penal Code there are 387 types of crimes, divided into two broad categories: serious offenses (delitti) and infractions (contravvenzioni) (Marongiu and Biddau, 2002). The Penal Code also assigns crimes to the following classifications: against the person; against the family; against public morality; against property; against the economy and public trust; against the nation and other social authorities and public order; and finally the catch-all category of "other crimes."

Official crime data are collected and processed by the National Institute of Statistics (Istituto Nazionale di Statistica – ISTAT) and published in the *Yearbook of Statistics: Crimes*. Several Italian research institutes, such as the CENSIS and the Doxa, usually carry out surveys for criminological research. These surveys gather public opinions about crime and measure how many people have been victims of crime. In 2006, recorded crimes increased by 7.5 percent over 2005. There was a strong increase particularly in the reports of swindling and computer fraud.

Crime data come from several sources: official records, self reports, and victimization survey. To augment official records, researchers rely on self-reporting and crime victimization surveys to uncover criminal activities unknown to the police, or the so-called "dark figures" (Barbagli and Gatti, 2002). Since 1993, ISTAT (National Institute of Statistics), in the annual survey on the "aspects of everyday life," samples nearly 60,000 people to determine who has been a victim of bag snatching, apartment burglaries, and pick-pocketing, and who has filed a complaint. Until 1997, the only source of crime data in Italy was based on the complaints made by citizens to the State Police, the Carabinieri and the Finance Guard, which were then forwarded to the Ministry of Interior, and finally presented in the ISTAT. Needless to say, such an official data source has many limitations, including only those crimes reported to the police.

Criminology

The historical preamble of the scientific inquiry into criminal behavior can be traced to the French Enlightenment movement of 1700 that advocated science and knowledge over ignorance and superstition. Cesare Beccaria's *Treatise on crimes and punishments* (1764) put forth the first liberal idea of criminal law embedded in the Enlightenment principles of reason, freedom, equality, and justice. The "Classical School" of criminal law was born. It stated that crime is an entity of the law and expresses the free will of the individual, and thus should be punished without consideration of psychological or social characteristics.

However, the study of crime was neither systematic nor scientific. This fundamental shift took place in the middle of the 1800s. The experimental and inductive scientific methods were applied to the study of the crime. The science of criminology was born in 1876 with the publication of *The Criminal Man* by Cesare Lombroso, who applied medical measurement and an analytical approach to the study of crime but paid little attention to the complexity of the problem. Although Lombroso's classification of criminal stereotypes is largely ignored these days, his criminal anthropology has led to tremendous growth in criminology by the introduction of multiple social, cultural, and biological factors.

Lombroso's ideas were advanced by the Positivist School of Criminal Law through the efforts of jurist Enrico Ferri (1856–1926) and of magistrate Raffaele Garofalo (1852–1934). In the treatise *Criminology* (1885) by Garofalo, the new discipline has been systematized from the legal point of view (Correra and Martucci, 2006). Upon the death of Lombroso, Enrico Ferri was a predominant figure. Between the 1930s and 1960s, the most prominent exponent of Italian criminology was Benigno di Tullio (1896–1979), considered to be the scientific heir of Lombroso. His vision was to develop a bio-classification in criminal behaviors based on medical models such as occasional criminal, constitutional, and mental illness.

Criminology as an independent academic discipline is a recent development. Upon the death of Lombroso (1909) and until 1963, an autonomous chair of criminal anthropology was absent in Italian academia. In 1936, in all the Italian universities, the courses of criminal anthropology were suppressed (Correra and Martucci, 2006). The chair of criminal anthropology at the University of Turin was subsumed under Forensic Medicine and entrusted to Mario Carrara. This union lasted until the age of Fascism (1931), during which the research on crime took on a distinctive political tone. Only in 1963 was a criminal anthropology chair reinstated at the University of Rome and entrusted to Benigno di Tullio. In the 1960s, thanks to the efforts of di Tullio, Italian criminology started to gain autonomy as well as academic recognition (Bandini *et al.*, 2003). Di Tullio was also credited with launching the Paris-based International Society of Criminology.

In 1957, the Italian Society of Criminology (Società Italiana di Criminologia) was established in Rome. Towards the late 1990s, specialized courses, master's courses, and seminars on crime and criminality began to proliferate in Italy. Currently, criminology is typically found in three academic disciplines: medicine, law, and sociology. It has gained a recognizable status and expanded to an international level. Today, there are about 50 courses on criminological subjects, four postgraduate schools of clinical criminology, and two doctoral programs (PhD) of criminology in Italian universities (Bandini *et al.*, 2003).

As a discipline, criminology has entered into regular academic instruction and been incorporated into the training of personnel employed in the security and crime control sectors. Criminology in Italy enjoys much autonomy and contributes to the professionalization of the security and social control occupations. It has become a profession that combines conceptual efforts with operational practices (Bisi, 2007).

In the early 1900s, researchers continued to carry on the traditions of psychiatry and forensic medicine. The discipline has long emphasized the clinical prospective (as was labeled "criminal anthropology"). Starting from the 1960s, the discipline has become increasingly open to contextual and relational variables and expanded beyond regular street crimes to include more complex topics such as white-collar crimes, illicit trafficking of people, and human rights violations (Bertelli, 2008).

There are many well-known research institutes in Italy with national and international recognition. In Turin there is the United Nations Interregional Crime Research Institute (UNICRI), formerly the United Nations Social Defence Research Institute (UNSDRI) until 1989. It was constituted in 1968 for research purposes. In Genova there is the International Center of Clinical Criminology, founded in 1975 thanks to the collaboration between the International Society of Criminology and a local university. In Milan, the National Center of Prevention and Social Defense (Centro Nazionale di Prevenzione e Difesa Sociale; CNPDS) conducts studies on criminological topics.

In Siracusa, the International Institute of Higher Studies in Criminal Sciences (ISISC) carries out studies and publishes research findings. In Messina, the "Intercenter," an International Center of Research and Sociological, Criminal and Penitentiary Studies (Centro Internazionale di Ricerche e Studi Sociologici, Penali e Penitenziari), sponsored by the European Council, promotes research and international meetings on topics related to justice, punishment, and treatment of criminals.

In Bologna, the "Centro di Studi sui Comportamenti Devianti e Criminali" (Ce.Sco.De.C.) works in connection with the university. At the University of Trento and at the Catholic University of Milan there is "Transcrime," an Interdepartmental Research Center on Transnational Crime. Moreover, in Rome, the Office of Studies, Research and Documentation at the General Management of the Institutes of Prevention and Punishment (Direzione Generale per gli Istituti di Prevenzione e Pena) at the Ministry of Justice promotes systematic research activities and publishing.

There are three main directions in the criminological discipline in Italy: 1) a didactic approach, essentially with cultural aims; 2) a formative approach, addressed to practical applications; and 3) a scientific research approach (Carrera and Martucci, 2006).

As for research methods, Italian criminology remains interdisciplinary, employing concepts and techniques from different disciplinary traditions such as psychology, psychopathology, and sociology. Crime research involves a clinical diagnostic approach, a technical investigation approach, and a qualitative and quantitative psycho-social approach.

Bandini *et al.* (1991, cited in di Martino, 2009) discusses five types of research commonly practiced in Italy: quantitative research, qualitative research, transversal or "cross-sectional" research, longitudinal research, and research with an experimental method. Criminologists in Italy are using multiple methods to explore criminal behavior and associated social variables.

The persistence of the clinical prospective and of the attention to the resocialization of the offender have sheltered Italian criminology from advances found elsewhere, especially in the United States. These differences between Italian criminology and that of other countries have become less visible in recent years. The development of international and transnational aspects in criminal behavior and the development in research methods increase common attitudes in different schools (Carrera and Martucci, 2006). In fact, during the last decade, sociological and legal approaches, as opposed to the clinical approach, have gained status in Italian criminology. In recent years, increasing attention has been paid to different economic crimes, organized crime, drug addiction, and so-called "new crimes" such as cyber-related and computer crimes (Carrera and Martucci, 2006).

Criminology in Italy examines a broad range of issues including criminal behavior, criminal bio-psycho-social characteristics, the dynamics of victimization, the processes of stigma, and the "perverse effects" of institutionalization, transnational crime, crime prevention, urban safety, and the various forms of institutional crime control (Bertelli, 2008).

According to the *European Sourcebook of Crime and Criminal Justice Statistics*, for the period 2000–3, Italy is placed between 22nd and 26th position (across different years) in terms of murder rates per 100,000 inhabitants among the 37 European countries covered. There are differences between North and South, principally owing to the role of mafia-type organizations (Maffei and Merzagora Betsos, 2007). Starting from 1880, murder rates in Sicily doubled those of Italy as a whole. Between 1975 and 2004, mafia-type murders numbered 6,144 (EURES-ANSA, 2005). A peak was registered in 1991 with 718 murders involving mafia crime (37.5 percent of total murders committed in Italy that year) (Maffei and Merzagora Betsos, 2007). Recently, a sharp decrease in mafia killings was recorded in Palermo (Chinnici, 2003), owing to government responses to mafia murders. In the North, by contrast, murders frequently occur within the family, involving elderly married couples. In general, as Savona (2007) points out, murders have decreased everywhere, while acts of violence have increased. This is a new phenomenon of "repressed violence" (Savona, p. 12) which involves more and more young people and that affects families, schools, sporting events, and the streets.

The most significant category of crime – like the rest of the world – is that against property (especially theft) (Maffei and Merzagora Betsos, 2007). The number of thefts reported ranges from 1,300,000 to 1,500,000 cases each year. Burglaries and car thefts are more frequent in the North. At the present, Italian criminologists have turned their attention to fear of crime and other related matters, such as victimization and crime prevention (Maffei and Merzagora Betsos, 2007). Since 1997, the National Institute of Statistics (ISTAT) has carried out a victimization survey every five years. The survey focuses on certain types of violent offenses, revealing the dark figures of such crimes and investigating the reasons for reporting or not reporting these crimes. Additionally, it attempts to measure public perception of safety associated with crime and victimization and the strategies of citizens to defend themselves and to prevent these crimes. The fear of crime seems to increase independently of the actual offences. More than 14 million Italians feel "totally or rather unsafe" to walk alone at night in their local street (Maffei and Merzagora Betsos, 2007).

Italian mafia organizations initially developed as regional enterprises and later expanded across the whole of Italy and abroad. Besides the world-famous Sicilian Mafia (dating back to the nineteenth century), the list includes the "Camorra" in Campania, the "Ndrangheta" in Calabria, and the "Sacra Corona Unita" in Puglia. These organizations have similar structures, based on a network of secret associations of "men of honor" governed by the code of silence (Maffei and Merzagora Betsos, 2007). They also infiltrate public offices and exert political influence. Over the years, mafia-type organizations have become more eclectic. The traditional crime of extortion from local businesses and shops has gradually being replaced by other profitable activities: loan-sharking, prostitution, the illegal importation of drug and cigarettes, robbery, kidnapping, smuggling of illegal immigrants, and international trafficking of artworks (Maffei and Merzagora Betsos, 2007).

Some studies have investigated the reasons for the success of these organizations from a political, economic and social point of view, attributing mafia crimes to a particular "mafia subculture," embedded in certain cultural traditions and in the weaknesses of human nature (Scalia, 2005). The fight against mafia-type organizations relies on a better understanding of their organizational structure and the defection of their criminal members. As Maffei argues, "mafia defectors are former members who leave the organization in exchange for more lenient judicial treatment and tailor-made protection program intended to provide protection, financial assistance and, in some cases, a new identity" (Maffei and Merzagora Betsos, 2007, p. 471).

Women traditionally were not involved in mafia activities. Since 1990, there has been an increase in the number of women imprisoned for mafia-related offenses as they have been assigned new key roles when their male partners are jailed to ensure that the fundamentals of mafia culture (loyalty, revenge, vow of silence) are passed onto the next generation.

After its emergence in the 1970s, Italy has defeated internal political terrorism. Between 1969 and 1982, 2,712 terrorist acts were recorded and 351 individuals were murdered in that context. At the present, as Maffei and Merzagora Betsos (2007) argue, the danger on the terrorist front is posed by the Islamic terrorist network linked to al-Qaeda, whose members are active in Milan, Turin, and the Emilia-Romagna region.

Sex crimes are underreported because victims are often unwilling to report them to the authorities. According to a telephone survey conducted by the National Institute of Statistics (ISTAT) in 1998 (based on a sample of more than 20,000 women aged 14–59), more than 82 percent of rapes and more than 93 percent of attempted rapes went unreported (Sabbadini, 1998).

Recently, new offenses of group violence and against minors have been introduced in the Code. Criminology has long studied these forms of violence, as a social phenomenon and as a potential threat to public confidence in the criminal justice system (Bandini and Gualco, 2000).

Drug trafficking is mostly a core business for mafia-type organizations. The number of foreign offenders for drug crimes has increased: in 1987 they were 1,543, and in 2004 they rose to 8,703. The drug market is dominated by ethnic groups that cooperate with local crime organizations. As Merzagora Betsos (Maffei and Merzagora Betsos, 2007) notes, local dealers often come from the Maghreb countries (Morocco, Tunisia, Libya). More than 50 percent of the total number of foreigner-committed crimes reported to the police was done by people from these countries.

Different theories have been proposed to explain the economic, political, and cultural causes of corruption in Italy. Research on white-collar crime has focused on the theories of "cost-and-benefits" and the interrelations between economic crimes and mafia-type organizations (especially in the South). During the early 1990s, the "Clean hands" campaign of judicial investigations – started by a group of prosecutors in Milan – was effective against a system of corruption that involved all political parties and hundreds of politicians, administrators, and businessmen. After this campaign, complaints for this offense have declined.

After the closing of the borders by traditional European countries of immigration (e.g. France, Great Britain, and Germany) in 1973, immigration began to redirect towards Italy (Melotti, 1993). Historically, Italy has been an emigrant nation. Consequently, crime by immigrants is a relatively recent phenomenon. Illegal immigrants are reportedly inclined to engage in criminal activities because they are not able to find regular jobs. Official statistics appear to suggest that immigrants are especially active in thefts and burglaries in shops and apartments (Maffei and Merzagora Betsos, 2007). A serious offense related to foreign criminality is prostitution rings. Especially in the North, prostitution has developed into a well-structured business.

As Bandinu (2003) argues, the criminalization attitude toward immigrants becomes more acute during political and economic crises, which create psycho-social instability, and in turn impact peaceful social coexistence. In this context, social stereotypes arise and produce "scapegoats" (the immigrants) and the evils of society are blamed on them. The immigrant phenomenon represents the litmus test of the changes of the Italian society, in regard to living together, public life, and the idea of State (Melossi, 2002). The uneasiness that Italian people feel toward foreigners finds a reason to exist in the suffering produced by their image, as a mirror that reflects Italian society.

In Italy, offenses by minors are mostly property related. However, in the 1980s and 1990s, violent crimes committed by minors were on the rise. Juvenile crimes also caught the nation's attention by their involvement in mafia-type organizations, especially in the South, where mafia organizations recruit youngsters for such jobs as drug runners and message carriers, motorbike riders, and drivers of motor boats for smuggling (Maffei and Merzagora Betsos, 2007).

Another line of research that has found fertile ground in Italy is ecological research. Research of this nature has been carried out in different metropolises; and findings suggest correlations between crime rates and urban degradation, accompanied by such variables as overcrowded housing, a lack of services, school facilities, commercial activities, public transportation, a lack of green spaces and socialization, immigration, and the presence of subcultures (di Martino, 2009). Such urban decay is seen in some Italian cities, such as Naples, Genoa, Palermo, and Catania. In the early 1980s, the historical centers of these cities became dilapidated and the rundown urban environments attracted high crime rates and other social problems. In recent years, local governments adopted policies for the redevelopment of these historical centers, and attracted migration towards new residential complexes located in the suburbs. The development activities have revitalized the historical urban centers, but it also moved many of the previous social problems from the city center to the suburbs, creating new social alienation and ghettoization.

Conclusion

Since the 1960s, criminology in Italy has attained academic recognition as an autonomous discipline. Overcoming the hegemony of the clinical approach and opening to a wider context, Italian criminology attempts to bridge the differences between other European countries and the United States. Although much of modern criminology originated in Italy, the country has been slow in advancing empirical research on deviant behaviors and their social reactions, or public opinion on criminal activities.

In Italy, the fields of study related to the work of the police, the work of the courts and organization of the prisons are still inadequate, compared to a few European countries or the

United States. Much of Italian criminology is still focused on the offense and the offender instead of on the social reactions to law violating behaviors (Barbagli and Gatti, 2002).

As noted by di Martino (2009), Italian criminology has been slow in applying empirical research on deviant behaviors and their social reactions, or public opinions on criminal activities. Furthermore, in Italy, quantitative studies on delinquency are few and often plagued with methodological inaccuracies (Bandini *et al.*, 2003).

Therefore, it seems important that the future of criminology in Italy should harmonize the different tools of data gathering. Extensive comparative studies have to be focused on obtaining comparable data in different social and cultural contexts (Bandini *et al.*, 2003).

Future research questions

1. Which cutting-edge topics of research must Italian criminologists currently consider carefully? Which of the most prevalent crimes are not currently being addressed?
2. Which methods are most effective for criminologists in Italy to use to reveal the "dark figures" (i.e. crimes unknown to police) of crime?
3. How can studies contribute to the fight against mafia-type organizations in Italy? What research is available that is not currently being used by practitioners? What are the gaps in the studies that need to be addressed?
4. What multi-lateral agreements does Italy need to more effectively investigate organized crime that crosses national borders?
5. The future of criminology in Italy should harmonize the different tools of data gathering to obtain comparable data in different social and cultural contexts. Which strategies and which tools could be used to achieve this goal?

Note

1 The education system in Italy is divided into five levels: pre-primary education, primary, lower secondary (that corresponds to the middle school), upper secondary (high school), and tertiary education (non-university and university). Primary and lower secondary levels form the first cycle, and upper secondary the second.

References

Associazione Antigone (Ed.) (2009). *Oltre il tollerabile. Sesto Rapporto sulle condizioni di detenzione in Italia.* Antigone, IV, 1. Turin: Edizioni L'Harmattan Italia.

Bandini, T. and Gualco, B. (2000). *Infanzia e abuso sessuale.* Milan: Giuffré.

Bandini, T., Gatti, U., Gualco, B., Malfatti, D., Marugo, M. I. and Verde, A. (2003). *Criminologia. Il contributo della ricerca alla conoscenza del crimine e della reazione sociale.* Milan: Giuffrè.

Bandinu, G. (2003). Immigrazione, devianze e criminalità. In C. Serra (Ed.) *Proposte di criminologia applicata.* Milan: Giuffrè.

Barbagli, M. and Gatti, U. (Eds.) (2002). *La criminalità in Italia.* Bologna: il Mulino.

Bertelli, B. (2008). Lo sviluppo della dimensione sociale della criminologia in Italia: l'insegnamento universitario della sociologia della devianza fra passato e futuro. *Rivista di Criminologia, Vittimologia e Sicurezza*, 3: 44–58.

Bisi, R. (2007). Discipline crimonologiche e problemi di formazione professionale. *Rivista di Criminologia, Vittimologia e Sicurezza*, 1: 1–8.

Chinnici, G. (2003). L'omicidio a Palermo. In M. Barbagli and U. Gatti (Eds.) *Rapporto sulla criminalità in Italia*, pp. 235–58. Bologna: Il Mulino.

Correra, M. M. and Martucci, P. (2006). *Elementi di criminologia.* Padua: Cedam.

di Martino, P. (2009). *Criminologia. Analisi interdisciplinare della complessità del crimine.* Naples: Edizioni Simone.

EURES-ANSA (2005). L'omicidio volontario in Italia. Rapporto 2005. Rome.

Fanchiotti, V. (2002) Le misure alternative. In M. Barbagli and U. Gatti (Eds.), *La criminalità in Italia*. Bologna: il Mulino.

Istituto Nazionale di Statistica (ISTAT) (2009). I consumi delle famiglie. Anno 2008, statistiche in breve. Rome.

—— (2009). Compendio statistico Italiano 2008. Italian Statistical Abstract 2008. Rome.

—— (2009). Annual report, the state of the nation in 2008. Summary. Rome.

—— (2009). Famiglia e società. Statistiche in breve. Rome.

—— (2009). Italy in figures. Rome.

Maffei, S. and Merzagora Betsos, I. (2007). Crime and criminal policy in Italy: tradition and modernity in a troubled country. *European Journal of Criminology*, 4: 461–82.

Marongiu, P. and Biddau, M. (2002). *World Factbook of Criminal Justice Systems*. Washington, DC: US Department of Justice, Bureau of Justice Statistics. Online at http://bjs.ojp.usdoj.gov/content/pub/ascii/WFBCJITA.TXT (accessed November 23, 2010).

Marotta, G. (2008). Ripensando al futuro della criminologia. *Rivista di Criminologia, Vittimologia e Sicurezza*, 3: 59–68.

Melossi, D. (2002) *Stato, controllo sociale, devianza, teorie criminologiche e società tra Europa e Stati Uniti*. Milan: Mondadori.

Melotti, U. (1993). Migrazioni internazionali e integrazione sociale: il caso italiano e le esperienze europee. In M. Delle Donne, U. Melotti, and S. Petilli, *Immigrazione in Europa. Solidarietà e conflitto*. Rome: Centro Europeo di Scienze Sociali (CEDISS).

Ministry of Justice, Research and Documentation Center (WODC) (2006). *European sourcebook of crime and criminal justice statistics*. 3rd edn. The Hague: Ministry of Justice, Research and Documentation Center. Online at http://www.europeansourcebook.org /esb3_full.pdf (accessed May 21, 2007).

Sabbadini, L. (1998), *La sicurezza dei cittadini: molestie e violenze sessuali*. Rome: ISTAT.

Savona, E. U. (2007). Introduzione. In Provincia Autonoma di Trento, *Transcrimine, Università di Trento e Università Cattolica di Milano, Ottavo rapporto sulla sicurezza nel Trentino 2006/2007*, Tendenze n.1. Online at http://transcrime.cs.unitn.it/tc/693.php (accessed November 23, 2010).

Scalia, V. (2005), I fenomeni mafiosi nelle ricerche del centro Giuseppe Impastato: 25 anni di testimonianza e rigore scentifico. *Rassegna Italiana di Criminologia*, 16: 285–304.

Sidoti, F. (2009). Premessa. in P. di Martino, *Criminologia. Analisi interdisciplinare della complessità del crimine*. Naples: Edizioni Simone.

United Nations Development Programme (UNDP). (2008) Human development report 2007/08. Online at http://hdr.undp.org/en/reports/global/hdr2007–8/ (accessed February 3, 2008).

41

South Korea

Current trends and issues in crime and criminal justice

Joon Oh Jang and Kyung-shick Choi

Introduction

Although South Korea's is deemed in general a safe society, crime is still an issue of public concern. In 2007, there were 1,965,997 crime cases in South Korea (Supreme Prosecutor's Office, 2008). The crime rate per 100,000 persons in 2007 was 3987.7, which included traffic violations. It has increased 2.5 percent in the number of overall crime in 2007, compared to figures for 1997 (Korean Institute of Criminology, 2008).

When considering only violent crime (aggravated violence, including murder, robbery, arson, and rape; and violence, including assault, injury, threat, intimidation, kidnapping, illegal detention, assault, and battery) and property crime (theft, fraud, embezzlement, stolen goods, breach of trust, and property damage) the crime rate per 100,000 persons becomes 1513.2. The crime rate of property per 100,000 in 2007 was 952.6, an increase of 39.1 percent from 1997. The crime rate of violence per 100,000 in 2007 was 560.6, an increase of 28.8 percent from 1997. The most frequent crimes are assault, injury, rape, and robbery, respectively. Among property crimes, theft and fraud are the most frequent (Supreme Prosecutor's Office, 2008).

Infrastructure

Located on the Korean Peninsula in Northeast Asia, South Korea is a long (1,100 kilometers) and narrow (250 kilometers) country, encompassing 223,098 square kilometers – almost the same size as the United Kingdom or Ghana (Ministry of Culture, Sports, and Tourism, 2009). Some 45 percent of this area, or 99,678 square kilometers, is considered cultivable, excluding reclaimed land areas. Mountainous terrain accounts for some two thirds of the territory, which is similar to Portugal or Ireland.

The Korean Peninsula is divided into two countries: South Korea (the Republic of Korea), which is a democratic and capitalistic state; and North Korea (Democratic People's Republic of Korea), a communist state. In addition to the mainland, the Korean peninsula includes some 3,200 islands. The peninsula shares its northern border with China and Russia. To the east is the East Sea, shared with Japan. To the west is the Yellow Sea.

As the world's 13th largest economy, South Korea's trade volume amounted to $728 billion USD in 2007, ranking 11th in the world. South Korea also has the fourth largest foreign reserves.

South Korea is the world's largest shipbuilding nation, and has been the industry leader for the past four years, accounting for 40 percent of the world's total shipbuilding orders. It is ranked third largest in semiconductor production (holding 11 percent of the global market share, particularly in terms of flash memory and Dynamic Random Access Memory (DRAM), fourth in digital electronic production, fifth in automobile manufacturing (producing over 3.8 million vehicles annually), and also fifth in textiles, steel, and petrochemicals.

Most South Koreans, especially politicians and media representatives, are sensitive to environmental issues. In 1990, the government established the Ministry of Environment with the mission of creating a sustainable and green country. The ministry employs measures to protect the country from threats of environmental pollution and diseases, and to enhance its international efforts to address global environmental problems.

Among the issues listed above, some may affect the occurrence of crime while others do not. Due to the geopolitical situation of South Korea – bordering with China, Russia, and Japan – transnational crimes, such as illegal migration, drug trafficking, and human trafficking, easily occur. For example, South Korea is a destination, transit, and/or source country for human trafficking. South Korean women are trafficked for commercial sexual exploitation to the United States, Japan, Hong Kong, Australia, New Zealand, and Canada. Meanwhile, South Korea is a destination country for women trafficked from Russia, Uzbekistan, Kazakhstan, the People's Republic of China (PRC), the Philippines, Thailand, and other Southeast Asian countries for sexual and labor exploitation (US Department of Justice, 2007: 129).

The geopolitical situation also raises criminal victimization of North Korean defectors living in South Korea. Until the end of 2008, South Korea received more than 10,000 North Korean defectors via China and Southeast Asian countries. North Korean defectors living in South Korea are more likely to become crime targets than native South Koreans because they do not have the educational and cultural backgrounds, which are necessary factors to adapt to the society. Some defectors become victims to fraud because they are not accustomed to a capitalistic way of life (Jang and Lee, 2006).

As of December 2008, there are 200,489 unauthorized foreign residents (Ministry of Justice, 2009). Many of them came from neighboring China and East Asia. Some of them are victims or perpetrators of human trafficking and drug trafficking.

South Korea, once known to be one of the world's poorest agrarian societies, has undertaken economic development since 1962 (Ministry of Culture, Sports, and Tourism, 2009). In less than four decades, it achieved what has become known as the "Miracle on the Hangang River." The economy has been transformed dramatically into an industrial society, developing rapidly from the 1960s, fueled by high savings and investment rates, and a strong emphasis on education. The outward-oriented economic development strategy contributed greatly to the rapid economic transformation. Based on this strategy, which used exports as the engine of growth, many successful development programs were implemented. As a result, from 1962 to 2007, the gross domestic product (GDP) increased from $2.3 billion USD to $969.9 billion USD, with its per capita GNI soaring from $87 USD to about $20,045 USD. In 1996, the nation became the 29th member country of the Organisation for Economic Co-operation and Development (OECD).

The economy showed a rapid recovery in domestic demand and exports from the recession caused by the global financial crisis in 2009. The global downturn, however, weakened domestic demand and severely affected GDP growth. In 2008, the GDP fell to 2.5 percent, well below the 5.0 percent of 2007 and the 2003–7 average of 4.4 percent. The pattern of growth throughout the year mirrored the progressive intensification of the global financial crisis and the consequent deterioration of the world economy. In 2008, GDP growth accelerated by a solid 5.8 percent in the first quarter, but then decelerated by 3.4 percent in the fourth quarter (Asia Development Bank, 2009).

According to the report by the Korean Statistical Information Service (2009), the average monthly household income in 2008 was 3.35 million Won ($3,300 USD) which has increased 4.5 percent annually since 2003. However, if the increase of prices of commodities is considered, then the household income has actually decreased 0.2 percent since 2003.

The Gini Index in 2006 was 35.1, ranking 85th out of 134 countries (NationMaster.com, n.d.). The Index has changed slightly in 2007 from 34.4 and to 34.8 in 2008 (Korean Statistical Information Service, 2009).

According to the national statistics (Korean Statistical Information Service, 2009), 17.1 percent of South Koreans in 2007 felt that they were relatively poor. In 2008, the percentage of those who categorized themselves as relatively poor slightly rose to 18.1 percent.

The largest occupational category in South Korea is the "clerk" classification, which is a white-collar job. The second largest one is that of "plant, machine operators, and assembler," followed by "salesperson," "skilled agricultural, forestry, and fishery worker," "professional," and "service worker," in that order.

The average unemployment rate during the period from 2002 to 2007 was 3.5 percent (Korean Statistical Information Service, 2009). These figures seem to be affected by a general assumption that the economic situation – especially poverty – was a major and fundamental factor impacting crime in the 1970s. Economic recession caused the weakness of government control, social disorganization, and in turn an increase in unemployment and poverty. Under such circumstances, people have more opportunities to commit crimes (Choi and Ki, 1999). Choi and Ki (1999) found an assertion in the 1970s that the increase in unemployment caused the increase in homicide six years later. However, this assumption was rejected by scholars in the 1980s (Chiricos, 1987; Cantor and Land, 1985). The relationship between poverty and crime was positive at one time and negative at another time. Chiricos (1987) argued that there was no relationship between unemployment rate and crime after he reviewed 63 empirical studies.

Although the effect of unemployment, poverty, and economic recession on crime is controversial, they do seem to affect the change in crime rates.

In South Korea, unemployment is one of the most significant variables to impact crimes. Jeon *et al.*'s survey on sexual assault (2007) shows that one third of a sample of sex offenders is unemployed and 16–20 percent of them are salespersons. The suicide rate is also closely related to unemployment. In 2004, 54.7 percent of those who committed suicide were unemployed (Park, 2007).

In regards to occupation, 32.1 percent of robbers are unemployed, 22.8 percent service workers, and 20.5 percent production workers, whereas 31.1 percent of thieves are production technicians, 21.3 percent service workers, and 11.5 percent owners of service businesses (Shim and Kim, 1990). Although it is difficult to assert a direct causal relationship between occupation/economic situation and crime, some studies show, to some extent, some relationship between them.

During the period from 2005 to 2008, the amount of goods exported has increased 13.5 percent on average annually, while imported goods on average increased 18.0 percent annually. The primary exports, in order of prevalence, are passenger motor vehicles, pulp and waste paper, transistors and valves, base metal ores, ships and boats, and petroleum products. The major import goods are crude petroleum, transistor and valves, natural gas, petroleum products, and automatic data processing equipment (Korean Statistical Information Service, 2009).

In 2008, South Korea produced 40,968 Tons of Oil Equivalent (TOE) of primary energy including coal, electricity, heat, nuclear power energy, and others (Korean Energy Management

Corporation, n.d.), while consumption per capita was 4.9 TOE. Most energy resources produced are coal and electricity, while coal and nuclear power are the most consumed energy. South Korea is only 17.2 percent energy independent and consumption continues to rise (e.g. increases of city gas, 15.2 percent; electricity, 13.5 percent; oil, 7.4 percent; and coal, 6.8 percent).

Standing at the apex of the executive branch, the President of the Republic of Korea, elected by a nationwide and direct ballot, serves a single five-year term with no additional terms being allowed (Prime Minister's Office, 10 August 2009).

South Korea's National Assembly is a unicameral legislature whose 299 members are elected to four-year terms by popular vote.

The legal system combines elements of continental European civil law, Anglo-American law, and Chinese classical thought (Jin, 2004). The highest court, the Supreme Court, consists of a chief justice appointed by the President and up to 13 other justices appointed by the President on recommendation of the chief justice with the approval of the National Assembly (Supreme Court, n.d.). Each justice serves a six-year term. The Constitutional Court rules on questions as to the constitutionality of laws. Other courts include appeals courts, district courts, and a family court. As of March 2008, there were 2,307 judges, 1,680 prosecutors, and 9,997 registered private attorneys (Ministry of Justice, n.d.).

As of 2009, there are six major political parties in South Korea: Grand National Party (GNP), the conservative, right-wing, ruling party; Democratic Party (DP), the leading opposition party with social liberalism; Liberal Forward Party (LFP), the third largest party with a conservative and right-wing ideology; Democratic Labor Party (DLP), a left-wing and nationalism oriented party; Renewal of Korea Party (RoKP), liberal and central; and New Progressive Party (NPP), a left-wing and social democratic party.

Between 2004 and 2006, telephone lines in South Korea were decreased from 26.6 million lines to 23.9 million lines, due to the increase in mobile telephones. During the same period, mobile telephone subscribers increased from 36.6 million to 40.2 million subscribers.

The rate of possession of television sets per 1,000 persons decreased from 458.0 in 2003 to 411.2 in 2005 and the rate of cable TV subscribers among 1,000 persons decreased from 282.2 in 2003 to 242.1 in 2005.

There are five major internet service providers (ISPs): LG Powercom, Korea Telecom, SK Telecom, Hanaro Telecom, and Samsung Networks. South Korea has one of the highest rates of Internet usage in the world (Life in Korea, 2009) at 7,220 users per 10,000 in 2007. Due to strong government support, it also has one of the highest rates of broadband connectivity, with most households being able to choose ISDN, ADSL, cable, or satellite in addition to traditional dial-up modems for connectivity.

In sum, telephone and internet use is frequently related to various types of crime committed. Recently, voice phishing – a type of fraud through telephone – has been a social problem among the general public. The scammers use a new form of identity theft, voice phishing, in order to obtain personal information via telecommunication after sending an email to online users telling them to call a telephone number to verify their personal information. The message normally says that your bank account will be closed due to a recent hacking incident. Then the scammers ask callers' security information. From April 2008 to February 2009, there were 266,263 cases of voice phishing reported to law enforcement agencies (Daum, 2009).

South Korea has been a target of cyber crime. It has the justifiable reputation of being one of the most wired nations in the world. After the Asian financial crisis devastated the South Korean economy in 1997, the Seoul city government, the national government, and the private sector made a concerted effort to move the country's economy from one reliant on heavy industry to one that included information technology – a shift that by most measures has been a resounding success. Today, an astonishing 95 percent of households have a broadband connection (Kim and Powell, 2009). The entire city of Seoul, whose metro-area population is over 10 million, is already one giant hot spot, with wireless access available from virtually anywhere within city limits for a small fee. Seoul has been named the world's most "advanced and efficient e-government" for several years by a UN sponsored e-government evaluation agency (ibid.).

However, South Korea is taking considerable risk by utilizing high technology, becoming a primary target by hackers, who challenge the advanced technology. The sophistication of computer criminal acts makes it difficult for government agencies to apprehend and prosecute cyber-criminals.

The recent case on Saturday, July 4, 2009 of cyber attacks against US and South Korean government websites is a good example. Cyber criminals launched sophisticated and powerful attacks against major US federal websites, knocking them offline throughout the weekend. The following Tuesday, the same types of attacks were made upon South Korean government and major commercial websites. In 2008, a total of 122,227 cases of cybercrimes occurred and were reported to the police in (National Police Agency, 2009).

As of 2007, South Korea has 103,000 kilometers of roads and about 78 percent of them are paved (Korean Statistical Information Service, 2009). The length of motorways (or highways) is 3,369 kilometers. The total length of railways is 3,125.30 kilometers and more than 1 million passengers use railways every day (http://blog.naver.com/kld5678, 2 October, 2002).

People

As of the end of 2007, South Korea's total population was estimated to be 48,456,369 with a density of 498 people per square kilometer (US Department of State, 2010). The capital city is Seoul with a population of approximately 10 million people.

The population grew 3 percent annually during the 1960s, but the growth slowed to 2 percent over the next three decades. In 2005, the rate decreased to 0.21 percent and is expected to further decline to 0.02 percent by 2020. The largest age group is under 15 years, followed by the group between 40 and 44 years, the group between 35 and 39 years, and then the group between 30 and 34 years. As a whole, the female population is larger than the male one.

According to OECD health data (2007), South Korea registered the greatest gain in life expectancy between 1960 and 2007, with an overall increase in longevity of 27 years, rapidly closing the average gap across OECD countries. In 1960, life expectancy in South Korea was 16 years below the OECD average. By 2007, it stood at 79.4 years, which is above the OECD average of 79.0.

Long-term inflows of foreigners to South Korea reached about 315,000 in 2006, an increase of almost 20 percent when compared to 2005. Net long-term migration of foreigners amounted to 132,000 in 2006, one of the highest figures ever recorded. In response to major changes in labor migration management, the migration of foreign workers has also gained importance. Under the Employment Permit System, foreign workers can work for up to three years in South Korea but must return to their origin country afterwards. In order to return to South Korea for another three years, the foreign worker must reside outside the country for at least six months (OECD, 2009).

South Koreans think of themselves as a homogeneous ethnic group although 0.1 percent of residents are foreign born. In 2009, there were 536,627 legitimate foreign-born residents in South Korea (Korean Statistical Information Service, 2009). Among those legitimate foreign-born residents, 31.1 percent were Korean-Chinese, 22.3 percent were from Southeast Asian countries, and 14.4 percent came from China. Although crimes committed by foreigners in 2008 make up

0.8 percent of the total crimes occurred (Supreme Prosecutor's Office, 2009), they are now an emerging social issue in South Korea.

South Korean culture includes a wide variety of religious elements that have shaped the people's way of thinking and behaving. According to a 2005 social statistics survey (Korean Statistical Information Service, 2009), 53.1 percent of South Koreans follow a specific religious faith. Buddhists account for most of the religious population (43 percent) followed by Protestants (34.5 percent), and Catholics (20.6 percent).

All South Koreans speak the same language with no dialect variations. They also write the same Korean alphabet. These have been decisive factors in forging their strong national identity (Ministry of Culture, Sports, and Tourism, 2009).

The South Korean education system consists of six years at elementary school, three years at middle school, and three years at high school. Elementary and middle schools are compulsory and the government pays school education fees for elementary and middle school students. High school graduates can choose to apply to two-year college or four-year university to attain higher education. About 80 percent of high school graduates go to college. In 2009, the Ministry of Education, Science and Technology introduced a comprehensive education fee support system that enables the integrated provision of tuition, meal fees, after-school program tickets, and communication expenses for students from low-income households (Ministry of Education, Science, and Technology, 2009). Before 2009, these types of support were separately operated.

Administration of justice

The South Korean criminal justice system is run by two branches of the government: the Executive and the Judiciary. While the court is a component of the Judiciary, the Public Prosecutor's Office and the police are under the control of the Executive branch. The correctional system is also under the Executive branch, with direct oversight from the Ministry of Justice.

There are three tiers of courts: the District Courts (including the specialized Family Court and Administrative Court), the courts of original jurisdiction; the High Courts, the intermediate appellate courts; and the Supreme Court, the highest court. The High Courts and the District Courts are divided into geographic districts.

The Supreme Court comprises the Chief Justice and 13 Justices, serving as the final and highest tribunal regarding civil, criminal, family, administrative, and military cases.

The Court Organization Act grants the courts general jurisdiction to preside over civil, criminal, administrative, electoral, and other litigious cases. It also decides on non-contentious cases and matters that fall under relevant provisions. In addition, military courts may be established under the Constitution as special courts to exercise jurisdiction over criminal cases in the military. The Supreme Court retains final appellate jurisdiction in all, including military, cases.

Although the Public Prosecutor's Office is under the supervision of the Ministry of Justice, which is under the control of the Executive branch, it is a functionally independent organization from the Ministry of Justice. It consists of a Supreme Public Prosecutor's Office, 5 High Public Prosecutor's Offices, 12 District Public Prosecutor's Offices, and their branches, each corresponding to a coordinate court. The Public Prosecutor's Office enjoys an independent status.

The national police system is a "central controlling" system in which the National Police Agency headquarters manages and controls personnel and budgets. Under the auspice of the National Police Agency, there are 14 regional agencies operating independently from the provincial governments.

Under the Ministry of Justice, the Correctional Service has four regional headquarters in major cities. As of March 31, 2008, a total of 47 correctional facilities were in operation: 32 correctional institutions and 10 detention centers, 1 vocational training correctional institution and 4 correctional branch offices. Since the 1980s, the emphasis of correctional administration has shifted from the punishment of offenders to correction and rehabilitation (Ministry of Justice, 2009).

Among four types of justice, South Korea seems to be a mixture of procedural justice, which emphasizes "fair play," and distributive justice, which emphasizes "fair share." South Korea also aims to implement the principles of restorative justice, which emphasize restitution and reconciliation between victims and offenders.

The main social control strategy relies on the rule of law. Every human right is protected by the constitution and relevant laws. However, public mentality plays an important role in social control. For example, protesters who organize violent demonstrations for their living needs are accepted by the public sympathy even though they violate the current demonstration law. Sometimes, public mentality is preferred to the rule of law.

Police, prosecutors, and judges have attempted to improve the human rights of criminal offenders for decades. Furthermore, every correctional facility has its own occupational programs to rehabilitate incarcerated offenders. Recently, the police and the courts are implementing the idea of restorative justice, with the assistance of the community. For example, juvenile offenders who commit property crimes are sent to reconciliation programs with victims and community volunteers.

Criminology

The most significant criminological and criminal justice research has been conducted by the Korean Institute of Criminology (KIC), founded by the Ministry of Justice and funded by the Prime Minister's Office. A part of that research is funded by other government organizations. In general, research is conducted by KIC itself or jointly with university professors, practitioners, and/or other research institutes.

Annually, KIC publishes 30–50 criminological and criminal justice books and reports. Research topics conducted and funded by KIC are selected by the National Advisory Committee. For example, the research on violent culture was one of the focal topics in 2008 and cybercrime in 2005.

Along with the major focal topics, KIC also conducts research on a single issue which is significant but has failed to attract the public attention. Research on arson and drink driving are good examples. Furthermore, KIC also produces the country's official criminological statistics, which are sent to the official site of the Korean Statistical Information Service.

Between 2004–8, KIC and relevant organizations have conducted research on crime and justice that is of current interest to South Korean society, such as criminal justice reform, including juvenile justice reform, cybercrime, violent organized crime, drug issues, correctional system improvement, crimes of inhumanity such as sex offenses, and the single issue of index crimes.

From 2004 to 2008, the Korean Ministry of Justice and criminal justice practitioners have concentrated their interests on criminal justice reform after some judges, prosecutors, and attorneys at law were found to have been involved in "unfair" criminal cases by using their extensive network of alumni and contacts. For instance, some adjudications of criminal cases at the court are affected by private attorneys at law who went to the same schools as the judges.

The focal issues of criminal justice reform in South Korea are 1) the improvement of legal services for the general public, 2) the introduction to law school education training program, and 3) the amendment of criminal laws related to the justice reform. For example, to protect people's rights from unfair legal procedure, Park (2004) proposed the reform of the court-appointed attorney system by raising the attorney's fee up to the appropriate level and introducing a legal aid system managed by the government. In this process, the Korean Ministry of Justice and the Korean Bar Association raised the issue to adopt the education system for the graduate school of law and amend criminal laws. Before this system, students used to attend a law school as undergraduates for four years. Now, the graduate schools of law in South Korea adopted the US system of law school. Research studies related to criminal justice reform and research figures in the three priority areas listed above have been studied by Park (2004), Ha (2004), Cho (2004), Kang (2007), Yoon (2008), and Oh (2008).

Restorative justice is, to some extent, a new idea in South Korea. Since the United Nations Office on Drugs and Crime raised this issue at the UN Commission on Crime Prevention and Criminal Justice in 2002, South Korea has begun to study and implement restorative justice in its reform efforts. For this, Kim (2004) developed the concept of restorative juvenile justice and feasibility of testing effectiveness in juvenile delinquency. Then, restorative justice started to be studied in earnest, beginning in 2006 with a pilot study to apply restorative justice to school violence (Kim and Lee, 2006) and continuing to include Kim (2004), Kim and Lee (2006), Hwang and Noh (2006), Kim (2006), Kim *et al.* (2007), and Kim (2008).

The KIC is the institution that the Prime Minister's office designated as the official organization for drug-trafficking research in 2002 and has taken the lead since that time (Kang, 2002; Kang and Lee, 2004; Kim and Kim, 2004; Kim *et al.*, 2005; Shin and No, 2006; Kang, 2007). Additionally, some universities as well as KIC are leading research organizations for organized crime (Toh, 2004; Tack, 2004; Kang, 2005; Hwang, 2005; Shin, 2006; Kang, 2007; Park, 2007; Cho *et al.*, 2007).

KIC has the best opportunities to approach correctional facilities officially and interview inmates when KIC's researchers conduct surveys at prisons. Due to this advantage, most research topics on corrections are conducted by KIC. KIC conducted seven projects on the correctional system in 2004, two in 2005, two in 2006, and one in 2007 (Park, 2004; Cho, 2004; Kim, 2004; Kim, Lee and Lee, 2005; Choi and Hwang, 2006; Jung, 2006; Choi *et al.*, 2007). Topics covered by those projects are various, from juvenile probation to rehabilitation of incarcerated women.

Research on cybercrime is very active because South Korea is one of the most vulnerable targets for cybercrime. Cybercrime research can be classified into two types: legal liability, reviewing laws related to cybercrime; and the current situation and environment of cybercrime (Choung, 2004, 2005; Tak, 2005; Kim, 2005, Hwang, 2005; Park, 2005; Lee, 2007).

Research issues on crimes against humanity are related to violation of human rights of minorities, including children, women, the elderly, and migrants. These types of research focus on current situations and countermeasures to solve problems (Hwang, 2004; Hwang, 2004; Yeon and Min, 2004; Jang, 2005; Jo, 2005; Kim, 2005; Jang and Lee, 2006; Cheon *et al.*, 2007; Jang *et al.*, 2008; Jeon, 2008).

There are some research surveys related to index crimes, such as murder, burglary, and robbery. Furthermore, there are surveys which are regularly conducted (e.g. a crime victimization survey). KIC conducts the South Korean crime victimization survey every three years (Jeon, 2004; Hwang, 2004; Park, 2004; Yeon, 2006; Kim *et al.*, 2006; Park, 2007; Jang and Yoo, 2007; Choi and Cho, 2007; Hong, 2008; Kang and Park, 2008).

There are different types of sampling in the research listed in the previous paragraphs. For some, a nationwide survey is conducted. For example, a crime victimization survey has been conducted every three years by collecting about 2,400 interviews from samples of households across the country. A juvenile victimization survey uses a similar kind of sampling strategy.

Second, some surveys collect samples by interviewing inmates and reviewing their criminal records. "The patterns and trends of homicide in South Korea" (Kang and Park, 2008) is an example. Researchers conducted face-to-face interviews with inmates who had committed murder.

Third, a particular sampling group is selected for a specific research topic. North Korean defectors, sex crime victims, and illegal migrants are examples. For example, the research study on North Korean defectors is based on interviews with 240 North Korean defectors living in South Korea (Jang and Lee, 2006).

Fourth, some research focuses attention on literature reviews and legal acts. Much criminal justice reform research is of this type.

For quantitative analyses, researchers use several kinds of statistical analysis, such as multivariate analysis, factor analysis, Lisrel, and so on, while the "HyperResearch" program is used for qualitative analysis.

Major datasets associated with crimes in South Korea including Index Crimes and Annual Survey are available at the website of Korean Institute of Criminology (http://www.kic.re.kr) and Korean Social Science Library (http://www.kossda.or.kr). Some of them are free of charge.

The key research institute on crime and criminal justice is the KIC established in 1989. Research on some issues, such as corruption and crime victimization of women, is conducted by the Korean Institute of Public Administration (http://www.kipa.re.kr) and the Korean Women's Development Institute (http://www.kwdi.re.kr).

Future research questions

1. Do some economic situations, such as poverty and business cycles, cause crimes?
2. What factors explain male-on-female sexual aggression?
3. Should prostitution be legalized in South Korea and for what purpose?
4. Should the criminal justice system in South Korea give preference to human rights over social order/stability?
5. Should the government provide more budgetary resources for the prevention of crime?

References

Asia Development Bank (2009) Asian development outlook 2009: rebalancing Asia's growth. Online at http://www.adb.org/documents/books/ado/2009/ (accessed December 7, 2010).

Cantor, D. and Land, K. C. (1985) Unemployment and crime rates in the post World War II United States: a theoretical and empirical analysis. *American Sociological Review*, 50: 317–32.

Cheon, Youngsil, Kang, Eun Young, Park, Hyungmin, Kim, Hyejeong, Hwang, Taejeong, and Jeong, Yuhee (2007), Types of sexual assault and measures against recidivism. Seoul: Korean Institute of Criminology.

Cheong, Wan (2005). The rational regulation of illegal and harmful information in cyberspace. Kyunghee University.

Cho, Byung-In. (2004). A study on the prison monitoring by civilians. Seoul: Korean Institute of Criminology.

Cho, Byung-In, Shin, Eui Gi, Kim, Kwang Joon, Kang, Seok-Gu, Yoon, Hae-Sung, Choi, Eung Ryul, Huh, Koung Mi, and Song, Bong-Kyu (2007). Countermeasures against organized violence crimes. Seoul: Korean Institute of Criminology, Dongkuk University, and Keimung University.

Choi, Insup and Kwang-Do KL. (1999). *Crime in the era of economic depression in South Korea*. Korea: Korean Institute of Criminology.

Choi, Soon Young and Cho, Jin-Uk (2007). Institutional control over the corrupt practices of civil servants. Korea Institute of Public Administration and Korea University.

Choi, Young-Shin and Hwang, Jung Im (2006). A study on the support programs for rehabilitation of incarcerated women. Seoul: Korean Institute of Criminology.

Choi, Young-Shin, Hong, Young-Oh, Lee, Bub-Ho, Jung, Young-Jin, Lee, Chang-Han, and Kim, Ahn Sic (2007). Treatment in the reentry process of prisoners. Seoul: Korean Institute of Criminology and Korea Correctional Service.

Choung, Wan. (2004). International cooperation for cybercrime prevention. Seoul: Korean Institute of Criminology.

Chiricos, T. G. (1987). Rates of crime and unemployment: an analysis of aggregate research evidence. *Social Problems*, 34: 187–212.

Daum (2009). Voice phishing cases. Online at http://blog.daum.net/ccpost/7829127 (accessed December 7, 2010).

Ha, Ta Hoon (2004). Direction of progress and application in suspects at pre-trial detention hearings. Korea University.

Hong, Young-Oh (2008). *Juvenile victimization survey in Korea, 2008*. Seoul: Korean Institute of Criminology.

Hwang, J.-T. (2004). *Cognition on the serious problem of current school violence*. Seoul: Korean Institute of Criminology.

—— (2004). Target selection of burglars robbers and thieves. Seoul: Korean Institute of Criminology.

Hwang, J.-T. and Noh, Seong-Ho (2006). *Facilitator's manual for juvenile restorative justice program*. Seoul: Korean Institute of Criminology.

Hwang, Man Sung (2004). The measures in the criminal procedure for protection of sexually abused children. Seoul: Korean Institute of Criminology.

—— (2005). Activate cooperation between criminal justice system and health care system for drug offender treatment. Seoul: Korean Institute of Criminology.

Hwang, Tae Jung (2005). Improvement of the legal system of personal data protection. Seoul: Korean Institute of Criminology.

Jang, Joon Oh (2005). Illegal migration between South Korea and China and its countermeasures. Seoul: Korean Institute of Criminology.

Jang, Joon Oh and Lee, Jung-Hwan (2006). Victimization of North Korean defectors in South Korea. Seoul: Korean Institute of Criminology.

Jang, Joon Oh and Yoo, Hong Joon (2007). Workplace theft in South Korea. Seoul: Korean Institute of Criminology and Sungkyunkwan University.

Jang, Joon Oh, No, Yong Joon, Yu, Hong Choon, Lee, Wan Soo, and Jung, Tae In (2008). Elderly crime and its victimization. Seoul: Korean Institute of Criminology and Sungkyunkwan University.

Jeon, Youngsil. (2004). Drunk driving in South Korea. Seoul: Korean Institute of Criminology.

—— (2008). The relationship between child maltreatment and juvenile delinquency. Seoul: Korean Institute of Criminology.

Jeon, Youngsil, Kang, Eun-Young Park, Hyungmin, Kim, Hye Jung, Hwang, Tae-Jung, and Jung, Eun-Hee (2007). Types of sexual assault and measures against recidivism. Seoul: Korean Institute of Criminology, Yeungnam University, and Kyonggi University.

Jin, Oh Seung (2004) Overview of legal systems in the Asia-Pacific region. April 10. Online at http://scholarship.law.cornell.edu/lps_lsapr/6/ (accessed March 31, 2010).

Jo, Eun Kyung (2005). Application of criteria-based content analysis (CBCA) to the Korean child sexual abuse victim statement. Hallym University.

Jung, Jin Woo (2006). A study on the unification of arrest system. Seoul: Korean Institute of Criminology.

Jung, Young-Jin (2006). Correctional treatment model for long-term inmates. Seoul: Korean Institute of Criminology.

Kang, Eun-Young (2002). An empirical study on drug abuse and demand reduction strategies. Seoul: Korean Institute of Criminology.

—— (2007). Strategies on the drug prevention and drug offender rehabilitation. Seoul: Korean Institute of Criminology.

Kang, Eun-Young and Lee, Seong-Sik (2004). Drug abuse and attitudes toward drugs in Korea. Soongsil University.

Kang, Eun-Young and Park, Hyungmin (2008). The patterns and trends of homicides in Korea (II). Seoul: Korean Institute of Criminology.

Kang, Seok Ku (2007). Freezing of the gangster organization fund. Seoul: Korean Institute of Criminology.

Kang, Suk-Goo (2005). The system for following illegal funds. Seoul: Korean Institute of Criminology.

Kim, Eun-Kyung (2004). An international review of restorative juvenile justice. Seoul: Korean Institute of Criminology.

—— (2006). A pilot study of restorative justice practices responding against the school bullying in Korea. Seoul: Korean Institute of Criminology.

—— (2008). A framework for juvenile justice reform in 21st century[//] : the effect of restorative justice practices. Responding against young offences. Seoul: Korean Institute of Criminology.

Kim, Eun-Kyung and Lee, Ho-jung. (2006). A pilot study of restorative justice practices responding against the school bullying in South Korea. Seoul: Korean Institute of Criminology.

Kim, Eun-Kyung, Kang, Eun-Young, Kwan, Oh-Seong, Kim, Han-Kyun, Park, Hyo Jeong, and Hwang, Man Seong (2005). Reforms of drug demand reduction and treatment system for drug offenders. Seoul: Korean Institute of Criminology.

Kim, Eun-Kyung, Kim, Ji-Sun, Lee, Seung Hyun, Kim, Sung Un, Won, Hae-Ook, and Lee, Ho-Joong (2007). A framework for juvenile justice reform in the 21st century (i): the new countermeasures of the actual and expected restorative justice. Seoul: Korean Institute of Criminology.

Kim, Hye Kyung (2005). The expression in cyberspace and criminal liability. Seoul: Korean Institute of Criminology.

Kim, Ji Sun (2004). Aftercare of discharged juvenile delinquent. Seoul: Korean Institute of Criminology.

Kim, Ji Sun and Lee, Dong-Won (2006). *Crime victimization survey in South Korea* (IV). Seoul: Korean Institute of Criminology.

Kim, Ji-Sun, Kim, Ji-Young, Park, Mi-Suk, and Hong, Young-Oh (2006). Crime victimization survey in Korea (IV). Seoul: Korean Institute of Criminology.

Kim, Ji Young. (2005). Elder abuse and generational conflict. Seoul: Korean Institute of Criminology.

Kim, Soung Yee, and Kim, Eun-Ah (2004). The development of treatment programs for drug offenders. Ehwa Women's University. Online at http://www.kic.re.kr/english/research/ebook_form.asp?chapter=2004c030 (accessed December 7, 2010).

Kim, S. and Powell, B. (2009). Seoul: world's most wired megacity gets more so. *New York Times*, August 24. Online at http://www.time.com/time/magazine/article/0,9171,1916302,00.html (accessed December 7, 2010).

Kim, Yang Gon, Lee, Soo Jeong, and Lee, Min Shik (2005). A study on the development of assessment instruments for juvenile probationers. Seoul: Korean Institute of Criminology.

—— (2005). Development of assessment instruments for juvenile probation. Seoul: Korean Institute of Criminology.

Korean Energy Management Corporation (n.d.). National GHG emission total information system: energy statistics. Online at http://www.kemco.or.kr/data/e_static/energy_chart/energy_static_view_main.asp (accessed December 7, 2010).

Korean Institute of Criminology (2008). Annual Report 2008. Public Relations & International Cooperation Center, KIC.

Korean Statistical Information Service (2009). Statistical database: population, household. Online at http://kosis.kr/eng/database/database_001000.jsp?listid=B&subtitle=Population, Household (accessed December 7, 2010).

Lee, Seong-Shik (2007). An integrating study for considering both causal and control factors across the types of youth cybercrime. Soongsil University.

Life in Korea (2009). Internet. Online at http://www.lifeinKorea.com/Information/Comms/internet.cfm (accessed December 7, 2010).

Ministry of Culture, Sports, and Tourism (2009). Exploring Korea. Online at http://www.korea.net/Korea (accessed November 25, 2010).

Ministry of Education, Science, and Technology (2009). Education for the future: science and technology for the future. Online at http://english.mest.go.kr (accessed November 25, 2010).

Ministry of Justice (n.d.). Justice system: overview. Online at http://www.moj.go.kr/HP/ENG/eng_02/eng_2040.jsp (accessed December 7, 2010).

Ministry of Justice (2009). Korea Immigration Service: statistics of unauthorized foreign residents. Online at http://www.moj.go.kr/HP/TIMM/imm_06/imm_2008_12.jsp (accessed November 25, 2010).

National Police Agency (2009). Cybercrime statistics. Online at http://police.go.kr/infodata/pds_07_total pds_03_01.jsp#none (accessed December 7, 2010).

NationMaster.com (n.d.). Economy statistics: distribution of family income: Gini Index (2006) by country. Online at http://www.nationmaster.com/graph/eco_dis_of_fam_inc_gin_ind-distribution-family-income-gini-index&date=2006 (accessed December 7, 2010).

Oh, Young Keun (2008). Reforming the Act on the Punishment of Sexual Crimes and the Protection of Victims Thereof. Hanyang University.

Organisation for Economic Co-operation and Development (OECD) (2007). Health data. Online at http://www.oecdbookshop.org/oecd/results.asp?TAG=&CID=&LANG=EN&PLANG=&SORT=sort_date%2Fd&STEM=true&SF1=Title&ST1=oecd+health+data%2C+statistics&SF3=SubjectCode&ST3=&st4=not+E4+or+E5+or+P5&sf4=SubVersionCode&ds=oecd+health+data%2C+statistics%3B+All+Subjects%3B+ (accessed December 10, 2010).

—— (2009). Country notes: Korea. International migration outlook 2008. OECD Publishing. pp. 256–7. Online at http://www.oecd-ilibrary.org/social-issues-migration-health/international-migration-

outlook-2008/korea_migr_outlook-2008-23-en;jsessionid=4pe6eqj0d733e.delta (accessed November 25, 2010).
Park, Hyungmin (2004). Arson in South Korea. Seoul: Korean Institute of Criminology.
—— (2005). A research on the online illegal and harmful website. Seoul: Korean Institute of Criminology. Online at http://www.kic.re.kr/english/research/ebook_form.asp?chapter=2005c014 (accessed December 7, 2010).
—— (2007). Trends and patterns on suicide in Korea. Seoul: Korean Institute of Criminology.
Park, Jeong Sun (2004). Delinquency in the making of juveniles in probation with a life course perspective. Seoul: Korean Institute of Criminology
Park, Kyung Rae. (2007). Exploring the income resource of Korean organized crime groups. Seoul: Korean Institute of Criminology.
Prime Minister's Office (n.d.). Government: executive branch. Online at http://www.pmo.go.kr (accessed August 10, 2009).
Shim, Younghee and Kim, Sung-eun (1990). Robbery and theft in Korea. Seoul: Korean Institute of Criminology.
Shin, Eui Gi (2006). Legislative introduction program of the United Nations Convention against Transnational Organized Crime. Seoul: Korean Institute of Criminology.
Shin, Eui Gi and No, Joo Ho (2006). Control of precursor chemicals of drugs. Seoul: Korean Institute of Criminology and Kyunghee University.
Supreme Court (n.d.). Judges. Supreme Court. Online at http://eng.scourt.go.kr/eng/judiciary/judges.jsp (accessed December 7, 2010).
Supreme Prosecutor's Office (2008) Analytical reports on crimes.
—— (2009). Analytical report on crimes. Online at http://www.spo.go.kr/user.tdf?a=user.pm.PmApp&chungcd=01000000&catmenu=030102&c=1001&seq=2116&x=19&y=5 (accessed December 7, 2010).
Tack, H. S. (2004). Reform policy on money laundering and organized crimes. Seoul: Korean Institute of Criminology.
Tak, Hee Sung (2005). The realities and legal regulations of the infringement of electronic information. Seoul: Korean Institute of Criminology.
Toh, Joong Jin (2004). Changing trends and policies in organized crimes. Seoul: Korean Institute of Criminology.
Tongil Ilbo (2002) (http://blog.naver.com/kld5678).
US Department of Justice (2007). Trafficking in persons report 2007. Online at http://www.state.gov/g/tip/rls/tiprpt/2007/ (accessed December 7, 2010).
US Department of State (2010). Background note: South Korea. Online at http://www.state.gov/r/pa/ei/bgn/2800.htm (accessed December 7, 2010).
Yeon, Seong Jin (2006). The trend of public official crimes in South Korea, 1964–2004. Seoul: Korean Institute of Criminology.
Yeon, Seong-Jin and Min, Su-Hong (2004) Preventing delinquency among runaway youths in South Korea. Seoul: Korean Institute of Criminology and Kyonggi University.
Yoon, Hae Sung (2008). Criminal special act amendment: industry, trade and scientific technology, information area. Seoul: Korean Institute of Criminology.

42

Mexico

The state of criminology and public safety

Mario Arroyo Juarez and Veronica Martinez Solares[1]

Introduction

In Mexico, crime, the criminal justice system and particularly criminological research, can be divided into two main axes. The first axis is an academic aspect that is very similar to other Latin American countries. It consists of the assimilation and acceptance of a positivist criminology which involves a series of isolated and fragmented studies by some key researchers from various scholarly domains, continuously subordinated to law, especially as a part of criminal science. The monopoly of the legal perspective in criminology has favored the dominance of legal discourse over empirical research. The second axis, which began in the early 1990s, took a different course from the criminological discourse and developed under the concept of public safety. Due to this perspective and to the notable increase in crime rates recorded in 1994, there was a boom in legislative activity, including the incorporation of public safety as a state responsibility in the Constitution. At this time, the first public security law in the country was created (that of the Federal District), as well as the General Law of Coordination of the National Public Security System, the Federal Law against Organized Crime and the Federal Preventive Police Act, among others. It was also in the early 1990s that scholars from disciplines besides law—such as political scientists, economists, psychologists and sociologists—started contributing to crime research. In this way, criminological discourse was displaced by other approaches whose only common ground is to take crime and the institutions as an object of study.

Mexico is the fifth largest nation in the Americas. Its total area is 1,964,375 square kilometers, of which 1,959,248 square kilometers is land mass area and 5,127 square kilometers islands. To the north, it shares a 3,152 kilometer border with the United States, while the border with Guatemala spans 956 kilometers, and with Belize, 193 kilometers. The population in Mexico is 112.3 million, of whom 51.1 percent are women, and 48.9 percent men. Its population is the 11th largest in the world and the third in America, only after the United States and Brazil. The average annual population growth in the period 2005–9 was 0.86 percent. The population density is 53 inhabitants per kilometer. The official language is Spanish; however, about 4.6 percent of the population speaks an indigenous language. Three quarters (76.5 percent) of the population is Catholic. In addition, 59.42 percent of the population is economically active and accounts for 93.59 percent of the employed population; unemployment stands at 6.41 percent and represents the highest percentage in the last five years (INEGI, 2009). Due to the worldwide economic crisis gross domestic product (GDP) has fluctuated in recent years, so while for June 2009 GDP was $854 billion USD, in the same period in 2008 it was $1,182 billion USD, thus decreasing 8.2 percent in real terms. The GDP (2007) per capita is estimated at $9,717 USD (IMF, 2009). Between 2006 and 2008, the proportion of people living in extreme poverty increased from 13.8 percent to 18.2 percent and the percentage of people below the poverty line in the country increased from 42.6 percent to 47.4 percent. The Gini coefficient (INEGI, 2008b) in 2008 was 0.482, while the mid-year current inflation is 5.96 (Banco de México, 2009).

Mexico is a federal republic composed of 31 free and sovereign states and one Federal District (Mexico City). Each state and Mexico City have their own constitution, local congress and autonomous judiciary. The president and governors are elected by direct vote for a period of six years. Therefore, the structure of the government includes the Federal Executive Branch (President of the Republic) and 32 local executive powers. The federal congress is bicameral with a Senate that is elected for six years, and a Chamber of Representatives, elected for three years. The states are divided into municipalities. Each municipality has an autonomous administration headed by a mayor, who is responsible for providing all public services to citizens, including public safety. The total number of municipalities in the country is 2,454 (INEGI, 2008a).

Administration of justice

The justice system is a mix of the United States constitutional system and the Roman-Germanic tradition, so it is considered as part of the civil law tradition and based on codes. Both the written Constitution and the organic design of the functions of institutions are in laws and codes because of the strict principle of legality. The main protagonists of the criminal justice system are the police, prosecutors, judges and prison system, described later, according to the Mexican constitutional sections. The Executive Power is responsible for preventing crimes through federal police (section 21), investigating them, prosecuting them, accusing, pressing formal charges and setting sentences through the prison system (section 18). The Legislature establishes what conduct is criminal based on social requirements (section 73-XXI), the basis of due process (section 20) and what penalties will be implemented (section 73-XXI). The judiciary is the establishment of administration of justice (section 17) and controls the constitutionality of acts issued by the two previous powers (sections 104, 105). In this context, the two main jurisdictions, federal and local, are defined by the Congresses. The Federal Congress has the authority to enact those behaviors that constitute federal crimes through the Federal Crime Code or special laws such as the Federal Law against Organized Crime, while state legislatures have the same authority, but on acts unrelated to the federation.

Since the beginning, citizens have had a difficult time understanding the criminal justice system, but especially since 1994. It has become a complex jigsaw puzzle, mainly because of the extensive number of constitutional amendments[2] and legal reforms, as well as their difficult implementation. Another relevant factor is the coexistence of two types of criminal systems: the traditional/inquisitorial system founded in 1917, and the adversarial/guarantor system, not yet widespread. As a federation, changes also occur frequently at the local level.

With the creation of the National Public Security System (through the 1994 law Ley General que Establece las Bases de Coordinación del Sistema Nacional de Seguridad Pública, or LGEBSNSP) Mexico began a period in which public safety became the focal point for preventive police officials, prosecutors, courts, those responsible for preventive prison, enforcement of sentences and treatment of juvenile offenders and those charged with protection of strategic facilities in the country. Essentially the National Public Security System began as a coordinating body for all three levels of government in the matter. On 2 January 2009, the law that created it (LGEBSNSP) was abrogated by the new General Law of National Public Safety System, which identifies it as the highest authority for coordinating the National Council for Public Security (NCPS). The NCPS has four working units national: the Administration of Justice, Administration of Secretaries of Public Safety or its equivalent, Administration of the Penitentiary System and Municipal Public Security. Its operating body is the Executive Secretariat of the National Public Security System that includes the National Information, Crime Prevention and Citizen Participation, and Police Certification and Accreditation.

Similar to most Latin American countries, police forces are divided, on one level, into two categories according to areas of responsibility: prevention and investigation. The role of the preventive police is to maintain order and public safety (sections 21, 115-III-h) while the investigative/ministerial police is responsible for investigating crimes under the command of the *Ministerio Público* (MP). Both police are civil institutions although there is a strong tendency in the country towards the militarization of police forces. A second level is the authority on which they depend. There are municipal preventive police forces, and state and federal police. The number of these different forces is imprecise depending on which source is consulted. In Mexico, there are between 1,661 (Garcia, 2006) and 3,000 (Reames, 2003) agencies in the three different levels. Thus, there are serious problems of coordination both in terms of operations and budgets. After ten years of formal existence of the Federal Preventive Police (PFP) from 1999, the Federal Police took over the power in 2009 to perform new investigations due to a constitutional reform in 18 June 2008. However, the concentration in a single agency of preventive and investigative powers is not yet a legal reality, although this occurs de facto via the Ministry of Federal Public Security (30 November 2000). In the course of federal reforms, the Federal Bureau of Investigation (*Agencia Federal de Investigaciones* or AFI), composed of investigative police belonging to the Attorney General's Office (*Procuraduría General de la República*, PGR), began operations in November 2001 despite their lack of a legal framework, only to disappear with the creation of the Ministerial Federal Police Reform dated 29 May 2009, after eight years. Neither the PFP nor the AFI, now both extinct, were ever evaluated on their performance.

Both federal and local *Ministerios Públicos* (public prosecutors) are the central operational authorities of the Attorney General's offices. They are responsible for both the investigation and the prosecution of crimes. Like the judiciary, jurisdiction responsibility changes from local to federal or vice versa depending on the type of crime. The Attorney General's Office has also been the subject of the regulatory sway as the Organic Law of 10 May 1996 was followed by another one on 27 December 2002, only to be substituted by a third on 29 May 2009, which seemed to be a domino effect of the constant constitutional modifications affecting the criminal justice system. Again, the arguments were focused on the crisis of insecurity in the country and strategies for combating drug dealing. On the other hand, the judiciary is divided into federal and local levels. The federal courts have jurisdiction over those crimes contained in the Federal Criminal Code and other special laws (like the Federal Law against Organized Crime and the Domain Extinction Act). It consists (section 96) of the Supreme Court of Justice, the Electoral Court; 188 collegiate circuit courts (21 criminal) each one with three magistrates dealing with the *Amparo* (Mexican *habeas corpus*), 76 unitary circuit courts (6 criminal) which include one magistrate each on charge of the appeals; and 307 one-magistrate district courts (54 criminal). With the constitutional reform in 2008 (section 16), there are seven Special Criminal Federal Courts in Searches, Bail and Intervention of Communication (Consejo de la Judicatura Federal, 2008). State judiciary systems follow a similar structure, but their jurisdiction differs according to the type of crime.

At the federal level, the decentralized administrative institution of Prevention and Social Rehabilitation of the Ministry of Public Security is responsible for detention centers and prisons. According to the Constitution, the levels of the prisons and detention are categorized according to the competent authority and legal status, sex and age of the inmate population. The first distinction is made by arrests at different authoritative locations.[3] Likewise, according to the legal status, detained but not convicted persons accused must be sent to jails, whereas sentenced individuals are sent to prisons; while men and women, adolescents and adults deprived of their liberty should be held in separate facilities. Another category is related to the dangerousness, in which case the centers will be minimum, medium and high security. In Mexico, there are 432 prisons of which 7 are federal, 10 belong to the Federal District, 323 are state, and 92 are municipal.

There are two criminal justice systems in the country. Each goes through a different process and institutions and has different functions. The first one is the inquisitive or traditional model founded in 1917. The second model is based on oral trials, similar to a North American model combined with the hearing process rules from the Chilean style (2008 reform).

In the first stage of the traditional model (see Figure 42.1), an individual reports a crime to the *Ministerio Público* (MP), preferably from the region where the crime occurred. Then the MP requests the judicial police[4] to make an investigation based on the report. There are many ways to proceed with the investigations and in some cases the investigators (judicial or preventive police) can have "probable cause" or enough elements to identify the suspect, for instance when the perpetrator was apprehended *in flagrante delicto*. In this situation, the suspect is brought and put under custody of the MP. In other cases, the MP conducts a preliminary investigation to decide whether a case should be pursued or not. If there is enough evidence, the case is brought before a judge. From the time of arrest or police detention, the MP has 48 hours (96 hours if it is organized crime) to determine whether the accused should be presented to a judge or if the case should be dismissed. The decision to pursue criminal charges against a suspect is called "*consignación*" (i.e. formal charges), and it is done when the investigation has finished and the MP has made an accusation. After formal charges have been made, the judge has 72 hours to hold a hearing to determine whether there is enough evidence against the accused for the crime pursued by the MP. The accused must be present in this hearing but the presence of the victim is not mandatory. At the end of the hearing, the judge will make a finding of probable responsibility

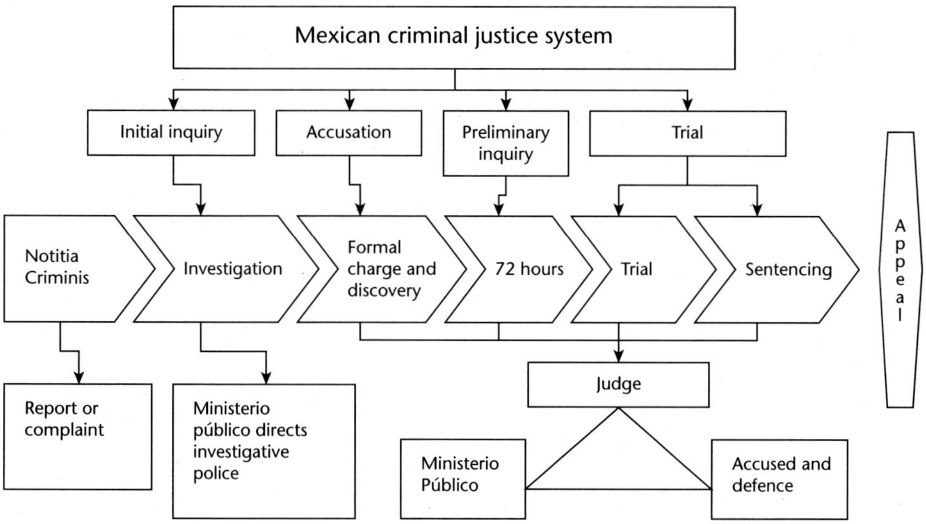

Figure 42.1 Mexican criminal justice system

or liberty due to lack of evidence. Depending on the crime, the accused may be released by bail bond or remain in custody. There is no bond for those accused of committing violent or organized crimes. Once the probable responsibility is determined, the trial will commence. The most well-known characteristics of the Mexican justice system are the practice of multiple hearings over a long period of time; however, the whole process takes place mostly in writing as there is an absence of "live" testimonies, "live" counter argumentation, "live" jury, and/or "live" judge.

Sentencing occurs approximately 15 working days after the final hearing. The various shortcomings in management, issues in processing, and systemic problems, have been documented by Zepeda (2004a). On the other hand, on June 19, 2008, an extensive criminal reform was published to deal with public safety and organized crime. A period of eight years was given for full implementation of the reforms, which include reforming local constitutions and several state laws to adhere to the new constitutional amendments. The current justice reforms include strategic and tactic crime prevention, public oral trials proceedings, pre-trial release, due process, discovery in early stages, plea bargaining, specific warrants, searches, and restorative justice. Undoubtedly, it follows the Anglo-Saxon model, but without juries and precedents. The Mexican government (Cámara de Diputados, 2009) devoted 0.52 percent of total GDP in 2007 to "Order, Security and Justice," and 0.73 percent in 2009.

Criminology

From the 1940s to the 1970s, Mexican economy and urban development overlapped with the debate on "law and order" in industrialized countries, but also with the revolutionary movements in Latin America, along with different perspectives on culture and ideology. The context brought a renewed interest in problems related to criminal matters. This particular state of the affairs created two schools of criminological thought. The first one, a positivist school of criminology, attached to the old tradition of the late nineteenth century, was particularly concerned as the study of offenders, the causes of crime, and a movement oriented towards public policy analysis, specifically towards prison policies. On the other hand, a more critical school of thought focused on studying the state and its control institutions. Incarceration as state policy served to encourage prison construction and the need for new control professionals: clinical psychologists, criminologists, social workers and forensic scientists. For instance, in September 1974, at the Autonomous University of Nuevo León, the first bachelor's degree in Criminology in Mexico was created. In 1975, Alfonso Quiroz, professor of many generations of scholars, founded the Mexican Society of Criminology, and in 1976 the National Institute of Criminal Sciences was established. To date, this institution has been the national leading institution working on criminological issues.

Due to the struggle for democracy in the 1960s and 1970s, there was the emergence of new publishers dealing with articles on criminology. The Fondo de Cultura Económica (Economic Culture Fund) and the publishing house Porrúa had been the main official publishers for Positivist criminology. Siglo XXI Editores, one of the new publishers at this time, started to publish books on critical thinking, ideas and studies to expose the power structure at the time and its excesses to explain the roots of the emergence of social upheaval and a dominant party authoritarian regime. Thus, books sharing the same perspectives were published first from Siglo XXI Editores in Spanish, such as *The law as obstacle to social change* by Novoa (1975), *Discipline and punish* by Foucault (1976) *Critical criminology* by Taylor *et al.* (1975), and *The future of prisons* by Morris (1978). Because there was a lack of native theoretical and empirical research in Mexico, Mexican criminology was also influenced by South American thought, and those books about their criminological research. Well-known authors such as Rosa del Olmo (Venezuela), Eugenio Zafaroni (Argentina) and Elias Neuman (Argentina) and all the conclusions of the authors remain respected. There were two opposite perspectives: the authoritarian states of the region, including Mexico, did not need public policy guidance on how to deal with the police or the criminal system, but rather strategies to maintain the *status quo* and to keep it under control even by using torture or enforced disappearance against all kind of social deviance, including offenders.

As mentioned before, criminology is not only the study of crime, but in Mexico, because of the lack of theoretical and empirical studies of its own, this discipline has evolved as an appendix of criminal science. Thus, it failed to develop and to be recognized as its own. Although trapped between the inheritance of Positivism and the combative critical criminology, there were few exceptions, and one of them was the National Institute of Criminal Sciences (INACIPE). INACIPE, as a creative space where individual efforts become notable, undoubtedly prevented criminology from becoming extinct in Mexico.

It was not until the beginning of the 1990s, when the Mexican authoritative state began to break down, that crime and its related institutions started to be studied and examined in a more consistent manner. The crucial year was 1994 for several reasons. In this way, the old and inefficient concept of "procurement of justice" had in front of it a new competitor in resources, in bureaucracy, the legislative arena, the academic arena and in empirical investigation. Added to these changes, the human rights discourse was another significant area of study that became part of the public debate. It is understandable that without an institutionalized criminology – in other words, without any human resources nor empirical previous investigations – the majority of the legal reforms and the creation of institutions and police reforms, prisons, etc. were made without any solid scientific foundation. The great diversity of subjects began to surface and be addressed by a large array of multidisciplinary experts, with multiple methods and different qualitative studies. Even today, we find a moot debate among academics, because each investigator has a monopoly on his/her subject. The emergence of drug trafficking and its transnational pervasiveness since 1985 have drawn attention to governmental and media interest. In a country such as Mexico where the media are considered a substitute for real scientific investigation, journalists' texts became the main source for the general public to understand the causes of crime in general or of a specific type of crime. Thus, in the 1980s and 1990s, we witnessed a proliferation of a type of literature termed "shadow criminology."

In Mexico, as in other Latin American countries and even in Spain (Barberet, 2005), research on crime, the criminal system or related public policies is not being addressed from a criminological point of view. Instead, crime is studied from a political science, legal, sociological, historical or even journalistic point of view. Books on criminology are not abundant; the majority were written decades ago and have undergone several editions. These major books continue to be used at the universities or at police academies. Some key titles are: *Manual de Criminología* (Orellana, 1978), *Criminología* (Rodríguez, 1981), *Criminología clínica* (Rodríguez, 1995), *Criminología. Introducción al estudio de la conducta antisocial* (López, 1991) and *Manual de criminología* (Barrita, 2006). A pioneering book is *Seguridad pública en México* written by Samuel González, Ernesto López Portillo and Arturo Yáñez (1994). In it, a first-time diagnostic on the police is done and some public policies are proposed. Each author has continued a fruitful career on their own. González has written on the criminal system and its reform (González *et al.*, 2005), on organized crime (González and Flores, 2007), and on the legitimate use of force (Mendieta *et al.*, 2009). Yañez has studied the Mexican police from a historical point of view (2000) and the institutional model on the federal investigative police (2006). López Portillo (2003) has researched the police in Mexico, their political functions and needed reforms. Luis Astorga, from the UNAM's Social Research Institute, is an authority on research on drug trafficking. His sociological focus was pioneering in the study of Mexican narco-trafficking subculture (1995). He also dealt with its regional and international impact (2003), and recently has researched the role that the militia plays in the drug conflict (2007). The point of view of critical criminology can be appreciated from a series of volumes titled *Ciudades seguras,* including*: Cultura, sistema penal y criminalidad* by Tenorio (2002), *Análisis y evaluación de leyes en materia de prevención delictiva* by Pérez (2002), *Percepción de la Inseguridad* by González (2002) and *Fenomenología de la delincuencia* by Kala (2003). With a broader vision and touching on subjects of relevance to the Latin American region there is: Rico, *Justicia penal y transición democrática de América Latina* (1997). There are other relevant and well documented books with a legal approach such as *Crimen sin castigo. Procuración de justicia penal y ministerio público en México* (2004a), *La justicia penal en la agenda del Estado de derecho en México* (2004b), and *Los retos de la eficacia y la eficiencia en la seguridad ciudadana y la justicia penal en México* (2006), written by Zepeda. Azaola has conducted a great many pioneering works on the study of crime from a gender and anthropological perspective, including *El delito de ser mujer* (1996b), *Imagen y autoimagen de la policía de la ciudad de México* (2006). Alvarado's (2008) *La reforma de la justicia en México* is a major publication of the state of criminology which shows different themes and points of view.

In Mexico there is no reliable system of statistics on public safety to allow proper, timely decision making. Most available public crime data correspond to the area of administration of justice, and consist primarily of information generated by the National Institute of Statistics and Geography (INEGI). The National Public Security System (with information provided by the local attorney general's office), is another source of information, although accessibility is strictly limited. The problem with statistics generated from these two sources is that they only cover part of the criminal world. Consequently, these statistics tend to be incomplete, biased and/or unreliable, especially if used for planning, research and public policy analysis. This has become more evident with the launch, and from the result, of victimization surveys. Victim surveys have served to grasp the scale of crimes in Mexico by focusing on another part of the criminal world, especially unrecorded crimes. The most recent and comprehensive polls are conducted by the Citizens' Institute for Studies on Insecurity (ICESI).

National Institute of Statistics and Geography (Instituto Nacional de Estadística y Geografía)

One of the main sources of information is the databases published and generated by the Instituto Nacional de Estadística y Geografía (INEGI). Within the catalogue managed by the INEGI, statistics are categorized by criminal matters with several variables; for example, the legal status of people incarcerated, such as accused or sentenced; type of crime committed; age; sex; place of residence; occupation; highest education level, and so on. This informational database is published annually, and it is offered in interactive format. The available information is from 1997 to 2008, including the two jurisdictions, federal and state levels. INEGI also handles other important issues such as domestic violence, and specifically child abuse, and other important data such as suicide, violence against women, violent deaths, accidents, homicides and suicides of juvenile offenders and prison population (http://www.inegi.org.mx).

National Public Security System

The National Public Security System is not the main source of public information. There are not many accessible data on this system, because access to most of the databases is strictly limited. The easiest way to access its information is through the statistical annex of the Annual Report that the representative of the Federal Executive branch presents each year to the Congress. Under the rubric of "Rule of law and security," national statistics are available, ranging from the budget spent under the "Order, Security and Justice" item, the amount of human resources by institution, arrested orders fulfilled by the police, number of expert opinions and number of reports lodged for the *Ministerio Público*, both the federal and state jurisdiction; as well as information on eradication and confiscation of weapons, vehicles, money and other matters related to this crime. The Statistics Section of local authorities displays the number of offenses reported by jurisdictions, types of crime, and information on the number of prison inmates who are under process and those that have already been sentenced. Both databases cover the last ten years (http://www.informe.gob.mx).

Citizens' Institute for Studies on Insecurity (Instituto Ciudadano de Estudios sobre la Inseguridad).

The Instituto Ciudadano de Estudios sobre la Inseguridad (ICESI) is a non-governmental organization established in 2002. To date, it has conducted six national victimization surveys: the first was conducted in 2002 and the most recent in 2009. Among these six surveys, the 2004–5 victim survey allowed Mexico to be included in the International Crime Victimization Survey (ICVS) for the first time. Victimization surveys conducted by the ICESI are known as the National Survey of Insecurity (ENSI) which is considered today as the most reliable source of information in Mexico concerning criminal victimization and perceptions of insecurity (i.e. fear of crime) (http://www.icesi.org.mx).

National Institute of Criminal Sciences

The National Institute of Criminal Sciences (INACIPE) was founded in 1976. It is the most authoritative institution on criminology in the country, even though it is anchored in the Mexican criminal sciences paradigm and thus has inherited the long-lasting legalistic tradition. However, there has always been a margin for the development of a true criminology. The INACIPE has produced very fruitful results in the areas of mentoring, training, research and publications. This entity has been publishing the *Iter Criminis* magazine since 1998, which specializes in the debate and dissemination of criminal law, criminal procedural law, criminology and victimology. Even though it is not a quality-controlled magazine and articles' standards vary, it receives contributions from practitioners and national and international academics which contribute to its timely relevance (http://www.inacipe.gob.mx).

Institute for Safety and Democracy, AC-Insyde (Instituto para la Seguridad y la Democracia, AC-Insyde)

The Instituto para la Seguridad y la Democracia, AC-Insyde (INSYDE) has three large portfolios: a) the Police Investigation and Reform Office; b) the Technical Service to Civil Society Office; and c) the Media and Violence Project. Its publications include collective works, with diverse methods and varied approaches. The criminological approach is not common, so more than scientific research, it includes essays with secondary sources that have the intention to orient public policy. They have a paper series that covers various topics, including police, human rights, violence and media (http://www.insyde.org.mx).

Economic Investigation and Teaching Center (Centro de Investigación y Docencia Económicas)

The Legal Studies Department of the Centro de Investigación y Docencia Económicas (CIDE) includes Public Safety studies and the Rule of Law Program (PESED). This program has as an objective the generation of empirical knowledge on themes related to delinquency, institutional applications, criminal justice and designing public policies that will impact the public debate on public safety issues. It is composed of four main areas: 1) network of specialists in public safety, police reform and human rights; 2) generation of statistical information; 3) key performance indicators; and 4) public expenses exercise program. Of most importance is the information from two sources: two editions of prison population surveys and a victimization and institutional implementation poll with five editions, most recently in 2008 (http://www.seguridadpublic acide.org.mx).

Conclusion

Criminology in Mexico is unlikely to be institutionalized and developed as an autonomous field in the near future. The emergence of other disciplines working on public security indicates that while crime and justice issues will attract public attention, they will be addressed without using criminological approaches, as has occurred during previous decades. The lack of empirical studies has been gradually covered by some researchers and institutions; however, the high politicization of crime and control issues by political parties and victims' organizations creates a narrow logic based on the sense of urgency, in which the high level of public visibility and short-term gains are more important than evidence-based approaches to crime reduction. It is possible to anticipate that criminology in Mexico will remain an isolated voice that is rarely taken into account to enrich the policy process. This trend may affect the development of the criminology itself, but mainly it may affect the quality and efficiency of security and justice services that Mexicans need and deserve urgently.

Future research questions

1. What is the impact of the budget allocation to security and the criminal justice system?
2. What must Mexico do to develop evidence-based criminological research that uses current international best practices?
3. The chapter outlines that there is not a strong relationship between criminology and the Mexican criminal justice policy process. Based on the state of the art of international criminology, how can the relevance of the academic discipline be integrated into the needs and resources of the Mexican government?
4. Which, if any, of the reforms in the police and the administration of justice systems have been effective? What performance measures are available to be used?
5. What role should academic research play in shaping policies, legal reforms and organizational transformations of the Mexican government's agenda?

Notes

1 The authors would like to thank Rika Chitose and Monica Chagoya for their assistance in translating the original Spanish manuscript.
2 With 136 sections, the Mexican Constitution has more than 500 amendments as of August 2009.
3 Those which are part of the federal, state and municipal authorities.

4 Now it is so-called federal ministerial police, and in local jurisdictions it is ministerial police, investigative police or scientific police.

References

Alvarado, A. (2008). *La reforma de justicia en México*. México: Colegio de México.

Astorga, L. (1995). *Mitología del narcotraficante en México*. México: UNAM-Plaza y Valdés.

—— (2003). *Drogas sin fronteras. Los expedientes de una guerra permanente*. México: Grijalbo.

—— (2007). *Seguridad, traficantes y militares. El poder en la sombra*. México: Tusquets.

Azaola, E. (1996a). *El delito de ser mujer*. México: Plaza y Valdés.

—— (1996b). *Las mujeres olvidadas*. México: Colmex/CNDH.

—— (2006). *Imagen y autoimagen de la policía de la Ciudad de México*. México: Ediciones Coyoacán-FLASUD-CIESAS-SSP.

Banco de México (2009) *Informes trimestrales sobre la inflación*. Online at http://www.banxico.org.mx/publicaciones-y-discursos/publicaciones/informes-periodicos/trimestral-inflacion/index.html (accessed November 25, 2010).

Barberet, R. (2005). Country survey, Spain. *European Journal of Criminology*, 2(3): 341–68.

Barrita, F. A. (2006). *Manual de criminología. Y otras disciplinas afines*. México: Porrúa.

Cámara de Diputados (2009). Servicios de investigación y análisis. Online at http://www.diputados.gob.mx (accessed November 25, 2010).

Consejo de la Judicatura Federal (2008). Informe estadístico. Online at www.cjf.gob.mx/secretarias/pleno/Info/IAL/IAL2008/AnexoDoc/AnexoEst/MAP_CN_08.pdf (accessed November 25, 2010).

Foucault, M. (1976). *Vigilar y castigar*. México: Siglo XXI Editores.

García, G. (2006)¿ Pour qué 1,661 corporations da la policía no bastan? Mexico: Diana.

González, L. (2002). *Percepción de la Inseguridad México*. México: Fondo de Cultura Económica.

González, S. and Flores, C. (2007). Violencia, corrupción y narcotráfico: el desafío de un México democrático. *En foreign affairs*.

González, S., Lopez Portillo, E. and Yañez, J. A. (1994). *Seguridad pública en México. Problemas, perspectivas y propuestas*. México: UNAM.

González, S., Mendieta, E., Buscaglia, E., and Moreno, M. (2005). El sistema de justicia penal y su reforma. Teoría y practica. *Fontamara*. May: 750.

INEGI (2008a). II Conteo de Población y Vivienda 2005. México y sus municipios. Aguascalientes: INEGI.

—— (2008b). Encuesta Nacional de Ingresos y Gastos de los Hogares. Online at http://www.inegi.org.mx/est/contenidos/espanol/rutinas/ept.asp?t = ming10&c = 3323 (accessed November 25, 2010).

—— (2009). Encuesta Nacional de Ocupación y Empleo (ENOE). Población de 14 años y más. Online at http://dgcnesyp.inegi.org.mx/cgi-win/bdiecoy.exe/618?c = 12898 (accessed November 25, 2010).

International Monetary Fund (IMF) (2009). Executive Board concludes 2008 Article IV Consultation with Mexico. Public Information Notice (PIN) No. 09/19. February 13. Online at http://www.imf.org/external/pubs/ft/scr/2009/cr0953.pdf (accessed November 25, 2010).

Kala, J. C. (2003). *Fenomenología de la delincuencia*. México: Fondo de Cultura Económica.

López, J. (1991). *Criminología. Introducción al estudio de la conducta antisocial*. México: ITESO.

López Portillo, E. (2003). *The police in Mexico: political functions and needed reforms*. In J. Bailey and J. Chabat, *Crimen trasnacional y seguridad pública: desafíos para Mexico y Estados Unidos*. México: Plaza & Janés.

Novoa, E. (1975). *El derecho como obstáculo al cambio social*. México: Siglo XXI Editores.

Mendieta, E., González, S. Buscaglia, E., Ventura, F., and Zingerman, G. (2009). *La fuerza de la razón y la razón de la fuerza. El uso legítimo de la violencia*. México: INACIPE.

Morris, N. (1978). *El futuro de las prisiones*. México: Siglo XXI Editores.

Orellana, O. (1978). *Manual de criminología*. México: Porrúa.

Pérez, A. (2002). *Análisis y evaluación de leyes en materia de prevención delictiva*. México: Fondo de Cultura Económica.

Reames, B. (2003) *Police forces in Mexico: a profile*. UCSD Center for US–Mexican Studies. San Diego, 2003: http://escholarship.org/uc/item/1sq4g254 (accessed November 25, 2010).

Rico, J. M. (1997). *Justicia penal y transición democrática de América Latina*. Siglo XXI Editores.

Rodríguez, L. (1981). *Criminología*. México: Porrúa.

—— (1995). *Criminología clínica*. México: Porrúa.

Taylor, I., Walton, P., and Young, J. (Eds) (1975). *Critical criminology*. London: Routledge.

Tenorio, F. (2002). *Cultura, sistema penal y criminalidad*. México: Fondo de Cultura Económica.
Yañez, J. A. (2000). La disputa por la modernidad: la policía en el siglo XX. In *La Policía en México, breve historia de un concepto y una institución*, pp. 91–126. México: Ediciones de la Policía Federal Preventiva.
—— (2006). *El modelo institucional de la Policía Federal Investigadora en México*. México: INACIPE.
Zepeda, G. (2004a). *Crimen sin castigo. Procuración de justicia penal y ministerio público en México*. México: Fondo de Cultura Económica.
—— (2004b). *La justicia penal en la agenda del Estado de derecho en México*. México: CIDAC.
—— (2006) *Los retos de la eficacia y la eficiencia en la seguridad ciudadana y la justicia penal en México*. México: CIDAC.

43

Nigeria

Social structure, criminal justice and criminology

Innocent Chukwuma[1]

Introduction

Nigeria's social, economic and political situations present a paradox on many fronts which impacts on crime. It is a country endowed with abundant human and natural resources and yet over 50 percent of its population live below the poverty line (Okafor, 2009; World Bank, 1996). Over the past decade, since elected civilian government was restored in May 1999 following 29 years of brutal military dictatorship, Nigeria has recorded impressive macroeconomic growth and stability (thanks to the rising oil price, its economic mainstay), and yet the country ranks very low on major global and even Sub-Saharan African development indicators – infant mortality, maternal mortality, quantity/quality of education, job creation, poverty eradication etc. (CIA, 2010; World Bank, 2009; Okafor, 2009; Saint *et al.*, 2003).

This chapter discusses the characteristics of Nigeria that may impact crime, the structure and philosophy of criminal justice administration, crime trends and scholarly contributions to understanding and responding to crime.

Infrastructure

Nigeria is located in West Africa and shares land borders with the Benin Republic in the west, Cameroon in the east and Niger and Chad in the north. It has a total mass of 923,768 square kilometers, extending from the Gulf of Guinea in the south to the Sahara Desert in the north (Encyclopedia of Nations, 2010; CIA, 2010). With a population of 151.2 million out of 782.5 million in Sub-Saharan Africa (World Bank, 2009), Nigeria is home to nearly one of every five citizens of the region and is the 32nd largest country in the world.

A 1990 estimate suggests that out of a total land area of 91 million hectares in Nigeria, 82 million is arable (Metz, 1991). However, only about 34 million hectares (or 42 percent of the cultivable area) were being cultivated at the time. Much of this land was farmed under subsistence agricultural techniques, called bush fallow system (Metz, 1991; Encyclopedia of Nations, 2010). The main natural resources of Nigeria are oil, natural gas, tin, columbite, iron ore, coal, limestone, lead, zinc and arable land. Out of these, oil and natural gas contribute 37 percent of the country's gross domestic product (GDP) (CIA, 2010) and have been a source of corruption, patrimonial politics and violent crimes in the country and also at the heart of environmental problems in

Nigeria, especially in the Niger Delta region where exploration by major global oil companies has led to devastating consequences on the environment (Okonta and Douglas, 2003). Other environmental problems confronting Nigeria include soil erosion in the east, desert encroachment in the north and deforestation in the south (Mongabay.com, 2010).

People

The Nigerian State has struggled since independence in 1960 to count its people accurately. At the root of the problem is the fact that population is one of the parameters used in the distribution of state resources (oil wealth or *national cake*) and so every state/ethnic group tries to outdo one another in ensuring that its population is high. The last census exercise, which was mired in controversy, was conducted in 2006 and estimated the population to be 140.4 million; 71.3 million male and 69 million female (National Population Commission, 2007). However, 2008 estimates from the World Bank suggest that the population of Nigeria is about 151.2 million with an annual growth rate of 2.3 percent (World Bank, 2009).

Nigeria has a three-tier federal structure: a federal government, with headquarters in Abuja, the federal capital territory; 36 states; and 774 local government councils. These large bureaucracies make Nigeria's federal structure unwieldy and very expensive to run as only a few states and local government councils are economically viable. Hence, the fratricidal battle for sharing of the oil wealth. There are 250 ethnic groups in Nigeria, with as many languages. Three of the groups are dominant – Igbo, Hausa-Fulani and Yoruba – and together constitute about 60 percent of the population. The official language is English, with Pidgin English widely spoken across the country. The dominant religions are Islam and Christianity.

Education is one of the areas where the Nigerian state is failing its citizens. In the 1960s and 1970s Nigerian schools were among the best in the world, producing world-class graduates and attracting scholars and academics from around the world. The story is different today as the quality of facilities and teaching in primary, secondary and tertiary institutions continues to deteriorate as a result of poor funding and mounting pressure on the schools to absorb more students to close the gap in enrolment of relevant age groups. According to the World Bank, the gross secondary school enrolment of relevant age group in Nigeria is 30.5 percent and that of tertiary school 10.1 percent. However, primary school enrolment is 93.1 percent and adult literacy of both sexes 70 percent (World Bank, 2009).

Every year about a million Nigerian youths register for university entrance examination to compete for about 100,000 positions in over 90 accredited federal, state and private universities (Olakulehin, 2009). Before sitting for the examination, about 90 percent of them are sure to "fail" because of limited spaces among other issues. With the neglect of formal diversionary programs such as technical/vocational education and skill acquisition centres, the options open for these young people are narrow: look for scarce jobs (Alanana, 2003); learn traditional hand skills that are divorced from the labor market requirements and rendered unprofitable by the energy crisis in the country (Kennedy-Darling *et al.*, 2008; Saint *et al.*, 2003); take to a life of deviance/crime (Omeje, 2005), escape to Europe/North America through inhumane routes (Amalu, 2008) or continue to take entrance examination into higher institutions every year until they either get in or give up and fall into preceding options (Nwagwu, 1997). The youth problem has exacerbated the level of crime in the country, particularly violent crimes such as armed robbery, kidnapping, ethno-religious violence and other forms of armed coercion outside the framework and control of the state.

Other major challenges Nigeria has are corruption and bad governance, which continue to deny the people service and accountability from their leaders, and the country is regularly ranked among the bottom in Transparency International's Corruption Perception Index (CPI) since 1995 when the data became available. In 1996, 1997 and 2000, Nigeria was ranked the most corrupt country in the world and has only marginally improved ever since (Transparency International, 2000).

However, Nigeria has made progress in macroeconomic growth and expansion of access to communication. Since 2005, Nigeria has witnessed a fairly steady growth in GDP at an annual average of 6 percent per annum (World Bank, 2009). The size of the economy in 2008 was $207 billion USD and the GDP per capita grew from $797 USD in 2005 to $1,370 USD in 2008 (World Bank, 2009). However, the inequality level in Nigeria is high with a Gini index of 42.9 (World Bank, 2009).

In communications, the number of people with access to telephone grew from 13 per 100 to 42 per 100 between 2005 and 2008, thanks to GSM revolution (World Bank, 2009). Similarly, the number of people with access to the internet grew from 5 million in 2005 to 24 million in 2008 and number of users increased from 3.55 persons per 100 to 16 persons per 100, representing a leap of over 400 percent within a period of four years (World Bank, 2009). However, with broadband internet service still out of the reach of most people in the country, internet browsing has remained a nightmare for the majority of users.

Administration of justice

The principal organs of Nigerian justice system are the Nigeria Police Force, courts and the Nigerian Prisons Service. There are other role players such as the Directorate of Public Prosecution (DPP), defense counsels and quasi-policing (specialized) agencies including the Economic and Financial Crime Commission (EFCC), Independent Corrupt Practices Commission (ICPC) and National Drug Law Enforcement Agency (NDLEA). They complement the functions of the three core agencies of justice administration in Nigeria.

The structure of justice delivery in Nigeria is heavily influenced by the country's British colonial experience. Formal policing began in 1860 and by 1930 had become firmly established based upon the colonial police model developed in India, which itself was modeled on the Royal Irish Constabulary (Brodgen, 2005). Thus, from its early days up to the present, the Nigerian police force was a paramilitary organization and very hierarchically structured. Until 1966, it existed side by side with local and Native Authority police forces in the western and northern part of the country respectively. The process of integration of the various forces into one police force was completed in 1972 (Tamuno, 1970). At present the population of the Nigerian police force is over 370,000 and the organization is divided into five command structure: a national headquarter command, 12 zonal commands, 37 state commands, 123 area commands and over 1,000 divisional command (Nigerian Police Force, 2000).

The police have wide functions and discretionary powers, which include prevention, investigation and detection of crimes, apprehension of offenders, protection of life and property, preservation of law and order, enforcement of all laws and regulations with which they are directly charged and to perform military duties (section 4, Police Act). In these official functions, there have been allegations of police ineffectiveness and inefficiency (CLEEN Foundation, 2008), disobedience of court orders (Fowoyo, 2010), detention of people for long periods without trial (NOPRIN/OSJI, 2010), torture of suspects (Human Rights Watch, 2005), extra-judicial killing (Access to Justice, 2005) and corruption (Human Rights Watch, 2010). However, police in Nigeria have enjoyed pervasive impunity in all such cases (Human Rights Watch, 2010).

However, in the past ten years efforts have been made by the federal and some state governments (especially Lagos State), donor agencies, non-governmental organizations and the Nigerian police force itself, to address human rights abuses by the police and improve effectiveness in the performance of their criminal justice functions through the establishment of presidential commissions and panels of inquiry, implementation of community policing strategies, revitalization of internal and external complaints mechanisms and establishment of human rights units in police stations. These efforts have resulted in dismissal, demotion and prosecution of thousands of police officers for misconduct such as human rights violations (Nigerian Police Force, 2000, 2004, 2005, 2006, 2007, 2008).

The first prison in Nigeria was established in 1872 in Lagos and prior to 1968 Nigeria had a dual system of prison administration: colonial federal prison administration, operational in eastern and western parts of the country and Native Authority Prisons operated under colonial supervision in the north (Awe, 1968; Alemika, 1988b). However, pursuant to the unitary policies of the military when they took over power in 1966, the Federal and Native Authority Prisons were unified in 1968 under the name the Nigerian Prisons Service. This move made the prisons an exclusively federal institution (Alemika, 1988b).

The Nigerian Prisons Service derives its operational powers from the Prisons Act 1990, which empowers it to take into lawful custody all those certified to be so kept by courts of competent jurisdiction; produce suspects in courts as and when due; identify the causes of their anti-social dispositions, setting in motion mechanisms for their treatment and training for eventual reintegration into society as normal law-abiding citizens on discharge; administer prisons farms and industries for this purpose; and in the process generate revenue for the government.

The Service is headed by the Comptroller-General of Prisons (CGP) who is responsible to the President of Nigeria through the Minister of Internal Affairs. There are 37 commands spread across the 37 states of Nigeria and Abuja, the capital, which are headed by comptrollers of the prisons. The total staff of the Prison Service is presently 24,000 (Nigerian Prison Service, 2009).

Nigeria has 145 conventional convicts' prisons, 83 satellite prison camps, three borstal institutions (i.e. youth prisons), one open prison camp, one staff college and four training schools. It also reportedly has 12 major farm centers, 124 market gardens, 9 cottage industries and 9 subsidiary farms for the training and rehabilitation of inmates (Nigerian Prison Service, 2009). The total prison capacity of the 144 prisons is estimated at 38,563. However, as of December 2007, the total inmate population was 42,030, of which 28,500 were awaiting trial and 13,530 convicts (Fapohunda and Jacques-Minnegheer, 2008). Overcrowding in urban prisons remains a major challenge of Nigerian Prison Services while other prisons are not used to their full capacity. As of January 2008, Ikoyi Prison in Lagos held more than two times its official capacity (Fapohunda and Jacques-Minnegheer, 2008). Because of overcrowding, the prison authorities have little time or space for rehabilitation and reintegration components of their mandate, focusing more custodial functions (Enuku, 2001; Alemika and Kayode, 1981). Reports from local and international human rights organizations and UNODC have alleged widespread abuse of prisoners' rights in Nigerian prisons (Amnesty International, 2008; UNODC, 2005).

Unlike the police and prisons services, which are exclusively federal institutions, the judiciary has two levels of court systems: (1) the Federal courts, which are basically the appellate courts[2] and (2) the state courts, which exercise judicial power over matters not covered by the Federal courts. The 1999 Constitution laid down provisions for the establishment and powers of these courts in Nigeria. The judicial institutions include: the Supreme Court, the Court of Appeal, the Federal High Court, the High Court of Federal Capital Territory Abuja, the High Court of a State the National Industrial Court, the Sharia Court of Appeal of the FCT Abuja, the Sharia Court of Appeal of a State, the Customary Court of Appeal of the FCT and the Customary Court of Appeal of a State.

In addition to courts created by the Constitution, there exist Magistrate Courts, District Courts, Area Courts and Customary Courts established in various states by state laws. These courts are of limited jurisdiction as specified in their enabling laws and appeals from them lie to the High Court, Sharia Court of Appeal or Customary Court of Appeal (Babalakin & Co., 2005).

Trials in the regular court system are open and generally respect due process safeguards, including presumption of innocence, rights to counsel of choice, to be present, to confront witnesses and to present evidence. However, low compensation for judges in many states, understaffing, poor equipment and corruption decrease the reliability and impartiality of the courts (Aremu, 2010).

A major problem plaguing the Nigerian court system is the congestion of cases in courts. It is not unusual for cases to drag at the magistrate or high court for three years and while the cases are pending, the defendants (of criminal matters) might be languishing in prison. The Nigerian formal justice system has remained punitive, oppressive and harsh against the poor and vulnerable, with little or no fundamental change in philosophy and law. The legal framework governing the functions of the police, prison and prosecution not only predate Nigeria's independence but also predate the United Nations, meaning that all the gamut of instruments the UN has churned out in the past 65 years of its existence to make the administration of justice humane and fair are yet to be factored into laws, polices and rules/operational procedures of justice administration in the country. Consequently, poor offenders are punished to the limits of the law and often sent to prison or the hangman, while those who can afford it hire the most expensive lawyers to free them from heinous crimes they may have committed by simply manipulating the system.

Some states, led by Lagos, have introduced alternative dispute resolution mechanisms such as the Multi-Door courts and Citizens Mediation Centers (CMC) to create rooms for restorative justice. These courts have been limited to civil and commercial matters and not extended to criminal cases, making it difficult for both the complainants and defenders to reach any restorative agreement once the matter has been brought to court, even if the complainant is desirous of it. This Victorian mindset of the Nigerian courts guided by the criminal law has alienated many victims of crime and made it very difficult for them to report to the police as they have nothing to gain apart from the initial natural vengeful feeling of seeing their assailant punished, which may take many years to come if the case is successfully prosecuted. Often the prosecutions are not successful due to either shoddy police investigation or witnesses refusing to show up in courts because of long delays before and during the trial process. The clearance rate of crime has remained low although there are no reliable official statistics on the issue to cite.

Criminology

Criminological studies on crime and the justice system are scarce. Most use qualitative methods. The main reason is that criminology as a discipline is still very nascent in Nigeria, even though the earliest graduates up to doctoral level date back to the late 1970s and early 1980s. With the possible exception of Salem University, a new private Christian university located in the central part of Nigeria, no university out of the more than 90 accredited universities in the country offers an undergraduate degree in criminology or the criminal justice system (Omale, 2009). There is also no organized society of criminologists in the country to promote the discipline, although efforts have been made several times to establish one (Iwarimie-Jaja, 2006).

Consequently, earlier studies on crime and criminal justice system were led by other disciplines, especially legal scholars and historians (Okonkwo, 1966; Awe, 1968; Tamuno, 1970). Of all the justice institutions, the police received the most attention. In his landmark study on the history of modern policing in Nigeria, Tamuno (1970) gave an account of why the colonial government preferred a police force estranged from the community through an analysis of the correspondence between colonial officials discussing the type of police to be established.

This pioneering work apparently spurred social scientists including criminologists to examine the colonial and military influence on police and policing (Ahire, 1991; Onoge, 1993; Alemika, 1993; Asemota, 1993; Rotimi, 1993), police structure, organization, administration and control (Ohonbamu, 1972; Igbinovia, 1980a, 1980b; Okereke, 1992a, 1992b; Onwudiwe, 2000); police performance (Odekunle, 1979) and public perceptions of and relationship with the police (Alemika, 1988a; Okereke, 1995; Adisa, 1999; Alemika and Chukwuma, 2000).

Criminologists were prominent in research on the prison system in Nigeria showing that that the system has been ineffective in protection offenders in custody, reforming or rehabilitating and reintegrating into the larger society on release (Adeyemi, 1977; Kayode, 1981; Igibinovia, 1984; Alemika, 1988b, 1993, 1997). For instance in a study of a sample of convicts in two Nigerian prisons, Etannibi Alemika of the University of Jos, north-central Nigeria, found patterns that were consistent with the literature from the West that young, poorly educated, and politically and economically disadvantaged groups are disproportionally represented in prisons. The study also exposed the arbitrary nature of sentencing practices in Nigeria because the courts appeared not to consider prior history of an offender (Alemika, 1988b).

In the last decade, a number of criminology-oriented studies have also been conducted to examine predisposing factors in violent crimes (Otu, 2003), receptiveness of restorative justice principles by victims of crime and officials of the justice system in Nigeria (Omale, 2009) and prevalence of gender violence (Odujinrin, 1993; Okemgbo *et al.* 2002; Ezechi *et al.*, 2004; Amobi *et al.*, 2002). In a study on the changing patterns of armed robbery in three selected prisons in the southeast of Nigeria, Smart Eqwu Otu tried to understand the predictive characteristics of contemporary armed robbery offence and offender, testing Sutherland's differential association theory. The result showed some patterns that contradict Sutherland's theory. He found that "contemporary armed robbers in Nigeria . . . are fairly educated and seem to have had stable family background including a well-practiced and active religious participation" (Otu, 2003, p. 395). He concluded that armed robbery in Nigeria was principally a product of imitation, learning and emulation and that other influencing factors include unemployment, availability of guns, being single male and economically active (Otu, 2003). Smart Egwu Otu is with the Department of Sociology and Anthropology, Ebonyi State University in the Southeast of Nigeria.

Another study examined the evidence of restorative justice and explored the opinions of victims of crime and the criminal justice professionals in Nigeria with regard to acceptability of restorative justice as an alternative to penal sentencing. It was carried out by Don Jon Omale, who teaches at the Department of Criminology and Penology, College of Peace and Social Sciences, Salem University, Lokoja, in the north-central part of Nigeria. The findings showed overwhelming acceptance in spite of official legislative thinking and news media's preference for penal populism. His study followed an earlier one by Okafo (2006), which used illustrative evidence of effectiveness of traditional justice system among the Igbos of south-eastern Nigeria to demonstrate that indigenous African justice system remains potent for social control in Africa.

Studies on gender-based violence have been led by public health officials, especially obstetricians and gynecologists rendering antenatal care to pregnant women in public and private hospitals in the country. These studies have used quantitative methodologies to establish the pattern, prevalence and frequency of gender violence (Odujinrin, 1993; Okemgbo *et al.* 2002; Ezechi *et al.*, 2004; Amobi *et al.*, 2002); age and socioeconomic groups most affected (Okemgbo *et al.*, 2002; Ezechi *et al.* 2004); and clinical management of cases (Aimakhu *et al.*, 2004). However, not much attention has been paid to the cost and other impacts of gender violence on the victims (especially women and children); police and criminal justice response to cases brought to their attention; and the effect on the economy, thus requiring further research by criminologists and sociologists.

Non-governmental organizations and UN agencies have also been active in research on crime and justice issues. These groups include the CLEEN Foundation, the Network on Police Reform in Nigeria (NOPRIN), Centre for Social Justice, Access to Justice, Prisoner Rehabilitation and Welfare Action (PRAWA) and Legal Assistance and Defense Project (LEDAP). The CLEEN Foundation has for the past six years focused on measuring crime levels in Nigeria and public perception of safety and justice institutions, especially the police through large-scale national crime surveys. The reports are published and distributed as open source materials on the internet as well as in printed form. The results show that violent crimes such as robbery have remained stable even though very high at the national level for the past five years, but fluctuate at the state and regional levels. For instance, in the 2006 survey the national average for robbery was slightly more than 10 percent, whereas in the Niger Delta states of Bayelsa, Edo, Abia, Rivers and Delta the average was more than 20 percent (Alemika and Chukwuma, 2007); see Figure 43.1.

When the study was repeated in March 2010, the national average remained stable at slightly above 10 percent. However, the state distribution showed a major shift, with Cross River State, which ranked below national average in 2006 coming first with 25.1 percent, followed by Benue, Kwara, Edo and Akwa Ibom states (CLEEN Foundation, 2010).

NOPRIN researches have focused on documenting patterns, prevalence and locations of police abuse of human rights in Nigeria. In a recent report jointly published with the Open Society Justice Initiative (OSJI), based on independent field monitoring and investigations at more than 400 police stations and posts in 14 states in Nigeria between 2007 and 2009, NOPRIN established high level of complicity of senior police officials and authority in egregious police abuse of human rights in Nigeria (NOPRIN and OSJI, 2010). The report corroborates earlier reports on police violations by Human Rights Watch, Amnesty International and more importantly, the Presidential Committee on Police Reform in Nigeria, headed by a former chief of police in Nigeria, Mohamed Diko Yusuf.

In its own research, the United Nations Office on Drug and Crime (UNODC) looked at issues of integrity and capacity within the Nigerian justice system. In a three-state study involving court officials and users, UNODC found that the majority of court officials believed that the court system was seldom affordable (UNODC, 2006). It also established that, on average, court users attend court over seven times before their matters are resolved and that:

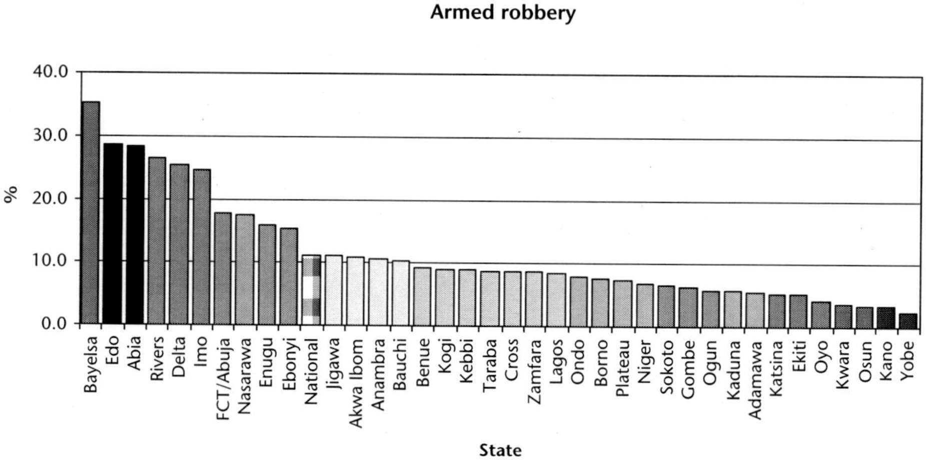

Figure 43.1 Armed robbery

> in states where geographical coverage of the court was low, especially in the north, incessant adjournment of cases caused unnecessary costs and time, encourages extrajudicial solutions as well as discouraged complainants from seeking justice or simply not defending their rights at all.
>
> *(UNODC, 2006, p. 70)*

Evaluation research is rarely conducted on the impact of government policies and practices on crime and justice, apart from those commissioned by development agencies such as DFID and USAID on specific programs they supported, which are largely qualitative and not rigorously done. Part of the challenge is the non-availability of reliable official statistics in an easily retrievable format and also the absence of a nexus between policy and research communities in Nigeria (Olomola, 2007). However, with a good dose of patience some data on crime and offenders can be collected from the police, prisons, courts and the National Bureau of Statistics (NBS). These are complemented by reports and datasets of non-governmental organizations. Table 43.1 provides the names of organizations that have some data on crime and justice issues in Nigeria.

Finally, funding of academic research in Nigeria is a major problem. There is the Education Trust Fund (ETF), whose mandate includes administering research grants for academic research. A combination of issues around the competitiveness of the grant allocation process and adequacy of available funds have denied many academics with interesting research proposals the funds to carry out their researches. However, international private foundations such as the Ford Foundation, Macarthur Foundation, Open Society Institute and bilateral and multilateral agencies such as DFID, USAID, EU, World Bank, etc. are active in Nigeria and provide some support but are geared mostly to short action studies lasting not more than a year to feed into their development assistance work. Some private companies in the telecom and banking sectors and rich individuals have started establishing private foundations to support charity work. Efforts are being made to persuade them to include funding for justice topics.

Table 43.1 Organizations and websites

Name of organization	*Website*
National Bureau of Statistics (NBS)	http://www.nigerianstat.gov.ng/
Nigerian Institute of Social and Economic Research	http://niseronline.org
Nigerian Institute of Advanced Legal Studies	http://www.nials-nigeria.org
Nigeria Police Force	http://www.npf.gov.ng
Nigerian Prisons Service	http://www.prisons.gov.ng
Nigerian Law Resources	http://www.nigerianlawresources.com
National University Commission	http://www.nuc.edu.ng
Social Science Academy of Nigeria	http://www.ssanigeria.org
Nigerian Communications Commission	http://www.ncc.gov.ng
Nigerian Education Trust Fund	http://www.etf.gov.ng
CLEEN Foundation	http://www.cleen.org
Network on Police Reform in Nigeria	http://www.noprin.org
Access to Justice	http://www.accesstojustice-ng.org
Project Alert on Violence Against Women	http://www.projectalertnig.org

Conclusion

In this chapter a discussion of Nigeria's characteristics which impact crime, criminal justice and criminology was undertaken. Nigeria's social, economic, political and governance challenges were implicated in the emergence of an army of able-bodied young people willing to fruitfully engage but alienated from the mainstream of society. Consequently, the youth problem has exploded in many typologies of violence and armed coercion outside the regulation/control of the state and over widening space and territories, which has continued to stretch the capacities of the already antiquated, brutal and corrupt justice system.

Criminological studies providing understanding, explanation, evaluations and suggestions on crime and justice issues are few and far between, largely traceable to the nascent nature of the discipline and inadequate research resources (finance and reliable official data). However, a number of criminologists and non-governmental organizations have distinguished themselves in a number of researches and may need collaborative research projects on topics of mutual interest with their colleagues in the other parts of the world to push the frontiers of the discipline in Nigeria.

Future research questions

1. With the increasing role of non-state actors in safety, security and justice provisioning in Nigeria, what governance arrangement would be helpful in enhancing their usefulness and mitigating their excesses?
2. What is the impact of domestic violence on family life and national economy?
3. To what extent have bilateral and multilateral justice reform assistance programs in Nigeria been effective and helpful in improving justice delivery?
4. To what extent are criminological theories developed in the West relevant in understanding and explaining contemporary forms of violent crimes in Nigeria?
5. What is the impact of police checkpoints and exercise of stop and search powers on crime and community in Nigeria?

Notes

1 With research assistance from Shola Omotosho.

2 Except in disputes between the federation and a state or between states, where the Supreme Court exercises original and exclusive jurisdiction; in questions as to whether a person has been validly elected to the office of the president of Nigeria, where the Court of Appeal has original jurisdiction; or in federal offenses where the Federal High Courts have original and exclusive jurisdiction (Babalakin & Co, 2005).

References

Access to Justice (2005). Breaking point: how torture and the police cell system violate justice in the criminal investigation process. Lagos: Access to Justice.

Adeyemi, A. A. (1977). Nigerian penal systems: a critical appraisal. *Lagos Notes and Record: The Journal of African Studies*, Vol. VI.

Adisa, J. (1999). A new Nigerian police image: its role in the next millennium. Text of a lecture delivered at a seminar organized for assistant inspectors, generals and commissioners of police by the Nigerian police force at the International Conference Centre Abuja, October 19–20, p. 6.

Ahire, P. T. (1991). *Imperial policing*. Milton Keynes: Open University Press.

Aimakhu, C. O., Olayemi, O., Iwe, C. A. B, Oluyemi, F. A., Ojoko, I. E., Shoretire, K. A., Adeniji, R .A., and Aimakhu, V. E. (2004). Current causes and management of violence against women in Nigeria. *Journal of Obstetrics and Gynaecology*, 24(1): 58–63.

Alanana, O. O. (2003). Youth unemployment in Nigeria: implications for the third millennium. *Global Journal of Social Science*, 2(1): 21–26.

Alemika, E. E. O. (1983). The smoke screen, rhetoric and reality of penal incarceration in Nigeria. *International Journal of Comparative and Applied Criminal Justice*, 7: 137–49.

—— (1988a). Policing and perceptions of police in Nigeria. *Police Studies*, 11(4): 161–76.

—— (1988b). Socioeconomic and criminological attributes of convicts in two Nigerian prisons. *Journal of Criminal Justice*, 16(3): 197–206.

—— (1997). Criminal violence and insecurity in Lagos State, Nigeria. *Africa Peace Review*, 1(2): 72–95.

Alemika, E. E. O. and Kayode, O. (1981). Some predictors of recidivism: a study of the inmates of a Nigerian prison. *International Journal of Comparative and Applied Criminal Justice*, 5: 187–95.

Alemika, E. E. O. and Chukwuma, I. C. (2000). *Police community violence in Nigeria*. Lagos: Centre for Law Enforcement Education.

—— (2007). Criminal victimization, safety and policing in Nigeria: 2006. Lagos: CLEEN Foundation.

Alemika, E. E. O. and Agugua, A. (2001). *Gender relations and discrimination in the Nigeria Police Force*. Lagos: Centre for law Enforcement Education.

Amnesty International (2008). *Nigeria: prisoners' rights systematically flouted*. London: Amnesty International.

Amobi, I. L, Okonkwo, P. I., and Adogu, P. (2002). Intimate partner violence among women of childbearing age in a primary health care centre in Nigeria. *African Journal of Reproductive Health*, 6(3): 53–8.

Aremu, I. (2010). Notes on judicial corruption in Nigeria. Illorin: Mustapha Akanbi Foundation. Online at http://www.mafng.org/symposium2/index.htm (accessed November 25, 2010).

Asemota, S. A. (1993). Policing under civilian and military administrations. T. N. Tamuno, I. L. Bashir, E. E. O. Alemika, and A. O. Akano (Eds.) *Policing Nigeria: past, present and future*. Lagos: Malthouse Press Ltd.

Awe, B. (1968). History of prison system in Nigeria. In T. O. Elias (Ed.), *The prison system in Nigeria*. Lagos: University of Lagos.

Babalakin & Co (2005). The judicial system in Nigeria. Babalakin & Co. Online at http://www.babalakinandco.com/resources/judicialsystem.html (accessed November 25, 2010).

Brodgen, M. (2005). The emergence of the police: the colonial dimension. In T. Newburn (Ed.), *Policing: key readings*. Devon: William Publishing.

Central Intelligence Agency (CIA) (2010) *The world factbook*. Washington, DC: Central Intelligence Agency. Online at http://www.cia.gov/library/publications/the-world-factbook/geos/ni.html (accessed November 25, 2010).

CLEEN Foundation (2007). National crime victimization survey: 2006 summary report. Lagos: CLEEN Foundation. Online at http://www.cleen.org/crimevictimisationsurvey.html (accessed November 25, 2010).

—— (2008). *Motion without movement: report of presidential committees on police reform in Nigeria*. Lagos: CLEEN Foundation.

—— (2010). National crime and safety survey: 2010 summary report. Lagos: CLEEN Foundation. Online at http://www.cleen.org/National%20Crime%20and%20Safety%20Survey%20(2010)%20Summary%20Report.pdf (accessed November 25, 2010).

Encyclopedia of Nations (2010), *Nigeria*. Online at http://www.nationsencyclopedia.com/Africa/Nigeria.html (accessed November 25, 2010).

Enuku, U. E. (2001). Humanizing the Nigerian prison through literacy education: echoes from afar. *Journal of Correctional Education*, 52(1). Online at http://www.nwlincs.org/correctional_education/articles/nigerian-prison-enuku.pdf (accessed November 25, 2010).

Ezechi, O. E., Kalu, B. K., Ezechi, L. O., Nwokoro, C. A., Ndububa, V. I., and Okeke, G. C. E. (2004). Prevalence and pattern of domestic violence against pregnant Nigerian women. *Journal of Obstetrics and Gynaecology*, 24(6): 652–6.

Fapohunda O. and Jacques-Minnegheer, D. (2008). Pre feasibility study on potential support for prison reform in Nigeria: final report. Abuja: Delegation of the European Commission.

Fowoyo, P. (2010). Lagos CJ carpets police over disobedience of court order. *Nigerian Compass,* May 20. Online at http://www.compassnewspaper.com/NG/index.php?option = com_content&view = article&id = 48805:lagos-cj-carpets-police-over-disobedience-of-court-order-&catid = 44:law&Itemid = 690 (accessed November 25, 2010).

Human Rights Watch (2005). *Rest in pieces: police torture and deaths in custody*. Lagos: Human Rights Watch. Online at http://www.hrw.org/node/11631 (accessed November 25, 2010).

—— (2010). *Everyone's on the game: corruption and human rights abuses by the Nigeria police force*. Lagos: Human Rights Watch. Online at http://www.hrw.org/node/92390 (accessed November 25, 2010).

Igbinovia, P. (1980a). The police in trouble: administrative and organizational problems in Nigeria police force. *Indiana Journal of Public Administration*, 28(2): 34–72.

—— (1980b). Police administration in modern Nigeria. *Police Studies*, 3(3): 33–45.

Iwarimie-Jaja, D. (2006). The need for the establishment of a Nigerian society of criminology. *African Journal of Criminology and Criminal Justice*, 2(2). Online at http://www.umes.edu/assets/0/22/910/16B0EF89-DA1E-4AFD-B385-56EB573F6E55.pdf (accessed November 25, 2010).

Kayode, O. (1981). Nigeria. In E. H. Johnson (Ed) *International Handbook of Contemporary Developments in Criminology*. Westport, CT: Greenwood Press.

Kennedy-Darling J., Hoyt, N., Murao, K., and Ross, A. (2008). The energy crisis in Nigeria. Online at http://humanities.uchicago.edu/orgs/institute/bigproblems/Energy/BP-Energy-Nigeria.pdf (accessed November 25, 2010).

Metz, H. C. (Ed.) (1991). *Nigeria: a country study*. Washington: GPO for the Library of Congress. Online at http://countrystudies.us/nigeria/57.htm (accessed November 25, 2010).

Mongabay.com (2010). *Nigeria*. Mongabay.com. Online at http://rainforests.mongabay.com/20nigeria.htm (accessed November 25, 2010).

National Population Commission (2007). 2006 final census results. National Population Commission. Online at http://www.population.gov.ng/files/nationafinal.pdf (accessed November 25, 2010).

Network on Police Reform in Nigeria and Open Society Justice Initiative (NOPRIN and OSJI) (2010). *Criminal force: torture, abuse and extrajudicial killing by the Nigeria Police Force*. Lagos: NOPRIN and OSJI.

Nigeria Police Force (2000). *Annual report, 1999*. Lagos: Nigeria Police Force.

—— (2005). *Annual report, 2004*. Lagos: Nigeria Police Force.

—— (2006). *Annual report, 2005*. Lagos: Nigeria Police Force.

—— (2007). *Annual report, 2006*. Lagos: Nigeria Police Force.

—— (2008). *Annual report, 2007*. Lagos: Nigeria Police Force.

—— (2009). *Annual report, 2008*. Lagos: Nigeria Police Force.

Nigerian Prison Service (2009). Command structure of the Nigerian Prisons Service. Online at http://www.prisons.gov.ng/pi.php (accessed November 25, 2010).

Nwagwu, C. C. (1997). The environment of crises in Nigerian education system. *Comparative Education*, 33(1): 87–96.

Odekunle, F. (1979). The Nigeria police force: a preliminary assessment of functional performance. *International Journal of Sociology of Law*, 6: 73–8.

Odujinrin, O. (1993). Wife battering in Nigeria. *International Journal of Gynaecology and Obstetrics*, 44(2): 154–64.

Ohonbamu, O. (1972). The dilemma of police organization under a federal system: the Nigerian example. *The Nigerian Law Journal*, 6: 73–8.

Okafo, N. (2006). Relevance of African traditional jurisprudence on control, justice and law: a critique of the Igbo experience. *African Journal of Criminology and Justice Studies*, 2(1). Online at http://www.umes.edu/cms300uploadedFiles/AJCJS/VoL2Issue1Okafo.pdf (accessed November 25, 2010).

Okafor, E. E. (2009). The use of adolescents as domestic servants in Ibadan, Nigeria. *Journal of Adolescent Research*, 24(2): 169–93.

Okemgbo, N., Omideyi, A. K, and Odimegwu, C. O. (2002). Prevalence, patterns and correlates of domestic violence in selected Igbo communities of Imo State, Nigeria. *African Journal of Reproductive Health*, 6(2): 101–14.

Okereke, G. (1992a). The social organization of Nigeria law enforcement: Its effects on police–public relations. Dissertation. Oklahoma State University.

—— (1992b). Police powers and law enforcement tactics: the case of Nigeria. *Police Studies*, 15(3): 107–17.

—— (1995). Police officers' perceptions of the Nigeria police force: its effects on the social organization of policing. *Journal of Criminal Justice*, 23(3): 277–85.

Okonkwo, C. N. (1966). *The police and public in Nigeria*. London: Sweet and Maxwell.

Okonta, I. and Douglas, O. (2003). *Where the vultures feast: Shell, human rights and oil in the Niger Delta*. San Francisco: Sierra Club Books.

Olakulehin, F. K. (2009). Policy formulation and capacity building for improved access to higher education in Nigeria. Online at http://www.educationdev.net/educationdev/Docs/n1.ppt (accessed November 25, 2010).

Olomola, A. S. (2007). An analysis of the research–policy nexus in Nigeria. In E. T. Ayuk and M. A. Marouani (Eds.), *The policy paradox in Africa*. Trenton NJ: Africa World Press Inc and Ottawa: International Research Idea Center.

Omale, D. J. O. (2009). Restorative justice as an alternative dispute resolution model: opinion of victims of crime and criminal justice professionals in Nigeria. Dissertation. DeMontfort University. Online at https://www.dora.dmu.ac.uk/xmlui/bitstream/handle/2086/2411/PhD%20Don%20John%20Otene%20Omale.pdf?sequence=1 (accessed November 25, 2010).

Omeje, K. (2005). Youth conflict and perpetual instability in Nigeria. *Africa Renaissance*, March/April.

Onoge, O. F. (1993). Social conflicts and crime control in colonial Nigeria. T. N. Tamuno, I. L. Bashir, E. E. O. Alemika, and A. O. Akano (Eds.) *Policing Nigeria: past, present and future*. Lagos: Malthouse Press Ltd.

Onwudiwe, I. D. (2000). Decentralization of the Nigeria police force. *International Journal of African Studies*, 2(1): 95–114.

Otu, S. E. (2003). *Armed robbery in southeastern states of contemporary Nigeria: a criminological analysis*. Dissertation. University of South Africa. Online at http://uir.unisa.ac.za/bitstream/10500/1189/1/Thesis.PDF (accessed November 25, 2010).

Rotimi, K. (1993). Local police in western Nigeria: End of an era. In T. N. Tamuno, I. L. Bashir, E. E. O. Alemika, and A. O. Akano (Eds.) *Policing Nigeria: past, present and future*. Lagos: Malthouse Press Ltd.

Saint, W., Hartnett, T. A., and Strassner, E. (2003). Higher education in Nigeria: a status report. *Higher Education Policy*, 16: 259–81.

Tamuno, T. N. (1970). *The police in modern Nigeria*. lbadan: lbadan University Press.

Transparency International (2000). TI Corruption Perception Index 2000. Berlin: Transparency International. Online at http://www.transparency.org/policy_research/surveys_indices/cpi/previous_cpi/2000 (accessed November 25, 2010).

United Nations Office on Drugs and Crime (UNODC) (2005). *Assisting the prison reform process in Nigeria: report of UNODC fact finding mission*. Vienna: UNODC.

—— (2006). *Assessment of the integrity and capacity of the justice system in three Nigerian states: technical assessment report*. Vienna: UNODC.

World Bank (1996). Nigeria: poverty in the midst of plenty. Washington, DC: The World Bank.

—— (2009). *2009 World development indicators online*. Washington, DC: The World Bank. Online at http://go.worldbank.org/U0FSM7AQ40 (accessed November 25, 2010).

44

The Netherlands

The state of criminology

Melvin R. J. Soudijn

Introduction

The official name of the country is the Kingdom of the Netherlands (which means low-lying countries), although it is colloquially known as Holland. This latter term stems from the seventeenth century, when the two prosperous provinces of North and South Holland were involved with international trade.

Infrastructure

In July 2009, the Netherlands had a population of 16,715,999. The country measures about 41,000 square kilometers and borders Germany to the east (577 kilometers), Belgium to the south (450 kilometers) and the North Sea to the west and north (451 kilometers). The country is a gateway to Europe because of its port of Rotterdam (the largest in Europe) and Amsterdam Airport Schiphol (the third largest in Europe). An important part of organized criminal activities, therefore, has resulted in smuggling and trafficking.

The country has a mild maritime climate in which significant rainfall occurs during the year. Summers are relatively warm. Winters can be fairly cold. Although this makes for arable land, Dutch farmers have also pioneered greenhouse cultivation. Because the climate is not suitable for cultivating drugs outdoors, growers of cannabis have also adapted these greenhouse technologies. This has resulted in the development of new cannabis strains with high potency.

About 2 percent of the working population is active in agriculture, 18 percent in industry and 80 percent in services. The total purchasing power parity has been estimated at $670.2 billion USD, with average growth rates of 1.8 percent and an inflation rate of 1.5 percent. The per capita income was estimated at $40,300 USD in 2008. Imports and exports account for $485.3 billion USD and $537.5 billion USD respectively. In the 1960s, the Netherlands discovered large natural gas reserves. This has resulted in over €200 billion in extra revenue, which also helped finance a generous welfare state.

The type of government is called a constitutional monarchy. That means the monarch appoints a council of ministers who initiate and ratify laws and policy. Following Second Chamber elections, the leader of the majority party or leader of a majority coalition is usually appointed prime minister by the monarch. The monarchy is hereditary.

Administration of justice

The judiciary consists of 61 cantonal courts, 19 district courts, 5 courts of appeal and one supreme court. The cantonal courts only deal with summary offences. The district courts pass initial sentence on indictable offences, and function as a court of appeal with relation to summary offences. The courts of appeal review sentences relating to indictable offences. The supreme court does not deal with the criminal facts but reviews the manner of proceedings and the lawfulness of lower courts' judgments.

There is no jury system. The judges are appointed for life by the Crown and irremovable (except for malfeasance). However, not all judges are occupied full time. Lawyers and legal scholars may be appointed as substitute judges to relieve professional judges of their caseload.

Law enforcement is primarily handled by the Dutch police. The police is organized into 26 regional forces (25 forces that operate at a regional level and 1 force, the Netherlands Police Agency, that acts on a national level). The latter includes departments for patrolling water, air and rail traffic, criminal intelligence and (inter)national investigation teams as well as diplomatic and security forces. In addition to the regular police forces, there are special law enforcement agencies for fiscal, military, economic and agricultural offences.

Prosecution is handled by the Public Prosecution Service, which is independent of the judiciary and falls under the authority of the Minister of Justice. Prosecutors are ultimately responsible for criminal investigations. Public prosecutors therefore have to ensure that the police observe all rules and procedures. However, as Tak (2003) notes, in practice, the police is allowed to deal with most cases without prior consultation with the public prosecutor except in more important criminal cases where the latter may give detailed instructions.

Capital punishment was abolished in 1870. The most severe penalty is life imprisonment which is rarely imposed and not compulsorily prescribed in the penal code. Fixed-term prison sentences range from a statutory minimum of one day to a maximum of 20 years. Alternatives to prison sentences are penalties such as electronic monitoring, community service and fines. Besides penalties the judges can also impose measures on offenders. These can range from confiscation of forbidden objects, confiscation of illegally obtained profits, obligation to pay compensation, hospitalization in case of psychiatric disorders or the treatment of drug habits.

Criminology

This section is divided in three parts. The first part deals with crime patterns based on survey data. What do Dutch citizens fear? How do they assess the chances of victimization? Second, actual crime figures are examined to verify whether public fears are justified. Because official crime figures also contain data about suspects, these are also discussed. Finally, this chapter concludes with a discussion on organized crime. Organized crime is difficult to capture in crime surveys or official numbers and therefore warrants a special discussion.

Since the 1970s, criminologists and policy makers have agreed that official crime statistics do not adequately depict citizens' real victimization or their fears of crime. One simple reason is that victims do not always report to the police, especially in cases of less serious forms of crime. In such cases they do not think the police can do anything and think that filing a report is too much of a hassle. These unreported incidents, therefore, constitute the so-called "dark figure." In order to fill these gaps in knowledge, crime surveys have been conducted to detect these "hidden crimes."

An important crime survey that measures the subjective and objective fears of crime in the Dutch population is the Safety Monitor State (available online only in Dutch). It is an annual standardized survey that started in 2006 and is handled by the Central Bureau of Statistics (CBS,

2008). At the beginning of each year, about 20,000 citizens are randomly sampled to be interviewed (often by telephone) about their experiences with crime. To measure subjective fear of crime, the respondents answer questions about public order and security risks in their own living environment and their fears of crime. The objective part of the survey asks the respondents in what specific way they became victims of crime in the preceding year. These outcomes are publicly available and used as background information on the development of public security and the functioning of the police. Some of these outcomes are presented below.

In 2009, about one in five of the population (older than 15 years of age) sometimes felt insecure about their safety. Compared with 2006, this fear of crime level has come down from 27 percent to 20 percent. About 3 percent admitted to feeling very insecure. Situations in which citizens felt insecure generally occurred outside of their own home. One in seven felt insecure at places where youths hung around, one in eleven at places of night-life entertainment and one in 20 in shopping malls as well as public transportation. The questionnaire also asked if people avoided certain places. One in eight admitted they would not open their door at night if they were not expecting a visitor.

The respondents also answered questions about the kind and the number of times they became a victim of crime in the last 12 months. The most reported case was damage to or theft from their car. This happened to 8 percent. Compared to the general rate of car ownership, this number rises to almost 12 percent. In actual numbers, this would mean about 1.3 million cases. About 4 percent of the population became a victim of bicycle theft. A few other notable percentages included the following: the destruction of property (5 percent), threats (3 percent), theft (3 percent), and burglary or attempted burglary (2 percent). According to the survey, about 25 percent of the general Dutch population became victim to one or several crimes in the past year.[1] However, not all crimes are reported to the police. According to the same survey, about one in three crimes were reported to the police. And about a quarter of all crimes had an official report prepared. One reason for making an official report was insurance related. To secure financial compensation, victims had to present a formal police report to the insurance companies. When the respondents were asked the reason why they *did not* report to the police, the common response was that it would not solve anything. Others judged it not important anyway.

These crime surveys show that the discrepancy between the occurrence of a crime and the actual filing of an official report is quite large. Some criminologists advocate only using crime surveys for guiding evidence-based policies and not the official police data. However, crime surveys also have their limitations. Consider the following questions. How do we know the respondents are telling the truth? What about specific crimes, such as fraud, that are not included in such questionnaires? How can we be sure that the interviewer and the respondent use the same definitions? For instance, one person might interpret verbal abuse as violence, whereas the other does not. What about minorities whose command of the official language is limited? Can they use interpreters? Or does the interviewer quickly select somebody else instead? Miscommunication can be an important factor in the difference between reported and officially recorded crime rates.

Elffers and Averdijk (2007) asked themselves such questions in their focus on the city of Amsterdam. They used a forward record check and a reverse record check to verify in what way the answers of the statements of the respondents to the Safety Monitor State could be verified. First, the researchers searched police databases to verify respondents' claims of filing a report. Second, they verified respondents' claims that they did not file a police report, when in fact they had. The findings showed that crime victim reports were not always reliable. Generally speaking, respondents did not always use the correct time perspective. For instance, a break-in that occurred three years ago was reported as if it had happened in the past 12 months. This is called a "forward-telescoping effect" and may have occurred in up to 24 percent of the reports. Backwardtelescoping happened in 7 percent, as people said they did not report a crime when in fact their names were found in police records. Sometimes a crime which occurred in another member's household was reported as if it occurred in one's own home (17 percent). Lastly, 29 percent of the respondents who claimed to have filed a police report were not found in the police files. Therefore, it is premature to simply dismiss police files.

We will now take a closer look at the Dutch crime data system maintained by the Netherlands Police Agency. This system contains two different sets of data. One part deals with reports filed by the police, based on reports received from victims. The other part contains crime suspects in a given period. This second part of the information is only recorded by the police and not available outside official channels. Because the Netherlands are relatively small, all data concerning known crime reports and suspects are centralized and reported annually. This results in a "national crime map," which gives insight into officially registered Dutch criminality and its suspects. These crime figures are extensively used by researchers and the Central Bureau of Statistics.

In 2007 the police recorded 681,198 crime incidents in 19 districts, about 564 crime reports per 10,000 inhabitants. Since 2002, the number of crime reports fell by 16 percent, although the drop stagnated in 2007. An exact comparison with the national crime survey is not possible, as the police data system uses seven broad categories. These include the following: theft without violence (65.4 percent), vandalism and public disorder (21.5 percent), violence against persons (10.3 percent), theft with violence (1.2 percent), other reports (1.1 percent), other sexual crimes (0.3 percent) and violent sexual crimes (0.2 percent).

As these crime categories indicate, the police differentiate between crimes with or without the use of violence. The reason for such differentiation is that crimes containing violence are subjected to stricter punishments than non-violent crimes. Such reasoning stresses the fact that police data are first and foremost collected for police purposes and not academic research. However, these broad categories contain many details, such as the specifics of the crime (including a more detailed description, time and place) and information about the victim.

The second large dataset is information about suspects. This information includes age, sex, nationality, place of birth, residence, recidivism and the suspected crime(s) according to the penal code. Because the details about victims and suspects can be tailored to specific questions, the police datasets are often used by academics. These range from practical applications to theory-driven analysis, as shown in the following examples.

As a practical example, research on bicycle theft comes to mind. Bicycles are a popular method of transportation in the Netherlands. The country is relatively small, flat and has compact cities. Therefore, taking a bicycle to and from school or work is a quick and easy travel solution for short distances. Bicycles are used by people of all walks and know no social boundaries. But the abundance of bicycles also attracts bicycle theft. Cyclists spend almost as much on their locks as they do on their bicycles. In 2007, the government announced an anti-bike-theft campaign to combat this rampant form of crime. According to the program, 750,000 bicycles were stolen in 2006. The campaign was to bring the figure down to 650,000 in 2010. Versteegh and van Mantgem (2007) used police data to test the feasibility of such an outcome. Their analysis showed that a focus on large and mid-sized cities would produce the best results. Because the database also records times, weekdays and places of thefts, certain hotspots could be targeted for increased police surveillance. The researchers also compared the bicycle suspects in 2002 and 2006, and found that they were getting younger. This finding suggests that drug addicts, notorious for stealing bicycles to produce drug money, are becoming less active because they are typically over 30 years of age. The police data also showed fewer drug-dependent suspects of bicycle theft.

An example that combines practicality with theory is geographic criminology. Police data also contain information on the time and place where the registered crime was committed. Using data on detected residential burglaries during the period 1996–2004 in The Hague and its environs, Bernasco (2008) was able to assert that initial and subsequent burglaries involve the same offenders.

Police data also make it possible to do research into the effectiveness of public safety policies. For example, Vollaard (2005) compared increases in police personnel and the effect of reducing victimization. He found that a 1 percent increase in police personnel per capita resulted in a 0.4 to 0.7 decline in crime and nuisance.

A theory-driven application of the police data is the catch–recatch method, also known as the capture–recapture method. This method can be used to estimate the dark figures of crime. This method was originally developed to estimate the size of a particular animal population in the wild. First a number of animals are caught and marked. These are then released back in the general population. On a later date, the population is sampled again (recatch) and the number of marked individuals of the first sample are counted. A comparison of the number of marked individual animals in relation to the sample size leads to estimates about the general population. Cruyff and van der Heijden (2003) tried to use this method to estimate the number of drivers under the influence and the number of people carrying illegal weapons. This turned out to be a complicated process with mixed results. One factor that weighs in the equation is the chance of apprehension. A drunk person is only breaking the law at the time he or she climbs behind the wheel. At other times his or her chances of apprehension for drunk driving are zero. But the chances of apprehension for a person who is carrying a weapon (or for that matter those without legal resident status) are much higher because he or she is continuously breaking the law.

Other researchers used the catch–recatch method to estimate the number of illegal residents in the Netherlands. Van der Heijden *et al.* (2006) estimated the size of the population of Dutch Antilleans that stay in the Netherlands without being officially registered to be about 3,000 in the year 2000 and 12,000 in 2003. Other research estimated the overall illegal population in 2002 at 112,000 to 163,000 people (Engbersen *et al.*, 2002).

Because police data go back over longer periods of time, it is also very useful to do research on criminal careers or life course criminology. Blokland (2005) used different sample techniques to track the criminal career of a group of over 4,000 Dutch offenders since 1977. This made it possible to study the way criminal behavior changes as individuals age. After 25 years, 65.4 percent of all individuals had been reconvicted for at least one offence. The average recidivist was reconvicted 9.4 times. However, the rate and shape of criminal trajectories differed significantly between individuals. All in all, four offender groups were distinguished. The largest group (over 60 percent), called sporadic offenders, had a very low conviction rate. Two fairly similar groups peeked during early adulthood. The fourth group (1 percent), called high-level persistent offenders, did not desist offending during adulthood. The study also showed that marriage functioned as a common predictor for falling offending rates.

Criminal research in the Netherlands is not limited to figures and statistics. Far from it. Researchers also make use of qualitative methods, e.g. in the areas of criminal subcultures (van Gemert *et al.*, 2008), delinquent youths (Weerman and Bijleveld, 2007) and minorities (Bovenkerk and Yesilgoz, 2004). In the next paragraph, we take a closer look at organized crime because this area of interest is especially hard to capture in quantitative figures.

Organized crime in the Netherlands is typically studied through qualitative methods, such as fieldwork by researchers or case studies of police investigations. For instance, Zaitch (2002) tried to understand how cocaine from Colombia was bought and sold in the Netherlands. His fieldwork took him from Amsterdam, The Hague and Rotterdam to Bogoto and Cali. In the course of his research he interviewed 8 Colombian drug couriers, 10 importers, 13 distributors, 3 retailers and 10 helpers and employees of cocaine entrepreneurs. One of his findings was the importance of reputation, which worked within and outside ethnic communities. Within the South American community, people who were deemed trustworthy could do more business than others. But outside this community, Colombian drug dealers could also capitalize on a reputation fed by popular media as fearsome criminals. An ordinary man called Escobar (which is a common Colombian name) successfully impressed his Dutch counterparts with his supposed connections to drug cartels.

Other field work has concentrated on human smuggling and illegal migration. Van Wijk (2008), for example, tried to find out how asylum seekers from Angola arrived in the Netherlands. Although Dutch officials often thought these people arrived clandestinely with the aid of human smugglers, illegal immigrants told van Wijk that they did not pay smugglers. Instead they often traveled legally to and within Europe. It was only because they wanted to bolster their asylum claims that they told Dutch officials stories about human trafficking. Other researchers talked with illegal immigrants from Turkey (Staring, 2003) or used interpreters to talk with Iraqis, Ethiopians and Somalis in the Netherlands (van Liempt, 2007). All of this research confirmed the importance of family and friends who assisted illegal migration. Such findings are repeatedly verified in other parts of the world (see, for example, Zhang, 2008).

Another method of doing research on organized crime uses the files that the police or other investigative authorities have collected for the prosecution of criminals. In this regard, the Netherlands has a remarkable position in the world due to its methods of police investigation and ease of access of this material for researchers.

Police files are sometimes seen as contaminated material because of biased evidence. But it is important to note that Dutch criminal investigations, in stark contrast to investigations in the US, do not make use of the very selective tool of plea bargaining. There is no jury system to "win over," nor are judges, public prosecutors or police chiefs dependent on elections. Instead, they are appointed on merit. Dutch cases also provide a great deal of "objective" evidence on offender behavior because of the extensive use of wiretaps.[2] The interception of telecommunications between criminals provides a great deal of insight into the way criminal activities are carried out and how offenders collaborate. As such, a "bug on the phone line" acts as the next best thing to the "fly on the wall" perspective. Furthermore, researchers in the Netherlands have full access to the original police files and are not restricted to second-hand information (e.g. interpretations of police officers).

One such study is the parliamentary inquiry called the Van Traa Report (PEO, 1996). This was the first overview of organized crime in the Netherlands. In this report, organized crime groups in the Netherlands are characterized by international smuggling activities: drug trafficking, smuggling illegal immigrants, human trafficking for sexual exploitation and other transnational illegal activities, such as money laundering and evasion of taxes. This stands in contrast to (American) mafia-type organizations that by racketeering monopolize certain economic sectors (e.g. waste disposal) or geographical locations (e.g. restaurants and bars in a certain district).

Still, mafia or not, policy makers have argued that criminals who want to invest their money in the legal economy by opening a bar, restaurant, shop, etc. should be stopped. The Netherlands follow the international rules on anti-money laundering regulation, in which banks and other financial institutions are required by law to report unusual financial transactions to a Financial Intelligence Unit. A study by researchers of the Free University in Amsterdam (Huisman and Nelen, 2007; Nelen and Huisman, 2008) showed that, following the example of Italy and New York, Dutch public administrators are also using their administrative authority to screen applications to operate certain businesses for possible connections with organized crime.

An important continuing study that relies extensively on police files are the Organized Crime Monitors by the Research and Documentation Centre (Kleemans *et al.*, 2002; Kleemans *et al.*,

1998; van de Bunt *et al.,* 2007). Through the use of systematic interviews with officials and analysis of case files, the Monitor focuses on such questions as: What is the composition of the crime group and how do offenders cooperate? What kinds of illegal activities do they engage in and how do they operate? How do they interact with the opportunities and risks of their environment? Because these Monitors combine empirical data with theory, they provide good insights into the workings of crimes that are organized.

In 1998 and 2002 the Monitor used social networking theory to examine criminal networks. The Monitors found that offenders cooperate in some projects, but the structure of their cooperation is fluid and changes over time. Social relations form the basis of criminal cooperation. Family, friends and acquaintances work together and introduce each other to third parties. In this way, offenders do not only find new opportunities, but also solve problems of cooperating in an environment fraught with distrust, suspicion and potential deceit. However, this does not imply that criminal associations do not have a structure or that the relationships within the organization are interchangeable and horizontal. In many cases, there are clear key players (nodes) on whom many other offenders depend because of their financial resources, technical knowhow or contacts. In time, other offenders may acquire their own expertise or contacts and become key players themselves. Another important aspect is the function of facilitators. They are money changers, underground bankers, financial service providers and forgers who operate in the periphery of criminal organizations. Because they render their services to several criminal organizations, they play an integral role in a criminal network.

Independent researchers can also request access to police files. For example, Klerks (2000) examined a specific crime group involved with cannabis, Soudijn (2006) examined 88 case files on how Chinese human smugglers were organized and Spapens (2006) examined 48 case files dealing with criminals producing and exporting synthetic drugs. Van Duyne uses case files and official records to estimate the threat of criminal profits on the legal economy (van Duyne *et al.*, 2009). He reckons that fears are mostly overblown. Foreign academics have also been granted access to particular police files for analysis. For example, cases dealing with *hawala* banking (also known as underground banking) in the Netherlands have been examined in collaboration with the American scholar Passas (Passas, 2004, 2005; van de Bunt, 2008). An interesting finding was that the common view of underground banking not leaving a paper trail was refuted by the evidence. House searches by the police turned up ledgers full of numerous transactions.

According to a study by Kleemans and de Poot (2008), the criminal careers of people in organized crime look different from those of most offenders. After examining the criminal careers of approximately 1,000 individuals involved in organized crimes, they found that there were no young offenders: none of the offenders were under 18 at the time of the investigation and only 7 percent were between 18 and 24 years of age. In total, about three quarters of the offenders were 30 years of age or older. On average, the offenders were approximately 27 years old when they came into contact with the Dutch judicial system for the first time. Only a quarter of all offenders came into contact with the Dutch judicial system before reaching the age of 20, and these were often the brothers, children or cousins of other crime group members. On the other hand, 40 percent of the offenders were aged between 20 and 30 when they first had trouble with the law, and 34 percent were older than 30 at their first contact with the judicial system. Furthermore, the authorities had no prior knowledge of approximately 28 percent of the offenders. It was not until the investigation that these offenders came within the scope of the Dutch authorities. These "unknown offenders" to a large extent were born elsewhere and came to live or reside in the Netherlands at a later date. With these characteristics, it is safe to say that the life-course development of organized criminals differs greatly from typical street criminal careers.

The study also showed that people became involved in organized crime through different paths: through existing social relationships, work and professional relationships, through leisure activities, certain life events or through recruitment. The researchers therefore stressed the importance of "social opportunity structures": social ties providing access to profitable criminal opportunities. Additionally, some participated in organized crime later in life as a consequence of life events, such as bankruptcy or serious debts. For example, a painter got through the first 56 years of his life without getting into trouble with the authorities. His criminal career began when, as a result of a life event (illness), he quit his regular job and through a friend became involved in the prostitution business. He was later convicted not only of trafficking in women, but also of aggravated assault and the possession of firearms.

Since the 1990s, the Dutch police have also employed researchers who publicize their findings on organized crime. A typical example is the report "Looks can be deceiving" (van Hout and van der Laan, 2008). In 2000, the government lifted the general ban on brothels in an attempt to decriminalize prostitution. Contrary to expectations, this did not eliminate abuses in prostitution. Human traffickers, pimps and bodyguards were still able to operate in the licensed window prostitution sector. The National Public Prosecutor's Office ordered a study of the modus operandi of one such offender group who exploited around 120 women. Using a technique called "scripting," the researchers dissected the prostitution business in all the necessary steps the offenders had to make in order to exploit illegal women for prostitution. These ranged from entering a country to having a place to stay and finding a place to work. It turned out that each necessary step brought the men and their victims out into the open. For instance, airliners transported the victims, housing agencies collected rent, managers in the red light district gave them a place to work. And of course, customers paid for their services. The police was never contacted because people didn't see or didn't want to see any exploitation. To counter this situation, different agencies and local government started to cooperate in raising their own awareness and sharing information. Criminologists employed by the government are thus actively involved in the improvement of society.

Key research and funding institutions in the Netherlands

1. Criminology is studied at the Erasmus University, University of Leiden, VU University of Amsterdam
2. The Netherlands Institute for the Study of Crime and Law Enforcement (NSCR): http://www.nscr.nl/
3. Research and Documentation Centre (WODC): http://english.wodc.nl/
4. Centre for Information and Research of Organised Crime (CIROC): http://www.ciroc.nl/en_index.php
5. National Rapporteur on Trafficking in Human Beings in the Netherlands (NRM): http://english.bnrm.nl/
6. The International Victimology Institute Tilburg (INTERVICT): http://www.tilburguniversity.nl/intervict/
7. The Netherlands Institute of Mental Health and Addiction (Trimbos Institute): http://www.trimbos.org
8. Centre for Drug Research, University of Amsterdam (CEDRO): http://www.cedro-uva.org/index.html

Conclusion

Criminology in the Netherlands is multifaceted. Research on crime in general makes use of crime surveys or police data. These datasets are tailored to answer specific questions or generate new theoretical ideas. Because of the availability of large datasets and (compared with other countries) ease of access to police files, criminology in the Netherlands has some unique perspectives to offer.

It is, however, tempting to compare the quantitative output of such studies with data from other countries, but this is not always as easy as it looks. Differences in penal law, judicial proceedings and, of course, statistical accounting can result in flawed comparisons. Qualitative research on organized crime faces the same problems. For instance, the Netherlands do not have a gang problem in which certain criminal groups try to dominate or control a specific area or trade. Instead, the Netherlands is faced with groups who concentrate on the trade of illegal goods.

Over the last couple of years, criminology has become a popular subject of study in the Netherlands. As students continue in this field of research, this will probably lead to ever more knowledge and understanding of crime in the Netherlands. But there are also dangers. Fundamental research positions are restricted to budget restraints. First indications show that most students of criminology end up in consultancy and governmental policy positions. Only time will tell if they can continue to do independent research or have to tailor their outcomes to the preferred policies. If that is the case, the success of criminology could also be its own undoing.

Future research questions

1 Using public administrators to screen applicants for criminal connections is intended to prevent money laundering. How effective (e.g. cost, time) is this method compared to regular police work?
2 Crime surveys and official police data are often out of sync. This suggests problems with compatibility. What methods are available to make these two datasets a better fit?
3 The prosecuting authorities in the Netherland make extensive use of intercepted telephone communications (wiretaps). The same authorities perceive the deployment of infiltrators in criminal groups as a more intrusive method. The method of infiltration is therefore used sparingly. Compare the drawbacks and advantages of both methods in light of potential human rights infringements.
4 The logistics of illegal activities could have a bearing on the structure of the cooperative ties of criminals. Analyze the structural characteristics that would result in meaningful comparisons between crime groups involved in different sort of crime (e.g. drugs versus human smuggling).
5 The career paths of criminals who are involved with international drug trafficking are likely to differ from repeat offenders. How does Merton's theory on anomie fit in?

Notes

1 Victimization, and subsequently, restorative justice, lie outside the scope of this chapter. For more information, see van Dijk *et al.* (2007, 2008).
2 Compare 62 wiretaps per 100,000 inhabitants in the Netherlands with 0.5 per 100,000 in the US (http://www.edri.org/edrigram/number2.14/wiretap).

References

Alemika, E. E. O. (1993). Colonialism, state and policing in Nigeria. *Crime, Law and Social Change*, 20, 187–219.

Amalu, C. (2008). Illegal migration – 59,000 Nigerians in transit countries. Vanguard Newspapers, August 8.

Bernasco, W. (2008) Them again? Same-offender involvement in repeat and near repeat burglaries. *European Journal of Criminology*, 5(4): 411–31.

Blokland, A. (2005). *Crime over the life span: trajectories of criminal behavior in Dutch offenders*. Leiden: NSCR.

Bovenkerk, F. and Yesilgoz, Y. (2004). The Turkish mafia and the state. In C. Fijnaut and L. Paoli (Eds.) *Organised crime in Europe: concepts, patterns and control policies in the European Union and beyond*, pp. 585–602. Dordrecht: Springer.

van de Bunt, H. G. (2008). A case study on the misuse of *hawala* banking. *International Journal of Social Economics*, 35(9): 691–702.

van de Bunt, H. G., Kleemans, E. R., and de Poot, C. J. (2007). *Georganiseerde criminaliteit in Nederland: derde rapportage op basis van de Monitor Georganiseerde Criminaliteit.* Den Haag: Boom Juridische Uitgevers.

Centraal Bureau voor de Statistiek (CBS). (2008). *Veiligheidsmonitor Rijk 2008: Landelijke rapportage.* Voorburg: Centraal Bureau voor de Statistiek.

Cruyff, M. J. L. F. and van der Heijden, P. G. M. (2003). *Benutting HKS en ontwikkeling vangst-hervangstmethoden. Een onderzoek in opdracht van het Wetenschappelijk Onderzoek-en Documentatiecentrum (WODC) van het Ministerie van Justitie* (Report). Utrecht: Universiteit Utrecht.

van Dijk, J. J. M., Groenhuijsen, M. S., and Winkel, F.W. (2007). Victimologie: Voorgeschiedenis en stand van zaken. *Justitiële verkenningen*, 33(3): 9–29.

van Dijk, J. J. M., van Kesteren, J. N., and Smit, P. (2008). *Criminal victimisation in international perspective, key findings from the 2004–2005 ICVS and EU ICS.* Den Haag: Boom Legal Publishers. (Onderzoek en Beleid, WODC, 257).

van Duyne, P. C., Soudijn, M. R. J., and Kint, T. (2009). Bricks don't talk: searching for crime-money in real estate. In P. C. van Duyne, S. Donati, J. Harvey, A. Maljevic, and K. von Lampe (Eds.) *Crime, money and criminal mobility*, pp. 241–74. Nijmegen: Wolf Legal Publishers.

Elffers, H. and Averdijk, M. (2007). *Aangeven aan te geven?* (NSCR Report). Leiden: Nederlands Studiecentrum Criminaliteit en Rechtshandhaving.

Engbersen, G., Staring, R., van der Leun, J., de Boom, J., van der Heijden, P., and Cruiff, M. (2002). *Illegale vreemdelingen in Nederland. Omvang, overkomst, verblijf en uitzetting.* Rotterdam: RISBO Contractresearch.

van Gemert, F., Peterson, D., and Lien, I.-L. (2008). *Street gangs, migration and ethnicity*. Devon, UK: Willan Publishing.

van der Heijden, P. G. M., Zwane, E., and Hessen, D. (2006). Schatting van aantal in Nederland verblijvende Antillianen die niet ingeschreven zijn in de GBA. Een "capture–recapture" – analyse in opdracht van het Ministerie van Justitie. Utrecht: Universiteit Utrecht, IOPS.

van Hout, M. M. J., and van der Laan, F. J. (2008). *Looks can be deceiving: the identification of human trafficking in the licensed prostitution sector.* Driebergen: KLPD-DNR.

Huisman, W., and Nelen, H. (2007). Gotham unbound Dutch style: the administrative approach to organized crime in Amsterdam. *Crime, Law and Social Change*, 48: 87–103.

Kleemans, E. R., van den Berg, E. A. I. M., van de Bunt, H. G., Bouwers, M., Kouwenberg, R. F., and Paulides, G. (1998). *Georganiseerde criminaliteit in Nederland* (No. Onderzoek en beleid, 173). Den Haag: WODC.

Kleemans, E. R., Brienen, M. E. I., and van de Bunt, H. G. (2002). *Georganiseerde criminaliteit in Nederland: tweede rapportage op basis van de WODC-monitor.* Den Haag: WODC.

Kleemans, E. R. and de Poot, C. J. (2008). Criminal careers in organized crime and social opportunity structure. *European Journal of Criminology*, 5(69): 69–98.

Klerks, P. P. H. M. (2000). *Groot in de hasj: theorie en praktijk van de georganiseerde criminaliteit.* Alphen aan den Rijn: Samsom.

van Liempt, I. (2007). *Navigating borders: inside perspectives on the process of human smuggling into the Netherlands.* Amsterdam: Amsterdam University Press.

Nelen, H. and Huisman, W. (2008). Breaking the power of organized crime? The administrative approach in Amsterdam. In D. Siegel and H. Nelen (Eds.), *Organized crime: culture, markets and policies*, pp. 207–18. New York: Springer.

Passas, N. (2004). Indicators of Hawala operations and criminal abuse. *Journal of Money Laundering Control*, 8(2): 168–72.

—— (2005). *Informal value transfer systems and criminal activities* (Cahier No. 2005–1). Den Haag: WODC.
Parlementaire Enquêtecommissie Opsporingsmethoden (PEO). (1996). *Inzake opsporing: enquête opsporingsmethoden, Eindrapport.* Den Haag: Parlementaire Enquêtecommissie Opsporingsmethoden.
Soudijn, M. R. J. (2006). *Chinese human smuggling in transit.* Den Haag: Boom juridische uitgeverij.
Spapens, T. (2006). *Interactie tussen criminaliteit en opsporing: de gevolgen van opsporingsactiviteiten voor de organisatie en afscherming an xtc-productie en-handel in Nederlan.* Antwerpen: Intersentia.
Staring, R. (2003). Smuggling aliens towards the Netherlands: the role of human smugglers and transnational networks. In D. Siegel, H. van de Bunt and D. Zaitch (Eds.), *Global organized crime: trends and developments*, pp. 105–16. Dordrecht: Kluwer.
Tak, J. P. (2003). The Dutch criminal justice system: organization and operation. Meppel: Boom Juridische uitgevers (2nd edition).
Versteegh, P. and van Mantgem, J. (2007). Fietsendiefstal daalt. *Secondant*, 5: 6–13.
Vollaard, B. (2005). *Police numbers up, crime rates down: the effect of police on crime in the Netherlands, 1996–2003.* CPB Document No. 75. The Hague: CPB.
Weerman, F. M. and Bijleveld, C. C. J. H. (2007). Birds of different feathers. School networks of serious delinquent, minor delinquent and non-delinquent boys and girls. *European Journal of Criminology*, 4: 357–83.
van Wijk, J. (2008). Luanda – Holanda: irregular migration from Angola to the Netherlands. *International Migration, DOI* (10.1111/j.1468–2435.2008.00485.x.).
Zaitch, D. (2002). *Trafficking cocaine: Colombian drug entrepreneurs in the Netherlands.* Den Haag: Kluwer Law International.
Zhang, S. X. (2008). *Chinese human smuggling organizations; families, social networks, and cultural imperatives.* Stanford: Stanford University Press.

Internet sources (all accessed August 5, 2009)

http://www.cbs.nl/nl-NL/menu/themas/veiligheid-recht/publicaties/publicaties/archief/2008/2008-veiligheidsmonitor-rijk-pub.htm

For general information about the Research and Documentation Centre, check: http://english.wodc.nl/. Here one can find numerous reports on research in crime. For the latest Organized Crime Monitor, see: http://english.wodc.nl/onderzoeksdatabase/fs200618-monitor-georganiseerde-criminaliteit.aspx.

Besides the CIA *World factbook* (https://www.cia.gov/library/publications/the-world-factbook/geos/nl.html), for all sorts of figures concerning the Netherlands see the English website of the Bureau of Statistics: http://www.cbs.nl/en-GB/menu/home/default.htm?Languageswitch = on. It has a special section dealing with security and justice: http://www.cbs.nl/en-GB/menu/themas/veiligheid-recht/nieuws/default.htm.

For information on the Dutch justice system in English, check: http://www.om.nl/vast_menu_blok/english/. It also has a special FAQ section on the Dutch drug policy.

45

People's Republic of China

The state of criminology

Liu Xiu and Jiang Tingyao

Introduction

This chapter will introduce China's national situation, and review the current major research topics in China's criminology society.

Infrastructure

The People's Republic of China has a land area of about 9.6 million square kilometers, the third-largest country in the world following Russia and Canada. China is bordered by Korea to the east; Mongolia to the north; Russia to the northeast; Kazakhstan, Kyrgyzstan and Tajikistan to the northwest; Afghanistan, Pakistan, India, Nepal and Bhutan to the west and southwest; and Myanmar, Laos and Vietnam to the south. Across the seas to the east and southeast are the Republic of Korea, Japan, the Philippines, Brunei, Malaysia and Indonesia. China's mainland coastline measures approximately 18,000 kilometers. Mainland China is flanked to the east and south by the Bohai, Yellow, East China and South China seas, with a total maritime area of 4.73 million square kilometers.

For three decades China's average gross domestic product (GDP) growth rate has maintained at an average of 9.5 percent and its economy has entered the ranks of the world's largest. China's economic development is also reflected in its poverty reduction. Between 1981 and 2004, the population below the official poverty line fell from 65 percent to 10 percent, lifting more than half a billion people out of poverty. The average disposable income per capita among urban residents rose from 6,860 yuan (roughly $680 USD) in 2001 to 10,493 yuan (roughly $1,500 USD) in 2005, at an annual increase of 9.6 percent; while the average net income per-capita among rural residents rose from 2,366 (roughly $338 USD) to 3,255 yuan (roughly $465 USD), with an average annual growth of 5.3 percent. The Engel coefficient (food expenses as a percentage of total consumer spending) fell from 39.4 percent in 2000 to 36.7 percent in 2005, gradually approaching developed countries' 30 percent. Among rural households, the Engel coefficient fell from 49.1 percent to 45.5 percent.

The Chinese Communist Party (CCP) is the biggest political party in China and has remained the ruling party since it established the People's Republic of China in 1949. There are eight other officially recognized political parties that serve consultative roles to the CCP. However, these are not opposition parties, nor are they seeking political power. In China, state power is exercised through the National People's Congress (NPC), the legislative body. The State Council (the executive branch of the government) is accountable to the NPC and its Standing Committee. The State Council has the power to formulate administrative measures, enact regulations, and issue decisions and orders within its functions.

China is the most populous country in the world, with an estimated 1.33 billion people by the end of 2008 or one fifth of the world's population. Since the late 1970s, China has implemented strict family planning policies in an attempt to control its population growth. By 2009, the annual rate of population growth had decreased to 12.14 per thousand. However, life expectancy has increased to 71.95 years, 5 more than the world average.

China is home to one of the world's oldest and most complex civilizations covering a history of over 5,000 years. The nation covers a large geographical region with customs and traditions varying greatly between towns, cities and provinces. There are roughly 56 different ethnic groups, with the Han being the largest. Chinese culture is a broad term that can be used to describe a wide range of cultural practices and customs. But the predominant social values are derived from Confucianism and Taoism. The official language is Mandarin.

Since 1950 China has provided nine-year compulsory education that covers more than 95 percent of China's populated areas. China's basic education involves pre-school, nine-year compulsory education from elementary to junior high school, standard senior high school education and special education for disabled children. The higher education system has been improved in recent decades. Many industrial polytechnic and specialized colleges have also been established. At this moment, China's education system continues to expand.

Administration of justice

The Ministry of Public Security (MPS) is in charge of securing and maintaining public order in the country. MPS is under the State Council. There are corresponding public security departments in provinces and autonomous regions. At the level of prefectures and counties and municipalities, there are corresponding public security bureaus. Then sub-bureaus are established in lower levels of jurisdictions. These are all part of the unified public security apparatus. The responsibilities of public security agencies in China include prevention, suppression and investigations of criminal activities and fight against terrorist activities.

The people's courts are the judicial branch of the state, the highest of which is the Supreme People's Court in Beijing. Local people's courts and special people's courts are located at different levels of corresponding administrative bodies. Higher people's courts are established in provinces, autonomous regions and municipalities. Then there are intermediate and basic people's courts at lower administrative levels. The Supreme People's Court, the country's highest judicial agency, is accountable to the NPC and its Standing Committee, and supervises the judicial work of the local people's courts, military courts and other special courts. The people's courts try all cases in public, except those involving state secrets, individual privacy or juvenile delinquency.

The people's procuratorates in China correspond to those of the people's courts. The people's procuratorates exercise the procuratorial authority in all incidents that endanger state and public security, threaten economic order and infringe on citizens' rights. Procurators examine all cases scheduled for criminal investigation, and decide whether a suspect should be arrested or not, and whether a case should be prosecuted or exempt from prosecution; initiate and support public prosecution in criminal cases; and oversee the activities of public security agencies, people's courts, prisons, detention facilities and reform-through-labor institutions. As is the case with the people's courts, the people's procuratorates exercise their own authorities prescribed by law, free of interference from any other administrative branches. Also the same in structure as that of people's courts, the Supreme People's Procuratorate in Beijing represents the highest level of this judicial branch in China. There are local people's procuratorates and special people's procuratorates at different administrative levels in local governments.

Criminology in China

Criminology in China emerged as an independent discipline in the early 1980s. In the 1990s, significant progress was made with the publication of large volumes of books and theses. In 1992, the Chinese Criminology Research Association was established, which greatly enhanced its professional and academic status. Much of the research focused on two main themes: (1) theoretical development, and (2) specific categories of crimes. Looking over the past five years, several main themes in Chinese criminology can be identified, which will be discussed in the following sections.

Unlike other countries, criminology in China is not considered an established academic discipline in the same class as sociology, psychology or economics. It is subsumed within the criminal law, under which it is treated as a secondary discipline as a branch of the law. Many scholars in China have striven to raise the status of criminology as a credible academic discipline. Well known among Chinese legal scholars and criminologists, Kang (1996, p. 30) attempted to define criminology as a legal science concerning the criminal facts, the study of which intends to explore criminal behaviors and their underlying reasons, and to devise effective countermeasures. However, there are other opinions on where criminology belongs. Many scholars in China believe that criminology, in theory, is a subsidiary of the criminal law; but it is at the same time a branch of sociology. The so-called "branch of sociology" refers to the fact that research on crime often concerns social facts. From this point of view, criminology appears to fit well with other social sciences. But the study of crime and criminal procedures seems to belong to the domain of law.

Wang (2004) argued that if criminology is placed within sociology, social policies on combating crime will then become the core of criminological research. But then criminology will be stuck in the quagmire of pointless social policies. According to Wang (2004), the most important task in criminology is to support the effort of building a better criminal law system. Only in the domain of law can criminology reach its fullest potential as an academic discipline.

More recently, a different perspective was proposed to define the role and task of criminology in China. Song (2004) proposed that crime represents the symptoms of a sick society (or abnormal society). The causes of crime reflect the underlying problems of an abnormal society and therefore concerned policies combating the crime are akin to medical remedies for the prevention and treatment of a sick society. Therefore criminology resembles a "social medical science," not in subordination to criminal law or sociology, or to some other social legal sciences in between.

Chinese scholars have currently reached a consensus on one principle about criminology: research on crime is different from that in criminal law. Criminologists regard crime as a social fact. The goal of criminology is to understand the phenomenon of crime and devise measures to control and prevent it. In the domain of criminal law, however, researchers are mostly concerned about legal procedures and penalty.

There are marked differences in how crime is defined by criminologists and legal scholars in China. Chinese criminologists have a more flexible and broader definition of crime. In comparison, legal scholars view crime as a violation of codified criminal law, which therefore invokes a system response that involves a penalty as prescribed by law. So the main task for legal scholars is to determine the precise description of every crime and provide guidance to judges on how to make decisions in sentencing.

But the main task of criminology is different. It seeks to answer three key questions: why people commit crime, what patterns crime forms and how to prevent it. Criminology makes inquiries not only into law-violating behaviors, but also transgressions that are not prescribed in law, such as acts that may be deemed as immoral but not necessarily illegal. Criminologists are also interested in preventing and controlling crime, except that the definition of crime is broader than that in criminal law.

In analyzing the term "crime," the chairman of the Chinese Criminology Research Association, Wang (2007), introduced the concepts of "value" and "domain." He argued that the understanding of crime varies based on different values and domains. His "value" argument states that social facts can be divided into two domains: the "scientific facts" and the "value facts." The former exists in the objective world, or the objective fact. The latter is subjective fact, which is assessed by our minds. He argued that the study of crime should allow diversity not uniformity because a unified concept of "crime" does not exist.

The view that crime can be beneficial to a society has its origin in the thesis of Emile Durkheim (1858–1917). Some Chinese scholars support this opinion and propose similar theories like "the benefit theory" and "the relativism crime theory." They believe that crime plays "a positive role" in the society. One such theory was put forth by Liang (2001), which points to two benefits of crime in a society. First, crime is beneficial to the society for its metabolism function, where society is compared to an organism such as a person or an animal. Society is activated by crime and purges its "wastes" to promote growth. Without crime, the development of a society will stop. Second, crime is an essential condition that makes a society possible; and any dramatic decrease in crime rate is only an act of self-deception or even suicide.

Other scholars have disagreed with this perspective. For instance, Yu (2007) from the China University of Political Science and Law proposed a different argument. He holds that crime should be classified as one type of "evils," among the worst elements of a society. Crime is a threat to society and should not be regarded as something beneficial. For thousands of years, all societies have been making efforts to get rid of crime. Over time, elaborate judicial systems are established in all societies to combat crime. New professions are created, such as judge, prosecutor, police, lawyer and corrections personnel, to bring peace and security to the public. Therefore, crime control actually consumes precious social resources that could otherwise be spent on other aspects of a society. Crime is thus a barrier to the development of a country as it incurs high costs of governance. The value of crime is negative, not positive, as it only harms a society and incurs costs. In no circumstance can crime serve as an impetus to social development.

In recent years, the field of criminal justice policy has attracted many criminologists in the country. In 2004, the Chinese government for the first time proposed a policy of "tempering justice with punishment and mercy." The main ingredients of the policy are as follows: serious offenses and minor offenses should be treated differently. Crimes that cause great harm to society shall be dealt with swiftly and sternly. But minor offenses, such as those due to recklessness or negligence, shall be handled with mercy. First-time offenders and juvenile offenders should be treated with leniency.

In the past several years, this policy has generated much discussion among Chinese scholars. Ma Kechang (2007), a well-known jurist in China, proposed that the official policy of "tempering justice with punishment and mercy" should serve as a guideline not only for criminal adjudications but also for sentencing and even criminal legislation. The policy should be applied to judicial, legislative and executive activities that concern criminals. Liu (2007) further contends that the previous "strike hard" policy (see glossary, p. 495), featuring periodic nationwide campaigns of intense police work at cracking down on criminal activities, can also be well absorbed into the "tempering justice with punishment and mercy" policy, which selectively targets serious criminal offenses.

Another hot topic in China's criminology is state aid and compensation for criminal victims. Chinese scholars have come to realize that the study of victims' rights will promote the reform and innovation of criminal legislation and judicial decision making. In 2007, state aid and compensation for victims in criminal offenses was listed as a main item on the annual work plan of both the People's Supreme Court and the People's Supreme Procuratorate. Sun Qian (2007), Vice Procurator-General of the People's Supreme Procuratorate, was influential in initiating legislative proposals for providing state aid and compensation for victims. In March 2007, he presented a proposal named "The state compensation for the criminal victim law" to the National People's Congress, which gained the approval for further consideration for legislative purposes. Sun believes that the establishment of a state aid and compensation system is important for China's current emphasis on building a harmonious society. It represents an important step towards advancing the constitutional rights of citizens and promotes the effective control and prevention of criminal activities. Such a compensation system can also help reduce the severity of criminal punishment and even death sentences. Qian (2007) believes that China's economic development has reached a stage where such a compensation system is financially feasible. Furthermore, people in China have come to recognize the victim's right to restitution. Past experiments with the practice of state compensation for victims have proved to be successful.

Wu Zongxian (2002), through his paper titled "Comments on restorative justice," first introduced the concept of "restorative justice" to China. The paper detailed a general introduction of the theory and practice in Western countries and discussed its applicability in China. As more papers have been published on this topic, restorative justice has become a hot topic among Chinese scholars both in criminology and criminal law. In 2004 the Restorative Justice Research Center was established at the China University of Political Science and Law. The center director, Professor Wang Ping, published a three-volume collection of papers on restorative justice in the three years from 2005 to 2007. The books included papers written by some of the well-known legal scholars and lawyers in China that explored restorative justice as a theory and practice and examined the challenges for its application in China. The three-volume collection marked a new stage in the development of China's criminology.

The Chinese judicial system has also experimented with restorative justice in practice and gained a lot of valuable experience. Many scholars now perceive restorative justice as a return of ancient Chinese judicial traditions that emphasized harmony and peace-making through reconciliation. Instead of seeking retribution, the restorative justice movement finds a balance among the interests of the victim, the defendant and the community. Many scholars have come to believe that restorative justice fits well with Chinese culture and should be promoted in China.

But some see it differently. Zou (2004) pointed out that restorative justice as a paradigm is immature and fragmented, not only in its application, but also in its constitutional implications. Therefore one must be prudent when studying and introducing this foreign theory into China's judicial system. Zhao (2005) cited three problems with restorative justice. First, it deviates from the basic principles and procedures of the criminal law in China; and the end result of restorative justice can sometimes be contrary to the victim's wishes. Second, it provides preferential treatment to minor offenders while it discriminates against other criminal offenders. Third, the behavior of the criminal is not necessarily corrected in a "restorative justice model" and because the criminal responsibility is sometimes unclear, the offender may bear no responsibility to the victim.

During the last 30 years, legal scholars and criminologists in China have published a lot of books and theses about organized crime in search of its causes and effective countermeasures. Among the best-known researchers on this topic is Professor He Bingsong at the China

University of Political Science and Law who believes that organized crime has been on a steady rise in China and has become diversified and regionalized (2003). More importantly, organized crime groups are being protected by local authorities. Some overseas Chinese criminal organizations have also moved into the mainland. Local gangs are also becoming organized and complex in their operations. Professor He (2003) argues that organized crime in China has entered a new stage and its activities are becoming more extensive, covering such activities as extorting protection money, drug trafficking, pornography or even murders.

Officially, the Chinese government has thus far acknowledged that only a few criminal groups have acquired so-called mafia-like characteristics in their organizational structure. However, there are no real mafia-type organizations in China. In Professor He's opinion (2003), the development of contemporary organized crime in China can be grouped in three stages. The first stage is the period from the late 1970s to the early 1980s when organized crime just began to emerge. The second stage is the period from the early 1990s to the late 1990s, when criminal organizations began to exhibit mafia-like characteristics. These groups include examples such as the crime organization headed by Ma Huichun in Pingyuan, Yunnan Province; the crime organization headed by Liang Xiaoming in Changchun, Jilin Province; and the crime organization headed by Zeng Qiqiang in the city of Foshan, Guangdong Province. The third stage is the period after 2000 when it seems that criminal organizations in mainland China have become more mature and complex.

According to Professor He (2003), a mafia-style organization should have four essential characteristics: organization, violence, money, and influence. Its main objective is to acquire political influence thus ensuring its ability to profit. They often intervene into the political spheres and economic affairs by committing violent crimes. Therefore organized violence is the main feature of mafia-style organizations, and the main business activities of these criminal organizations often include crimes involving firearms, drug trafficking, cross-border smuggling, and money laundering. He (ibid.) further proposed a "self-organized" theory of mafia-style organizations. Mafia-style organizations originated from some persistent conflicts in a society, such as social inequality and tensions between the poor and the rich. Aside from these root or internal causes, there is also the universal desire to make money, which serves as an external driving force to bring about criminal organizations. He further posits that an appropriate circumstance for the development of mafia-style organization requires two elements. One is political corruption, and the other is weakened social control. A social environment with these two elements is a hotbed of mafia-style organizations to grow and mature. When these internal, external and environmental factors converge, mafia-style organizations will appear (ibid.).

It was not until the 1980s when scholars in China first began research on terrorism. After the September 11th events, Chinese scholars have intensified their efforts in understanding terrorism and proposing countermeasures. Chinese scholars are paying particular attention to two terrorist organizations in China: the Tibetan Youth Congress (Ruan, 2007; also, see glossary, p. 495), and East Turkestan Islamic Movement (Xia and Wang, 2004; also, see glossary, p. 495). Much has been published in recent years about these two groups.

Over the years, Chinese scholars have also systematically examined such topics as the definition of terrorism, constitutional response to terrorism, criminal justice response, judicial process of terrorist offenses, legislative improvement, crime causes, characteristics of crime, prevention and conformity measures (Wei, 2007). Among these topics, the definition of "crime of terrorism" has attracted much attention because of its significant legal and judicial implications. Researchers argue that a clear definition of "crime of terrorism" enables the judicial system to respond decisively to terrorist activities and the international community to improve its shared understanding of the tasks at hand.

With the success of the Chinese economy and open-door policy, cross-border crimes have become more serious than ever before, posing a threat to the nation's social stability and economic security. Common cross-border crimes in China include smuggling of various commodities, drug trafficking, human smuggling, cross-border organized prostitution rings, associated graft and bribery crimes, and terrorist activities. Chinese scholars again have engaged in discussions on its concept, characteristics, patterns, causes, development trend, investigation measures, jurisdiction, prevention and conformity policy.

Juvenile delinquency remains a major research topic among criminologists in China. For instance, more than ten books related to juvenile delinquency and juvenile legal proceedings were published in the most recent five years. Many articles have also been published on juvenile delinquency. These publications reflect the progress made by China's research community on juvenile delinquency and efforts towards an integration of juvenile delinquency theories and legislative and judicial practices. This progress is also reflected in the growing separation between the juvenile justice (including juvenile law, juvenile procedural law and juvenile correctional practices) and the regular justice system for adults.

Three trends in China's juvenile justice system are worth noting. First, the Chinese legal system and academics alike are studying success stories reported overseas and in neighboring justice systems, such as those in Hong Kong and Taiwan. Such learning has led to a series of systemic changes in China's juvenile justice system that include greater emphasis on surveillance and protection, social integration, non-custody measures, risk assessment, juvenile probation and adequate adult participation. Second, the research community is paying more attention to basic theoretical issues, as the juvenile justice system has gained its independence from the adult justice system. Third, the central government is drafting plans towards establishing a national juvenile judicial system, reflecting improvements in our collective appreciation of the uniqueness in societal response to juvenile delinquency.

Currently, the Internet industry is burgeoning in China and many youngsters spend a lot of time online. Because the online community remains largely unregulated and unfiltered in China, both officials and academic researchers have shown great concerns about the exposure to negative influences of young web surfers. The relationship between Internet use and juvenile crime has drawn much attention among researchers in China. For instance, in July 2005, the 14th annual conference of the Chinese Criminological Research Association was held. Internet use and its negative impact on juveniles was listed as a special topic that drew wide discussions. Some scholars (Chai, 2005) at the conference believed that exposure to negative content online can cause psychological problems that lead to delinquent behaviors. Such causal speculations include (1) youngsters' sexual crime tendency as a result of exposure to pornography; (2) youngsters' violent crime tendency as a result of exposure to violent online content, especially violent video games; and (3) youngsters' fraud crime tendency caused by the weakened sense of morality and ethics in the virtual world.

The Notice on Operation of Community Correction Pilot Work identifies the official policy on the tasks and scope of community corrections. It requires the People's Courts, People's Procuratorates and public security agencies at different administrative levels to implement community corrections jointly and smoothly (Chinawebinfo.com, n.d.). It stipulates that community corrections may be applied to a limited number of convicted offenders, such as those put on probation or released on parole or permitted to temporarily serve the sentence outside prison are allowed to receive "community corrections." Under community corrections, offenders are assisted by government agencies, social organizations and volunteers to correct their behavior and return to the normal life. In 2005, the Ministry of Justice added 12 more provinces in the central and western China to the list of jurisdictions where community corrections can be practiced. Currently a total of 18 cities and provinces are allowed to implement community corrections (18 November 2009).

The community corrections system is still in a pilot stage with many unresolved issues and problems. The issue of community corrections has become a hotly discussed topic, with legal scholars and criminologists trying to propose and explore its legal boundaries, administrative implications and legislative requirements.

From time to time, villagers and urban dwellers gather to protest against some events of perceived injustice. These events involve hundreds or thousands of agitated people who demand fair treatment or justice to their problems. Often these events involve rival sites and can escalate into violent outbreaks or riots. Although the Chinese government remains sensitive to such riots and protests, it lacks an effective mechanism to resolve these disputes and control riots. The number of riots and protests has been on a steady rise in the recent decade. In 1993 there were only 8,709 such events in China, but in 1999 this figure was more than 32,000. In 2003 it quickly increased to 60,000; in 2004, 74,000; in 2005, 87,000; in 2006, 90,000 (Yu, 2008). In recent years, protests and riots have become common in most parts of China. These events not only cause social instability and harm the local economy, but also undermine the legitimacy of the government. Legal scholars and criminologists therefore have felt the urgent need to study these events and explore effective response strategies.

In the past, these events were commonly viewed as "social frustration-venting events" – people expressing their angers and frustrations over an adjudication by some local authorities that they considered unjust or unfair (see glossary, p. 495). In March 2009, a high-level forum was held by the Juvenile Crime and Judicial Research Center, the Criminal Psychology Research Center and Tingdu Law Firm in Beijing, where prominent legal scholars and criminologists gathered to discuss the pressing issues involving "group events." Professor Pi Yijun from the China University of Political Science and Law introduced the concept of "social hostility" as a psychological condition prescribed to the collective sentiments behind the riots. Professor Pi argued that psychologists can contribute significantly to the understanding of "group events." However, in mainland China, the word "hostility" can easily be portrayed as a confrontation between two opposing social classes, which has political ramifications. Professor Pi justified its use as an academic viewpoint referring to some kind of antagonism, dissatisfaction and mistrust among the populace. Such hostile sentiments are common in today's society, reflecting dissatisfactions between an individual and a group, and between the masses and government agencies. Professor Pi added that such hostility would rise when people's demands were not met, and these charged emotions were not without reasons. It is natural for a society to have contradictions and confrontations within the people, especially when a mistake is made by an official entity. When people become dissatisfied or disappointed at the government, public sentiments are likely to escalate into these "group events." Therefore, it is important for government agencies to give attention to negative public sentiments because such antagonistic moods tend to arise from concerns about the credibility of the government and its transparency and fairness.

Most researchers borrow or transplant methods from other disciplines such as sociology, law and psychology. Based on a review of publications in recent years, predominant research methods in Chinese criminology are as follows:

Qualitative research methods are most used in the Chinese criminology research community. The methodology consists of a set of research methods as follows: inductive analysis, dialectical analysis, generalized analysis, comparative analysis, historical analysis and assumption approach.

By comparison, quantitative research methods are mostly used in actual data gathering and analysis. The methods include pattern analysis, correlation analysis, mathematical models and statistical analysis. In the past, the Chinese criminology community paid little attention to quantitative measures, as few studies and publications were based on such methods. It was not until recent years that the Chinese criminology research community realized the importance of the quantitative approach and applied them in analyzing crime patterns and causes.

Chinese criminology scholars tend to favor conceptual analysis over empirical research. This imbalance between so-called theorizing and data gathering is due to several factors. First, most researchers are not familiar with empirical research methods, as methodological training and statistics are not included in law school education in most colleges. Second, crime statistics are controlled by the government and are considered state secrets and therefore generally kept away from the public. For example, statistics on death sentences are considered high state secrets and never released to the public. Difficulties in accessing official data prevent researchers from conducting systematic assessment of any crime situation in China. Third, researchers are resource poor and lack basic support to launch field work. Crime research typically receives little funding from the government.

The Chinese Criminology Research Institute was founded in 1992, under the auspices of the Supreme People's Procuratorate, and is housed in the College of State Prosecutors. There are seven branches in the institute: (1) Crime Prevention Committee; (2) Crime-Sociology Committee; (3) Crime and Correction Psychology Committee; (4) Crime Measures in Border Areas Committee; (5) Criminals Transformation Committee; (6) Juvenile Law Education Committee; and (7) Occupational Crime Prevention Committee.

The Criminology Association, a branch under the Chinese Law Association, is another visible academic organization. Its tasks include (1) engaging in investigation, theory discussion, academic publications, translation and introduction of international research findings; (2) holding seminars and conferences; (3) organizing and promoting international exchange activities; (4) undertaking research projects and providing consultation to external entities; (5) publishing criminology anthologies and maintaining communication among members; and (6) recruiting new members. The Criminology Association currently has more than 2,200 members, most of whom are professors, scholars, experts and researchers in legal professions.

Many large universities, research institutes and judicial bodies also have their own institutes to study crime-related issues; for example, the Crime Prevention Institute inside the Ministry of Justice, the Fourth Departments under the Ministry of Public Security, Crime Problems Research Center in Peking University, Crime Prevention and Control Institute in Nanjing University, Criminology Institute in Chinese People's Public Security University and Juvenile Crime Institute in East China University of Political Science and Law. The China University of Political Science and Law (CUPL) also has several such research entities: the Terrorism and Organized Crime Research Center, Juvenile Crime and Judicial Research Center, Restorative Justice Research Center and Forensic Psychology Research Center.

Funding for criminological research remains limited because criminology is subordinate to the science of criminal law and thus attracts little attention from funding agencies. Generally, research funds come from the following outlets: (1) Academy of Social Sciences (which is affiliated with each provincial and major municipal government), or ministries that concern with public security and crime control; (2) cooperative projects on crime prevention and control provided by public security agencies, people's procuratorates, and people's courts; (3) support provided by foreign governments or research organizations; and (4) funds raised by researchers themselves. The general view is that criminology, much like its cousins in the humanities, produces no direct economic benefits and therefore is unlikely to attract any financial support from businesses or government agencies alike.

Conclusion

After a 30-year development, criminology has made reasonable achievements in China. The field of research has extended; the number of scholars has increased. As a result of an unsound academic discipline and lack of empirical research methods, criminology played a limited role in the whole society system. Only a few valuable and practical applications were taken by the government. However, Chinese criminology scholars realized the need for improvement in the study of criminology in China. The implementation of advanced methods of criminology is more emphasized through trying to learn from their Western counterparts in the same field. The study of criminology in China will be more advanced and mature to match the international practice.

Future research questions

1. How can we promote the function of criminology for society and the government in China?
2. What are the problems of and resolutions to the methodological strategies of criminology in China?
3. What other important topics should Chinese criminologists investigate?
4. Further explore the weaknesses and strengths of the "Strike hard (Yan Da)" policy in China.
5. How should criminologists study riots and protests in China?

Glossary of uncommon words

Strike hard (Yan Da): The "strike hard" campaign is a national campaign launched by the Chinese government periodically to crack down on the serious criminal offenses within a specified timeframe. Initiated and directed by the Central Committee of the Chinese Communist Party and the Chinese central government, the campaign is orchestrated by local governments. The campaign typically has two priorities: (1) to crack down on serious crimes, and (2) to hand out harsh sentences to criminals caught during the campaign. There have been a total of three "strike hard" campaigns in China's recent history. Such campaigns reflect the political reality in a communist country where political power is absolute and centralized. The first "strike hard" campaign was introduced in China in 1983, the second was in 1996 and the third was in 2001.

Tibetan Youth Congress: Established in 1970, the group has made its name in advocating an independent Tibet at all costs. The group was considered a power base for the Dalai Lama. As part of the "Tibetan government in exile," the organization is currently considered a terrorist organization by the Chinese government. On 14 March 2008, the Tibetan Youth Congress was accused of instigating unrests and riots in Tibet, Gansu and Sichuan Province, causing extensive damage and deaths.

East Turkestan Islamic Movement: In 1996, it was founded by Maimaitiming'aizilaiti in Turkey, with its headquarters in Istanbul. The organization aims to establish the East Turkestan Islamic Kingdom in China's Xinjiang Autonomous Region, Kyrgyzstan and Kazakhstan. Considered a terrorist group by the Chinese government, the group has been accused of plotting several violent terrorist attacks. It receives funding from robberies, drugs and weapons smuggling activities, and from Al Qaida. It was recognized as a terrorist organization by United Nations on 11 September 2002.

Social anger-venting events: The term was proposed by Yu Jianrong when he was delivering a speech at the University of California, Berkeley. These are essentially mass protests that often escalate into riots. According to Yu's analysis, these events have four characteristics. First, the events are caused by incidents, as signals of seeking help from government authorities or administrative lawsuits. Second, organizers cannot be found and participants have no direct relationship with the initial incidents. Protesters vent dissatisfaction at perceived unjust decisions made by government officials or corruption. Third, misinformation conveyed mainly by words, messages and the Internet is used to stir up public sentiments that escalate to a larger scale. Lastly, illegal or criminal acts such as beating, smashing, robbery and fire settings may occur.

References

Chai, C. (2005). Juvenile crimes research and harmonious society building. *People's Procuratorat*, 9: 13–15.

Chinalawinfo.com (n.d.). Community corrections would be practiced in the whole country in China. Online at http://vip.chinalawinfo.com/newlaw2002/slc/slc.asp?db (accessed 18 November 2009).

He, B. (2003). *The interpretation of the crime of mafia-style organization*. Beijing: China Attorney Press.

Kang, S. (1996). *The general theory of criminology*. 2nd edition. Beijing: Peking University Press.

Kechang, M. (2007). The location of the criminal policy of tempering justice with punishment and mercy. *China Law Study*, 4: 117–22.

Liang, G. (2001). From absolutivism to relativism: the function of the crime. Beijing: *Law Scholars*, 2: 11–19.

Liu, H. (2007). The scientific location and judicial application of the criminal policy of tempering justice with punishment and mercy. Beijing: *The Law*, 2: 21–5.

Ping, W. (2005–7). *Restorative Justice Forum* (1st, 2nd and 3rd vols., published in 2005, 2006 and 2007). The Masses Press.

Qian, S. (2007). The thought on the construction of the state compensation system for the criminal victims in China. *The Law Study*, 2: 53–62.

Ruan, C. (2007). *Terrorist crime research*. Beijing: Peking University Press.

Song, H. (2004). A prospective of research on crime and the disciplinary nature of criminology. Shandong: *The Shandong Police School Journal*, 2: 93–103.

Wang, M. (2004). The position and nature of criminology as a discipline. Beijing: *China University Education*, 8: 35–6.

—— (2007). The concept of crime: in or outside the criminal law. *Law Study*, 2: 3–20.

Wang, Q. (2007). *Research on community correction*. Beijing: Intellectual Property Rights Press.

Wei, L. (2007). Cross-border crime and harmonious society. *Criminology Collection*, 5: 410–16. Beijing: China Procuratorial Press.

Xia, Y. and Wang, Y. (2004). Generalization of researches on terrorist crime definition in Chinese academic field. *Law and Business Research Journal*, 1: 129–38.

Yu, J. (2008). Political situation in China and my dream. Online at http://view.news.qq.com/a/20081204/000038_3.htm (accessed 18 November 2009).

Yu, Z. (2007). *The value of the crime*. Beijing, Peking University Press.

Zhao, J. (2005). The conflicts between the advantages and disadvantages in restorative justice. *The Law*, 5: 113–15.

Zongxian, W. (2002). Comment on restorative justice. *The Jiangsu Police School Journal*, 3: 69–85.

Zou, J. (2004). A brake on the restorative justice. Shanghai: *The Eastern China Political Science and Law Journal*, 6: 39–44.

46

Russia

An overview of crime and criminology

Yakov Gilinskiy

Introduction

Criminality is an element of society. The state of criminality is reflected in the crime trends, which reflect the society in which it exists. For many decades Russia and Russian criminology existed in conditions of isolation from the world and its science. Russian criminology dates from the 1870s to 1890s. From the 1930s to 1950s, during Stalin's totalitarian regime, criminology, sociology, genetics, cybernetics, and others were "forbidden science." Russian criminology only began to reappear during the Khrushchev's "thaw" (1960s) and began actively to develop and to join the world of criminological science at the time of Gorbachev's perestroika (1986–91).

Infrastructure

Russia, or the Russian Federation (RF), resulted from the breakup of the USSR in 1991. Russia's 17-million square kilometers of land mass shares borders with Norway, Finland, Estonia, Latvia, Byelorussia, Ukraine (to the west), Georgia, Azerbaijan, Kazakhstan, Mongolia, China (to the south), and North Korea, Japan, and USA to the east. It includes many climatic zones: from permafrost in the north to subtropics in the south, from black earth to Siberian and Far-Eastern taiga, from the Baltic Sea and Arctic Ocean to the Pacific Ocean and Black Sea.

The huge territory supports many kinds of land use: agriculture, timber cutting, pasture, different spa resorts, national parks, and mineral industry. There are numerous natural resources: mineral oil, natural gas, coal, ferrous and non-ferrous metals, precious metals (gold, silver, and others), bauxite, diamonds, amber, and others.

But there are complicated environmental issues. Many pollutant emissions, including atmospheric, water, and air pollutions, are the result of outdated techniques, outdated technology, and violation of safety measures.

The gross domestic product (GDP) was $1,746 billion (trillion) USD in 2006 and $1,164 billion (trillion) USD in 2009. The reduction in GDP is the result of the contemporary world economic crisis. GDP per capita was $8,230 USD in 2009.

There are varying data on poverty in Russia, which causes confusion. According to the World Bank data, poverty increased during 1997–99 from 24.1 percent of population (35.3 million people) to 41.5 percent (60.5 million people), and decreased to 19.6 percent in 2002. Various Russian experts (for example, Janitskiy, 2004) consider that 20.8 percent of the population

(29.8 million people) has an income lower than the official living wage in 2004. Other data suggest that about 30 percent of the Russian population have incomes lower than the official living wage (World Bank, 2005).

> The ever-growing economic polarization of the population – visible in the stark contrast between the impoverished majority and the nouveau riche minority (the "New Russians") – is a [source of social conflicts]. The ratio between the incomes of the 10 percent least prosperous and the 10 percent most prosperous [(the "coefficient of decile")] increased from 1:4.5 in 1991 [to 1:16.8 in 2007], according to the official data. In the opinion of experts, the actual ratio between the incomes of the highest and lowest 10 percent is as high as 23–25 in Russia as a whole (Russian Federation, 1999) and 40–60 in Moscow. For comparability, this coefficient is 3–4 in Denmark, Finland, Sweden, and 10–12 in USA.
>
> *(Gilinskiy, 2009, p. 261)*

The Gini index (i.e. index of economic inequality) in Russia increased from 0.289 in 1992 to 0.422 in 2007. According to Ol'kov (2004), during 1990–9 the index was at its maximum in 1994 (0.409) and the number of homicides was at a maximum too (32,300); the index was at its lowest in 1990 (0.218) and the number of homicides was also lowest then (15,600).

> Technological backwardness and the incompetence of the domestic production and service sectors have manifested themselves in the course of the reforms . . . [T]he class of the excluded (Lenoir, 1974; Young, 1999) constitutes the social basis for various forms of deviance including crime and organized crime.
>
> *(Gilinskiy, 2006, p. 262)*

The inflation rate decreased from 18.8 percent in 2001 to 9.1 percent in 2006 and increased to 13.3 percent in 2008. The unemployment rate decreased from 13.2 percent in 1997 to 6.2 percent in 2008, which is associated with crime reduction.

Foreign trade turnover of Russia was $735 billion USD in 2008. Main imports include machinery and equipment, trucks and passenger cars, medicines, clothes, shoes, software, and environmental and other consumer commodities. Main exports are mineral oil, natural gas, coal, and ferrous and some non-ferrous metals (e.g. aluminum, nickel, native copper).

There are some joint energy systems in Russia: Central, Northwestern, Volga region, North Caucasian, Ural, Siberian, and Far Eastern. Ten nuclear power plants exist in Russia. The production volume of electrical energy was 997.3 billion kilowatt-hours in 2007.

According to the Constitution of the Russian Federation there is a division of powers. The Russian Federation is a presidential republic. The President is the head of State, and there are presidents in republics, such as Bashkiria, Dagestan, Tatarstan. The Federal legislature is a parliament (or *Federal'noe Sobranie* – the Federal Assembly) which consists of two chambers: the upper chamber *Soviet Federatsiy* (the Federation Council) and the lower chamber *Gosudarstvennaja Duma* (the State Duma). The *regional legislatures* are called *zakonodatel'noe sobranie* (legislative assembly) or parliament.

The Federal executive power belongs to the government with a Prime Minister. Regional executive power lies with the governor (or mayor in a city) and the government (administration).

There are many commercial communications companies and a state telephone service. Many radio and television broadcasters were established after the breakup of the USSR. Unfortunately, state television exerts a prevailing influence and unofficial ("internal") censorship exists. The internet is widely used, with several internet service providers and about 46 million users.

Russian railways extend 154,000 kilometers, including 75,300 kilometers of electrified lines. The network occupied is second, only to the US. There are more than 20,000 locomotives and more than 550,000 freight cars and more than 70,000 passenger cars.

There are 701,000 kilometers of motor roads, including 597,000 kilometers of asphalt surfaces ("highways"). But the quality of Russian roads is bad (i.e. uneven, holes). An old Russian proverb exists that explains the road situation: "There are two Russian troubles: fools and roads." There are more than 38 million vehicles.

There are 1,623 airports in Russia; the largest are Domodedovo, Sheremetjevo, Vnukovo in Moscow, and Pulkovo in St. Petersburg.

People

The population of the Russian Federation rose from 102.9 million in 1951 to 148.7 million in 1991 and fell to 141.9 million people in 2009. Seventy-eight percent of the population live in the European part of the country and 22 percent in the Asiatic sector (i.e. West Siberia, East Siberia, and the Russian Far East) (Gilinskiy, 2006, p. 260).

The Russian population is aged or aging. More than 20 percent of the population in 2005 were pensioners and only 17 percent children. Approximately 47 percent of the population is male and 53 percent female. Three quarters of the population (73.1 percent) live in urban areas (Vishnevski, 2006).

According to Vishnevski (2006), the growth rate (per 1,000 population) was 12.1 in 2009. The death rate (per 1,000 population) was 15.0 in 2009. Life expectancy in Russia in 2005 was 59 for males and 73 for females. In Western Europe (2005) the figures were: males, 76, and females, 82. This is a national catastrophe for Russia.

Every year more than 12 million persons enter Russia and more than 11 million persons depart from Russia. Migrants totaled 258,193 in 2007 and 257,148 in 2008 (Vishnevski, 2006).

The number of HIV-positive individuals was about 325,780 people in 2005 or 228.2 per 100,000 of the population (Vishnevski, 2006).

There is a variety of different nationalities. Russians make up 80.1 percent of the population, with Tartars composing 3.3 percent, Ukrainians 2.1 percent, Chuvashians 1.1 percent, and less than 1 percent of each of the other groups. There are more than 100 languages spoken by different nationalities and ethnic groups in Russia (Vishnevski, 2006).

The Russian Federation is a secular State with freedom of conscience. Official statistics on religion do not exist. According to various sociological surveys conducted by the Lewada-Center, about 65–7 percent of the population is considered Orthodox, 5–6 percent is Muslim, 6–10 percent is atheist, and 1–2 percent is representatives of other faiths. But only 30 percent of population attends church.

Russia's educational system includes primary (elementary) education (grades 1–4, children aged 7–10); main general education (grades 5–9, children aged 11–15); secondary education (grades 10–11); primary and secondary professional (vocational) education; higher education (university, institute, or academy) and post-graduate study. According to general media, the literacy rate for ages 9–49 is 99.8 percent. There are about 61,000 schools (gymnasias, lyceums), and 1,068 universities (institutes, academies). A bimodal system of higher education (bachelor and master's degree) has been introduced.

Administration of justice

The police of Russia, known as the Militia, was set up a month after the coup d'état of October 1917 and continues to this day. The entire Militia in Russia is under the direction of the Ministry of Internal Affairs (MVD), as are the internal forces (e.g. army) and specialized police forces (e.g. railroad, air, and river militia). The penitentiary service was transferred in 1998 to the Ministry of Justice.

The Militia in the republics are directed by the republican Ministry of Internal Affairs, and in each territory, region, city, or district they are directed by the main board of internal affairs, as established by the Constitution and law of each region. The current directives, functions, and structure of the Militia are laid down in the Russian Law "On the Militia," passed on 18 April 1991 (with subsequent modifications).

The Militia is organized into two main sub-divisions: the Criminal Militia and the Militia for Civil Safety (or Public Order) at the local level (Law "On the Militia for Civil Safety," 1993). The Criminal Militia include the Detective Service, the Economic Crime Prevention Service, scientific–technical specialists, operational investigators, and others who supply material for the criminal investigation. The Civil Militia include the Duty Service, the Service for Securing Civil Order, the State Automobile Inspectorate, the Security Service, divisional inspectors, temporary detention guards, the prevention service, and others. The Criminal Investigation Service is a separate unit under the Ministry of Internal Affairs.

There are different data on the size of the Russian Militia: the Militia forces stood at about 540,000 and that of the internal forces (e.g. army) at about 278,000 in 1995 (Everyone's Newspaper, 1995, No. 51); the police ratio per 100,000 population was 1,224.58 in 1994 (Newman, 1999); and the staff of the system of the Ministry of Internal Affairs RF was about 1.5 million in 1996 (Dolgova, 2000).

According to the Constitution there are several levels of legal institutions (Art. 118, Part 2):

- The Constitutional Court of the Russian Federation;
- The Supreme Court of the Russian Federation;
- Courts of the subjects of the Russian Federation (e.g. supreme courts of the republics; regional – *krai*, *oblast*, *autonomous regions* courts; Moscow and St. Petersburg city courts;
- Area (district), city courts;
- Military courts;
- Arbitration courts (e.g. the Supreme Arbitration Court; arbitration courts of the subjects of the Russian Federation).

Military courts are included in the common legal system. Arbitration courts resolve disputes between juridical persons.

Unfortunately, contemporary Russian justice is not independent. First, many judges are very corrupt (e.g. Sungurov, 2000; Timofeev, 2000). Second, many courts are dependent on politicians and the authorities. For example, often the Basmany court (i.e. *Basmany*; it is one of a number of districts of Moscow) decided a case in favor of the authorities. And *Basmany court* is a common noun now.

Finally, there are so-called *mirovye sud'i* (magistracy). They consider more minor cases (e.g. administrative, civil, minor criminal delinquency).

There is the Office of the Public Prosecutor. The goals of this institution are protection of law and order and uniform use of law; defense of the rights and freedoms of people; and defense of the legal interests of society and state. The General Prosecutor is the head of the Office of the

Public Prosecutor. There is an Office of the Public Prosecutor in each of the 83 subjects of the Russian Federation, in each region, city, and district. Important functions of the prosecutor are the oversight of public order and legality, criminal investigation, and prosecution.

The correctional service (Federal Service for the Implementation of Punishment – FSIN) is a department of the Ministry of Justice. Presently, there are 755 correctional colonies, 62 educational colonies (for minors), seven prisons, and 225 jails. The number of convicts is more than 890,000 (May 2009) or 631 per 100,000 population. The prison population is second only to the US.

The problem of an effective social response to crime is especially important for contemporary Russia: on the one hand, currently, it has one of the highest rates of homicide and other serious violent crimes, suicide, alcohol abuse, and corruption in the world. On the other hand, there are old repressive forms of social control ("war on crime," "war on drugs," and so on) that are not effective. Unfortunately, retributive justice prevails in Russia.

Social control of criminality remains very severe in contemporary Russia. The new Criminal Code (CC) of the Russian Federation (RF) from 1996 contains very harsh punishments: death penalty (Art. 59 CC RF), life imprisonment (Art. 57), and deprivation of freedom for 20 to 30 years, depending on the number and timing of crimes committed (Art. 56). There were no such punishments, such as life imprisonment or 30-year sentences, in any previous Criminal Code, including during the Stalin period. Since 1997 there has been a moratorium on the death penalty, but the Russian parliament has not ratified this.

It is necessary to add that while crime-fighting is conducted (with doubtful success) mainly against street crimes, the huge layer of respectable crime (i.e. white-collar crime) still remains outside the fields of fight. When it is dealt with by the police and condemned by the court, respectable crime functions as a scapegoat to demonstrate the successful struggle against criminality. It is known as the problem of selection in criminal justice.

There has been a tendency to reduce alternatives to detention in penal and sentencing practice: the quota of corrective labor without deprivation of freedom has decreased (from 26.4 percent in 1988 to 4.7 percent in 2007); the quota of fines has decreased (from 15.7 percent in 1986 to 12.8 percent in 2007). The imprisonment rate (per 100,000 of the population) in Russia is very high (more than 625 in 2007). The conditions in penitentiary institutions are terrible. The extremely harsh regimes in secure institutions experienced by those awaiting trial or under a conditional sentence contravene human rights: bad food; the spread of tuberculosis; torture of those awaiting trial/under investigation in so-called "press cells"[1] to procure confessions of guilt; mass beatings, etc. (Gilinskiy, 2006, p. 287). Life in institutions for the deprivation of freedom (prisons and "correctional colonies") is unbearable and the possibilities for "correction" are nil (Moscowskaja Helsinskaja Gruppa, 2003).

Criminology in Russia

Criminology as any science is international, a world science. But it is well known that for many decades Russian criminology existed in conditions of isolation from the world science and under rigorous political and ideological control. Consequently, Russian criminology and the works of Russian criminologists are not well known abroad.

There are five stages in Russian criminology (Gilinskiy, 2009). First was the "pre-Revolutionary" period from the nineteenth century up until 1917. This period included the "origin" of criminological ideas and studies (Radishchev, 1802; German, 1823), and forming of the discipline (Foinitchky, 1889; Duchovskoi, 1897) and its development (with anthropological and psychological contributions by Dril (1846–1910); and sociological contributions by Gernet (1874–1953) and others). The sociological perspective dominated, especially the multifactor school. Liberal Russian criminologists come out in defense of crime prevention and opposed the death penalty (see, for example Gernet, 1913). The second period ran from 1917 to the 1920s to 1930s. Old bourgeois criminology continued to develop in the new conditions. Studies of the personality of criminals dominated in this time period (due to the impossibility of social causes in a happy socialist society). Many bourgeois criminologists were repressed by the end of this period.

The third stage was "Stalin's epoch": criminology was prohibited de facto, and criminological studies were absent. But there was rudimentary criminological knowledge in criminal law and "criticism" of "bourgeois" criminology.

Fourth was a "stage of revival" from Khrushchev's "thaw" (1960s) to Gorbachev's perestroika (1980s). In 1963 the Institute for Research of Crime Causes and Crime Prevention (Moscow) was founded; in 1964 criminology was included in the educational program of the schools of law. A great many empirical criminological studies were organized in two Russian regions in the 1970s under the leadership of A. B. Sakharov (Sakharov, 1979)

There are two main points of view: an official and legal view, which parallels theoretical and empirical criminology. The West is certain that in the Soviet Union there was only one, official "communist" point of view: crime is the result of the vestiges of bourgeoisie consciousness and the capitalist system. However, during the 1960s in the former Soviet Union a legal "parallel" of theoretical and empirical criminology actively evolved without the Communist party or State approval, accumulating its empirical data step by step, advancing and defending a theoretical explanation, uncommon for the Soviet ideology of a crime as a social phenomenon conditioned by social factors (i.e. social and economic inequality, social conflicts and strain, social and economic conditions, etc.). The concepts of Durkheim, Merton, Sutherland, the Chicago School, labeling theory, and others were all applied to Soviet conditions.

Only a few scholars whose work has gradually weakened and destroyed the stereotypes of official ideology and helped to create a national criminology can be cited: Avanesov, Bluvstein, Gilinskiy, Karpets, Khochrjakov, Kogan, Kudrjavtchev, Nikiforov, Sakharov, Spiridonov, Vitsin, Yakovlev, Zabrjansky, and others.

The fifth stage corresponds to contemporary times (from the late 1980s). The freedom to teach and carry out research, to foster professional contacts with foreign colleagues, appeared only at the end of the 1980s and in the beginning of the 1990s, thanks to the Gorbachev's perestroika.

The main topics of contemporary Russian criminology include organized crime, violent crime, corruption, hate crimes, economic crime, drug trafficking, human trafficking, and social control over crime (Gilinskiy, 2006, 2009; Luneev, 2005).

Main research methods are statistical analyses, surveys of the general population, victims, experts and prisoners, and interviews. Comparative studies are widespread (Gilinskiy, 2000; Paoli, 2001, etc.). Criminologists actively use mathematical methods (factor analysis, correlation analysis, and others) to analyze the results of research (Ol'kov, 2007; Jusichanova, 2005; Skifskiy, 2007). Unfortunately, official police statistics are not complete and the dark figure of crime (latent) is very high. Therefore the analysis of latency is an important part of research (Inshakov, 2007). Statistical data are published online on the site of the Ministry Internal Affairs (MVD) and in the corresponding annual publication "Crime and delinquency, statistical review" of the MVD and the Ministry of Justice. Moreover the full data of the recorded crime and criminals are published in the annual publication of the Russian Criminological Association under the editorship of Prof. A. Dolgova.

The main research institutions are the Research Institute of the General Prosecutor's Office of the Russian Federation (Moscow), the Research Institute of the MVD (Moscow), Center of Deviantology (Sociology of Deviance) of the Sociological Institute of the Russian Academy of Sciences (St. Petersburg), Saratov's Center of Research of Organized Crime and Corruption, and others.

The trends in recorded crime from 1961 to 2009 are:

- "The rate (per 100,000 inhabitants) of total recorded crimes decreased in 1963, and remained at a low point during Khrushchev's 'Thaw' between 1963 and 1965, then rose slowly and steadily between 1966 and 1986. Gorbachev's Perestroika occurred between 1986 and 1988. In the second year of Perestroika (1987) the crime rate suddenly went down, and it stayed at this lower level in the following year, but from 1989, after the end of the Gorbachev era, the crime rate started a rapid increase, which continued for a five-year period, taking it from 816.9 in 1987 to 1887.8 in 1993; after 1993, the rising trend flattened strikingly, with some further increase in 1999, and brief dip in 2002" (Gilinskiy, 2006, p. 262). The crime rate rapidly increased from 2003 (1,926.2) to 2006 (2,692.3). The later decrease in 2007–9 is very difficult to explain now. The majority of the criminologists think it is a decrease in recorded crime, but not a real decrease of crime. There is great hidden crime, due to non-reporting from the police.
- "A sustained rise in the rate of homicide (including attempts) also started in the late 1980s: the rate increased from 6.3 in 1987 to 21.8 in 1994 and leveled off thereafter" (Gilinskiy, 2006, p. 262), reaching 22.5 in 2002. Later it decreased in 2006–9 to 12.5.
- The trends in rates of other kinds of crime is analogous: it was at a minimum during the Gorbachev period, increasing again from 1994–5, decreasing for a short period, increasing again from 1999–2003 and decreasing after 2006. The period of the Khrushchev "thaw" also saw a reduction in the crime rate.

But we must consider the following facts to get an accurate picture that the real number and rate of crime is much higher than official statistical data, similar to other countries. For example, one criminological study shows that on average the rate of actual crime to reported crime during 2001–6 was for homicide 1.40, for grievous bodily harm 1.50, for rape 4.17, for theft 6.56, for robbery 2.25, for assaults with robbery 1.08, for bribery 73.16, etc. (Inshakov, 2007).

Organized crime, one of the main social problems in Russia, has generated primary studies under the direction of Dolgova (2003), Gilinskiy (2003, 2004, 2006, 2009), Gilinsky and Kostjukovsky (2004), Ovchinsky (2001), Repetskaja (2001, 2007), among others.

Organized crime is not simply the aggregation of criminal groups and the criminal offences committed by them. It is built into the social system and affects its components, mainly the economy and politics. Organized crime is identified with illegal entrepreneurship, business, production, and distribution of goods and/or services. The formation and development of organized crime is the world process. It is a particular case of well-organized management at the subsystem level (economics, politics, etc.). The main characteristics of organized crime as a social institution are the following: long life; stable functioning; performance of certain social functions (i.e. satisfaction of demand for illegal services or goods due to their deficit, job creation, redistribution of means, etc.); the use of work code or certain norms; professional language (slang); and allocation of roles (Gilinskiy, 2009; Gilinskiy and Kostjukovsky, 2004).

The process of institutionalization of organized crime started in Russia (the Soviet Union) from the beginning of the 1960s and finished by the end of the 1970s or the beginning of the 1980s. Russian organized criminal groups widely integrated into international organized crime by the beginning of the 1990s.

Yet the newer tendency is for crime bosses to aspire to make their activities legal, perhaps by a gradual transition through semi-legal activity, by infiltrating the power structure of legal businesses, with the aid of money laundering. Moreover police structure is now replacing organized criminal groups, likely to, for example, protect drug traffickers.

Violence is an old Russian problem (Tsytsarev and Gilinsky, 2004). There are primary studies under the direction of Antonjan (2002), Gilinskiy (2008, 2009), Pobegailo (2008), and others. The rate of violence is very high in Russia. The official police-recorded homicide rate (per 100,000 population) increased from 6.3 in 1987 to 22–3 in 2001–5. However, the medical statistics (World Health Organization, 1996; Questions of Statistics, 2004) are more exact than police data, at approximately 10 per 100,000 higher than police data.

The number of crime victims in contemporary Russia is huge. The total number of victims was 1,446,588 persons during 1987–2007. In addition, 25,000 people are declared missing every year and are never found (MVD RF, 2009). In the military, most of soldiers die due to "violent, unregulated hazing rituals ('dedovshina' [the abuse of power by older soldiers that often takes sadistic forms]), accidents related to military service and suicide" (Gilinskiy, 2006, p. 272).

In addition to violent crimes, such as homicide and assault, other criminal activities are associated closely with the use of violence. For instance, in the climate of wild capitalism, violence is viewed as an acceptable means to solving problems between business competitors.

The term "hate crime" first appeared in 1985 (Jacobs and Potter, 1998). There are many manifestations of hate crimes (i.e. from vandalism to murder and genocide). The term "hate crime" is used in two ways. In the broad sense it is all crimes committed with the motive of hate; for example, the murder of a hated husband or wife. In the narrow sense it is the crimes committed with motives of a national, racial, religious hate, or enmity nature. This definition is included in some articles of the Criminal Code of the Russian Federation.

There are many hate crimes in Russia and very few registered cases. For example, only 9 cases were registered according to Art. 105, part 2 "l" in 2001; in 2002, 10 cases; in 2003, 11 cases; and in 2004, 10 cases (Babichenko, 2005). Police and those holding power prefer to qualify these cases as "hooliganism" because it is more "gentle." Russian non-governmental organizations announced the following data on victims of hate crime: 2004, 49 people killed, 218 people injured; 2005,47 people killed, 417 people injured; 2006, 56 people killed, 552 people wounded (Verchovski, 2007, p. 111). According to Moscow's Office of Human Rights, 74 people were killed in 2007 and more than 317 people were wounded.

What is the "ideology" of Russian contemporary Nazis, fascists, and skinheads? It is "Russia is for Russians!", "Migrants go home!", "Fight the blacks!"

Who are the victims of hate crimes? There are citizens of China and India, Egypt and Cameroon, Uganda and Mali, Israel and Lebanon, Ghana and Senegal, also so-called "persons of Caucasian nations," Asians, and Gypsies. Most often they are students of the Russian universities or legal and illegal migrants. Hate crimes occur most often in Moscow, St. Petersburg, Voronezh, and the Krasnodar region (i.e. a region in the south part of the European part of Russia) (Verchovski, 2007).

What are the means of hate crimes? Most often there is an unexpected armed attack of a group of skinheads or fascists with knifes, bats, or metal rods. They try to kill "foreigners" by cutting their throat (Gilinskiy, 2009: 233).

> There are many definitions of corruption. Perhaps the shortest of them is: "the abuse of public power for private profit" (Wewer, 1994, p. 481). The UNO offers an analogous definition (Resolution 34/169 of the UN General Assembly, 17 December 1979). There are many forms of corruption, such as bribery, favoritism, nepotism, protectionism, lobbying, illegal distribution and redistribution of public resources and funds, [illegal ability to finance political structures, extortion, allowance of favorable credit (contracts),] the

famous Russian "*blat*" – different services for relatives, friends or acquaintances [Ledeneva, 1998].

(Gilinskiy, 2006, pp. 280–1)

There is corruption in all countries, but the dimensions of corruption are diverse. Corruption, common in Russia, permeates all organs of power and establishments. The Index of Perception of Corruption (from Transparency International) for Russian was 2.7 in 2002, and has decreased to 2.1 in 2008. It is 147th out of 180 countries. That is, Russia has become more and more corrupt.

The INDEM foundation suggests that the corruption market was $319 billion USD in 2005; the data from the General Prosecutor's Office shows $240 billion USD in 2006. It is 1.5 times more than the national budget of the Russian Federation.

Every day different Russian newspapers and magazines publish who (name, position) received a bribe when, and how much money or "service" was involved, and there is no reaction from those in power.

Corruption in contemporary Russia is an element of the political system, a mechanism of the political regime. There are two levels of corruption: "lower" ("face to face") and "upper," the great corruption networks. The study of the INDEM foundation shows that there are extensive corruption networks in the Ministry of Internal Affairs, the Federal Service of Security (FSB) and the State Committee of Customs Service. The military is also very corrupt. Each corrupt network includes three structures: commercial or financial, state officials, and "group of defense" – police, FSB, prosecutor's office (Satarov, 2002).

On the "lower" level, an average bribe (for a policeman, doctor, teacher, and so on) ranges from $20–120 to $1,000–5,000 USD per occasion. The scale of bribes in corruption networks is greater. There is also another system for calculating the bribe, "otkat"; that is to say, the official gets 3–10 percent or 40–60 percent of the total amount of the contract or agreement.

Corruption paralyzes all positive, creative activities. Corruption of police, the prosecutor's office, and judges is particularly dangerous. "Corruption of judges is one of the most powerful corruption markets in Russia . . . Corruption of judges penetrates different corruption networks on a different level of power" (Satarov, 2003).

The Center of Deviantology (Sociology of Deviance) of the Sociological Institute of the Russian Academy of Sciences studies organized crime and corruption in Russia. Our respondents (informants) commented as follows on the contemporary situation: "The average businessman is extremely involved in crime . . . One has to bribe for everything . . . one cannot deal with taxation inspection without a bribe . . . A bribe is inevitability in the sphere of business . . . Tax inspection is highly corrupt" (Gilinskiy, 2009: 279). One has to bribe when registering a business, when renting premises from state bodies, when acquiring licenses for their utilization from state bodies, for obtaining low-interest bank credit, when reporting to tax inspectors when completing customs formalities, etc. Additionally, the amount of the "tariff" for fire-inspection is more than the tariff of the sanitary inspection, but less than the tariff of the customhouse. But this is not only a problem for businessmen. Bribes must be paid in education institutions, in medical institutions, in different administrations, in the police, and so on to receive the services.

Corruption is the "normal" way to solve problems in contemporary Russia. Corruption is the most serious problem in Russia, because all other problems remain unsolved when anything can be bought and sold.

Human trafficking is a global problem, and all types of trafficking exist in Russia. Moreover, Russia takes first place in the list of the world trafficking (Erokhina and Buryak, 2003). This is no surprise, because there are many poor, unemployed people in Russia, especially women and youth.

Trafficking in the form of forced prostitution of minors occurs in various contexts in Russian cities: on the street (i.e. average age being 16–17 years); on highways (i.e. very young girls, including children of 12–15 years of age); in railway stations, hotels, and clubs (i.e. 14–17 years of age); in "public houses" (i.e. illegal in Russia); through "call services"; and others (Gurvich *et al.*, 2002). In addition, trafficking of children includes those trafficked for pornography and illegal adoption.

The Center of Deviantology of the Sociological Institute of the Russian Academy of Sciences studied the commercial sexual exploitation of children in St. Petersburg and Northwest Russia, including Vyborg, Petrozavodsk, and other areas (Gurvich et al., 2002). The main users of children's sex are the "new Russians," city "authorities" and foreign visitors, particularly from Finland, but also from Sweden, Germany, Norway, and England. Child pornography is the least studied and most highly profitable sphere of the commercial sex trade. The street children are the most vulnerable and sought after for victimization (Gurvich *et al.*, 2002).

Forced labor has also been and continues to be prevalent, particularly for male victims.

Social control over crime is a very important topic in Russian criminology. Social and economic inequality, a criminogenic factor, generates social conflict, dissatisfaction, envy, and deviation (Gilinskiy, 2009, pp. 380–445). Unfortunately, repressive social control is used to exclude Russian citizens, and occurs through the selection process in the police and criminal justice system, thus increasing the deviance and crime rates. There are many scientific studies of this problem (see, for example, Gilinskiy, 2006; Luneev, 2005).

Conclusion

There is long, yet inconsistent, complex history of Russian criminology dating from the nineteenth century. After Gorbachev's perestroika, national criminology is penetrating world science. The main topics of contemporary Russian criminology are organized and violent crime, trafficking in persons, hate crimes, and corruption. Rational and effective social control over crime is currently an important reality. Modern Russian criminologists actively co-operate with foreign colleagues, participating in joint exploratory projects.

Based on the research cited in this chapter, this author concludes and/or agrees with other recommendations that it is very important to change the basic strategies of social control:

- Recognize the irrationality, ineffectiveness of reprisals;
- Change from retributive justice to restorative justice;
- Change the strategy of social control from "war" to "peace" or "harm reduction" and "peace-making" (Pepinski and Quinney, 1991);
- Search for alternative (non-repressive) measures of social response (e.g., fines, community service, electronic control, etc.);
- Make crime prevention the priority.

Future research questions

1. The number of crimes reported in official statistics is considerably lower than the number of crimes known to police. What are the reasons for police withholding crime numbers and how can the problem be fixed?

2. What would be effective strategies to encourage the study of white-collar crime and corruption by the new generation of Russian criminologists?
3. How is Russian corruption comparable to corruption in other countries and what makes some aspects of it unique to Russia?
4. How might research be used to prevent hate crime in Russia?
5. Will restorative justice practices need adaptation to the culture and history of Russia?

Note

1 "Press cell" – it is a cell that can be found in all institutions. In such cells prisoners selected by the administration beat, torture, and rape other prisoners to obtain information from them or to make them compliant to the administration.

References

Antonjan, J. (2002). *Violent crime in Russia.* Moscow: NII MVD (in Russian).

Babichenko, K. (2005). Discrimination and hate crimes: qualification and prevention. Doctoral dissertation. St. Petersburg: University of MVD (in Russian).

Dolgova, A. (Ed.). (2000). *Corruption and the fight with corruption.* Moscow: Russian Criminological Association (in Russian).

—— (2003). *Criminality, its organization and criminal society.* Moscow: Russian Criminological Association (in Russian).

Erokhina, L. and Buryak, M. (2003). *Trafficking of women and trafficking of children for sexual exploitation in social and criminological perspective.* Moscow: Profobrazovanie (in Russian).

Gernet, M. (1913) *Death penalty.* Moscow.

Gilinskiy, Y. (2000). Analysis of statistics on some forms of social deviation in St. Petersburg from 1980 to 1985. In H. Leifman and N. Henrichson (Eds.) *Statistics on alcohol, drugs and crime in the Baltic Sea Region,* pp. 175–98. Helsinki: NAD Publication. 37.

—— (2003). Organized crime: a perspective from Russia. In J. Albanese, D. Das, and A. Verma (Eds.) *Organized crime. World perspectives.* Ch. 6; pp. 146–64. Upper Saddle River, NJ: Pearson Education, Inc.

—— (2004). "Exclusion" as a global problem and social basis of crime, drug abuse, terrorism and other deviance. In *Works of St. Petersburg's juridical Institute of General Prosecutor's Office RF.* N6 (in Russian).

—— (2006). Crime in contemporary Russia. *European Journal of Criminology,* 3(3): 259–92.

—— (2008). Social violence: theory and Russian reality. *Russian Criminological Outlook,* 2: 224–35 (in Russian).

—— (2009) *Criminology: theory, history, empirical basis, social control.* 2nd edn. St. Petersburg: Juridical Center Press (in Russian).

Gilinskiy, Y. and Kostjukovsky Y. (2004). From thievish *Artel* to criminal corporation: the history of organised crime in Russia. In C. Fijnaut and L. Paoli (Eds.) *Organised crime in Europe. Concepts, patterns and control policies in the European Union and beyond.* Vol. 4. pp. 181–202. Dordrecht, Norwell: Springer.

Gurvich, I., Rusakova, M., Pyshkina, T., and Yakovleva, A. (2002). *The commercial sexual exploitation of children in St. Petersburg and Northwest Russia.* Stockholm: Save the Children.

Inshakov, S. (Ed.) (2007). *Latent criminality in the Russian Federation 2001–2006.* Moscow: UNITY-DANA (in Russian).

Jacobs, J. and Potter, K. (1998). *Hate crimes. Criminal law and identity politics.* Oxford, New York: Oxford University Press.

Janitskiy, O. (2004). Modern and its waste. *Sociological Journal,* 1–2 (in Russian).

Jusichanova, E. (2005). *Modelling of criminogenic processes in the subjects of the Russian Federation.* T'umen: Vector Book (in Russian).

Ledeneva, A. (1998). *Russian economy of favours: blat, networking and informal exchange.* Cambridge: Cambridge University Press.

Lenoir, R. (1974) *Les exclus, un français sur dix.* Paris: Seuil.

Luneev, V. (2005) *Criminality XX Century. The world, regions and Russian tendencies.* 2nd Edn. Moscow: Wolters Kluwer (in Russian).

Moscowskaja Helsinskaja Gruppa (2003). *Position of prisoners in contemporary Russia* (2003). Moscow: Moscowskaja Helsinskaja Gruppa (in Russian).

MVD RF (2009). *State of crime in Russia.* Moscow: MVD RF (in Russian).

Newman, G. (Ed.). (1999). *Global report on crime and justice.* New York: Oxford University Press.

Ol'kov, S. (2004) About profit and harm of inequality (criminological study). *State and Law*, 8: 73–8 (in Russian).

—— (2007). *Analitical criminology.* Kazan: Poznanie (in Russian).

Ovchinsky, V. (2001). *The 21st century vs Mafia.* Moscow: INFRA-M (in Russian).

Paoli, L. (2001). *Illegal drug trade in Russia.* Freiburg i. Br.: Iuscrim.

Pepinski H. and Quinney, R. (Eds.). (1991). *Criminology as peacemaking.* Bloomington: Indiana University Press.

Pobegailo, E. (2008). *Selected works.* St. Petersburg: Juridical Center Press (in Russian).

Questions of Statistics (2004). Main social-economic indicators on RF for 1999–2004. *Questions of Statistics.* 9: 73.

Repetskaja, A. (2001). *Transnational organized crime: characteristics, causes, strategy of control.* Irkutsk: IGEA (in Russian).

——(2007). *Criminal market of Russia.* Saratov: Saratov's Center of Study of the Organized Crime and Corruption (in Russian).

Russian Federation (1999). *Human development report.* Moscow: UNDP.

Sakharov, A. (Ed.) (1979). *Methodological and methods questions of the study and prevention of criminality in a large city.* Moscow: Institute of General Prosecutor's Office (in Russian).

Satarov, G. (2002). *Diagnosis of Russian corruption: sociological analysis.* Moscow: INDEM (in Russian).

——(2003). Rusty justice. *Native Notes*, 2 (in Russian).

Skifskiy, I. (2007). *Violent crime in contemporary Russia: explanation and forecasting.* Tumen: Vector Books (in Russian).

Sungurov, A. (Ed.) (2000). *Civil initiatives and corruption prevention.* St. Petersburg: Norma (in Russian).

Timofeev, L. (2000). *Institucional corruption. Sketch of theory.* Moscow: RGGU (in Russian).

Tsytsarev, S. and Gilinsky, Y. (2004). The roots of violence in modern Russia: a psychocriminological analysis. In L. Adler and F. Denmark (Eds.) *International perspectives on violence.* (Ch. 13; pp. 225–40). Westport, CT, London: Praeger Publishers.

Verchovski, A. (2007). *Upper strata and masses of the Russian nationalism.* Moscow: Center "Sova" (in Russian).

—— (Ed.). (2006) *Demographic modernization of Russia 1900–2000.* Moscow: New Publishers (in Russian).

Vishnevski, A. (Ed.) (2006). *Demographic modernization of Russia 1900–2000.* Moscow: News Publishers (in Russian).

Wewer, G. (1994). Politische korruption. *Politic-Lexicon.* München, Wein: Oldenbourg Verlag.

World Bank (2005). *World Development Report, 2005. A better investment climate for everyone.* New York: Oxford University Press.

World Health Organization (1996). *World Health Statistics. Annual Report.* Geneva: World Health Organization.

Young, J. (1999). *The exclusive society: social exclusion, crime and difference in late modernity.* London: Sage Publications.

47

Sierra Leone

The quest for justice and social cohesion

Christopher E. S. Warburton

Introduction

Sierra Leone has a checkered history of contacts with two European nations prior to the nineteenth century, Portugal and Britain. It became a Crown Colony in 1808 and gained its independence from Britain on April 27, 1961. This chapter presents the socio-economic indicators that are essential for understanding criminological work on Sierra Leone. These indicators include national income concentration, social and physical infrastructure, and the administration of justice. This chapter shows that crime and internal conflicts pose challenges for the realization of justice and social cohesion in the country. It ends with a brief analysis of empirical research on criminology in Sierra Leone and possible sources of funding for extended research.

Infrastructure

Sierra Leone is a West African nation with 71,620 square kilometers of land between Guinea and Liberia. Freetown, the capital city of Sierra Leone, is close to the Equator, about 900 kilometers, but the country has two distinct seasons: the dry season, from mid-November to April, and the wet season thereafter. The heaviest precipitation occurs in July, August, and September, with the greatest amount of rainfall along the coastal area.

The country is endowed with iron ore, gold, diamond, platinum, chromite, bauxite, and rutile that have constituted the backbone of its economy since the 1920s. The first diamond was discovered in 1930, subsequent to which mining began. Rich natural resources have also brought about major problems such as illicit mining, corruption, and smuggling. The ten-year war, which started in 1991, is largely attributed to the quest for diamonds, which was instrumental in financing the war for its duration.

Land ownership raises equity issues as a result of: (a) the way its use is regulated in the interior and (b) the way its resources are depleted because of corruption and illicit exploitation. Sierra Leonean land ownership law is pluralistic. Proprietary ownership of land is legal in the city and its adjoining surroundings, but not necessarily in what was once considered a British protected territory, where land is obtained through leases. This practice was strongly engrained in customary law (Unruh and Turay, 2006; Unruh, 2008). An attempt to reform the legal dualism was made in 2005 with the passage of the Lands Commission Act.

To the extent that proprietary rights cannot be exerted in the leasehold areas, the disincentive to invest in land in the interior creates a push-factor for outward migration that worsens the conditions of the interior including inadequate medical facilities, poorly equipped schools, and unemployment. As such, demand for land in Freetown and its adjacent areas with freehold law has increased exponentially. This demand leads to encroachment and arrogation, which are oftentimes encouraged by corrupt government officials. Unchecked urban encroachment is expedited by official corruption, which increases the pace of deforestation in Freetown (Munro, 2009).[1] Deforestation hastens the decline of sustainable economic conditions.

Sierra Leone is one of the world's most impoverished nations with a per capita gross national income of $770 USD (evaluated at purchasing power parity, PPP) in 2008 and PPP per capita gross domestic product (GDP) of $900 USD.[2] Its national income, which is estimated to be $2 billion USD in 2009, has a three-year average growth rate of 5.3 percent. Per capita national income of $770 USD translates into approximately $2 USD a day.

There is tremendous income inequality and instability (Warburton, 2008). Economists and social planners often use the Gini coefficient (GC) to measure income concentration.[3] The CIA estimated the Sierra Leonean GC to be 0.629 (in 1989). If income concentration is high (a reasonable presumption because of the increasing level of poverty), then the correlates of poverty (the proportion of families or individuals with per capita income less than the per capita poverty threshold) and crime are most likely high also.

The income disparity is made worse by inflation. The annual rate of inflation (consumer prices) between 2007 and 2008 was 17.5 percent. However, since the prices of fixed baskets are used to compute inflation (the Laspeyres Index) and not the Paasche Index or GDP deflator, inflation might be slightly exaggerated. Inflation reduces standard of living or increases the cost of living, thereby making it difficult for the poor to provide for their basic needs. Unable to maintain price stability, the monetary policies of the past decades pose tremendous challenges for the current government.

The government of Sierra Leone is made up of three branches: the executive, the legislature (Parliament), and the judiciary. The President is the head of the executive arm and Commander-in-Chief of the armed forces. The President is the guardian of the Constitution, and guarantor of the national independence and territorial integrity of the state, and relations with foreign nations. The executive consists of the President, Vice-president(s), cabinet members and deputies. The President determines the size of the cabinet.

The legislative power of Sierra Leone is vested in the Parliament, which consists of the President, the Speaker, and Members of Parliament. The legislature makes laws for the peace, security, order, and government of Sierra Leone. One Member of Parliament is elected for each district under the principle of universal adult suffrage. The country is made up of 12 administrative districts and 146 chiefdoms. Twelve members of the legislature are Paramount Chiefs who represent the country's 12 administrative districts.

The judiciary interprets the laws of Sierra Leone under a dual court system that deals with *general law* (British oriented law) and customary or local law. The historical and contemporary developments of the general law courts have been heavily influenced by the common law tradition of England (Thomson, 1999). The courts are organized on the basis of jurisdiction (geography, subject matter, and hierarchy) and venue, and legal disputes are classified into the conventional categories of civil and criminal. The court system has jurisdiction over criminal cases in a five-tier structure: (i) Local Courts, (ii) Magistrates' Courts, (iii) the High Court, (iv) Court of Appeal, and (v) Supreme Court. Yet the government has not always been stable.

The All People's Congress (APC) had a long and despised reign over the country under the leadership of Siaka Stevens (1968–85) because of the economic and political conditions that were created – economic dependency, odious debts, overvalued currency, inflation, and authoritarian rule under a one-party state from 1978 to 1991. One-party rule was originally flirted with by the then dominant alternative ruling party, the Sierra Leone People's Party (SLPP), but it never came to fruition. Sporadic incidents of student and worker protests and abortive coup attempts to usurp the authority of the APC government (treason or high crime) created a climate of political instability in the country. Before the outbreak of war in 1991, transient political instability paled in comparison to the savagery and brutality of war crimes that the nation endured.

Two successful coups occurred in the 1960s, two abortive coup attempts were made in the 1970s, and two successful attempts coincided with the ill-fated ten-year war that started in 1991. These coups, successful or not, reflect desperate discontent among some segments of the populations and oftentimes are fueled by ulterior motives and ethnic patronage (Cox, 1976; Kposowa and Jenkins, 1993).

Currently many international or multilateral organizations have rules that inveigh against high crime, encourage international peace and security, and promote democracy and liberalization. Sierra Leone is a member of some of these organizations that have facilitated the restoration of calm within its borders. Prominent international organizations of which the country is a member include the United Nations (UN); the International Monetary Fund (IMF); the World Trade Organization (WTO); the African Union (AU); and the Economic Community of West African States (ECOWAS). Membership to these international organizations imposes responsibilities and obligations for the development of international law (harmonization of municipal law with conventions or treaties), the interpretation of international law, the promotion of international cooperation, and the administration of justice through treaties and international or hybrid tribunals.

The channels by which international law can shape municipal law take at least two tracks: (i) *stare decisis* (adherence to precedents that can guide judicial decisions, otherwise known as common law) and (ii) *pacta sunt servanda* (nations are bound to keep obligations they make when there is no fundamental change in circumstances). Since treaties are contracts and not laws when they are not self-executing or need further legislation to be internally operative (for a judiciary to apply them), they can only be applied as law when the intention of the signatories is to make them internally operative (O'Connell,1965)

Various statutes of Sierra Leone reflect a commitment to the ideals of international organizations in the fight against international white-collar crimes to promote international peace and security and attain economic development. These include the Anti-Corruption Act (2008), which legally defines and outlaws corruption; the Anti-Money Laundering Act (2005); the Banking Amendment decree of 1996 to prevent unlawful risk-taking; and the Environmental Protection Agency Act (2008), to ensure a cleaner environment and sustainable development. The language of the Sierra Leonean statutes is generally consistent with those of the US Foreign Corrupt Practices Act 1977 and amendment in 1988; the UN Convention Against Corruption (2005); the 1986 US Money Laundering Control Act; the cross-jurisdictional initiatives of the Basel Committee on Banking Supervision; and the 1976 US Resource Conservation and Recovery Act (RCRA).

People

Sierra Leone has a population of about 5.7 million people who speak diverse languages, but English is the official language. The population consists of 18 ethnic groups, of which the Mendes account for 35 percent of the population, the Temnes for 32 percent, and the Limbas for 8.4 percent. Temnes, Limbas, Yalunkas, Korankos, Lokos, and Susus have numerical strength in the Northern Province and tend to be generally supportive of the APC. Mendes, Golas, Gallinas, Krims, Sherbros, and the Bullom people have numerical strength in the Southern Province and tend to be generally supportive of the SLPP. The Creoles, a minority group, are mostly found in the Western Area, while the Kono and Kissi people can be found in the Eastern Province.

Ethnicity tends to be a prima facie indication of political allegiances and ethnic differentiation is highly politicized (Cox, 1976; Kandeh, 1992). The Creoles, who were assailed and murdered in large numbers by the indigenes in 1898 (as part of an insurrection against a tax on Huts and Western civilization) are preponderantly apolitical and committed to their historical niche of professionalism as educators, lawyers, bankers, entrepreneurs, and health providers. Their exit from politics was expedited by the British policy of marginalization as a punishment for their outspokenness and "disloyalty."

It did not take too long for ethnic rivalry and political ineptitude to be on worldwide display. The first ethnocentric high crime (treason) in the country occurred in 1967 (six years after independence) when the Brigadier, Lansana (a Mende), of a rapidly Africanized force seized political power to ensure the political hegemony and preservation of the SLPP and his ethnic privileges. If the coup was surprising, the efforts to create a predominantly Mende bureaucracy and military leadership were not.

> During Sir Albert Margai's period of rule a fusion of senior army officers and leading members of the civilian elite became the order of the day. Thus of the nine most senior officers in the army, seven belonged to extended families whose members played a prominent role in Sierra Leone political life . . . On the most elementary level, a common ethnic identity helped forged bonds between military officers and civilian *big men.*
>
> *(Cox, 1976, p. 65)*

In 1962 and 1964 fewer Temnes held cabinet positions relative to Mendes when the SLPP was in power; similarly in 1973 and 1988 fewer Mendes held cabinet positions relative to Temnes when the APC assumed power (Kandeh, 1992).

It became clear in 1967 that the multiple shenanigans of the SLPP gratuitously fed the APC with unsolicited talking points with which to defeat the SLPP in elections. As a result, when the elections were held in 1967, the SLPP lost; at least by the determination of the Governor-General who declared the APC as the winning party. The unbearable loss forced the Brigadier, Lansana, to seize political power. His cabal of loyalists was charged with treason, treason felony, and misprision of treason [treason by acquiescence] (Joko-Smart, 1973). From 1967 to 1991 civil–military relations in Sierra Leone had tawdry co-existing functions.

Military action and conflict resolution in the twenty-first century espouse expected ethnic alliances. Empirical analysis by Humphreys and Weinstein (2007) suggests that members of the Mende ethnic group strongly associated with the leadership of the Civil Defense Force (CDF) and the ruling government (though not at the conventional levels of acceptance) and were more likely to reconcile and reintegrate, rather than Sankoh (a northerner) and his Revolutionary United Front (RUF) band of rebels. Analogously, officers and members of the Mende tribe were more likely to complete the disarmament, demobilization and reintegration (DDR) program at a faster rate relative to other groups. The CDF eventually joined forces with the then government when the country returned to civilian rule in 1996. Location fixed effects actually provided more indications about reintegration potential than individual-level attributes.[4]

The war has hastened the pace of migration from the interior, and Freetown is under considerable population pressure, given the available livable space relative to other areas such as Koinadugu or Bombali. With the exception of the Southern District, which had a marginal net gain of less than 1 percent between 1985 and 2004, and Freetown, which had a net gain of about 3.24 percent increase in population, other districts had a net loss of population (Sesay *et al.*, 2006). The 2004 census data revealed that 32 percent of the population will have to be relocated in order to attain a completely uniform distribution of population in Sierra Leone. To fully understand the problem of disproportionate population concentrations, it might be instructive to take a look at a few examples of space and population densities. In 2004, Koinadugu had an area of land of about 12,121 square kilometers, but a population density of 22. Bombali had an area of land of about 7,985 with a population density of 51 and Freetown had an area of land of about 82 square kilometers with a density of approximately 9,426 (Sesay *et al.*, 2006, p. 19). By all accounts, migration to Freetown puts tremendous pressure on the available land. The consequences of such imbalanced population concentration are a *fait accompli* – unemployment, vagabondry, theft, burglary, prostitution, inadequate social services, and overwhelmed law enforcement agencies.

The number of youths who did not work but actively looked for work within a four-week period was twice as high in the Western Region (10.2 percent) relative to other regions of the country in 2004 (Government of Sierra Leone, 2007, p. xix). Unemployment in the Northern Region was 5.5 percent, the Eastern Region, 4.5 percent, and the Southern Region, 3.8 percent.

Of the reasons provided for unemployment, job unavailability featured prominently. "No work available" recorded rates of over 75 percent in all the regions while seasonal inactivity was high in Southern Region (11.4 percent), followed by Eastern Region (3.8 percent), Northern Region (3.7percent), and Western Region (2.8 percent) (Government of Sierra Leone, 2007, p. 29). The Youth Commission Act (2009) is intended to address the growing problem of youth unemployment. International cooperation with the government of Sierra Leone also attempts to reduce youth unemployment. Additional problems identified by the government study include delinquency, social instability, prostitution, drug abuse, idleness, burglary, and larceny. Reliable crime statistics are not easily obtainable and the perceptions of crime are varied, but about 65 percent of those surveyed by Statistics Sierra Leone (Government of Sierra Leone, 2007) thought the crime situation did not improve from 2006 to 2007.

Another problem associated with the crime problem in Sierra Leone is the low level of education. Large numbers (68.9 percent) of heads of households had no formal education (in 2004); 2.7 percent have some primary education, 15.2 percent have some secondary education, and 8.3 percent have post-secondary education (Government of Sierra Leone, 2007, p. xvi). The adult literacy rate (those who are 15 years and over and can read and write in any language) for Sierra Leone is 36.9 percent. The adult literacy rate for males is 47.9 percent and 27 percent for females. At 25.1 percent, the Northern Region has the lowest adult literacy rate while the Western Region the highest at 70.7 percent.

Literacy rates in the Western Region are higher because of income differential and access to academic institutions. About 53.8 percent of secondary school age children have access to secondary education in the Western Region, unlike the Southern Region (30.6 percent), the Northern Region (25.3 percent), and the Eastern region (27.4 percent) (Government of Sierra Leone, 2007, p.15). It is worth noting that 30.4 percent of households have difficulty paying tuition. Without adequate free public education, poor people are confronted with the competing choices of providing food and medicine and dealing with the prohibitive costs of texts, uniforms, and transportation.

Administration of justice

Sierra Leone has a pluralistic legal system that is made up of (i) *general law*; (ii) customary law; and (iii) Islamic law. *General law* refers to enactments of the Sierra Leonean legislature and English law as they have been adopted in Sierra Leone.

> English law is incorporated into the legal system of Sierra Leone by means of the automatic application of specific Acts of Parliament as Imperial Statutes, the re-enactment by the Sierra Leone Legislature of certain Acts of Parliament, and the direct application of the common law, doctrines of equity, and statutes of general application in force in England on the first day of January 1880 [when Sierra Leone became a Crown Colony].
>
> *(Joko-Smart, 1980, p. 87)*

The local Courts Act of 1963 defines customary law as any rule other than the *general law*, which has the force of law in any chiefdom of the provinces, applicable to a particular case, conforms with natural justice and equity, and not incompatible, directly or indirectly, with any enactment applying to the provinces, including amendments of customary law made in accordance with an enactment. In a similar manner, the Court Ordinance of 1881, section 38, requires the courts of Sierra Leone to observe and enforce any law in the Protectorate that is not against natural justice, equity, and good conscience. As a system of law, the *Sharia* does not apply in Sierra Leone in the same way as the *general law* and customary law; it may apply either as part of statute law or as part of customary law (Joko-Smart, 1980; Tully,1994; Thomson, 1999).

Crimes in Sierra Leone are mainly classified according to the English common law tradition into three broad categories for restorative justice – justice in the conventional form, which punishes criminals and seeks to make whole the victims of crime, including society: (i) treason [high crime]; (ii) felony; and (iii) misdemeanor.[5] The Treason and State Offences Act of 1963 made treason a statutory offense that departed from the British prescription before independence in 1961. In the words of Thomson, "Sierra Leone's existing law of treason is, therefore autochthonous." (1999, p.177). Treason consists of (i) preparing or endeavoring to overthrow the Government of Sierra Leone by unlawful means or attempting to usurp the executive authority of Sierra Leone by force; and (ii) suspension, alteration, or repeal of the national Constitution by means other than the authority of Parliament (Section 108(8) of the 1991 Constitution). Treason is one of the most severe crimes in Sierra Leone and it is punishable by death.

Policing, a critical component of justice administration, is under reconstruction after years of neglect, inadequate compensation and corruption. Culp (2007) notes that police crime reports and other statistics from January 1991 to June 1996 virtually disappeared. Offender records, including fingerprint files and crime evidence, were missing, lost, looted, or destroyed in most police stations. However, Baker (2008) finds that for the top four crimes – assault, larceny, fraudulent conversion (the conversion of accessible assets and documents into fraudulent use), and wounding with intent – the data did not show much change since the 2002 Crime Survey. Culp identifies three phases for the reconstruction of the police force: (i) the rebuilding of infrastructure – the provision of basic supplies and equipment; (ii) the training and education of police officers; and (iii) the integration of the force with the other sectors of the criminal justice system – the courts and prisons.

Post-war policing crisis has made the theory of fragmented policing – the notion of informal policing by communities and youths in a proactive way – much more viable. Fragmented policing is an ancillary theory of the argument that Western-style policing (an imported brand of policing) may not necessarily be suitable for all conditions and circumstances in Africa. Critics of fragmented policing are uncomfortable with the magnitude of the shift of policing from the state to private entities, but given the limitations of size and skills of state police forces across Africa the idea is becoming much more appealing.

Once people have been arrested under the presumption of innocence, they have to be tried in courts of law. The Local Courts are at the lowest level of the court system and they have jurisdiction over minor criminal cases, mostly involving customary law. Elders of local areas or territories who are proficient in customary law preside over cases in the local courts. The Magistrates' Courts, like the Local Courts, have limited jurisdiction, but they are courts of record with both original and appellate jurisdiction over facts and law. As original courts, they perform important roles in the hearing and disposition of lesser criminal charges punishable by imprisonment or a fine.

In the Magistrates' Courts, the trials can be conducted by jurors or judges. Summary proceedings are trials of criminal charges without a jury. Magistrates' Court may commit a defendant to be tried on indictment (jury trial), if the circumstances of the case evince an aggravating or compelling factor. The High Court, Court of Appeal, and Supreme Court form the Superior Court of Judicature in Sierra Leone and all Superior Court judges are appointed by the President on the advice of the Judicial and Legal Service Commission. The powers of the High Court are original, appellate, and supervisory. As an original court, it hears and determines all types of criminal cases, especially those involving treason and such serious felony charges as sedition, murder, manslaughter, rape, robbery, burglary, larceny, forgery, and conspiracy to defraud. Cases in the High Court are normally tried by judges and jurors, but on exceptional occasions the Director of Public Prosecutions or the Attorney General may request a trial by judge alone on an *ex parte* application. The High Court also functions as an appellate court when it hears and determines appeals from decisions of Magistrates' Courts that had been tried under limited jurisdiction or as District Appeals Courts.

The Supreme Court of Sierra Leone is the highest Court of the land and it has appellate and other jurisdiction as may be conferred upon it by the Constitution of Sierra Leone or any other law. Major supervisory role of the Supreme Court, like other superior courts, involves the issue of writs (legal orders): (i) *Mandamus* (compelling the lower courts to perform a lawful duty); (ii) *Certiorari* (compelling the lower courts to produce records of its proceedings for review); (iii) *Prohibition* (compelling the lower courts to refrain from proceeding with a matter that is *ultra vires*, beyond their legal authority); and (iv) *Habeas corpus* (an order to inquire into the legality of the detention of any person within Sierra Leone).

Treaty arrangements allow the government of Sierra Leone to use international tribunals for the interpretation of international law. Tribunals with the authority (usually by treaty) to apply municipal and international law are legitimate hybrid tribunals. The Special Court for Sierra Leone (SCSL) is a hybrid tribunal. The Special Court for Sierra Leone was set up jointly by the Government of Sierra Leone and the United Nations after the Government of Sierra Leone asked the United Nations (UN) to establish an international tribunal to prosecute those who were responsible for serious violations of humanitarian law during the civil war.

Unlike the restorative genre of justice already presented, justice also may take a cathartic form of truth telling and forgiveness so that society can forgive and forget the past for progress and social cohesion. This form of justice is known as "transitional justice," but there is widespread disagreement over restoration and reconciliation. The Truth and Reconciliation Commission in Freetown (2003) was used to reinforce the mutually inclusive principles of punishment and forgiveness that are inherent in the principles of restorative and transitional justice. Other reintegrating measures include the Disarmament, Demobilization, and Reintegration (DDR) program and investment in education for readmission into society.

Criminology

A small group of scholars in the West have been studying crime in Sierra Leone for years. Major research topics in the past five years in Sierra Leone can be classified under the following broad categories: (i) the causes of war and war crimes; (ii) international tribunals and positive externalities; (iii) demobilization and reintegration; (iv) crime and policing; (v) violence and macroeconomic instability; and (vi) corruption and deforestation. Kposowa (2006) attributes the war to the erosion of the rule of law that can be explained in the criminological language of the routine activities theory suggested by Cohen and Felson (1979). Humphreys (2005) argued that the impact of natural resources on conflict cannot be entirely attributed to weak states.

Culp and Warburton (2010) estimate the prospects of deriving benefits from domestically seated tribunals based on available funding for contractual services, general operating expenses, and supplies and materials. By linear programming algorithm, they find that Sierra Leone derived external benefits from the domestically seated tribunal and that justice can be better served with sufficient and expeditious funding of hybrid tribunals. More pointedly, apart from deriving infrastructural benefits, assessed contributions are much more efficacious than voluntary contributions when courts are domestically seated for the administration of justice.

The pioneering work of Humphreys and Weinstein (2007) focuses on the source of variation in the key explanatory variables that are used to measure reintegration and whether or not the DDR programs provide efficacious results. They address the issue of why some individuals have been able to successfully reintegrate after conflict at the micro level because it is practically difficult to identify the effects of DDR programs on peace building at the macro level. Among other things, they find that 86 percent of combatants in their sample broke ties with their factions, 84 percent found permanent occupation, 62 percent expressed confidence in electoral politics, and 93 percent reported no problem. Other empirical studies include Adam *et al.* (2008), Baker (2008), and Munro (2009).

Adam *et al.* (2008) found that after violence, aid reduces the need for the government to resort to seigniorage, thereby reducing inflation. More surprisingly, over and above these effects via income and inflation, postwar aid has a direct effect, perhaps through strengthening confidence in the maintenance of peace. Other pertinent research addresses the issue of whether Western-style policing is suitable for all conditions in Africa, including Sierra Leone. Baker (2008) speaks to this issue in his paper on community policing. Munro (2009) argues that deforestation in Freetown is intimately linked to corruption.

There are various sources of data that can be used for research purposes in criminal justice and criminology. The Mining Annual Review (various years), the Metals and Minerals Annual Review (various years), and the Diamond Registry (based on US Geological Survey data) provide data for the diamond production. The data provide estimates of total diamond production, including diamonds that are exported clandestinely in the underground economy. The oil data is derived from measures reported in the BP Statistical Review of World Energy/BP Statistical Review of the World Oil Industry (various years), PennWell Corporation's *Oil & Gas Journal*, the US Department of Energy, the OPEC Bulletin, and *Petroleum Economist* (Humphreys, 2005). Other data sources for criminological work on Sierra Leone include: Statistics Sierra Leone, the World Bank's World Development Indicator (WDI) online, Transparency International, and the International Monetary Fund's (IMF) International Financial Statistics (IFS).

Fulbright and MacArthur grants support criminological research work on Sierra Leone. Fulbright provides grants for Sierra Leoneans to pursue graduate study in the US and post-doctoral research and teaching opportunities in Sierra Leone. The Fulbright US Student Program offers fellowships for US graduating college seniors, graduate students, and young professionals to study abroad for one academic year. The Fulbright US Scholar Program sends American scholars and professionals abroad to lecture and/or conduct research in a wide variety of academic and professional fields.

MacArthur is one of the US's largest independent foundations. The Foundation fosters the development of knowledge, and makes grants and loans through four programs: the Program on Global Security and Sustainability, the Program on Human and Community Development, and the General Program.

There is an apparent dearth of indigenous criminologists in Sierra Leone partly because the tertiary educational institutions in Sierra Leone do not have the infrastructure, programs, personnel, and curriculum to train or prepare Sierra Leoneans for research in the field of criminology. Sierra Leonean scholars usually have formal training in the areas of economics, law, politics, history, and other disciplines that are not directly related to criminology. The paucity of Sierra Leonean criminologists is not only noticeable at home, but abroad; mainly because before arriving abroad Sierra Leonean scholars already have preexisting academic training that is compatible with their current research interests, for example Kandeh (in political science), Kposowa (in sociology), and Judge Thomson (law and criminology).

A significant problem is that policy makers have made no significant investment of resources in the diversification of the curriculum or programs of the University of Sierra Leone since it was established in 1827. A marginal improvement worthy of acknowledgement is the law school. The University of Sierra Leone has a law school in which students train to become lawyers and law enforcement officials, but not necessarily criminologists. This is problematic because the cultural context of criminological fieldwork is usually lost.

Invariably, a very good understanding of the culture of any society is important to understanding the contextual concept of crime and the context of intellectual formulations; for example unfamiliar language, geography, and cultural practices are obvious impediments to fieldwork and the interpretation of local customs. As such, criminology is a great area of opportunity for international investment that can shed light on the causes of crime, how crime can be prevented in an impoverished society like Sierra Leone, and social cohesion. Foreign assistance will be particularly valuable in developing the infrastructure to train criminologists who can undertake and facilitate meaningful fieldwork in Sierra Leone with a very good understanding of the cultural nuances, geography, and languages of the country.

Conclusion

Sierra Leone has attracted much attention from the world in recent years because of the atrocities committed by ethnic conflicts and armed warlords. Although the country has stabilized significantly in recent years and a functioning government and judicial system have emerged, there are still tremendous challenges on the fragile democracy. Criminology has not emerged as a strong academic discipline in Sierra Leone, but many Western researchers have shown interest in applying their knowledge and expertise in examining crime and social control issues in the country.

Future research questions

1. Under what conditions can pluralistic laws achieve justice and social cohesion?
2. What is the role of international law in the development of municipal laws against nonviolent crimes?
3. Evaluate the argument that transitional justice and hybrid tribunals may be necessary but are insufficient conditions for social cohesion.

4. Is the socio-economic condition in Sierra Leone unsuitable for the Western form of policing, or is it corruption that is corrupting the imported form of policing?
5. To what extent can infrastructural development and reverse-migration reduce crime (conventional and nonviolent) and achieve socio-economic development for social cohesion?

Notes

1 White-collar crimes are nonviolent crimes that inflict no immediate physical injury on anyone, but are usually costly to society. The phrase was popularized by the American sociologist, Sutherland; see also Norris, 1903; Bonger, 1916; Braithwaite, 1985; and Podgor and Israel, 2009.

2 PPP is an exchange rate mechanism used to correct for differences in the ratio of the prices of nontraded goods to those of traded goods between two or among more countries. A set of prices for goods and services prevailing in the countries are used to construct the exchange rate; see World Development Indicators online and Central Intelligence Agency (CIA) World Fact Book for data on economic indicators.

3 Nations are conventionally divided into three categories of income inequality: Low GC < 0.40; medium 0.40–0.5, and high GC > 0.50; see Perkins *et al.* 2006, p. 197.

4 Fixed effects estimation is an empirical method of estimation, which takes into consideration the varying attributes of cross-sectional units. It is a binary process of estimation that can also be estimated by taking the variations from cross-sectional averages.

5 Section 1 of the English Criminal Law Act of 1967 contemporaneously abolishes the distinction and introduces a new concept of arrestable offense; see Thomson, 1999, p.37.

References

Adam, C., Collier, P., and Davies, V. (2008). Post-conflict monetary reconstruction. *World Bank Economic Review*, 22(1): 87–112.

Baker, B. (2008). Community policing in Freetown, Sierra Leone: foreign import or local solution? *Journal of Intervention and State Building*, 2(1): 23–42.

Bonger, W. A. (1916). *Criminality and economic conditions*. Boston, MA: Little Brown.

Braithwaite, J. (1985). White collar crime. *Annual Review of Sociology*, 11, 1–25.

Cohen, L. E. and Felson, M. (1979). Social change and crime rate trends: a routine activity approach. *American Sociological Review*, 44: 588–608.

Cox, T. (1976). *Civil-military relations in Sierra Leone: a case study of African soldiers in politics*. Cambridge, MA: Harvard University Press.

Culp, R. (2007). Post-conflict rebuilding of the police: lessons from Sierra Leone (June 1). Online at http://ssrn.com/abstract = 1467123 (accessed August 6, 2010).

Culp, R. and Warburton, C. (2010). Can domestically seated war crimes tribunals generate positive externalities? A case study of the Special Court for Sierra Leone. In G. Andreopoulos, R. Barberet, and J. Levine (Eds.) *International Criminal Justice Critical Perspectives and New Challenges*. New York, NY: Springer.

Government of Sierra Leone (2007). Core Welfare Indicator Questionnaire Survey (CWIQ) 2007. Final Statistical Report. Freetown, Sierra Leone: Statistics Sierra Leone.

Humphreys, M. (2005). Natural resources, conflict, and conflict resolution. *Journal of Conflict Resolution*, 49(4): 508–37.

Humphreys, M. and Weinstein, J. M. (2007). Demobilization and reintegration. *Journal of Conflict Resolution*, 51(4): 531–67.

Joko-Smart, H. M. (1973). Sierra Leone. In N. Rubin and E. Cotran (Eds.). *Annual Survey of African Law*. Vol. 3. Portland, OR: Frank Cass.

—— (1980). The place of Islamic law within the framework of the Sierra Leone legal system. *African Law Studies*, 18: 87–102.

Kandeh, J. D. (1992). Politicization of ethnic identities in Sierra Leone. *African Studies Review*, 35(1): 81–99.

Kposowa, A. (2006). Erosion of the rule of law as a contributing factor in civil conflict: the case of Sierra Leone. *Police Practice and Research*, 7(1): 35–48.

Kposowa, A. J. and Jenkins, J. C. (1993). The structural sources of military coups in postcolonial Africa, 1957–84. *American Journal of Sociology*, 99(1): 126–163.

Munro, G. P. (2009). Deforestation: constructing problems and solutions on Sierra Leone's Freetown Peninsula. *Journal of Political Ecology*, 16: 104–22.
Norris, F. (1903). *The pit*. New York, NY: Doubleday.
O'Connell, D. P. (1965). *International law*. Vol. 1. Dobbs Ferry, New York: Oceana Publications.
Perkins, D. H., Radelet, S., and Lindauer, D. L. (2006). *Economics of development*. 6th edn. New York, NY: W. W. Norton and Company.
Podgor, E. S. and Israel, J. H. (2009). *White collar crime in a nut shell*. 4th edn. St. Paul, MN: West Publishing.
Sesay, I. M., Kamara, A. A., and Ngobeh, J. J. (2006). 2004 population and housing census: analytical report on population distribution, migration, and urbanisation in sierra leone. Freetown, Sierra Leone: Statistics Sierra Leone.
Thomson, B. (1999). *The criminal law of Sierra Leone*. Lanham, MD: University Press of America.
Tully, J. J. (1994). The place of Islamic law in Sierra Leone. *The Muslim World*, 84: 3–4, 301–16.
Unruh, J. D. (2008). Land policy reform, customary rule of law and the peace process in Sierra Leone. *African Journal of Legal Studies*, 2: 94–117.
Unruh, J. D. and Turay, H. (2006). Land tenure, food security, and investment in post-war Sierra Leone. Livelihood Support Programme (LSP) Working Paper 22. Food and Agriculture Organization of the United Nations.
Warburton, C. E. S. (2008). When is transitional justice successful? An econometric approach. Proceedings of the Activating Human Rights and Peace Conference, Southern Cross University, New South Wales, Australia, pp. 395–415.

48

Turkey

The state of criminology

Ali Ozdoğan

Introduction

The state of criminology in Turkey, as in other countries, cannot be well understood without discussing the socioeconomic and political context of the country. In this chapter, after discussing the context, the system of administration of justice and the state of criminology are described.

Infrastructure

Geographically located in the southwestern area of Asia and the eastern area of Europe, Turkey's Asian and European parts are divided by the Marmara Sea and by the Bosporus and Dardanelles Straits. In addition to the Marmara Sea and the Straits, Turkey's coastline of 8,333 kilometers borders the Black Sea, the Mediterranean, and the Aegean Sea. Turkey has a land area of 783, 562 square kilometers and total land borders of 2,875 kilometers with Bulgaria, Greece, Georgia, Armenia, Azerbaijan (Nahjivan), Iran, Iraq, and with Syria.

Turkey's terrain is rugged and has a relatively high elevation. The average altitude is 1,132 meters and 90 percent of the country is above the sea level. The highest point, Mount Ararat, which is the probable legendary landing place of Noah's ark, has an altitude of 5,137 meters.

The seas surrounding Turkey, the rugged terrain, and the mountain ranges are the primary factors affecting the variation in climate, arable land, flora, ecology and environmental issues, and use of natural resources of the country. The country lies between the temperate and sub-tropical climate zones with an average rainfall of 646 millimeters annually.

The ruggedness of the terrain is the primary factor affecting the size of the arable land, of which 10 percent has permanent crops. The arable land of Turkey comprises approximately 36 percent; vegetation covered land (e.g. forests, maquis), 30 percent; meadows and pastures, 28 percent; water surfaces (e.g. rivers and lakes), 1.5 percent; and other lands (e.g. rocks, settlements), 5 percent of the country's total land, which is about 78 million hectares (Doganay *et al.*, 2005).

Although the arable land comprises 36 percent of the total land, only 30 percent of the arable land has potential for irrigated agricultural practices, and 15 percent of the arable land has irrigation systems. In other words, currently, only about 5 percent of the country's total land is available for irrigated agricultural practices (Doganay *et al.*, 2005).

Turkey is a world leader in terms of agricultural production. It is the world's largest producer of hazelnut, fig, apricot, cherry, quince, and pomegranate. Turkey has been one of the few countries self-sufficient in food production since the1980s. Yet the share of the agricultural products within the total production in the Turkish economy has declined since the 1980s. To prevent that decline, the government initiated several incentive programs, such as negative interest rates for agricultural loans, fertilizer and pesticides subsidies, and so forth. In addition, a 20-year project, the Southeastern Anatolia Project (GAP) is nearing completion with a cost of more than 30 billion dollars. The GAP, which included the irrigation of about 1.8 million hectares of land and the construction of 22 dams and 19 hydro-electric power plants, has brought prosperity to the agricultural and power sectors in the southwestern part of Turkey. The power plants built under the umbrella of the GAP project have a total installed capacity of 7500 megawatts, which meets about 20 percent of the country's electric power demand (Yazici and Koca, 2010).

Turkey currently is the producer of about 60 different minerals including coal, iron, copper, chromium, antimony, mercury, gold, barite, borate, celestine, emery, feldspar, limestone, magnetite, marble, perlite, pumice, sulfur, clay, and uranium (CIA, 2009). The richest mineral reserve, approximately 70 percent of the world's total, is borate (Kistler and Helvaci, 2006).

The extraction of natural resources and industrialization has become the sources of both economic prosperity and environmental pollution. The lack of adequate regulations for protecting the environment has resulted in water pollution; air pollution in urban areas; deforestation; oil spills from the ships passing through the Bosporus; and land degradation and soil erosion. The air pollution has declined in the recent decades, because coal consumption has increasingly been replaced by natural gas in urban areas. The soil erosion, which started thousands of years ago, is one of the most important environmental problems affecting three fourths of the arable land in various levels of severity (Gormez, 2007).

Turkey established the Ministry of Environment in 1991 and subsequently merged to become the Ministry of Environment and Forestry. The biggest successes of that organization is perhaps the significant reduction in air pollution particularly in the big cities (e.g. Ankara and Istanbul), and establishment of new water treatment facilities (Gormez, 2007).

Turkey is a newly industrialized country with an emergent market. The World Bank (2008) classified Turkey as an upper-middle income country with $11,900 USD Gross Domestic Product (GDP) per capita (PPP). Turkey's GDP (PPP), $903 billion USD, had the fifteenth largest GDP-PPP in the world. It is a founding member of the Organization for Economic Co-operation and Development and G-20 countries, and has a Customs Union Agreement with the European Union (EU).

Poverty is an issue. According to the CIA *World Factbook*, 20 percent of the population lives under the threshold of poverty. A statistical analysis demonstrated that the poverty was positively related to the educational level of the head of household, and negatively related to the number of children in the household and living in rural areas (World Bank and State Institutes of Statistics, 2004).

In addition to poverty, another social issue is income inequality. Turkey is a high-inequality country: the Gini index indicates that the distribution of family income is 43.6, which is in the rank of 49th in the world. The Gini figure demonstrates the inequality in terms of income. The consumption inequality, 33.6, is smaller than the income inequality (World Bank and State Institutes of Statistics, 2004).

The inequality is a little higher in urban areas than in rural areas. Yet the difference between the urban and rural is not the primary factor affecting the inequality. The primary factor driving the inequality is the regional differences. Eastern and Southeastern parts of Turkey are markedly poorer than the rest of the country (World Bank and State Institutes of Statistics, 2004).

Both poverty and inequality are closely related with labor issues, such as employment status and type of occupation. For example, the likelihood of poverty among the individuals with permanent work is 12 percent, while the likelihood of poverty among the individuals with a casual type of work is 44 percent. Poverty rate among the employees working in agricultural, construction, mining, manufacturing, and wholesale and retail trade sectors are 36.5, 36, 3, 17, and 18 percent, respectively (World Bank and State Institutes of Statistics, 2004).

The labor force involves about 25 million individuals. Unemployment rate is high: 9.9 percent in 2007 and 10.8 percent in 2008. Moreover, in 2008, 4 percent of the labor force is underemployed. The distribution of labor force among the agricultural, industrial, and service sectors are 29, 25, and 46 percent, respectively. The minimum monthly wage, 300 euros, is higher than in nine EU countries (Cosar *et al.*, 2010).

The largest industry is textile and clothing, which constitutes about 17 percent of the total industrial capacity. The other large sectors are oil refinery (14.5 percent), food (10.6 percent), chemicals (10.3 percent), iron and steel (9 percent), automotive (6.3 percent), and machinery (6 percent). Turkish industry includes the largest TV set producer in Europe, the 4th largest shipbuilder sector in the world in terms of number of ordered mega yachts, the 15th largest automotive producing sector in the world, and the 3rd largest construction/contracting sector in the world (Cosar *et al.*, 2010).

Turkey primarily exports textiles, clothing, food, raw metals, and transport equipment. The major destinations of the export are Germany, UK, UAE, Italy, France, and Russia. Turkey primarily imports machinery, chemicals, semi-finished goods, fuels, and transport equipment; mainly from Russia, Germany, China, US, Italy, France, and Iran. The volume of the exports is about $140 billion USD, while the volume of the imports is about $194 billion USD (CIA, 2009).

Energy, probably, is the most difficult challenge for Turkey's industry. More than half of the energy consumed is imported. Rapid urbanization and fast economic growth has rapidly increased the power demand in the recent decades. This increase in power demand continues by 8–10 percent each year. The hydroelectric power plants built under the GAP project are aimed to reduce the foreign dependency on power. Currently, Turkey, with 30,000 megawatts per hour installed electric energy capacity, has little dependency on foreign electrical energy. Yet Turkey depends on foreign sources to meet almost 50 percent of the country's demand for oil, and almost 90 percent of the natural gas demand (Yazici and Koca, 2010).

Turkey is a democratic republic with a parliamentary regime. Turkey has a civil law system primarily derived from the French and Italian legal systems in the 1920s when the Turkish Republic was founded on the ashes of the Ottoman Empire.

Turkey has a unicameral legislative system. Article 7 of the Turkish Constitution outlines the structure of the legislative branch of government, the Grand National Assembly (i.e. Parliament). The Parliament has 550 representatives who are elected by popular vote to serve five-year terms.

The courts constitute the judicial branch of the Turkish government, as described in Article 9 of the Constitution. Article 138 states that no authority may influence the courts or judges relating to the exercise of their judicial power. Both legislative and executive branches have to comply with the judicial decisions. Article 139 of the Constitution secures the tenure, salary, and other rights of judges and public prosecutors. In short, judges and public prosecutors have the most powerful positions, in terms of their independence.

Article 8 of the Turkish Constitution states that the President and the Council of Ministers, including the Prime Minister, are the head of the executive branch. While the President is not politically responsible to the Parliament, the Council of Ministers is responsible to the Parliament. The Prime Minister is appointed by the President from among the members of the Parliament. The Council of Ministers is appointed by the President based upon the nominations of the Prime

Minister. The President either approves the names of the ministers nominated by the Prime Minister, or makes changes as he or she chooses.

The tradition is that the Prime Minister is the leader of the majority party in the Parliament, and the Ministers are selected from among the members of the Parliament. The Prime Minister is responsible for ensuring the coordinated and harmonious working among the ministers. Each minister, according to the Constitution, is accountable to the Prime Minister. The Prime Minister ensures that the ministers fulfill their obligations in accordance with the law.

The election law requires that if a political party failed to obtain 10 percent of the ballots cast, it cannot have seats in Parliament. Therefore, in 2009, only four of the 49 political parties held seats in the Parliament. The threshold was designed to pave the way for only the strong parties, and to curb the number of marginal groups entering Parliament.

The four political parties seated in Parliament are the Justice and Development Party (AKP), which is the current majority party, Republican People's Party (CHP), Nationalist Movement Party (MHP), and Democratic Society Party (DTP). Political parties are the primary political pressure groups. The other effective political pressure groups include the businessmen's associations and, to a lesser extent after the coup d'état in 1980, the unions.

Another set of actors affecting the policy and politics, to some extent, is the international organizations with which Turkey is associated. These organizations include the EU, UN, NATO, IMF, G-20, OECD, CERN, IAEA, FAO, INTERPOL, Europol, OSCE, SECI, UNESCO, WTO, and WHO, among many others.

There are about 17 million fixed telephones (as of 2009), 64 million mobile cellular phones (as of 2009), 11.3 million internet users (as of 2006), and 120 radio and 750 TV broadcasting stations (The World Bank 2008). The state monopoly in telecommunication and broadcasting sector started to decay due to the emergence of the private TV and radio broadcasting stations in the late 1980s and, internet and GSM mobile phone service providers in the early 1990s. The state currently maintains its monopoly primarily in two telecommunication services: the internet backbone which serves as a bridge between country and global internet system; and the fixed line telephone system. The liberalization of these services has been an ongoing process since 2004.

Despite the existence of all transportation modes, the highway system carries most of the transportation burden. It carries about 92 percent of freight, and 95 percent of passenger traffic (United Nations Economic Commission for Europe, 2004). The country's highway network is about 400,000 kilometers long, of which 100,000 kilometers are paved roads and 2,000 kilometers are motorways.

The airway is the second largest mode of transportation for passenger traffic. There are 103 airports, of which 6 are international. Yet most of the international air traffic flows through three airports: Istanbul, Ankara, and Izmir. There are about 300 airlines that serve Turkey.

The railway is the weakest mode of transportation. The total length of railroads is about 11,000 kilometers. The railroad system is state owned, and it has suffered lack of renovation tied to lack of funding for many decades. It is predominantly used to carry minerals and bulk commodities over long distances.

Shipping plays a vital role in the Turkish economy. There are many small and large ports of which 21 are international and 5 are state owned. These ports mainly handle international cargos of steel products, petroleum, raw materials, semi-finished materials, chemicals, and food such as tea, hazelnuts, and so forth.

People

Turkey's population is about 77 million according to estimates in 2009. Turkey was ranked 18th in the world in terms of its population size. Two thirds of its population is within the 15–64 years range. The people below 15 years old comprise about 27 percent, and the people above 65 years old comprise about 6 percent of the whole population. The median age is about 28 years old. The life expectancy is 70 years for a male, 74 for a female, and 72 years average (Karabag and Sahin, 2009).

Population growth rate is about 1.3 percent. On average, there are 2.21 children born per woman; and there are 18.66 births and 6.1 deaths per thousand people. Another factor contributing to the expansion of the population is migration. The migration for the country is 0.56 migrants per thousand. The country is ranked 64 for the rate of migrants. Most of migrants are from the countries where various forms of political crises have occurred. These are Iraq, Afghanistan, Iran, former Soviet Union countries (e.g. Georgia, Azerbaijan, Chechnya), and Balkan countries (e.g. Albania, Macedonia, Kosovo) (Karabag and Sahin, 2009).

Turkey's population is 98 percent Muslim and the remaining population is Christian and Jewish. Turks, the majority ethnic group, comprise 75 percent of the entire population; Kurds, 15 percent; and the remaining 10 percent have different ethnic backgrounds including Macedonians, Albanians, Circassians, Bosnians, Arabs, Georgians, Greeks, Bulgarians, Azerbaijanis, Armenians, Jews, Gypsies, and others. Each ethnic group has its own language. Yet the newer generations have a tendency to lose their ethnic language, as Turkish is the common language for communicating with most people within the country (Gungordu, 2006).

The literacy rate is about 88 percent. This rate is almost 100 percent for the people under 15 years old. There is an imbalance between the literacy rate of males and females. It is 95 percent among males, and 80 percent among females. The education expenditures comprise about 4 percent of the country's GDP (Cosar and Bildirici, 2010).

There is no salient disease reported. The HIV/AIDS prevalence rate is less than 0.1 percent (Karabag and Sahin, 2009).

Administration of justice

The administration of justice is organized around three institutions: law enforcement, the court system, and the correctional system. After summarizing those three institutions, the section summarizes how justice is handled.

There are four law enforcement units: the Turkish National Police (TNP), Gendarmerie, Coast Guard, and Customs Protection. The major law enforcement units report to the Ministry of Internal Affairs and the customs protection reports to the Ministry of Customs. In addition, each municipality has its own guards, which have some law enforcement functions.

About 180,000 uniformed and 40,000 civilian personnel work for the TNP (Goksu *et al.*, 2008); 60,000 professional and 220,000 individuals who are fulfilling their mandatory military service work for the Gendarmerie; and 2,200 individuals work for the Coast Guard. There is one police per 382 citizens in urban areas, and one Gendarmerie per 81 citizens in the rural areas (Cerrah, 2008). The number of citizens per total number of law enforcement personnel is 146 (Cerrah, 2008).

The TNP is a civilian institution, and the Gendarmerie and Coast Guard are the military institutions, structurally part of the Turkish Armed Forces. Jurisdictional responsibility is split: country waters are the jurisdiction of the Coast Guard; the rural areas, where about 30 percent of the country's population lives, are the Gendarmerie's jurisdiction; and the urban areas, where about 70 percent of the population lives, are the police jurisdictions.

The TNP, which follows the Turkish public administration system model, has a strong centralized structure. Founded on March 20, 1845, the TNP modernized itself in 1930s by enacting two major acts, the Powers and Duties of Police Act (Law No. 2559, PVSK) dated

July 4, 1934 and the Security Organization Act (Law No. 3201, ETK) dated June 4, 1937. Those acts regulate the structure, powers, duties, responsibilities, and personnel of the TNP. The head of the TNP reports to the Minister of Internal Affairs. His selection process requires nomination by the Minister of Internal Affairs, recommendation by the Prime Minister, and approval by the President. Five deputies, who lead the Headquarters of Legal Consultancy, Board of Inspectors, Intelligence and Special Operations, Directorate of Public Relations, Police High School, and Police Academy, report directly to the chief of the TNP. The departments under the supervision of the deputies include the police offices in each province, and about 30 headquarters including Organized Crime, Counter-terrorism, Forensic, Financial Affairs, Human Resources, and Training.

The TNP, Gendarmerie, and the Coast Guard are in charge of maintaining order. For this purpose, the law enforcement units are in charge of preventing, detecting, and investigating crime under the authority of the state attorneys. State attorneys, under the administrative authority of the Ministry of Justice, have the most powerful positions in the organization of criminal justice.

There are four different court systems in the judicial branch: Constitutional Court, Administrative Courts, Military Courts dealing with the cases related to the military personnel, and Judicial Courts dealing with the civil and criminal cases.

The Constitutional Court has jurisdiction to examine the constitutionality of any laws, decrees, rules, and procedures. The cases can be brought to the Constitutional Court through three different ways: the President, Parliamentary groups of the majority or the strongest minority party, or by a petition signed by minimum of 20 percent of the total members of the Parliament.

The Administrative Court system includes Administrative Courts, Audit Courts, and Regional Administrative Courts. These courts have jurisdiction to review all administrative decisions.

The Military Court system has jurisdiction to try the cases related to offenses committed by the military personnel or on military bases, or offenses related to military duties. The Military High Court of Appeals is the appellate court for reviewing the verdicts given by military courts. Another military court is the High Military Administrative Court of Appeals which has jurisdiction for judicial review of the administrative decisions related to military, even if such decisions are made by civilian authorities.

The Judicial Court System includes at least ten different courts with different competence and jurisdictions. The Civil Court of the Peace is the lowest civil court with a single judge. It has jurisdiction to try cases where the amount is less than 2 million Turkish liras, and claims such as eviction cases for rentals by lease, and other issues assigned to the Court by the Code of Civil Procedure and other laws. The Civil Courts at First Instance has jurisdiction to try all civil cases except for the cases assigned to the Civil Court of the Peace. Specialized in cases about commercial transactions and activities, the Commercial Courts with three judges are branches of the Civil Courts at First Instance. The Penal Courts of the Peace are the lowest criminal court with one judge. The second type of criminal court is the Penal Courts of First Instance with one judge. The third type of criminal courts is the Central Criminal Courts with three judges and one prosecutor. These courts have jurisdictions to try the offenses punishable by at least five years of imprisonment, according to the Turkish Penal Code. The Execution Investigation Courts with one judge have jurisdictions over disputes arising during the execution of judicial decrees and civil sentences. The Court of Cassation is the highest court of appeal. This court has specialized chambers.

All types of courts mentioned are sometimes divided into several branches in accordance with the need in their jurisdiction. In addition, in accordance with the need in a city, there are lower courts dealing with various issues such as traffic offenses, juvenile delinquency, land disputes, and so forth.

There is at least one Civil Court of the Peace, one Civil Court of First Instance, one Penal Court of the Peace, one Penal Court of First Instance, and one Execution Investigation Court in every district. There is at least one Civil Court of First Instance, one Penal Court of First Instance, and one Central Criminal Court in every city. There is only one Cassation Court, located in the capital city, Ankara.

As of December 2008, Turkey had about 103,000 inmates incarcerated, of which 44,000 were convicted in court, in 384 correctional facilities including three juvenile training facilities, two juvenile prisons for the inmates between 12 and 18 years old, and four women's prisons. In four prisons, there are hospitals specializing in psychological illnesses. Some of the correctional facilities have industrial facilities to improve the inmates' job skills, and to provide income for the inmates. All correctional facilities have libraries and conference rooms, as well as the other essential facilities for living.

The Controlled Freedom Act legislated in June 1, 2005 reformed the correctional system by bringing the restorative justice model to the correctional system. The Act basically founded an institution which supports the released inmates to continue their education and to obtain a job. The job support includes providing job training, and a low interest rate loan for the former inmates who intend to start a business.

There is a parole and probation system in the Turkish correctional system. The inmates who demonstrate good behavior are conditionally released from prison.

Inmates have the right to have access to all legal periodicals and online education at elementary, high school, undergraduate, and graduate levels, as well as the other basic rights including meeting with his/her lawyer, requesting psychological and social counseling and a medical doctor, exercise of his/her religion, access to the internet, TV and radio, using a public phone, and so forth. The correctional facility provides accommodation for the inmates to continue their education. The inmates have the right to have visitors once a week. The inmates can choose to work and are paid in the prison's industrial facilities.

Reactive policing has been carried out since the formation of the justice system. Proactive policing is relatively new. The underdevelopment of proactive policing is compatible with the underdevelopment of non-governmental institutions and civilian review boards, and with the strong centralization in the justice institutions. Yet this administrative and legislative infrastructure has been changing since the late 1990s.

The legislative, philosophical, and administrative foundation of proactive policing has been founded in the recent decade. The EU accession process including the harmonization of the rules and procedures according to the EU recommendations and directives, and increasing quality and education level in the TNP personnel, has been the primary factor in bringing proactive policing into practice. The TNP funded hundreds of its members to pursue their graduate degrees in the popular universities in Western countries. There, proactive policing was practiced to some extent and thus this has been a contributing factor in developing this philosophy, including establishing community police units, meetings with representatives of the community, and policies to develop trust between community and law enforcement, which has increased the volume of the 155 (i.e. US equivalent of 911) calls from citizens to inform the police, and increased authorizations of the recent legislation for law enforcement to conduct proactive investigations.

Legislation passed in July 2005 (i.e. Law No. 5397) authorized the TNP and Gendarmerie to gather information upon approval of a judge, before an incident occurs. In the law, the incidents for which the proactive investigation is authorized are listed as homicide, drug trafficking, human trafficking, terrorism, treason, organized crime involving violence, and robbery.

Another source of proactive policing is the informal social control mechanism. Turkey has roots of strong informal social control mechanism in its culture and individual relations. For example, in the traditional culture, a youth does not smoke a cigarette in the presence of an older individual, even if that older individual is a stranger to him/her and that older individual smokes a cigarette. Although such traditional norms and values have lost their practice by the emergence of the modernization and globalization of values, they are effective in most sectors of the public at various levels.

The handling of justice in courts and correctional facilities has been improved in the last decades. Today, the practices in courts and correctional facilities comply with the European Convention on Human Rights.

Restorative justice in the correctional system is working to some extent. Some correctional facilities have factories where the inmates are working and gaining experience for a specific job. In addition, the job training courses in some correctional facilities aim to produce skilled people for industry. The job experience and job training programs accelerate the integration of the inmates into the community.

Criminology in Turkey

As in Europe, criminology in Turkey was primarily studied in law schools until the 1990s. In addition, some psychological aspects of criminology were studied by medical doctors. Sulhi Donmezer, Timur Demirbas, Feridun Yenisey, Fusun Sokullu-Akinci, and Mustafa Toren Yucel are some of the many prominent Turkish legal scholars who contributed to the legal aspects of criminology. I. Hamit Hanci, Ozcan Koknel, and Atalay Yorukoglu are some of the prominent medical doctors and psychiatrists who studied criminology. Criminology with a sociological aspect was initially studied by several sociologists in the 1990s. Yusuf Ziya Ozcan, Tulin Icli, Ali Caglar, and Recep Gultekin are some of the frontier sociologists who studied criminology with a sociological view.

Since the 1990s, the Turkish Police Academy has been the primary home for criminological studies. The Police Academy is a university with research institutes that grant academic degrees, including a Ph.D. in the areas related to criminal justice, criminology, and security. Currently, the Police Academy has almost 100 young researchers studying criminal justice and criminology. The Police Academy publishes an academic journal, *Turkish Journal of Police Studies*, which contains articles about criminal justice and criminology.

Given that terrorism has been the major social problem since the 1950s, terrorism related studies have taken a greater portion of the criminology studies. In 2007, the workshops sponsored by NATO and the Turkish National Police gave rise to three volumes about terrorism. In these books, there are many articles examining terrorism from a criminological point of view. Oguz (2007), Ozsoy (2007), Alkan and Citak (2007), Ozer (2007), Ors and Cetin (2007), Gunes and Ozeren (2007), Gultekin (2007), Kayaoglu (2007), Koseli (2007), Simsek (2007, 2009), Teymur, Sahliyeh, Yayla and Yilmaz (2007), Gultekin (2007), Gozubenli and Akbas (2007), Ozdoğan (2006, 2008), Caglar (2006), and Icli (2006) examine the social, economic, cultural, political, and global factors for producing terrorism at the individual, family, and group levels. Nikbay, Smith, and Mus (2007) examine the factors such as gender, age, education, prior arrests, outstanding warrants, and target's characteristics on terrorist suicide bombers. All these articles have a criminological perspective to terrorism, and they predominantly use quantitative methods.

In 2007 and 2008, in a project by the Turkish Scientific Research Institute (TUBITAK), Aydemir *at al.* (2008) surveyed 4,500 people in ten provinces of Turkey, to investigate the social factors affecting the radicalization process of the terrorists abusing religion. They determined the provinces where the survey was conducted, by looking at the statistics showing the most likely hometowns of the two terrorist organizations, Turkish Hezbollah and Islamic Movement; for example, two statistical pieces of data: 97 percent of the convicted members of the Islamic Movement and 53 percent of the convicted Hezbollah members were born and raised in the provinces of Batman, Urfa, Mardin, and Diyarbakir. Accordingly, the project team determined their sample geographical locations as those four cities as well as Istanbul's two provinces, which attracted immigrants from those four cities. The findings demonstrate that poverty, lack of education, weakness of family and tribal ties mostly because of immigration, lack of religious knowledge and practices, and immigration are the primary factors associated with the members of the Turkish Hezbollah and Islamic Movement, which are religion-abusing terrorist organizations.

Criminological research is definitely not confined to terrorism. There is much research related to crime in urban areas. In 2007, TUBITAK funded a project headed by Halil I. Bahar that tried to obtain the profile of purse snatching. They surveyed 1,360 people in Istanbul's four provinces (i.e. Eminonu, Beyoglu, Kadikoy, and Sisli) where purse snatching is a serious problem. They found that the victims of purse snatching are spending more time outside than the others who are not victimized, and they are more likely to be female. They also found that police visibility and trust between police and citizens are significantly associated with the lower numbers of purse snatching.

In 2008 and 2009, a project supported by the TNP, Turkish Ministry of Interior, and International Strategic Research Institute (i.e. USAK) investigated the citizen's security perception in Istanbul, which is the largest city and has a population of 12 million. The project team, headed by Halil I. Bahar and Suleyman Demirci, examined the combined effects of the "broken windows," "routine activities," strain, and social control on the crime rates. They conducted surveys and expert interviews to collect data, and they used both statistical and crime mapping (i.e. GIS) tools to analyze and report the findings. They interviewed 100 experts from non-governmental organizations, media, and academia. During the survey research, 5,400 person were randomly selected and administered the security perception survey. The survey results demonstrate that 62 percent of the respondents replied that crime is a serious problem for the city (i.e. Istanbul); 50 percent replied that crime is a serious problem for their neighborhood; 72 percent have confidence that police are competent in solving crimes; 97.3 percent feel more secure because of the security camera system (i.e. MOBESE) operated by the police in the city; and 67 percent believe that people in the city are helpful to each other. The results show that homeless youth, purse snatchers, and traffic violations are perceived to be the most threatening factors in both residential and commercial zones. The interviews demonstrated that citizens' confidence in the police and physical conditions, such as street lightning at night, are the most important factors deterring criminals (Demirci, 2009).

A survey has been a commonly used instrument of data collection for criminological research in the last decade. Finding secondary data for criminological research is difficult because criminological research was rejuvenated in the 1990s after an interregnum that lasted many decades. Currently, the major source of secondary data is Turkish Statistics Institute (TUIK), and Command and Control Headquarter (AKKM) of the TNP, as well as the international institutions, such as World Bank and UN, storing data about the socio-economic conditions for almost all countries. The TUIK data are accessible through the internet and the TNP data are obtained through written request to the TNP.

The data collected in criminological studies are usually analyzed by using quantitative methods. Turkish researchers started using advanced statistical tools, such as time series analyses, within the last several years.

Most of the research in the last decade has been funded by the TUBITAK. As part of the Turkish government's EU harmonization policy, TUBITAK raised its funding resources from around 35 million Turkish liras per year to approximately 1,000 million new Turkish Liras per year from 2003 to 2008.

The Turkish researchers in criminology are affiliated with the research institutes in the Turkish Police Academy, Turkish Academy of Drug and Organized Crime, think tanks such as USAK and International Strategic Research Forum (ISREF), and sociology departments in several universities, including Harran University and Middle East Technical University, among others.

In sum, the criminological research in the last decade has increased considerably, both in terms of the numbers and quality of the research. The engine behind that increase contains the components, such as the Police Academy's focus on the research, increasing funding opportunities for research, and Turkish National Police's policies promoting postgraduate education for its members.

Future research questions

1. What are the criminogenic conditions fostering the elite clandestine organization, Ergenekon, in Turkey?
2. Why is the PKK terrorism persistent in Turkey, despite the huge counter-terrorism efforts? What are the individual motivations and deprivations, and structural conditions such as ethnic and linguistic heterogeneity, previous land reforms, agricultural mechanization, industrialization, and urbanization?
3. How and to what extent is a Turkish Muslim youth radicalized, and how is he or she alienated from the West?
4. What are the criminogenic conditions affecting immigrant Turkish workers in Europe?
5. What are the cultural factors deterring crime in Turkey?

References

Alkan, N. and Citak, M. (2007). Youth and terrorism. In H. Durmaz, B. Sevinc, A. S. Yayla and S. Ekici (Eds.) *Understanding and responding to terrorism*, pp. 285–304. Amsterdam: IOS Press.

Aydemir, S, Kara, Z. K., Yilmazer, A. F., Akguc, S., and Okten S. (2008). *Turkiye'de Dini Kullanan Terorun Sosyal Sebeplerinin Arastirilmasi*. Sanliurfa: TUBITAK Projesi.

Caglar, A. (2006). Religion-based terrorism in Turkey. In R. Orttung and A. Makarychev (Eds.) *National counter-terrorism strategies*, pp. 145–54. Amsterdam: IOS Press.

Central Intelligence Agency (CIA) (2009). *The world factbook*. Washington, DC: Central Intelligence Agency. Online at https://www.cia.gov/library/publications/the-world-factbook/geos/tu.html (accessed December 8, 2010).

Cerrah, I. (2008). Democratization of policing: the case of the Turkish police. In M. Haberfeld and I. Cerrah (Eds.) *Comparative policing*, pp. 183–222. Los Angeles: Sage Publications.

Cosar, N., and Bildirici, M. (2010). *Turkiye Ekonomisi*. Ankara: Seckin Yayincilik.

Demirci, S. (2009). *Istanbul Ili Mahalle Guvenlik Algilamasina Etkin Eden Unsurlar: Karar Agaclari Model Calismasi*. Unpublished manuscript.

Doganay, H., Ozcan, N., and Sahin, C. (2005). *Turkiye Cografyasi*. Ankara: Gunduz Egitim Yayincilik.

Goksu, T., Sozen, S., and Cevik, H. H. (2008). Turkiye. In H. Huseyin Cevik (Ed.) *Karsilastirmali polis yonetimi*, pp. 406–37. Ankara: Strateji Gelistirme Baskanligi.

Gormez, K. (2007). *Cevre Sorunlari*. Ankara: Nobel Yayincilik.

Gozubenli, M. and Akbas, H. (2007). Adaptation of community policing in Arab and Muslim communities in response to terrorism. In S. Ozeren, I. D. Gunes, and D. M. Al-Badayneh (Eds.) *Understanding terrorism: analysis of sociological and psychological aspects*, pp. 207–18. Amsterdam: IOS Press.

Gultekin, K. (2007). Women engagement in terrorism. In S. Ozeren, I. D. Gunes and D. M. Al-Badayneh (Eds.) *Understanding terrorism: analysis of sociological and psychological aspects*, pp. 167–75. Amsterdam: IOS Press.

Gunes, I. D. and Ozeren, S. (2007). Theory of prism; individual capital and frustration. In S. Ozeren, I. D. Gunes and D. M. Al-Badayneh (Eds.) *Understanding terrorism: analysis of sociological and psychological aspects*, pp. 27–32. Amsterdam: IOS Press.

Gungordu, E. (2006). *Turkiye'nin Beseri ve Ekonomik Cografyasi*. Ankara: Asil Yayincilik.

Icli, T. (2006). *Türkiye de Terör*. Unpublished manuscript.

Karabag, S. and Sahin, S. (2009). *Turkiye'nin Beseri ve Ekonomik Cografyasi*. Ankara: Gazi Yayinevi.

Kayaoglu, M. (2007). Does inequality trigger terrorism? In S. Ozeren, I. D. Gunes and D. M. Al-Badayneh (Eds.) *Understanding terrorism: analysis of sociological and psychological aspects* (pp. 99–108). Amsterdam: IOS Press.

Kistler, R. B. and Helvaci, C. (2006). Boron and borates. In J. E. Kogel, N. Trivedi, and J. M. Barker (Eds.) *Industrial minerals and rocks*. 6th edn. pp. 171–86. Littleton: Society of Mining, Metallurgy, and Exploration, Inc.

Koseli, M. (2007). The poverty, inequality and terrorism relationship: an empirical analysis of some root causes of terrorism. In S. Ozeren, I. D. Gunes and D. M. Al-Badayneh (Eds.) *Understanding terrorism: analysis of sociological and psychological aspects*, pp. 109–19. Amsterdam: IOS Press.

Nikbay, O., Smith, C. J., and Mus, E. (2007). Suicide attacks as a devastating terrorist modus operandi: an updated evaluation of Turkish cases. In O. Nikbay and S. Hancerli (Eds.) *Understanding and responding to the terrorism phenomenon*, pp. 73–90. Amsterdam: IOS Press.

Oguz, E. (2007). Family case approach in understanding and combating crime in general and specifically terror. In H. Durmaz, B. Sevinc, A. S. Yayla and S. Ekici (Eds.) *Understanding and responding to terrorism*, pp. 271–84. Amsterdam: IOS Press.

Ors, H. and Cetin, H. C. (2007). Characteristics of global terrorism. In S. Ozeren, I. D. Gunes and D. M. Al-Badayneh (Eds.) *Understanding terrorism: analysis of sociological and psychological aspects*, pp. 85–95. Amsterdam: IOS Press.

Ozdoğan, A. (2006). Where do terrorists come from? In R. Orttung and A. Makarychev (Eds.) *National counter-terrorism strategies*, pp. 21–42. Amsterdam: IOS Press.

—— (2008). Social fragmental origins of terrorism. *International Journal of Comparative and Applied Criminal Justice*, 32: 111–19.

Ozer, M. (2007). The impact of group dynamics on terrorist decision making. In S. Ozeren, I. D. Gunes, and D. M. Al-Badayneh (Eds.) *Understanding terrorism: analysis of sociological and psychological aspects*, pp. 63–75. Amsterdam: IOS Press.

Ozsoy, I. (2007). Terrorism: a socio-economic analysis. In O. Nikbay and S. Hancerli (Eds.) *Understanding and responding to the terrorism phenomenon*, pp. 55–70. Amsterdam: IOS Press.

Simsek, Y. (2007). Terrorism and migration in Turkey between 1992 and 1995. In S. Ozeren, I. D. Gunes and D. M. Al-Badayneh (Eds.) *Understanding terrorism: analysis of sociological and psychological aspects*, pp. 144–60. Amsterdam: IOS Press.

—— (2009). Profiling PKK terrorists. In S. Teymur, H. Ozdemir, O. Basibuyuk, M. Ozer, and M. Gunbeyi (Eds.) *Combating terrorism*, pp. 271–86. Washington: The Turkish Institute for Security and Democracy.

Teymur, S., Sahliyeh, E., Yayla, A. S., and Yilmaz, I. (2007). The recruitment process of terrorist organizations. In S. Ozeren, I. D. Gunes, and D. M. Al-Badayneh (Eds.) *Understanding terrorism: analysis of sociological and psychological aspects*, pp. 161–6. Amsterdam: IOS Press.

United Nations Economic Commission for Europe. (2004). *Transport situation in Turkey in 2004*. Online at http://www.unece.org/trans/doc/transsitdocs/2004turkey.pdf (accessed October 20, 2009).

World Bank (2008). World economic indicators database. GDP(PPP) 2008. Online at http://www.world bank.org (accessed October 20, 2009).

World Bank and State Institutes of Statistics (2004). Turkey Joint Poverty Assessment Report (vol.1). Chapter 3. Turkey: Human Development Sector Unit, Europe and Central Asia Region and State Institute of Statistics.

Yazici, H. and Koca, M. K. (2010). *Turkiye jeopolitigi*. Ankara: Pegem Akademi Yayincilik.

Index

Page references in bold denote boxes, figures and tables.